P9-CJV-754

A Child
of the Century

SELECTED WORKS BY BEN HECHT

Novels:

Erik Dorn

Fantazius Mallare: *A Mysterious Oath*

The Kingdom of Evil

The Kingdom of Evil, Being a Continuation
of the Fantastic Journal of Fantazius Mallare

Gargoyles

The Florentine Dagger

Humpty Dumpty

Count Bruga

A Jew in Love

Miracle in the Rain

I Hate Actors

The Cat That Jumped Out of the Story

Nonfiction

1001 Afternoons in Chicago

A Guide for the Bedeviled

Charlie: The Improbable Life
and Times of Charles MacArthur

Perfidy

Gaily, Gaily

Letters from Bohemia

Plays

A Flag Is Born

With Charles MacArthur:

The Moonshooter

The Front Page

Jumbo

Twentieth Century

BEN HECHT

A Child of the Century

Primus

DONALD I. FINE, INC. • NEW YORK

Library of Congress Catalogue Card Number: 85-070637

HARDCOVER ISBN: 0-917657-42-X
PAPERBACK ISBN: 0-917657-41-1

MANUFACTURED IN THE UNITED STATES OF AMERICA

10 9 8 7 6 5 4 3 2 1

THIS BOOK IS PRINTED ON ACID FREE PAPER. THE PAPER IN THIS BOOK
MEETS THE GUIDELINES FOR PERMANENCE AND DURABILITY OF THE
COMMITTEE ON PRODUCTION GUIDELINES FOR BOOK LONGEVITY OF THE
COUNCIL ON LIBRARY RESOURCES.

To Jenny

Illustrations

Contents

Introduction

I HAVE IN MY KEEP one copy of *A Child of the Century*, and it sits now at my elbow, its covers gone, its copyright missing, nothing left of its commemoration, even its title page lost to some ill wind or forsaken ashcan. In the thirty-one years since it broke out as a bestseller, I have owned a good dozen of this book in hardback and at least a score in paper. All were gifts to friends and enemies, dolled up as loans but with no hope of return. What enemy worth the name—forget about friend—would give back a Ben Hecht? Particularly this baby you hold in your hand today, thanks to Donald I. Fine, Inc. This fabulous life you could otherwise not have obtained without practically offering your body. O rare Ben Hecht! It had a double meaning until Donald I. Fine, Inc. came along. O rare Don Fine!

Devotees of Ben Hecht will understand what a true Hechtian lead I have just written, albeit more in substance than style. They are sure to recall Walter Burns in "The Front Page" after Hildy Johnson captures the Red Menace Earl Williams and hides him in a rolltop desk in the criminal courts pressroom in Chicago. Hildy knocks out a lead graph and reads it to Managing Editor Burns, who is incredulous: "Where's the *Examiner*, doesn't the *Examiner* get *any* credit?" Hildy says, "Hold your horses, it's in the second paragraph." Walter Burns sneers. "The *second* paragraph? Nobody reads the second paragraph, you dumb bastard."

O rare Don Fine, you betcha! In a world in which too many publishers can't read and not many editors will, Donald not only doubles in brass and not only reads, he reads for trouble. Which is to say he actually gets as excited over a good line as those marketing-major publishers get over the bottom line. And maybe more excited, though maybe it's best not to push this too far. I can hear Bennie in my mind's ear exhorting me at least to wait for the promotion budget, he's still a publisher for chrissake!

Well, the Jews have a word for it. *Dayenu*. Sufficient. As in the Passover prayer: "If He brought us forth from the Land of Egypt and did not open the Red Sea it would have been *dayenu*"—sufficient. The logic appears faulty, you say? Any prayer that's made it for 3,000 years, over bitter herbs and unleavened bread yet, is *dayenu*.

Donald Fine would love to open a Hecht Renaissance with this sparkling new edition of *Child*. He knows how to get mad and he is mad as hell that Ben Hecht has disappeared from the stalls, that his work is ignored by the academy, that even before his death (1964) a generation had grown up knowing only that he was a Hollywood screenwriter. If they knew that much.

What a joy it will be if the Renaissance happens. If we can walk into a bookstore and find such haymakers as *Count Bruga*; *Erik Dorn*; *A Guide for the Bedeviled*; *Gaily, Gaily*; *A Jew in Love*; *A Book of Miracles*; *Perfidy*; *1001 Afternoons in Chicago*; *A Treasury of Ben Hecht*. Plus the stage and screenplays, never yet compiled.

I am believer enough to think it will happen, that this book will *make* it happen, that Ben has at long last found a publisher "demented enough to let me present all my works, maturely edited, in a score of fat volumes."

But if it should end here, with *A Child of the Century*, it would have been *dayenu*. For this is an autobiography like no other, written with more wit, *brio*, juice, style, clout than all those Hemingways, Fitzgeralds, Faulkners and other erstwhile icons could have put together in a millennium. The reason is simple: To write a great autobiography you have to live it. And while most writers are lucky to live half a life and are seldom comfortable doing it, Ben Hecht lived in a dozen worlds, enjoying them as if he were a citizen of each. Acrobat, magician, poet, newspaperman, playwright, author, screenwriter, propagandist—Hecht was all of these and then some. Which is probably why, the way ironies iron out, he had to title the first chapter of this book, "Who Am I?"

Across the years I became impatient with people who never heard of Ben Hecht or knew only that he wrote some great movies like "Scarface" and "Notorious" and "Wuthering Heights" and of course the quintessential newspaper play "The Front Page." But the truth is, I didn't know even *that* much about him when somebody handed me *A Child of the Century* in the fall of 1955 in the lounge of the Yale Law School. I was a fledgling on the road to becoming Clarence Darrow, but in the meantime I was holding forth on how Franklin Delano Roosevelt stood by and allowed the Jews of Europe to go up in smoke while he sat there in the White House smoking Camels.

I had absolutely no documentation to support this charge against my childhood hero Roosevelt, but I believed it completely. A few months earlier, an aging aristocratic Jew from Cuba, a man with a goatee, a walking stick, a cape and shining eyes, had been a guest at my house in Passaic, New Jersey. The occasion was a cocktail party my parents threw for his granddaughter, who was about to marry my best friend.

Eisenhower was in his first term, and the father of the groom-to-be said, "Isn't it a shame we don't have a great man like Roosevelt in the White House." Nothing more ordinary could have been uttered in those days where we lived. FDR was still mourned, particularly by the Jews, by every Jew I knew. The day he died I happened to have been at the bird store buying seed when I heard the news on the radio and I ran home to tell my grandmother, and my grandmother cried and said, "What will happen to the Jews?"

But now this old gentleman from Cuba stood up grandly and said, "I am leaving!" There was panic in my living room, nobody could figure what was going on except that somehow the marriage was about to be over. In the confusion, my father whispered something to the old man and he sat down. (Later I found out it was a Masonic sign, my father did something that kept him there out of Fraternity.)

"I remain because of my host," the old man said. "But I wish to register my shock that in a Jewish home the name of Franklin Roosevelt can be spoken in anything but disgrace."

He talked for no more than five minutes. He was born in Belgium, he said, and he made money in the diamond business and left Europe with the advent of Hitler and ended up in Cuba. When the extermination of the Jews started, he began using his fortune to save the Belgium Jews.

"I was able to help relatively few," he said. "But there were many like me and we did what we could. I brought them into Cuba and had to pay the dictator to keep them in camps until we could make arrangements in Argentina. In camps! You know why? Because your friend Roosevelt would not allow them in America. That's why there are Jews now in South America. Because he would not help, he would not lift a finger to save our people. And you sit here and praise him. You knew nothing of this? You were all blind? Or you wanted to be blind?"

Nobody believed him, though they were happy to agree. The marriage, after all, had to be saved. I say this without rancor, these were my parents, these were my friends. None of us was prepared for anything within light years of this. Yet I was sure he was right, this old man with the shining eyes. Such is the arrogance of youth, and maybe the genius.

But not all youth, surely not those listening to me go at FDR that night in the Yale Law School lounge. Wow, did they let me have it. Jews mainly, Jews telling me how crazy I was, how irresponsible, how dare I say this about Roosevelt, what proof did I have?

Except there was one Jew, a dark-haired fellow with half-mast eyes, a first-year student from Tucson, Arizona, named Jack Waltuch, who was hanging around the rim of this scene wearing an enigmatic smile.

Waltuch waited until my critics drifted back to the library and then he said, "If you just read Ben Hecht's autobiography why didn't you tell those guys, were you ashamed of the source of the Roosevelt story?"

I had no idea what he was talking about, while he couldn't believe that someone could grow up and get into Yale Law and not know Ben Hecht and yet talk about FDR and the Jews. Waltuch shook his head as if I were a hangover and said, "Wait here." And went up and brought me his copy of *A Child of the Century*.

It was all there about FDR and the Jews, more shocking than anything I was ready for, loaded with details, proof beyond a reasonable doubt by the man who lived it. Ben Hecht had been cochairman of a group I never heard of, The Emergency Committee to Save the Jewish People of Europe. It was this committee—opposed by the Jewish Establishment—that finally succeeded in getting FDR to set up the War Refugee Board. Too little too late, but it did save a couple of hundred thousand Jews and in doing so raised the horrific question of how many more could have been rescued had Roosevelt not been, in Hecht's bone-chilling phrase, "The humanitarian who snubbed a massacre."

Today the word is definitively in on Roosevelt and the Jews (see, for example, David S. Wyman's massively documented work, *The Abandonment of the Jews*), but it took three decades after *A Child of the Century* and forty years after Ben went after FDR. Hecht did not wait to write a book, he attacked in full-page ads while the massacre was going on. If there is a synonym for courage, spell it Ben Hecht.

I have left something out here, I am quite aware, and nothing less than the spirit, gaiety, joy and exuberance of the hero. For this I make no apology, only amends. The book is before you, so the amends will be short, but something needs to be said else one might get the idea that we are dealing here with mainly a polemicist. In truth, we are talking about one of the great raconteurs of any time, one of the loveliest storytellers, a man who lived with passion and wit. And so attracted to his table the best of his generation. This book is loaded with marvelous tales of Chicago, New York, Hollywood, of H.L. Mencken, Sherwood Anderson, John Barrymore, Harpo Marx, Charles MacArthur, Fanny Brice, Dorothy Parker, Gene Fowler, Jed Harris, Herman Mankiewicz, Constance Collier, David Selznick, Billy Rose, Kurt Weill—and that old reliable, Etc.

Hecht is no name-dropper; if anything, most of these luminaries were more a part of his life than he of theirs. That many were household names, far more famous than Ben Hecht, was of no import to him, and in reading this book it will be of no import to you, only an oddity. Or as Hecht writes: "As a man embarked on his memoirs, I am not depressed by this lack of fame, nor should the reader be. For though fame is a help in selling books, it is of small use in writing them."

Ben Hecht was never one for heroes, but he did have H.L. Mencken, his "Alma Mater." Mencken was the first to publish his short stories in *The Smart Set*—Don Fine will certainly have to do a collection of Hecht's stories; they are simply in the top-drawer of all American short fiction—and Ben recounts here a walk he had with Mencken down Michigan Avenue in Chicago during a Republican National Convention. When the Sage of Baltimore needed a water closet. And the nearest john was a half-mile off.

But Hecht remembered an old whorehouse, ready now for the demolition hammers. On the wall above the toilet, Mencken read aloud a quatrain written there in indelible pencil:

> O Lady of lustful gyrations
> O Vandal of velvet and vice,
> O Creature of carnal elations—
> Why will not a two-spot suffice?

It was entitled "Three Shy" and signed, boldly, BEN HECHT.

"You have a true poet's heart," Mencken said. "A love of women and a lack of funds. And I can say I never read a poem under better conditions."

It is smart to be wary of anyone who tells you a book changed his life, but I have to say I was never the same after reading *A Child of the Century*. What I met here was what I suppose everyone looks to meet in a book: a kindred spirit, a brother and a wise one. A brother who had been everywhere and done everything, who caught the nature of man in its ultimate evil and still loved the morning, a worldly romantic who never let sanity get him down. A brother who could write that his late-coming religious faith dispelled the only illusion he ever had. "I believe in God," Ben Hecht says here, "because I have lost my faith in reason and the progress of thought."

And then there is the newspaper game, foremost the newspapers, of course. I would never have left the law for journalism were it not for this book. I thus joined generations of newspapermen who caught the bug with "The Front Page," Hecht and MacArthur's lovesong to the Chicago of their flaming youths. I was a little late for that one, so I got mine with *A Child of the Century*. If there was a way to do a computer take-out on how many newspapermen have gone into the racket on account of Ben Hecht, I wouldn't be a bit surprised that you'd find just about everybody who meant anything in the profession and most you never heard about.

Well. Don Fine is going to accomplish one thing for sure with this coup, this event in publishing. He will bring a new bunch of kids into newspapers who will kill to get that story. Who'll get it right. Who'll get it into the paper. And even if they wear the Harvard tie, the hat will be over the eye.

Hell, just one like that, it would be *dayenu*.

P.S. I met him only once, two months before he died. I was a rookie reporter on the New York *Post* and I gave Leonard Lyons a scoop. Lennie asked me, "What can I do for you, kid?" I told him, introduce me to Ben Hecht.

It was the day Lyndon Johnson made his first State of the Union speech, February, 1964. Ben was living in a small duplex on West 67th Street in Manhattan. After pouring drinks, he said, "Did you see the President this afternoon?" I hadn't but I didn't say why. The reason being I was honing up to meet Ben Hecht.

Ben said, "I watched him like he was a potato bug. And he's the most evil man we've had in the White House during my lifetime."

I thought, uh-oh, this guy's around the bend. We are talking now before LBJ sent all the troops to Vietnam; this was the Great Society Lyndon who managed to pass the Civil Rights Act and the poverty stuff, everything Jack Kennedy hadn't done. So I looked at Ben Hecht as if *he* were a potato bug.

He smiled and said: "His eyes filmed over when they played the National Anthem. Any man who'd cry during the National Anthem . . . well, I won't live to see the results, but you will."

O rare Ben Hecht. Yessiree!

—Sidney Zion

"But there is a spirit in man. . . . Fair
weather cometh out of the north . . ."
Book of Job

For a number of years I have thought of writing a book about my-self. I deferred the project, believing that I might become brighter and better informed about my subject as I grew older. Waiting, I stayed silent.

This vanity of expecting too much of myself has often thrown me into long silences as a writer. I was, in my dreams of self, never quite finished with becoming what I hoped to be and, thus, inclined to hold my tongue as unworthy of my future wonders.

I have decided to put away such convenient humility and accept myself as completed—wonders and all. Perhaps I am even a trifle over-done, for I have less anger in me and less love than I had a few years ago, and my sentences have grown a little longer. Obviously, if I keep postponing the task, no book at all will come to pass and the empire I call myself will vanish without its ideal historian to chronicle it.

So I set myself to work.

I intend to write an autobiography of my mind and salvage not only some of the thoughts that have gone through it, but discover as fully as I can its capabilities. Insight has been mine, and understanding and vision. Were I able to put down a fraction of the thinking I have

1

done, the moods I have tumbled through, the truths I have held fleetingly by their tails, I would, I am certain, emerge as one of the geniuses of my time.

For we are all geniuses—we who live. In fact, it would be almost impossible to live without being one.

It is as writers that our genius disappears, or at best shrinks to a few stuttering and remembered anecdotes.

MY LACK OF FAME

WHEN a great man or an historic figure writes of himself, he can start right off with tales of his nursery days, his first adventures on his bicycle and all such memory-album trivia. We know who it was rode the bicycle and hid under the veranda from his nanny. His rompers do not fool us. It was the Conqueror of India or the Great Philosopher who altered the course of human thought. The name that signs such a book turns us into eager backstairs eavesdroppers.

No such name is attached to this volume. Although I am known here and there as a writer not without wit and fecundity, the information is a bit spotty and I can rely little on reader snobbery. Had I contented myself with writing books, as I started out to do when I was seventeen, I might have acquired a more definite identity than I seem to have, among the critics if nowhere else.

I can understand the literary critic's shyness toward me. It is difficult to praise a novelist or a thinker who keeps popping up as the author of innumerable movie melodramas. It is like writing about the virtues of a preacher who keeps carelessly getting himself arrested in bordellos.

The drama critics under whose attention I have come from time to time are in a similar dilemma. They are fierce fellows who have never tasted defeat in the shooting gallery which is their battlefield. And they are never so fierce as when confronted by a man of letters with a Hollywood address. There is no critic so soupy-minded he does not feel hotly superior to the creations of the movie capital.

There is yet another matter that troubles my all-too-human critics. This is the legend seeping through newspaper and magazine offices that I collect great fortunes from the movie studios as a scenarist. As a result, my emergence in print or behind the footlights (and even on the screen) often brings down on my head envious sneers at my riches, as if I were an embezzler or an apostate looking for absolution in the sacred courts of art, and being righteously denied it.

The fact that I am, and have been for twenty-five years, a man without a bank balance, owning neither stocks nor bonds, always broke, always battling my way out of debt, without money laid up for a rainy day and without even an insurance policy to provide for my family after I die, has kept me grinning wryly at this legend of my riches. Impostor I have been, but in the world of dollars, not of words.

And even though I have managed by my pamphleteering on the subject of Jews and their rights to Palestine to anger the whole of Great Britain to the remarkable point of being officially boycotted (as if I were a one-man enemy country), this achievement has brought me more financial discomfort than notoriety, or any other version of fame.

I am lodging no complaint against all these matters but making it plain, I hope, that whatever importance I can offer the reader I must attain under his nose in these pages.

FAME IS A DUBIOUS SPOKESMAN

As a man embarked on his memoirs, I am not depressed by this lack of fame, nor should the reader be. For though fame is a help in selling books, it is of small use in writing them. And though a reader may be pleased to eavesdrop on the reminiscences of famous people, he will rarely come away from such volumes with more than a three-dollar nodding acquaintance.

The reason for this is that famous people are usually too sensitive of their fame to write anything of themselves that may jeopardize it, such as that they are bored, frightened, bewildered or hollow as the drums that acclaimed them. Great ones, when they take to autobiography, are chiefly full of tidings about their pedestals and how they got on them, and how modestly they occupy them, and how many other people on pedestals they know.

THE FIREFLIES OF FAME

THERE IS also a new sort of fame in our day that has never quite been known before. It is a fame seemingly invented out of whole cloth, based on nothing and needing only a press agent to keep it alive. This new species of fame does not wait for a man to win a race or a worldly prize before riveting its neon light on his head.

People in our day become famous who are no more than advertisements, and they advertise not genius but existence.

They are famous for stopping in hotels, for holding hands in public, for speaking to each other, for having babies, for getting invited to parties. This is true not only of movie stars but of statesmen and mountain climbers. So deep is the limbo into which industry, politics and overpopulation is shoving us, that we ask of fame that it makes us aware of men rather than supermen.

A depersonalized citizenry avid for identity has invented this new type of fame. The lonely city dwellers, whose human faces are lost in the shuffle of world problems and mechanized existence, elect representatives to live for them.

As a result our new type of famous ones rhumba for us, answer erudite questions on the television for us, cohabit for us, marry and divorce for us, go to cafés for us and even lie in hospitals battling diseases for us. We are less interested in their talents than in their publicized routines. We have no hankering to be awed by their genius (which is, perhaps, lucky for both us and them). We find pleasure not in how much they surpass us but in how much they resemble us.

I do not bemoan this phenomenon. The hunger that spawns celebrities out of nobodies is less disturbing to me than many other kinds of fame making—particularly the intellectual snobbery that from age to age keeps alive the names of stale and unreadable authors. In fact, most literary fame is not a matter of honest laurels worn by the dead, but dishonest boasts of culture made by the living.

The importance to which I aspire in these pages is possibly the opposite of fame, real or spurious. It is that sharpness of identity that those we know intimately have for us.

Who cares about the moods or problems of a stranger, however glamorous he is? But when a brother speaks, all he says is vital. His troubles, confusions and adventures are our own. It is not a blood tie that makes him important and meaningful to us; it is the fact that we know him well.

It is this importance I hope for.

HOW, THEN, TO BECOME A BROTHER

THE READER has certain expectations of an autobiographer. He expects such a self-coddler to be a chronologically-minded fellow, to get himself born, baptized and surrounded by relatives in orderly sequence; to get himself married, appointed to something or other and emerge bit by bit as a rounded character formed out of deeds, discourse and social contacts.

I intend to write no such tourist's guide of myself. For my hope is not merely to write *about* myself but to turn myself into a book.

All my life I have been haunted by a phrase read in my youth in one of Joseph Conrad's books—"the soul of man." I grew up with this phrase tugging at my elbow. And I secretly measured literature, people or events by whether or not the "soul of man" was in them.

The "soul of man" meant to me the urgent rivers of emotion on which humans have always traveled—the dark torrents of mania, greed and terror; the bright streams of love and brotherhood. Beyond the monkeyshines of his politics and the inanities of his verbal worlds, this "soul of man" has beckoned my attention, stimulating and horrifying me and occasionally filling me with pride. This pride was less for man's achievement than for his persistence, for his Phoenixlike rise out of evils, his own and nature's.

For three thousand years, until the middle of the nineteenth century, nearly all the thinking about the human soul had to do with its immortality. Philosophers from Lucretius to Kant pondered the problem of what part of the human being hopped off to Heaven or Hell after he was shoveled into the ground, and of what this part was made —molecules, flux, natural gas or the breath of God.

This concern with the immortality of the soul of man, with its survival in a place no one has ever seen, is part of the wasted energy of the mind, like its concern with witches, angels and demons.

I do not know if any part of me will manage to slip through the undertaker's fingers and go gallivanting off into mystic space. And I shall never, even when I lie dying, ponder this question. I shall die with my eyes turned earthward, for I am a creature of earth and nowhere else.

MY FRIEND, THE OCEAN

THE PACIFIC OCEAN that lies a few yards beyond my window in Oceanside, California, and the curving sky above it make a hypnotic geometrical design at which I never tire of looking. The summer morning is like the inside of a diamond.

An ocean is likely to be a troublesome collaborator for a writer. Writing at its side is like writing in a temple surrounded by statues of heroes. I am inclined to sit and ponder the mighty problems of evolution in a set of unwieldy phrases.

During the day the ocean, when I stop admiring it as a scenic companion good for my health, becomes a classroom full of eras. The great and awful past of the world rides effortlessly on its waves. It is still a fresh and virginal sea bespeaking the fact that Time is a futile embrace.

The mind of man is much like the ocean. It, too, has remained fresh and active despite the cataclysms that have afflicted it. And I, too.

In the night the ocean becomes a theologian and debates with me the existence and nature of God.

Looking at the rain of stars across incomprehensible space I inquire, "If there is not a God involved in this methodical business of spinning planets, what else is there?"

Do I see a house, I am certain instantly that someone built it. An intelligence conceived it. Hands constructed it.

My certainty that an intelligence is behind the construction and upkeep of the universe is a little less spontaneous. It wavers a bit. But it is there.

Obviously it is an intelligence that can conceive of me more easily than I of it. When I consider that all the theologians, physicists, poets, saints and philosophers have not succeeded in a hundred centuries in arriving at the dimmest understanding of this universe-spawning intelligence, I am inclined to question the existence of human reason rather than that of God.

MY DEBUT AS A LAMB

I AM a little surprised to find myself, contrary to the habits of my life, writing now of God as if He were an interstellar fact rather than a human aberration. Stiff-necked and vain of my self-sufficiency, I spent most of my years convinced He was no more than a synonym for the collapse of thought.

But like most children of nature when Time has bitten into them, I come to pillow my head on His mystery.

As a matter of fact, in the days of my heresy the question never was —did God exist? It was always how could I relate myself to Him, without feeling I had struck all my intellectual colors and enrolled myself as another Simple Simon in the lowest grade of human meditation.

I have found my answer, and I shall put it down as clearly as I can. My thousand and one days and nights will have to wait upon my clarification of this issue. A man who writes of himself without speaking of God is like one who identifies himself without giving his address.

I remember my early God aversions with approval. A man who in his youth embraces God is likely to be a sickly fellow with no more than a trickle of sex in him; or a creature full of low impulses that need concealing.

I was no such citizen. I spent my youth enjoying my senses and increasing my mind. I had no more spiritual life than a monkey in a tree. I was an apostle of human reason. As such, I looked on God as an enemy. He had an ugly history on our planet, comparable to the most virulent bacteria. All the deadly sins appeared tó be His trainbearers, chief among them being brutality.

Accordingly, I orphaned myself from His side. My faith in reason did not deny His existence, it revolted against Him. The reading of history and the observing of my fellows had convinced me that the presence of God in the human head induced lunacy and outrage, and dammed the progress of reason. I believed that the secret of human salvation lay in people's changing from the disordered worship of the unknowable to the reasonable study of the known.

My conversion has nothing to do with the acquiring of illusions. In fact, my belief in God dispelled the only illusion I ever had and, therefore, I can say it embittered me more than solaced me. I believe in God because I have lost my faith in reason and the progress of thought.

I believed once, like Voltaire and Carlyle, that the ills of the world could be cured by thinking. I see that belief now as an emptier superstition than any that ever bent the knee to the most gargoyle of gods. On what evidence of progress was it founded? What baseness in man did thinking ever oust? What grace has reason ever added to the behavior of my species? When and where did it ever transform with its magic the wretched human passion for inhumanity?

An incense of sweet words hangs like a secondary sky over the world. But the feet of man can no more enter it than he can walk with his boots on into the Biblical Kingdom of Heaven.

I see my own century, heir to five thousand years of reason, still torn by irrationality, still blood-soaked and floundering.

HOW MY EGOISM DIED

A SIMPLE FACT entered my head one day and put an end to my revolt against the Deity. It occurred to me that God was not engaged in corrupting the mind of man but in creating it.

This may sound like no fact at all, or like the most childish of quibbles. But whatever it is, it brought me a sigh of relief, a slightly bitter sigh. I was relieved because instead of beholding man as a finished and obviously worthless product, unable to bring sanity into human affairs, I looked on him (in my conversion) as a creature in the making. And, lo, I was aware that like my stooped and furry brothers, the apes, I am God's incomplete child. My groping brain, no less than my little toe, is a mechanism in His evolution-busy hands.

And thus I lay my long-treasured egoism on His altar, set fire to it and watch it disappear. I murmur a sad prayer in its smoke. I am no special creation divorced from the chemistries of other seeds. My talent for thinking has no more standing in the eyes of nature, or influence upon it, than the breathing of the algae. Along with the bugs and beasts and invisible gases, I am in the process of being used, whether in some Plan or in some equally mysterious absence of Plan, I have not the faintest idea. I am the sport of Time and Space and of various involved laws which nobody has succeeded in understanding. And I am as mindless toward my creator as are the tides of the sea or winds of the sky. We all obey. We do little else, despite the noises we make.

I have gained little from my new understanding of God but a sense of proportion, and one not in my favor. I recognize my notions as a sort of religion, one that apologizes for humanity with the credo "It is not done yet. It is only begun."

HOW I AM LEARNING TO HOPE
WITH A NEW SET OF WORDS

OBSERVING in history and in the newspapers and hearing at dinner tables the wretched and impractical whinnying of the human mind, observing my fellows still unable to say hello to one another without baring their fangs and fingering their bludgeons, I see that human reason has moved so imperceptibly in the last five thousand years that it is not yet possible to tell in which direction it is going—forward or backward.

There is even the possibility that it is not moving at all and that God has seen fit to abandon His experiment with the mind of man as He saw fit to scrap some of His earlier and too-horrendous fauna of our planet. The one thing that is certain about God is that He makes mistakes. The mind of man may be another one of his unsatisfactory experiments destined to disappear or to evolve into something more practical—like the automatism of bugs.

These musings—on a June day—divert me, for it is always pleasant to think, however abysmal the topic. But I know them for what they are—the ancient human despair with humanity. If I had no wit or words I might weep over what I know. So foul, man. So deep his pain. So miserable and futile his efforts to live by his reason. His psyche, which was able to stand up valorously against the early terrors of the jungle, sickens in the streets of civilization. He was the intellectual among monsters. Among ideas he becomes the savage.

This is our brief history—that ideas make monsters out of us. They reanimate our most savage instincts. Our minds are the arsenals from which we constantly rearm our instinct for killing one another.

Knowing this, seeing all the world about me crawling with ideas as if a new species of brute had entered it, watching and hearing the travail of humanity tearing at itself, I summon my new faith to soothe me. A hope flickers. I turn to God with what I know. If I am something that He has invented, and not too well, He will certainly understand if I enter His presence mocking us both a bit.

A LUCIFER AT PRAYER

MY ACCEPTANCE of God does not bring with it any love of Him. It may later. I can already understand this love of God. It is the despair with everything else. It is the heart looking for a home that can find none in the hostility of humans.

My obeisance to God in my fifties is cool, sad and detached from any mass demonstration. I could no more think of going into a church and praying and singing than of running around in an Indian war bonnet.

I prefer giving homage to God's wonders rather than to Him for the good reason that such homage will not disorder my vocabulary or darken my lucidity. Therefore I honor His incredible sky, His legerdemain of color and light, His physicist tricks of life within life; and, a bit sadly, even the bird of thought that flaps with lame wings and seeks to soar out of my hormones into my skull.

The nature of my faith also keeps me from addressing Him, as a vain and pathetic waste of time. My knowledge of God informs me, with fine clarity, that He does not love me. He loves my species, perhaps. He is interested, craftsmanlike, in its continuation, I hope.

As an infinitesimal child of God, I shall not waste my brief time heckling Him with incantations. Rather should I heckle the world, which has a smaller and more visible ear.

"AND THOU SHALT LOVE
THE LORD THY GOD."

NOTHING used to irk me so much as religious writing. Confronted by its rhapsody and rigmarole, I would wince too much at its nonsense to be fetched by the fine literary clothes it sometimes wore.

Among the things that for years kept me from believing in God were the disreputable arguments offered by the various Holy words of His existence. The discouraging chatter of Testaments, Scriptures and Korans and of all their commentators and annotators has, I am certain, kept half the world Godless since the Greeks; the half that tried to think.

That hundreds of millions of otherwise intelligent people accepted the hoaxes of religious writing as Truths, that its nursery tales were acclaimed as wisdoms, used to send me running from all works of divinity as from a plague.

I have another attitude now toward religious writing. When I meet in print the eurythmic saints and prophets, I do not flee their noises. I linger and I listen. I have no brotherhood with their desperate words or wanton manners, but the ferment that produced these is there in my own soul. It is the ferment of incompletion. We are all children in the womb and we are smitten by the dream of form and substance not yet achieved by us; but in the offing.

My parent, God, is busy with all of us, the hosanna howlers and me alike. There is a finger, not my own, prodding faintly at my interior and working patiently away in me.

Perhaps this is all that the saints and prophets had to say in their own ways—that we are ungrown, unfulfilled and that God still models us.

THE LORD IS—HOW MANY?

IT APPEARS that, despite my insistence on my ignorance, I have, like all writers who tamper with theology, answered who God is, what He does, how He operates—and why. I desire to withdraw all my answers. I have no answers. I have a knowledge, as of the name of a city, but lacking all other information.

I am reminded of a Negro I saw hanged in the Cook County Jail in Chicago. He was a dentist and had grown a little vague about things while awaiting execution. He stood on the gallows in a medical frock coat, his wing collar missing (a décolleté required by circumstances), and smiled oddly at the audience gaping at his last moments. Though the rope was around his neck, he was not entirely certain where he was or what was happening. Before springing the trap, the sheriff at his side inquired of the doomed dentist, as was traditional, if he had anything to say.

The man with the rope around his neck smiled and answered in a faraway, polite voice, "Not at this time."

I, too, reserve comment.

Since I have made so many mistakes in loving humans I could see, feel and smell, how addled would be my conception of God, did I have any.

I sit beside my ocean and recite a first catechism.

That God has managed to survive the inanities of the religions that do Him homage is truly a miraculous proof of His existence.

The knowledge of God must be so deep in the human soul that none of the religions have been able to destroy Him. This is truly a thing of wonder.

If without love, awe, song, ritual or reverence, then how do I worship God?

I think of Him.

MY PEDESTAL OF SAMENESS

EXCEPT for my relation to God I have not changed in forty years. I have not become different as an adult. I have not assembled a character for myself out of the exterior world. I have no fabricated ego loud with answers. I have found no truth. The best I can do is guess. In my fifties, my head is as full of queries and confusions as any dog's in a new house.

Looking on most of the adults around me, I see this difference—I am as I was; they are as they have made themselves, or been made.

They are worldly people with a talent for belonging together. They depress me and make me often feel lacking in a sort of social sanity. I frequently envy them. They know always what to do, these adults born of no-child. They know where to go, how to amuse themselves, how to captivate one another, for whom to vote, where failure lies, where triumph waits. I know none of these things.

And they are as immune to my boon companion, ennui, as a turtle to rain.

I am without their resources. They can enjoy belonging to "noble" enterprises on sale in the press and over the "air" and at their social rallies. They can glow with hates and loves as spontaneous as the whoops of a baseball fan. And they are never mentally alone, for the opinions of the church, state and editorial writers are their constant buddies.

It is otherwise with me. When I feel shallow, which is most of the time, nothing can distract me from the disturbing fact. When I am dull it is impossible for me to pretend I am not. I cannot draw on the world to amuse me or live for me or succeed for me. I must draw only on myself.

Being as I was when a child, I am unable to feel proud, successful or important. All in all, my opposites in the world, who outnumber me considerably, seem to have the better of the bargain. Except that I have hours in which I know this is not entirely true. *My* enemies are all without. I have none within.

THE HALF-ALIVE ONES

I HAVE some further notions about my opposites—the men and women in whom I can detect no relation to the soul of their childhood. When I was a newspaperman I greeted them as they got off trains and tagged along with them to hotel suites. It was my chore to interview them, for they were the people who ran the world. They were armed with certitudes and as alike mentally as the teeth of a comb. They were the mindless, moodless hunters of success. I could not then understand how men and women who differed in no way from the dullest of failures I knew in my daily life could be such thumping successes.

Later I understood. They were successful for the same reason that their kind were usually failures. Their success was founded on the fact that they were not themselves. They had borrowed identity from the world and not out of their own souls. This feat produced equally the leader and the led.

I have found most "greatness" in people to be of this quality. Lacking individuality, they can only become big with the world. They feel their importance as their only identity.

Of true greatness there is a fine definition in the Old Testament. It is told in Exodus that Moses spent forty days with God and that when he returned to the common ways of man his face was radiant —but he did not know it.

To such radiance I have always bowed.

A PEEP AT DEGENERATION

WHEN YOUNG I used to wonder by what black magic the wild question-asking of youth was changed into the tame answers of adult-hood. I saw later that this was not a process of education but of suicide.

What a world we would have if youth could retain its bulging quiver of arrows! How soon all the cock robins of sham and swindle would lie dead! A renaissance would dawn in which no fool would be safe, rather than our present continuous senescence in which fools nearly always emerge as leaders. But as well dream of a world in which all women stayed beautiful.

Youth is our brief sanity. It is our fleeting performance as individuals. The rest, for most of us, is suicide.

Youth destroys itself for various reasons. Chiefly, it seldom has the talent to sustain itself. Its brain is short-winded. Its revolt piddles into a murmur and an apology.

There is another thing that destroys youth. Unholy impulses sometimes twitch at its nervous system. A knowledge smites the young that the being they were born is too odd for them to use. They must re-make themselves in order to function normally, possibly even to avoid arrest. Theirs is then the job of covering up undesirable material as we used to do in school when we slipped our geometry book jacket over a volume of badly printed erotica.

This sort of "improvement" of our dangerous or unusable selves goes on in the world constantly. Folk with topsy-turvy libidos escape occasionally into the arts. But most of them seize on the "sanity" of the world behind which to hide their sickly innards. They give to this outer "sanity" the adoration of converts who have been saved. They become the storm troopers of all clichés. Instead of thinking, they echo.

This genius for echoing is to be found also in people honorably put together by biology but too weak to resist the tidal wave of education. The destruction of self and the substitution of loud and empty certitudes is not only an inner necessity. It can be an outer demand. We throw away who we are and become everybody else.

Our civilization is like an implacable advertising campaign determined on overcoming all individual expression. Civilizations have always been that, but no era has ever before had as many propaganda whips for bullying and megaphones for deafening. Never before have a civilization's current errors and patchwork philosophies been so remorselessly slapped into all souls.

The individual healthy enough to think his own thoughts is numbed by the pandemonium around him. He must seem not an individual but the most rabid of anarchists if he would "think for himself." This he is not. He lets go his individuality, and the sales campaign claims him. He goes staggering to market after the intellectual panaceas and bonanzas advertised.

Robbed of self, he becomes like his neurotic brother, a man of echoes. He becomes a vociferous part of the advertising campaign that destroyed him—a solid citizen, an unquestioning member of society. And what a society!

The collapse of rationality in my century is the result of this defeat of human individuality. The smallness of man—his personal baggage of mood, thought, gossip and art—has been run off the map by the bigness of the crowd.

The crowd has taken over, everywhere, the business of human thinking and human destiny. Individual man is being remade as a faceless part of Democracy, Socialism, Communism and Fascism. Although at variance in mood and practice, all modern political systems make for the same goal posts—how to run the world most conveniently for the crowd.

As a member of the crowd, I have no objection to conveniences. I like a good postal system and fine plumbing. I like burglars to be caught, prices to be controlled, the streets to be cleaned.

Although disaster is on every horizon, my food supply is still neatly handled, and I am soothed as a mindless crowd-man by a hundred conveniences never known before in the world. And though I could do just as well without them, I nevertheless like them all.

In my country there is not yet darkness, but a twilight. Individualism is not yet an offense punishable by death or exile. It is frowned on, harassed and made to seem a potential crime against the Democratic State. Its practitioners, in fact, behave like criminals and move furtively through society. They do not cry out at the unreason, illogic and shabby hypocrisy around them.

I will give a small example of mass-man thinking. Over the radio I heard the following advertisement of a movie. Cried the announcer, "James Stewart plays the role of a convict, who while serving time in jail invents a new automatic rifle destined to save the lives of millions."

A thousand such sickly paradoxes as "the war to end wars" and "armament for peace" assail our ears daily. Statesmen, educators and scientists speak the same indecent "black is white" prattle demanded by the mass-man. Rationality drifts away in a twilight of politics.

Within this twilight, the sick of soul, the echoers, live in an illusion of sanity. Hate boils around them. Their old admonisher—God—has fled their hearts. They are up to their hocks in an era that specializes in killing—and preparing for killing. And all this seems fine and correct to them—and even noble.

When the atom bombs fall and destroy most of them, they will die with this illusion of a sane world still intact in their blasted noggins.

OF SMALL SOULS

IF I HAVE NOT BEEN a willing member of the world of adults, it was not entirely due to high-mindedness on my part. The sickness called loneliness was in me—a sickness as unalterable as one's face.

There have been many adventures in my life, and I have bombinated through one decade after another usually giving the impression that I was a happy and lucky fellow. I have been envied for my gaiety and my many preoccupations. These existed, but I, somehow, did not exist as part of them.

At the core of my living was a curious inability to live. I could seldom lose myself in anything I did or anything that happened. The books, plays, stories, movies I wrote; the causes to which I contributed and even helped lead left no ownership in me once I was done with them. They disappeared when they were completed.

A similar lack of adult paste in me kept me from attaching myself to many people. However friendly I seemed, in my heart I was seldom part of them—or they of me.

When I have gone to parties I have more often than not felt full of secret social deficiencies. In the presence of adults who make a pleasant habit of foregathering, of living off one another's personalities or of merely basking in amiable surroundings, my deficient self has always stuck in my eye.

And I have often seen it sticking in other people's eyes. For, although outwardly my gift of tongue and talent for stimulating others make loneliness seem no part of me, people know a lonely man and shy from him. Their instincts warn them against him. He is a fellow who will lessen their pleasures, by merely looking at them. He will embarrass them in their amiable and chattering drift through the days by turning his unbelieving smile on them.

I have sat thus isolated among people whose talk was filled with small intimacies, and, peri-fashion, I have listened to them chuckle and chat as if this vague and tiny dialogue were part of a great love affair they were experiencing.

And such it is—the love affair of the social soul. It blooms on the ability people have to be interested in nothings, to find pleasure in congregating as human ornaments, in advertising themselves as hat, fur and smile wearers: in knighting each other with hellos and posturing before one another as glowing disciples of conformity.

I have witnessed like a reporter the delight people are able to evoke in each other by standing shoulder to shoulder, cocktail glass in hand, as full of ad lib prattle as a chorus during a stage wait. But the gabble of such powder-puff folk has been as difficult for me to enter as might be the discourse of a room full of Einsteins and Whiteheads.

Yet, even as I write dourly of this baaing of the beribboned sheep of society, tossing my adjectives at its cliché-castrated satyrs and clothes-spayed Venuses, the hoopla of its homosexuals and its froth of comradeship—the truth is: My loneliness has often looked at these ineptly twittering social folk wistfully.

And a deeper truth is: that it is a preferred loneliness. I prefer something else to the friendships and social warmths I could not have. I prefer love.

Love is the only relationship of which I am capable, with a man or woman. All other contacts seem vain and dreary to me, as they did when I was a boy.

"AMOUR—AMOUR—"

OF ALL the worlds in which a man lives, the most difficult for him to understand—and remember—is the world of love.

If you ask a man how many times he has loved—unless there is love in his heart at the moment—he is likely to answer, "Never." He will say, if his heart is loveless, that often he had thought he loved, but that, victim or hero of love, he was mistaken. For only love can believe in love—or even remember it.

Such a man, forced to recall himself as a lover, will admit to folly or youthful oddity outgrown. Ah, he will say, there was little sense to it!

Little sense, indeed! His soul was in it, his sanity and mania wrestled over it. He narrowly avoided murder and suicide because of it. The successes and failures of his life were molded by it.

And all that was sweet in living lay in its warm hours. In those hours he bloomed like a field of poppies, his heart opened to rain, wind and light; he looked out of himself with new eyes; he visited humanity and beheld the nearness of God. Yet, grown old, he smiles at love as if nothing had happened. Loveless, he occupies his age like a castaway washed up on an empty shore, who gratefully calls the vacant sand his home.

Cold is the memory of love, colder than all other memories, stripped like skeletons are the scenes of its embraces that come to mind, its bedrooms are without furniture, and its streets are empty. The tender and antic flesh of love is not in them, and its soul is gone.

Remember amour—and it is death you see, not love. Your heart kneels at many graves, and where you loved most wildly the silence is deepest.

I begin now to write about love. It is a long and intricate subject. I shall tackle it in bits, hoping they will eventually come together and present some sort of human picture. If they do not, it will not be because the bits are at fault. It will probably be because some of them are missing.

MY SEA-BOTTOM UNIVERSITY

A MAN does not need to remember his actual amours in order to·
write of them. What remains alive of love is something deeper than
the flickering chronologies of passion recollected. It is information
that accumulates, information of self, of women and of the sea bottoms of the soul. Events grow dim, dramas vanish, paramours wilt
in memory and their bloomless faces disappear. The soul is left
empty; only the intelligence is served. At least, that is how it has
been with me.

And so, I offer my informations to the reader.

In most of the things a man does in his life, a certain amount of
awareness is essential, or he will not do them well. The opposite is
true of his love-making. For that he has a need of unawareness. In
fact, his ignorance of what he does as a lover—or why he does it—
is often the factor that enables him to do it.

One explanation is that a man nearly always loves for other reasons than he thinks. A lover is apt to be as full of secrets from himself as is the object of his love from him.

A man's ignorance of himself as a lover is based also on the fact
that love is like the appearance of a new language in his head. It is
the language of his secrets, of his buried needs and unspoken loneliness. Though the lover speaks this language well, and all his hungers cry out in it, he has only the dimmest knowledge of its meanings.
As the wind blows through a ripening field, so does the language of
love speak through him. And often it speaks despite him. When its
speech is done he can remember it only as one remembers the corner
of a dream.

A definition of love is hardly ever more than a sly diagnosis of
the definer. Nevertheless: To fall in love with a woman is to fall in
love with life and with oneself. It is to overflow with hope and dread,.
to discover the only solution for ennui. Love is the only gateway out
of solitude. It is the sudden hilltop of companionship and it adds
a sense of genius to living.

A love affair may be small, but the love that launches it never is.
Whether it ends quickly or lasts forever, this love comes out of the
same deeps of one's being. One brings a full self to all beginnings.

It is the woman and the circumstances of the relationship that start deterioration. In the beginning, however doomed or feeble the mating may be, the heart rejoices like an out-of-work actor who finds himself suddenly cast as the hero in an epic. Life is suddenly endowed with dialogue. Its routines are transmuted into joy and gallantry and the sadness of too much dream.

The need to be loved remains in a man despite his accumulating cynicism and experience. The bent and weather-beaten tree will continue to offer its fruit to the touch of summer, and so will the heart.

A man's desire to hear the intimate cry of another's heart never lessens. When he hears it, something more remarkable than peace, honor and solvency appear in his life. He buds again through love. He comes into a sort of spectacular existence in another's need of him. His humanity fizzes in him because another soul desires him. Love is the magician that pulls him out of his own hat.

There are degrees and variations in this miracle—but thus love is born—always as the sweetest and most promising of human adventures close to earth's creatures and the budding of the soil.

WHO IS EVER VIRTUOUS?

I HAVE had less commerce with women than most men, even discounting their lies on the subject. This is because I married early a woman who was able to hold the attention of my various selves.

The secret of a long love affair such as I have weathered with my wife is a simple one. One of its participants must be perfect. The constancy and honor omitted in my own make-up have held me in a never failing embrace during a quarter of a century. My unchanged gaiety of heart and harum-scarum sense of security owe their existence, greatly, to this embrace.

I needed never the world to love me but only a world of one. With this achieved in this marriage, I was able to flourish without frustration, dislocation or disillusion.

Or such, at least, would have been the case had I not been born with a talent for disdaining the blessings of Providence. Why will a man who has all he wants go play beggar on a street corner? And why does a man whose wounds are healed go looking for a rain of spears in which to run? And why must a man lucky enough to have found happiness go hunting in dark byways for misery and disquiet?

Men have romantic answers for these questions. They need new adventures to refresh their hearts, glands and talents. Their personalities would stale and their wits wither did they not renew themselves with younger Venuses.

I hold no such theories. No dream of rejuvenation has ever urged me to new loves. I have found, however, that fulfillment does not remove desire, that finding a journey's end leaves untouched the impulse to travel. And that there is a hunger in a man that stays alive as long as he can find food for it. This is also true of an animal in a pasture.

What I have to write now of love is independent of the life I have lived happily beside one woman. Did I know only what that long adventure taught me I would write only of the fine facts of human fulfillment.

Fortunately, or unfortunately, I know other facts.

SAILOR—BEWARE

LOOKING into my nature, I have no wish to reform myself or tinker with my "subconscious" and persuade it to alter its patterns. My interest is that of the traveler who, on the last leg of a troublesome journey, finds rueful diversion in studying a map of the traveled territory. Such, and no more, are to me the uses of psychology; not to improve one's habits but to know oneself. Even here, care is needed. Too much knowledge of self can be as unwise as not enough, for our ability to function often depends on how much of ourself we do not know. Even our sanity may be based on this ignorance.

But a right amount of self-knowledge does many good things. It keeps us from worrying too much about what others may think of us. It adds humor to our vanities and sprinkles our spirit with humility.

The word humility makes me pause. It is a word usually missing from the manners of psychology. All other sciences contain it and are often based on it, including even the unreadable science of theology.

The psychologist, alone, writes as an All-knower. The fact that his equipment is a mirror rather than an algebra table makes his task seem easier than that of other scientific investigators. Although it is still to be recorded that a man looked at himself and saw more than a rumor.

Nevertheless, the psychologist's books are stiff with certainties and repetitions. The brightest of them seem to have no more than a dozen sentences at their command—a dilemma which makes psychology at times seem less a science than a love affair between a man and his secrets. The same self-infatuation that keeps a woman looking into her mirror for hours holds the psychologist to his task. He swoons rather than writes, and his repetitions have in them the fanaticism of a lover bewitched.

I shall try to remember this. And if by chance I am writing here the truth of what I am, I shall keep both doubt and humility on tap; and a blue pencil. If I write the truth it is only because my mind is nimble enough to glimpse a feather of it falling and not because the great eagle has come to roost on my head.

I SERENADE A VIRTUE—MY OWN

MOST OF the virtues I own can be debated—chiefly that they are inconstant and that I have been as often without them as with them. Kindness, tolerance, integrity, modesty, generosity—these are usually attitudes that events permit us. They are our holiday moods, and we are as proud of them as of fine clothes we have hung away to wear on occasions.

But there is one virtue which has been an active part of my being since I can remember. It is a lack of fear of other people's minds.

It began, possibly, in my relation to my mother. I was eager always to please her, but her opinions never affected me. I never measured myself by them.

The rest of the earth's population has made no more impression on me than did that first dear one. Since my boyhood I have sought always to please, but out of a kindness in me, never out of a fear or respect for what was in others. And I have never been afraid of what others might think or did think of me—if I failed to please.

"I REMAIN, YOUR LOVING SON"

My MOTHER, however, is responsible for a great deal of the trouble and confusion that women have brought into my life—and I into theirs. She is long dead but she still continues, like some ghost at the tiller, to run the boat she fashioned.

My mother was a woman of astonishing virtues. Not only I but her husband and nearest kin were astonished by them. She was a woman of beauty, but it was goodness and honor that were her most striking features. They stared out of her a bit fiercely and gave her a haughty air. With her firm shape and her bold blue eyes she looked, in my youth and hers, a bit more Valkyrie than Venus.

Yet she was the most childlike of women, naïve and girlishly in love with excitements such as dancing, swimming, parties at which people sang and toil of any kind. She had an infatuation with chores. The expenditure of energy was the chief meaning of life for her. I remember her as at her happiest cooking for a horde of guests, polishing the house till it shone or moving breathlessly under the lights of an amusement park.

Among my mother's more disturbing virtues was a passion for truth-telling. She was terribly vain of the fact that she "couldn't tell a lie." In fact, she was vain of all her virtues and disdainfully conscious of their absence in others. Luckily, one of her virtues was the commandment, seemingly issued by her, that people should "mind their own business." This prevented her from expanding as a moralist and a social nuisance.

It was odd that this woman, born as a peasant on a farm in southern Russia and come of a long line of humiliated Jews, should have acquired such a baggage of pride or faced a life of poverty with such a sense of security. Her fine character never faltered. She disdained sentimentality, bristled at flattery, sneered at hypocrites, and God—whom she respected—was less to her than honesty.

Such was my mother, Sarah, who without words or kisses adored me from my infancy under the misapprehension that I was fashioned in her image. She never sought to instruct or improve me. She deemed me moral and upright as herself, as a queen might deem her son to be of royal blood.

I was too devoted to her, and too fearful of her, ever to disillusion her. I never gave her even a hint of what sort of unroyal fellow I actually was. She would probably have loved me no less had she known. But that sort of gamble was beyond me in the boyhood days when I fashioned myself into a liar for her sake.

"A CHILD IS CRYING"—FOR MAMA

I GREW UP with a need to keep my mother's qualities alive in my world. Unfortunately, this need extended to finding these qualities in any woman who touched my fancy. Here a world of troubles beset me, for I was full of a foolish talent for imagining my mother's virtues existed in women who, until my advent, had been getting along happily without them.

Haunted by the ideal of my mother, I never waited for her actual counterpart to hoist sail in my presence. Instead, the moment a woman looked at me tenderly I imagined her, forthwith, to be the spiritual twin of my mother.

And when I learned I was in error I committed a more inexcusable second error of not retiring in good order. Rather I gave myself to a mission. I set out fanatically to induce in my paramour my mother's qualities of truth, honor, and incorruptible decency.

How curiously they looked at me—those girls who, expecting Casanova, found Savonarola in their arms! And how patiently they listened to my insistence on virtues in them which I made no pretense of having in myself; and on a fidelity and devotion which must have sounded oddly unreasonable coming from a man who was not only married but never out of love with his wife.

I asked for more than my mother's virtues in these bewildered ladies. I asked, too, for her manners.

My mother had prided herself on her unpossessive attitude toward me and her respect for my independence. She had asked neither obedience nor loyalty as proofs of devotion. Even my presence was unnecessary to her serenity and strong spirit. When I was away from her (later) she demanded neither letters nor telephone calls. Nothing I did or did not do depressed her with a sense of being unwanted or outgrown.

Whenever we were, happily, under the same roof, the house became animated for me. My ennui vanished, watching her ever-busy hands. She buzzed like a beehive and never seemed dependent on me in any matter. I quarreled with her over card games, laughed at her naïvetés and her angers. I teased her and called her names that made her turn purple with rage—hypocrite, miser, liar, cheat and buttinski (all the things she was not). Her bristling retorts kept me laughing for hours, until she too would join me in outbursts of gaiety.

But the interest we found in each other's company was only a small part of our relationship. From the time I was nineteen, we grew away from each other. We parted, lived at times at different ends of the continent, seemingly without awareness of each other. Yet she was always the most important person in the world to me, as I was to her. The thing that held us together was the knowledge in both of us that she guided me. However exotic and away from her my activities became, we both knew that in some inexplicable way all I did was related to her.

Such was my happiness with my mother. In my illicit love affairs I looked for a similar delight. In them I kept alive a concept of love I had fetched unchanged out of my boyhood. This was to be loved a bit madly and to owe no allegiance to one's love, to be admired above all other humans and remain indifferent to such admiration, to be the core of the loved one's existence and she never more than a generality in one's own life; to possess and never be possessed.

I recognize now this fretful and lopsided credo for what it is. Just so does the child demand and ignore its mother, demand her inviolable fidelity and dream constantly of its own independence.

I have a childhood photo of me, with my arms clasped smugly about my pretty mother's neck, that seems to express all these things.

And yet the grown-up enlargement of this charming picture is not so simple as that.

IN SEARCH OF THE "UNKNOWABLE"

MY ADVENTURES with women have their root in my relation to my mother—but to a different mother than I have put tenderly into words: to an Enigma Mother. The truth about my mother and me is that I loved her, but that there was no knowledgeable person for me to love.

My mother was full of such observable virtues as I have described. But these qualities did not create a character for me. They seemed, rather, to hide one. Throughout her life my mother was as mysterious to me as a creature from Mars. She was an enigma I loved and could never know.

Most enigmatic was the mask of virtue she wore. I looked vainly for the human face behind that mask, for a creature like myself, astir with lust and deceit. The mask remained impenetrable. I believed in it, as I always must. Yet my first awareness of people told me there was no such person possible as my mother seemed. For one thing, a virgin could not have two sons, nor sleep nightly with a devoted husband, nor walk with such pride of figure. Nor could a woman who had worked with her hands since childhood be that void of greed and envy.

Although I saw my mother as perfect, I could not believe in perfection. Her virtues were natural to her, but belief in virtue was unnatural to me. So might a duckling look on its hen mother under whose wing it had been accidentally hatched—and become haunted with the difference between them. In its soul such a duckling would insist on the mother being a duck and not a hen. It would grow up with an unsolved problem—how to make them both ducks so they could swim together.

ETIOLOGY OF AN IDOL SMASHER

THERE was no possibility of my removing my mother's mask, but removing masks in general became an intellectual passion with me. My first literary works were of this nature. I disbelieved with a violence that made me seem an embittered philosopher long before I had become even a man of intelligence.

I sought to remove the mask from the world, to look behind it, to disprove loudly the virtues it proclaimed. Obviously no philosopher but a thwarted young Oedipus was at work. My earliest writings were full of an excited contempt for all moralists. I dedicated myself to attacking prudes, piety-mongers and all apostles of virtue.

I did not confine my attack to literary assaults but supplemented them by looking for the virtue mask on a particular human face—a woman's face. Having found it or, more usually, imagined it there, I proceeded to remove it and stare my fill at all that lay behind it.

An unfriendly onlooker might say that I pursued women with the purpose of destroying them. My objective seemed to be the noisy and fatiguing business of disproving the virtues behind the new mask that said "I love you" to me. There was a double victory involved. I proved first that the unthinking girl who said she loved me was unfit to take my mother's place. Secondly, in unmasking the girl I unmasked my mother. I satisfied myself fleetingly that my mother's virtues were a fraud and had never existed. And thus, in my soul, removed for a painful hour the barrier between us.

VENUS ON A RACK

I HAVE APPEALED to a number of women by my mother-haunted misconception of them. My eagerness to believe that a woman who loved me (or seemed to) was a rare vessel of truth and honor usually exercised a potent magic over her. For women are nearly always eager to pretend they are as they first dreamed of being, before experience slapped their ideals out of shape and men robbed them of their virtues.

Given an admirer bent on misconceiving them as creatures of virtue and honor, and on demanding of them these defunct qualities, they will fall weirdly to work on themselves. Thus the qualities I desired in a woman who sighed at me always came to bloom, not as gardens springing from the earth but as flowers produced, seance fashion, out of the air.

A great deal of clamor goes into such reclamation projects. Apparently before a woman could become what I wanted her to be (or, rather, fail to become that), she had to yield her entire case history into my hands. For I have never had the more amiable talent of half knowing a woman, of accepting a few obvious moods as her spiritual meaning and a half dozen anecdotes as her identity. I have envied other men's gifts for enjoying women as adventures that called for nothing more than some sexual prowess and good manners. Their stories of high times experienced without psychological mayhem have made me sigh and wish for another soul in my body. To love a woman without first having to drag her through the keyholes of one's subconscious, to be content with the amount of love she has to give and not sit keening for volcanoes to erupt; and to have no need to destroy one's pleasures—these are recipes for amour I could never follow.

To such as myself—for there must certainly be more than my own dizzied noggin in the category—the fact that a woman says she loves him ceases to mean anything after a week or so. He becomes, then, full of curiosity concerning how much of her loves him, how deep her love goes in her life, and what else does she love.

This involves a type of exploration for which the mind has almost no talent. Short of telepathy there is no way of entering, sure-footedly, the existence of another. The battering ram and the torture rack are only makeshift substitutes. But they have to suffice.

HEAD DOWN, HEELS UP, IN A STORM

I HAVE WRITTEN somewhat facetiously of a thing which in life has no hint of facetiousness about it. However whimsical a discussion any love affair may make, it is as humorless as a lynching bee in the making. And even in its beginning there is always the overtone of the ending—the promise of betrayal and good-by.

I wrote in my youth, "There is a cry that rises from all endings."

I have heard this cry often and sat with its mournful echo in my heart. And while it lasts there is nothing as painful in the world. It is a sound that drains life out of the day. The air darkens. Not only yesterday but tomorrow lies dead. This time of ending is not an event ever to be disparaged. I do not disparage it now; I suspect only its permanence. Such healthy suspicions, however, are no part of the headlong panic of the lover, involved in an amour that must end. Even in the midst of love he tampers with constant woe.

He loves through apprehension. He can never enjoy what he has but must live with the expectation of its destruction. This is due to many psychic factors, and one realistic one—the man's false posi-

tion in a love affair—since most such love affairs happen to men
after they are married.

I have known some fifty husbands well enough to know somewhat
of their love life. Of the fifty, not one was faithful to his wife. A few
of these errant mates were given merely to casual infidelities and
looked upon their extramarital bed companions as no better than
whores to be paid and forgotten. But most of the husbands I have
known indulged in no such easy diversions. They went in for en-
tanglements. Of these latter, count me one.

The husband thus entangled operates out of a false mood which
he does his best to keep out of the picture. He makes love as if the
relationship were a permanent one—and he permanent in it. He
knows his own impermanence but behaves as if it did not exist. He
will work away on his love affair until it reaches the point of "leave
your wife and come with me." In fact, this unreasonable demand is
usually his objective. If it is the sort of affair that is not heading
toward such a denouement it is too minor, too unsatisfactory, to
interest him. He will discard it with a confused sense of having
wasted his time.

As a "leave your wife" affair, it has the stimulation of importance.
It also gives him the illusion of being loved wildly and hopelessly—
and unreasonably. Knowing he will not leave his wife, the man brings
to his beyond-the-home-fires amour the knowledge of its doom. He
knows the time of "choice" will come. And he knows he will choose
his wife.

The other loved one will then vanish. He lives with this vanishing
in his mind.

He watches for evidences of her love waning or turning elsewhere.
He pounces on these evidences and battles them avidly. While she
is his she must be wholly his, a woman dedicated to him. He cannot
afford to give her the leeway of a wife or a permanent companion.

He must fill their brief time with a concentration of devotion, as
if to make up for the years of non-love and no relationship that
wait around the corner.

And during this moody business, self-knowledge is of no use to
him. He may know the subconscious pattern that operates him. He
may know all about masks and his need to remove them. And he may
even know the basic lie of his love affair—that it is not to his wife
he is unfaithful but to his paramour, that it is on her dreams he

has placed doom. But such knowledge will not ease his day. His subconscious may be doing the operating, but it operates a man. He has the skin, hair, teeth and heart of a lover and not a Case History. And his battle cry of Love Me Forever is wrenched out of the only heart he has.

But I would be writing like a moralist and liar if I let the picture stand thus—full of woe, idiocy, torture and shame. There is a totally other look to this same picture. It all depends on who looks at it—and when it is looked at.

Love is in many ways at its best when it is born doomed. Passion without the future of home and fidelity plucks the roses a little more desperately while it may. Its sky is full of fiddles and its days leap about like a ballet dancer. Its impermanence gives it not only an extra life but an extra dimension. In such a love, one postures, invents, acts, and thus the dimension of art is added to kisses. It is a muddle head and a liar who kisses, but also an artist. He creates for himself and sometimes for his bewildered lover a beauty beyond truth and reality.

AN OPEN LETTER TO SOME LOST LENORES

It is difficult to evoke a vanished love affair. A little pain stands guard at the gate of memory and speaks, "Keep Out."

It being evening and I being alone, I walk by this woeful sentinel for a look at the place he guards. I look—and there is nothing to see. What is he guarding? Is this vacant place in the soul—The Love Affair? It is empty and silent as a wasteland. No cries of passion echo in it. No sound of long-ago sobbing is to be heard. Yet the woeful sentinel repeats his warning, "Keep Out."

But this is my ghostland to roam in as I will. I speak to its emptiness with magic words—"I knew you who lived there. I knew your every secret. I lived on your graces. I breathed with your soul and you fed me. I speak again. Sting me with your kisses. Let me burn against your skin. I am back beside you. I repeat my vows to you. 'Nothing will ever be as wonderful as this hour. It will leave a light forever!' "

A room appears. It has curtains. There is a bed in it. A lamp shines in its corner. The magic words have produced some scenery. I inspect the premises and wait. There were once people in this room—two people. I repeat the words of the past to the empty room—"Till I die, I'll love you till I die. There will never be anyone beyond you. Here is Forever."

A woman appears in the bed. But there is a mistake. This is not the one who wept with love, whose face was a fairyland, whose body was a bed of coals on which I burned alive. This one lies on the bed and smiles mockingly at me. "I'm not yours any more. I belong elsewhere. I went away. What do you want of me?"

I answer, "I want to see you again as you were when you loved me."

She shakes her head. Her smile remains mocking. I plead.

"I know it ended. I know what happened after we left each other. We went into other arms and other worlds. Our forever vanished. But so will everything else in my life. Don't mock me because our love is dead and we are both alive. I come back to a shrine. Let me see you again."

The stars return to her face. Her arms curve toward me. This is the one—the rapture-smitten mouth. These are the eyes that adored me. How tender the throat was! How sweetly the breasts glowed—like the lanterns of a bacchanal! And how intimate her touch was, as if her hands were part of a dream in my head; and all her existence was a pulse that beat inside of me. Her words come from the ghostland—"I am yours. Hold me."

But the arms that curve upward remain empty. There is only one in the bed. Where is the other?

Ah, bed that will not hold me again, bed behind the wall of time—wait for me. Someday I will come back to all my unrealities. In that moment when I am dying, in that last little corner of my life when death reaches to close my eyes, I will love again. I will love again with a hundred hearts and bring all my forevers back to their vanished beds. All that I ever loved will become equally real. There will be no truth or untruth. My last breath and my last thought will give thanks equally to all that has been—to all who loved me—to all the forevers that died before me.

FOOTNOTES ON WISDOM AND FOLLY

As A CHILD of my century I have learned a number of things. They are not necessarily things I am or qualities I own. They are my tastes.

I have learned—

That a wise man remains himself, however foolish his fate.

That a wise man does not judge himself or others by things that happen. He knows that most evil is an accident and that calamities are as impersonal as the feet that step on ants. (I do not speak of the calamities that are always with us and that are actually our character.)

That a wise man does not judge the hour but the year. He mistrusts his anger and knows it for a bruise that will be healed. He knows that when it has healed it belongs to memory, not judgment.

That a wise man knows he has only one enemy—himself. This is an enemy difficult to ignore and full of a cunning lacking in the enemies outside. It assails one with doubts, fears and disgusts. It always seeks to lessen, and leads one away from one's goals. It is an enemy never to be vanquished but constantly outwitted.

That a wise man never measures anything by what he feels for it. A woman is not as wonderful as his love, a dollar is not as big as his need for it.

That foolish people look for importance in their friends. The smaller a man is, the happier he is when he sits beside superiors of any sort—even those who may despise him. It is a happiness that never lasts. A beggar, however well treated, ends up full of misery and curses.

That a wise man will not trust too much those who admire him, even for his wisdom. He knows that an admirer is never truly satisfied until he can substitute pity for his admiration and disdain for his applause. Our admirers are always on the lookout for evidences of our collapse. They find a solace in the fact that our superiority was transitory and that we end as they do—old and useless.

That a wise man will always allow a fool to rob him of ideas without yelling, "Thief." If he is wise he has not been impoverished. Nor has the fool been enriched. The thief flatters us by stealing. We flatter him by complaining.

That a wise man, asked how many women have loved him, will divide his conquests by ten, subtract half from the remainder, erase the result and answer, "Only the woman who still loves me, which makes one."

That a wise man cannot evade pain or rage, but when they come to him he treats them as visitors and not as permanent relatives. A man who suffers too long or remains too long angry is not at grips with any enemy, but coddling a disease.

That a wise man will not try to pretend he is improving with age. He knows that the years diminish him, that time rots his body, cools his blood, darkens his brain and, like a furtive embalmer, prepares him for his winding sheet.

That a wise man is never impressed by other "wise men." I noticed early that pompous people have actually less a high opinion of themselves than a desire to create such an opinion in others.

Overproud people are also wasted on me, as are faces with granite expressions. I know that excessive pride is a sort of paste that holds an inner rubbish in place. It is also a bid for applause that people make who have done nothing.

Fools who specialize in deep silences also fail to disturb me with their grimness or their pauses. I find the pantomimes of stupidity no more impressive than its oralizings.

I know a man is hollow who play-acts importance, graceless when he tries to make me feel ill at ease, and a fool if he tries to impress me rather than interest me.

I know that a man who struts in my presence hopes to find in my eyes an importance missing in his own.

People who glow with success I have found among the most charming of humans. But those seemingly successful ones who try to bulldoze applause out of me, I know for impostors. They have not found success but are still looking for it.

The same is true of piety or of happiness or of wisdom. Their true possessors do not need me as an audience.

I know that a man who tries to convert me to any cause is actually at work on his own conversion, unless he is looking for funds under the mask of some fancied nobility.

I know that a man who shows me his wealth is like the beggar who shows me his poverty; they are both looking for alms from me, the rich man for the alms of my envy, the poor one for the alms of my guilt.

And last: That a wise man saves his good manners for disaster. A fool practices them when they are useless.

Such are some of my tastes. I have not always been guided by them, but they have been with me even when I have lain beside Jonah at the bottom of the sea.

MY INVISIBLE FLAG

The results of my "wisdom" have been mostly negative. I have failed to acquire a large group of friends, or any noticeable contingents of admirers. I am aware here and there of some fellow eccentrics who are pleased by my work or personality. Mainly, I am confronted by numerous and sharp-spoken people (professional critics among them) who, mysteriously, do not admire me. They have filled my ears and eyes for over thirty years with reproaches and disdains, and I have remained for that time without response to their opinions of me.

It is not because I value what I am so highly that I have been indifferent to others' appraisals. But I can imagine no achievement or praise that could alter the ennui in which I exist, or add the smallest permanent dimension to my life. I have had both success and failure. They were like meals, digested and forgotten.

My imperviousness to the judgment of others is my sole virtue, however (perhaps my sole wisdom), and one on which it pleases me to linger. It is a small valor but, to me, a vital one. It is the only self-pleasure I can rely on in my solitude—the knowledge that my thoughts and my behavior have, in however minor a degree, proved the existence in me of this sort of fortitude.

Although I have no more than tasted of it, I know that valor is the most voluptuous of sensations a human being can experience. It is as deep a satisfaction as a woman or a God can contribute to the soul.

Valor, unsung by others, still sings itself to its possessor. It is the memory of secret victories, of pains felt without flinching, of faiths kept in silence and losses never mentioned that gives the valorous man that fitness for life which the cowardly and the nerve-racked never can understand.

The secret heroisms with which the human soul confronts the dreary attack of living enable us to live in triumphant peace with boredom as well as with vicissitude. Valor is the only form of self-love that helps a man and does not weaken him for existence. It teaches him how to recover from illness, defeat or despair; for valor dictates that however much of a man may die, the part of him which survives must remain always healthy and untouched.

Of physical valor I know less than of this other kind, and think less of it. Misadventures have brought me several times close to death. (And what misadventure is there more ominous than age?) At such times the prospect of dying aroused neither protest nor terror in me. This is a small boast and one which more than half the world can make as truthfully.

If a man has enough sanity for living, he has no great aversion to dying. A sane soul is always packed and ready to go—in fact, sometimes a bit too ready.

The Roman, Marcellinus, being ill, asked of a Stoic if he should permit himself to die. The Stoic answered, "Not only evil and calamities but the mere satiety of living should make a man wish to die."

I am certain Marcellinus himself died full of resignation and content, as do most of us without the aid of such fine precepts. Despite the hysterics that surround the bedrooms of literature, we sane ones depart usually like grateful guests from a house in which we have been well, if confusingly, entertained.

I have known, however, people of great physical valor who have not had enough intellectual courage to cross a street against a traffic light. Taboos paralyze them where physical danger leaves them unmoved. Conventions or the expectations of the crowd mind bring them to their knees. They are unable to think except in homage to other thoughts.   .

I have come now to an end of my mental introduction. It was my intention to sketch my mind for the reader before giving outline to my person and experiences. I consider the sketch not done but indicated. I shall fill it in as I go along. For, as has been written, there is only one plot—the human mind. It is a plot without denouement, for it is endless.

FAMILY FACES

My mother, Sarah.

My father, Joseph.

My mother's parents, Mr. and Mrs. Swernofsky.

My Tante Chasha.

My Tante Chasha's nervous husband, Uncle Harris.

My Uncle Joe on his way to work.

My Uncle Issy, before he became a
millionaire.

My Aunt Millie.

My mother and her two devoted sons, Pete and I.

My brother Pete in half patent leather shoes.

The author featuring his Racine high school senior-class pin, inscribed with class motto (in Latin): "By perseverance."

CHICAGO FACES

Rose Caylor as "Bub McNair" in a drama of the backwoods, *Dawn of the Mountain.*

The author covering a news story for the Chicago *Journal* in 1911. An event he is unable to remember.

The author's only picture as a busy Foreign Correspondent in Berlin, 1919. The other enfevered journalist is Richard Little of the Chicago *Tribune.*

My guide and mentor, Sherman Reilly Duffy.

A 1919 Chicago journalist resting from his labors.

Sherman Duffy and his leading disciple, Bennie Hecht, in 1913.

My cynical compañero, Wallace Smith.

My fellow brothel-dweller, E. H. (Ned) Griffith.

Richard J. Finnegan, when he won his spurs on the Chicago *Journal*.

Kaiden Kazanjian

Our Sindbad of booksellers, Adolph Kroch.

J. P. McEvoy, the first literary man I knew who wasn't a financial idiot.

George Wharton, "Dour and witty/ He kept a whole city/ Roaring with laughter."

I am surprised to see he wore glasses, but this was Christian Dane Hagerty, D'Artagnan of the A.P.

My first managing editor, the gallant Martin J. Hutchens of the Chicago Journal.

Marie Armstrong Hecht.

Margaret Anderson. First there was Mrs.
O'Leary's cow, then there was Margaret.

Victor Georg

Sherwood Anderson and the author
drawing a bead on Chicago's Literary Renaissance—1916.

Sherwood Anderson. "Swatty," our
entry for Balzac.

Stanislaus Szukalski.
"I put Rodin in one pocket,
Michelangelo in another,
And I walk toward the sun."

Maxwell Bodenheim, who used to sing—
Down our river banks with spring.

Jannelise Rosse

Herman Rosse, who helped me love Chicago's
warehouses, bridges and clouds.

Carl Sandburg, our Orpheus.

Eugene Hutchinson

The Chicago *Daily News*—before the hammers turned it to dust. The empty Local Room shades on the fourth floor are down, and the building itself, waiting its doom, has shrunk to a third of the size it was when I worked in it. *(left)*

Henry Justin Smith. Such reporters as get to heaven are given a desk in Editor Smith's Local Room. *(below)*

Lloyd Lewis and Henry Smith, surveying a beloved Chicago—to which they alone of all our literary tribe remained true. "This rock shall fly/From its firm base as soon ere I.'

Ashton Stevens, our drama critic who smiled when he called you a son of a bitch.

My City Editor on the *News*, "Nix-crackin Beit," Brooks Beitler.

Pascal Covici, in whose Washington Street Book Store and Publishing House we were all geniuses.

Vincent Starrett, our Local Room
sonneteer.

Burton Rascoe, whose snickersnee
flashed on our battlements.

Henry Blackman Sell. He invented
our Book Page.

Our critic, Harry Hansen, who read
books like a miser counting nickels
and loved them almost as much.

Leo Dietrichstein, who starred in my first play, but blasted my career as an actor. (Somebody did.)

Keith Preston. Martial, the Roman, loaned him a silver bow and arrow.

Charles Collins, in the days when I loved all critics.

MY EMPIRE OF THE FIVE HILLS

MY BOYHOOD was centered around five locales in the Wisconsin town of Racine—the basement of my mother's store, the great lake in front of my window, the gable-windowed bedroom where I slept, the barn behind our house and my neighborhood's tree-shadowed streets after dark. I shall write of these all, for in them are the original treasures of my existence. I have added but little to them. In fact, I doubt whether they all remain.

I have less talent for coping with my disintegration than most men, for I am too related, still, to my beginnings. They are a yesterday that refuses to recede, and scorns burial. I do not grow used to my infirmities, my lessening hair and teeth, my diminishing vigors. Things which would have wrenched cries of anguish from my youthful self—still wrench them from me.

As I look upon the five hills of my youth I know, indignantly, that I shall never run up to their tops again. This indignation is my last fidelity to youth. When I come to die, I know I shall be less disturbed by that final demise than I was by the many funerals of my selves which preceded it.

In many of my present days, the eagerness for life—so wild in

37

my boyhood—disappears entirely. At those times no disillusion or pain saddens or disturbs me. I find myself, rather, without the wings of self, and lie against the earth like those crippled sea birds I watch on the sand who have been blown down out of the sky.

These desireless times that come to me are like an erasure of identity. When they come, the day has no meaning or shape and the future seems as dim and dead as the past.

Sitting on this roost of amnesia, I try to remember the trick of living. I try to recall what it was made me able to feel close to things and eager to move from day to day. And I discover (anew) that it was never ambition or the hope of pleasure. It was the tune in me and the certainty that my mind was crowded with life. In my head was a rabble of companions ready always to roister on the hilltops.

The companions are still there—when the fogs of age lift, and youth, like a sun traveling backward, throws its sudden light into my mind. In this light I can perceive that I have not altered. I still love what I loved and I still value what I valued. If the roistering on the hilltops is less, my soul is still there. It follows along like those bards of the Huns who, in love with battle but too weak to swing the barbarian sword, remained in the fray and walked beside their chieftains singing of their glories.

CONCERNING CHIEFLY THE LIFTING
OF A DRESS

THE BEGINNINGS OF SEX, like the beginnings of everything else, are always the best. There are no adolescent masterpieces on the subject to prove this, or even to remind us of the truth. The writing about sex is done by citizens of maturity. These will sometimes write of early love, but, when they do, it is chiefly with a fatherly humor, or worse—with the bugged-out eye of the scientist.

As for most of us, we keep ourselves intact by dismissing contemptuously our outgrown selves. If we have minted the fine ore of our boyhood into a few scurvy coins, these become the coins of our realm. We live by these and gauge our riches and importance by them.

Such is the propaganda of maturity that the very words "puberty" and "adolescence" bring to our mind a farce of pimples and confu-

sions. Not awe and rapture, not the bursting of a dike and the over-
flooding of our senses.

There have been numerous improvements in my sexual pleasures
during the many years. Love, drama, aesthetics have been added to
them—and bedrooms. And yet would I not often have sacrificed
willingly all such improvements for the original and untutored embraces of my boyhood?

These occurred usually in the besooted basement of my mother's
store, where she fancied me honestly engaged as a furnace tender.
My mother's store was on Main Street and offered hats and outer
garments to the ladies of Racine. It employed four women clerks
whose thirst led them at intervals down the dark basement steps
to the only water faucet in the store. I waited at this water hole.

Sex in boyhood is distinguished by a marvelous silence. I would
as soon have thought of whistling in a cathedral as of speaking to a
woman I was embracing—or trying to embrace. The jabbering
comes in later years. There is no time or room or breath for such
footling things as words in the beginning.

It was not fear or stealth that kept me silent. It was that there were
no words in me then to express the wonders of the quarry that came
to my water hole. Although I have grown more proficient in expression, I doubt whether my present words can do much better.

The beginnings of sex are deeper than a mere introduction to
sensations. In these beginnings all the thrill of earth's novelty that
has been assailing us from the first days of our toddling comes to its
magical climax. The full orchestra plays; all its strings, brasses and
timpani sound. It never plays again, not in that fashion.

I do not remember distinctly the belles of my first sex adventures. Their faces and names are vague. As for character, they never
had any beyond the staggering fact that they were female. They
float in my memory like distant banners of lingerie, corset covers
and mystic garters. Sluts and second-maids and school trollops
though they likely were, no Sultan's brides could seem dreamier to
recall.

What I remember of them chiefly is their sharp mystery and the
unbelievableness of a breast in my hand, and the sight of a white
thigh above a stocking top smiting me like a lightning flash. I remember that the breath of another human against my mouth was
as bewildering as being born, and that a yielding belly set me

adrift in Arcady. Lust was not a means of expression but a voyage, a Flying Carpet voyage of discovery. It was not sex but Woman I discovered. It was another soul in myself that seemed to have its hiding places under the dresses and inside the blouses of these softer people.

There was no satiety. Sensation was not the goal of my embraces. Sensation departed, leaving me with undiminished enthusiasm for the feast. The hunger stayed in my eyes, hands, nose and ears. I wrote once:

> *Young, startled, timid and obscene*
> *In my first masculine endeavor*
> *I could have, froglike, lain between*
> *That little peasant's thighs forever.*

I have a theory about this beginning of sex. In our first contact with the female we discover the ghost of our own lost femaleness, lost perhaps in our biologic past. And we turn dizzily and briefly into hermaphrodites. This may or may not be the fact of the case, but it has in it the quality of the boyhood sex I remember. In those embraces, my own familiar body seemed of minor importance, and what was happening to it of secondary consequence. The woman and all her slightest movements, tremors and sighs was the star of my duets. I was more she than myself. Completion was what I found in another.

My identification with the female has always been present in me. *She* sang the melody of passion and *her* heart and thought, inflamed with need for me, were what I called love. When that need bloomed, I was happy. When it waned, I sickened. When it vanished, I felt cast out. And it was always not a woman I lost, but myself. I grew small and empty as if my identity had lessened. I became an orphan again.

I have written of my pursuit of a maternal enigma in other women. What I write now is no contradiction of that part of me. There are other parts, and no man's relation to women or to the world is dictated by any single part of him, unless he is an out-and-out lunatic. The sane man is balanced as is the earth—in the midst of a hundred catastrophic pulls, each one enough to wreck it. Combined, they form a mystic unity and hold it lawfully in place.

CONCERNING ANOTHER SORT OF WISTFUL MALE

I HAVE had some friends whose love of woman was not mere identification but a psychic somersault into femininity. They did not find the missing female in the female but in themselves.

Such a lover becomes more and more feminized as his "love" deepens. He adores his inamorata's contours and sex characteristics because he actually wears them like an invisible skin over his maleness. He is fascinated by all her activities. He directs them. He finds the right hairdresser for her, the right clothes for her to wear, the right handbag to carry, the correct shoes, gloves, etc. The smallest of her needs obsesses him. He adorns her and manipulates her.

In order to do all these things he has to select a woman practically mindless or, at least, one much inferior to himself. It is difficult to enslave th᷑ tastes of an intelligent woman.

Having burdened himself with the sort of weak and moody personality that will not resist his more clever intellect, the lover-who-would-be-a-woman achieves his final triumph by tossing his own intelligence overboard and thinking with the mind of his paramour. He adopts her point of view toward himself as a man, shares with her her contempt of his "sins," his lies and duplicities. He never sees into her "crimes," but like a trembling criminal stands perpetually before the bar of her "justice."

He understands why he has "offended" her. He whips his male self with her derisions and accepts himself as a creature full of spiritual deficiencies. His "guilts" keep him tossing and desperate. But there remains a secret triumph in him. He is thinking like a woman, and however inferior or preposterous her thinking may be, it is a woman's—and as mystically pleasing to him as the handbag he vicariously carries and the breasts he vicariously flaunts.

Of this sort of identification I have been innocent. I have been happy to leave my femaleness to the woman and enjoy its existence in her.

TALE OF THE YOUNG CALIPH'S TRAUMA

BETWEEN THE AGES of eleven and sixteen I kept a diary, chiefly of my amorous adventures. The tale I have to tell is in this manuscript, which I still own, but which has never been of any use to me as a source of material. For I wrote this diary in code, inventing a series of scrambled words and algebraic signs to record the more interesting of my adolescent activities. By this ruse I sought to outwit my mother, who was a great hand at house cleaning. Short of burying an object, there was no way to keep it out of her ever-busy hands. I succeeded in outwitting myself as well, for I have lost the key to my code. In fact, I doubt if one ever existed.

The mysterious and unreadable entries in my diary stare at me today with a double secret, the secret of what they mean and the secret of my faith in my boyhood self. I obviously improvised the code from day to day, certain in the knowledge that I would never change and that my mind would always know exactly what I had done with "3 B Mzo" and what "awning with glass onimus X" connoted. Who could imagine in those golden times that I would ever commit the bitter folly of forgetting them!

Mrs. Anderson was one of the drinkers for whom I waited at my water hole. She was a plump and happy matron, recently married to a traveling salesman, and my mother's most important saleslady.

Mrs. Anderson endured my wooing around the water faucet while she slaked her thirst in a manner that all but frightened me off. She laughed. Fearful that her laughter, which rose like a happy fountain the moment I laid hand on her, would attract the ear of my mother and bring her down on us like a regiment from above, I stood mumbling desperately to her to be silent. My mumbling only increased her laughter.

In the third month of my siege, Mrs. Anderson finished drinking out of the tin cup one afternoon, hung it back carefully on its nail— and failed to laugh. Instead she spoke to me quietly with words that left me stunned. Mrs. Anderson suggested that I call on her at home that evening, and gave me careful instructions.

I was to arrive outside her door with a large suit box under my arm, as if I were delivering a purchase to a customer. I was to ring the bell. When Mrs. Anderson appeared I was to look at her without recognition and ask if Mrs. Jones lived there.

If her husband, Mr. Anderson, the traveling salesman, was home, my dream of delight would answer that there was no Mrs. Jones at this address. But if this blurry but vital personage, the husband, was still on his travels, Mrs. Anderson would answer by taking me into her arms.

With this Boccaccian plot arranged, Mrs. Anderson flitted back up the stairs to her duties. I was left with my ears ringing, and unable to swallow. A rendezvous in a bedroom—with no furnace gases or coal dust! And a bed—undreamed of arena for sex!

I arrived upstairs pale and intense. I stole one of the cardboard boxes used for the wrapping of major purchases such as suits or coats and made off with it on my bicycle. I hurried into the barn back of our house. Here I carefully filled this box with two bricks, several paint rags, a few wooden sticks and a large discarded sponge that had been used to swab down horses. I felt that the box should weigh what it would did it contain an actual suit. The rags and sponge were added to keep its contents from rattling around in an unsuit-like fashion.

At seven o'clock of a warm summer evening I set off, being due at the gates of Paradise at eight. Mrs. Anderson's house under normal impetus was forty-five minutes away, but I allowed fifteen minutes for a puncture. It may be the fault of memory or the speed with which I traveled, but I recall none of the scenery of that ride. The moon lit up the world. The pavements were dark with tree shadows. There was wonder in the night.

Clutching my weighted box, I arrived dripping and exhausted forty minutes too soon. I marked time on a near-by lawn, flattened under a lilac bush and getting my wind back; and my eyes glued to the dial of a gold-cased watch for which I had given thanks to my parents at my Bar mitzvah a year ago.

At seven fifty-seven I sprang from the earth, the weighted cloak and suit box under my arm. On the dot of eight I rang the Anderson doorbell.

A radiant Mrs. Anderson appeared. She was encased in a voluptuous kimono, and an odor not of this world attended her. I stood sniffing, mute and awed. Mrs. Anderson finally asked me in an irritated voice what I wanted. I inquired hungrily if a Mrs. Jones lived at this address. Mrs. Anderson answered curtly there was no such party residing there and slammed the door on me.

I returned to my bicycle under the lilac bush, half unconscious with grief. It was obvious (although I could not yet believe it) that Mr. Anderson had come home from his travels and that the voluptuous kimono and the odors of Araby that rose from it were for him and not for me. I lay a long time under the bush, chewing up handfuls of lilac leaves and staring at the curtained windows of the festive-looking Anderson house.

I rode back to my home and, although a good bicycle rider, I had an accident. Coasting down a hill, I hit a six-inch railroad track and went over the handle bars. I landed on my forehead and acquired an enormous bump. But I was too preoccupied for pain. I picked up the loaded suit box and resumed my pedaling homeward.

My mother was entertaining friends. Seeing me with a bump like a miner's lamp protruding over my brow, she demanded to know what had happened. I answered honestly that I had fallen off my bicycle. My mother then spied the cardboard suit box to which I was still clinging. She asked what I was doing with it, and before I could quit her presence she had pounced upon it.

She opened the box with a grimness in her lovely face, for it seemed obvious to her she had caught me in some mysterious theft from the store. There was a silence in the room, as in a great court scene, as the contents of the box emerged—the bricks, paint rags, old sticks and tattered sponge.

Invention failed me. I was unable to explain the presence or meaning of these objects. I recall a room full of laughing people, my mother's relieved but perplexed face. And the moral of my tale is that for the more than forty years since that night I have never held a rendezvous with a married woman.

THE FIRST LIGHT ON A HILLTOP

IN THOSE boyhood years of anonymous passion, of thunderclap rendezvous, of females worshiped for an hour and forgotten immediately forever; of leaping over dark back-yard fences in wild flights from parental wraths (parents seemed always to return from Wednesday evening prayer meeting or visits to the Bijou Theater hours before they were logically due); in those days of first adventures which seem to me to have been lived in the time of Cellini and the Medici, so full were they of scurrying and conspiracy, I made another debut. I fell in love.

Our first love is often our first and only adventure in idealism. If there is anything noble in a man's love history it is this trip to fairyland he makes in his half-articulate youth.

In the midst of those years when the female body was a new world dawning, I experienced a sudden and overwhelming emotion for a woman as bodyless as a sunbeam. She was of my age, gentle-faced, happy-spoken, and with the stare of childhood lingering in her wide eyes. She was womanly to look at, but I saw no woman when I looked at her. Her body consisted only of her finger tips and a smile.

During the time of my love, which lasted a year, we were constantly together, for we shared the same house. We were alone in the dark for hours. But in her presence, or dreaming of her, the thought of sex remained as alien as the thought of murder. She had no flesh to explore. She was without legs and breasts for me, and without the promise of pleasure. There was a deeper mystery about her than in all the eroticism I had discovered.

What this mystery was I have since found out, or at least found words with which to discuss it. But in that day it was as inscrutable as the star-pitted summer skies, to which it seemed oddly related.

We walked in the leafy-shadowed streets together at night and stopped, where the shadows grew deeper, as if jointly lassoed. We spoke little and embraced not at all. We sometimes grew too faint to move, and sat together on veranda steps and looked at the night sky flying away over our heads.

We played cribbage on a lapboard between us, and our kneecaps touching made the game almost impossible. We went on sleigh rides in large wagon sleighs filled with hay and singing classmates, but we seldom sang. We lay on our backs, our arms touching, and watched the dark spaces waving above us, and our hearts felt the pull of the moon and stars as if a tide were rising in us.

My chief memory of all this is its pain and sexlessness. It was a love that desired nothing but itself. And yet another was necessary to it. It was a love that never brought us together. Yet when we were absent from each other I had a sense of amputation. Although I owned nothing of her, my heart thumped with unbearable loss when I saw her looking at another face than mine. Her voice speaking to some other boy seemed to be reading my death warrant.

I recall that this was also a time of great fears. All the childhood shudders I had known returned again. I was afraid to look into mirrors when alone. I was frightened of empty rooms and of darkness. The electric light in my attic bedroom was a weak one and failed to drive the shadows out of its corners. I rigged up a system of cords and pulleys which enabled me, while I lay in my bed, to move the bulb into all the dark corners.

A nightmarish dream of my childhood returned. In this dream three witchlike figures flew through the screaming air, and then turned and swooped toward me with extended talons.

Yet during this period of terror and exacerbation, I felt the happiness I was never to feel again until years later when I met and married forever the woman whose eyes were like this first one's.

THE VANISHING OF LOVE AND MARRIAGE

I LEAVE my five hills, for a space, to offer some notes on love and marriage.

Nothing has changed more in my time than these two institutions. I am no longer an ideal field worker in amour but, from what I hear, see and gather, virtuous love has passed practically from our scene. I would look with surprise on a couple "keeping company" for a month who have not been to bed together or, more likely, shared carnally the back seat of an automobile.

As for marriage, its new name is liaison. Not even religious people any longer regard it as the bond indissoluble. It has a flyaway roof and an exit march. Divorce is its twin.

There is possibly a connection between our loosened sex habits and the impermanency of our marriages. Men and women who love lightly and regard sex as a back-seat divertissement are not the ones to go in for "until death do us part" mergers.

But I am giving aid to a theory which I know to be utterly false. This is the theory that a virgin can hold a man more firmly than her unvirginal sister. Here is as big a myth as the one that she can get a man more easily. The fact is, rather, that female virginity has wrecked more marriages than it has cemented. The twitters and inhibitions accumulated along with a protracted virginity are apt to unfit a girl forever for the easygoing lechery required in a healthy marriage. Insistence on chastity is much the same as trying to train men to be soldiers by teaching them to be afraid of firearms.

The increasing collapse of marriage is as intricately motivated as the approaching demise of the Capitalist System, and there is a relation between these deathbeds. Industry and its ever-growing cities and suburbs are in the picture. Marriage was never at its best in the metropolis full of Babylonian diversion. Its bastion was always the lonely farmhouse, the snowed-in bedroom, the chore-exhausted soul of the soil tiller.

What is most responsible, however, for the vanishing of "old-fashioned love" and permanent marriage is the masculinization of women—and the accompanying effeminization of men. This male-izing of women has been the most significant event to happen in my time, one that more than all our other "revolutions" has changed the vital qualities of our living. Yet it appears to have attracted hardly a commentator. It is somewhat as if the Japs had landed in California and captured the U.S.A. unnoticed.

HOW WOMEN LOST THEIR SEX
IN MY TIME

I CAN RECALL as a newspaper reporter in 1912 covering the police court trials of women arrested for smoking cigarettes, for shopping without their corsets on—their jiggling torsos were considered hostile to the peace; for using profanity, for appearing on bathing beaches without stockings, for wearing odd garments in the open such as slacks and shorts, for kissing in public, for wearing a man's hat, for sitting alone in a café or drinking in a saloon, for driving an automobile without a male in attendance; for putting too much paint on their faces or cutting their hair too short.

I actually covered the trials of such defendants as listed above, including another I hesitate to mention—so preposterous does it seem today. But I was there in the Chicago Avenue police court to report the following newsworthy event. In alighting from a Clark Street car at North Avenue, a young woman had revealed an expanse of leg that had fired the civic wrath of a high-school principal onlooker. Forthwith he had summoned a policeman, gathered witnesses and filed a complaint. The next day he stood by triumphantly to see the culprit fined ten dollars for indecent exposure.

Those were parlous times for moral slips, the worst blight of all being the unwritten law, supinely accepted by the male, that if he lured a hitherto chaste female to bed, the sin was his and he had to marry her. What was more, if he did not, the town was full of whisky-nosed judges ready to send him to jail in the name of woman's honor.

But the high-school principal, the judges, the reverends and their ilk did not have the situation entirely in hand. There were "advanced thinkers" who busied themselves rabbit punching at morality. Novelists and playwrights were knocking the wind out of the public by presenting radical heroines who had been to bed with some man before their marriage and who, in their cunning plots, refused to "pay the price" of their lapse.

The current morality was also under nightly attack in all the conclaves of artists and Radicals, among which I was to be found after the age of sixteen. Its overthrow was one of our major missions. It was a time before youth had been politicalized, militarized or science-ized. It was an Era ending, and we who were young in it believed that most of the ills of the world would be cured if the girls went to bed with us, honorably and fearlessly; and if our hypocritical elders would cease their caterwauling about Sin.

Our campaign, which was not without casualties, for we were being constantly arrested (along with the lady who got off the street-car) for "indecent exposure" in our books and paintings, may have had a small influence on the general collapse of female virtue which ensued. But it would be vainglory to cry for more than a thimbleful of credit. A score of other armies, unseen by us, were in the field, all with cannon aimed at virginity, modesty, fidelity and—as it turned out—femininity.

The principal forces that altered womankind had little relation to art or literature. They were the forces of industry and war, mostly the former. Factory, office, political and military machines raided the long-intact middle-class harems, plucked the *Kaffeeklatsch* and the sewing-bee veils off the girls and landed them breathless and aglow in all the ancient male compounds. During the thirty years of its full and equal life among the males much has happened to the female sex. Its morals have vanished, its breasts have shrunk, its hips are bonier, its voice is hoarser, its hands are stronger, its eyes are smaller, its face is less chubby and its behind has flattened out. It smokes and drinks like a man, tells dirty stories in mixed company, follows all the male crafts and trades, and it can sin to its heart's content without losing social or amorous prestige.

This masculinization of women has also been accompanied by an equivalent feminization of men. The process is not as far advanced as among the ladies, it being harder to grow breasts than to lose them. Masculinity is also a more basic physiologic matter than femininity, which, at best, was always made up half of humbug and low mental devices for the ensnaring of mates.

But there is a change already discernible in the male. A gabbiness is on him in business, in politics, everywhere, except in the arenas of love. Here he has become a bit silent, perhaps because he is no longer in the presence of grateful ignoramuses, but of connoisseurs. His haberdashery has paled, his sports clothes are stamped with turtles, birds and flowers, and a basso or even baritone speaking voice has become a rarity. His hands are thinner, his eyes larger, and a beard or large mustachio look almost as eccentric on him as they would on his aunt.

A YES TO MARRIAGE

OUT OF my own marriage and many unions similar to it that I have known, I bow to wedlock, before I turn state's evidence. It has been, it can be, and will continue to be a fine business for two remarkable people to enter—particularly if they are violent and fearless, and invincible as Charlemagne or steadfast as Dido.

A happy and lasting marriage requires many things, but basically genius. It may be the genius of character, of self-hypnosis, or wit, or merely that of endurance; but genius must be there. Its presence will not prevent those domestic typhoons which blow through all bedrooms in which men and women become settlers. But it will rebuild the debris and restore the broken windows.

Of all the types of genius, the genius for gallantry is the best equipment for insuring permanence in a male and female relationship. Most lasting marriages are actually no more than that—a lifelong exercise in gallantry.

A strong man finds pleasure in giving his strength to one who is weaker, which a woman usually is. Sometimes this weakness is no more than age which unfits women for living by themselves. How would a man feel if his wits left him altogether in his forties? That is often how a woman feels whose beauty rusts and whose shapeliness goes awry in her maturity. There are always vivid and desirable young women to go to bed with a husband, whatever his age or shape. But not even in her daydreams can a wife, oxidized and a bit overstuffed by time, trump up a personable lover to come panting after her. The years reduce her more and more to one gallant fellow— her husband.

Sometimes women, particularly chaste and honorable ones, suffer from a lack of worldliness or social talent. Obsessed by their chores, they acquire the soul of a country cousin. Their wings clipped, they twitter and hop around, and like invalids forget the areas of life beyond their small routines.

And sometimes women, dedicated to a man and his comforts and activities, become victims of the malady of unused self. They substitute loyalty for ambition, maternalism for personality growth, and acquire, through marriage, the empty and puffy look of political prisoners of state.

Whatever the woman's weakness is, the man feels its pull and finds pleasure in being its medication, in completing the life of another. And, in an odd way, completing his own life by thus lending his strength to a lesser comrade. For he might not be so strong if someone did not need his strength; so steadfast and touched with valor if these qualities in him were not important to another.

In a like manner it is sometimes the wife who completes the life and character of a husband. She does this by a sturdy belief in him which baffles most onlookers and often makes her seem a gullible zany. She does it by sustaining her man when the monotony of living dulls his spirit, and his talents droop, and his friends begin to shy from him as a bore. She does it by continuing to love him honorably when other women have "dishonored" him. And she does it, most wonderfully, by lending him the flash of courage missing in him when events crowd to lay him low.

This give and take of manna is interchangeable in a lasting union, for if there is such a thing as "the art of peace" in the world, it consists of the heavy burden lifted together, or the task of life accomplished together—and such also is "the art of friendship."

ERRATUM?

THE KEEPER of my logic, editor of my reiterations and vanguard of all my critics—my wife—catches me here in what she considers a curious omission. In discussing the fine things that bind married folk, I have omitted childbearing and child-rearing—much, says she, as if I were discoursing on the lives of monks in a monastery or bachelors indulging in some light housekeeping with their passing sweeties.

As the father of two daughters I should be able to speak with a trace of authority on this subject. The omission was not a mental lapse but a sort of argument in absentia. I grant the point that it is an argument which will be better understood if I make it.

Of my two daughters, one is married and has produced recently a grandchild far away in Brazil. The other of my daughters threatens me with no such exposure. She is not yet eleven years of age and, as far as I can make out, has the character of genius. She is radiant, has my mother's infatuation with toil and pursues her youthful tasks with the determination of a pioneer opening a new land. Her name is Jenny.

My older daughter, who has seen fit to add the title of grandfather to my name, is a creature of much charm and beauty and innumerable talents. I have considered her always among the most pleasing of mortals and can recall no anger or even distaste that she ever aroused in me. Her name is Edwina, although she has always been called Teddy. I mention these facts and my love for my daughters as part of my argument, which is—that the rearing of children may be a bond between some married folk; it has never been one to me.

I have observed that children are as likely to wreck marriages as to cement them. My first marriage, in which a child appeared after a year, lasted three years in all. I had been married the second time for most of my life before offspring entered the union.

This is a tenuous and debatable point but, nevertheless, a point at hand. I evaded parenthood for more than twenty years because I preferred marriage without children. In the back of my head was the half-certainty that a child would endanger or lessen my happiness.

Having a thing in common is not the same as a man and woman having each other. A child is always a lover's rival and usually another child's undoing—which is the same thing, for lovers are in part children with the demands of childhood lingering in their embraces.

The appearance of a golden-haired genius in my wife's arms of recent years was not much different than would have been the appearance in them of a rival who combined the wit of Portia, the lyricism of Pushkin and the glamour of Prester John. I resigned instantly as king of my household and enrolled as a freeman in a democracy. As in a democracy, I voted but influenced no important events.

My new daughter introduced, to give her her due, a new dimension in the lives of her parents. At thirty this dimension might well have been a disturbing one. In my fifties I find it a gift and a delight, for the other dimensions were too solidly fixed for annihilation.

The most sensible biologic reason for marriage is obviously that of having children. But marriage is no biologic matter. If it were we would probably be without it as are most of the animals, who meet only to reproduce—and then depart each other's presence in pursuit of more pressing matters.

Marriage is biology multiplied by economics, history and a sort of human inertia or habit pattern. It is also a social matter, a long party for two and a merger of personalities that has in the long run little to do with sex and less with the fruits of sex. In marriage a woman "fulfills" herself by childbearing, a man does not; nor does a marriage "fulfill" itself by producing children, nor even cement itself.

A sensitive husband is more likely to abandon his wife if he can leave her with a child to solace her than if she is childless. And rarely is a man held to his hearth by the fact that he owes his protection to his young.

There may be men with other attitudes. I speak only of my own sort. We are fathers as we are husbands—usually by accident. Our children in order to interest us have to entertain us, the same as do our wives, friends or paramours. We have for our children a special affection born of their smallness, weakness and need for us (although what a child's need for its father is, has never been entirely clear to me). But we have neither rapturous sense of possession toward them nor identification with them. This is the mother's relation.

I expect to astonish no one by these observations, not even my wife. I include them only because others, as she did, might misunderstand their omission.

A NO TO MARRIAGE

HAVING PAID my respects to fine marriages, I turn to some less fine. Most marriages that I have seen are not as I have chanted. They are usually wearied disasters, epilogues of ennui. And they are based, as a rule, on the profitless generality that misery loves company, or is too poor to buy solitude.

Married folk are held together most frequently by disillusion and a need for revenge. Disillusion between a husband and wife can inspire years of debate. It is nerve-racking but stimulating. It is often the only mental excitement in the lives of a married pair. It keeps them together in the unended argument of which is worse, which is guiltier, stupider, more insensitive and a bigger nuisance.

Revenge also will hold a pair within barb shot of each other, for revenge is empty without the constant presence of its victim. An injured soul will not always flee its tormentor. It sometimes finds a peculiar solace in remaining and belaboring its Torquemada with its sufferings. The necessity a man and woman have of proving that each is only a source of pain and misery to the other can consume a lifetime.

The secret of most such marriages may well be that a man (or woman) prefers a concrete enemy within the gates to the wild host that menaces beyond them. It is easier to fight a wife than a boss, a critic, a world of injustice and a knowledge of insufficiency; and it is easier to battle a husband than have at the indifference of life or the sorrows of age.

Age itself is one of the prime cements of marriage. Age often frightens both contestants off from trying their luck in new arenas. A fidelity based on a sad little farewell to life and sex ensues.

WHY MARRY?

MANY INSCRUTABLE and wanton forces bring men and women together. I itemize some of them.

There is a great tribe of men who do not marry women at all, but marry fetishes; who promise to love, honor and obey a coiffure, an odor, an overmeaty breast.

There are fortune hunters and misfortune hunters, romantics playing blindman's buff and lonely hearts looking for someone with whom to play cards.

There are jilted men who marry somebody else rather than commit suicide.

There are men who marry in order to convince themselves they are men.

There are men too shy to undress in front of strangers, and men weary of undressing before strangers.

There are men and women who marry because they have nothing else to do with themselves.

There are politically-minded young men who marry party constituents. (This is particularly true of Communists.)

There are men who marry because they want to be like their father, and others who want to be like their mother, and still others who want to be like everybody else.

There are men who offer marriage as a bribe to women they could not otherwise seduce, and men who marry women as the only way of pulling them out of other men's beds.

There are men who marry kitchen stoves and vacuum cleaners, and men who get trapped into wedlock by a female determination stronger than their own love of freedom.

All these get married or hurl themselves into more disorderly liaisons. As to why women get married, I will peep into that subject on a separate page.

THE BED OF ECHOES

A LARGE CONTINGENT of men are led into wedlock by the recurrence of the first desireless love of adolescence.

Passion can send us into befuddled pursuits of women who seem, in our fevers, to have cornered the market on thighs and buttocks. But this other form of attachment, the revival of our boyhood genius for adoration, moves us, I think, more deeply and certainly toward mating.

For in this love, our interest is in ourselves and not the woman. She is a sort of magic tuning fork held above our souls that sets them to humming their perfect note. She does no more than hover beside us, as she once did in our boyhood, and we expand. We bloom, we jibber-jabber, we grow big with dreams, lies, personality. Our own inner beauty overwhelms us.

When we were boys, this beauty, stirred by the hovering one, was a vague sweeping thing having to do with starlight and the other mysteries of day and night. We had no selves to love then, so our love poured out upon climate and astronomy. Now *we* are there, and we lift a curtain, turn on a spotlight and come striding into it. We experience a second birth, and this one also through the power of a woman.

Dizzied, grateful and with an almost filial respect, we marry the one who has re-created us.

And here, or hereabouts, the business often ends. The re-created one collapses. The song of self that piped him to the altar or into a grand passion is heard no more. Nature's objective has been achieved. Or the shopkeeper's objective—flushed customers in need of new carpets, curtains, chinaware and mattresses.

There usually follows for such matings a crescendo of unreality. The male, though deflated after the first bloom of union, refuses to give up. He tasted honey in his soul. He will not concede it was only a thimbleful and not a gallon. And he clings to the memory of this taste, to the memory of his love.

A great part of our emotional life consists of such echoes—echoes of desires, plots and plans which have long ago expended themselves. The lover will continue to speak out of his memory of love, a bit hollowly, like a voice coming back out of a cave. He does this out of fear of seeming "less" than he was. He does it out of a foolish hope that if he pretends enough, a magic will happen and make his pretending true. He does it out of the need to keep his mate "fooled" into adoring him. This is the last sad pleasure of the unloving heart— to be loved.

In one guise or another, I have found myself in these caves of echoes. But I have never remained long in them. I have known love to die. The death of love can hold one spellbound for years. I have sat mourning at graves. But I have wandered off when I heard my voice growing too hollow.

A FEW BY-PRODUCTS OF MARRIAGE AND SOME DRAMATIS PERSONAE

WITH TIME, marriage often becomes more a business than a mating. I have seen married couples who seem like president and vice-president of a busy corporation. I am willing, in their presence, to concede that copulation is as out of place in marriage as at a board meeting.

I have seen marriages in which the participants do not appear ever to have met or revealed any desire to be introduced to each other. They arrive at parties like a pair of diplomats without a language in common. They sit politely at dinner tables without glance, word or ear for each other. The only evidence they offer of being married is that they arrive and depart at the same time.

This tribe is equally silent on its own hearth. There is no visible enmity or criticism in their silence. They are two people who have exhausted all interest in each other, whose hearts, minds and sex organs have achieved a mutual coma. They hang like flies motionless in a web.

I have seen couples who have chiefly the relation of opposing attorneys in a courtroom toward each other. Given a jury of two or more listeners, each will offer eloquent and derisive evidence of the other's villainy, stupidity, cowardice, venality or selfishness.

I have known couples who, unable to tolerate the sight or sound of each other, devote all their energies to trapping guests. Their dinner tables are always filled with strange nervous people who have never seen each other before, having been run down and bagged on different heaths.

I have found myself often at such repasts, and have sat twitching for hours while husband and wife tried to turn me into entertainment. Little entertainment is possible in these arenas of boredom. The guests usually end with a distaste for each other similar to the aversion between the married couple hosting them. And they leave on the single note of comradeliness—that nothing can ever drag them to that house again, where everybody felt at his worst and performed at his lowest.

I have learned not to feel sorry for such hosts and hostesses because I have seen that their dinner parties are never failures in their own eyes. A remarkable industry enables them to recruit always new "friends" and, with the butler serving and the radio going and eight harassed and fidgety people staring into their soup—there is victory enow. A battle has been won, not lost. The married pair have managed to lessen their boredom by grandly sharing it.

Such couples have another trick by which they manage to keep married in the grinding teeth of incompatibility. On those evenings when they run out of dinner-table quarry for their homes, they "go places." They toss from theater opening to theater opening in a fever of ennui and are an untiring safari of two in quest of new cafés, "interesting" spots and other people's doorbells.

I have known marriages that are held together solely by the twin themes of sin and its reform. A husband will dislike a wife so much that he must spend all his time in saloons and shabby amours. He must totter home drunk and sexually depleted four days out of the week. The other three days are then devoted to his "reformation."

A strong-willed woman can keep "reforming" a man in this manner for several decades. After a husband has betrayed his wife a hundred times, his load of guilt is such that he is ready to cling to marriage like a sinner grasping at an altar rail. He needs no further nagging. The distaste for the wife that drove him to sin is exchanged for respect for her—as the loyal angel who, through thick and thin, has been trying to make a better man of him.

Infidelity will often renew married people's interest in each other, as it will in themselves. Sometimes these brink-of-divorce couples endure for ages. An unfaithful husband is often full of tenderness for the one he deceives, and sometimes of a roguish concupiscence, as if she and not his paramour were his partner in sin. Or he becomes a marital "sugar daddy," loading his betrayed wife with jewels and extra servants and unexpected gifts from furriers, as if he were extracting endless blackmail from himself.

As for the errant wife in marriage, she is usually tolerant and witty. Whenever I hear a woman offering fond banter to her mate, I know she has another bed for more serious exchanges.

When such marriages end in divorce, the severance is seldom due to the immorality of the mated ones. It is brought about usually by the clamoring morality of the third party in the love mix-up.

Pity is the rottenest cement to be found in "Love among the Ruins." I have known husbands to cling to their wives for the very reasons they should abandon them—because they have grown fat, become dull, turned into chatterboxes or lost all traces of looks and allure. In some mystic way, such a husband, full of stray guilts, will hold himself responsible for the collapse of his wife's shape, beauty and intellect. Although unfaithful to her, he will return monotonously to her increasing homeliness and unfemaleness. Poor wives!

> And dotingly they earn their fees
> Performing in their little lairs
> And trying wistfully to please
> Their wand'ring mates with wifely snares
> Of custards and economies
> And raisin sauces, sighs and prayers.

(I wrote the above, not Browning.)

Men often have confided to me that they "returned" to their wives from "tender" sentiments. The pity involved in these returns, more often than not, is no pity at all but the secret need of the Don Juan husband that fetches him home. His marriage represents to him the true haven for his basically unsexual self—a haven in which he does not have to be a man but can stay a husband. (And even a battered and unfeminine wife is socially a more becoming companion than a homosexual friend.)

The child-parent relationship is at the bottom of a good percentage of marriages, and these sometimes make the most charming of unions. A husband married to a "mother-image" may betray her sexually, but his heart will never lose its need for her. She will remain into old age a companion who stirs his youngest and fairest emotions.

The "mother-substitute" is often a paragon among wives. She will possess without throttling, adore without demanding usurious adoration in return. She will heal the hurt of living in a man and see him always not as one who has outraged her by his sins but as one who needs her because of them.

However—being wives and husbands, and not mothers and sons, these pleasant companions sometimes erupt into ugliness and violence, when their parting usually seems doubly tragic.

In the case of women married to "father-substitutes"—the idolatry of the "daughter-wife," her gentle voice, her proud and mystic silences are soothing to experience and observe. The rub lies in the "father." Men do not make as pretty marital-parents as do women.

A "father-husband" is likely to deteriorate under such adulation into smugness and social lunacy. Perhaps this is because men are lacking in father instincts and basically are never fathers, as mothers are mothers.

A man fancies himself a "father" when he finds a fellow human being who will senselessly admire his faults, or mistake his footling estate for greatness or power. He becomes rather a child than a child's superior in doing this. The result often to be seen in "daughter-father" marriages is a union of two children—one charming and the other much less so.

Finally, there are marriages that are more reunions than unions. Men and women who have shared grief, calamity or fine times find a need for each other as a mutual memory team. They consort like alumnae. Sometimes it is no more than youth they have lost. There is solace in living with a woman who has known one's moist brown curls and remembers one as a man of vigor and fine hopes. Most sentimental marriages that reach the silver- and golden-anniversary stages have this as the source of their sentiment. They survive on memories of yesterday.

Such are some of the marriages I have noted in the twilight of the institution.

THE CALIPH IN HIS PALACE

I RETURN to the second of my hills, my boyhood's attic room with
its gabled windows that overlooked the great Lake Michigan across
the street.

When I was in the hospital a year or two ago, with illness threatening to put an end to me, a few thoughts trickled through the
half-dream of dying in which I lay one night. One of them was of
this attic room. I hoped, if I died, to go there again.

In this room I remember no one but myself. My mother paid it
an occasional visit, and once a week a stocky hired girl came in
cautiously after making sure of my absence and cleaned it with a
feather duster. It grew amazingly dirty in the four years I occupied
it.

Being under the roof, with nothing between it and God but a
layer of moldy shingles, the room was impossible to heat in the
winter. In the summertime it blistered like a wooden oven. When it
rained, large drops spattered through its ceiling and little rivers ran
down its walls. All these things were highly satisfactory. Its hardships distinguished my room from all other rooms and gave it an
unmatchable character.

There were several pieces of carpet of different colors in it which
I had nailed to the floor myself. There was a wooden bed, a bureau and a bookcase. There were no chairs, but there was an abandoned kitchen table in one of its corners. The table was covered by a
black velvet cloth with a silver fringe that reached to the floor all
around it. On the front of this fine velvet drape my name was sewn
in large letters made out of the same silver fringe. I had at one
time planned to make my living as a magician.

On the table were most of my belongings, for I liked them always to be visible. They are visible to me now, and they are truly a
magic paraphernalia, for the favorite objects of many years, enough
to fill a room, rest amazingly on that table.

There were carnelian marbles called "canuks" and costing as high
as twenty cents apiece. In the wintertime these were kept in cups of
lard to preserve their beauty.

There were horse chestnuts lying in glasses of vinegar, a fluid which helped to harden them. The chestnuts had holes in them. They were, when ready for competition, swung on the end of a string and brought down, hammerlike, on rival chestnuts.

There was my sloop, "The Pirate," three feet long, which I had made and rigged myself. In the summertime this craft was sailed in the bay behind the breakwater. Tin sailors were fastened in its shrouds and glued to its decks. I owned a brass cannon six inches long that was able, with a proper charge of gunpowder, to send a bicycle ball bearing a hundred feet. This cannon, planted on the shore of the breakwater bay, fired its ball bearing at the passing pirate ship and sometimes tumbled its tin sailors from their positions into watery graves. The cannon, sailors and reserves of gunpowder were also on the table.

Lying on the table was a dancing skeleton, three feet tall, with detachable head and ribs made of tin. Black threads moved its joints.

(My violin, music and music stand were in my mother's sitting room downstairs, partly because of my distaste for them and partly at my mother's insistence. She refused to take my word for the amount of violin practicing I did each day and demanded that my sawing away on that unpleasing instrument be done where other ears could corroborate it.)

On the table lay also my twenty-two caliber rifle (not a repeater). Beside it were my canvas cartridge belt, sewed for me by my mother, and holding fifty bullets, and my deer-handled hunting knife with its leather holster. These I had earned by selling subscriptions to a magazine called *The Youth's Companion*.

Other objects of great charm and import beckon my memory, but too dimly for inventory.

The walls of my room were hung with numerous framed pictures of Sherlock Holmes. They were the covers of *Collier's* Magazine, in which the adventures of Mr. Holmes were being printed for the first time. No sooner did any drawing of the great, gaunt detective appear, there or elsewhere, than I rushed it into a frame to hang on my wall.

All these were important possessions, many with the nostalgia of childhood lending them secret glamour. But the great thing in my room was the throne in which dream and marvel sat. This was my bookcase.

My love for this bookcase is still sharp in my senses. I have never loved any other object since in that way. My bookcase was a sort of extra continent in the world. Its wood and glass spoke to me of the new wonder that had come into my life, the wonder of books. It was made of dark "mission" wood and had four doors full of little leaded cathedral-like windowpanes. Behind these panes, as in a perpetual durbar, stood my books.

I was only twelve when this object was carried into my room, crowded out of the lower floors by the ever-increasing clutter of the house.

HARRY, THE CALIPH'S FIRST VIZIER —AND HIS FAMILY

THE HOUSE was a large one with a rabbit warren of rooms in it. It was painted a chocolate brown with white trimmings. It was alive with useless turrets and capricious contours. It belonged to a woman named Mrs. Costello, who ran it as a rooming and boarding house. She was the widow of Dan Costello, who had been P. T. Barnum's partner and a famous acrobatic clown.

Besides my family, there were a dozen guests in this house. All but ourselves were transients. They were circus folk, retired from their sawdust world, but springing constantly out of their retirement toward lesser roles in smaller and smaller tents. Occasionally the entire troupe of a visiting dramatic repertoire company invaded the other rooms on the attic floor. Lying in my bed, I would hear them singing at a midnight party and roaring jokes at each other on the way to the corridor bathroom.

Mrs. Costello was in her seventies, possibly eighties. She had been a bareback rider of renown. I remember her as the busiest, most nimble-footed, least-idle human being I have ever known. Despite her great age, she was shapely and slender. She had black eyes that still glittered like spangles, and she wore a shining black wig. She whisked up and down the stairs like a ballerina.

Her energy was a contrast to the behavior of her son, Harry, who was in his forties. He was my first mentor, and I write his name with tenderness.

Harry was a trapeze performer. He lay all winter in his bed in an overheated little back room, reading "nickel novels" and drinking beer. In the spring he rose from his bed and started getting into condition again. Harry was the first to stir ambition in me. He aroused in me the desire to be an acrobat. For three years, until I was fourteen, Harry instructed me in a routine as a "single." The trapeze hung in the barn behind the house.

I kept my trapeze practice secret from my mother. I had an uncle named Breitbart who was a strong man in a circus. My mother spoke always slightingly of his vocation, and I was moved by this fact to hide my ambition from her.

In the summer of my fourteenth year, Harry and a troupe of acrobatic jacks-of-all-trades got together enough money to take a one-ring tent show on the road. I went as part of the troupe.

My mother frowned when I told her I was going along to play the fiddle in the band. She was unable to remember any fiddles in a circus band. I assured her firmly that Harry was breaking a long precedent in my honor and that I was going to play as a soloist. This satisfied her sense of reality.

I did my soloing on the trapeze for the next two months until bankruptcy overtook our circus. On the way to Fond du Lac it mysteriously disintegrated—its tent, its blue-painted rows of flap-down seats, its thousands of feet of heavy ropes and various pieces of unsatisfactory equipment, all disappearing along with all my genial and arthritic colleagues of the sawdust.

Harry and I rode back to Racine with our pockets equally empty. He seemed in no way shaken by his troubles and was eager to go into the fishing business with me as a partner. He returned, however, to his bed, his "nickel novels" and his bottles of beer.

Many years later Harry committed suicide by shooting a gun off in his mouth.

Of Mrs. Costello, I remember chiefly her emotional interest in a nephew named Frankie. Frankie was dead, having been drowned some forty years ago at the age of fourteen while canoeing on a picnic. He remained, however, much in evidence. Two pairs of his baby shoes hung on the wall of the big parlor in which the tall mica-windowed stove glowed all winter. A cap he had favored, a dozen photographs of him and a pair of black curls under a glass frame completed the little wall shrine of Frankie. Under it was a piece of a printed page, in a black frame. It was the epitaph written by Abd-ar-Rahman, Caliph of Spain, for his tomb.

I looked up Abd-ar-Rahman in the Public Library when I was fifteen, and had been long familiar with his fearsome last words. He was a hero and warrior famed for the twenty-two thousand silk carpets of his palace, its twenty-two thousand silk tapestries, its myriads of golden goblets and jewel-encrusted automaton birds that sang. His hundred and fifty thousand soldiers were dressed in precious fabrics, with belts of gold and rubies. His twelve thousand horsemen carried scimitars shining with emeralds and pearls. The palace of the Caliph Abd-ar-Rahman and the gardens of Zehra were the most beautiful that had ever been known. The Caliph himself reigned for fifty years in a time of ever-mounting glory and power.

His epitaph, hanging under Frankie's cap, baby shoes, photographs and curls, read:

"I have now reigned above fifty years in victory and peace, beloved by my subjects, dreaded by my enemies, respected by my allies. Riches and honor, power and pleasure have waited on my call, nor does any earthly blessing appear to have been wanting in my years. During this life of wonder I have kept count of the days of happiness which have been given me. They number fourteen. O man, place not thy confidence in this present world."

MY FATHER AND HIS ELEPHANTS

FOR A WHILE the most minor of princelings occupied my bookcase—Henty, Brady, Alger, Oliver Optic, and the authors (whose names I have gracelessly forgotten) of Jack Harkaway, Fred Fearnot, Dick Merriwell, Diamond Jim Brady and Nat the Naturalist.

But on my thirteenth birthday a tremendous event took place. Four large boxes filled with books arrived in my room. They were gifts from my parents, but personally selected by my father under the advice of a scholar who was one of his brother Elks.

My father was a man who had read almost nothing, looked at no paintings and listened to no music. But he had a love of the arts, particularly literature. He hovered like a peri without the gates of beauty, smiling apologetically on all the wonders he was never to know and telling great lies about his relation to them. These lies were his dreams. His soul had been formed by ancestors in Persia centuries ago in the time when that land lay scattered, with Bajazet and all his glories gone, and its voluptuous eras of conquest ended in a beggar's cloak.

My father's ancestors had come wandering out of this old-clothes wagon of history. They had strayed into southern Russia. But my father remained a man from Shiraz. Silk-covered elephants and the endless pennants of the Commanders of the Earth haunted him and gave him certain delusions that were like golden threads in his modesty. Given a credulous ear, missing in his own family, he would lay reckless claim to erudition and pedantry, to worldly riches and high political connections. My father did not have to meet people to know them. If he only saw them to smile at, or better yet, heard them in a "hall," he went away their crony.

He worked hard as a designer of women's clothes, having risen to that estate from lowly tailoring tasks. Outwardly, no man from Shiraz had come to the U.S.A., but only another tall, gaunt Jewish cloth cutter.

But now in our Wisconsin town he drew pictures of beautiful women. He drew them without their heads, hands or feet, they being pictures of "new styles." But they were beautiful women, nevertheless, and finely drawn, with every piece of braid, loop of lace and curve of body accurately put down. In addition to his drawing and pattern cutting, my father had launched, at this time, his long, unprosperous career as an industrialist. He had built a factory in which ladies' garments were made. He toiled and planned, traveled and sold "lines." But he was not of the tribe of realists. He savored success before it came. He rolled in millions when only pennies were in the safe. The chief and busiest department of his factory was always an air castle. He had never any profits to share with his family, except the happy smile of his daydreams. Tall, lean, straight-backed, childlike, misinformed, his dark eyes gentle and confused, his wide mouth firm, he retold in miniature the lies of Don Quixote.

Yet it was my untutored and impractical father who bought me the books in the four large crates. Though he never read any of them, they were forever inside his head, fully digested. He had seen and touched them. It never occurred to him, I am certain, that he had worked hard for the money that paid for them.

HOW HAPPY WAS THE NEW LAND

MY FATHER WAS, like most daydreamers, a shy man. He was not present at the uncrating of the books. He turned his back on the great joy he had given me and sat downstairs with my mother. Alone, I wrenched nails and ripped at boards like one fallen upon a desert island treasure.

The first to emerge was a fifteen-volume set of Shakespeare, maroon-colored, flat-backed and bearing gold titles.

Next there appeared Charles Dickens in thirty green volumes.

There followed a fifty-two volume *History of the World* in stiff blue-black covers with silver lettering.

Thirty brick-red colored volumes of Mark Twain appeared.

Then came a noble-looking set of books in half-morocco called *The Home Study Circle Library*. There were twenty-five of these elegant fellows. They contained excerpts from Macaulay, Plutarch, Boswell, and biographies of great musicians, painters, scientists, courtesans and prime ministers.

The last set was *The World's Famous Orations* in fifteen tall, gray tomes.

By evening I had looked at the illustrations in all the volumes, and they stood ranged on my bookcase shelves looking as beautiful as they were, an army with banners.

I have tired of the look of many things, but never of books. I have kept them always in my bedroom so I could see them from my bed as I used to in this attic room. They still surround me at night, and I look at them tenderly and without thought as I fall asleep. They are the mind of man arrayed like dragoons and Javanese dancers. They are as symmetrical as ripples on a river. When there is only moonlight on them, they shine with mystic life. They are the only real ghosts. How dead the world would be without these dead ones! I sometimes say aloud the names of the authors on my shelves, as I do of loved ones who have died. They dreamed of being remembered. There is as deep a charm in conferring immortality as in achieving it.

AND HOW WONDROUS WERE ITS WORDS

IT WAS Shakespeare I read first. I lay in my attic at night, eyes held to the blurring pages. The plots meant nothing. The characters were indistinguishable, even male from female. I had no idea who was king or clown, villain or hero, or to what purpose they battled and slew. But I met and recognized the nobility and precision of language. The words leaped from the paper and seemed to hang in the air like feats of magic.

The magic of words still remains for me. I prefer them to ideas. They are a more precious currency. No ideas have ever filled me with wonder. Phrases have. Ideas become quickly impoverished. Their value, never great, fades with usage: The word has a hardier mintage.

Phrases, not ideas, are the tools for re-creating life. Ideas lie on a perpetual rubbish heap, waiting to be salvaged, dusted off and flaunted anew as riches. The mind, searching pompously for truth, pokes among the fineries of yesterday, rearrays itself in what it has outgrown, parades again in remodelings. The ideas of yesterday, to-day and tomorrow are the same, and they add nothing to the meaning of life.

It is phrasing alone that can bring fresh gifts to the spirit. When we describe accurately a mood, a mountain, a desire—when we put down with that combination of diligence and dream the words that are the true souls of things observed—we add to the stream of life.

ON READING VERSUS WRITING

IN THE LAST TEN YEARS I have reread Dickens and Twain. They were as good as I thought them in my first encounter. They could not be better.

Two such jolly and bitter men! How these chuckling, weeping, roaring fellows haunted my pillow! What a carnival they unloosed in my attic room! It was not to be believed.

Schopenhauer declaims, "What palace ever rivaled in magnificence the dingy hole where Cervantes wrote *Don Quixote!*" We *read* the great storytellers in as fine a place.

Villiers de L'Isle-Adam, the Parisian writer, who lived like an alley cat, ate stale fish, went hiccuping and threadbare through fifty years of penury, who wrote with frostbitten fingers on cigarette papers, spoke from his hovel when dying: "Farewell. I have lived the richest and most magnificent of men."

We who read can die with a similar boast.

Shakespeare had been to me warriors and kings, plumed in words; earth and sky become a mirage of words, and thoughts, like falling stars, swooping before my eyes. Twain and Dickens were cornucopias. Populations tumbled out of them.

I have always preferred reading fiction to writing it, not alone because it is easier. The sad thing about writing fiction is that unless one writes classics one writes in a closet. Nothing can disappear like a book. I remember reading some time ago an account of the origins of man. In it the author discussed the vanishing of the Neanderthal race, a species of human being who seemingly had ceased suddenly to exist, as if they had been spun off the earth by an accelerated movement of our globe on its axis. The Cro-Magnon race had popped up out of nowhere and taken its place. The author, a learned and unbiased man, debated from this whether the Neanderthal race had ever existed at all. That is how a book one has written can disappear.

I have written much fiction. The characters I made up are still alive, but they inhabit no world—only a closet. A foot beyond is limbo. They do not walk or caper in people's minds. They continue to utter their many fine sentences, to weep, joke and make love—but in the closet always. Like all writers who have tried hard, I dream sometimes that the closet door will open.

WHY I HAVE NO TASTE

I PREFER fine books and an exalted style and masterful probings. But when I read the other books, the ones sprung from equally ardent but smaller heads, I feel no lessened pleasure. I supply, as well as I can, what is missing. I skip what is too untrue. I am content with their smaller ambition. I do not praise them after they are closed, but while I read them I am as pleased as if no better books existed.

When I was a literary critic in Chicago, writing in the most icono-clastic publication of our times, *The Little Review*, run by Margaret Anderson, I could never attack books. I wrote only of books I could praise. I was ready to undermine in print such institutions as mar-riage, democracy and heaven. But books I could never sabotage, any more than I could publicly hiss actors.

My chief drawback as a literary reviewer was not kindness, how-ever, but an inability to read any book through the assaying scale of my culture. When I read David Graham Phillips I was not aware of having read Gogol. When I enjoyed Paul de Kock, I had no memories of the pleasures of Stendhal. Each one, at his own time, was as good as the other. And with such an attitude one can never go far as a critic.

I used to argue about this with my friend, Sasha. He was Alex-ander S. Kaun, a smoldering Muscovite come to Chicago after some ineffectual bomb-throwing in the north of Russia. Despite this po-litical activity, he was, basically, not a politician but a man of letters. He later became Professor of Russian Literature at the University of California in Berkeley. I never saw him in his cap and gown, for he died before my travels led me to San Francisco Bay.

In his pre-professorial youth, we argued during all-night sessions such as only political caucuses hold nowadays. In that time, sweet pause before chaos, literature was a more burning issue than it is at present. It is now a bauble in the hands of publishers, critics and readers. It was then a secret flame in the hands of the dedicated.

My point of view infuriated Sasha. I professed not to see any dif-ference between a beautiful object and an ordinary one. I said that I liked all books in the manner that I liked all girls who were pre-sentable. When with a girl of moderate allure, I did not disdain her because there were lovelier specimens in the world. Rapture might be limited, but criticism was surely out of place. And what did one gain by making oneself constantly toe the mark of preference—except fewer delights? In loving, or reading, a man was a fool to sit in judg-ment when he might lie in pleasure.

This aesthetic was lineal descendant of my young self in the attic room where I had found no difference in the charms of Nick Carter and Hamlet, nor outside the room, between hired girls and high-school princesses. A mediocre book or woman never lessened my opin-ion of myself.

I have outgrown some of this wholeness. But culture that deprives one of the many joys of being uncultured still seems to me a misuse of the mind. I have railed often against books in discussions with their readers. But it was actually against the readers I was fomenting. The books were innocent.

A GARLAND OF IGNORANCE

Aside from this first astonishing gift to my mind contained in these four crates of books, my parents' interest in my education either never existed or was too vague for me to remember.

I recall that my mother had been determined I should become a great violinist. She had not the faintest interest in music herself and was actually depressed by the sound of fiddle playing. But in the New York ghetto where I was born, Jewish mothers dreamed en masse of their sons turning into Kubeliks, standing on the stage with long hair and soulful eyes and earning a thousand dollars a night sawing away at a fiddle. Such was the only greatness Jewish parents could envisage for their offspring in Jew-tabooed Russia. On the wings of music alone could the little circumcised one flap his way into the wonder world beyond the Old Country ghetto. And my mother harassed me with this un-American concept through my childhood.

Her aberration kept me chin glued for years to the fiddle, despite my aversion to that skimpy instrument. Not until I appeared as a virtuoso in an Orchestra Hall concert in Chicago at the age of twelve did my mother's fixation relax. She attended the concert and, despite the applause I evoked, came away thoughtful. She said nothing, but it was obvious she felt there was something a little shameful about a man standing alone on a stage playing a fiddle. It might be a fine thing to do in Russia but in Chicago it seemed a mistake.

Thereafter I continued to take violin lessons but I no longer had to lie about my hours of practicing. I no longer had to wash my bow every month or compete with my more musically talented Brooklyn cousin, Irving, who not only could play circles around me but was gifted as an eccentric dancer and a boy soprano.

Aside from my vanished musical career, my parents seemingly had no interest in my cultural future. They never asked after my interests as a scholar nor discussed what sort of marks were on my report cards, and there was never any talk of what I was going to grow up to be. The fact that I was going to school and that I stayed awake half the night reading books of every sort set me apart from them. They looked on me as one launched on a life superior to any they had ever known.

For my parents were both ignorant of learning, as were my many aunts and uncles. Now that they are all, or nearly all, dead, I remember this ignorance tenderly. It seemed to keep them always young and loving.

There is one virtue open to "ignorance" which can make it as endearing as the fairest of wisdoms. This is the virtue of grace. The ignorance of my parents was always graceful. Others' education did not humiliate them and set them to plotting secret revenges. They looked on all evidences of a more ornate existence than theirs with the delight of sight-seers. I never knew them to argue against learning, to envy riches, to be pouting or competitive in the presence of their worldly betters.

My parents were not alone in this ability to smile eagerly rather than bark angrily at finer worlds. I have often found this graceful manner among the unpropagandized poor. They are critical only of what they know—one another. They are ready to applaud a philosopher (if they ever run into one) as amiably as a sunrise. Both are matters beyond them. People without concepts lack the bellicosity and envy which concepts inspire.

It is the half-informed, the possessors of a few rags of learning, a few mismated shoes of opinion, who are the combative ones. In the world of ideas, a dollar of thought makes a man instantly a millionaire; a single opinion lands him jowl to jowl with Aristotle.

I do not make a theory out of the manner in which my parents loved and ignored me. I see in it only the fact that it is possible to serve a child without intrusion, guidance or fret for his tomorrow.

MY LONG FLIGHT FROM SCHOLARSHIP

WITH THE SET of *The Home Study Circle Library* books I come to the beginnings of my scholarship.

I read these volumes with an enthusiasm approaching madness. I was driven almost crazy with delight by meeting Beethoven, Caesar, Lucretius, Leonardo da Vinci, Mozart, Dr. Johnson and all the other mandarins of my planet. I gasped at their genius. Their adventures overwhelmed me. Their victories left me out of breath. No mind could have embraced more passionately those pages I turned.

Yet, no sooner was the book closed than, as if by some black magic, all disappeared. No date, no quote, no antic, no shred of them stayed in my head. I could not have answered, a week after gloating over him, whether Telemachus was a Greek or Roman, a hero or villain, what he had done or in what age he lived. The "Home Study Circle Library" seemed to fall into a pit without a bottom. It made a fine racket while it fell. But it vanished into silence.

This was no weakness of an adolescent mind. It was a failing the years have not removed. I read Plutarch every five years, and Gibbon. Also Prescott, Suetonius, Tacitus, Graetz, Dio, Josephus, Lecky and a dozen other gold mines of information. And they are always new to me. I have never been able to keep their facts printed in my head. The same is true of books of entomology, astronomy, physics, oceanography, biology. I read, my mind glows, understands, adores and forgets. I seem to be able to get no further as a man of erudition than my father, who read almost nothing.

Like all handicapped people, I keep on the lookout for evidences of superiority in my handicap. I find some. I have discovered that a man of intelligence does not need a memory, and that memory may be a dangerous ally, not only for writing but for living. There are people who stand like watchmen with drawn guns guarding their warehouses of memory. They are not afraid of anybody robbing these warehouses. What they fear is that somebody will try to put something new into them. What they know seems to give them a fierce face against knowing anything else. Their sense of completion is challenged by new authors, new facts, new ideas. They "live" in their well-stocked memory as in a world all solved for them.

As for me, I own no warehouses. I have forgotten not only books, but the scenery of life. I remember almost nothing of the excitements that moved me into various activities. When I look back, I see a curtain down. It requires effort to raise it.

Having no active memory, I bear almost no grudges. All that is past seems unimportant to me, and toward those who hindered me

I have a blank mind and heart. I often have met people who considered me their enemy because they had either wronged or opposed me. I have greeted them with enthusiasm because I recalled only the interesting fact that they had once been in my life.

The same is true of people who have liked or aided me. These, too, I greet with enthusiasm but I seldom can remember that they were "on my side." Friends and enemies alike wear the same look after many years, and have the same value. For a moment or two the past does not seem so dead in their presence.

It is not altogether a pleasant thing to be without memory, however, and I do not recommend it promiscuously. To know less as one grows older, to remain after the ingestion of thousands of books as one was—practically unlettered; to find no after-enjoyment in one's jobs; to sprawl much of the time as vacuous as a cretin in a sandbox—this is no situation for a timid spirit. My partial amnesia has demanded of me almost a constant fortitude. It is difficult to sit emptily in an empty world and remain cheerful.

I have known rewards, however. Just as books seem always new to me, so do events. No memory makes me into a critic. I do not compare, I enjoy—when there is anything to enjoy.

Then, too, if I lose in not having a memory, I make up for it in my talent for remembering. Given a reason for remembering something, such as the present one of writing, I am a fisherman of prowess.

P.S. AND AN ACTUAL ESCAPE
(For which I remain forever grateful)

MY SCHOOL DAYS ended when I was sixteen, although other plans had been made for me. Who made these plans I do not remember, except that neither I nor my parents could have been responsible; neighbors, possibly, and some acquiescent bounderism on my part no doubt.

I enrolled in the summer of 1910 in the University of Wisconsin. I spent my first two days lurking about in the fraternity house to which I had been pledged, fascinated by the high stiff collars my brothers-to-be insisted on wearing on the premises, despite the heat and the fact that there were no womenfolk to badger them. I was unusually silent, for these high stiff collars undermined my ego. On the second evening one of the students informed me he was off to keep a date with a chorus girl with whom he was going to spend the entire night, as he put it, pasted together. This phrase is all I remember of my college days, which ended abruptly the next afternoon.

On the third morning I went to an office and selected a course of education with the amiable tag "Arts and Sciences." At the lunch table, one of the high collars, who also wore a gold lion's head stickpin in his tie, asked me if I had chosen my branch of learning. Thus openly invited to discourse by one of the flossiest of my hosts, I answered with a gush of confidences. I said that I had, but that I was greatly worried because, as far as I could make out, the university had nothing to teach me. I had already read nearly all the books listed in the Arts and Sciences prospectus.

After lunch my sponsor in the club, Jack Davies, with whom I had played football in high school, led me ominously to his room. He explained I would have to apologize to the house at the dinner table for having insulted the university. I agreed to do this.

At six o'clock I started downstairs to speak my piece of apology to the stiff collars. But I was unable to enter the room in which they sat waiting as stonily, I was certain, as a gallery of Cauchons prepared for the entrance of the heretic maid, Joan. Instead, I made for the front door and bolted into the summer evening. I trotted through the streets of Madison, full of misery. An hour later I was on a train going to Chicago—and out of universities forever.

I MEET THE TRIBE OF HALF-MEN

I WAS INTRODUCED to politicians by my set of *The World's Famous Orations*. These whoop-dee-doos startled me. They were unlike the language of Shakespeare, Dickens and Twain. It was many years before I learned they were no language at all, but the prattle of con men and the whine of beggarly souls pleading for the alms of power and salary.

Although the politician is the most obvious of intellectual rogues, it takes a long time to understand him, for when we are young we look at him with our hopes. We do not see him as the buzzard who swoops down, feasts and grows fat on the follies of the hour. He seems benign and dedicated to the task of keeping our civilization functioning. (But his function is quite otherwise. It is to send a civilization burning like a strawstack.)

The orations chilled my eagerness for reading. I scowled on the gray and growingly repugnant volumes that had seemed so elegant when I first unwrapped them. There may have been a Pitt or Burke among them, or Robert Emmet. There must have been a Lincoln. But they were swallowed up and outweighed by the unsavory monster of oratory, the world verbigerator who borrows sonorities, rhetorics and rhythms, as well as moral fineries, for his kindless, truthless purpose. I did not know that if the world ever passed into the hands of the politicians, as it was to pass, they would do what they have always done—destroy it.

The hydra-tongued gabble of politics filled my attic room. What boy could know that it was the voice of human disintegration? I was young, in love with my rain-soaked ceiling, and the orators seemed only dull.

WINDS THAT BLEW

I LOOK at the diary I kept as a budding citizen of Racine, Wisconsin. Each of the diary entries begins with the name of a day and an announcement concerning the wind. There is no date. I obviously imagined that time was standing still.

The top of a diary page reads: "Thursday. Light winds North by Northwest." Another page begins: "Monday. Strong Wind. Northwest changing to Due West."

When my mother went to visit in Chicago, I wrote her letters with the same prefatory pronouncements on the wind: "Friday. Medium Wind. North by Northeast." My mother saved them. I have them before me now. Ah, Friday. Ah, wind that blew North by Northeast.

This obsession with the day-by-day direction of the wind left me after I moved to Chicago. If I write what I now think of it I shall likely seem a bit softheaded. But when does that ever stop a man?

My theory is that much as we reveal our savage origins as infants, it may be that as boys we point like magnets to the historical types we are. The savage no longer peers through our unreasons as in our infantile pulings, but there is to be glimpsed in our youth-drunk souls a page of history that refuses to turn over. Such is my personal notion of heredity.

The authorities state that we have all come riding out of caves and forests on a river of sperm. Our souls, say the soul-spokesmen (together with our coloring and measurements), come bobbing down the zigzag course of this river. I add to this information the possibility (there is nothing wrong with believing in foolishness) that certain eras appear to leave a special print on our genes. We have, each of us, a thousand and one ancestors all decently entombed in the vaults of our blood stream. There is always one of the pack, however, who comes out of his winding cloth to say hello.

Such an historical imprint revealed itself in my boyhood. I knew where I had come from when I first saw the great Lake Michigan in front of our house. It was the sea.

A year later I was sailing on this lake in a boat built in the Costello barn. It was eighteen feet long, had a flat bottom, twelve-inch decks, the tallest mast our money could buy, a vast gaff-rigged sail, and a jib almost as unmanageable. It had a centerboard, an oaken rudder, and was caulked watertight with cotton and white lead. It was painted pea-green with blue trimming.

There were three others in the crew, Ken, Chuck and Harry. They all admired our ship, were eager to sail it, and as able as I; they contributed all their available fortunes no less than I did to its maintenance. But there was an itch, a compulsion, in the matter for me. I became captain of the boat because I was on it all the time. My three aides bowed to the fact that I *had* to be aboard, sail hoisted in wind or in calm. They didn't. They could do other things. I appeared beside them when a northwester rose, hounding them out of other pleasures, for I needed one of them then for the jib. At night I sneaked from my room to go sleep in the would-be cockpit. I organized secret midnight sails when there was no wind. I faked treasure maps showing gold buried by the Indians near the village of Evergreen, eight miles from our boathouse, and piped my gullible mates into all-day and all-night cruises that cost us drubbings at home—me, the worst.

My story is, it was neither boat nor wind nor water that lured me, but a ghost. The ghost was in me. It bade me sail. It chortled with phantom glee at the lap of water against the wooden hull, and at bow foam flying, at wings of sail bellied, and mast stays humming. It luxuriated, ghost-fashion, in the leap and thump through three-quarter seas and in the gurgle around the rudder. I did not sail the lake. I haunted it.

So great was the power of this ghost that it almost shaped my life. I clamored to enter the United States Navy and spend all my years on its frigates. My father, consulting a brother Elk as always, learned I needed to be recommended by a senator for appointment to Annapolis. He was on his way toward finding one perhaps when my desire went cold. I discovered there were no frigates in the navy, no sailing ships at all in fact, and that all its mighty vessels were run by steam like locomotives. I withdrew from the navy. The ghost in me had no feeling for steam.

THE CUTLASS IN MY SOUL

IT WAS not too bright a ghost, and, for many years, when I sought to put an identity to it, it wagged foolishly at a hundred spoors.

But one day, in a book of maritime adventures, I pinned it down, and knew its old berth and shipping papers, and proved its name—to my own satisfaction at least.

Out of Sicily my ghost had once sailed, in the year 1300. It was one of the conquering flotsam crew of Catalans, Goths, Gauls, Huns, Swabodians, Russians and Turks. The crew had no flag and belonged to no kingdom but the planks of a deck. Stateless, flagless, with only the waves for allies, it was known as the Great Company—and as the Great Company it battled the two Catholic empires of Europe and, for good measure, the new Empire of Mohammed.

My ghost was among them. It was present at the sacking of a hundred cities. It fought for Christian and against Christian, for Moslem and against Moslem. With its wild companions it stormed the Bosphorus, stood in the fortress of Gallipoli on the Hellespont and overthrew the armies of Byzantine emperor and Turkish sultan alike. Its captain was Roger di Flor, renegade Knight Templar tossed out of civilization.

One can talk oneself into such things, I know, and as a reporter I have met numerous zanies who insisted the spirit of a Pharaoh or a Caesar was spelling out words and dreams for them. I can only plead that other people's lunacies do not deter me from my own. No other of the thousand names in history ever whistled to me to join its crew so piercingly as that of Captain di Flor.

What a captain he was! On calmer reflection I may not desire to cleave my enemies in half, from head to crotch, with a single slice of my sword, as did the mighty Roger. No impulses to loot Africa and Europe bother me. And yet—have I not still the wish—a little wish—to face all the kings of the earth and bring the world to heel as one of the riffraff crew drawn up behind that invincible captain, Roger di Flor—the man without country who brought Christian and Moslem empires alike to their knees—my ghost's commander and its beau ideal!

As I write, there occurs to me for the first time (so help me God) the significance of my ghost. It is a Jew. Who else but a stateless Jew, first cartographer, first wanderer of the seas, belonged more in the Great Company—an outcast soldier under an outcast flag?

Who else could have been so happy under Roger di Flor that he must remain alive for six centuries to take roost in the soul of a Wisconsin boy who haunted a lake?

This ghost did not leave me after my boyhood. It stayed with me—to chuckle with glee one day in 1941 at a lunatic project brought me by two strangers from the Holy Land. This project was to drive the British and six of their satellite Arab countries out of Palestine. A little to my surprise, I agreed. And the old stateless, flagless ghost of a Jew in me rejoiced.

For once more Roger di Flor's henchman was on familiar ground. Flotsam from the four winds, ragtag and renegade from all the empires, excommunicated by all the popes, and with no nation for friend or home, the Great Company (that never numbered above fifteen thousand men and women) became a Power in the world. Kings pleaded for its good will. The weak wooed its succor. The strong gave it a wide berth. And in its midst my ghost rejoiced, beholding in all this the destiny of the Jew.

I step into the present—1950—The fight for Israel's freedom is won. I speak to Captain Bader, one of the captains of Jerusalem who had been a fighter in the Irgun Zvai Leumi in the first days of its challenge against the British Empire. I ask the young Captain one question of which I am still ignorant.

"What was your ordinance? Tell me with just what material and money resources you went into the war against the Empire of Great Britain?"

Captain Bader thoughtfully replies: "With three hundred pounds, with four hundred men, with forty revolvers, with five or six rifles, one submachine gun, three tons of explosives, and a donkey."

He adds wistfully: "The donkey was important. The poor donkey, with a pack of explosives on his back, was the first to give his life for the cause."

And so . . . as I write . . . we become closer friends, my ancestral ghost and I. I would rather that David, Saul or Solomon had taken up residence in me. But my spooky mariner is good enough to keep my soul alive with the whoop of Jewish destiny.

In my boyhood there were no such Messianic whoops in me. At that time, smelling with its new mortal nose the odors of wind and water, this ghost set up such a roar for its captain and its past as kept my craft, "The Seabird," turning circles for three years, with me glued happily and thoughtlessly to the helm.

GABRIEL'S TRUMPET BLOWS ABOVE
A FEW STREETS

I HAVE KNOWN men returned from shooting lions in Africa to sit and listen enviously to the tale of a trip to the zoo. And to have nothing in their mental game bags to match it.

The adventures of our first youth are this trip to the zoo. For in boyhood, though we go nowhere, our hearts storm the world. Every walk is an exploration, every move out of the house a sortie and an assault.

When I look back on my first self I am struck by the present insensitivity of my soul. That I could have been what I was and become what I am without suffering acutely over such change is a miracle of insensitivity. It is the miracle by which we live—this talent for dying without a sense of loss, this faculty of admiring what is left.

We do not weep for life spent, we do not shudder at death approaching. We are, luckily, a dull, thick-skinned lot.

Mortality would be unendurable to a truly sensitive or imaginative mind. It sometimes is unendurable and produces the protest of poetry. But most of us do not turn into poets with raging vocabularies. We become ruins without regret. Time is, indeed, the nimblest of God's magicians. While robbing us of life, it keeps us grinning with its promises. It deftly removes our existence and leaves us applauding (with limp hands) the shortening hour not yet taken.

I record these facts without too much complaint. Being a sane man, I feel grateful for my ever-diminishing sensitivity. It enables me to look back, without mourning, on the succession of graves, like those in a military cemetery, under which a legion of my selves already lies.

Toward the end, I imagine that memory plays a different part in our lives. Instead of bringing regrets it prepares us for dying. I think that when I am cooled and hunched beside the clouded window of age, I shall start a pilgrimage. I shall go tiptoeing among my headstones. I think I shall be lonely for all the dead selves beneath them. And I shall feel an urge to join them. Such a desire has already appeared at the door of my house and stands outside like a mendicant with a secret, waiting humbly to be welcomed.

But at this moment I am not yet dying and my memories of the past toll no bell in my heart—and do not summon me to join them. I turn to my past as a merchant still in business, pausing to take inventory of his riches. Here are the early wares of my nature.

I owned a sailboat. I set nets in the lake at evening. I raised them at dawn, removed two hundred perch and several pickerel, cleaned them before going to school and sat through six hours of algebra, English and ancient history covered with fish scales and reeking like a rotting wharf. Then I hurried out with my three first mates of "The Seabird" and, dragging a loaded cart after us, we sold fish for ten cents a dozen to the housewives of Racine.

I froze the Costello back yard into a skating rink, played ice polo on it, went hunting sparrows in the trackless snow and popped away with my rifle at the telegraph pole insulators. I built bonfires twenty feet high out of autumn leaves; lay panting fully clothed atop the best-dressed girl in my class, who would permit no intimacy that involved even the slightest disarrangement of her garments.

I manufactured horse-radish, chiefly out of potatoes stolen from a near-by garden. There were no horse-radishes to steal. Those we had to buy.

Bottles were difficult to get. But at last we discovered a heaven of bottles. This was the city dump, a mile outside of town. We gathered bottles, washed the spiders, bugs and curious growths out of them under the faucet and filled them with our horse-radish. Our customers were a hardy tribe. None perished.

We dug caves in the lake bank, lined them with timbers and sat in them motionless for hours, proud of our invisibility to any enemy eye.

I went to the funeral of a rich boy whose sister had rolled with all the neighborhood under the park bushes at night. Her dozen seducers stood bareheaded beside her young brother in his coffin—and ever after no crew member of "The Seabird" laid hand on Florence again.

We built huts behind the breakwater, caulking them watertight, for the waves broke over their tar-papered roofs during a nor'wester. Once a mighty billow battered our front door open, rolled in and exploded the red-hot stove which kept us cozy. We escaped with no more than eyebrows gone.

I owned a camera, large as a valise, and photographed the ditch-diggers at work on the gas mains in our street, hoping to sell a hundred prints at ten cents apiece. By the time I had the photographs on paper and each in a neat cardboard frame, my sitters had been called to other gas mains. This was my first bout with bankruptcy.

We manufactured hydrogen; why, I do not remember. But jars of it filled the barn. There were also jars of oxygen, handmade. Into these we dropped bugs and mice and noted excitedly their short but happy lives.

We engaged in Indian battles of a highly realistic sort. We were armed with bows and arrows and five-foot spears. The arrows were tipped with rags soaked in kerosene. We sent them flaming at each other's hiding places. The spear ends were made of sharp tin. There were no casualties, but once, during a scouting operation on the lake bank, I spied one of my tribe struggling at the practice of sodomy with an enemy figure. They lay, war forgot and knickers down, in the tall grass. I was shocked and fled. I was not learned enough at the time to know that sodomy was a diversion peculiar to warriors who favored the bow and arrow, as witness the habits of the world-conquering Persians and Turks.

I dreamed of occupying a bed with a girl and hopefully escorted a candy-store clerk to her home, three miles beyond the town, walking all the way. She lived in a hovel in a field alone with a deaf mother. Her father had recently died.

In the dark bedroom, she undressed shyly. To cover my mounting confusion, I poked around the room picking up and examining various objects. One of them turned out to be a fiddle, strung and easily tuned. Tucking the instrument under my chin I played, sobbingly, Schubert's "Serenade." The effect was unexpected. The candy-store clerk burst into tears. It was her father's violin, and my playing reminded her of her dead parent, whom she had promised on his deathbed to be a good girl. I left after a half hour of vain debate, having learned for all time the dangers of violin playing.

We wore pirate headdresses and ravaged the far-flung orchards of Squire Walker. Each of us had a pirate motto. I remember my own: "Never Come Back Empty-Handed."

We gave shadowgraph performances, chiefly of a doctor operating on a patient with saw, chisel and hammer, and removing from his interior balloons, bedsprings and coils of rope. I performed, also, as a magician, with the aid of my younger brother, dressed up in a small George Washington suit, discovered somewhere.

These performances were given in the Costello barn. Here I made dark lanterns out of gourds, hammered at sailboats and an iceboat, stored my oxygen menageries, and practiced feats on the trapeze. Harry Costello trained me while a dozen battered, happy-looking acrobats, balancers and contortionists wandered about and worked on their routines.

In the barn I also helped paint the long blue circus seat benches with their folding backs, readying them for the road. In the one-ring Costello Show, I performed on the trapeze in black trunks and a white silver-trimmed blouse with ballooning sleeves. After the performance I sat for hours stamping the throwaways with the name and date of our next stop.

We tried to blow streetcars off their tracks on Fourth of July mornings by putting little hills of potash and torpedo powder on the rails. We kept rabbits and doves; pestered the carpenter in the sawmill for materials for hut and ship repairs; went hopping ice cakes on the lake. The iceboat was the one thing in which Harry's genius failed me. It never sailed. It went scurrying before the cold wind, refusing to turn, tack or be halted. It passed beyond the ice and went flopping into open water. Leaping off, we watched it vanish with mournful hearts.

We went looking for canvas to patch the sail of "The Seabird." I borrowed the iron crank that rolled down the awning of my mother's store, and we raided Main Street one night with stepladder and scissors. We rolled down several similarly operated awnings and cut large squares of needed canvas out of them. There was great mystery in Main Street the next morning over these awnings with meaningless big holes in them.

We formed an orchestra of five—violin, piano, cornet, flute and drum—and I was thus able to put my fiddle to sensible use. We received two dollars an evening as an ensemble. We played chiefly in Wagner's Saloon.

We bicycled to Milwaukee, twenty-five miles off, stopping to scout in Kenosha. In Milwaukee we watched musical-comedy performances (among them Dick Carle in *Jumping Jupiter*) and spoke to strange, elderly girls, offering to give them rides on our handle bars.

My name first appeared in the news, and I read the item with delight, after I had recovered from my mother's loud anger. The item related that I and my crew of three had been saved from drowning during a sudden storm by the prompt action of the lifesavers' cutter in the harbor.

I played football on the high-school team as right end and collaborated on our class play with our left end, a colored boy whose father owned a small restaurant. We were inseparable, as collaborators often are, for several months.

I ran on the track team and had on my wall a framed newspaper photograph of me winning the mile in our interstate high-school meet. The photographer had made an error I found easy to overlook. I had neither won nor even finished the race. At the moment of being photographed, fifty feet in advance of the field of runners, I was about to plunge headlong off the track into a faint. But the record of glory on the wall of my attic room lost nothing by this lack of truth.

New books were on my bookshelves—among them Bret Harte,

Hornung, Richard Harding Davis, Hawthorne, Gogol, Gorki, Balzac, Maupassant, Poe, Thackeray and a man of marvels named Dumas.

We watched the upper windows of a mansion at night, grouped in silence behind tall bushes on its lawn. Behind these upper windows the elderly and idiot daughter of one of our town's millionaires undressed without pulling down the shades and stood naked and cackling foolishly before being put to bed.

And the pages of my diary still try to reveal my unflagging sex activities around the water hole, in caves, hallways, barns, cupolas, under trees and bushes. A typical entry reads: "Wednesday. Calm. No Wind. Met 4 minus X. Who says? Sixteen XB but RWZ = 31. Sbird has leak in bow." . . .

I see again the red automobile I owned and drove for a summer. It was a two-cylinder Santos-Dumont model with its door in the back. My father had taken it in payment for a debt. I wrecked it one afternoon by running it into the pyramid of cannon balls beside the Civil War statue in Monument Square. I have never driven an automobile since.

I serenaded girls beneath their windows, my mandolin strumming in the night. I spent hours singing in groups around parlor pianos, hunting frogs to sell, swarming around soda fountains, playing mumblety-peg, cracking jokes, kicking footballs, throwing baseballs, snowballs, stones and sticks, and sitting on dark curbings in long discussions which I can neither remember nor imagine.

I was my school's cheerleader after a broken ankle and collarbone had unfitted me for the gridiron. I walked, jumped, ran, played a thousand games and was introduced finally to the comforts of love in a bed by a spinster who patronized our fish and horse-radish industry. Thereafter I clamored vainly at her door for a month, but either her fears or my ineptitude as a lover had lost me a mistress and a customer.

I sat in trees devouring cherries, apples, peaches and pears. I dried bags of hazelnuts over the stove in winter, raided cabbage fields and made hundreds of dark lanterns out of gourds; lay all day under currant bushes stripping their branches; denuded hundreds of yellow raspberry bushes on the lake bank and engaged in battles of burrs and wild cucumbers. I manufactured phosphorus out of chemicals stolen from the high-school laboratory and spent months making large matches.

I went on hay rides, sleigh rides, bicycle rides, train rides, boat rides, and watched the vaudevillians at the Bijou Theater and the real actors at the Opera House, where *The Bells* and *Richelieu* and other wild dramas were enacted. I sat swooning with love for my Latin teacher, who wore a tight skirt and a starched white waist. I sat in the first row of the class, my legs extended and the words "I love you" chalked on the soles of my shoes for her to see.

I lay motionless for days reading books, tried to learn to dance, copied my weekly English theme out of a Chicago newspaper that ran a daily "Evening Story" and received, thus, my highest marks as a scholar. I burst into long trousers, went to parties at which I was sometimes the wittiest boy ever beheld and as often the most oafish, tongue-tied guest who ever suffered against a wall. I built snow forts, sported in blizzards, was overjoyed by cloudbursts, learned to ski on skis made out of barrel staves. I lay dreaming during heavy summer hours on hilltops, staring at cloud galleons, and the sky was part of my flesh. The wind blew out of my bones. At night the star clusters were my eyeballs. I was related to everything—to a dead fish, a crushed worm, a wall of green water breaking over my boat. I went leaping after grasshoppers and butterflies, breasts and pelvises, print, and Time itself. I knew no other way to live than to worship each new burst of sun over the horizon. My prayers were yells, my hymns were squeals and curses. I yearned, swelled, wept, ravished, splashed through mud and rolled in flowers—and was never injured, and hurt no one.

All this is not like a life I lived, but like a book I read or a dream I had. Looking on all its dimmed pantomime, on all the ghostly teeming hours of the past, I say, like someone unconvinced, "That was I."

AMBASSADORS FROM JERUSALEM

OF JEWS I shall write considerably before I am done with this book. Jewishness is one of the subjects on which I am most informed by experience and emotion. Thus there will be a parade of Jews. And there will be in the parade some Jewish politicians, a fledgling sect but already expert in chicaneries.

I have believed in a nation of Jews and worked for that belief. But there are moments when I think wistfully of the lost innocence of the Jews, when the only politics they knew was the management of heaven. Nations rose and fell, blood baths drowned the earth; jackal heroes screamed its peoples on to carnage; unsated neurotics in togas, gold braid and high hats slashed at the veins of life, crying, "Glory! Glory!" And with this evil the Jews had nothing to do. They were the birds that got tumbled out of their nests when the winds blew hard. They had no more to do with the historical winds of the world than to die in them, an innocence they are now happily done with.

The Jews are now politicians. They have a country of a sort in Palestine, which may be snatched from their fumbling hands by morning. They have a government of a sort. At the time I write there is only one thing certain about the Jews, exchanging their two-thousand-year-old dream of statehood for reality: Their politicians are as unpretty as those of many of their enemies. I pray that when I am writing the chapter of their doings, God will give me the wit of Sholom Aleichem or some small part of it.

Here I write only of the first Jews I knew. They were the best, the cream of my parade—my relatives, who came from Chicago, Cleveland and New York to visit my family in Racine. I say they were the best, not because my ego demands the finest origins. I say it because it is true. What family is not the best?

I know there are terrible families who sometimes attack one another with axes. I have read, also, that most of the nervous collapses and sexual disorders that overtake people are due to the shocks that mothers, fathers, sons, daughters, uncles and aunts give each other. Our scientists have been busy since Freud uncovering the sweating toads of family neuroses. I do not deny them a word. It is all true, including the ax murders, incest, swindles, bed-wetting and having to be kept in bathtubs.

But there are families without neuroses or homicidal lusts for each other. In short, there are families of love. These seldom appear in books, for the same reason that healthy people do not appear in the medical records. In a world that is not noted for its beauty of soul, these families make up for many things, even for atom bombs. When the atom bombs have left all our cities curled up like clinkers in a grate, these families will come crawling out of the silence and the drifts of dust, and build little fires and start cooking.

The sea minds its own business. After the storm it settles down to small waves and a bright look. These families are like the sea. They are modest, helpful and eager. They send gifts and telegrams of congratulations, never more than ten words long. They suffer for one another and celebrate one another's successes. They criticize a little, and why not? When people become big they sometimes forget who they are. But if the success is big enough they end all criticism and grow proud, as if they had elected a President (even if the President forgets who elected him).

Such was my family. I know the dangers to the reader of writing about one's family. The worst thing about an autobiography is usually the uncles and aunts one has to meet. A fatuousness comes over the writer as soon as he starts introducing his relatives. He begins pumping away at their characters and spreading anecdotes before us like a child excitedly emptying his pockets of rubber bands, bird feathers and favorite round little stones. I shall try to remember this.

But why do I write about my family at all? Considering that they were people who attracted practically no attention in life, what interest can they have in print? There is not even an inventor among them. And where do they fit into the writing of a man who is trying hard to be a thinker?

I will answer these logical questions with a confession. I write of them because I am in love still with all of them, the dead and the living. It is a love affair that shaped my brain. Possibly it even created it. I mean that if it had not been for this love affair I might never have known how to love anybody. I would have judged people by their thoughts, their expressions of opinion on foreign treaties and presidential candidates. And, who knows, I might have gone mad.

Though I shall write a full account of my relatives, I shall not go to all their noisy, food-smelling homes or waste time on their local color—the potpourri of tenements, sweatshops, card games, weddings, circumcisions, synagogues, wakes and a never-ending kitchen festival.

I shall, instead, bring them all from Chicago, New York and Cleveland to Racine on a Fourth of July morning thirty-eight years ago, place them where they once sat, on the back porch of the Racine Hotel overlooking the great lake, drinking beer, roaring with laughter, stripped to their undershirts, and in uncorseted kimonos, and vying with one another in a sort of Yiddish *Canterbury Tales*. Thirty-

eight years ago! But what I saw and heard never changed. It aged
and died. It grew sad with the troubles of gall bladders, livers, kidney
stones, swollen feet and palsied hands. But its heart never changed.
The love that was on the hotel back porch never vanished.

MY TANTE CHASHA AND UNCLE HARRIS

My Tante Chasha was my father's sister, married to my mother's
brother, Uncle Harris.

My Tante Chasha was tall, swarthy, fat, proud and profane. She
wore diamond rings and earrings. A gold-pinned watch, gold-
rimmed glasses and a diamond brooch made a Christmas tree of her
pillowy bosom. Her eyes were small and black, her mouth wide and
her face was like a handful of little apples. She was childless but
considered herself my true parent because, in her doting opinion,
my mother was too cold a woman to love me properly.

My mother usually answered this accusation with a derisive snort
and, if I was handy, a slap at my head.

Until I was fifteen my Tante Chasha was constantly trying to bite
my ears and was avid to rub my back in the evening with witch hazel.
She horrified my mother by informing me in Yiddish during a lull
on the hotel porch that I should always shun small women because
they had large vaginas. She answered my mother's cry of "Chasha,
don't talk like that. I forbid it!" with a sneer that a boy should not
grow up in ignorance.

My mother and tante glared a great deal at each other, but never
fought. They seemed to be afraid of each other, but this was only
respect, for theirs was the strongest friendship of two women I have
known.

As a child in New York's ghetto, I used to be whisked away almost
daily to entertainments by my Tante Chasha, who thus hoped to
shatter my allegiance to my home. Once, at the Buffalo Bill show, I
watched the long-haired hero of the plains sitting on his white horse
and shooting at glass balls that were being tossed into the air. I noticed that he missed half of them and that they landed whole on the
ground. I called my tante's attention to this and told her I wanted
them. She rose instantly and pushed her way down into the arena.

She was picking up the glass balls and sticking them into her bediamonded bosom when a tribe of Indians on horseback appeared, ready to charge to massacre. They charged only as far as my Tante Chasha and pulled in their mustangs to keep from running her down. My tante looked up at their crazily painted faces, cursed them in Yiddish, finished gathering the glass balls and returned to my side in a storm of hisses and hurrahs.

At seven she had taught me a dozen different card games, including my favorite, pinochle. I used to stand in the alley outside her bedroom and throw sticks at her window, trying to wake her up before her accustomed hour, which was noon, with cries of "Tanya, get up." Thirty years later I ordered a blanket of flowers for her coffin with that message spelled out in roses, but it was not used because it was an orthodox funeral at which flowers are not permitted.

Once awakened, my tante would sit half the day in nightgown and my uncle's slippers, her short hair rumpled like a pirate's, and play cards with me until my mother came to feed us both.

In later years, when I came as a new Chicago journalist to live in my Tante Chasha's house for a few months until I could afford private lodging, I objected once to the bareness of her walls, which were without pictures. My tante frowned. When I returned that day from my toil, I found the flat ablaze with "beauty." A dozen plaster busts of George Washington and several Indian chiefs of various tribes stood on the floor in the corners of my bedroom, and on the table beside my bed and on the dresser in front of it. She had bought out the complete stock of an Italian statue peddler whom she had spotted walking with a basket on his head.

Once, playing cards with my tante, I admired the green and gold brocade portieres that hung between the dining and living rooms. They were a wedding present from the old country. She climbed on a chair, snatched the portieres from their rods and began cutting them up with a scissors. In an hour she had made me a dressing gown out of them. Years later I wrote my first novel, during evenings after work, attired in this splendid robe.

Long after the time on the Racine Hotel porch, my Tante Chasha moved to California. She lived in a bungalow near the sea. I wrote her a letter once a year.

After seven years I came to the Coast to make my debut as a writer of movies. I called on my tante the first day. My letters were all in frames hanging on the wall. Under them stood vases of flowers.

My tante told me on this visit that she had started dying a few years ago. One night, feeling herself at "the end," she had lain down on the floor, placed two lighted candles at her head and pulled a sheet over her face and body. My Uncle Harris, returning from his favorite pier with a fine string of halibut, had found her laid out in this fashion and sat beside her weeping all night and pleading with her to get up and live. His pleas meant nothing to her, my tante related to me. However, after lying in state for several hours with her eyes tightly shut, my tante had risen of her own accord.

She had decided to defer her death until she saw me again. The cerements, candles and other props of the tomb had been put aside to await my arrival in Hollywood. Now that I was here, and she had seen me—she smiled defiantly at my mother standing beside me—she was ready to die. But first we would all sit down to the dinner she had cooked of the fish Uncle Harris had captured out of the ocean.

Three days later I sat beside her in a hospital. Her body was full of surgical punctures as an emergency measure to save her from dying of dropsy. She breathed with difficulty. I assured her she was improving, and in a few weeks she would come East with us to visit in my home in Nyack.

My Tante Chasha smiled fondly at me and spoke:

"When I was a little girl there was a holy man who lived in the woods outside our village. He got sick finally, sitting by himself, talking to God. And I used to bring him chicken soup in a pot. I walked through the woods at night with the soup. Nothing ever frightened me—the trees, the devils, nothing."

My tante panted and looked at the tubes that were draining something out of her. She continued in a hoarse voice, "One night I came to the holy man's house in the woods and I opened the door. It was dark inside but I could hear him in the bed. I said to him, 'It's Chashela. I'm here with the soup.' He called out to me from the bed, 'Stay outside with the soup, little girl. Don't come into the room. The Angel of Death is here.' 'Where?' I asked. 'On the wall,' he said, 'over there. He stands on the wall.' I looked on all the walls and I couldn't see anything."

My tante's eyes rolled to their corners. "But now I see him," she said. "Right on the wall. Like the old one saw. Standing where he said. Waiting for me." Her small eyes looked intently at me. "Give me a kiss," she said. After the kiss her hand pushed me weakly from the bed. "Go away," she whispered. "The old bastard is here." She closed her eyes and was dead an hour later.

On the back porch that Fourth of July in Racine she informed me that she had shut down her husband's ladies' tailoring establishment because she had caught him pinching his customers' behinds while fitting suits on them. I remember my mother crying out, "Chasha, don't talk like that in front of my son—about my own brother!" "I'll trade you the son for the brother," my tante snorted and glared at my Uncle Harris. "Women, may their bellies rot! Grabbing such a broken-down cripple of a man as my Hershela! Their bowels should burn in hell—and his, too." "Disgusting talk!" my mother bristled. "Talk!" my Tante Chasha sneered, "I won't talk. I'll break his rotten bones for him if I catch him again." And she winked at me and held out a small jeweler's box. It contained a signet ring with my initials on it. I could have it for a kiss—in front of everybody.

My Uncle Harris smiled tolerantly. He had an elegant air, watery blue eyes, and he kept his mouth pursed like a man full of sardonic ideas. He never uttered them. He was handsome, blond and snub-nosed like my mother, and with her same air of hauteur. But he was a comic version of my mother. He held his little finger crooked like a society man from Moscow. It never took part in his tea drinking, hand shaking, or card playing. He wept easily, despite his proud air, and gave off mysterious and dramatic sighs when he entered a room or sat down to play cards. He adored his wife and lived in terror of her long after she was dead.

For my seventh birthday he had made me a Cravenette overcoat that hung fashionably almost to my toes. A small brown derby hat went with it. He escorted me, thus arrayed, to a photographer, and my picture was taken in the Cravenette overcoat, the derby hat and a large minstrel-man bow tie around my neck. I held a pair of white gloves in my left hand. A boy's size ebony walking stick hung idly from my right. My Uncle Harris looked at me proudly.

"I want you always to be a little gentleman such as you are now," he said. "Don't forget."

Chasha died when my Uncle Harris was in his seventies. He remarried three times, but Chasha's ghost bedeviled his honeymoons, and the marriages ended in "settlements." The ghost appeared for the first time while he was driving Chasha's first successor to their new home. Seeing it, my uncle closed his eyes and put the brakes on quickly so as not to run the ghost over. When he opened his eyes, the police were all around. The traffic had halted. My uncle learned that a boy had been run over. Without waiting for further details, he threw himself into the arms of a policeman and confessed that he had run over the boy in order to avoid Chasha's ghost in the road. The police led him weeping into a cell.

It was revealed at his trial a few days later, however, that his car had been fifty feet away from the injured boy, and that innumerable witnesses had seen the guilty automobile hit the boy and speed off. The jury immediately released my uncle. He fell to sobbing and embraced all the jurors, kissing them with the wet and fulsome kisses that were his specialty. So potent were his tears that the jurors also wept noisily, and so did the judge. I was there, and helped to make the "settlement" with the bride, who was waiting to take him home.

There were two other unfortunate divisions of furniture, bungalows and dwindling cash. After he was eighty, my Uncle Harris tried no more marriages. He sat down instead to finish his memoirs, begun as soon as Chasha's departure had set him free to write. Once, while living at my mother's flat, he had insisted on her reading them. She read only a dozen pages and her face purpled. She flung the manuscript to the floor.

"Shame on you, Harris, a man of your age writing such things!" she said.

"Every word is true," my uncle answered. "In Kremenchug there was not one girl who did not sleep with me before I was seventeen. Go on, read, I beg you, Sarinka. It is exactly as it happened."

My uncle lived on in a small hotel room in Los Angeles, where he sat and played cards with men not quite so old as himself and read them at night the true account of all the women who had loved him. He died one night as I was writing about him.

TANTE ETA AND UNCLE MAX

MY UNCLE MAX had a drooping Cossack mustache that hung down his chin in two black points. He had Chinese eyes, and his right forefinger was missing. He had shot it off himself to evade service in the army of the Czar. Inducted despite this heroic action, my Uncle Max had deserted his Muscovite regiment and gone over to the enemy, the Turks. He had spent most of his youth in the Turkish land, infatuated by the musical genius of its people. Do not ask me what war this was. There were no historians on the back porch that Fourth of July morning.

This tall, Chinese figure of my Uncle Max sat beaming on his wife, my Tante Eta. She was a sister of my father, and of Chasha, and, like her, childless. Uncle Max beamed with so great a love that he was considered a foolish man, even by my mother, who admired fidelity as man's highest talent. Nevertheless, she was always a little embarrassed by my uncle's unwavering look of devotion, which he kept fastened publicly on my Tante Eta.

We all admired his fierce, warrior ways. He drank his tea out of a red-hot glass and refused to ride in elevators or on anything but horse-drawn streetcars. He knew all of Caruso's arias note by note. In his own home he sat in silence, his Eta beside him, playing over and over again the records of the great tenor. His phonograph played nothing else. I was told at the time that if it were not for the silver plate somewhere in my Uncle Max's throat, put there as a re-sult of some ailment befallen him in the land of the Turks, he would have been, himself, one of the great singers of the world. Occa-sionally a few notes, sonorous and dramatic, burst from my Uncle Max's throat, to be followed by a heavy sigh and a sardonic chuckle, a slow wiping of both halves of his mustache and a melting look at his Eta.

My Tante Eta was as large as her sister, Chasha. But she was beautiful, or at least she moved in an aura of beauty. When my Un-cle Max looked at her she seemed to be on a stage as if she too were part of an opera, and there was music playing around her.

My Uncle Max, returned from the delightful land of the Turks, had found her in Odessa. What she was doing there no one ever told me. Nor do I know what my Uncle Max was doing in Odessa. But I have seen their photograph as bride and groom, my Tante Eta tall, shapely, with a black-browed oval face as serene as a freshly laid hen's egg; my Uncle Max slim and a few inches taller, and looking at her as fiercely as if he were about to storm a city.

That had been many years (and many pounds) ago. But on the

back porch in Racine the love that had riveted their eyes on each other as they stood before the Odessa camera had not abated.

My Tante Eta and Uncle Max, after years of marriage, had no friends. They sat together night after night in their New York or Chicago home. They walked together in the parks, for my Uncle Max had a disdain for theatergoing or card playing. (This last failing exiled him from my family, who did almost nothing else—except work.) They listened to Caruso's records together. They ate together and they went to bed together. So odd, lonely and silent a pair were they that my family, who could make gossip and scandal out of the most unpromising of material, could never muster a tale about Eta and Max.

On this Fourth of July, amid the chatter, telling of tales and beer drinking, they were the only silent ones, except for my Uncle Max's surreptitious bursts of *"Vesti la giubba"* or *"Celeste Aïda."* My Tante Chasha looked sneeringly at her sister.

"Look at her," she glowered. "How she sits there! This cow that thinks it's a little bird! Fatter than me, with legs like a pair of pillows! Pheh! Who can help feeling ashamed of such a sister?"

At night my Uncle Max spoke to me, as he had often done in words that never changed.

"You are looking at the sky," he said slyly, his Chinese eyes twinkling. "Who is up there, do you think?"

"I don't know," I answered, as I had always answered.

"Let me tell you," my Uncle Max said. "God. That's who is up there. Nobody else. He made everything. The stars. The moon. The sky. But now I will ask you something. You are an American boy going to school. So maybe you can tell me. Who made God?"

"Such a foolish question!" my mother snorted. "I'm surprised at you, Max."

"It stands in the Talmud," my Uncle Harris would begin, and Chasha would cry out, "If my nephew wants to find out what stands in the Talmud he will read it. I don't want any fools to tell him. Quiet, Hershela, and mind your own business!"

And my mother said, "Please, let's not quarrel about religion. It's unbecoming."

I knew little of my Uncle Max and Tante Eta in that time. Uncle Max, the fierce Cossack, devoted lover and Caruso disciple, worked in a tailor shop. He was a cloth cutter and always poor.

It was not until many years later that the love story of my Uncle Max and Tante Eta became for me the idyl that still haunts me when I think of them.

My Uncle Max called on me in the Chicago newspaper office where I worked. He had grown thin. His coat hung scarecrow fashion from his broad shoulders. His face had become white. All that was left of its fierceness were the drooping points of his mustache.

He limped as he came to my desk. The doctor had told him he had "water on the leg" and would die soon. He asked me if, out of my high position in the world as a newspaper reporter, I could help him get a free bed in the county hospital.

"I'm sorry to bother you." The mustachioed white face smiled ruefully at me. "But who else is my friend? After all, when you were a boy we used to talk about God. And your Tante Eta loves you. Other people can talk more about it, but take my word for what I tell you."

I started telephoning for a doctor and hospital space.

My Uncle Max beamed at me.

"A great businessman couldn't telephone more people," he said proudly. Then he made me take a vow. His Eta must not be told how sick he was. Everybody must lie to her—I, the doctor, the hospital. Unless he was assured of this he would walk the streets all day until he dropped dead.

He looked around the busy newspaper office and then leaned over and whispered to me, "I don't want my Eta to feel bad. Please."

I vowed silence.

I called on him in the hospital where he had lain dying for several weeks. Eta was beside his bed. I remember their talk.

"Max, it's time for you to come home," said my Tante Eta. "You've been in the hospital enough, I think."

"Another few days are not going to hurt me," my Uncle Max said. "After all, when have I had a rest? And if we have a nephew who can arrange such fine things, let's enjoy them and ask no questions."

"But you say you're feeling good," said my Tante Eta, looking at him nervously. His face was now whiter than the pillow.

"Good!" My Uncle Max beamed. "Never better!" He let out a few of Caruso's powerful notes and winked at me.

The last time I came to the hospital my tante and uncle were holding hands. His face was turned to her, but his eyes were closed. He was dead.

Some years later I called on my Tante Eta in New York. I was on my way to Germany as a foreign correspondent. I found my tante in a tiny basement restaurant in the ghetto. She was its proprietress. She cooked, swept, washed the dishes and waited on the six tables.

It was raining when I stood in the doorway of this basement eatery. My Tante Eta, carrying plates of noodle soup to three patrons, saw me. She finished her mission and then held out her work-reddened hands to me.

We embraced. I was placed at a table, and my tante served me as she used to do in her own home. She sat watching me eat and asking softly questions about my family. Then, with a shy smile on her oval face, she arose and went to a table on which a phonograph stood. She turned it on and the little basement restaurant became full of Caruso's passionate voice.

The phonograph played for an hour, and my tante held my hand and kept looking into my eyes with so wild and deep a love that I knew her forever.

"You remember?" she whispered as each record started playing. "You remember?"

She died a few years later, after many misadventures, including the amputation of a leg. The look of her smooth oval face and her large childlike eyes as she listened to the music on that rainy night has never left me. And I still answer, as I did across the last food she served me, "Yes, I remember."

On the hotel veranda that Fourth of July in Racine, my Uncle Max astonished the family by crying out suddenly in his fiercest tones, "Eta! Show them!"

My Tante Eta blushed and then held out her hand for us to look at. A new diamond ring was on her finger.

UNCLE JOE AND TANTE LUBI

THE OVERSIZED ONE who looked like a Roman senator, tall, curly-haired, imperious-eyed, actor-faced, and with a voice meant rather for roaring than speaking—was my Uncle Joe. He was also my mother's brother.

The roar, the imperiousness, the noble lift of the large head were all a mask. My Uncle Joe was a child with a single talent, toil. No Carthaginian chained to an oar ever toiled harder.

My Uncle Joe made ladies' garments in a loft. Twenty, sometimes fifty, sometimes two hundred men and women worked for him, all cursing this slave of toil as a slave driver. My Uncle Joe was the Boss, but his idea of a boss's position in the scheme of things was an odd one. He sat in the midst of his embittered employees, putting out more work than any five of them. He toiled never less than twelve hours a day. In the busy season he toiled all night. Like my mother he grew flushed and sprightly with toil. He knew only one other joy—attending banquets.

There was another odd detail in my uncle's character as boss. He came to work always in his finest attire. He wore a frock coat with satin lapels, an ascot tie with a big diamond sparkling in its folds. He carried an ebony stick with a carved ivory handle. A gold watch chain strong enough to moor a stout vessel was looped across his vest. His trousers had stripes in them. His shoes shone like a pair of new coffins. And he wore a silk hat, the tallest ever seen in Canal Street.

Thus dressed, he walked up the five flights of stairs to his sweatshop each day at dawn and fell to roaring and toiling as if under penal sentence.

There was little greed in my Uncle Joe's industry. He made money, lived well, saved nothing, lost everything and continued to toil on into his seventies and eighties without shrewdness or regret. He had no love for power, no eagerness for wealth. He loved only toil, and that with a gambler's fervor.

Idle on a rare holiday, he sat with his big, calloused hands limp, his mouth curled in a Punchinello smile, drinking quart upon quart of beer and his eyes loving everybody.

In my ghetto boyhood in New York he had made me Lord Fauntleroy suits of black velvet with pearl buttons, cutting them and sewing them with his own hands and presenting them to me as if I were a favorite doll.

He sat on the Racine porch that Fourth of July, gurgling words in a half-cockney, half-Yiddish accent sometimes difficult to understand. His greeting to me never varied. His face, cheery as an emperor's, would boom and gurgle out, "Come, mine nephew! Stand up! Let's see! He's a big boy now, eh? A very big boy. How far can he swim, tell me?"

In his youth my Uncle Joe had swum the Dnieper River in flood, swum up streams and through torrents, dived like a pelican, walked on his hands on the bottom of the sea and left a memory of aquatic marvels in his village near Kremenchug. All this was hearsay to me until his eightieth year, when I beheld him in his favorite element for the first time.

He arrived unexpectedly one summer Sunday at my home in Nyack. I was entertaining a group of formal and elegant visitors, a French duke with a monocle among them. We were sitting around the swimming pool in the garden when my Uncle Joe came crashing out of the syringa bush near by like a bear after honey.

I was pleased, snobbishly, that of all my relatives it was my Uncle Joe who had appeared. No French aristocrats could match his imperious look or come close to him for physical grandeur. He stood, a handsome and majestic figure, as he beamed on the duke and all, and, unable to follow the complicated names I was offering, interrupted the introductions. "Please to meet you, everybody. It is always an honor to meet mine nephew's friends. And now, if it's all right, I would like to take me a swim. On a hot day like this everybody should be in the water." He confided this to a young lady as haughty as she was beautiful. With a practiced tailor's look at her fine size thirty-two contours, he added, "Come on, we swim together."

"I'll get you a bathing suit, Uncle," I said.

"I don't need no suits," my Uncle Joe boomed. "I got on mine underwear."

My Uncle Joe undressed behind the syringa bush, puffing and grunting, for he was not only eighty but grown portly. And for the next half hour, stripped to a baggy union suit, he entertained us with diving, swimming under water, walking on his hands on the pool bottom and bellowing out of the agitated deeps like a herd of sea lions.

Exhausted, he came to rest dripping beside the Duke of Vallambrosa and downed several bottles of beer. Then, fascinated by the nobleman's monocle, my uncle suddenly inquired, "What country are you from, can I ask you?"

The duke answered, "France."

"That's a good country," my Uncle Joe beamed at him. "I have a broa-in-law whose whole family comes from that same country. He thinks very highly of it."

(He was referring to my Uncle Issy Dreyfus.)

On his eighty-third birthday I asked Uncle Joe what period he remembered most happily in his life.

"In Canal Street when I owned my shop," he answered. "When I used to come in early in the morning, in my fine coat, with my ivory cane and my silk hat. And all my working peoples in the shop would say, just when I was opening the door, 'Aha! Here comes the swine!' Yes, sir, that's what they called me when I was young and strong and dressed up with a diamond in my tie. Yes, mine nephew, those were happy times."

My Uncle Joe's wife, Tante Lubi, was on the Racine porch with him. She was a short, stocky woman with her face as brightly painted as a rocking horse, and a rainbow-dyed coiffure above it. Her ears, bosom and fingers glittered with diamonds. She spoke in a sharp squealing voice in a Chauve Souris accent. When she addressed her husband her voice became so top-heavy with arrogance and contempt as to make her words entirely unintelligible. My uncle had only to begin a tale or offer a comment to set my Tante Lubi cackling at him in a sort of hiccuping frenzy of contradiction.

Great battles took place between my Tante Lubi and Tante Chasha. One of them had only to speak and the other came whooping into action. Once they even came near to murder. This happened during one of their honeyed truces when my tantes had whisked off to Karlsbad, Germany, without their husbands.

(There, the legend was, eternal youth lay in the baths and with it a cure for the mysterious disease which seemed to afflict all my relatives—"neuralgia.")

During a poker game on a hotel veranda on a Swiss alp, my

Tante Chasha had lost her head, picked up the fat but smaller Lubi and dropped her down the mountainside. Ever after, my Tante Chasha referred unreasonably to my Tante Lubi as a harlot. Only the presence of my mother, whom they both respected, held them on this Fourth of July to elaborate sarcasms.

My Uncle Joe, through forty-five years of her unflagging verbal assaults, loved his wife tenderly. He loved her not as Max did Eta, but as a humble coachman might love a princess come to share his lot. He regarded her as a woman of matchless wit, beauty and greatness. There was some ground for Uncle Joe's awe, for I have seen a photograph of my Tante Lubi taken before her wedding. She was slim, wore a Salome skirt and stood with a tambourine haughtily raised and ready to bang on her head. And she was also, throughout her marriage, president of an organization that arranged benefits in all the Yiddish theaters and raised money for "worthy causes."

My Tante Chasha often charged that Lubi stole all the money raised by the benefits to buy herself diamonds and the favors of young men who otherwise would not spit on her. But this we all knew to be an unbridled lie.

It was to my Tante Lubi that I owed my first introduction to the arts. At her home in my childhood I met the great Yiddish actors of the day. They came, after their performance in the theater, to play poker all night and eat, chiefly out of a huge bowl full of a heavenly food made out of sauerkraut, goose fat and onions all chopped together.

I remember some of the actors, the great Boris Thomashevsky among them, arriving at the poker game still in their costumes of purple tights, red mantles and swords dangling at their sides.

MY TANTE MILLIE AND UNCLE ISSY

MOST OF THE TALK on the Racine porch was of the missing relatives toiling in faraway cities of the U.S.A. My mother spoke of her two sisters, Becky and Millie, and I heard again what a genius had been lost to the theater when Becky became a dressmaker. Nobody, not even Bertha Kalich, could recite dramatic poems about dying husbands and runaway wives like Becky. I remembered her witty face, not fair and snub-nosed like my mother's, but sharp and Hebraic and full of mockery. Beside it was the jester face of her husband, Uncle Louie, who went through a lifetime of poverty and domestic tragedy flinging jokes around him.

Of my Tante Millie the family spoke with caution, for she had become high-toned and educated since her husband, the "Frenchman," had turned (to the wonder of all who knew him) into a millionaire. And my mother said, proudly, that in her last letter her sister Millie had related that she had ridden on a horse through Central Park.

My Tante Millie's husband was Isadore Dreyfus, a French Jew who wore tight checked pants and gambled with dice. He had started out as one of the family—even lower, for he had driven a pickle wagon and had been known in the Bowery as Issy Pickles. True, it was his father's own wagon he drove, the vehicle of a thriving pickle and olive importing business. Nevertheless, a pickle wagon driver was not a man to be suspected of future greatness. When my Uncle Issy's French-speaking family disowned him for courting the daughter of a lowly group of Russian-Jewish tailors, my Tante Chasha took him to her bosom, perhaps literally, for she was never a woman of half measures. And my uncles all gathered around him and explained to him the secrets of cloth, style, patterns and all the phases of garment-making.

How this misfit in the garment industry had risen to become a leading national manufacturer of ladies' clothes was a black mystery to my family of insolvent experts. But there he was, living on Riverside Drive with oil paintings on his walls, butlers, nursemaids, fancy automobiles and a dozen models marching in and out of his showrooms.

"I hear the tenor he is sending to Europe to learn how to sing is going to be a second Caruso," said my Uncle Harris in a tone that clearly conveyed the opposite meaning.

"He has a perfect right to spend his money as he wishes," said my mother.

"Gambling," said my Uncle Joe respectfully. "That man is a grand gambler. Pinochle with thousand-dollar bills I've seen him play."

"Gambling!" my Tante Lubi squealed. "What you know from gambling? From anything? No! Please don't discuss!"

"A fine millionaire," my Tante Chasha sneered. "How many times this millionaire has be-pissed himself in my bed!"

My father said, "He ain't the only man who can make a million dollars in the world." And he looked sternly into the distance.

Max and Eta had no comment. Millionaires were too far away for them to consider.

Years later, when my Uncle Issy lay sick, reduced to a skeleton, his riches all but gone, gasping asthmatically, boil-tormented and unable to hold a lamb chop on his stomach, my relatives who had survived still regarded him as the Fortunatus among them. And such, in truth, he was. With agonies of various sorts harassing his vitals for ten years, and driven by small means during that time into half-shabby little family hotel suites, my Uncle Issy remained always true to his star of great fortune. His interests continued to be those of a rich man in search of diversion and culture. He gambled with nickels instead of thousand-dollar bills. Bedridden, he listened to races and ball games over the radio. He smiled at elegance and beamed fraternally at all moonshooters. Cooped up in his diseases and deprived of all ventures, employees and spear carriers, he remained what he had been in his heyday—a top-of-the-world fellow.

My mother's sister, Millie, who was his wife, attended him in his last years like a court of nurses, cooks, scrub women and Scheherazades. No potentate ever received more homage than my Uncle Issy on his long death bed with only one heart to serve him; or ever died with a sense of superiority more intact.

On the morning of his funeral, my Tante Millie stood alone with me in her hotel suite bedroom. Her finger tips were cracked and bleeding from the years of toil and tension. But her hair was more beautifully combed than any of the throng of younger mourners in the parlor, and she retained, on this last of many evil days, the erect, proud air of a lady of fashion.

"I want you to remember if you write about him," she said with a faraway smile, "he was a grand man."

MY UNCLE JAKE

I RETURN to the porch, to all my relatives in their heyday, and I hear again the story of Uncle Jake—Uncle Jake, the lowliest of the relatives, the dweller in slums, but the hero of our family. He was my mother's eldest brother.

My Uncle Jake lived on the top floor of a tenement in Pitt Street with a Galician wife named Mary and a brood of children. These cousins of mine, in the pre-Racine days, introduced me to the joys of poverty. We broke windows together, lit fires under sagging clotheslines, hunted cats with big rocks and tried to frighten my be-wigged grandmother (the one who died laughing) into chasing us down the tenement fire escapes.

My Uncle Jake's wife, with erratic notions of sanitation, had stuffed mattresses into the windows of the bedrooms of her flat (to keep the dirt out). There were no chairs around the large oaken table in her dining room, and my Uncle Jake and his family ate standing up.

When my mother, on a visit, inquired what the reason was for this uncouth housekeeping, her sister-in-law answered: "Do you want us to sit down like the Irishers?"

My Uncle Jake worked as a presser in my Uncle Joe's sweatshop. He had been given this position after coming out of the hospital, where, I was told, he had lain on ice for two months after being beaten to the earth by twenty policemen.

My Uncle Jake's beginning as a presser was the end of his career as a hero. He had been Saul and Bar Kochba. Though he pressed garments for fifty-five years until he died at ninety, it was never as a presser that the family spoke of him.

In the time before my mother and her people had left the farm outside of Kremenchug where their family had gone barefoot and raised geese for four hundred years, my Uncle Jake had been the pride of the Swernofskys and of all the Jews who lived in that far part of the world. His brothers, Harris and Joe, had risen from goose tenders to tailors, and all the others of the family had learned a trade, even my grandfather, who exhausted himself daily hailing God in the synagogue. But my Uncle Jake had stayed aloof from all this. He plucked no geese, sewed on no cloth and prayed to no God. He had only one interest in life. Tall, with aquiline jutting face and a high head covered with the tight curls of a hero, he walked the streets of Kremenchug in the night looking for Cossacks to battle.

Kremenchug was a garrison town, and Jew-baiting was one of the Cossack sports of those days.

My Uncle Jake battled Cossacks as often as he appeared in Krem-enchug. He walked into their cafés, drew their insults and laid them low with his fists. He was a powerful man, stronger even, my family told me, than the famed Uncle Breitbart who made his living in the circuses allowing trucks to drive over his body while he "bent the crab" over a board of protruding spikes. My Uncle Breitbart was finally vanquished by a too-heavy truck which forced his back down on a spike. Blood poisoning ensued and killed him. Uncle Jake, on the other hand, survived the Cossacks with no damage to himself.

He had joined reluctantly in the Swernofsky migration to the new world, for he had found an ideal life in the old, breaking the heads of Jew-hating Cossacks. Arrived in New York City, where there were no Cossacks, and apparently only Jews, my uncle became an idle man who walked the streets in vain. His two brothers supplied him with food and tobacco, a roof and such diversion as he asked for. He sat in their kitchens and smiled at the tales of his valor which they never tired of telling to new neighbors.

Finally my Uncle Jake got wind of a new enemy. This was no enemy of Jews and therefore a little hard for him to understand. He sat in halls and listened to descriptions and denunciations of this enemy. It was an enemy who afflicted the poor and wronged the workers. Thus, while all the family were engaged in trying their best to become Capitalists, my Uncle Jake became a Socialist.

My Uncle Jake would rise from his grave and smile at me reproachfully if he could hear me use this word to describe him. For it is a little word full of small arguments.

In the halls where my Uncle Jake sat listening to orators there was a larger argument that held his attention. Hoodlums hired by the bosses broke into these halls and sought to scatter the men and women of the sweatshops who were trying to organize themselves into unions. My Uncle Jake worked in no sweatshop nor had he ever felt the distress of toil or exploitation. But his strength and his sense of justice knew only one cause—that of the lowly. When the hoodlums sent by the bosses entered the halls, my Uncle Jake rose always to face them. The needleworkers of the East Side saw again the hero of Kremenchug in action. As he had fought for Jews without knowing their God or their synagogues, so he fought for the poor, because he was one of them.

The end of his battles came in a parade. A Socialist named Barondess was running for Congress, and a parade of his admirers marched behind a band through the streets of the ghetto. My Uncle Jake marched with them.

A troop of policemen appeared. They had orders to scatter the parade. A fight ensued in which the paraders with their banners were driven from the street—all but Uncle Jake. He stood his ground, with law-abiding Jews from all ends of the world observing him out of their tenement windows, and shamefully battled the police. He fought alone until the twenty of them brought him to the earth, and he was taken to the hospital with broken bones and in a great fever, and laid away on ice for two months, so my family said.

When he came out of the hospital he was still strong, but he had put aside the spear of Saul and the sword of Spartacus. He lifted instead the gas-burning iron in my Uncle Joe's shop.

"You had ought to see him," boomed my Uncle Joe. "All the day on his feet. He never sits down. And that iron that I can't hardly lift he holds like a feather."

"Jake is a fine man," said my Uncle Harris, "but too hotheaded. In Kremenchug a hundred times I had to save that man's life."

"Look who is saving somebody's life!" said my Tante Chasha. "My new hero from the Moneshtana!"

"A fine man," sighed my Uncle Joe.

"What you talkin'?" Tante Lubi shrilled. "What you know? My cousin from Odessa! Is twice so good-looking."

"I am proud of my brother Jake," said my mother staunchly, as if she were settling an argument.

"I would like to tell you a story," said my father, looking shyly toward me. I had been drinking in the old tale of my Uncle Jake's valor.

"Joe!" cried my mother, quick to know the symptoms of an approaching lie. But it was, as always, too late.

"When I was coming to this country"—my father slid happily into a favorite whopper—"I wore a white suit and I had to sleep in the trees, not to be arrested on account of the wrong passport I had. I slept in the trees all the way from Minsk to Hamburg."

"Joe, please!" My mother's face was turning purple.

"Let him talk," said his sister Chasha. "What is he, a cow in a field?"

My mother became silent, her face burning.

"From Hamburg I took a ship," said my father, "which carried only a few passengers. The whole ship was loaded with coconuts. Then came the shipwreck. The whole ship got on fire and everybody had to jump in the ocean. I was swimming around in the water when I saw a crate of coconuts. I got on top of it and saved myself. But the trouble was I got hungry and I had to start eating the coconuts. Finally it got to a point when there was only enough coconuts left in the crate to keep it floating. If I ate one more it would sink. If I didn't eat, I would starve to death."

My Uncle Joe listened fascinated to this dilemma, which he had often heard before.

"So what did you do?" he demanded hoarsely.

"What did I do?" My father smiled at me. "I sat there, figuring which is better, to starve or to get drowned? And a ship came along and saved me."

My mother, who had left the porch at the first mention of the coconuts, returned. And the talk moved on to tales of ghosts in Kremenchug who turned keys in the door and stuck pieces of straw through the keyholes.

I have another story to tell of my Uncle Jake before I say good-by to him. During the years of his ironing I saw him only at funerals. He appeared whenever a member of the family was being buried. When the grave was filled and the mourners were moving away, my Uncle Jake remained behind. I used to stand beside him as he lingered. As we left each grave, he would say gently, "Why didn't He take me? I am older than the one who is buried there." At my mother's grave he patted my hand and said, "She was the best of us." At my father's grave a few years later he smiled at me and said, "He was too lonely without her."

But my story is of the time he came to visit me in Nyack. He was eighty-five. He sat upright without noticing my living room and spoke in a slow and gentle Yiddish.

"I would like justice," my Uncle Jake said. "An unjust thing has been done to me, and I would like you to change it, please."

I asked what had happened.

"For fifty-five years," he said, "I have worked for my brother Joe as a presser. He has had many different shops, and he has made much money. But I have not wanted any of his money. What he has made belongs to him. All that belongs to me is my job, and the iron. Wherever he has moved his shop, I have gone along and I was the presser. I have been on time every morning, and I have not been sick one day. This is what has happened. Last week I go to the shop. I climb the stairs. And the door of the shop is locked. But I hear my brother Joe is inside. He opens the door and he looks at me and says, 'Jake, there is no more work. You will have to go home.' Like that. After fifty-five years. I answered him, 'You are not doing right. You remember, in Kremenchug, when the widow Slotkin's horse got too old to work, she did not send him away. She opened the gate, and put him into a pasture. Me, you send away —where?' "

I promised to talk to my Uncle Joe and remedy the injustice if I could.

The next day Uncle Joe said to me, "Mine dear nephew, what can I do? The shop is closed. After fifty-five years, I ain't boss no more. I have lost all my money. How can I give Jake a job when I got no job mineself? I have always had a job for him since I was a young man. In big shops. In little shops. But now—I am no better than he is. I got no shops, no money, no job. What can I do? How can I give him justice?"

I tried to find my Uncle Jake. But there was no telephone in Pitt Street. And because I failed to reach him in time a woeful and comic thing happened.

My Uncle Joe had one worldly achievement that matched his imperious air. He was the president of the Kremenchuger *Verein*. This was an organization of men and women who had once lived in and around Kremenchug. Since nobody had migrated from Kremenchug in the present century, all the members of this circle were people bowed with years. The *Verein* held monthly meetings and gave banquets.

My Uncle Joe's role as perpetual president was as important to him as Vespasian's. A document three feet square hung framed on the wall of his bedroom in Washington Heights, proclaiming with ribbons and gold badges who Joseph Swernofsky was in the *Verein* —President.

In all the years of his ironing, my Uncle Jake had never appeared at any of the meetings of the Kremenchugers. A week after his visit to me, he presented himself to his first gathering. He was known. The wispy-faced and bent old men from long-ago Krem-enchug knew him as the citizens of Gaza had known Samson. They rose from their chairs to honor him as he came into the hall.

My Uncle Jake made a speech to the Kremenchuger *Verein.* It was the same speech he had made to me. The ancients listened, ap-palled. Their eyes looked furtively at their president, who still wore a diamond in his tie, who still roared with lordly tones at their banquets.

There was nothing my Uncle Joe could do but hang his head. He could not summon the courage to tell his lifelong admirers that he was a bankrupt, without a shop, a man brought low by adversity. He had been for sixty years the Rothschild of the Kremenchugers, their great nabob of industry and top-hatted Capitalist.

"It was a terrible thing for me," my Uncle Joe said to me a few days later. "Jake, mine own brother, accusin' me of this terrible thing! And I got to keep mine mouth closed. The election for the new president is coming up next month. You think they are going to elect for president a man without a shop? So I had to make them a promise I'm going to take him back. Where back? Never mind. I am walking all day through the garment district looking for a job for mine brother Jake. But it's no use even if I find one. He is too proud to work for anybody but me."

EVENING

THE SUN went down and the fireworks on the lake front began. My mother and father, my uncles and tantes, sat looking with wonder at the exploding skyrockets, the bursting Roman candles. A new case of cold beer appeared on the porch. My mother brought out fresh plates of peppered beef, sour pickles, salami, smoked white fish, twisted bread and other ghetto delicacies. There was no Jewish delicatessen in Racine. My family had arrived for the visit with suitcases full of spicy Yiddish foods.

When it grew dark, my family sang. I heard Yiddish songs as I watched the fireworks that celebrated the birth of freedom.

I leave them singing on the back porch.

Many years later I became a propagandist for Jews. I attacked their enemies—the Germans and then the British. I joined in the many-sided and confusing battle for a Jewish homeland in Palestine. I wrote books, plays, advertisements, rhymes, essays and money-raising letters for Jews. Swallowing my long aversion to the lowest of the arts, I even made speeches.

I did all these things partly out of my own needs. But much of what I have done as a Jewish propagandist has been done because I loved my family. It was they who were under attack by the German murderers and the sly British. It was they who, long dead, suddenly set up a cry in me for Palestine. Although I never lived "as a Jew" or even among Jews, my family remained like a homeland in my heart. I have carried them with me through all the streets of my native land.

They remained also a sweet counselor in my brain. When I hated too much the poison and folly of the world, when I have sat at bay like an inkfish spitting invective and seeing only the fangs of life around me, my family has brought a grin and sanity back into my soul.

I leave them on the back porch singing, all still young, all dizzied with fireworks and a new language, all full of beer and turbulence and undaunted lusts. And I say, if ever a man had guardian angels —they were mine.

Book Three

CHICAGO

I RETURN to Chicago, the tall marching town shouldering its sky-scraper spearheads.

I come back with almost the same mood I brought to it more than thirty years ago—to look on wonders.

Wonders to be; and now wonders that were. I once looked forward and I now look back, and between these two looks is most of my life.

So one might watch a speeding automobile approaching and vanishing and remain standing on a lonely corner with the thought in one's head, "My God, that was me in that car! I have come, I have gone."

I encountered many things in the city of my first manhood. I met torrents that spun me around, tides that drowned me and comets that pulled me across the sky. I had many adventures. I found there also a first understanding of myself—that I was in love with life. The child's joy I had first felt watching the symmetry and colors of sky, day, night, remained to delight me in the city.

This delight has never left me, and it has altered little. It is the only thing of continuity in me, that I have been always in love with the pulse of existence. Now after long immersion in the brutishness and lunacy of events and with the vision in me that tomorrow is a hammer swinging at the skull of man, I still glow with this first love. I have only to look at the sky, to see people in the streets, to see oceans, trees, roads, houses, to feel and smell snow and rain, and listen to wind—I have only to open my senses and I am again as I was in my boyhood—and in my Chicago time—delighted to be present.

My years in Chicago were full of this mothlike avidity that kept me beating around the days as if they were shining lamps. When I look back to that time I see the city as I saw it then, all at once; no separate streets, neighborhoods or buildings, but a great gathering of life, an army encamped behind windows.

At sixteen, the windows of buildings became a new poetry in my mind. Their sameness, numerousness and metronomic sweep excited me. I thought of windows as if they were in the heads of people rather than in the walls of buildings.

The walls of the city, the buildings that slid off into space; the rooftops of houses like a tangle of decks of ships at anchor; the smoke of chimneys making awning stripes across the sky; the porcelain-lettered names on windows telling the story of trades and crafts and people behind counters; the Noah's Ark streetcars and the taxicabs like tattered couriers and the firecracker signs that hung in the air in a continuous explosion—all these things gave me a similar elation.

Most fascinating of all that I met in the city was the crowd. I had read no books about it yet, nor heard of its bad repute. Watching it flow like a river, wriggle like a serpent, scatter like a disturbed ant-hill, I had no thought of its mindlessness. I saw only life in its face and the valor of survival in its movement. The feet of this crowd had come walking out of endless yesterdays. My heart applauded the long unbroken march.

I used to stand glued to the sides of buildings watching the crowd more avidly than I have watched any performance on the stage. And some such thoughts as these would come to me, "As it moves now it has always moved, wave on wave of humans thrusting their legs forward, their secrets draped in immemorial cloths. The great thing called survival hovers over the bobbing fedoras and jiggling breasts and gives them a dramatic look, as if their little walk from doorway to doorway were the winning of a glamorous battle."

My instinct never looked on the crowd as a history-figure. It did not come marching out of the events of history but out of the caves of existence. Watching it, I thought of a seed that could not be stamped out by glaciers, drowned out by floods or devoured by saber-toothed tigers.

There were no Governments in my crowd and no Philosophies. It carried no scar of Time on it. It was my family grown too big to embrace and too numerous to count.

CONFERENCE BETWEEN GHOSTS

My years in Chicago were a bright time spent in the glow of new worlds. I was newspaper reporter, playwright, novelist, short-story writer, propagandist, publisher and crony of wild hearts and fabulous gullets. I haunted streets, studios, whore houses, police stations, courtrooms, theater stages, jails, saloons, slums, mad houses, fires, murders, riots, banquet halls and bookshops. I ran everywhere in the city like a fly buzzing in the works of a clock, tasted more than any fly belly could hold, learned not to sleep (an accomplishment that still clings to me) and buried myself in a tick-tock of whirling hours that still echo in me.

But before I begin the tale of these antic years, my curiosity makes me pause to look at two people, the one of whom I write and the one who writes. I have boasted I am unchanged. I withdraw the boast. The young man of whom I write inhabited a world that was unthinkable without him. Tomorrow never existed for him. He felt a childish immortality within the day he occupied.

He saw people shot, run over, hanged, burned alive, dead of poison and crumpled by age; he attended deathbeds, executions, autopsies; he counted corpses in disasters, he even haunted the county morgue in quest of data and tidbits, and still there was no knowledge of death in his hours, no whisper of it anywhere in the word "future." Neither literature nor reality awoke his sense of being mortal. His relatives began dying, friends collapsed and were shoveled into the earth, and he continued as unaware of death as if it were a language no teacher could bring to his tongue.

Put beside that young man whose name and the remains of whose face I bear, I am quite a ghostly fellow. Not he who is long gone but I who still exist am more the spook. For his activities were solely part of living, mine are divided between living and dying. What he could not imagine, I think of a great deal of the time, and when it is not in my head it settles in my mood, and I can even feel it as a sudden brake on my laughter—the world without me—that strange, busy and eerie activity from which I shall be absent. The sky will be in place, the automobiles will run, the crowds will move in and out of buildings, the great problems will blow like threatening winds through the mind of man, and I shall not be there.

I can recall the hour in which I lost my immortality, in which I tried on my shroud for the first time and saw how it became me. This is a queer thing to be writing about, having promised exuberantly the tale of my youth in Chicago. But the tale must wait on the teller. My youth speaks to me, and I see myself not as I was but as I am.

The knowledge of my dying came to me when my mother died. There was more than sorrow involved. I felt grief enough, and my heart felt the rip of a dear one dying. I carried her image in my eyes, seeing her when she was no longer seeable. Her vanished voice echoed in my head and the love she bore me struggled painfully to stay alive around me. But my heart did not claw at the emptied space where she had stood and demand her return. I accepted death for both of us.

I went and returned dry-eyed from the burial, but I brought death back with me. I had been to the edge of the world and looked over its last foot of territory into nothingness. I had seen mortality and it remained in me like a disease. It changed my knowledge of life. Its delights were never quite able to fool me again. The secret of death appeared in all the faces around me. I knew they were citizens of two worlds, of the small vanishing one of light and noise, and of the vast endless one of darkness and silence.

The passing of time, which had once been a happy and unimportant thing, became a matter of meaning. There was a plot to the rising and setting of the sun. Life was passing. The days were dropping from me as if I were shedding my life. Time was my blood ebbing.

THE GOOD-FAIRY LIQUOR SALESMAN

IT WAS the third of July, 1910. I stood before the box-office window of the Majestic Vaudeville Theater waiting to buy a ticket for the matinee. I had run away from Madison, Wisconsin, the day before. I had slept on a bench in the Chicago railroad station until morning, walking all morning through the coffee-smelling Loop, bought a new tie and debated with myself whether I should notify my mother of my decision against further education. I had won the debate. I intended to notify her after a few days. I had fifty dollars in my pocket, my university budget for July. After the money was spent (although how to spend fifty dollars far away from the needs of boats, huts and Indian warfare was a mystery to me), I would return to Racine with a fine crop of lies concerning mishaps at the university—pickpockets, desperate gamblers who cheated. I was certain the right story would occur to me. A university was an institution so far removed from my mother's experience that she was sure to believe anything I told of it.

A voice called my name as I was paying for my theater ticket, and terror almost sent me flying. But at sixteen, one does not yield too quickly to panic. One has dignity and the beginnings of courage toward one's guilts. I turned with pounding heart but unbroken ranks and saw a man with a large red nose beaming at me. Logic told me it was a relative, for who else would know me?

It was an uncle distantly related, a penumbra uncle who might never see my parents for the rest of his life. Hope came to me. Not only was this uncle's nose red, but his belly was big, his eyes were bloodshot and he did not look as if he would live long.

"I recognized you by your eyes," the uncle said. "They're like your mother's. How is she?"

"Fine," I said.

"And your father?"

"Fine."

I thought of darting into the theater and trusting to luck that this vague uncle would forget so brief an encounter.

"And what are you doing here?"

"I'm going to a show."

"So I see." The red nose beamed. "I mean what are you doing in Chicago?"

A sudden lie occurred to me, one that would do service not only now but later when I faced my parents.

"I'm looking for a job," I said.

"Any particular kind of a job?"

"Not exactly."

"Come on with me. Maybe I can fix you up with something."

"I just bought a ticket to the show. I'll see you afterwards."

"Afterwards is no good." The bloodshot eyes smiled. "Get your money back for the ticket and come along."

I turned in the ticket and walked off reluctantly beside the big belly and the red nose. A conversation drifts out of a long-ago street.

"Do you know my name, young man?"

"It's Mr. Moyses."

"That's right. Manny Moyses. You don't drink, do you?"

"You mean whisky?"

"Yes, that's what I was referring to, young man."

"No, I don't drink that."

"Is that so? And you came to Chicago in this heat to hunt for a job?"

"Yes, sir."

"What would you like to be?"

"That depends on the offer, I think."

"Well, have you been trained for anything—like a bookkeeper or salesman?"

"I've been trained to be an acrobat."

"You don't say so! A tumbler, eh?"

"No, on the trapeze."

"That's crazy."

"If necessary I can play the violin."

"That's kid stuff. It's not practical. Come on. I've got something better for you."

"Are we going anywhere in particular?"

"Yes. We're going to call on one of my best customers. You've got to be smart, boy. Now I'm in a business where people are always glad to see me. I'm a liquor salesman."

Fifteen minutes later he said, "Here we are."

I looked up at a gray stone building with extra large windows. One of the windows was lettered in gold, "Chicago Daily Journal."

I hesitated. The smell of the near-by river came to my nose.

"I'd like to do something on a boat," I said.

"That's no good, working on a boat. Come on, now. Don't be scared. And let me do the talking."

"Certainly. I'll be exceedingly glad to."

We rode up a large elevator into a urinous smell of ink. A door read, "John C. Eastman, Publisher." We entered.

A man with a mat of gray hair, a large red nose like my uncle's and almost the same sort of bloodshot eyes, sat at a desk. He said, "Hello, Manny, what have you got today?"

"Something special, John," said my uncle. "I've brought you a hundred-and-twenty-proof genius. Just the thing your great newspaper needs. This is my nephew, Bennie Hecht."

"How do you do, Mr. Hecht." The bloodshot eyes peered at me. What kind of a genius are you?"

I was left dumb by my first "mister."

"He's a writer," Uncle Moyses answered, and a greater lie I had never heard.

"Can you write poetry?" the other red nose demanded.

"He can write anything," my genie uncle answered recklessly.

"I'm giving a party," Mr. Eastman confided, "and I want a poem written about a bull who is nibbling some God-damn grass in a pasture and swallows a God-damn bumblebee by mistake. The bee goes down his throat into his stomach and after two days of hardship comes out of his ass in a big load of bull shit. Mad as hell, this God-damn bumblebee crawls out, dusts himself off, jumps on the bull, and stings the be-Jesus out of him. I want that written in a poem. Think you can do it, Mr. Hecht?"

"Give him a pencil," Uncle Moyses answered proudly.

"I want a moral on the end," Mr. Eastman explained, "about not keeping a good man down."

Both red noses left. I heard them laughing in the hall, and I sat at the publisher's desk writing a poem. I was nervous about using dirty words but decided to utilize Mr. Eastman's vocabulary.

When he came back an hour later the poem was finished. It was six verses long with a "*L'Envoi.*" He read it slowly.

"That's all right," he said. "I can use it at the party. Come along, Mr. Hecht."

I followed beside him to the second floor. We entered a large barnlike room full of desks and long tables, piled with typewriters and crumpled newspapers. There were many men in shirt sleeves. Some of them were bellowing, others sprawled in chairs asleep, with their hats down over their eyes. The smell of ink was sharper here.

Mr. Eastman took me to the largest roll-top desk I had ever seen. There was an awesome railing enclosing it. At this desk sat a man with a mat of gray hair, a red nose and another pair of bloodshot eyes. I was introduced to Mr. Martin Hutchens, the managing editor. Mr. Eastman said, "I hope you can find a place for Mr. Hecht on your staff, Mr. Hutchens."

Mr. Hutchens took a long look at me. I wondered what had become of my uncle.

"Journalism is a high calling," announced Mr. Hutchens in a loud growl. "I ask chiefly of a newspaperman that he devote himself to his craft, which is one of the finest in the world."

He stood up. Mr. Eastman had disappeared like my uncle. Mr. Hutchens led me to a flat-topped desk that swarmed with telephones, baskets, spikes and smeared paper streamers. A tall man with an imperious face was standing at this desk. He had an eagle beak and the look of a captain running a ship.

"Mr. Ballard Dunne, this is Mr. Ben Hecht," said Mr. Hutchens, "a new journalist who will assist you."

Mr. Dunne turned a look on me like a searchlight.

"Mr. Dunne will be your city editor," Mr. Hutchens added. He stood for a moment regarding me with a sort of increasing surprise. Then he walked abruptly away.

"Have you had any experience on a newspaper?" Mr. Dunne asked.

"Only today," I said.

"Indeed! What did you do today?"

"I wrote a poem for Mr. Eastman about a bull," I said.

"As a rule we prefer prose in our columns," Mr. Dunne muttered. He turned and frowned at the distant desk behind which Mr. Hutchens already sat glaring at a newspaper. After a moody silence Mr. Dunne addressed a handsome black-haired man sitting on the other side of his table. I had not noticed him before.

"Mr. Finnegan, this is Mr. Hecht," said Mr. Dunne, and the searchlight eyes played on me again. "Mr. Finnegan is our assistant city editor. You will report to him at six o'clock tomorrow morning."

I was amazed that so omnipotent a man could make so great a mistake. Tomorrow was the Fourth of July, a day sacred to torpedoes on streetcar tracks, cannon crackers and hundreds of little explosives. I sought to correct Mr. Dunne's lapse.

"Tomorrow is the Fourth of July, a holiday," I said.

"Allow me to contradict you, Mr. Hecht," replied Mr. Dunne. "There are no holidays in this dreadful profession you have chosen."

I nodded and waited for something more to be said. But I seemed to have vanished. I stood for several minutes staring out of limbo. Then I walked away. Mr. Finnegan had smiled at me, and I left quickly to keep from bursting into tears.

ROBINSON CRUSOE IN A NEWSPAPER OFFICE

THERE WILL BE no end to this book if I continue unreeling memory spools. For I have come to a part of my life that is as vivid still in me as if it were happening. I have forgotten whole months and years, almost whole lives. But of this time I remember minutes and words, smells, grimaces, the quality of air I breathed, the expression of faces and every move and turn I made. And I do not lament this time as one does a lost love. I enjoy it as one of the few proofs of my existence. Whatever I have become, that youth who sat breathlessly in the *Journal* local room was what I was meant to be.

Many habits were formed by those days, and points of view which I have never outgrown or improved upon came to roost in my head. I shall write of these later. I would like now only to relive that swift time without adding present ornament to it.

I had been dropped willy-nilly into a world that fitted me as water fits a fish. It was a world that offered no discipline, that demanded no alteration in me. It bade me go out and look at life, devour it, enjoy it, report it. There were no responsibilities beyond enthusiasm. I needed nothing else than to remain as I always had been—excited, careless, bouncing through rain, snow, hot sun and vivid streets. I have never seen my Pumblechookian Uncle Moyses again to this day. But I stare at his big belly and red nose with never-ending gratitude.

And here is what befell. I went to live at my Tante Chasha's flat.

I arrived in the *Journal* local room each morning at six. There was much excitement the first day. Jack Johnson and Jim Jeffries fought for the world's heavyweight championship in the West. Men moved in and out of offices, bellowed at each other, broke into sudden sprints, grew suddenly profane. Some were normally dressed. Others wore dirty aprons. I wondered what kind of journalists these could be. Mr. Dunne, a pilot guiding the paper to its deadlines, stood up at his desk at eleven-thirty. Some fifteen men had all started pounding typewriters at once. Mr. Dunne didn't sit down until two-thirty. Mr. Hutchens remained at his desk bowed over reading matter. He was obviously too important for anybody to speak to. Mr. Finnegan's handsome face became covered with ink blurs. His cascade of black hair became uncombed.

I sat at a long table on which stood some twenty typewriters. There was one in front of me but I didn't use it. There had been a typewriter in my mother's store. I had learned to run it. But I sat in front of this one with my hands in my lap. I had nothing to write on it.

I sat in this fashion for two weeks. No one spoke to me. I gave up looking eagerly at the faces around me. And as far as I could make out nobody looked at me. There were a lot of useless things in this big room—disabled typewriters, broken chairs, a wrecked dictionary stand. I was apparently in this category of impractical objects.

But though I sat marooned each day from six A.M. to three P.M. and ate a sandwich for lunch alone in a restaurant where no newspaperman ever appeared, I remained almost out of breath with excitement. The smell of ink, the drunks coming in with seven A.M. hangovers and sucking therapeutically on oranges, the clanging of a mysterious bell above Mr. Dunne's head, the air of swashbuckle—hats tilted, feet up on top of typewriters, faces breathing out liquor fumes like dragons—these matters held me shyly spellbound.

I had received my first pay after working three days. A plump boy bulging in knee pants and with a large-nosed swarthy face had come to me on Saturday and given me a message from Mr. Finnegan. This was Harry Romanoff, head copy boy, who in later years became one of Chicago's most turbulent journalists.

"Mr. Finnegan says you should go get your pay," said Harry. "Saturday is payday."

"Where do I go?"

"Follow me."

I stood before a grilled window and a stranger handed me a small sealed envelope. Inside it were twelve dollars and fifty cents. I had received money before for working but never in sums exceeding a single dollar. The pile of bills that came out of the little envelope bewildered me as if a chestful of pirate gold had opened under my nose. I wondered if it were my half salary for the three days or my full weekly wage. Still undecided, I returned Monday to my place at the long table and sat in a swoon of riches. The next payday answered my confusion. My full wage was twelve dollars and fifty cents. I was not disillusioned. I returned again to the long table to sit, breathe the inky air and wait as one waits for a race to begin. I noticed that when my colleagues were not typing, sprinting, bellowing, dozing or sucking on oranges, they read newspapers. I considered imitating them for a while but decided against it. My name might be called from the now-distant peak where the imperious Mr. Dunne had his being, and I would be too engrossed to hear it. It was better to take no chances. I remained poised, attentive, my hands in my lap.

And then one day at ten-thirty A.M. I heard my name. It boomed from the faraway Mr. Dunne.

"Mr. Hecht!"

I stood up, controlled a desire to show how fast I could run, and walked to the city desk. A man was watching me. He stood behind a glass-paneled door, holding a curved pipe in his teeth. He had black hair, a curl of it ajiggle on his brow like a spring, and he looked like an Indian. I had seen him before. He was always standing holding the curved pipe in his teeth and puffing on it. I passed the glass-paneled door and the Indian face smiled at me.

Mr. Dunne looked at me solemnly.

"How are you getting along, Mr. Hecht?" he asked.

"Very well."

"How do you like being a journalist?"

"I like it very much."

"Mr. Finnegan tells me you are in the shop every morning on time."

"Oh, yes. Six o'clock."

"Keep it up," Mr. Dunne smiled. "And now would you mind running down and getting me a can of tobacco. Dill's Best. The fifteen-cent size."

I returned in three minutes out of breath and gave Mr. Dunne his can of tobacco.

"Thank you very much," he said.

I went back to my place at the long table and sat quivering as if with some major achievement. Something had started. My name had sounded in the world of men.

Another event followed. The Indian face that smoked the curved pipe came out from behind its glass panel and walked across the big room toward me. I looked up and saw a pair of smiling eyes.

"Greetings and salutations," said the Indian face.

I could think of no answer to such odd words.

"My name's Duffy, Sherman Reilly Duffy."

"I'm Bennie Hecht."

The Indian face puffed on the curved pipe and considered something.

"I thought I should talk to you about your hat," it said, finally. "Where did you acquire it?"

"In Racine, Wisconsin."

"I suggest, if you are to continue in your career as a newspaperman, that you get another one, Bennie."

My heart turned over at the sound of my boyhood name. No one had spoken it in this new world. I looked at the dark strong-nosed face, and it smiled, sneered, blew smoke out of a mouth corner and grimaced aloofly, all at the same time. The hat under discussion was a flat-topped fedora, shaped like a round cheesebox with a brim that curled up evenly. It was a trifle too small when my hair wasn't cut, and I had to keep pulling it down.

"That hat is incomplete without a ribbon fluttering from its side," said Mr. Duffy. "I would take steps if I were you."

He returned briskly to his post behind the glass-paneled door.

"ARE YOU READY, DIAVOLO?"

I BOUGHT a new hat and suddenly, before another week was done, I was a curious combination of ruffian, picklock and enemy of society. Mr. Finnegan, handsome and smiling, sent me forth each dawn to fetch back a photograph of some news-worthy citizen—or die. The citizen was usually a woman who had undergone some unusual experience during the night, such as rape, suicide, murder or *flagrante delicto.*

In that time the camera was not as active or efficient as it is today. There was also a prejudice against printing pictures of corpses in the news columns. The picture chaser was thus a shady but vital figure. It was his duty to unearth, snatch or wangle cabinet photographs of the recently and violently dead for his paper.

While maturer minds badgered the survivors of the morning's dead for news data, I hovered broodingly outside the ring of interviewers. I learned early not to ask for what I wanted, for such requests only alerted the beleaguered kin, weeping now as much for the scandal coming down on them as for the grief that had wakened them. Instead I scurried through bedrooms, poked noiselessly into closets, trunks and bureau drawers, and, the coveted photograph under my coat, bolted for the street.

These burglarious activities seemed only too reasonable to me. I had dreamed of being many things in Racine—the "human fly" who walked upside down across a rigging high in the circus tent, the pirate who ravaged rich coastal towns, the figure that flew from trapeze to trapeze, the bespangled hero of the carnivals who stood high on a ladder ready to dive into a small tub of water as the drums rolled and a voice below called—"ARE YOU READY, DIAVOLO? . . . . . !" Diavolo was ready.

In the adventurous months that followed, I was frequently pursued, once by a new widower who kept firing a pistol at me, and who arrived in the *Journal* local room with two cartridges undischarged. I had hardly time to hand Mr. Finnegan the photograph of the man's suicide wife, posed coyly in a bathing suit some years before, and dart into the composing room for refuge and a new world of entertainment I had encountered there.

Here Mr. Bill Boyer, head compositor, presided as master of all the dirty jokes and bawdy tales that I was to continue hearing with scarcely a variation for the next twenty years. Mr. Boyer was partial to me as a listener for I had then heard none of them. His aproned, burly figure, his bald head, his ink-smeared hands and the fine odor of beer that rose from him when he laughed at my laughter still come to tell me I once knew Silenus.

My picture stealing filled Mr. Finnegan and Mr. Dunne with pride. They never inquired into the methods by which my contributions to the day's journalism had been obtained. But their grins were broad when I stood before them with my loot.

Only once do I remember Mr. Dunne regarding me with some nervousness. This was when I appeared at his desk lugging a gilt frame, four feet square, that contained the hand-tinted photo enlargement of a mustachioed Pole, mysteriously shot to death in his bed in Aberdeen Street. It had been the only likeness of the deceased in the basement flat.

I had spotted it hanging on the parlor wall directly above the dead man, who had been laid out on an ironing board balanced on top of two chair backs. The mourners were gathered in the kitchen, refusing to discuss the tragedy with a cluster of policemen.

In climbing up to unhook the heavily framed likeness, I had been forced to stand on the ironing board on which the original lay. It had toppled over, dropping both of us to the floor. My bruised nose was still bleeding, and I was unable to speak—exhausted with a mile run from the scene—when I lifted the large frame to Mr. Dunne's desk.

"Have Bunny Hare make a copy of that thing," he said coldly, "and then see that it gets back to the man's family. I don't approve of major burglary and mayhem." After studying my bleeding nose a moment he added, "I must ask you, Mr. Hecht, to exercise more discretion in your work—and try using your wits more."

My salary, however, was raised to fifteen dollars.

A few months later Mr. Finnegan offered me advice. He had noticed me slipping some equipment into my overcoat pocket before leaving on an assignment. I now carried a pair of pliers, a "jimmy" and a large file.

"I'd go a little easy if I were you," Mr. Finnegan said. "You're not going to help the paper any by doing time in Joliet."

Mr. Finnegan was Irish and prescient. The file did not earn me a striped suit, but it got me my first beating.

I was sitting one dawn with a policeman in a rooming-house bedroom. He had been left to guard the body of a murdered young actress that lay nude and hatchet-hacked on the bed near us. The policeman had instructions to see that nothing was touched until his superiors arrived.

It was half light outside. I sat on an old-fashioned trunk that had belonged to our corpse-companion, and I kept its police guardian chuckling with a selection of Mr. Boyer's dirty stories. While talking I worked away with my file, silenced and hidden by my overcoat. I was filing through the staple lock on the trunk. I was certain there would be innumerable photographs of the hatchet victim inside it. I worked eagerly because, despite the missing segments of the body on the bed, it was obvious that it had been a young woman of great beauty. The photograph of a beautiful young woman as the victim in a murder case was the finest manna that could fall on Mr. Dunne and Mr. Finnegan.

I had filed more expertly than I knew, for, abruptly, the trunk's padlock dropped to the floor. At the noise, the policeman jumped to his feet. I continued telling him Mr. Boyer's tale of the married man who came home unexpectedly and found his wife and sister-in-law in bed with a three-legged man from the circus. But the policeman pulled me from my perch, beheld my villainy and started swinging fists at me. I stood my ground, demanding a look into the now-opened trunk before my unscrupulous rivals from the Hearst paper showed up. But I was thrown out, with a lump over my eye.

HOW I OUTWITTED TWO
LONG-AGO DEMONS

THERE WERE a number of picture chasers like myself loose on the city in 1911. But my only important rivals were two who worked on the Hearst paper, the Chicago *Evening American*. A more ominous pair of rogues have never crossed my path, for which I thank God. They broke my heart again and again, for toil, plot, cheat, rob, climb and swindle though I might I was often no match for their combined cunning. They were named Roy Benzinger and T. Aloysius Tribaum.

Mr. Benzinger had a glass eye which he would pluck out of its socket while pleading with some already hysterical parent for a likeness of her ravished and throttled daughter. The gesture usually gained him five minutes of uninterrupted search while his hostess lay in a faint. Mr. Tribaum was an even more intimidating fellow to collide with on a picture chase. He was an albino with a puckered scar extending from ear to ear across his throat. His colorless eyes were undetachable, but he had other unethical ruses. He was able to pose as a policeman, an insurance adjuster, a fire chief, a gas-main inspector. His genius as an actor seemed to me truly Satanic. He was full, also, of an adult cruelty and bluster when addressing the grief-stricken, and often I stood by, curdling with impotence as he cursed his way to the family album, snatched from it the picture he wanted and skittered off with a leer at my empty hands. I had no way of matching such ruthlessness. Yet once I shook him on his throne.

On a cold winter morning in Oak Park the entire press had been locked out of a cottage in which a mother and two sons were sorrowing over the death of a seventeen-year-old girl. She had killed herself in a suicide pact with a married minister of the neighborhood. No cajoling or deviltry could gain any of the journalists admission. The two sons were husky and beside themselves with grief, shame and rage.

As the day darkened, and heavy snow began falling again, I still hung about. I had been jumping up and down to keep from freezing since seven in the morning. It had been a lonely stretch, for none of the journalists in that time spoke to me. They had an aversion for picture chasers, who were considered as lowering the standard of their calling, and increasing its hazards besides.

At five o'clock my heart suddenly beat high. The moment for which I had waited through ten hours of cold and hunger had come. My two Hearst rivals were pulling up stakes and taking their frostbitten persons back to town. They threw a last look around to see where I was, but I was crouched behind a snowbank and apparently gone from the scene.

Left alone, and with an hour before the picture-chasing crews of the morning papers would appear, I went to work. I climbed the side of the cottage with a half-dozen boards under my arm. I placed the boards over the mouth of the chimney and packed them tightly with snow. Then I lay on the roof and waited. Smoke began seeping out of the cottage windows. The front door opened. A billow of smoke sailed out. The mother and her two sons, gasping and coughing, came hurrying into the street. One of the sons ran for a telephone to call the fire department.

I slid from the roof and pried open the kitchen door of the emptied cottage. Five minutes later I was bounding through the heavy snow with a photograph in my pocket of the Oak Park Juliet who had died for love.

This event was a climax in my career. My salary went up to seventeen dollars and fifty cents a week and my picture scoop was discussed in several saloons. Walter Howie, the great city editor of the Hearst newspaper, sent for me, via my albino rival, and invited me to join his crack staff. I sent back word that I was incapable of such treachery as he proposed.

VIGNETTE OF A HEADLESS MAN

DURING THE TIME of my picture chasing, the thought of writing anything for the *Journal*'s columns remained as foreign as the thought of reading them. The appearance on the front page of a two-column photograph I had brought to the office exhausted my interest in the newspaper, except for the limerick contest on the back page. Daily awards up to fifteen dollars were being offered for the best last line to unfinished limericks. I worked on last lines constantly while in the office, for money troubles had begun to beset me. Despite my weekly seventeen dollars and fifty cents I was broke half the week and often went without lunch or without a pipe to smoke.

This was due to unconsidered investments in books. Salesmen appeared at the gate of the local room. They carried suitcases full of book backs. These they opened, accordion fashion, to reveal irresistible phantom sets of Turgenev, Tolstoy, Hawthorne, Kipling, De Musset, Smollet, Sterne, Flaubert, Maupassant and others. I bought all the sets that were offered, not even scorning the poetical dramas of Swinburne. I paid a dollar down on each set, signed a document obligating me to pay fifty cents every Saturday on each purchase and found myself facing bankruptcy. With five, ten and finally fifteen sets of books to support, there was often not enough left out of my wage after the Saturday collections to carry me through Wednesday.

This siege of hunger came after I had left my tante's bed and board, with exotic results I shall set down later. Now I grew thin and desperate, and I became ambitious to make money. The limerick contests had brought me only a single third prize of five dollars. I began to feel dissatisfied. I had found out recently that reporters who wrote stories for the paper received higher salaries than any picture chaser could ever command, however accomplished he became.

Also I had felt the first sting of criticism. In the years to come, I was to be flayed and eviscerated by critics, and I learned how to steady my nerves against their assaults. But this first challenge of my honor and sufficiency (into which all criticism degenerates for its victims) shook me like a betrayal. To work wildly and with all one's forces, to pitch one's heart like a gift to God knows whom, and to earn a slap in the face and the title "idiot" is an almost fatal shock when first felt. Grimly and shakily one gets used to the bleak phenomenon of defeat. One learns that there is a curious incompetence in one's talents, and that the betrayal comes not from the outside but from an inner Judas. The critics are only bystanders with a little salt for one's wounds.

The first sting of criticism in my life befell in this way. I was returning to the office one morning with a photograph in my pocket of a woman who had been held up by two bandits. Suddenly there was a great commotion in the street ahead of me. A Negro was running toward me, waving two handfuls of money in the air as he vaulted along. Behind him came a press of roaring people. I was to learn in a few minutes that the Negro was full of hashish and that he had walked through the plate-glass window of Jesse Binga's Negro bank, terrified a dozen men and snatched a bundle of money from the teller's cage. Now he screamed and laughed as he sped toward me. He was soaring through clouds of bliss on wings of gold. Leading the posse at his heels was a powerful-looking man in a butcher's apron. He sprang forward swinging a meat cleaver. The Negro's head vanished suddenly. His trunk remained erect for several instants spouting blood like a fireworks piece. Then it fell.

I was immediately alert. Within five minutes I had all the facts and names of the story. I was at Thirty-fifth and South State Streets. Instead of going to a telephone and calling my paper with the news of the wild event I had witnessed, I lit out on foot for my office. I spurned streetcars and taxis and ran almost as dementedly as had the Negro who had lost his head.

It was a four-mile stretch to the *Journal*. I arrived at Mr. Dunne's desk in a precarious condition, my eyes protruding with exhaustion and unable to speak. Imagining me the victim of an acute disease, Mr. Finnegan helped me into Mr. Duffy's department. Here I was served a drink and managed, before a doctor was called, to blurt out my story of the decapitated Negro, the hashish, the bank robbery, the greenbacks floating in blood.

Mr. Finnegan stood scowling at me.

"The story came in twenty minutes ago from the City News Bureau," he said coldly. "Next time try to remember you are living in the twentieth century with easy access to the telephone."

Mr. Finnegan gave me no assignment for a week. I sat reliving my stupidity, unaware that spring was in the streets. Then I heard my name called, and I shuffled to the city desk. Mr. Finnegan spoke to me as if I had never done anything wrong.

"Here's a woman who's being sued for divorce and charged with sleeping with twenty different men," he said. "Her husband's detectives have tracked down five different love nests she favored. Get her picture and also an interview with her. I'm not sending anybody else to cover it. It ought to make an interesting feature story—if you can keep it from being too dirty. Think you can handle it?"

"Yes," I said. "Do you want me to telephone it in?"

Mr. Finnegan laughed and I felt whole and human again.

"No," he said. "I want you to write it."

MY LITERARY DEBUT

Mrs. Bertha Chandler was a soft, shapely and purring matron of thirty-five. She fed me lunch, sewed a rip in my sleeve and talked as no woman had ever talked to me before. Her tears never stopped, her voice trembled and choked. At several points we wept together. For Mrs. Chandler was apparently the victim of an inhuman and half-mad scoundrel—her husband. She had never betrayed her mate with any man. She had never even dreamed of such ugly behavior. But Mr. Chandler's mind had begun to fail. His dyspepsia had turned slowly to madness. This was understandable in a man approaching sixty-five. The tale of her sins was a lie sprung out of this madness.

"I would rather die before kissing another man," Mrs. Chandler wailed, "and Fred knows this. But he has talked himself into something. He is mad—mad!"

At one o'clock I shook hands with Mrs. Chandler and promised her the power of the press as a champion. Overcome, she embraced me, covered my face with kisses and held me tightly against her uncorseted body. My rage at her husband's villainy was such, however, that only thoughts of avenging her came to my head.

I sat at a typewriter in the local room for two hours writing the story of Mrs. Chandler. I still remember the lead: "We think that one of the greatest injustices ever done against a pure and noble woman has been done to Mrs. Bertha Chandler by a madman who calls himself her husband and protector."

I sent the story to the city desk, page at a time. The bulging Romanoff, head copy boy, stood beaming at my side as I wrote. I wrote seventeen pages. And as I wrote I saw an unprecedented thing happening. Mr. Finnegan read each page carefully and then handed it to Mr. Dunne. Mr. Dunne, in turn, pored over each sheet, obviously not skipping a word, and then carried the "take" in person to Mr. Hutchens at his desk. Mr. Hutchens' eye remained glued with similar fascination to my writing. As if this were not enough triumph for my first flight as a journalist, Mr. Hutchens handed the accumulated pages to Mr. Boyer, who chanced to be passing. I watched Mr. Boyer, eyes wide with wonder, read my copy. At this point Mr. Duffy came out from behind his glass panel and joined my group of literary disciples. I was on page eighteen, with the story of Mrs. Chandler's sweetness, purity and woes still only half told, when Mr. Duffy came up to me. He stood looking at me, his pipe held to his mouth, his lips puffing, his eyes twinkling, sneering and glaring all at the same time.

"That's enough of that," he finally said.

"I'm not through yet."

"Don't be a horse's ass," said Mr. Duffy. "Come on, we'll go have a drink."

I heard a guffaw from the far end of the room. Mr. Murphy, our police reporter in for a chat with Mr. Dunne, was reading my story. Mr. Murphy laughed loud and long and cried out in delight, "What God-damn Gussie Mollie wrote this crap?"

This query and another look at Mr. Duffy puffing on his pipe told me the truth. I was a clown belaboring a typewriter. I had poured out my heart and talents and earned the title idiot again.

"Come on, we'll have a drink," Mr. Duffy repeated. "And don't worry about being fired. I'll see to it nothing of that fatal nature happens."

The crime of writing unprofessionally was one I was to outgrow quickly. But that other idiocy—that of mooning over strumpets as virgins, of perceiving honor and truth where not even their ghosts remained, God forgive me—I am still not done with it. My record as a reporter was a preview of my record as a man. I grew hourly keener toward understanding men. My mental nose could smell out the doubts in an archbishop, the fears in a banker, the insecurities, cruelties, lonelinesses and depravities asimmer behind the male façade. But to women I brought ever a Phoenixlike illusion.

I can hear Mr. Duffy's words in the saloon booth a half hour later, as he ogled his fourth highball: "Read Rabelais. There's a man who knew women for what they are. Puff adders. Gila monsters. I suggest you study the blue-nosed Mandrill in the zoo, a monkey that sports an ass like a rainbow. Which is a damn fine definition of a woman, if I do say so myself. As my friend Gene Field wrote in his ditty 'The French Crisis,' there is only one honest feature to the female." And Mr. Duffy quoted tenderly, " 'Here's to her orifice of sin—that lets her liquefactions out and other factions in.' We'll drink to it."

Mr. Duffy drank, and added:

"In addition to reading Rabelais, I suggest you learn how newspaper stories are written. This is done by reading newspapers, particularly the Chicago *Daily Journal,* which I notice you have not deigned to peruse as yet."

FULL SAIL, HULL DOWN

I HAVE MOVED my writing board from the Pacific Ocean to the Hudson River. With the world outside strapping on its armaments and arguments for another war, and with civilization threatening to explode again, I sit and beam on the dim little harlequinade of my youth. And an urge, as of largess, lifts me. I desire to make others happy with a happiness that was once in me. As the poet seeks to give to others his pictures of birds flying, trees budding and rain falling, so do I offer my little remembered antics and hope to evoke the joyousness that was in them. Unlike the saints, I have never had visions of heavenly bliss and have therefore never cried out the raptures of kingdom come. But of earth I have had visions. It is these visions that enrapture me as I look back on the buzzing, fevered comedian who once carried my name.

How it happened that that wistful booby I have described turned into a good newspaper reporter able, as Mr. Duffy phrased it, to distinguish his ass from a hole in the ground, belongs to the mysteries of nature. I can remember, however, that in the six months that followed my experience with the nymphomaniacal Mrs. Chandler (for that is what a gaudy divorce trial revealed her to be) I came to fame as a journalist. The fame was confined to the small space around Mr. Dunne's desk, but I could imagine no greater world to conquer. It was also somewhat undeserved, for it was not my talents as a news gatherer I offered my paper but a sudden fearless flowering as a fictioneer.

I have made up many bold plots in my work as writer and movie inventor, but none was ever more bold and dream-headed than the stories I fetched back daily out of the Chicago streets as "exclusive news" for the *Journal's* columns.

Mr. Finnegan had become irked by the sight of me hovering hawklike around the edges of his desk. My picture-chasing work was usually done by ten-thirty. And he had said to me one day, "Go out and see if you can pick up a story."

"Where should I go?" I asked.

"Anywhere," said Mr. Finnegan fretfully. And thus I was launched. The "news stories" I brought back in the months that followed gave

Mr. Finnegan, Mr. Dunne and Mr. Hutchens all the delusion that they had hatched a journalistic wonder. Tales of lawsuits no court had ever seen, involving names no city directory had ever known, poured from my typewriter. Tales of prodigals returned, hobos come into fortunes, families driven mad by ghosts, vendettas that ended in love feasts, and all of them full of exotic plot turns involving parrots, chickens, goldfish, serpents, epigrams and second-act curtains. I made them all up. I haunted police courts, the jails, the river docks, the slums. I listened to the gabble of sailors, burglars, pimps, whores, hop-heads, anarchists, lunatics and policemen. Out of their chatter I wove anecdotes worthy of such colorful characters. And to give reality to the people of my "scoops" I raided the family album in my Tante Chasha's flat.

One by one all my relatives, particularly the female ones, appeared in the columns of the *Journal* as spies, heiresses, Isoldes, King Lears, Monte Cristos, Evangelines, Hedda Gablers and the relicts of Enoch Arden. There were also "scoops" innocent of relatives. These were harder to cook up. But here Mr. Finnegan came unwittingly to my help. Fascinated by my unexpected knowledge of the city and insight into its news sources, he assigned a photographer to assist me in my Haroun-al-Raschid enterprises. I have known two photographers well in my life—this one, Gene Cour, and the camera genius of Hollywood, Lee Garmes. Because they shared the same natures, I hold photographers among the most winsome of folk in the world.

Gene was older than I. His good-looking face was blue-spotted from a powder explosion. His polka-dot smile is still in my heart. He joined innocently and expertly in my quest for "news." My concepts of journalism stirred a delight in him that made us brothers. Together we schemed and toiled in a make-believe world of dramas. We produced "scoops" now that shook the rival city rooms of the town.

One of the first of these was the story of an outbreak of piracy on the Chicago River. We persuaded a fat tugboat captain named Garrett and a policeman named O'Toole that fame and fortune would come to them if they loaned themselves to our project. Gene photographed the captain, gun in hand, the tugboat "Martha Graham" and the policeman. The illustrated story of how Captain Garrett and Officer O'Toole had fought it out on the river waters with a small black pirate craft seeking to board and loot the "Martha Graham" in the dead of the night was devoured by the *Journal's* editors.

and readers alike. In the brisk battle reminiscent of the days of the Spanish Main, scores of shots were exchanged. The seamanship of Captain Garrett finally won the day. Heading his ship into a hail of fire he rammed the river buccaneer, overturned it and sent it to the bottom. Officer O'Toole, as shown in the photograph, was still dragging the river for the pirate bodies.

I recall also the story of the Runaway Streetcar. A motorman had fainted at his controls, and his streetcar, filled with screaming passengers, had hurtled wildly through the streets. I remember Gene's photograph of terrified pedestrians waving their arms at a passing streetcar, and I remember the "staging" of the picture. It had involved an outlay of five dollars. I am unable either to recall or to figure out now in what manner I made this fantastic lie sound plausible enough to be accepted as news, how or with what data and witnesses I could have backed it up. But I remember it in print on the front page. And I remember Mr. Hutchens, ever loyal to his staff, defending me a little incoherently against an outraged representative of the traction company, come to demand apologies and denials:

"Your organization, sir, is already in sufficiently bad odor with its grafted franchises and boodle politics." Mr. Hutchens' bloodshot eyes flashed at the traction mogul. "I advise you not to add to your crimes that of libel against the press. And in conclusion I can tell you, I would rather take the word of any of my reporters than the sworn testimony of all the millionaires of Chicago."

I wince now, but in that younger day I felt a simpler emotion. I would have died for Mr. Hutchens had he asked me.

Another of my stories was flashed on the city in a seven-column front-page headline: "Earthquake Rips Chicago." A four-column cut of a great fissure opened by the quake on the Lincoln Park beach accompanied the story. Gene and I had spent two hours digging the fissure. There was other corroboration—housewives who reported dishes spilled from pantry shelves and broken, stenographers who reported the top of the Masonic Temple to have swayed dangerously, and several male citizens who had been thrown to the ground by the impact of the quake while at work in their shops. These were, of course, all my relatives, this time with their true names and addresses attached. For several days, during which an angry rival press sought to belittle the *Journal's* great scoop of the earth's upheaval, my aunts, uncles and cousins stood firm in their memories of terror and shock. My Tante Chasha was widely quoted as having thought the end of the world had come.

An unfortunate incident put an end to my news fabrication. I was not too depressed by it, although it resulted in a week's suspension without pay, for I was growing up rapidly, and the praises I drew from my editors were beginning to embarrass me.

The scoop that undid me concerned the love plight of a "Rumanian princess." Rather than marry a prince whom the royal family of Rumania sought to force upon her, my princess had escaped to America with the man she loved and was now toiling happily as a waitress in a Greek restaurant in Wabash Avenue. "I am a woman married to the man I love," she said, "and that is better than being a loveless aristocrat."

One of the most beautiful photographs ever to appear in the *Journal* illustrated this moving tale. It showed the princess in several poses, one a large ravishing two-column cabinet photograph captioned "Royalty Scorns Kingdom for Love." The other pictures revealed the ex-royalist waiting on table and washing dishes in the restaurant kitchen.

At two o'clock our publisher, Mr. Eastman, appeared in the local room. Mr. Eastman's appearances were rare and always ominous. He seemed always to be walking sideways with his head down as if he were making leeway in a stiff wind. The wind appeared stiffer than usual this two o'clock. Mr. Eastman was waving a copy of the Home Edition in his hand. He listed for Mr. Hutchens' desk and stood bellowing over his startled editor.

"Who put this God-damn thing in my paper? This God-damn whore on the front page! That's Gloria Stanley! Every God-damn fornicator in Chicago knows her! Jesus Christ, what kind of a whorehouse gazette are you running, Martin? The whole God-damn Union League Club is laughing at me! Get that whore out of my paper! And I want to see the pimp-headed sonofabitch who disgraced my front page. I'll murder the foul bastard!"

I heard the last of it as I slipped warily into the composing room. Mr. Duffy found me an hour later still huddled behind a linotype.

"I've been having a hell of a time with old Hutchens," he said. "Sweet Christ, you ought to know better than to go slapping that Jezebel into the paper."

"I didn't know she was so well known," I said. "She told me she'd only been in that profession for a few weeks. And she was in a convent before."

"Jumping H. Sebastian God!" Mr. Duffy took the pipe out of his mouth and stared at me. "She's the God-damnedest, busiest, well-known whore and———in the whole of Christendom." He resumed puffing sadly on his pipe. "Jeezoo, how long are you going to stay wet behind the ears?"

I had no answer. He went on, "I think I've straightened the contretemps out for you. You're to keep away from the office for a week. I think all parties will have cooled down by that time, and you'll be able to resume your nefarious activities next Monday. Now go out the back way before anybody catches sight of you."

And Mr. Duffy crossed himself, as was his habit in times of stress, accompanying the holy gesture with his special prayer, "Ales, wines, liquors and cigars."

When I reported for work a week later Mr. Finnegan studied me with his jaw muscles working.

"I'm taking a hell of a chance sending you out on an assignment," he said.

"No, you're not," I said.

This was my vow to become an honorable and truthful newspaperman. During the twelve years I continued in that calling, I kept my vow, as reasonably as I could.

A ROOST IN GOMORRAH

I WAS SEVENTEEN, and a great desire was on me to live in the world alone, separate from even the finest of relatives. Sitting next to me at the long table in the local room was a young man of nineteen. He was Ned Griffiths, later to become E. H. Griffiths, a director of movies in Hollywood. In that time he was nineteen, Ned was the handsomest youth I had ever seen. He looked like Lancelot. He was tall and blond, with a poet's elegance on his face and the frost of knighthood in his manner.

We had one thing in common. We were the two friendless figures on the paper. None of the men who tumbled in and out of the office ever paused to include me in their hail-fellow palaverings. I was too young and, perhaps, too peculiar. They smiled at me when I caught their eye. I remember Al Johnson, who had been a strong man in a circus; Larry Malm, who had taken permanently to drink the night of the Iroquois Theater fire as a result of finding himself in a wagon with twenty-five charred corpses piled on top of him; and Jimmy Murphy, who lived in open fear of having me assigned as his assistant on his police beat.

Outside the office, Mr. Duffy alone spoke to me and bought me a drink occasionally. But generally when my day was done in the office, I wandered off to my tante's flat, disinherited.

Ned's loneness was the result of his looks. His beauty exiled him from the intimacy of his fellows. In vain he went without ties, affected a torn raincoat and neglected shaving. The staff gave him as wide a berth as they did me. Mr. Finnegan was dark and handsome, but the fine look of his face was a familiar one. It was to be seen in orators and statesmen. Ned was the frontispiece to a fairy-tale book, and he could make a whole barroom feel ill at ease by merely entering it.

We had little else in common than our aloneness in a turbulent scene. I had not learned to converse at the time, and when not reading my fifteen sets of books, was content to sit and stare at people. Ned was even more reticent, for his head was echoing with poetry. I had introduced myself shyly to him when he came on the paper. A second conversation revealed that we were both living in the homes of aunts. We decided to go look for a room together.

It was a spring day. We walked down North Dearborn Street and had reached the eight-hundred block without finding a rooming house to our liking. We paused in front of a building more high-toned than any we had seen in our walk. It had a marble balustrade leading to its carved front doors. Its windows were richly draped. There was no "Room to Let" sign in any of them, but we decided to inquire nevertheless.

A remarkable-looking woman answered our ring on the bell. She looked like a society dowager, and we both blushed for our crudity in summoning her to the door.

"What were you looking for?" the society dowager asked.

"A room," Ned said, smiling suddenly like a Welsh Valentino.

"I don't take gentlemen roomers"—the woman smiled—"but perhaps I have a place for you boys."

We were shown to a room on the third floor. Two cots were in it and two armchairs and a bureau. There was a magnificent red carpet on the floor. White lace curtains hung over the window.

"Will four dollars a week be all right?" the woman asked.

"Apiece?" Ned asked.

"No, for both of you," she said. "Bring your things whenever you want. This is your home."

My Tante Chasha cursed and screamed, but I pried my books and scant wardrobe loose from her loving grip the next day. Ned and I settled in our new home. In the evenings we occupied the two large armchairs and read. Ned was reading Oscar Wilde. I had bought a new set of books—Victor Hugo.

Our work done, we had no friends to meet, and no money to spend, and the city itself was, as yet, no match for the book pages we turned day after day, night after night. We never saw our landlady at all.

We planned furtively a larger social life for ourselves. We bought a bottle of liquor and several glasses and stood them on the bureau in preparation for any callers we might have. None came. The bottle remained unopened. And we continued our silent little reading society on the third floor of this elegant Dearborn Street mansion.

Then one night I leaped to answer a knock on our door. A beautiful young woman in an evening gown said there was a call on the telephone for Mr. Hecht.

"It's probably from the office—an assignment," I said to Ned. "Some disaster."

I followed the young woman to the second floor. We entered a beautiful vestibule.

It was Mr. Duffy on the phone. He was inviting me to join a party going on in the barroom of the Virginia Hotel near by.

"I'm with my friend, Ned," I said. "Why can't you and the party come to visit us? We have liquor and everything in our room."

"What is the address of your abode?" Mr. Duffy asked, and I felt a twinge of misgiving for having asked him. He sounded drunk. I gave the address nevertheless. There was a pause, and Mr. Duffy asked me to repeat the number. I did.

"Has your habitat a marble balustrade outside?" Mr. Duffy asked.

"It has," I answered stiffly. "You can't miss it."

"H. Sebastian God!" Mr. Duffy croaked. "I'm bringing the party right over!"

Ned and I shaved, opened our bottle of liquor, arranged our books in neat piles on the floor and waited our debut as hosts.

"Did you know," I said casually to Ned, "that Mr. Duffy is not only a great sporting editor, but a great scholar as well?" As I talked, a din came to my ears. Voices were howling and singing, men's voices with feminine squeals of glee and agony. The tumult was on the floor below.

Ned and I peered over the stair rail. We saw Mr. Duffy and his party in a horrible state of drunken madness. I rushed down the stairs.

"We're here!" I yelled. "You're on the wrong floor. Mr. Duffy, for God's sake!"

Mr. Duffy was dancing with our landlady, the society dowager, beating out the dance rhythm with hearty blows on her rump. It was she who was doing most of the gleeful squealing. Ferdinand Fisher, to whom Mr. Duffy had once introduced me, identifying him as the "literary flower of the South," was standing in the splendid vestibule of the dowager's home. He looked aloof and pensive, and I was about to appeal to his reason when I noted that he was pissing in the large umbrella stand near the open door. The other two members of Mr. Duffy's party were lost in Laocoönian embraces with two beautiful young women in evening gowns.

Mr. Duffy spied me and cried out, "I want you to meet the God-damnedest sweetest old whore who ever gladdened the soul of man—my darling Frances, the sweetest bitch of all time."

"Be your age, Sherman," the dowager squealed, "and stop acting like an orangutan. You're frightening the poor boys to death."

Neither Mr. Duffy nor his party ever visited our room. They stayed the night in the more luxurious quarters provided by the dowager. Ned and I sat alone among our neat piles of books. What we thought, felt or discussed is not in my memory. I recall only that when we moved out the next afternoon, the gray-pompadoured Frances and three beautiful women watched us from the doorway as we walked down the stairs, our arms loaded with books. And I remember also that as we paused to say good-by, Mr. Duffy's darling Frances and the sweetest bitch of all time placed four bills in my hand, the forty dollars we had paid for the ten weeks' room rent.

Good Duffy was pleased for many years to tell the tale of how he found me living a babe in a brothel, an innocent in a world of sin.

The next morning he handed me the only poem he ever wrote. It was dedicated to me. It read:

> Oh, see the merry moron.
> He doesn't know a damn.
> I wish I were a moron.
> My God, perhaps I am.

AND A GOOD SONG RINGING CLEAR

ALL MY LOVES were for men in my first Chicago years. I would as soon have thought of loving a stuffed owl as a woman in those teens, and been as little capable of it.

This love of men in my youth increased and strengthened me. It put an armor on me and a wit into my soul. And most of all it preserved my childhood. In a world of men we can remain children more easily than under the economic and emotional proddings of the female.

The psychoanalysts, whose findings are always interesting, write exhaustively and often darkly of male intimacies. They submit that masked sex urges bring males together for beer drinking, card playing, choral singing, and other comradely hi-de-hos. I, too, have seen open proofs of the psychoanalyst's most libelous theories concerning convivial males. Damon and Pythias are no gallant innocents to our new scientists, and not always to me.

Yet I who have known a good quota of men, flared like a powder keg in their presence and cavorted brightly at their sides, have no memory or knowledge of any libido stirring. If there was any sex at the bottom of my love of men, it was too involved for my noticing. I would deny it altogether except for my prejudice against absolutes.

In speaking thus of myself I am reminded of the peasant traveler in Rabelais. He was walking the road with his two young daughters slung over his shoulder, one resting on his chest, the other on his back. Another wayfarer, interested in his burdens, inquired:

"Are they virgins?"

The father sighed.

"I can vouch for this one," he said and pointed to the one under his nose.

I vouch, thus, for the side of myself I know. Its other meanings hang out of sight, and I give them neither bill of health nor libelous identity.

WHY MEN LIKE EACH OTHER

MY ATTACHMENT to men has never been as deep (meaning troublesome) as to women, although usually it has lasted longer. My love of men has had one basic superiority to my love of women. Men have never wounded my heart or left me frustrated and lessened by withdrawing their fondness for me, or outgrowing it.

In my youth I preferred relationships with men. It was as I grew older that I sought more after the ego disturbances which women can provide. Women, apparently, become more important to the male as he ages. They sting, whip, shock. They offer condiments to help along a lessening appetite for life.

No matter how close I have been to a man I have never made a jackass of myself over him, which is to say a poet or a fantast. This is one of the things fortunately lacking in male friendships—the opportunity to play-act, to overstate, to lie, to be illusioned and disillusioned. In loving a woman, a man suffers an inflammation of his vocabulary. He primps, dances, minces, exaggerates and enjoys all these departures from his sane self as much as does any actor rousing bravos from the stage.

In loving a man, one does not have to contort oneself into a hundred pretenses of devotion and fidelity in order to wrest a cry of ardor from his lips; not unless one is looking for ardor. I have loved men for their looks, their talents, their spiced personalities, their gallantry, their verbal style, but never because I needed them.

And I have never felt jealousy toward a man. As a result, I have never been cruel, mean, dishonest or vengeful to males, nor have I ever uttered an hysterical word in a man's presence. No wonder men like each other and swear by each other as nobler animals. They see only each other's best sides.

Men can betray each other, but a man's betrayal of me was always the end of our relationship, not, as it often is with women, some more kindling for the flame.

These are the secrets of the charm men can have for each other—a sort of love without pain or anger. Friendship between men is a goad to their gallantry, a stimulation of their virtues and seldom a locked-horns conflict of their insecurities. The beauties men find in kinship lie in the pleasure of being known and not judged, of being admired and not bagged and clapped into a marital zoo, of being intimate without the inconvenience of turning into a Siamese twin, of finding oneself magically devoid of lies and deceits; and of being able to walk off without leaving a suttee fire in one's wake and a load of guilts pressing on one's heart.

Of the things men give each other the greatest is loyalty. I come now to the first deep friendship of my life.

MY FRIENDS, THE PRESS

My world suddenly filled with friends. I lunched daily at a crowded round table in King's Restaurant. A four-piece orchestra played on a balcony the gayest and most yearning of waltzes. To its strains, masticating reporters sat denouncing Mr. Dunne and Mr. Finnegan. They denounced also the mayor, the chief of police, women, literature, politics and morality.

I contributed happily to the denunciations. Of these conclaves, I remember nothing except that I, the least embittered young man on earth, sat and took gleeful part in the destruction of the world. My memory is that all the thunderers and sneerers shoveling away at chicken à la king, with the *Chocolate Soldier* music melting in their ears, were no more bitter than I.

There was the reporter who had written a book called *The Lights and Shadows in a Chorus Girl's Life*, the reporter who had been to London and smelled of high-priced cologne, the reporter who had tried for several years to become a priest, the reporter who had mysterious connections with a West Side pawnshop and was an authority on the underworld, the reporter whose father was a general in the U.S. Army and who phoned in his story of a court trial with the opening words "The State's Attorney won a Fabian victory today."

There was the reporter who was taking a correspondence course in embalming (hoping thus to rise in the world), the reporter who stood in the local-room window during a thunderstorm and defied God, if there was a God, to strike him (and the city editor) with lightning, the reporter who drew geometrical figures on paper illustrating some peculiar Hindu concept of the sexuality of the universe, the reporter whose wife was always dying, the reporter embittered by gonorrhea, and the reporter who, like Charlemagne in the land of the Saracens, had futtered an entire whore house of twenty-five damsels in one night; and there was the reporter who was collecting first editions of George Moore and Arthur Symons, and the reporter who wore a derby and seemed through twenty years of chasing fires a well-dressed impostor.

Scores of them return vaguely to my mind. But there is nothing vague in my memory of their combined quality. They sat, grown and abuzz, outside an adult civilization, intent on breaking windows.

There was, I am sure, neither worldliness nor cunning enough among the lot of us to run a successful candy store. But we had a vantage point. We were not inside the routines of human greed or social pretenses. We were without politeness. There was a feast all around us. We attended it as scavengers. We picked up and examined the debris of murders, suicides, family explosions. Our noses were full of the odors of chicanery and human fatuousness.

Around this table in King's Restaurant we who knew nothing spoke out of a knowledge so overwhelming that I, for one, never recovered from it. Politicians were crooks. The leaders of causes were scoundrels. Morality was a farce full of murders, rapes and love nests. Swindlers ran the world and the Devil sang everywhere. These discoveries filled me with a great joy. The waltzes played. Mabel, the beautiful waitress, served us and punched our checks for fifteen and twenty cents less than we had eaten. There were no thoughts yet in my head. But I was gay with birth pangs and drunk with a superiority that could flaunt no more than a soiled collar and an outlaw's guffaw.

DUFFY AND HIS COURT

THE WORLD, however, was not entirely a shambles. There was one great man in it. He was the pipe-smoking, fetlock-jiggling, Indian-faced figure behind the glass-paneled door—Sherman Duffy. He read Latin, French, Spanish. He was an expert horticulturist. He wrote articles about irises. In his home in Ottawa, Illinois, he bred acres of irises, the finest in the land. And there was no man as witty, worldly or full of wisdom. A Phi Beta Kappa key hung from his vest pocket. He could drink more than anybody on the paper, even Mr. Hutchens, who disappeared sometimes for ten days and had to be hunted in all the Turkish baths of the county.

Notables crowded the cubbyhole office where Sherman reigned as sporting editor. Prize fighters, wrestlers and their managers; sportsmen, raconteurs, gamblers, press agents, promoters, athletes and ex-athletes, all in gaudy clothes, all full of juice and jest. I worked afternoons in sports (for no extra pay). I kept the box scores during ball games, wrote "new leads" for afternoon sporting events.

When the telegraph keys in the adjoining room stopped clicking, and Egg-head, the operator, emerged with his last line of copy, and the day of killings and jack-rollings, infidelities and safe-blowings, lumberyard fires, embezzlements, con games, pitchers' duels, track meets and box scores was done, I went out on the town with Duffy. I was his shadow, his court and his student body. I sat beside him in saloons while he swapped anecdotes with adventurers from China and Peru, and other guzzling rubbery-faced journalists in old-fashioned stand-up collars who had been everywhere and seen everything.

Great wits crossed swords with my champion. There was Arthur James Pegler, the salty and verbally crackling father of Westbrook, the mighty columnist-to-be. Pegler, père, was the inventor of the blood-and-thunder rhetoric which became known as the Hearst news-writing style. He wrote once, in a magazine tale, a description of the thing he had helped create: "A Hearst newspaper is like a screaming woman running down the street with her throat cut."

There was Christian Dane Hagerty, Associated Press veteran of the Boxer Rebellion in China, who looked as if he had stepped out of Carbon de Castel's grenadiers, who had loved a princess in Cathay, been lost in Tibet, prowled for twenty years through faraway places as avid for news as a saint for the sight of his Maker. And there was the tall, owlish-faced, nose-twitching prince of humor, Richard Henry Little, who had scooped the world on the Battle of Port Arthur, a towering, vague and elfin man convulsing his fellows with

comic and improbable phrases and himself usually expiring of love
for some unyielding damsel. Duffy always hailed Richard Henry's arrival at our table with the same cry, "Behold Ichabod—the genus of
Famine descending on the land!"

There were also the dramatic critics, the *Journal's* Doc Hall, blond
and scholarly grave-digger for Thespis, Percy Hammond of the *Tribune*, and Charles Collins of the *Post*—wits and sophisticates all, who
dared say, whenever the theater alighted in Chicago, who and what
was genius in this flossy international realm. There was the cynical
Eddie Mahoney, our assistant city editor, who was writing a book that
was a meticulous report of everything women said, did, cried out, sang
or moaned during the moments of orgasm. This book, he said, was
going to revolutionize the art of fornication and put an end to all its
shallow mysteries, and he added to his work from week to week.

There was Eddie Moore, music critic, darkly silent as are those
whose heads are full of the incommunicable wisdom of music. And
there was Ashton Stevens, of Mr. Hearst's drama page, dressed like a
young duke with a flower in his buttonhole, an epigram, like a
lozenge, always on his tongue. There was Caliban Harris, a sports
promoter with a Scotch burr and a mastery of Anacondian invective,
and Larney Lichtenstein, a benign manager of prize fighters, fat and
loving as a character in a Christmas pantomime. There was Harry
Hochstadter, Duffy's chief assistant and a mighty barroom brawler,
who sat grinning in his cups like a sleepy Bar Kochba. And God
help our enemies—pimps, gunmen and bruisers alike—when the
battle shophar blew.

And there was George Wharton, of the Associated Press, whose
like I have never since heard in the world, not even in the runaway
wit of George Jessel. Wharton did not speak, he entertained. Laughter sounded always around his Buddhalike figure, but never his own.
For he was dedicated solemnly to the destruction of sham. The comic
spirit was his weapon. He transformed all that was pompous or
bigoted into hilarious caricature. The world wore a clown's cap in his
words. His astringent waggery launched a generation of conversa-
tionalists in Chicago.

There were a score of others, bibulous, mocking and high-
mannered. They were Duffy's friends, not mine. I sat among them
like a stowaway on Parnassus. And I heard language. It was the language of wandering scholars, of wit that had found no paper, of

genius with wings of alcohol. It was the language of Dickens, Twain, Carlyle and Rabelais come out of book covers and gladdening bars, city rooms and whore houses.

I was silent among my betters, but no ears ever listened with more delight. The language of those revels still echoes in me. It is the great event I remember of my first years as a newspaperman. The whiplash phrase, the flashing and explosive sentence, the sonorous syntax and bull's-eye epithet—if I have any literary forebears, these barroom confabulators are mine.

I SEE A MAN HANGED

A CRY entered my mind one summer dawn. It is still there. I hear it when I read about the conferences between nations that seek to avert a war. I hear it on Christmas mornings when the children come into my lane and sing carols in the snow.

There were two brothers, Ignace and Manow. Ignace was strong and fierce. Manow was slight and gentle, and he still had a boyish smile.

The two brothers went out one night and held up a truck farmer bringing in a wagonload of his produce to the city market. The farmer fought for his radishes and tomatoes, and the two brothers killed him.

The police found the brothers. They were placed on trial, and on the witness stand Ignace confessed to the murder. He begged for his brother, Manow, to be spared. He, Ignace, was the strong one, the wild one. He alone had done the killing, he said. Manow had only stood by, unable to stop him. He wept for his brother. Manow was innocent, he said as his tears dropped, Manow was good.

I took notes as Ignace spoke and wept. The deep love in him that sought to save his brother made a good story. I wrote it and went back to cover the rest of the trial. I watched both brothers stand before the judge for sentence. The judge ordered the state to hang both brothers by the neck until they were dead. I heard Ignace cry out, "Hang me—yes! Me only! Not Manow. Let him live! He is good. Let my brother live!"

Ignace put an arm around his boyish brother, and I heard him whisper, "Don't be afraid, Manow. I will save you—before I die. I will save you."

This, too, made a good story.

On the morning of the hanging I sat in the tall slotlike room of the Criminal Courts Building with some fifty other men. We were there in one capacity or another to see the brothers Ignace and Manow hanged on the county gallows.

There was only one noose dangling over the closed gallows trap. The brothers were going to be hanged one following the other.

The door in a balcony above us opened, and the first of the brothers appeared. He walked with the sheriff on one side and a priest in purple on the other. Behind him the heavy shoes of the deputies and doctors clomped in the death march along the iron balcony.

At the sight of the dangling noose the strong, fierce Ignace stopped. He held out a stiffened arm as if he were warding off an unbearable apparition. A cry of terror came from his throat. Then hoarse wild words sounded:

"Hang Manow!"

The deputies dragged him to the gallows. The calling continued, a whimper, a plea, a deep cry for another fifteen minutes of life. When his arms were being tied to his sides, Ignace was still moaning and roaring.

"Hang Manow!"

They hanged Manow after the white-sheeted figure of Ignace had stopped turning on the tautened rope.

I sat looking miserably at my typewriter in the local room.

"What's the matter?" Mr. Finnegan asked. "Did the hanging upset your stomach? Start writing and it'll go away."

An hour later I told Duffy.

"It wasn't the hanging that made me feel sick. It was the way he yelled for them to hang his brother. He'd loved Manow and tried to save him. And then, just to live a few minutes longer he started begging them to hang Manow first. For God's sake, how can a man change like that?"

Duffy puffed his pipe and grinned at my whitened face.

"You'll find out that's the easiest thing people can do," he said, "change into swine."

And he quoted moodily from Dostoevski:

"Man survives where swine perish, and laughs where gods go mad."

CITY, COME BACK TO ME

THEY ARE STILL THERE, the streets of Chicago—a little cleaned up and with more windows than ever. I walk through them when I stop over between trains from New York to Los Angeles. I look furtively for landmarks.

There is one in Madison Street near Clark, a very busy spot. I look at the curbing and find the exact foot of it on which I used to sit, near the hydrant, when too drunk to continue on to Mr. Dunne and the local room.

I eavesdrop on a young figure, hatless, a beautiful thatch of hair catching the March wind, and not bad looking, either. Eyes a bit too large, and a face somewhat too innocent seeming, particularly beside the hydrant. I hear—

Eleven-twenty A.M. Forty minutes to the Home Edition deadline. Great gods and little fishes! I have to write a story. It seems unusually cold for March. I must have forgotten my underwear in Miss Bennetti's bedroom. I must learn not to dress in such a hurry. A beautiful girl. But Miss Bennetti can't be as innocent as I think, or she wouldn't have insisted on my going to bed with her—after knowing me only an hour. She must be a woman of some experience. On the other hand, maybe she drank all those Martinis because her conscience hurt her for doing what she did. Besides, she was suffering from grief over Mr. Ericson's rotten conduct. I'll never forget her tears. But I must learn to drink only five Martinis and stop. After five this sort of thing always happens. If I get up and walk I'll probably be run over and killed.

I listen to this young rake beside the hydrant, his feet literally in the gutter, and I watch what he does. He writes. He covers sheet on sheet of grayish copy paper with carefully penciled words, using a volume of Anatole France as a desk, *The Sign of the Reine Pédauque*, which, unlike his underwear, he remembered to take with him. I can see the words on the gray paper. "Cupid, who usually works with a bow and arrow, hurled a bombshell into the City Hall today with the arrest of John Ericson on a bastardy charge filed by Miss Dorothy Bennetti, 2934 Calumet Avenue. Mr. Ericson's campaign for sheriff on the Democratic ticket suffered a compound fracture—"

The figure finishes writing and holds up a half-dozen sheets of paper to the March wind. A mounted policeman, who has been looking down from his saddle at the drunken scrivener, reaches for the copy. The figure by the hydrant beams and utters the words, "Mr. Dunne, second floor. Tell him I broke my ankle."

"I'll tell him," says the mountie, and his horse clatters off for far-away Market Street and the waiting city desk.

I study the landmark, salute the hydrant and the great-souled cop who carried my news to Ghent, and walk on. It is an aging fellow who prowls the streets of Chicago, between trains, and his heart says, "You are mine. I know you better than anything in the world." But the city looks back at him like a busy stranger. No bellboys wink. No policemen grin. No judges, lawyers, whores, bartenders, house dicks, book clerks, aldermen, bank presidents or elevator starters call his name.

And sour things have happened to the hotel lobbies. They have new carpets and streamlined furniture. The registration desks have been moved, rather idiotically.

And the railroad depots! More sabotage! They are full of new marble and glass partitions and vast spaces. How can the reporters find their way to the trains? They must be a very methodical sort of journalist. We had a few in my time. They wore glasses and bought houses in the suburbs.

I walk full of ghostly complaints. Why was it necessary for this city to grow, to change, to spawn new towers, bridges and a cement lake front? There were more than enough! But as I walk and stare, the strangeness falls from my town. The falderal added by a generation grows dim, and the unchanged friend of my youth glitters its windows at me and hails me with its thousand and one doorways.

BOY ABOUT TOWN

I HAVE LIVED in other cities but been inside only one. I knew Chicago's thirty-two feet of intestines. Only newspapermen ever achieve this bug-in-a-rug citizenship.

I once wore all the windows of Chicago and all its doorways on a key ring. Saloons, mansions, alleys, courtrooms, depots, factories, hotels, police cells, the lake front, the roof tops and the sidewalks were my haberdashery.

Frown on me now or give me a stranger's eye, good town; or cackle meaninglessly over my head and hide like a runaway bride in a forest of stone walls—I know you still. Listen!

A man lay on his back in Barney Grogan's saloon with a knife sticking out of his belly, and I made notes.

A naked woman with a smoking gun in her hand knelt and moaned beside a dead dentist, "Why did I do it? I loved him so!"

And there was a dentist arrested for raping a patient during office hours whose crime was immortalized (for one edition) by the headline, "Dentist Fills Wrong Cavity."

Clarence Darrow in his poor-man's suit, baggy pants, floppy jacket, stringy tie, sang his song of humanity to the jurors trying an ex-chief of police for shaking down whores, pimps and madams. He said: "My client, after twenty-five years on the police force, is a poor man." His client, Chief Healy, went free.

Teddy Webb's sweetheart called the police and told them that the fearsome bandit was lying in a bed in Cottage Grove Avenue with another woman. Four policemen darted forth to capture the wanted killer. They nabbed him as he was trying to pull his pants on, but one of the cops dropped dead of heart failure in the excitement. Chief of Police Scheuttler came on the scene and fired a bullet into the armpit of the dead policeman and saved his honor.

A fire gutted the Stockyards and seven firemen died trying to shoo the bellowing cattle out of the flames.

A man stood naked in front of the Congress Hotel screaming that the world was coming to an end, and he bore out his contention, in part, by dropping dead when the police laid hands on him.

The school board was arrested for graft. Investigators revealed the new county hospital had pillars stuffed with straw instead of cement and was menacing the lives of all who entered it; and the assistant keeper of the morgue died of poison from eating the leg of one of the corpses in his custody.

A minister of the Gospel and his paramour died in the basement of his church, overcome by escaping gas. The impassioned reverend had kicked open a gas jet while doing homage to Eros. Preoccupied by love, he had smelled no other fumes than those of Paradise and given up the ghost while still glued to his parishioner.

And another minister, several miles to the west, discovered horns on his head, put there by his wife bouncing beneath a baritone in the choir. She pleaded wildly for forgiveness, which her reverend husband agreed to grant her provided she proved her repentance by crawling on her hands and knees the full four blocks around his church. This she did, inch by inch, as the cameras clicked and a beaming husband welcomed her to his bosom again at the altar.

The mayor of the city, William Hale Thompson, was accused of stealing all the money out of the treasury and giving it away to friends.

The yellow cabs fought the checkered cabs, and passengers were tossed into the gutter. The Hearst Chicago *Examiner* fought the Chicago *Tribune*, and each publication sent stern and muscled minions through the rush-hour streetcars to snatch the rival paper out of passengers' hands, and, on resistance, toss the readers into the gutter.

Attorney Charles Erbstein, examining his client on trial for murder, said, "I ask you now to try on this hat which was dropped by the killer as he fled from the scene." The defendant tried on the hat. The jury laughed. There is nothing more quickly humorous than a hat three sizes too small perched on a big man's head. "Ropes" O'Brien, the state's attorney, cried out that a strange hat had been substituted for the state's "Exhibit A." But how to prove such a thing to a chuckling jury? Mr. Erbstein's defendant, a prominent murderer, walked out of the courtroom a free man.

Banker Kirby sat in the witness chair in Judge Landis' Federal court trying to convince the Savonarola-faced jurist that he had lost his money to some confidence men in a wire-tapping race track swindle—and not buried it somewhere for future personal use. Judge Landis refused to believe the defendant. "Where have you hidden the ninety thousand dollars that belong to your depositors?" he rasped, grimaced and glared. "This court will not be satisfied until you have confessed the hiding place of the money that belongs to the poor people of your neighborhood." After three days of broken cries that he was no cunning thief but the victim of swindlers, Banker Kirby gave up the uneven debate and pitched dead out of the wheelchair in which he had been brought to court. Two months later a wire-tapping con man, Harry Strossneider, confessed the swindle of the dead banker.

A linen fetishist tore up all the bed sheets in the storerooms of the

Sherman Hotel and was captured as he lay sexually exhausted on the fire escape.

A janitor ravished a child behind a coal pile in a Halstead Street basement, and Theodore Dreiser wrote a play about it called *The Hand of the Potter*.

An automobile salesman killed a reluctant customer by bashing in his skull with a baseball bat, and died gamely on the gallows, so we wrote.

Carl Wanderer was hanged for killing his wife and a Ragged Stranger whom he had hired to hold them up as they were coming home from a movie show; and with the rope around his neck, Carl sang a ballad called "Dear Old Pal of Mine."

Blackie Weed, a white man, died on the gallows for killing a representative of the gas company and a policeman come to collect a bill he had already paid. The receipted bill was his only defense. Blackie, a firm man, spat at the cross the priest held up for him to kiss, a moment before the trap was sprung.

And a Dr. Hugo succumbed on the gallows in the oddest manner of all the seventeen I saw twisting in their white sheets on the end of the whining rope. Sheriff Hoffman, always eager to hear a confession of guilt from the guest he was scheduled to hang, made a deal with the doomed doctor at four A.M. of his final morning. In return for a full confession, he granted the medico a last request—a ladies' make-up kit. I hurried through several brothels, secured a "vanity" case and darted back with it at five A.M. to the death cell. Dr. Hugo had time to rouge his cheeks and lips, mascara his eyes, pluck his brows and heavily powder his neck before the death march started. He stood thus on the gallows, painted and simpering and oddly triumphant. The sheriff, unnerved by this indecency to which he had committed himself, worked fast. The doctor went through the trap in jig time. Out of him, hanging and turning in his death throes, there came a woman's high falsetto screech.

And on Wabansia Avenue two men were burned to death while trying to stab each other in an argument over a pinochle game. They were found in the charred rubble, each with a knife in his blackened, unfleshed hand.

A lover tied his beloved to the bedposts on the fifteenth floor of the Morrison Hotel and whipped her to death for not loving him enough. Then he jumped out of the window into the noon traffic.

A machinist shot and killed his wife and then killed himself, leaving a note: "Nobody else will ever have her." This tale took a strange turn when an alert undertaker, preparing the bodies for burial, announced that the "machinist" was a woman, fully equipped in every respect. And thus I was introduced to the marvels of psychiatry.

Federal Judge Carpenter listened to evidence contending that the "Oceana Roll" was a piece of musical plagiarism. And he handed down the judgment that since the "Oceana Roll," to which he had listened with an open mind, was not music, it could not be a musical plagiarism. Case dismissed.

But not so the "Oceana Roll," or the tide of jazz that came rolling to town with it. A colored band up from New Orleans appeared for the first time in a white café, operated by Ray Jones on the South Side. Turkey Trots, Bunny Hugs, Stomps, Blues, Grizzly Bear Hugs, the music that was not music filled the joints and cat houses of Chicago. Only New Orleans and Memphis had heard these brassy, snorting, wailing incantations before. Now South State Street heard them, and North Clark and Archer Avenue; West Harrison and the lava bed precincts beyond. And a new tribe of hopped-up horn tooters was born, to provide a faster, wilder obbligato for love, crime and liquor.

Titta Ruffo made his debut singing *Pagliacci* in the Auditorium Theater, where I was present as a third-string music critic on Saturday matinees. Titta sang the Prologue, beating his clown's hat against the curtain as he hung on endlessly to the last note—and two thousand operagoers exploded. The fire department was summoned. Hysterical women were lowered from the gallery windows. Police checked a panic and Titta sang on. The first and only musical criticism I wrote carried a seven-column headline on page one, "Scores Injured in Baritone's Debut."

A month later the same wild scene was repeated in the same theater, and on the stage stood a black-haired, slim and beautiful prima donna named Galli-Curci. Like Titta's debut, her first appearance left the town shaken as if by an invasion.

There were swindlers, funerals and weddings; a rash of bichloride of mercury suicides, and the arrest of Mrs. Ginnis, who ran a nursery for orphans in which she murdered an average of ten children a year.

Counterfeiters sold ten-dollar bills for eight dollars to the America-infatuated immigrants in Maxwell Street and were captured by Captain Porter of the U.S. Revenue Department.

Captain Porter was hidden in an attic space above the room in which the criminals were printing the money. He watched them through a hole he had poked in the ceiling plaster and waited for reinforcements to make the arrests. After a thirty-hour wait, the captain's back teeth came afloat and his kidneys demanded emptying. The Revenue Department investigator pissed cautiously but at some length into a corner, whereupon the plaster, thus treated, dissolved, crumbled and fell noisily on the counterfeiters below. And there was nothing for Captain Porter to do but widen the hole he had pissed open and hurl himself singlehanded on the miscreants below. All were bagged.

Yellow Kid Weill darted about togged out as an old widow lady, an old-fashioned fan and reticule in his hands, and swindled suburban bankers and other shrewd financiers.

And Leo Koretz, prince of thieves, sold millions of dollars of non-existent Central American oil to the profit-hungry tycoons of Chicago. He entertained five hundred of them at a dinner in the Congress Hotel one evening. During the dinner, newsboys came clamoring into the banquet hall shouting, "Extra Paper—All about Leo Koretz Oil Swindle! Koretz Exposed! Millions Lost in Koretz Swindle!" It was all a banquet jest.

Mr. Koretz himself, with the aid of one of his heaviest investors, Arthur Brisbane, the Hearst Philosopher, had arranged the jest. A front page had been "faked" on copies of Brisbane's paper, the *Examiner*. Koretz had written the "story" himself, putting into it every truthful fact of his skulduggery.

When the banqueters recovered from the shock of hearing the dreadful news and reading the tale of their idiocy and bankruptcy on the front page, Mr. Brisbane, whose prowess as a sage was great in that day, rose and reassured the company. "It's a joke," he cried from the speaker's table. "We did it just for a lark. Mr. Koretz is a great and honorable financier." And the ace journalist, putting his arm around the swindler, led the hall full of dupes in the singing of "For He's a Jolly Good Fellow." Mr. Koretz killed himself in his jail cell a year later. He was waiting trial for his five-million-dollar swindlings. One of the many women he had known and kept in opulence was still loyal to him. She brought him a five-pound box of chocolates. Mr. Koretz had diabetes. He ate up all the chocolates and died.

A colored man named Henry knelt in his Desplaines Street basement flat and prayed to God to save Chicago from its sinful ways. God heard the prayer and sent His Wrath to punish the wicked city. His Wrath was Henry, who came out of his flat with three loaded guns and shot dead eight Polish workingmen starting out on their day's toil. The workingmen fell in front of their doorways, their lunch boxes in their hands. The police came to get Henry, but Henry the Wrath of God smote them for five hours. He barricaded himself behind a bureau. His wife, singing hymns, loaded and reloaded his rifles. One policeman was killed, and three wounded. Henry, untouched behind his bureau, cried out, "Hallelujah! Thy Will be done!" each time he fired. At one o'clock the police dropped dynamite through a hole in the roof and blew up several buildings. In the debris were the remains of Henry Wrath of God and his loyal hymn-singing wife.

Orators spoke at luncheons, thousands of them. Presidents, vice-presidents, senators, royalty, geniuses, billionaires, lecturers, beauties and dowagers, priests, educators—made an unending parade before my reporter's pencil, ninnies all, talking through their hats, which is the only way "greatness" dare speak for publication.

Revivalists bellowed, organs played, Evangelist Rodeheaver blew his hot trumpet and men and women were saved and cured of paralysis and blindness. And the Stockyards' owners imported Billy Sunday to divert their underpaid hunkies from going on strike by shouting them dizzy with God.

A psychoanalyst (like a first robin) appeared with a beard and a Viennese accent. His name was Dr. Stekel and he brought the good news to town that chastity was a disease responsible for most of the lunacy in the world, especially among ladies.

Jim Colisimo, genial owner of half the whore houses in town and possessor of one of the greatest collections of rare cheeses in the world, was shot and killed in a phone booth. The great cortege of jurists, politicos, financial and industrial nabobs was halted outside the gates of the Catholic cemetery. Burial in Catholic ground had been denied the corpse by the local priesthood. For five hours officials of the city pleaded with Pope Pius over the transatlantic telephone. The connection was bad and the Pope irritable. A great jurist finally informed the press, "He hung up. Let's take Jim some other place." And Jim's bullet-riddled remains were wheeled off to a heathen grave.

Tommy O'Connor skipped out of his cell in the county jail while the sheriff was testing the gallows on which he was to hang in the morning. A thousand cops combing the town failed then and ever after to find any trace of Tommy. Straining a number of points in this story, I wrote it as my first movie, *Underworld*.

Jack Johnson, the colored World's Champion, was married to a white girl, Lucille Cameron. They waited in the South Side parlor surrounded by an excited wedding party, and none of the pictures we took could be used, because Lucille had sat soothing her powerful but nervous groom by tenderly stroking his genitals.

Trains were wrecked, hotels burned down, factories blew up. A man killed his wife in their Sedgwick Avenue flat, cut off her head and made a tobacco jar of its skull.

Beautiful women jumped off the top of the Masonic Temple, the High Bridge in Lincoln Park and the Frances Willard Building in La Salle Street.

A surgeon named Dr. Pratt was arrested for removing unnecessarily some nine hundred uteri.

A butcher in Division Street killed his wife, ground her up and distributed her to his sausage-loving customers. The presence in one of the sausages of a wedding ring bearing his wife's initials led to his arrest and hanging.

And these things went on every day in these streets, and I was there among them. I could cover a hundred pages with lists of fascinating cadavers. They all clamor for cataloguing. But I stop my pencil and sit sighing among my phantoms, and feel pleased. What better is there to sigh for than happiness, yesterday's or tomorrow's. And that was happiness. Skyscrapers banged at a cymbal sun. The headlines of murder, rape and swindle were ribbons round a Maypole. The Elevated squealed hosannas in the sooty air. The city turned like a wheel. The chimney smoke lay in awning stripes against the white clouds. The days leaped away like jack rabbits. Nights sprinted across the Illinois sky, and a jack pot of moons tumbled out of the heavens. Swiftness was in all the hours—yet nothing moved. Everything stood still and was changeless, for it was youth. Youth holds time like an arrow in its hand. The hand and arrow stay motionless.

BLACK TIES AT THE OPERA

ATTIRED IN TUXEDOS, Duffy and I went to the opera where I sat, fidgeting and yawning and looking for some bedizened heiress who might fall in love with me and make it unnecessary for me to work the rest of my life. This dream of never working is one I brought with me to Chicago on the July day that plunged me into forty years of toil—in the teeth of which it still persists.

Every night of the "season" found us, thanks to Eddie Moore's free tickets, under the bombardment of kettledrums and sopranos. A peppery bantamweight named Cleofonte Campanini directed. With the lights down, a heady smell of perfume in the air, an occasional bosom popping out of an evening gown and Maestro Campanini's orchestra swaying in the pit like a black-and-white armada of sound—the Auditorium Theater seemed a fine place to be.

Duffy, as tuneless as a barbarian, went to the opera for social reasons. It was the only Society Event he admitted into his life. Of music he said firmly that "it was good for the soul—it chasteneth the sinner." Entering the theater he furtively crossed himself as he did before all minor ordeals and murmured his "ales, wines, liquors and cigars."

Between acts Duffy's tuxedo mingled with other tuxedos and he introduced me loyally to most of the swells milling around in the foyer. I was able to contribute no more than a moody hello to these flossy folk who seemed always full of rapturous tidings for each other. They came together in the foyer with the elation of lovers meeting, and I found it as impossible to talk to them as I would have to the explosive tenors and divas darting about on the stage.

When we rode off following an after-theater snack, shared with some of Duffy's society friends, he held forth on the life histories of the "rich and great" with whom we had sipped wine. In addition to letting me know where they had come from, whom they had married and who originally had made all the money they now owned, he discoursed on their general qualities.

"Society people," he said, "are terrible bores if taken in too-great doses. They can't talk for sour apples. They toil not, nor can they spin yarns. But they all smell pretty and are inclined to be lacking in morals, which is something highly in their favor. Their ladies, if properly approached, will go to bed with you quicker than the lower classes—and without pay."

I was impressed.

"In addition to smelling pretty," said Duffy, "and emulating the busy mink in amour, the rich and great have an important function in the world. They are the patrons of the arts and, by God, they keep beauty alive by being rich enough to pay for it and having nothing else much to do but sit around on their ornamental behinds and admire it."

I was not impressed by this second piece of information but not inclined to debate it. At that time I was as grateful that Duffy had high connections in the community as that the doors of ten-dollar bawdy houses swung open merrily at his knocking. I was pleased, unquestioningly, to follow him where I might not have trod otherwise. Drunk or sober I trailed my Socrates through all his groves.

THE LOST TRIBE OF SWELLS

SINCE that romantic time when, beside my friend, I first saw the world of blue-bloods, like a Fabrizio del Dongo on Napoleon's battle-field, I have learned it was the ground of Waterloo we stood on. Not mine but the swells!

Who could have imagined in the 'teens of our century that all the power and glamour of riches would be gone out of the U. S. A. in a few decades! I am aware that there are still people who wear tuxedos and voluptuous evening gowns. But I am speaking of a class, the class of the well-to-do, once the Republic's favored citizenry.

I write (re-write) in 1952 this footnote to the swells. It is election year. The press and television are boiling with political insult. Democrats and Republicans are yelping at each other and laying twenty years of criminal ineptitude at each other's feet. The language is theirs, not mine. Every minority is crying its problems and its needs, including small, sad groups of Red Skins who are without moccasins for the coming winter.

Only one group is silent—the affluent. Had all the nabobs of the Republic had their heads lopped off on a Union Square guillotine, the silence could not have been more complete. No Democrat or Republican speaks for the swells or for riches or for that most vital of units in the land—the Capitalistic Class.

I hesitate, myself, to bring up the subject out of a fear that I may sound demented. Surely so mighty a swindle as is being perpetrated on the U. S. A. could not take place without anybody but me noticing it! What I have seen happening and continue to see happening is the extirpation of the American rich man and his flossy cousin the upper middle class gentleman of means. And in this cruel work Republican and Democrat, left winger and right winger are pulling together. Being politicians, they all espouse from one angle or another the new politics—which in Russia or the U. S. A. is to build a State and the devil take its citizens.

During the present flap-doodle race for the Presidential plum, all sides have put up the boogieman of Communism as a reason for whatever zany program they've adopted. The facts are as plain as flies in a pail of milk. The issue of Communism is rolled out to hide the lunatic expenditures to which both Democrats and Republicans are committed, the costly armies of occupation and the costlier business of trying to wheedle two hundred million Europeans into liking us and staying on "our side."

And not a sane man cries out. And not a single patriot. The word Communism is apparently powerful enough to flatten out all sanity and patriotism. Nobody says to Hell with the Communists, let them have the stale cake of Europe—if Europe wants to be eaten. Nobody points out that other people's revolutions are none of our business. Nobody points out that Communism is the kind of government that a half billion people in the world are potty about, and that we can no more overthrow this half billion than kick the moon out of the sky.

As a result of this terrified silence, the looting of the U. S. A. continues. And I behold, apparently all by myself, a nearly bankrupt nation, taxed to the point of individual insecurity and despair, not having courage enough even to cry out for the only honest remedy. The lowliest peasant of Czar Romanoff's time was a bolder fellow. The peasant at least had a few songs about his last beast being led away by the tax collector.

The silence in which this genocide of the tribe of the American well-to-do is taking place is a thing no American could have believed twenty-five years ago. The well-to-do are the caste to whose economic philosophies we are supposedly pledged. Their political plundering constitutes as definite a Revolution as Marat ushered in one 14th of July. And good God what a racket the aristocrats of that time sent up!

Looking at the boozy and reveling delegates to the nominating conventions in Chicago, I pondered: The homes these very delegates owned—a legal right deep and emotional in our civilization—were no safer today from our greedy government than the homes of the Armenians were once from the Turks.

I thought of the numerous house owners I know whose houses had been snatched from them by unforseen tax liens and "disallowances." I thought of men of talent and repute tumbled from their hard-earned places without trial or accusation, but by novel laws and by an almost secret tax collecting machinery. I thought of all the big and little demagogues pouring their hysterias into the word Communism and succeeding in making their public cower before this far-away word more than before "bankruptcy," "hunger," "homelessness." I thought of the tax collectors who had been exposed recently as swindlers and bribe takers. And I thought of the financial look of our country, its mortgaged homes, unpainted and in disrepair, its evaporated bank balances and nest eggs. And thinking of all these matters I came to the conviction that not I but the nation was demented, driven whacky by the word Communism as the nations of Europe were once thrown into a century of witless, suicidal Crusades by the word Infidel.

It cannot be that all our Capitalists are as blind to their fate or as dithering as the political con men who dart over the air waves yelling, "Jiggers, the Commies!"

But I heard not a voice from their midst.

They were silent—which is perhaps as well, for in the preceding two decades of their downfall, their combined power, including that of all the newspapers they own, has not been enough to get a dog-catcher elected.

The only expression left to them—even lower than the peasants' moody singing under Czarism, is, apparently, bribery of the tax collectors, or a secretive outwitting of the Tax Department.

Such are the "rich and great" of 1952. They sit in one of the good-bye holes of History, counting their fingers and trying, a bit bravely, to have a good time, not as rich people but as obedient victims of the God damndest Indian Rope Trick of a revolution ever to tumble a nation.

SOME BOOKISH THOUGHTS

A SMALLER MATTER here interests me—my waning love for reading novels.

I read now coolly. A bitter, strident book with saber phrases such as Robinson Jeffers' *The Double Axe* will slap at my mind again, as all books once did. And Norman Mailer's *The Naked and the Dead* will stay alive in me after I have closed its covers—all its aching, slime-flecked humans keeping up a pantomime in my head when I lie in the dark; and Thornton Wilder's *The Ides of March* left the poet Lucullus sharing my early breakfasts for a week or two.

But most books vanish as I read them. Their populations find no home in me, nor I among them. The explanation I favor is that novels are unable either to surprise or inform me. Their language is coarser and nearer to life, if not to beauty. Their people are scurvier and thus closer to reality. My eyes meet again the outcries against injustice, the answers back to the torture of living. Organs lust, plots twist, characters writhe, psychology comes up with sea bottoms in its teeth, good and evil battle it out on a mat of phrases, and Truth pipes as hopefully as ever, "Behold me!"

But these worlds of ink and paper grow yearly dimmer.

"Read on," says my mind. "Books are your last loves. They will be the last youth you will know."

I obey and note, gratefully, the progress of novels. The banalities and kindergarten hubbub that marked the novels of my youth have been siphoned off almost entirely into the movies.

The most obvious progress in books is in the frankness they bring to the investigation of love. The modern novelist, rid of asterisks, has lifted biology from under the counter where Fanny Hill and Justine blushed in secret. His heroines are nude as eels. Their legs fly open like compasses; and he is expert at a sort of bimanual examination phraseology. The Arabians once startled the Occident by their bold investigation of the female in their literature. They wrote of a heroine that "her buttocks were like twin moons" and that "her navel would hold an ounce of olive oil." Our modern novelist can smile at such superficial information. He is a fellow full of learning about ovaries and vaginismus, and he goes after his girls with the thoroughness of a map maker.

He is also teeming with all the new findings on the subject of coy testicles and reluctant yoni. His lovers do not lust after one another only, as was once the naïve fashion. They hunger, on the side, to bed with their parents, brothers or sisters, and make goo-goo eyes at members of their own sex.

This Freudian understanding of the horrors of courtship was missing in the first five thousand novels I read. Matters are otherwise in the new books. In them the love-driven duo begins on page ten with an experimental bout between the sheets. They emerge on page twenty pale and in a trauma, and the author usually has the devil's own time bringing his hero up to the mark again. This may all be closer to the ways of life than the hearty leg-twining that marked George Moore's *The Lovers of Orlay* and most of the other fiction of that time. I do not debate the point. If there is something wrong with sex, it is just and proper for readers to be told about it.

Perhaps I have hit on a reason for my waning love of novels of which I was not aware before—that they have substituted gynecology for romance. I doubt it. If gynecology had been the plot of books in my youth, I would have devoured them, rubber gloves and all, as avidly as I did the pre-Freudian fictional valentines.

The truth remains that the change that matters is not in books but in myself. However brighter and stronger they are now, they all lack one fascinating character. I am not in them. I read, but I do not participate. It was once different. I worked in Chicago, but I lived, a little madly, between book covers.

BOOK ADVENTURES IN CHICAGO

IN THAT TIME, the people, deeds and places of books were as real as the world I could touch. Bazarov was as alive as Mr. Finnegan; the Abbé Coignard was as close and palpable as Duffy. Reading was part of the day. I read constantly. I read on my way to cover stories, while waiting for cardinals to die, murderers to hang, embezzlers to confess, fires to ebb, celebrities to speak. Raskolnikov, Lord Jim and Thaïs went with me into the police stations. Stavrogin, Des Esseintes and Salammbô; Zarathustra, Sanine, Prince Bezukhov, Père Goriot, Candide, Julien Sorel and Oblomov; Tess, Maggie, Odette and all that magic company were ever at my elbow.

And I bought books as a drunkard orders drinks. I found pleasure not only in reading them but in watching them grow and fill bookshelves and crowd chairs out of corners and lamps off tables.

The blue-eyed Marcella Burns, Lorelei of unread treasures in Mc-Clurg's bookstore, sold me scores of them and kept me thin with poverty. And there was Walter Hill, who trafficked in first editions as costly as sapphires and whose stock I raided for items beneath his notice. He rid his shelves carelessly of such dross as Walter Pater sets, Goethe sets, Burton and Casanova sets and such strays as Crébillon and Merezhkovski.

There was also the Marco Polo of Monroe Street, Papa Kroch, in his first hole-in-the-wall bookshop. On Papa Kroch's counters lay all the latest loot of elegance and art. Smiling, young and gleaming-eyed, this merchant of Monroe Street did not sell me books. Rather he waved a wand and the wonders of de Gourmont, Huysmans, Pollard, Mallarmé, Wedekind, D'Annunzio, Villiers de L'Isle-Adam, Strindberg and Proust sprang into being.

And there were the Powner secondhand bookstores which Charles Vincent Emerson Starrett, renowned later as Vincent Starrett, and I hounded like a pair of porch climbers. We hoped to spot valuable "first editions" on the Powner twenty-five-cent bookshelves, snake them off and resell them at great profit to Walter Hill.

They are in my room now, all the books I once loved—Andreyev, Lamartine, Aksakov, Butler, Borrow, Hudson, Wells, Keats, Euripides, Daudet, Brandes and rows on rows of poets, anarchists, moonshooters, hell-divers, wind-chasers and star-counters. In an "attic" that adjoins my room several hundred small-framed pictures of the world's great authors hang in a mass on the walls. I glance at them every day and notice that most of them have beards—and think of them all as Chicagoans.

EUROPE IS CALLED TO MY ATTENTION

ANOTHER GUIDE in the pursuit of books in the days when I became a part of their ink and buckram was a tall man with a small, wanton red beard. He was Doc Knapp, and he wrote the editorials for the *Journal*. He had come from Colorado, off the *Rocky Mountain News*, where he also must have been an editorial writer, for it was difficult to imagine Doc Knapp grappling with anything less than world problems.

Duffy, fetched by the sparse and wiry red beard, called him Doc Yak; and Doc Yak he is in my grateful memory. I see him walking through the local room in a knock-kneed and imperious gait, conveying his fulminations to Mr. Boyer, the head printer. His copy went directly from his lordly hand to the linotype.

His was an alien figure full of faraway enterprise. He stirred no envy among us despite rumors of his great salary, but he drew our stares. He was the part of the paper that *thought*. Among a troupe of performing terriers, a canine that talked would have attracted a similar somewhat bewildered notice.

None of us in the local room read Doc Yak's "thoughts," though they were printed daily in type twice as large as the rest of the paper's reading matter. "Cassandra croaking in the wilderness," Duffy called him. A sweet wilderness it was—an office, a city, a nation fascinated only with itself; the last Narcissus years of America.

Doc Yak, riding like Don Quixote, head down, against battlements we could not see and clashing swords with ogres invisible to us, was no sensible part of our paper.

It was when books began piling up around my typewriter that he first noticed me. The bearded visitor from Mr. Eastman's third floor would pause at my desk on his return from the composing room where he had left the linotype clattering with his jeremiads. He would stand beside me, his long arms folded, and smile at the books. He had read them all and, like me, he loved them all. I chattered excitedly about "Anatole's irony" and Dostoevski's "psychological depth," and Doc Yak listened to my juvenile findings as if I were James Gibbon Huneker himself. Unlike Duffy, who battered away at my misconceptions and gaucheries, Doc Yak never offered me contradictions. He seemed to be smiling on me from afar, as if I were a littler Doc Yak of long ago in Colorado. My bumptiousness toward this learned and superior man still makes me squirm when I recall it. Luckily an incident occurred to end my patronizing of our Doc before I had passed from his ken. I am happy to remember that in the last years I saw him, I looked on him always with the respect of which he was worthy.

I had interviewed hundreds of famous men by this time, but I had never known any. Famous men were a tribe apart, like the people who got shot or hanged or swindled or abandoned by their lovers. I considered them fair game rather than impressive folk. In writing news stories about famous transients I tried always to tumble their high hats. My instinct was that I owed my paper a comic version of everything that came my way—except corpses. I held the theory that the essence of good reporting was to make important people ridiculous.

Doc Yak had been standing editorially for some months with the Greek phalanx holding off the Bulgarian hordes. Accounts of the Greco-Bulgar war had attracted my eye, adversely, for its communiqués often crowded my best efforts off page one. I remained ignorant, however, of its reasons and objectives. A look at Doc Yak's editorial columns would have lifted my ignorance in a twinkling. But there was something too alien about a war in Europe to arouse enough curiosity for this. The Greek-Bulgarian fracas (as Duffy called it) was on a par with a soccer game being played by oddly uniformed athletes in a stadium too distant to be news.

"Would you care to go to dinner with me this evening?" Doc Yak said one day, standing lonely beside my typewriter, his arms folded, his beard at a higher angle. He added, "It will be necessary for you to shave."

We entered a large hall in which some thousand men and women sat. I followed Doc Yak confusedly to the speaker's table where two empty chairs were waiting at its center. We sat down in them and, as we did, the thousand men and women stood up and filled the banquet room with applause. Doc Yak arose, smiled at the banqueters, bowed slowly to the left and to the right, and sat down to his soup.

I was unable to eat. I stared at Doc Yak with saucer eyes. The lonely Doc Yak to whom hardly anybody ever spoke on the paper, who had only me to take with him to his great hour—here he sat with a world cheering him. Duffy would never believe it. Mr. Condex, a Greek gentleman who manufactured cigarettes, stood up as master of ceremonies and talked of Doc Yak as if he were George Washington and Lord Byron. He recited, as if Doc Yak had written them, the lines:

> The mountains look on Marathon—
> And Marathon looks on the sea;
> And musing there an hour alone,
> I dreamed that Greece might still be free.
> For standing on the Persian's grave,
> I could not deem myself a slave.

Other men spoke and recited. They told of Doc Yak's vision, scholarship and humanity. They spoke English with the Greek accent I had learned to associate with low comedy. But there was nothing comic about these speakers or the thousand who cheered their words. They were men of passion, a passion that arose out of no streets or prairies I had known. Yet it seemed suddenly close to me.

At the end of the speeches Doc Yak was given a decoration that described him as a Friend of Greece and a Champion of Civilization.

That evening was my first glimpse into the faraway Pandora's box of Europe. I had interviewed many Europeans, one an Irish lass from the County Cork who had survived the sinking of the *Titanic*. She had told me how the Irish immigrants had rushed from the steerage into the emptied first-class salon as the great ship was going down. Ogling the fine surroundings, they had massed around the grand piano and sung their native songs, going down to their watery graves in a room of plush and marble never beheld before. But that had not been Europe—only people. Nor had the "comic" whiskered scientists, the weirdly accented sirens, the mysteriously angry travelers in square hats and dark cheviot suits, whom I had interviewed by the gross, been Europe.

Here in the banquet hall cheering my friend Doc Yak, Europe sat, however, and I saw it plain. I looked, wondering, on a roomful of people full of passion for something far away, ready to die for a cause invisible to my Chicago eye and, strangest of all, loosing hosannas for a man from Colorado who wrote editorials nobody read.

MY FLIGHT FROM PHILOSOPHY

THERE WAS one tribe of writers who, even in those uncritical years, repelled rather than attracted. These were the philosophers. They seemed, chiefly, to have made up a new language by torturing familiar words beyond their understandable meanings. I found in them only a guessing game and a ruined vocabulary.

I have learned, since then, not to judge a philosopher by how readable he is. A better criterion would be: how unwelcome is the philosopher's seemingly harmless pastime of thinking to the churchmen, politicians, and other majorities of his time.

There are times and countries, Thomas Mann said, when the only place for an honest man is in jail.

Socrates, by his death, helped create a time in which his disciples asked troublesome questions and answered them in innumerable volumes. Voltaire held the Catholic Church at bay. Such victories were also Spinoza's and Anatole France's. Such was Georg Brandes in his time. Freud, writes Ernest Jones, was "of those who troubled the sleep of the world." And such, also, was my hero, H. L. Mencken, in my century.

But anarchs such as these are few in the annals of philosophy. I doubt if there are a dozen. The rest swim elegantly in the fashionable currents of their time and are left stranded and rubbishy looking when their currents are dried up, and other fashionable currents have replaced them, full of other notable philosophers.

There were some I read with pleasure who were too tired to be philosophers. Among them was Remy de Gourmont, who pleaded with men of intellect not to translate thought into action.

And there are the laureled notables who, though they seem to be writing eruditely and aloofly, are doing nothing more than exhausting their minds in holding together the biases and errors in which they live. Such, to my mind, was Santayana.

There are also those mystical enthusiasts who go so far in unclarity that they become as exciting as melodrama, or an "underground" movement. I remember encountering excitedly the first Time-Space burst of philosophical shrapnel and with it the beginning of the "let's stop trying to be artists and let's have fun as men of action" battle cry. This was Professor Henri Bergson with his *élan vital*, this also was Nietzsche, so seductive at times with his heels-up-head-down-in-a-storm ideology, and his mad call that aped the wind and rain of freedom:

"They who follow me must first forget me."

Nietzsche excited me, for I was ever ready to follow writers who beckoned me as poets, not as constables ready to lead me off into the cells of their belief.

(I knew then, as I know now, that there are wiser men than I in the world, but their wisdom becomes useless to me if I must be cowed by it. What is wisdom in them becomes, then, cowardice in me.)

The arch scoundrel of them all was Spengler, who masqueraded a national press agentry in the robes of philosophy. Only compare Mencken's life-long quarrel with his own beloved America to Oswald's frenzy for his native Germany, a frenzy that helped prepare his land for World War II. Spengler, with the aid of Time-Space patter, managed better than any of his philosophical predecessors to run the soul of man off the map. His Decline of the West advised us that Homo sapiens was a bug imbedded in history, that there was no sense in this bug, and that he might as well surrender his whole baggage of poems, paintings, protests and daydreams, since they were getting him nowhere, and become a powerful State. Music was the only thing worth listening to, said Oswald, with a press agent's eye to the fact that music was the only thing the Germans were able to create that made any sense to the rest of the world.

Alas, Oswald, Time, which you prophesied would write the real live Drama to take the place of our "lifeless" Grecian decadence, has told its tale, and with no German accent, and not in a Homburg hat either.

TWO AMERICAN HEROES

IT IS IMPOSSIBLE to live without contemporary heroes. The most self-contained of us will elect a Napoleon or two of our own time and call them Sire.

My obeisance to the two earth-shakers of my teens may not have passed muster as true hero worship, since I had no call to fetch them followers or be injured in their service. Yet it was, by my lights, hero worship on two counts: One, they could do no wrong; two, they seemed a little better than I was.

I hailed a quality they both had—although, if I remember rightly, they despised each other. This was the quality of exuberance, of bouncing up and down from sunrise to sunset like a pair of lads on a trampolin. One of them was a physical-social exuberant; the other an intellectual one. Had the brain of one been hooked up with the glandular system of the other, a great man would have resulted, the like of which history has not known since Alexander and Caesar. My two heroes were Theodore Roosevelt and H. L. Mencken.

Of Teddy's ideas and political projects I have, to this day, only vague information. I never read any of his books and was too preoccupied at the time of his bid for power to notice much of what he was talking about. The defeat of his efforts to sweep all the Democrats and Republicans from their roosts and fill them with Bull Moosers did not impair his status in my eyes—any more than his success would have increased it. It is not necessary for a Don Quixote to capture actual fortresses. The manner of his assault is all that counts.

My hero worship of Teddy, unlike that of Mencken, had a trifle of condescension in it. I knew that my hero was a ham actor and a grandstand player. But the truth is that on two occasions I bellowed myself hoarse for Teddy. And during my active hero worship of him, I wrote thumping ballads about his spirit, his prowess and even his fine looks. These appeared on the front page of the Chicago *Journal* in the time he was heading the Bull Moose political party, and were a novelty in political reporting, if not in poetry.

My hero, Teddy, was of a different cut from any of the scores of politicos I interviewed in those days. They had struck me all as mealy-mouthed job hunters, full of a Uriah Heepish oil for the journalists or cooing at them like Just Folks copybooks. But there are men who do not go shopping or begging for laurels but seem to have in them a sort of magnet for their attraction. The genius for exciting the mob is as much a part of them as excitement is part of the mob.

And so I shall not skip the teeth-flashing Teddy because he removes an oddity from my self chronicle. It would be a little too odd to grow up in a Republic without having loved a single mayor, governor, senator or President.

HOW I YELLED FOR TEDDY

I SHALL CONFINE my reminiscences of my hero to the two times I stood on my feet cheering him. The first time was the day he bolted the Republican Convention assembled in Chicago to nominate a presidential candidate. I have covered several of these incredible fish fries by which the Republic decides its alleged political destiny. They are among the most mindless spectacles ever achieved by the politics of any land. Reason is appalled and the certainty born of them that our nation is not capable of surviving another two years, whoever is elected.

But this convention which Teddy and his Bull Moosers bolted was an affair I remember with as much delight as I do Otis Skinner playing Hajj the Beggar in *Kismet*.

The bolting began before noon. Delegation after delegation arose and marched their state banners out of the Coliseum. I watched the intrepid delegates as they paraded down Michigan Avenue to Orchestra Hall, a distance of two miles.

The badge-bedecked and ribbon-streaming grocers, salesmen, shopkeepers, ward heelers and boodle fanciers who had come from far-flung caucuses to Chicago as delegates paraded like Heroes moving to man the barricades. The facts that there were no barricades, that the most tiddlywink of battle cries distinguished this revolt, that the ideological difference between an impassioned Bull Mooser and an impassioned Republican could be determined only by a micrometer—these facts cut no ice. Cliché had thrown down the gauntlet to cliché. A do-or-die partisanship had sprung up out of nothing, and one as pointless as the dissension which tore the Byzantine Empire with the rivalry between the Red and the Blue chariot drivers.

Orchestra Hall filled up with these fake fire-eating delegates. They sang, cheered, stamped until the walls bulged. On the stage orator upon orator bastinadoed the Republicans and proclaimed their Bull Moose Teddy, the Light of the World.

For two hours the speechmakers winded themselves holding the fort waiting for Teddy to appear. No Teddy appeared. Such a hunger grew for the sight of him and such a fear was born that he might ditch his Comanche-lunged disciples and go back to the Republican white folks in the Coliseum, that panic flirted with these first Bull Moosers. Their singing and whooping alarmed policemen a block away. And still no Teddy showed.

During the last of these waiting hours I was with my hero in his hotel suite. He sat on a couch, beaming and tossing whisky after whisky down his gullet. He also pretended to be writing a speech. He grinned at us, ordered us to stop whispering, chewed up his pencils, drew pictures of comic elephants on the note paper, opened a second bottle of whisky and wrote nothing.

So happy and footling a fellow human I had never yet seen. His campaign managers, however, grew nervous. It would be bad politics to produce a sort of rubber-legged Leon Errol into Orchestra Hall. The press of the world was on hand to record every hiccup and stagger.

My hero waved aside his advisers, who despite their sobriety and practical words seemed to me also men of small understanding. It was obvious that my hero knew what he was doing. He was enjoying himself. He was enjoying the screaming, potentially treacherous mob waiting to crown him on the Appian Way. He was a man who could not only drink the common liquor of the world, he could drink also the hour, savor it, gargle it like a connoisseur—and swallow it without sputtering.

Finally, clutching a handful of blank note pages, Teddy stood up. He had drunk his fill. It was time to proceed now to his tryst with destiny and allow the boys to slap the Bull Moose crown on his head.

I hurried to Orchestra Hall ahead of him and wedged myself into one of the balcony boxes reserved for the press. I was full of concern. My devotion to Teddy would not be shaken by what I expected—the arrival of a weaving and babbling souse. But one does not like to see one's hero fall on his face, unless his name is Charlie Chaplin.

Senator Hiram Johnson of California was astride the podium, a mighty orator, a man unafraid of lightnings. He stood socking home anew the marvels of their Leader, and the hoarsened delegates rose anew to cheer the tale of Teddy's genius and valor. Senator Hiram knew what I knew, that any moment now might produce an addled or leaping drunk. His eyes watched the stage wings as he bombinated, as so did six thousand eyes of the hysteria-moaning audience.

My hero appeared. He came not out of any stage wings like a tardy actor but straight off the street into the auditorium—and alone. No adviser was at his side and no steadying hand. He walked down the center aisle as casually as some wayfarer hoping to find a seat. And he walked as sure-footedly as a mountain goat. No weave was in him and no hint of alcohol touched his smile or manner.

For a few minutes the audience could not believe that this aisle saunterer—this stray citizen who seemed to have lost his way and was moseying around arguing with ushers and waving his hand good-naturedly at a pal here and there—was their Theodore Roosevelt, Light of the World. The knowledge that Teddy had not only arrived but *was in their midst* smote the assemblage all of a sudden, as if a firecracker had exploded under all their seats. Up the three thousand leaped and out of them came a roar that lasted for seven minutes—the longest, loudest unbroken roar ever to that time heard under an American roof.

So loud was the noise that it was difficult to see Teddy. I made him out dimly as he scaled the stage, coming upon it like an acrobat. And I saw him stand, his empty note pages in hand, grinning at the dervishes in front of him. Why they roared, I knew not then or now, nor why I roared, nor why the roar would not end but seemed to feed on this erect and grinning figure with teeth flashing from behind a walrus mustache. It grew louder like a succession of Wagnerian chords. Without rhyme or reason we stood roaring, our throats turned into megaphones of love. After four minutes, Teddy raised his hand for silence. I was for an instant horrified. That our hero should show so cloven a hoof as modesty and try to cut short his acclaim was unthinkable. No hero ever checks an ovation. It is only near heroes who are afraid the ovation will not last long enough who raise a pusillanimous hand for silence.

But I had misjudged our Teddy. He would as soon have thought of stopping our roars of love as of shooting down his grandmother. Our hero had raised his hand—but not for silence. He had raised it to throw the empty sheets of note paper into the air, to show his disciples that so overcome was he by their adoration that he was not going to speak to them from any notes. He was going to speak—when they allowed him—from a grateful and overflowing heart.

The scraps of empty note paper, tossed violently into the air, fluttered down around his head and as they fell the roar deepened, took on new and wilder instrumentation. And another three minutes of bedlam bulged the walls.

I have no memory of what Teddy said, when finally he spoke. I remember his voice as almost a comic squeak. And I recall his fist sawing the air as he orated. But his words were unimportant, to the three thousand as well as me. We sat back glutted, voiceless and blissful. We had beheld a hero.

TEDDY'S BULLETPROOF EGO

THE SECOND TIME I cheered for Teddy I cheered the words he spoke. It seemed to me I would never hear finer words said by a man, and, perhaps, I have not.

There was no historic stage wait this time. Some five thousand men and women sat in silence in the Milwaukee auditorium. They had come to hear Teddy Roosevelt speak, but it was doubtful whether he would.

On his arrival in Milwaukee that forenoon, Teddy had been shot by a would-be assassin. The bullet had plowed into his midriff. He had been taken, bleeding, to the hospital. Surgeons had cut him open and probed for the bullet and been unable to find it.

We in the audience were uncertain whether we would see and hear our Teddy orate this night or listen to a bulletin announcing his death. At ten o'clock a group of men came out on the stage. They were escorting a pale-faced, walrus-mustached figure to the speaker's stand. It was Teddy.

Surgical bandages wrapped the thick torso under its short cutaway coat. Teddy's voice was fainter and squeakier than I had ever heard it. He held up his hand for silence this time and we gave him the auditorium instantly. He looked as if he might topple over, if we kept him standing too long.

I have never checked my memory of his speech against the records of that night, so I do not vouch for its literal accuracy. However, these are the words I remember.

"Friends and fellow Americans," said the walrus mustache grinning at us. "I was shot this morning and the doctors haven't yet removed the bullet from my insides. They are going to operate when I get back to the hospital. I came here to tell you only one thing. I want you to know that whatever happens to me I have had a hell of a good time on this earth, for which I am grateful alike to my God, my friends and my enemies."

Long after Teddy's ambulance had clanged back to the hospital with him in it, we were still on our feet cheering.

And why was I full of hoorays for Teddy Roosevelt? Why did I respond so worshipfully to his exuberance? Was I admiring myself in a large, gaudy mirror; applauding the quality that was at the bottom of my own character?

I doubt this easy answer. There is a life force in hero worship beyond personal psychology, a sort of racial optimism that keeps the human tribe from drifting into psychic defeat and melancholia.

Hecuba, moaning to the Trojan women, spoke a famed denial of hope in the strophes of Euripides.

"That mortal is a fool who, prospering, thinks his life has any strong foundation; since our fortune's course of action is the reeling way a madman takes, and no one person is ever happy all the time."

Granted; but it is this cry of despair the hero denies for us. He is no madman reeling and without goal. He is no structure without foundations. He is no soul overcome by the confusion and dreariness of living. What we see of him glittering in the spotlight is a winner, a human who has met destiny and pinned its shoulders to the mat, a happy man.

Such was my relation to the popeyed hero of San Juan Hill, of Doubtful Rivers, forgotten causes and tattered political phrases. I rejoiced to see in high office not a sage or statesman but a happy man always ready to enjoy himself swinging the world by its tail.

I CAST A VOTE

THAT THERE ARE no statues of H. L. Mencken in our public parks
is proof of the fact that history rarely honors those who make it. It
saves its pedestals for the puppets who are made by it. A politician,
a general, a money grubber—all of them usually nobodies who got
run over by some Major Event—these are hoisted on pedestals for the
nurses in the park to admire and the pigeons to bedeck.

It is just as well there are no statues of Mencken. He has watery
eyes, a round wistful face, a dubious waistline and despite any pose
the sculptor might invent for him, he would still look like a queru-
lous and defeated alderman. It is different with Shakespeare, Goethe
and Voltaire. The first was an actor and knew the art of make-up. His
pointed beard alone was enough to insure him park space forever.
Goethe was actually an artist's model. Of all the literary men who
flourished in the two centuries before ours, he seems to have been the
only one with a set of weight-lifter's muscles and a face that did not
resemble a deputy sheriff in need of dentistry. As for Voltaire, he
managed to end up looking like Old Mother Witch—a character that
has always allured the artist's brush and chisel.

My hero, Mencken, belongs with these literary great in the statue
world, but I am reconciled not to behold him in the parks. I am even
reconciled not to spot him on my friends' bookshelves, nor to see his
name shining in the literary-page firmaments. Such honors can well
go to those in need of them. I know where Mencken's statue is. It is
the U.S.A.

No single American mind has influenced existence in the Republic
as much as did his. That he influenced us without declaring wars,
starting panics or drumming up a job-hungry constituency to help
him is fine proof that brave words can still lift the soul of man.

MENCKEN—THE REPUBLIC'S ONE-MAN
RENAISSANCE

MENCKEN'S INFLUENCE is varied. He invented novelists, the best of
them Sinclair Lewis, who lambasted the small and pompous greeds

into which the Republic had fallen. Feeding off the Menckenian spinach, his disciples grew great of sinew and fell upon the Philistines.

And my hero waded into the battle himself, not like a philosopher in a frock coat but like a barroom brawler with his shirt sleeves up. He fought with every weapon that came to hand, from Excalibur to a bung starter. He attacked Baptists, Methodists, Y.M.C.A. secretaries, parrot-cackling university professors, Rotary Club orators, theologians and moony poets. Yet none of these was his target. He was after the soul of the Republic, sunk to its intellectual knees and kissing the rump of every platitude on the calendar.

The vain, the smug, the shallow winced before his single shillelagh. His blows sought out big and little fools alike. The buncombe of politicians, the flatulence of mindless parsons, the dreary bragging of property-drugged shopkeepers, the rantings of quack Messiahs, the bad writing, the shabby thinking, the yapping of America's boom-town credos, were the enemy at which he kept pummeling. The cant and drivel of an unlicked nation magnificently stuck on itself, the half-idiot bluster of a people who did not need wit or honesty or culture to land them as a world Top Dog, drew his wrath and felt his banging phrases.

No coast-to-coast syndicates carried his voice, and the magazine in which it was to be read (along with his books) never swept the country. He was comparatively an unread prophet even in his heyday. But like a true prophet he functioned through his disciples. College boys and girls read him and carried his sneers at humbug into their classrooms and farm-land parlors. Newspapermen read him and filled the corners of the press with his cynicism. Budding novelists, playwrights and essayists read him and dramatized his derisions, flung fiction heroes into darkest garden-club America and watered far away arid places with Menckenese. And, curiously, politicians, orators and financiers read him, as Machiavelli was read by the truth-hungry rascals of his day. These leaders felt the tickle of his fierceness, tried on his grins and shed a part of their sham.

There was another thing he did even more useful to the nation. He reformed the American language, particularly its literary language.

The narcistic drone of words into which the highbrows of the land had fallen felt the impact of the Mencken sentence and never recov-

ered, entirely. The glossy phrasings of the professors, the larded
paragraphs of critics and philosophers seemed, alongside the
Mencken prose, void of human look. Mencken brought the sounds
and smells of the street into his writing. Prose became a language to
be understood, not guessed at, for among the shams to whose destruction he was dedicated was the sham of abstruseness. His rhapsodies
never said good-by to lucidity. He stuck to clarity as he stuck to syntax. A hooliganism livened the deepest of his cogitations, and he
backed up his thinking with similes and metaphors as unfancy as
those of a sailor in rut.

My lifelong interest in Mencken was kept going by his unfailing
wit. Neither his enormous erudition nor his roaring anger could
smother the raillery in his brain pan. He was opposite to the stuff
that saints are made off; he was of the genus that laughs. He sought
not to uplift the weary and the sick of mind. He was out to peddle his
own health.

The health of a strong mind is potent magic always, and
Mencken's was one of the healthiest heads that ever came butting
temples down. Mencken's hilarity turned boogiemen into clowns.
The villains he attacked all ended up as zanies in a comic strip. Nor
did he posture among his victims as a knight on a white horse. He
was always on foot, his own shirttail flying, and an ingratiating, half-
clownish look to his own rig.

He fought his times not as a man outside of them. He was the philosopher hatched out of a newspaper office and not the classroom. It
was never an ideology that paraded itself in his writings. It was
always a man named Mencken who spoke, a tough, human fellow
whose words were salted and juicy with his own personality.

I write this about Mencken without his books open in front of me,
and with no intent of playing critic to his works. He was the hero-
mind of my youth and as such I celebrate him now. His ideas and
points of view were to be found sometimes in other men—Nietzsche,
Pollard, Huneker, Bierce, Brandes, Schopenhauer, Voltaire. But
they existed there like a retired army idling in full dress. Mencken
put battle suits on them and sent them forth in my century.

As I grew older I fell away from Mencken. The pessimism at the
bottom of his thinking was not in my nature. In pointing out his pessimism I indulge myself in no contradiction of his exuberance and
laughter.

No pessimism was ever more thorough and serene than Menck-en's. His soul had made its peace early with the fact that God was a fraud, that the human race was a hopeless tangle of inanities; and that the only good in life was the derision and laughter one could bring to it. There was no secret piety tucked away in this pessimism. It never flirted with hope or looked for angel chins to chuck. It was the pessimism of a surgeon with a steady hand who could not be seduced into admiring the disease he was attending—humanity.

There came a time when the Menckenian sanity deserted me. Un-Menckenian woolgatherings seduced me. I was unable to stay rea-sonable and to view unreason with contempt alone. Compassion came to me, compassion even for the stupid, the hypocritical and the ugly. Compassion is not necessarily a thing to boast about. Perhaps we learn compassion for human failings when we get our first glimpse of them in ourselves, and perhaps it is ourselves we nobly forgive and not our fellow men.

Although no longer Mencken's disciple, I have not added ingrati-tude to my heresy—as disciples often do when they "outgrow" their masters. In fact, did I have a choice, I would prefer to have remained entirely what I am now only in part—ruthless toward the stupidities of religion and all human humbug. But the fanaticism that makes a Mencken was denied me.

MY MENCKENIANA

MY WIFE (the first one, Marie) was giving a dinner party somewhere in 1917. Eight guests were waiting the bell. At seven-thirty our cook, whose knitted bag was stuffed with my I.O.U.'s, appeared in the living room and announced that the butcher and one assistant were in the kitchen demanding payment for a meat bill and refusing to allow her to start cooking the porterhouse steaks until such pay-ment had been made.

I followed Marie and the cook into the kitchen and learned that we had run up a meat bill of over three hundred dollars. My salary at the time was forty dollars a week. I had no bank account of any sort. I owed, according to remarks I heard fall now and then, three thou-sand dollars.

Pleading failed to swerve the butcher and his aide from their plan. They gathered up the pile of uncooked steaks and left. Our guests were informed of the sudden famine and they, too, left.

I retired thoughtfully to a small room where I kept a typewriter, couch and rack of pipes. Spurred on by the picture of the predatory butcher making off with the steaks and of our eight guests wandering off hungrily into the night, I sat down to write my first commercial short story.

I write now with a pencil but in those sharper days I wrote everything on a typewriter—including poetry.

I wrote for two hours and at ten P.M. mailed a manuscript called "The Unlovely Sin" to H. L. Mencken, Smart Set Magazine, 25 West 45th Street, N.Y.C. Six days later a light blue envelope bearing the magazine's title arrived. It contained a short, congratulatory letter signed, "Yours in Christ, H. L. Mencken," and a check for forty-five dollars. I had expected at least a thousand but adjusted myself quickly to this lesser sum. If these convict labor prices were all that the great Mencken could afford to pay for literature he admired enough to print, my task was clear. I would have to write twenty-five short stories instead of one before I netted a thousand dollars. This I did in the next few months.

I met Mencken several years later in Chicago. He had come to cover the Republican National Convention at the Coliseum as a correspondent for the Baltimore Sun. It was summertime and the city thirsted in the first throes of Prohibition. Mencken visited my house and went away with nine bottles of homemade beer sticking out of all his pockets. As he left he assured me I was the white hope of American letters.

The next day I walked with him from his hotel to the Coliseum. We were on Michigan Avenue and well past the hotel zone when Mencken demanded a water closet. There were no empty cabs to flag, the city being overrun with visiting politicians and their families. The nearest lavatory of which I knew was a half mile off, unless the great man cared to take his chances in Grant Park across the boulevard.

"It's that fine beer you gave me," said Mencken. "Three of the bottles exploded while still in my pockets but I drank the other six. For Christ sake, don't tell me a big city like Chicago hasn't got a water closet on every corner!"

I stopped, having remembered something. We were passing one of the town's old whore houses. The place was partially boarded up and ready for the demolition hammers. I led Mencken inside, up a deserted stairway, to a remembered water closet.

On the wall above the toilet, Mencken read aloud a quatrain written there in indelible pencil.

> *O Lady of lustful gyrations,*
> *O Vandal of velvet and vice,*
> *O Creature of carnal elations—*
> *Why will not a two-spot suffice?*

It was entitled "Three Shy" and my name was signed boldly on it.

"You have a true poet's heart," said Mencken as we departed the derelict brothel, "a love of women and a lack of funds. And I can say I never read a poem under better conditions."

Some years later when I was collared by the Federal law for writing a "lewd, obscene and lascivious" book and defiling the U.S.A. mails with its transport, I cast among the men of note I knew to appear as witnesses at my trial.

My attorneys, Charles Erbstein and Clarence Darrow, were of the opinion that the best way for me to beat the case and keep from being sent to jail was to have a dozen men and women of literary eminence inform the jury that the book in question, *Fantazius Mallare*, was a fine work of art.

I knew scores of such eminent folk well and pleasantly. Most of them had read the book and written me letters praising it and commending me for its writing. Nevertheless, approached to be witnesses in a Federal court, they all beat a retreat. They explained, as if they had all been coached by the same hand, that they could not afford to jeopardize their standing as citizens, fathers, mothers, husbands, etc., by coming out in the open and defending a book that had the word "pissing" in it.

The one eminent one who came forward, unsolicited by me, and offered to step on the anti-Federal barricades—and also pay his own railroad expenses to and from Chicago—was H. L. Mencken.

NIGHT IN THE CITY

THE WRITING on the wall of the Michigan View Hotel which I showed to Mencken was the merry obit to a world that had vanished from my life long before the Sage of Baltimore appeared in it.

This little world of ornate parlors and over-perfumed bedrooms comes dimly to my mind. Whores in their bright gowns and negligees appear, festooned like Ophelias.

It is a world more difficult to recall than my nursery time, for I am further removed from it. I recall chiefly my activities as a reformer in those carnal precincts and the fact that the whores I knew always wept.

Elsewhere, I was less purposeful and more like my colleagues, drunk and staggering on Saturday nights from saloon to saloon, sitting among bawds and pimps in Colisimo's Café and Mike Fritzel's Friar's Club. We went in loud groups, bawling songs and obscenities to Sunset No. 2 and The Entertainers. There whites and blacks danced together and wiped out the color line with liquor, music and sex.

I was hail fellow with thieves dividing their night's loot among their vulturous ladies in basement dives. Knives flashed, fists suddenly beat at limp faces. Hop-heads gibbered around us, and we reporters were all part of a cancan, with oath and music and the whip of alcohol keeping us going. I remember that men cursed each other like lovers and shouted filth and defiance at each other and embraced in sudden peace pacts.

When we came finally whooping into the brothel parlors, I grew apart from my companions of the night. I had no stomach for the insults they bellowed at the brightly gowned girls. I winced at the wild slapping of buttocks, at the angry-seeming embraces. Looking in the eyes of the noisy, rouged girls I thought I saw pain. As the free-for-all love preliminaries quickened I became silent as if in the presence of cruelty.

I was aware, without understanding its meanings, of the underhanded comradeship between men that made fornication seem less than laughter. Male allegiance appeared to increase as the moment neared for the hop-skip into the bedrooms. Loud derision for the female and all she had to offer was the measure of wit and masculinity. Full of brave jest, my friends gallumped off to bed as with a common enemy.

There were also serious and furtive men, who sat dry-lipped and gulping as if waiting to commit a crime. And there may have been some like myself, trapped by friendship into deeds not in their nature. If so, I noticed little, for I was busy hiding my own unfitness for the scene by playing drunkard and whoremonger with all the vocabulary at my command.

In the bedroom my heart always ached for the young and pretty girl with whom I lay. I felt sad to see something as wonderful as youth and beauty so ignobly employed. My own "sins" failed to enter my brooding, for I was wise enough to know that it was not I who was the whore. I asked questions out of an eagerness to know what sort of girl lay smiling beside me. The older ones, those in their twenties, laughed at me, but I was rewarded at times by a gush of tears. I would then sit up in bed and listen for an hour to a tale of seduction and downfall sobbed out by my bed companion.

I usually heard the same tale from different girls—a priest had deflowered them at fourteen, a father had beaten them; sickness had overtaken them and while they lay between life and death the doctor had crawled into bed and ravished them; and, finally, a rich man appeared and promised to marry them but, instead, he abandoned them in a strange town—and after that nothing mattered.

The tales were lies, but the tears were not. They were tears of confusion. Staring into the night beyond the window, the young whore would wonder what made her a whore, and why she was different from other girls. Some mystery had brought her to the brothel, and the mystery had power to frighten while she was still young.

I remember how friendly and motherly these flesh outcasts were, how kind to the foulness and stupidity of the men who fell on them; how they accepted, dully and sometimes gracefully, the drunken leavings of male personality—its hatreds, nauseas and frustrations. And even me they beamed on, despite my idiotic insistence on virtue of some sort—and tears.

At five A.M., when the business of the night was done, the girls—five or six of them—gathered around the glass-topped dining table that stood in the parlor. Here I sat often with them talking my head off, usually about books I had read. They doted on such high discourse and rewarded me with many anecdotes of their lives.

Their talk became my well-worn dictionary to be used forever— much as reporters' talk still is in my ears with its special language. There was Queen Lil, the white-haired madam, regal, profane, with a jutting lavender-painted face and a limp to her massive body. She walked with a large, silver-handled cane. Her limp and cane had always fascinated me.

"How'd you get hurt?" I asked her one night.

"It's my God-damn foot," she said. "I'll tell you, kid. I come to this town when I wasn't no older than you. I was a girl of seventeen. I come from a ranch in Nevada. And I wind up in a whore house in a couple o' months—a God-damn wooden shack in a muddy street. Fifty cents a crack, and the boys linin' up like it was a bargain. Which it was, the dirty sonsobitches. Well, I'm lyin' in bed one morning, and I got the window open because it's spring. I'm lyin' there alone, naked, enjoyin' the breeze and lookin' out of the window. And all of a sudden a bird hops on the window sill. And the God-damn bird starts chirpin' and hops over to my bed and, so help me Christ, this God-damn bird hops up and lights on my foot. I got so God-damn mad all of a sudden I couldn't see straight. This bird chirpin' on my foot like I was some God-damn apple tree. So I reached and got my gun out of the drawer. I brought it with me from Nevada. And I draw a bead on this sonofabitch of a bird and I pull the trigger. And I shoot myself right in the foot. I blow my own God-damn big toe off. So I've been limpin' like a bitch ever since."

KINSWOMAN OF DOLORES

I HAVE FELT a scholar's gratitude toward the whores I knew in my youth. They provided a minimum of fun but they sharpened my wits for years to come. They enabled me to understand women who otherwise might have seemed full of enticing mysteries.

These were women who were far from harlotry socially. But the whore was in them. The limp faces of the bordello girls of my youth peered at me above their family dinner tables. I saw the same sharp eyes and flaccid lips of the whore in women who sat safely among their kin; in women who wept too much when a lover wooed them; in women full of proud postures that crumbled at a first crude grab at their bodies.

Of these women who are sometimes our hostesses, sweethearts or wives, Duffy would say, "A whore at heart and a bitch about the house."

In my youth I learned that it was the absence of sex in a woman that was at the bottom of whorishness; and that the mystery that turned a girl into a whore was often her contempt for her femaleness.

I have found much the same psychology in the glamour girls who parade their romances in the fine cafés. The same absence of sex is in these promiscuous ladies who not only manage to keep their bottoms out of brothels, but who win for themselves the reputation of "great lovers." They peddle "love" instead of simple fornication but, like whores, they know the trick of service. They are desperate performers in bed, as are most frigid women. They work like a combination masseuse and contortionist to snare a month or a year out of a male.

These sultry-spoken, sexless sweethearts clawing away at their beloveds and pouring on them the illusion of passion are the heroines of most of our newspaper reports of wrecked marriages. They are usually the steaming and voracious Other Woman for whom the husband bolts his barnyard—for the harlot's jackdaw nest.

THE FEMME FATALE

MY TEACHERS, the sad and gaudy whores of my youth, informed me of one of the secrets of many a modern woman—perhaps a good half of womankind—the whore's cousin.

I have met this tribe under many circumstances—sometimes, luckily, for no more than a hello. But so well-instructed a graduate was I from Madam Lillian's Classes that I knew their true name quickly.

As with most men who are full of powerful information about women, my knowledge was never of much help in keeping trouble out of my life. It enabled me, however, to understand it and kept me from being too mystified by it.

The Jew can seldom descend into sin without some Talmudic counselor at his elbow—even such a Jew as I. For this reason (I can't think of any other), I quote here Rabbi Moishe Leib, the Wonder-Rabbi, who wrote quite a while ago, "The trouble that women bring us cannot be avoided by improving our mind, but only by making our character more noble."

Possibly Rabbi Moishe is a symbol of my advancing years and came to help me out with a moral attitude needed for this chapter. I am a respecter of symbols and shall let him sit. Quiet, Rabbi.

I was discussing the secret of certain modern women, and how I learned of it in my youth. In the brothels I had noted a strange fact. It was that the whores had the same contempt for their female-ness that their male callers had. Whore and customer shared the same desire to make a bitch out of Venus and roll her in the gutter. The whore liked the insults she received. They were directed against her femaleness. She found "solace" in helping men outrage this femaleness. For the mystery inside her was that she despised her-self for having been born a woman instead of a man.

I have known only a few "Lesbians," but of these other shadowy anti-women in whom the desire for a missing malehood is constantly aboil, I have known a number. They are as often married as single. And they are as often virgins as debauchees. In fact, they are likely to be the fiercest of virgins, hating deeply the thing that threatens to complete their horrid status as woman—sex.

As spinster-virgins such castration sufferers stay fairly intact. It is as wives and lovers that they are likely to grow full of complica-tions. As wives they are restless as the devil, drink heavily, gam-ble anxiously and are willing to sample other beds. They are inclined to spend much time altering over and over the look of their homes, particularly their bedrooms (unable to alter the scenery of their thighs); they are apt also to develop endless female complaints, and end by having themselves uselessly hollowed out by surgeons. They are wives who must dominate in marriage, who must criticize the male without pause for being a male. The least troublesome of such wives are those who sneer openly at sex, consider it a wretched, coarse business, and will have none of it.

Out of wedlock, these anti-women follow the whore's therapy for their ailment. They seek to soil the female in themselves by hopping from bed to bed and experiencing out of a hundred love affairs only the sickly pleasure of having treated their femaleness with disrespect.

In this latter tribe are to be found the trouble bearers against whom Rabbi Moishe Leib wrote that there was no armor but a noble character. He meant that a man should avoid them. No man can quite do that (including Rabbi Moishe Leib, or how would he know about these matters?) for the *femme fatale* is as inevitable in a man's life as his first bicycle. She is not only inevitable but she is often preferable, and some men refuse to do without the bruises and distresses which come from this anti-woman, and can never have enough of them.

On this point Rabbi Moishe Leib turns somewhat Yogi in his writings and counsels, "A man should put his thoughts on virtue and remember as little of evil as is possible. Thus will he find peace."

I consider this a very questionable pronouncement based on the clergyman's fallacy that a human being wants peace. This fallacy is dear to all who retire from the world, particularly the aged. The truth is that no one wants peace until it is forced on him. In my own case, having somewhat outgrown the time of deviltry, I find pleasure in revisiting it with my mind. The evil of women, Reb Moishe, is a happy thing to remember in the years when it has become harmless and instructive.

I continue with my strumpets—the ones beyond the brothel. There are many educational differences between the real prostitute and her gallivanting sister, the "glamour girl." The most important difference lies in their ability as actress. A woman who is able to act well, and loudly, steps from whoredom into romance—a very dangerous step for the male. She becomes one of the tribe of painmakers, the "other woman." She is the alluring and tormenting one after whom the male heart wanders as after a shape of mist in a dream. Over this mirage of the "Loving Female," the thirsting male heart lets out the Biblical moan, "Oh, the river that was dried; oh, the fountain that was sealed!"

THE WORST OF THEM ALL

THE OTHER WOMAN is often a woman of compelling charm and considerable beauty. Grace and wit distinguish her and make her memory not too unpleasant. But there is one variety of the tribe that leaves only a shudder in its wake. This is the child-woman siren. Here Rabbi Moishe Leib is right. It is worth going to the pain of developing a noble character to avoid one.

The real child-woman is seldom a creature with a childish mind. Such pests are menacing only to semi-senile men. The true child-woman is likely to be a lady as sharp-witted and bright-spoken as Portia. Her childishness is entirely a matter of character. Tricked out with finery, and great worldliness, this fascinator operates romantically as an infant. She pants, weeps, snivels and has fits like a two-year-old child—a bad one. This noisy and preposterous infantilism is her way of signaling that her soul is wounded.

I have noted a number of these complex ladies in action and their performances are as alike as if they had all been graduated from some Moscow theater acting school—in the same year. Their objective is unvarying. It is to make a man feel "guilty and responsible."

They would rather sob and snivel than talk, for they operate out of infant memories of how effective their gushing tears and whoops of nasty sound used to be. And despite their high I.Q.'s, they would rather talk without sense than with it, hoping to be coddled again for their cute unreasonableness and for the endearing inferiorities that marked their babyhood.

Their cuteness is not to be discouraged. It is their better side. They have another quality which has resulted in more homicides than all the other villainies of women combined. As a newspaper reporter, I interviewed some twenty woman murderers. My memory is that nearly all of them had been urged to their deed by this same quality —a genius for being persecuted.

Disasters threaten the baby-souled inamoratas from morning to night. The actual disaster is, possibly, that they are a woman and not a man. But such musings are broken reeds of rebuttal. A sensible word uttered to these crisis-mongers is certain to double their colic. The world is in a plot against them. It is full of big and little conspirators at work on their physical and social doom. They are helpless before this onrush of adult calamities, as helpless as they were in their little cribs—and as cunning.

Thus they win whatever their foolish points are by the same ruses the aboriginal infant uses. They are powerless and full of needs; and it is the same noisy powerlessness with which they unhorsed all the menacing adults in their babyhood.

How those grownups suffered and pleaded when attacked by the weeness of that long-ago infant! How guilty those adults felt! How eager to appease! And what delightful presents they heaped on the little wailer!

Eagerly these baby-souled wenches work to bring the little tyrant of the crib back into their throats and tear ducts. And when the tears are over and the convulsive griefs gone from their heaving bellies, what a lovely thing is their sudden, grateful infantile smile! How sweetly they cuddle and how tenderly they talk through their noses as they ask little favors from their daddy-lover!

God spare all men females who talk through their noses! Who fall apart when criticized; who explode into blubbering when rebuked; and around whom a man has to walk on tiptoe as around a screechy and alerted infant ready to be-shit herself at the first wrong move of its near and dear ones! Of all the *femmes fatales*, they are the least rewarding, the most unmanageable. It does the male no good to see through these cooing, wheedling, overgrown two-year-olds, full of superficial despairs and cunning hysterias. It does him no good to note that their love is shallow and greedy; that they are forever aglow with themselves, preoccupied and fascinated with their bathing, their pimples, their bowel movements, their nap-taking.

Rabbi Moishe Leib is out of my head, and in his place has appeared a fictional hero of my youth. I have forgotten his name and the name of the book in which he flourished—but I salute him with reverence. He was a colored man of fine stamina, and in the middle of the book he left his sweetheart with whom he had been living in a grand passion for two years. On the pillow beside her sleeping head he pinned a farewell note. It read, "Dear Milly, your troubles begin to amaze me."

INTERRUPTION

MY WIFE here informs me that there are more imbecilic child-men in the world than child-women (of the sort I have been lambasting). She points, in fact, to half of my male friends, who are writers, actors, agents, press agents, producers, painters and flimflammers of many kinds. They whine, they throw fits, they rush from the room when the wrong company appears, they are unable to carve a turkey, they get drunk and can't find their way home, they have to be coaxed into taking baths, they fly into rages when criticized or contradicted and they sit for hours on end silently playing cards—just as babes of three occupy themselves with building blocks.

They also pout, weep, refuse to shake hands, and pour into wifely ears the endless tale of how the world abuses and misunderstands them.

My wife's findings may be true, but I remain unable to respond to them. I have never been the victim of these baby males. I have never had to dandle them, humor them or pretend, with my stomach turned, that I loved them.

My good madam will have to write her own book about them.

THE ACCESSORY MALE

I HAVE WRITTEN of all these Isoldes a little one-sidedly, omitting the phoniness of the party of the second part, the grease-paint Tristan who makes possible the full performance. Of this two-faced wooer who sneaks to his trysts with breaking heart and coat collar turned up like a con man on the lam, I shall write little here and possibly little elsewhere. He is a fellow I salute and understand.

I will say, in his behalf, that he is also a fellow who understands his Isoldes, including even the infantile tyrant. He does not cry out too long against their perfidies. Poor gentleman, what sort of leg has he to stand on for such bellowing? When the end of the great love in which he is tossing comes into sight, when he begins to note (again) the dropped cues, the abstracted stare in Isolde's passion-drenched eyes or the unedited screech of infant demands, his heart clouds with pain, true enough. And his vitals feel the match put to them and he bangs his head against the night. For he would live again, be young again and grow wings where only gray hairs sprout.

Thus, unlike the perfidious one, he knows pain. But he also knows *her*. Unless he is a chump with his brains ascramble, he knows that impermanence was what he sought in his Isolde. He knows that how-ever real and deep his love for her was, it was a love designed to ornament his life and not to mold it, his life being already molded into family and business patterns. Nine times out of ten, the curses he hurls on his beloved who loves him no more are edged with gratitude. She has enabled him to return to the honest arms of his wife and the normal ways of his office. This he does, nine times out of ten, full of marital good will. The tenth time is another story.

How the devil Duffy knew about these ladies I shall never know, Duffy being now dead. He never married or had, as far as I knew, any unfortunate love affairs. Yet he knew. Long before I found out, he told me.

"Whores are the best," he said. "They are good beasts, no more. Damn their souls, if you must, but you can say for them they never hurt you. When you grab a Jezebel, you know what you've got—noth-ing. You can see through a whore and laugh and kick her in the ass—to the delight of all parties. But when you grab the other kind, you grab trouble. A whore's heart in a lover's smile—that's the thing that makes men shoot themselves. If you're very lucky, Bennie, you'll maybe grab a woman. But don't ever bank on it. Women are as rare as hen's teeth. By God, it's my humble opinion that there aren't any women, real ones, on the planet, from pole to pole."

As I write these words of Duffy's, spoken long ago in a saloon that is no more, it comes to me that there was, possibly, more plot to Duffy than I ever knew. One does not learn pain and perfidy out of book reading—neither Duffy nor I.

TALE OF CHRISTIAN DANE HAGERTY'S TRIUMPH

LOOKING into those days when I was young and indifferent to the inhumanities which I brought bird-dog fashion to my city editor, I see many adventures in which I move like a dimming figure in a dream. I select two of them to tell—a happy boast of a newspaper-man's prowess and an account of the nether world of sin, always on a reporter's doorstep. One is a story of ideal morality, the other a story minus morality. This is a distinction I make today, for in the time when they happened all stories were alike to me. I cannot re-member feeling any righteousness toward any of the sinners, per-verts or murderers of whose deeds I was the daily chronicler. In those days I belonged to life as uncritically as a rain barrel belongs to the rain.

No other profession, even that of arms, produces as fine a version of the selfless hero as journalism does. Unlike the profession of arms, journalism does not coerce and discipline its own into selfless-ness. The journalist's dedication to his craft is based on his own na-ture, the one he brings to it as a duck brings its webbed feet to the pond.

What I write is no blanket description of newspapermen. It in-cludes only the kind I once knew and admired because I was some-what like them. They were young, whatever their age. Their profes-sion allowed them to remain exactly what they were—either stupid, elegant, profane, aesthetic, crooked, idealistic. And the newspaper-men were accordingly full of a fierce gratitude toward their profes-sion as toward perfect and indulgent parents.

A good newspaperman, of my day, was to be known by the fact that he was ashamed of being anything else. He scorned offers of double wages in other fields. He sneered at all the honors life held other than the one to which he aspired, which was a simple one. He dreamed of dying in harness, a casual figure full of anonymous power; and free. For the newspaperman, the most harried of employees, more bedeviled by duties than a country doctor, more blindly subservient to his editor than a Marine private to his captain, considered himself, somewhat loonily, to have no boss, to be without superiors and a crea-ture always on his own. As Duffy said, "Socially, a journalist fits in somewhere between a whore and a bartender but spiritually he stands beside Galileo. He knows the world is round."

This tale which I shared with Chris Hagerty is one of many sim-ilar adventures I remember out of which Charles MacArthur (out of this same rain barrel) and I wrote the play *The Front Page*. It may be that journalism and journalists have changed, along with everything else of charm in the world, but here is what they were on a March day in 1912.

The telephone rang in Mrs. Farrington's brothel—later the Michigan View Hotel at Twelfth Street and Michigan Avenue—at five-thirty A.M. on St. Patrick's Day. Eddie Mahoney, my assistant city editor, had tracked me down. He was at his *Journal* desk and informed me with excitement that the city of Dayton, Ohio, had been wiped out by a flood, that all its inhabitants were very likely drowned and that he was giving me this opportunity to shine for the first time as a real "Staff Correspondent."

"The cashier's office is closed," he said. "You will have to get fifty dollars somewhere for expenses and catch the six-thirty train for Indianapolis. If you can make it I'm sure Finnegan will let you cover the story alone."

I spent a half hour rousing the girls in the place and pleading for expense money. At six I was on my way to the depot with forty of their hard-earned dollars in my pocket.

The barroom of the Claypool Hotel in Indianapolis was crowded with staff correspondents from Chicago and other cities, all heading for the scene of the flood. They had come to a halt in their trek because all the bridges leading to Dayton had been swept away by the flood. The Eagle River was a torrent impossible to cross. All railroad service to Dayton was halted. By tomorrow the Eagle River would be navigable and train service resumed. These facts were passed around by my colleagues.

I sat among them until midnight, listening to brave and salty tales of other catastrophes covered by the staff correspondents in the barroom. At midnight I feigned weariness and started for my room. Instead, I left the hotel and entered the freezing street. I walked along the torrential river for two hours looking for a fording place. I found one. It was a high railroad span. The river had risen almost to its open tied tracks but the trestle bridge still stood. I snooped around in the blackness among the deserted shacks until I found a lantern. I lighted it and started out.

The flooding water made a noise like a charging army as I approached the shaking span. A tall, fattish figure was walking behind me. I held up my lantern. It was Christian Dane Hagerty—Hagerty of the Associated Press. My dreams of a scoop went down in the flood. Hagerty at my side was the same as having all my sleeping rivals tagging along with me. The A.P. served all the papers whose staff correspondents were swapping yarns in the Claypool barroom.

"I'm going to cross the bridge," I said. "I don't think you'd better come along. It's risky. You can see it's shaking already."

I noticed that Hagerty, like myself, was without an overcoat despite the almost zero weather.

"I've been following you for an hour," said Haggerty. "I yelled at you a few times, but you're evidently deaf."

"I'm not deaf," I said.

"Glad to hear it," said Hagerty. "I knew a deaf newspaperman in Africa once. Wore my fingers out talking to him. Get going. And keep the lantern raised."

I started miserably across the bridge. The river was still rising. The water roared a few feet under me, threatening to sweep the shaking structure into the night. I walked quickly, holding the lantern high. Hagerty walked behind me.

I was eighteen. Hagerty was fifty-five. I could still run a mile in five minutes, sprint a hundred yards in eleven seconds. Hagerty's belly was large, his waist line gone, his voice hoarsened by the river of whisky that had flowed down his gullet. His eyes were bloodshot. He breathed through his mouth. His feet kept slipping between the railroad ties. There was an even chance this wheezing old man would break a leg or topple off the railingless bridge.

But when I stepped off on the other side, Hagerty was still a few feet behind me.

Snow covered the ground. No trains were running.

"Dayton is that way." Hagerty pointed in the dark. "Get going."

I walked in silence, listening hopefully to Hagerty's difficult breathing. He panted, coughed, spat out phlegm and stayed a few feet behind me on the railroad bed.

"Want me to carry the lantern?" he asked.

"No, it's my lantern," I answered.

Hagerty laughed.

"I saw you steal it," he said. "You remind me of a Chinese I met in the Boxer Rebellion."

I knew there was no stopping a newspaperman in the grip of a reminiscence, come hell or high water, but I cautioned him nevertheless.

"You'd better save your wind," I said.

"I hate walking," Hagerty said. "It's always a bore." He coughed, spat and continued to wheeze out between gasps and stumbles a tale of faraway China. "This young Chinese of whom you remind me stole a silver filigreed flowerpot from the palace in Peking—among a lot of other fine antiques. I met him on the road loaded down with loot and ended up buying the silver filigreed flowerpot from him. You'd never think he was a thief from the way he bargained over that pot. He insisted on giving me a bill of sale, too, to make the transaction legal, he said. Well, that flowerpot ruined the finest romance I ever had. I was in the interior trying to run down the Boxer leader who had taken to the hills, and I met a Chinese princess in a sort of fairy tale palace, far away from everywhere. A wonderful girl. I fell in love with her and wanted to marry her. Never saw any woman as beautiful before or since. But I had to get back to Peking. I gave her the silver filigree flowerpot as a present and told her I'd be back.

"A week later a messenger arrived in Peking. He handed me a box and a note in Chinese. The flowerpot was in the box. The note said I was never to appear in the princess's presence again. She hated me for the joke I had played on her. She had accepted the silver pot in good faith—but when she had pissed in it she had discovered it was full of holes and had ruined a fine carpet. There was no sense in my trying to tell her it was a flowerpot and not a piss pot. She had already been shamed, and I knew the Chinese soul."

The wheezing anecdote came to a sudden stop. Two Italians were on the roadbed ahead of us trying to lift a handcar onto the tracks. We joined them, and I heard no more of the Chinese princess. We helped hoist the flatcar into place.

"Going to Dayton?" Hagerty asked. They were, and if we would take our turn pumping the car we could come along.

I looked at Hagerty in the lantern light. His face was purple. He looked frozen, spavined and on his last legs.

"Go ahead," he said to the two Italians. "You start and we'll relieve you in fifteen minutes."

In fifteen minutes Hagerty and I were pumping the car. I pumped as fast as I could. My nose was frostbitten, my head was dizzy with weariness. And my wind was beginning to bother me. But Hagerty, fifty-five, kept bending his fat belly and muscleless back over his end of the car pump.

We came to a double track, and the handcar shot on around a turn. Hagerty stopped pumping.

"Wrong track," he said. "Dayton's over there. See those lights. They're Miami Junction, just outside Dayton. There's a telegraph station there."

The Italians insisted on taking the wrong track. They were headed for wherever it led.

"Better walk," said Hagerty.

It was almost dawn. We started down the railroad bed toward the distant window lights. No more anecdotes came out of Hagerty. I stole a look at him dragging on silently behind me. Hagerty, the A.P. hero of the Boer War, the Russo-Jap War, the Boxer Rebellion, the Spanish-American War and of a score of other notable calamities, would never make Dayton, Ohio. The hero's legs were wobbling. Exhaustion twisted his face.

"Want to rest?" I asked.

"Keep going," said Hagerty.

A shot rang out! Several more followed. Bullets sent up sprays of snow a few feet from us.

Hagerty dived off the roadbed into a snowbank. I followed. We lay together, hidden and choking in the deep snow. We heard voices and some more shooting.

"What the hell they shooting at us for?" I asked.

"Deputies," Hagerty panted, "shooting down looters."

"We're not looters," I said.

"They don't know that," Hagerty said.

"I'm going to tell them," I said.

"You God-damn dumb cub," Hagerty said, "stay put. And keep out of sight. If they see us they'll pinch us and throw us into the can—either that or the morgue."

Fifteen minutes later we started again but not on the easy road-bed as targets for any murderous deputies. We plowed along through the deep snowdrifts at the foot of the embankment, out of sight.

"It's about another mile," I said, turning for another appraisal of Hagerty. He had stopped moving.

"Go on, kid," he said. "You've lost me. I can't go any further."

I rejoiced and felt sorry.

"Go on," Hagerty said again, "it's your story. That's Dayton down there. It looks like quite a flood."

And Hagerty looked at the distant waters that covered a city like another Moses at the Promised Land.

"I'll send somebody back to get you," I said. Hagerty nodded. He looked like a dying man. But he did an odd thing for a man dying. He walked to a telegraph pole and started climbing it. I stood watching him, sure he had gone mad. I watched his paunchy, exhausted body lift itself foot by foot up the pole. When it reached the cross-bar, one of its legs went professionally over it. Hagerty had been a telegraph repairman before he took up journalism. He removed a pair of pincers from his pocket. The mechanics of what he did are still unknown to me. But at six A.M. on March 18 in the Chicago office of the Associated Press a bulletin arrived. It read:

"Dayton, Ohio—A.P. Everywhere.

"Hagerty."

His message sent, Hagerty slid down the pole and passed out in the snowbank.

I reached the Miami Junction telegraph station alone and told of Hagerty "dying." Three men went back after him.

A dozen telegraph operators were sending out messages. The head operator refused to let me file a story. He had instructions that no message of more than two words was to be sent by any one sender. The messages going out all read the same. "Am safe." And a signature was attached.

I talked to the head operator, drank hot coffee, heard a hundred fascinating details of the flood—horses swimming into second-floor windows, houses floating away with families on the roofs.

"Can I use your typewriter?" I asked.

"It's no use," the head operator said. "You can only file two words."

Hagerty would arrive in an hour. He would somehow send a story out. He was a man not to be trusted to stay silent.

I wrote six pages of double-spaced copy on the typewriter, as the telegraph keys kept clicking their "Am safe" obbligato.

"Just read it, even if you can't send it," I said to the head operator.

He read my copy and tears filled his eyes. His face flushed. When he had finished the last page he called out, "Take a rest, Jim. I'm going to use your key."

I had written a story about the heroes of the Miami Junction telegraph station—the twelve men who had sat for thirty hours without leaving their posts, without knowing if their own families were alive or drowned, and tapped out the thousands of happiness-bringing "Am safe" messages to other relatives. The names and descriptions of each of the twelve heroes were in my story.

I saw Chris Hagerty again twenty-four hours later.

I had spent the day in a canoe, paddling through flooded Dayton, interviewing other boatmen and gathering data on the catastrophe. Toward evening I had fallen asleep in the canoe. Rescuers had found me and taken me to the National Cash Register plant where the Red Cross had set up its headquarters.

I woke up on a refugee cot, in a strange nightgown, with a tag around my neck. I began yelling for my clothes and brought a nurse down on me. She insisted I was one of the victims of the flood and refused to "discharge" me until I was examined by a doctor. I answered I was a newspaperman, a staff correspondent for the Chicago *Journal* and had a story to file for the first edition.

Humiliation robbed my voice of conviction. I stood yelling in my skimpy refugee's nightgown, as unlike a journalist as could be imagined.

A familiar figure appeared. It was Hagerty. He was gathering data on the flood's refugees. There were hundreds of them on cots around me.

"Tell them," I begged, "will you! Tell them I'm a newspaperman and not a God-damn refugee."

Christian Dane Hagerty smiled at my getup for a moment and then nodded.

"He's a newspaperman," Hagerty said, and we walked out together.

TALE OF THE MURDERER AND THE TWO ODALISQUES

I CHOOSE the dolorous tale of Frank Peebles to tell chiefly because there is a great deal of snow in it. I have always been partial to tales in which snow falls deeply and endlessly and paints a ghostly summer on the trees, in which snow lies piled in white and useless hills and brings into the world the faraway look of another planet.

The snow had been falling on the village of Plano, Illinois, for five days, and there was no village left but only a long snow house in which a few lights twinkled; among them the light of a saloon and the light of a blacksmith's forge. A wind blew with teeth on it like a saw. When it smote the snow-piled prairie land around Plano, the earth began to snow upwards.

Moving through funnels of snow and in and out of snowy Taj Mahals were three bloodhounds and nine men and a tenth figure which was both man and bloodhound—this being myself. We were tracking down an old farmer who, the night before, had murdered Plano's sole harlot.

This grain grower had fled his wife and home and sported a week with the Jezebel, drinking and dancing with her in the Plano saloon and rolling with her in her Devil's bedroom when all the Christian lights of Plano were out for the night.

And then when his loins were emptied, a great guilt had seized on this wayward old man. He had looked with horror on his soft-bellied companion, on the

> Cold eyelids that hide like a jewel
> Hard eyes that grow soft for an hour:
> The heavy white limbs, and the cruel
> Red mouth like a venoromus flower; . . .

And he had atoned for his sins by swinging a rock at the head of the child of Satan who had lured him from his honest ways. She lay now on a table in the back room of the Plano post office with all her fierce midnights and famished morrows done, her head bashed in, and a horse blanket over her death-stiffened body. Society moved through the blizzard behind the three bloodhounds crying vengeance.

In the afternoon I detached myself from the footling, frostbitten posse circling the snow-piled prairie and went back to snuggle beside the blacksmith's forge. We watched the snow together and drank out of a whisky bottle I had bought.

"Poor old Frank," said the blacksmith. "He never done wrong before. Lived here since he was born in the same house. He was never a man for moving around like a lot of people. Honest and upright, never owed a cent. And now he's out there in the snow with the hounds after him. It's a thing I don't like to think about—poor old Frank hiding in the snow from a parcel of hounds."

As the blacksmith spoke, a conviction came to me and I hurried out of the warm smithy.

The day was darkening. I pushed against the wind into the snow-covered prairie that lay glittering like a white ocean as the night covered it.

I had had a vision of where farmer Frank Peebles of the bloody hands was hiding. He had gone home. Where else was there to go in this blizzard-tumbled night? Where would Dostoevski have sent him in such a tale—or Thomas Hardy? Home, with his soul whimpering for the fireside he had betrayed, with his frightened old-man's eyes yearning for honest and familiar walls.

An old woman with a bloodless face sat beside a lamp in the kitchen window of the Peebles' farmhouse. This was Mrs. Peebles looking out on a blizzard and a vision of a husband hanging by the neck until dead.

"He's bound to come home," I told her, "if he hasn't come home already."

"He ain't here."

"Then he will be."

"He won't dare come here."

"There's no other place for him."

Mrs. Peebles stood up. None of the people hunting Frank in the snow was as fierce and full of hatred as this woman who had slept with him for thirty years. She took the lamp, and we explored the farmhouse together. No murderer cowered under beds or crouched in dark closets. We returned to the kitchen, and I sat with the bloodless-faced Mrs. Peebles. We sat at the window that overlooked the prairie and waited for a shadowy figure to come leaning against the wind and moving toward the farmhouse.

The hours passed. The night grew wilder and the snow more

ominous. But my heart turned from the scene and began to ache. Thoughts came to me that had no place in the mind of a man-hunter. I yearned for Babe, whom I had left behind in my rooming-house bedroom.

Like Farmer Peebles I, too, had a Jezebel. Murder, horror and the agony of sin of which I had been conscious all day only added to her charms. I saw no lessons in dead harlots under horse blankets or in disasters smiting the wicked. My mind went wistfully beyond the blizzard and posse and came to rest at Babe's side. My bosom was straitened, and I desired to be with her.

Babe was a brothel girl who had "given up" a life of sin to come live with me. She was seventeen, with blue-black hair, and her body when it lay naked looked as if it were bathed in moonlight. She had been "reformed" for two weeks. They had been fine weeks. I had read books to her every night. She was illiterate and had never before met the printed word. She lay nude and listening like one bewitched. I had encouraged her to weep over her vile life in the whore house, now done forever. I had listened to her vows of eternal virtue and of eternal fidelity. She was the first woman to say she would love me forever and that no other hands but mine would ever touch her until she died. We whispered these finalities as we clung to each other. I was the shepherd filled with love, and she the sinner washed white as the lamb. Our nights were tender and sweet with a piety which, Duffy would have said, was a "new name for it."

I had taken her to fine restaurants and to the theater, where Duffy and Dick Little frowned on me, for it was a breach of good conduct to flaunt a whore socially. No argument could convince my friends that it was a lamb at my side and not a contaminating trollop. I quarreled with my mentors and gave my allegiance to my bride of love.

There was a milk train passing through Plano at one A.M. My yearning triumphed over my sleuthing instincts. I abandoned my vigil. I caught the milk train for Chicago and sat in the dim coach smiling tenderly at the vision of the little Thaïs who waited for me.

It was not yet dawn when I stumbled, half-frozen, into my rooming house. My room was on the third floor. I opened its door. Babe lay in my bed. Beside her lay a man with a large mustache. Sitting in my sole possession, a large leather chair bought with two months' savings, sat a second man, waiting. His lips and cheeks were rouged.

I looked on this hellish sight from the doorway, unable to move or speak. I saw Babe's white face and her black staring eyes through a fog of tears—my own and hers. I heard her cry out in a voice of true pain, "Honey, please! It don't mean anything! It don't mean anything—what you see! Don't go 'way!"

I walked the streets to the *Journal* building, and the Swinburne rhyme that had come to me in the Plano morgue continued its chant in my head,

> O *lips full of lust and of laughter,*
> *Curled snakes that are fed from my breast . . .*

The local room was empty and still dark. I lay down on the copy boys' bench and slept. I failed to hear the arrival of the new assistant city editor, Mr. Eddie Mahoney, and the clatter of typewriters and cries of rewrite men woke me not. Mr. Finnegan, who was now city editor, arrived at seven. There was no longer a Mr. Dunne. Thus the world disintegrates. Mr. Dunne had vanished into that limbo which gobbles up without trace all ex-newspapermen.

I opened my eyes at eight, and Mr. Finnegan listened to my report of the man hunt and to my theory concerning farmer Peebles' hiding place. When I was done with my pen pictures and boasts, Mr. Finnegan handed me a small A.P. dispatch. It read that Frank Peebles, the slayer of Gladys Renshaw, had been captured by the police. He had been found in his own farmhouse. He had lain hidden in its attic during the hours the bloodhounds had hunted him in the blizzard.

"This old coot of a murderer was in the house all the time you were waiting for him," Mr. Finnegan sighed. "You'd make a good detective if you only had sense enough to know what you were doing. And to stay on a job and not come running back to the office like a homesick kid."

Little Mr. Finnegan knew.

And little I remembered before the day was over. I had sat for hours under the eyes of a desperate murderer who might have been written by Dostoevski, in a blizzard Whittier could not have surpassed. And I had met infidelity and degeneracy in a bedroom out of Baudelaire. And all these shocking matters were as quickly forgot as a cinder in the eye. The waltzes played in King's Restaurant.

> O *garment not golden but gilded,*
> O *garden where all men may dwell,*

O tower not of ivory, but builded
By hands that reach heaven from hell; . . .

Babe was gone. The old man who had sported with Jezebel and cracked her skull was hanged. And I went on, rolling my rain barrel down the street.

MY FIRST HOURS OF LITERATURE

WHEN I WAS SEVENTEEN and an established reporter, my parents moved to Chicago. My father's Wisconsin try for fortune had piddled out. His factory and store had collapsed, a trusted partner had made off with all the money and my father was back in Chicago again, no longer a budding garment mogul but a designer looking for a job.

My mother applied herself to cooking and cleaning as if she had never presided handsomely in the front lines of salesmanship. In a back room of this flat I set to work on novels and short stories.

It was a secretive work. I showed my writing to no one. My first novel, about a blind man who fell in love with an ugly woman he considered beautiful, struck me as idiotic after I had typed two hundred pages of it. I burned the manuscript and started on a more practical tale, a short story of which I still remember the opening sentence, "Steve Grogan staggered out of Minnie Sheema's brothel with the wind in his hair, a wad of tobacco in his mouth and a bullet in his heart."

Mr. Grogan followed my blind hero into the fireplace.

I wrote on blissfully month after month without a plot in my head, not a character there or a sense of style or even anything to say. It never occurred to me to write about anything I had seen, heard or felt. Instead, imitations of Kipling, Bret Harte, Dostoevski and De Maupassant crackled brightly in the fireplace. I burned everything I wrote like a fugitive disposing of incriminating documents.

To destroy what I wrote seemed the logical thing to do, not because I thought the writing bad but because it was finished. There was no ambition in me and no dream of fame held me bowed and scribbling over my bedroom desk. The appearance of words on paper delighted me as a new set of toys did in my childhood. I loved to form them, to watch sentences build, to see phrases come into existence and the mysterious architecture of thought raise its penciled sky line.

The juvenile distaste for authority that led me to think of myself as my own boss and so decided me to become a writer was abetted by no consciousness of any talent for writing in me. Not till the H. L. Mencken tuning fork awoke the iconoclast in me, did I know who I was. Nevertheless, unhandicapped by the fact that I had as yet nothing to say, I continued to write like one possessed. And I continued to find a persisting delight in writing.

After many years this delight remains. I understand it partly now. It is a sort of narcism that finds pleasure in staring into the contents of one's own head.

I have seen weight-lifters in front of mirrors studying devotedly the bunching of their muscles, and I have watched dancers in rehearsal halls married tenderly to their hopping images in the glass. They are no more narcists than those of us who fall to inspecting the insides rather than the outsides of ourselves.

When I came to write books and stories intelligent enough to merit publication, my delight in putting words on paper remained unchanged. The desire to please others and become famous was (unfortunately) never strong in me. I continued to write because writing pleased me, because it enabled me to remain "independent" and because it kept always fresh the quality I had most enjoyed in my childhood—the talent for diverting myself with my own imagination.

Yet in the days when I wrote my auto-da-fé manuscripts there was a small daydream in the back of my head. It came to me when my mother would stand, puzzled, watching me throw my scribbled pages into the fireplace.

"Why don't you let Mr. Duffy read what you've written before you burn it up?" she asked. Pride and hope were in her words, and I dreamed of fame for her sake. I remembered a couplet attributed by Plutarch to the mother of Themistocles—a woman who had been lowly born.

> Let the Greek women scorn me, if they please—
> I was the mother of Themistocles.

"THE HARP THAT ONCE THROUGH
TARA'S HALLS—"

DESPITE the secrecy in which I wrote, Duffy and Doc Yak got wind of my literary toil, probably from the shining-eyed misconceptions of my mother. They became full of guidance and warnings.

Doc Yak, standing over my typewriter in the local room one afternoon, pronounced suddenly words that were to stay forever in my head—"Define your terms, young man, and stick to your meanings. That's the secret of writing."

Duffy spoke up one evening in a favorite barroom.

"When you write never get too fancy. Never put one foot on the mantelpiece, and be sure your style is so honest that you can put the word shit in any sentence without fear of consequences."

Mr. Finnegan also became aware of my literary side. He began to favor me with page-one assignments that called for adjectives and nuances. I wrote three columns on the funeral of Sammy Meisenberg. Sammy was a soldier under General Pershing in the Pancho Villa Mexican campaign. Sammy was the only American casualty in the capture of Vera Cruz.

The Jews of Chicago's West Side followed Sammy's hearse as if escorting a new Maccabee to the grave. I wrote of the thousands of mourners as if they were all my aunts and uncles, describing them humorously and lovingly. A Jew had died for his country—their new country—and the people of Chicago's ghetto walked proudly under American flags. I recall of the story chiefly that my name was printed above its lead in bold-face type. It was my first by-line and it stirred a patriotic fervor in me equal to Sammy Meisenberg's. I would gladly have died for Mr. Finnegan and the *Journal*.

I was sent out to interview men of intellectual stature. Among these I remember Theodore Dreiser. Mr. Dreiser's novel *The Financier* had recently been published. He was at the time a writer celebrated by H. L. Mencken and hardly anyone else. The literary arbiters of the Republic had pronounced him a verbose and turgid fellow incapable of fine style and crudely obsessed with pornography.

Smarting under these canards, the moody Dreiser received me with a bilious eye, imagining I was of the tribe of critics. When I told him I was a reporter come to get a story about *The Financier*, which my city editor, Mr. Finnegan, considered one of the finest histories of Chicago ever written, the dour novelist forgot the circle of boils on his neck and the love troubles which were afflicting him almost equally, and spoke for several hours of the city I loved.

His information on Chicago from 1880 to 1905 was staggering. I was depressed by it and felt, as I listened, that I would never become a novelist, for I was incapable of knowing anything so thoroughly.

The interview ran for two columns on the front page and carried a seven-column headline proclaiming, "Dreiser Exposes Chicago."

A month later I received a letter from Dreiser. He was in St. Louis and had met there a woman eager to invest a hundred thousand dollars in the new Western enterprise of movie making. The movies, wrote Dreiser, were going to take the place of literature in the U.S.A., and fortunes were going to be made out of them. He offered me a junior partnership in the producing company he was going to organize, with the woman's money, and awaited my arrival in St. Louis.

I showed the letter to Duffy, Doc Yak and Mr. Finnegan and received my first financial advice from my elders.

Dreiser was a fantast, they said. The movies were a flash in the pan and I would be making a horse's ass of myself if I succumbed to any such get-rich-quick scheme as he outlined. It was good advice, though poor prophecy. I remember gratefully the three wise faces of my friends beaming at me and, like three fairy godfathers, presenting me with another ten happy years of printer's ink and poverty.

My secretiveness as a writer did not extend to rhymes. Apings of Kipling, Robert Service and Swinburne often startled the front-page readers of the *Journal.* I bombarded Mr. Finnegan with ballads and quatrains about politicians, corpses, freedom, Christmas orphans, survivors of storms at sea, beloved animals run over by streetcars and poverty's flowing tears. An outcry in behalf of human valor or Irish Freedom usually passed from the Finnegan hands into print.

My lyre had another string—not meant for the public. The bulk of my metrical output consisted of lewd rhymes chiefly for Duffy, Doc Yak and the Sports Department. Mr. Boyer, the head printer, was an important and appreciative member of my audience.

My last and sunniest memories of the *Journal* are the writing of rhymes in Duffy's office. I wrote them on a typewriter between the re-

write of telegraph "takes" of a baseball World Series in Philadelphia. Waiting for the further doings of Eddie Cicotte or Chief
Bender, I tackled the sexual problems of the Caliph Haroun-al-
Raschid in rhyme. I had promised Duffy and Doc Yak to put Burton's *Arabian Nights* into verse, a project that kept the entire Sports
Department lyrically agog through happy summer afternoons. My
muse lured the dog-watch journalists away from the windows
overlooking the hotel across the street, a hostelry in whose bedrooms
business executives could be seen banging their secretaries, if one
kept an eye constantly peeled.

The rhymes were bawdy, and Mr. Boyer often honored them by
printing them on his linotype and distributing copies among his
favorite whore houses. I was sometimes greeted in these places by
poetically smitten wenches who had memorized pages of my doggerel and would stand at my embarrassed side reciting them to the
customers. I recall hundreds of lines, but four will be enough to
identify the strains of my muse.

> *One night the Caliph Haroun lay with member wan and wee,*
> *Regarding his bedraggled tool sad and reproachfully,*
> *"Alas, poor Lucifer," he sighed, "how fallen now ye be*
> *And fit for no more enterprise than languidly to pee."*

At times I departed the *Arabian Nights* and fell to rhyming
Rabelais—

> *Mrs. Hans Carvel, but recently wed,*
> *Blushingly made herself ready for bed.*

And there was a notable time when Duffy sat translating from the
Latin of Apuleius, and I batted out *The Golden Ass* in scores of
rhymed pages, as he read. I recalled the episode where the Roman
lady yielded herself to the hooved embraces of the rose-cropping
quadruped, and her grateful cry of, "O ass, you have touched my
heart!" I interpreted this as a salute to the animal's super genitalia
and wrote—

> *No lady knew such bliss before, for since the world began*
> *To touch the heart of woman is a trick denied to man.*

I remember a rhyme not meant for Duffy or Mr. Finnegan—but
handed nervously to the beauty who had appeared on our staff as its
one "girl reporter."

This was the second girl reporter to work on the paper. The first one had been brought to it by me. Her name was Clara, and I had persuaded her to give up her life of sin in Madam Farrington's brothel and turn to journalism.

I had spent two weeks showing her the ropes and secretly writing the copy she sent to the city desk. Clara was lovely and well mannered and would have easily been able to become a journalist if not for the quirk in her character which had originally thrown her among the red lights. Mr. Hutchens, entering the composing room unexpectedly late in the afternoon, had spotted this fine-looking lady journalist on an improvised couch with one of the printers. Several others were hovering about awaiting their turns.

It was a year before Mr. Hutchens would permit another female on the staff, and when he did he took pains to check her antecedents. As a result our second girl reporter was a creature of such virtue as had never before crossed a newspaper threshold. She came of good family in the social suburb of Highland Park and was learned in music, painting and French literature.

I had been fascinated by her from the first hour of her appearance at her desk. I was fetched by the fact that she wrote all her copy on a typewriter with a green-inked ribbon and that she read books during her leisure. They were French books, and this left me agape. Most of all, I was bewildered and allured by the phenomenon of virtue. Since my arrival under my uncle's wing in Mr. Eastman's office I had never met or consorted with a "good woman."

I had known Marie two months when I handed her a sonnet, most of which I remember—

> *For one blind moment, I would yesterday—*
> *An Orpheus mad, and thou Eurydice—*
> *Have wandered into Hades after thee;*
> *With Perseus then I would have rushed to slay*
> *The fiery dragon that beset my way*
> *To thee, Andromeda; and 'neath thy spell*
> *With Paris I had held thee though Troy fell*
> *And sworn by thee that all my Gods were clay.*
>
> *For one blind moment yesterday*
> *That we two jested smilingly away.*

FAREWELL TO ARCADY

I sat on the edge of Mr. Finnegan's desk at the summer's end. Tears were in my eyes. I told him I had received an offer from the Chicago *Daily News* at a salary of forty-five dollars a week, fifteen more than I was now earning. Harry Hansen, a pensive, meticulous news reporter, was being sent to Germany by his paper to take charge of its Berlin office. Harry had met me in Madison Street and told me there was an opening on the *Daily News* staff. I had paid a treacherous visit to the *Daily News* local room and spoken to a tall, lean man with a gaunt terra-cotta face and a romantic-looking mustache. This was Henry Justin Smith, the managing editor, as reserved as a chief justice and as moody as a poet on a rainy day.

I told all this to Mr. Finnegan. My feeling of disloyalty was so great that I was unable to look at his smiling, handsome face.

"I know you can't pay me anything like that here," I said. John C. Eastman, the *Journal*'s owner, had proclaimed often that any reporter who thought he was worth forty-five dollars a week did not belong on his newspaper. "I don't want to leave the *Journal*," I said. "And I wouldn't, either, if it were just a matter of a fifteen-dollar raise for myself. I'd rather stay here than work anyplace else. But I need more money because Marie and I are going to be married next week. So I think I'll have to say good-by."

And good-by again. That was the end of my boyhood. I stood looking then, as I look now, on the dusty shambles of a local room, on the sweet, familiar figures who had beamed on my ineptness, fervor and asininity with the kindest faces in the world. I stood amid beginnings that would never know me again. I knew that what I was would never exist again. There were other worlds. I had touched them and sensed them. But this world, the world without pain or sadness, the world without fear or guilt or malice—the undaunted world of heedless days—was never to be found again.

The smiles of the faces I knew grew blurred. The windows blurred. The glass-paneled door behind which the pipesmoking Indian face of Duffy beamed, good Duffy who had told me the right kind of hat to wear—blurred, and vanished.

OBIT FOR A NEWSPAPERMAN

ONCE on the *Journal* a reporter died whose name I forget. I remember that he was reddish-haired, round-faced and a great chuckler, and that all his clothes were always unbuttoned—vest, coat and overcoat.

Mr. Finnegan asked me to write our colleague's obituary for the paper.

"I'll get all the dope on him from Enoch Johnson," I said. "He knew him best."

"Never mind any dope," said Mr. Finnegan. "I just want four or five lines. And nothing fancy, if you don't mind."

"Can you use eight lines?" I asked.

"No more," said Mr. Finnegan.

I wrote the first four lines in rhyme. They read:

TO A DEAD NEWSPAPERMAN
We know each other's daydreams
And the hopes that come to grief
For we write each other's obits
And they're Godalmighty brief.

This obit will be longer.

Sherman Reilly Duffy died a few years ago in Ottawa, Illinois, where he had been born, where his father, Christopher Columbus Duffy, had reared him on Montaigne, Shakespeare and the Old Testament, where he had crossbred irises, studied Latin and loved his family.

He often took me home with him on week ends, and I experienced evenings of politeness and charm. Despite my youth, I was treated with curious respect by his three lovely sisters, Jane, Helena and Chrissy, by the white-maned, roaring patriarch, Christopher Columbus, by the Mother Duffy and by the young adventurer son of the family, Guy. This was because I was Sherman's protégé, and Sherman was as wise a man in their eyes as in mine. We played cards, sang around the piano, told stories and photographed the irises and the Illinois River.

In the thirty-odd years after I walked out of the *Journal* local room for the last time, I saw Duffy rarely and heard from him almost never. This circumstantial estrangement ended the year Duffy died. He sent me a manuscript of an autobiography he had written while he lay painfully giving up the ghost in an Ottawa hospital. In it he related the friendships, opinions and adventures that fifty years of journalism had brought him. It contained many stories about me, all told with accuracy and tenderness. Reading the pages, I learned that the four years I had spent as Duffy's protégé had remained as alive in his heart as in mine. He writes:

> I still like to remember my most entertaining and satisfying day during my twenty-year service as sporting editor. This was on the old Chicago *Journal*, and at the time Ben Hecht was sitting in on afternoons as my assistant, keeping box scores, reading a little copy and writing running stories of the ball games as the score by inning descriptions came over the wire.
>
> Someone had given me a fine new edition of *The Golden Ass* of Apuleius, a Latin text. Ben was curious about the work, with which he was not familiar. I sat down this summer's afternoon and began translating a line at a time between pieces of sporting copy and passed them over to Ben. He sat at his typewriter and, as I supposed, was transcribing the translation. He was doing so but in verse. He had the singular faculty of turning out verse on a typewriter almost as easily as he did prose, and Ben was a speed merchant at turning out prose copy. By the time the sporting extra was sent to press we had a beautiful metrical version of *The Golden Ass*. . . . I realize that it is now forty years since I first met Bennie, with his funny Little Boy Blue hat and fiddle—he could fiddle very well, too. I begin to believe I am really getting along in years.

But more fascinating than our mutual memories of the past was the character of the man who sat propped up in the hospital bed tapping out his gentle saga on a typewriter, tapping it out without search for any other phrases than had been always in his head and with fingers moving swiftly—for nobody, sick or well, could run a typewriter faster than Duffy. Of this character, Duffy was as unconscious as a child might be of its charm and courage. He describes in sprightly and mocking phrases the disease that was ending his life.

They are the same phrases with which he gladdened the ear of my youth. He had peritonitis and was "blown up like a blimp." He was unable "to button his pants" across his enlarged belly, "whose general contour would have befitted a woman about to hatch out twins."

Then follow pages of witty and detached reporting of an operation, during which his "guts exploded like a gas main," of the removal of a growth from his transverse colon, of the vanishing of his "hellish bellyache" and of his delight to find on opening his eyes that "I hadn't winged my way to a harp and the Great White Throne but like Jacob of old had wrestled with the Angel of Death and won at least four straight falls."

In all the three hundred swiftly typed pages Duffy wrote while he lay dying, there is not a single complaint against life. Of no one does he speak with animus, of no one with envy. The successes of his friends who flew the coop in which he remained an aging and more and more insolvent reporter delighted him.

The fifty years of which he chats and jollifies were all years of charm. No fame came to Duffy, and money remained always a legend to him. He had put no pennies by for the rainy days of age. At seventy, after fifty years of honorable and accurate newspaper work, he was still dependent on his weekly check for food and lodging. And there was no bank balance to provide for private nursing. He mentions the penicillin injections which kept him alive for a time with a pensive sense of extravagance. "Five dollars a shot," he writes, "and, perhaps, worth it."

After he was sixty, Duffy found difficulty in hanging on to the career he had entered at twenty-one. Aging reporters are not popular with editors. He tramped the newspaper offices, pipe in his teeth, looking for a job. Unable to find one, he became a political press agent. Finally his profession relented. He was allowed back into its revered circles, but shoved into the limbo of "obit editor."

I saw him once between trains to California, sitting in a corner of the Chicago *Sun* local room. He was sixty-eight. His sleeves were rolled up, as of old. His eyes were snapping with a wit to which there was no one to listen. The friends of his youth were all dead or far away. There was no one to remember Sherman Duffy, the great editor, barroom Socrates and hail-companion of heroes from all ends of the earth. The reporters around him saw only an old man

with a pipe, hitting seventy and full of mysterious and archaic japer-
ies.

The annals of journalism recite usually the doings of reporters on
big stories, of their braving shot and shell "to get the news," of their
grit and ingenuity in the presence of stirring events. I add to these
annals the story of Duffy's last assignment, for I see in it more than a
deed of valor. In it is a whole life of valor, of that mocking selfless-
ness which is the gold badge of the good newspaperman.

At seventy-two Duffy sat in the University Club of Chicago taking
notes on a meeting of the University of Illinois' trustees, the institution from which he had been graduated fifty-one years before with
Phi Beta Kappa honors. This was a piddling assignment, a tiny task
at the bottom of the city desk's list of daily trivia to be checked. But
Duffy sat sternly by, doing his errand-boy chore as attentively as if
he were covering a world peace conference. Forgotten by his time,
by his own kind, even by his city editor, he sat taking down the "remarks of those present" in a shorthand learned in his youth. The
fact that the story he wrote of the event would be less than fifty words
and would appear, if at all, on the bottom of some back page, did not
enter his mind. He was pleased to be sitting where he was, still a
newspaper reporter at seventy-two, and he brought to the smallness
of his task the dignity earned by a lifetime of important toil.

It was while sitting in a corner of this club, with his unlighted pipe
stuck between his teeth, that the "hellish bellyache" smote him.
Death had already entered him as if a bullet had lodged in his gut.
Peritonitis was already there.

I see him standing up, unable to straighten out due to the agony
in him, and I hear him speaking in a polite whisper to one of the
trustees. "I think I have enough for a good story. I'll have to run
along now." And out he crawls, the claw of pain at his vitals, to a
telephone. "City Desk? Duffy talking. I've got some tidbits here on
the meeting of the Illinois University Trustees. Would you mind taking them over the phone? I don't think I'll be able to get to the office. No, no—perfectly sober and in my right mind. I have what seems
to be an important bellyache. Can't understand the damn thing.
Never been sick a day in my life. Thanks, it's not much. Just a stick or
two."

And Duffy recites his tidbit notes to a bored young rewrite man
who frets silently at the facetious phrases that interlard them. The

sweat of pain is on Duffy's face as he utters them, but Duffy can no
more keep the humor of phrase out of his talk than he could keep
from breathing. They will both end at the same time.

His last story telephoned in, Duffy steps into the street. Fever
brings a wobble into him and he thinks of a doctor, but the only doctors he can remember are long dead. Suddenly this town in which he
has worked for fifty years seems friendless to him. It is big, vast; its
familiar face is beclouded. In fact, it doesn't look like Chicago at
all. The Chicago of Mangler's saloon, and Stillson's and Vogelsang's,
of the great World Series games, of *The Chocolate Soldier* at the
Garrick Theater, of Dick Little, George Wharton, Joe Sheehan and
Tetrazzini "standing on her hind legs" bellowing out the final aria
of *La Traviata*. It is a town of strangers, and Duffy, with his belly
swelling up like a balloon, takes his hellish pain to the friendliest
place he knows—the depot from which the trains leave for Ottawa.

This exit Duffy makes from Chicago has in it the same quality that
marked his old friend Chris Hagerty's hair-raising trek to Dayton,
Ohio. The selflessness of the good newspaperman distinguishes it.
No wounded warrior ever left a battlefield with more modesty or
more grace than Duffy, who rides home now to die. There are no
new words of panic in his head. He writes in his autobiography that
"the damn Humpty Dumpty bellyache grew worse after I clambered
aboard the train, but I made the trip with no great difficulty."

He writes, "Arrived in Ottawa, I called for a medico, who
thumped my distended carcass, which gave off sinister vibrations
like 'The Drums of Oode.'" This was an Austin Strong one-act play
we both saw in the vaudeville theater in 1912 in which the Hindu
"terrorists" kept beating their menacing war drums off stage and
upsetting the English colonel and his daughter who had recently inherited the whole of India.

Duffy continues, "The medico said, 'Good God, get this man to a
hospital.' So the stretcher-bearers and ambulance came and carted
me off."

Thus Duffy reports aloofly and facetiously, and thus I report on
Duffy. Reading his book, and his last pages of copy, I meet the same
Duffy I left looking at me through the glass-paneled door of his
Sports Department. There may be many people in the world whose
hearts are as innocent and valorous as was Duffy's. If there are,
then the world is a nicer place than it seems at times.

Book Four

I WAS A REPORTER

A PRESSED VIOLET

A GAUNT, shabby-looking man in his late fifties stands in the doorway of my Nyack room. He surveys me with lowered head. His pallid eyes are rolled upward in a smile of sickness and mockery.

The albino face with the look of frostbite on its skin grows solemn as it studies me. It becomes stern with memories. The eyes regard me as if I were a grave with withered flowers strewn across it.

I do not hurry my guest, for he is a poet. I stay silent as he poses in the doorway until a jack-o-lantern smile distends his mouth, exposing a number of missing teeth. Then I invite him in.

He enters slowly as if drama were in his feet, which are flat and ill-shod. He pauses, bows sardonically, sits down, extricates a pint bottle from a hip pocket, takes a long swig from it, emits a fiercesome and salivarous cackle and speaks in a voice I remember well, a voice with a slight stutter, and full of taunt and triumph, as if every sentence it uttered were a victory won.

"And how is my cynical friend on this exquisite winter morning? Still writing?"

The word "writing" issuing from the grin-spread face of my visitor becomes a harpoon of sarcasm.

Having spoken, my visitor's face grows rigid. It stares with melancholia. He sits, unaware of me, like a man lost in some private Hell.

My visitor is Maxwell Bodenheim, the poet whose fine poems once infuriated critics, embittered editors, estranged readers and earned him, nevertheless, a curious sort of fame. When all other acclaim had been denied him he became remarkably renowned as a failure.

There have been poets in my time who sang more wildly, who dreamed more deeply and loved life more knowingly. But my friend Bogie was never lost in their shadow, for he seemed never to compete with their strophes. He came no nearer to the poets than he did to life, but appeared to stand by himself, lonely and obsessed, like a fisherman bent over a favorite stream. And he fished with cobwebs.

My visitor's status as a poet, however, is of small interest to either of us on this winter morning. He has brought an entire Art Era into my room and he sits mournfully and shabbily in its midst. It is the Era that was our youth. It contained days of brightness and an American literary renaissance—a small one, but our own.

During its quick and vivid years—there were hardly nine (1913-1922)—Chicago found itself, mysteriously, a bride of the arts. Not gangster guns but literary credos barked. New novelists, poets, painters and critics dotted its pavements and illumined its name.

Maxwell Bodenheim's visit passes without reference to any name or event of our past. Yet memories like galleons in full sail loom in my head. I am certain he, too, sits watching them. But neither of us offers them a hail.

We speak instead, irritably and at loggerheads, of the present. He is full of contempt for the Capitalistic System, as he well may be, for he never tasted a spoonful of its blessings. Hunger, disease and fantastic poverty have been his portion of his native U.S.A.—these and the tomblike disdain of critics. It is easy to understand his preference for some other scheme of things.

I sit listening with little patience to his radical beliefs. Here was one of the great conversers of my youth. Not only poetry came out of the brain under this mop of blond hair, but derisions of sham and garrotings of fraud were its constant product. It was a brain mysteriously learned, although it despised nearly all it read. And it was a brain with a jeweler's eyepiece for the flaws of reason.

I remember this brain as I sit listening to its present utterances. I recall its youthful and nimble verbiage, its never-ending spray of epithet and simile in which it hung like wit in a rainbow. And I do not need to visit the ruins of Karnak to know to what levels time reduces greatness.

Alas, politics! It can give refuge to male talent as the brothel offers roosting place for female beauty.

Yet all this talk of radicalism and its wonders is no new thing born in my friend Bogie's soul in its twilight. It was there in the glare of his youth, but it had other meanings and other words. In his youth Bogie loved what was hurt and in pain. His heart sought out bums and prostitutes to comfort. He looked with tenderness on homely and callous-fingered working girls, and his derisive mind was full of a queer respect for all people who worked hard and had little.

Misfortune and illness have removed the fineries of his poet's spirit. Politicians have provided him with a ready-made vocabulary to take the place of moonlit phrases and jack-in-the-box metaphors. But despite the great change in his speech, I am aware as I listen to this aging Bodenheim that he is faithful to himself. What he once loved he still loves. Unable any longer to love it with talent, he loves it almost illiterately—the thing that is hurt, the lowly human.

But I notice sadly that despite his advocacy of radicalism there is small dream in him of any lovelier tomorrow. He is not like the Radicals we both knew in our youth who looked blissful-eyed at a time to come of justice and honor; who were neither Reds nor politicians but daft knights with no other program than to battle for the disinherited.

My friend speaks without eagerness of a Communist tomorrow. He is not even thinking as he speaks. But being a poet he cannot live without hope or without calling something beautiful. Stubbornly, against all the dictates of his mind, he recounts the blessings of Communism—and remains forlorn and unblessed.

As the windows darken, my visitor grows tired of our lame political debate. His cadaverous face stiffens again as it did when he first sat down. He stares with melancholia at the darkly falling snow and begins to weep. His tears do not surprise me.

"I am tired of living," he says. His voice is childlike and without mockery. "Honestly, Ben, I am sick of the whole thing. I know of no sensible reason why I should not commit suicide and put an end to this whole stupid nonsense. Beauty, art, poetry—yes, I am even sick of poetry, sick of pretty words staring at me. I hate them —all the pretty words. I'd commit suicide tonight except that I am in love with my wife. She is very sick and full of suffering. And she needs me. Yes, Ben"—the lips peel back, the stained teeth make a death skull grimace and his voice grows prouder—"that poor little Grace needs me. And she loves me. I can't imagine why—can you? A scarecrow body and a dead soul! But she does! Would you please call her on the telephone and tell her I'll be home in an hour. Yes, I'm going straight home."

My old friend rises and looks at the snow coming down in the dark. A smile touches his tear-wet mouth and he whispers, "The falling snow is like a wreath of daisies in the night."

ENTER—THE MUSES

OF THE SWARMS of young men and women in a great city there is a handful only who make the declaration to themselves and to their usually nerve-racked families that they are artists. It is a fine declaration, however silly-seeming are its voices. For whoever sets out to conquer the world of the arts seeks only to conquer himself, to loot his own brain of whatever riches it holds and to offer these as spoils to mankind.

Most other forms of ego increase are parasitic or destructive. The arts alone produce a harmless power and a harmless fame. No one suffers from the success of a symphony, painting or work of literature. No one has been "exploited" by its production; no one has been injured or lessened by its birth.

Art is the magic whose lonely trick here and there keeps the notion going that the human soul is full of wonders. This magic has ebbed in our time and its trick is less and less to be seen.

Everything else in our century seems to have increased but this one word—art. Power, science, death, production, despair, government—these words have grown fat in the past fifty years. The word art has a leaner look than ever since the middle ages. It has become almost a synonym for homosexuality, incompetence and idleness.

Despite the popularity of concerts, exhibitions, ballets and printed matter—or, perhaps, because of it—the artist is a vanishing figure and the arts are becoming a branch of the Advertising Business. Never was the public so "artistic" and never was there so little mystery and magic entering the world.

There are, in fact, no arts. There are only entertainments. Our talents, like our waterfalls, have all been harnessed to make life pleasanter for the Public. The iconoclastic or anti-public artist exists no more than an anti-public traction company.

In Russia all individualism in art has been forbidden by law and is punishable as crime. There are no such laws in the U.S.A. Here our individualism has dried up and blown away by itself. In an increasing statism such as ours, no less than in the more advanced statism of the Russians, individual expression is the enemy to be scotched. The Russians scotch it with a firing squad. In the U.S.A. we scotch it with an investigation, fear and envy.

My announcing the death of American art may be premature. It may be that I am not in touch with its underground. Somewhere beyond my ken possibly there are still candlelit rendezvous in the big and little towns where youth gathers to kick the hell out of syntax and sanity. But I doubt it. Such American revolters as I know in these days are a two-faced lot. They revolt on week ends. The other five days are full of box-office dreams.

The public is a big loser in this disappearance of art anarchists. Not that the public looked much at their masterpieces while they lived or derived a nickel's worth of pleasure out of their mystifying literature and music. But unbeknownst to the public these disorderly few were the headwaters of the world's diversion. Without their anarchy to freshen the public's entertainment, it must grow constantly duller. Without visionaries to steal from, the box-office entertainment servers must offer staler and staler dishes.

There is a bigger loss. The young artists who fight the clichés of their time may create few masterpieces but they contribute vitally to our civilization. They keep the clichés from overrunning us. In the absence of their young courage, elderly fears rule the day.

I have in mind our front-line patriots who have plunged our nation into near terror and near bankruptcy with their fear of Communism. They must seem a shaggy lot to youth, yet no youth cries out against them. Our youth, with its anarchy seared out of it, goes along sourly with these terrified elders.

Élie Faure in his *History of Art* stated the case neatly at the beginning of our century. The stamping out of the artist, he said, is one of the blind goals of every civilization. When a civilization becomes so standardized that the individual can no longer make an imprint on it, then that civilization is dying. The "mass mind" has taken over and, said Faure, another set of national glories is heading for history's scrap heap.

The stamping out in our time is almost done. I have only to remember how different things were in my youth to see how far it has gone.

WHO WAS SYLVIA?

IN MY YOUTH the word art had a meaning it has completely lost. I shall try to give its 1910-1925 definition.

If you did not believe in God, in the importance of marriage, in the United States Government, in the sanity of politicians, in the necessity of education or in the wisdom of your elders, you automatically believed in art. You did not automatically plunge into the worlds of painting, music and literature. You plunged *out* of worlds, out of family worlds, business worlds, greed and ambition worlds. You did not necessarily stay out of them forever. It might happen that you got married, grew a paunch, bought an automobile and, what with one pressure and another, forgot all about art and drifted back into cozier bourgeois orbits with no damage done other than a memory of foolishness outgrown.

But as long as you "believed in art" you remained orphaned from the smothering arms of society. You shaved only when you wanted to and you felt a contempt in your head like a third glass of wine for all that was popular and successful. Mediocrity might wear a crown and rule all the rest of the world, but at your side it was a beggar. You were divorced not only from the crowd but from all its gods. And you selected gods to worship as lonely and disinherited as yourself.

And this befell because the wish to bloom as an individual is all that art was. It was a rare wish and came to few. The numerous professions claimed their millions; art touched only its hundreds.

The mystery of its touch belonged to biology as much as to aesthetics. It was usually not a consciousness of latent talent nor an ambition to shine in the world that summoned youth to the arts. Talent and ambition, as often as not, came after the call. They were part of the equipment of the professional.

Nor was it even any particular yearning for beauty that stirred the young soul of the proclaimed artist. That, too, came later—if at all.

The mystery was chiefly this—that there was seemingly a tiny proportion of the human family born without greed, who entered life without fear of tomorrow, without an urge to lose themselves safely in the known and practical worlds of their elders.

These were, in the past, automatically the artists.

A NIGHT IN THE SPRINGTIME

IT WAS a spring night in 1913. I walked north in Clark Street heading for a Cass Street rooming house. Marjy Currey had told me there would be a party there. It was Marjy who usually gave parties in the reconstructed Chinese laundry in Stony Island Avenue which was her spacious abode since her divorce from a young man named Floyd Dell, a Chicago literary critic in a Windsor tie who had treacherously gone to New York City to become a novelist.

I had some misgivings about this Cass Street party. Its host was an Advertising Man. He worked as a copy writer for Taylor-Critchfield & Co., a notoriously successful institution. One did not consort with advertising people, and I would have to keep my evening's diversion secret from Duffy.

The Cass Street room was crowded and dimly lighted by several candles, strategically placed around the host's chair.

I knew most of the merrymakers who, on my arrival, were already sprawled on the floor. I learned, as Marjy handed me a water glass full of gin, that our host was going to read to us some stories he had written as soon as everybody quieted down. This struck me as a wretched imposition on people forgathered to have a good time—and typical of the ways of the advertising world.

Sasha (Professor Alexander S. Kaun to be) was talking to three girls on the floor. Gaunt, young and compact as a lightweight pugilist, he greeted me with an inhospitable snort as I sat down among his listeners—for Sasha considered any young ladies in his presence, whatever their numbers, his private quarry. A bit ruffled, he continued to talk.

"In Moscow," said Sasha, "when we used to attend a party, the hostess, a beautiful woman, would appear completely nude except for a pair of gold slippers. This was a test of our dedication to the Revolution. Our souls were too filled with the dream of Russian freedom to respond to a naked woman. But now I have forgotten all the revolutionary speeches that were made at those parties. I remember only her breasts—two heavenly pillows. It is sad to confess this, for it shows how my soul has degenerated."

A slim, golden-haired youth with pale blue eyes and the pensive face of Christ in the Hofmann painting stood over us. A soiled and bulging brief case was under one arm. In the other hand he held a corncob pipe in which a foul tobacco called "nigger hair" smoldered and reeked.

"Are you prepared to listen to the exquisite prose of our host?" asked Maxwell Bodenheim. "Or would you prefer the briefer torture of one of my sonnets?"

He cackled, inspected our host with malevolence and sat down beside one of the girls. He spoke to her in an abruptly dreamy voice, "Your hair is like a wistful sunrise. Will you marry me, Valerie?"

"I've said yes a number of times," the girl answered.

"I am a miser counting yeses," Bodenheim smiled.

Another guest entered the room. He was young, with a small pointed red beard. He wore a flowing black cape with a silver buckle at its neck. He carried a heavy cane and walked into the room limping.

He was Michael Carmichael Carr, an English painter come from Italy, where he had worked with Gordon Craig manufacturing puppets to replace actors in the new era of drama dawning and made love to duchesses on bluffs overlooking the Mediterranean. There

was a legend of one who, heartbroken over some defection of
Mike's, had jumped off and drowned.

"I didn't know you had hurt your leg, Michael," said Marjy.

Mike beamed.

"A bullet through the right calf, nothing too serious," he said,
"particularly since it is a phantom bullet."

He unbuckled his cape and sat down among us, a tumbler of
gin in his hand.

"I had to break an engagement last Wednesday with a lovely and
fabulously rich young woman who is devoted to me," Mike said. "I
gave as an excuse that I had been shot in the leg by an old political
enemy from Rome. She lives on the North Side—and I start limping
as soon as I step north of Randolph Street."

A fourth girl joined our group. She was blond and pretty and
recently arrived from Aurora, Illinois, where she had been employed
as a telephone operator. She had given up her job and all memories
of Aurora, including her American farmer parents, and taken the
name Fedya. She sat among us and heard nothing we said. Her blue
eyes looked unwaveringly at our host in his candlelighted chair. A
year later a love-addled Fedya was to ride a white horse over a high
cliff in Laguna Beach, California, and die on the ocean rocks below.
But on this night there was no one happier among us. She smiled,
her lips parted and her eyes closed as our host looked at her—a
bit truculently, for we were taking a long time to quiet down.

Bodenheim whispered to her:

"Your face is an incense bowl from which a single name rises."

A wispy, elderly woman, as thin and white as a penny candle, sat
near us in a chair. Bodenheim rose and bowed to her and in a voice
surprisingly empty of sneer spoke to her. "I hope you have recovered from your cold and are enjoying the blessings of a dry nose."
He smiled with what he fancied was a show of gallant interest. In
reality he looked as desperate as a bank robber facing a reluctant
vault. The elderly woman was Harriet Monroe, editor and publisher
of a magazine called *Poetry*. In this magazine and nowhere else in
the world, poetry of the sort that Bodenheim wrote was printed
—and paid for.

Beside Miss Monroe stood a tall, bony woman named Eunice
Tietjens who wrote Japanese poetry (in English); and a young Italian writer of great Baudelairian promise. He had recently been ar-

rested in Lincoln Park for unbuttoning his pants and exposing himself before a plain-clothes policewoman who was taking the evening air. Bodenheim considered this unfair tactics.

"Anybody can become famous," he said, "if they wish to resort to cheap publicity."

He glowered at the Italian youth, later to die in a madhouse in his native land. Miss Monroe's heart had been stirred by the young man's troubles, and she had been publishing pages on pages of his phosphorescent prose poems.

Returning to our group on the floor, Bodenheim said, forgetting his pussyfooted wooing of *Poetry*'s editor, "I do not quite see the connection between the public flaunting of one's penis and the publication of two hundred lines of hogwash describing the moon. But Miss Monroe, no doubt, has sharper eyes than mine and perhaps dreams of becoming a policewoman." He cackled, slapped his thigh with his palm, cried out "Oh, boy," and beamed in triumph at a red-faced Miss Monroe and her outraged court.

A slight disturbance began in a shadowy corner occupied by Jerry Blum and a girl named Dorothy. She was a very thin girl with black hair and not to my liking, for it was rumored she carried a small dagger thrust in her garter and had drawn blood from several young and over-amorous writers.

Jerry had returned recently from the South Seas, where he had gone to paint and sleep on the ground, for he had a phobia against beds. He was short, strong-bodied, dark-haired and smiling. I had noticed him sitting on the floor smoking a sort of Chinese pipe with a stem five feet long. But now he had put aside his pipe and was talking to Dorothy in an angry voice.

"I can't bear to have women sitting next to me with clothes on," Jerry said. "Either take off your clothes or go 'way. Clothes are ugly, stifling and insulting."

Dorothy, fully attired, joined our group and Jerry took up his curious pipe. Many years later I visited the greatly gifted Jerry in the state hospital where, in a cell-like room, he sat smiling amid chimeras. "No more canvases?" I said to him. "No," he answered lucidly enough, "since no one ever bought my paintings, it is nobody's loss if I just sit still and imagine them. And enjoy them myself, as I used to do when I put them on canvas."

The candles continued to light up our host, and eventually the guests became silent and sat looking at him as if he were an actor on a stage. His rugged-looking face with its wide mouth and glowing black eyes smiled at the shadowed figures in his room. Under its wing of flat black hair, it looked like an Italian face, the kind you saw behind barber chairs. It was odd that such a face should be called Sherwood Anderson.

Our host addressed us and I became aware that this rugged-seeming man was a gentle, almost womanish fellow. There was a tremor to his lips, and his large, handsome face seemed to flutter when he spoke, as did his voice. He changed as he spoke from a barber into a swami. One hand reached out and waved rhythmically at us, in a gentle, patronizing fashion. His voice caressed us and I heard a fine writer speak for the first time.

"I was going to read you a book I've written called *Windy McPherson's Son*," he said, "but it's a very long manuscript and kind of heavy to hold. So I'll read you some stories I've written about a town called Winesburg, Ohio. They're not really stories. They're just people."

We waited silently as our host moved a candle nearer his pen-written pages.

"Down the street ran George Hadley . . ." Sherwood Anderson began reading.

MY FRIEND SWATTY

SHERWOOD and I became friends. I learned that his nickname was Swatty, that he had run away from a schoolteacher wife and two children in Ohio, that he had owned a factory there which had burned down, bankrupting all who had invested in it, and that he had wandered for several months through cornfields and prairies, a victim of amnesia. He had arrived on foot in Chicago wearing a shaggy beard and still uncertain of his identity, but nevertheless landed a job immediately as a copy writer for Taylor-Critchfield & Co., where his inability to remember his name or where he came from stamped him as a genius in his employer's mind and resulted in his getting a bigger salary than anybody else writing copy for the firm.

I learned also that he had never been to any school, but that his wife, Cornelia (abandoned in Ohio), had taught him spelling and punctuation after their marriage. She had induced him to read a few books, over which they had quarreled violently because she liked them and he did not. He had left her because he considered reading a dangerous thing and books a corrupting power; and he had read no books since, nor was he ever going to.

Of these and a hundred other tales Sherwood told about himself, I believed almost nothing. But whether they were lies or truths made no difference. The man who told them was full of a compelling salesmanship. I sat always fascinated.

I stopped thinking of him as a barber or a swami. He became a gypsy full of larceny and guitar music. He laughed at me a great deal with a sort of water-whistle laugh that covered a full octave as it bubbled almost continually out of his heavy throat. Almost everything I said seemed to miss its point as he listened. To the fanciest and most melodramatic of my police-station and hanging-chamber anecdotes, he would answer with a patronizing chuckle, "Life is more important than that." And he would go off into a dither of owlish words: "Life is something precious. You've got to look at it like you look at a baby. You've got to hold it that way."

But when he spoke such patter, his words were somehow alive with secret meanings. He seemed always trying to convey these deeper meanings, and not quite succeeding. And therein lay the power of his personality—that he was unable to talk lucidly, as he was always unable to write clearly. The failure became not his but his listeners'. Vocally or in print he made the same effect. When he talked his features seemed to tremble with some inner delicacy of mood. His writing contained a similar tremble. Listener and reader both went from his presence with the sense that something superior and profound had been offered them—and not quite understood by their lesser spirits. The effect on girls of those half-woozy and purring hints of hidden sublimities was even greater than Sasha's Russian revolutionary songs.

Sherwood insisted one evening that we take a few weeks off from our respective jobs and write a play together. I was writing one-act plays, after hours, with a Princeton graduate named Kenneth Sawyer Goodman. Kenneth's father was a millionaire lumberman and allowed us to use his board of directors' room in Michigan Avenue as a studio. Sherwood knew of this and disapproved.

"You don't want to collaborate with a millionaire," he said, "except in business."

"We have big plans," I said. "Why don't you join us? After we've written enough plays, Kenneth is going to build a People's Theater in the slums around Maxwell Street and bring good drama to the masses—free."

"The masses have enough trouble," said Sherwood, "without you and Kenneth Goodman trying to make them artistic."

The theater Kenneth talked of was built after he died, but not in Maxwell Street among the poor. It stands behind the Art Institute on Michigan Avenue as an imposing marble monument to his eager beginnings as a playwright.

I deserted Kenneth and the board of directors' room and went to work in Cass Street with Sherwood. We began a play about Benvenuto Cellini, a character with whom Sherwood had identified himself, almost on first hearing his name. We finished a first act and I became dubious. The act was a hundred and twenty typewritten pages long instead of the customary fifty, and Sherwood insisted on adding more speeches to it. I knew little about playwriting, but Swatty seemed to know less. Moreover, he refused to go to a theater and see a play, or read one between book covers. He maintained a play could be as long as we wanted it to be and that people who went to the theater were all pernicious idlers and would be grateful for a drama that ran eight hours.

After three weeks of Cellini, I went back to Kenneth and the board of directors' room. Writing with Kenneth wasn't as much fun, but sane and practical little plays came out of it. Besides, I had concluded that Sherwood did not want to write a play. He wanted to walk up and down his room, reciting our lines and pretending he was Cellini.

I continued to visit Sherwood and listen to his increasing stack of unpublished manuscripts and I became awed by his attitude toward the magazine and book publishers who kept refusing to print his work. He chuckled over them as fools and laughed each time the mailman brought a rejected manuscript.

"They want me to become a hack full of plots about virtue and success," said Sherwood. "Maybe I would, but I don't know any plots. Anyway, there are enough literary hacks in the land without me. So I'll keep on being what I am. When they finally publish me, I may even be a little sad. Because it's fun to be an artist—like this. And keep on writing because you know you're an artist, not because anybody has told you so."

Yet of this tender-minded man who was the hero of the young Bohemia I had found, its poet, sage and chief Promise, I remember one of the cruelest episodes of my youth—in fact two of them.

There was a phone call for me in the *Daily News* local room one rainy autumn afternoon. A girl told me that Sherwood's mistress had tried to kill herself an hour ago in her Oak Park home. I knew Sherwood's mistress and admired her. She earned her own living and was full of jollity. The girl on the phone had saved her life by getting a doctor over in time with a stomach pump.

"But she's still going to do it," said the girl. "She's going to do something terrible. She's screaming now. Please come out and help me."

I arrived in Oak Park an hour later. Sherwood's mistress had broken away from her friend and was wandering in the rain-dark woods beyond Oak Park. I went after her and found her after a long search. She was sitting on a railroad embankment, rain-soaked and silent, and waiting for a train to come along and run over her.

I led her away and we talked all night. Sherwood had been her lover for two years. She had adored him, devoted herself to him. They had never quarreled. He was a great artist and she had loved him, nursed him, coddled him, loaned him money and never failed him in his dolorous hours.

"And then," Sherwood's mistress spoke, "for no reason this happened. Not that he left me or stopped loving me. A man is entitled to leave and stop loving, a man like Sherwood. But he walked out of here two weeks ago, kissed me, said how sweet I was, how he loved me. And that was all. I didn't hear from him for several days. I called him at his office. His secretary answered that Mr. Anderson was too busy to speak to me. I went to the office to see him. He refused to see me. I went to Cass Street. He wasn't there. He's moved. I wrote him letters. They came back unopened—with my address in Sherwood's writing on the envelope. That's why I've gone crazy. Why should he do this? What made him hate me so? He must have heard something wrong, some horrible lie about me. I can't live like this. It's too awful to sit all day and night and not know what's happened, what my crime is. If he'd only speak to me once —and tell me why—I could face it. But this way I can't."

I told Sherwood's mistress I would have lunch with him and find out everything for her. With this promise in her ears the tormented girl fell asleep and I left Oak Park.

I lunched with Sherwood as I had promised. We talked of his newly published book—his first—*Windy McPherson's Son*. I had written a two-column review of it for the Chicago *Evening Post's* book page, run by the eclectic Llewellyn Jones—at that time the sole critical lighthouse of the town. I had also written Mencken a letter pleading with him to reconsider his evaluation of Sherwood Anderson. Mencken had dismissed Windy McPherson briefly in his *Smart Set* magazine monthly discourses as a feeble imitation of Theodore Dreiser. And Mencken had written back that he would keep a weather eye open for the Anderson genius after this.

Sherwood was delighted with my activities. He beamed on me through the lunch, his eyes tender with fellowship. I brought up finally the topic of his mistress. He listened to my story of her grief and attempted suicide with seemingly little interest.

"I knew you wanted to talk to me about B——," he chuckled when I had finished. "I could tell from your voice when you called up. I'll tell you why I left her and if you want to tell her you can. I decided two years ago that I wanted to see what it was like to have an affair with a thoroughly homely woman—with a homely face and a homely body. I wanted to see how a man would feel— pretending to be in love with that sort of a woman, sleeping with a woman who bored you to death. Well, the experiment is over. You can tell B—— what you like but that's the whole truth. I just decided to quit two weeks ago—and I just feel that talking to her or listening to her once more—would be too much."

I returned to Oak Park that evening and told B—— a tall tale. Sherwood, I said, had fallen in love with another woman and was so sick and guilty about it that he hadn't been able to face her, B——.

"He's been drinking steadily for two weeks," I said, "and worrying about you and afraid to face you and your pain. He hasn't written a line and may probably lose his job. He begged me to tell you not to call him for a month or write to him, until he can get hold of himself again. You know how Sherwood is?"

"Yes," said B——. "I know how Sherwood is. He's different than all other men. He's a genius. And I'll do what he wants."

The other cruel episode I remember had me for its victim.

My first novel, *Erik Dorn*, had just come off the presses. I had received three advance paper-backed copies. I gave one immediately to Sherwood. My friend Swatty was now a literary force in the Republic. Prizes had fallen to him, and his name was almost as big as Dreiser's in the world of writing.

I had written reams of copy about the art of Sherwood Anderson, before and after his fame. I felt happy joining him for lunch, for I had heard he had read and liked my book. So had Mencken. But I was more eager to have my friend Swatty in my corner. Mencken wrote only for the *Smart Set*. Sherwood would be able to whoop it up for me in a half-dozen periodicals which had come to consider his word as artistic law.

Flushed with these visions of logrolling, I sat down opposite Sherwood in our favorite restaurant—a noisy place full of shirt-sleeved working people. Sherwood handed me back the white-and-purple-striped copy of my novel and laughed at my eagerness.

"It's all right," he said, "not bad at all. I read it with real interest."

"Thanks," I said.

"But I've got something important to tell you," Sherwood said. "It's a big idea that came to me last night about you and me. We've been friends now for seven years. That's a long time to be friends. It kind of wears off and loses its point, friendship does. My idea is that we become enemies from now on. Real enemies. You do everything you can to injure me. Attack me, denounce me, try to steal my girls, ravish my wife—anything you want. And I'll do the same to you. That way we can have a lot of fun—instead of just piddling along as a couple of fellows getting more and more bored with each other."

And Sherwood looked at me with a chuckle.

"I'll begin with your book, *Erik Dorn*," he said.

I never saw Sherwood again until some twenty years later—two days before he died. I read his books and found myself mentioned in them occasionally—with a sort of good-humored contempt. He was pleased always to make me out older than himself—and refer to my "adventures" in the Spanish-American War. And he once devoted a lecture to me, a report of which revealed that he was happily continuing the feud with which he had hoped to dam my career.

I did not join the feud and when I saw him again in my favorite New York saloon, Twenty-One, I sat down with him as if not two decades but two weeks had passed since our last sight of each other. His laugh was intact. The intimate purr, the glowing eyes, the delicately trembling features—these were all the same. He had grown paunchy, gray-haired and a sort of pelican pouch had been added to his neck, but it was my friend Swatty, unchanged from that first night in Cass Street.

He was off in the morning for South America, where he was going to live for the rest of his life. He had sold his small-town newspaper, and was spending a last evening in the U.S.A. These things he told me. We drank wine again together, laughed loudly over a few long-ago names. The magic I had felt in him in his youth seemed unchanged.

Yet I felt a change. I was writing a daily column for the New York newspaper *P.M.* The next day I handed a story of my reunion with Sherwood to Editor Ingersoll. I had written in the story that Sherwood was a man leaving not a country but life, and that he was like a wearied animal going off to an unfamiliar place to die.

The day my column about Sherwood was printed there was a small box "precede" to it. The "precede" announced that Sherwood Anderson had died the night before on shipboard bound for Brazil. He had swallowed the toothpick in an hors d'oeuvre sausage and punctured a vital organ.

SOME CRITICISM—AND A CAROM SHOT

Sherwood Anderson was one of the finest poets of our time. His short stories and novels are nearly always a sort of overgarrulous poetry. He had little literary discipline and hardly any technique. He was unable to dramatize episodes or relationships except in the naïvest fashion. His plots, when they existed, were childlike and usually seemed like lies.

He was also incapable of realism. Things he had seen and known, including people, escaped his memory. He had truly an amnesia, not only for the weeks of his wandering among the Ohio corn, but for all the years of his living. He was a bad observer and a forgetful listener.

All he wrote was invention. He dreamed up life, psychology and characters. His soul was too busy with an inward stewing to take on impressions from without. The world entered him obliquely and deviously and was translated instantly into Sherwood Anderson.

But behind all this fantasy that masqueraded as small-town realism and great psychological sex lore was always the strumming of Swatty's gypsy guitar. It was this undernoise, this never-ceasing song beneath, that filled his fictional woolgatherings with beauty and even sanity. Life, as he had confided to me, was something precious—a secret, a dream, a child in hiding. And through his pages, even the most garbled of them, there was the reach of the poet for mysteries.

When he wrote poetry openly, as in *Mid-American Chants*, Anderson lost his gift. He could only be a poet when he was telling lies—inventing plots and characters that had no existence this side of the moon. To make such fantasies sound real, to sell their Mother Goose people as human beings who belonged on our planet, poetry was needed. It was always on tap in Anderson, a mystic sales talk that threw out hints of sublimity and purred with love.

He wrote without eye to reader, critic or royalty returns, except once when he concocted an almost idiotic dime novel about gangsters and rumrunners. He looked only into himself. Unlike most of his imitators or disciples, of whom Ernest Hemingway was the best, he did not hitch his poetry to ten-twenty-thirty melodrama. Nor did he ever weave his tales around gaudy escapist figures that are always the heroes of lucrative entertainment. Unlike Hemingway *et al.*, he did not grandly play the poet while busily wooing the box office. He was never hack and artist, too. From the day he started writing in Cass Street to the night he stepped on the Brazil-bound ship, he remained always the lonely, faraway liar with a secret he could not quite express, and a song that hinted of it.

ART IN A BLUE SUIT

SHE WAS BLOND, shapely, with lean ankles and a Scandinavian face. Sasha, a little embittered by her beauty and chastity, called her Diana, the frigid huntress. I forgave her her chastity because she was a genius.

During the years I knew her she wore the same suit, a tailored affair in robin's-egg blue. Despite this unvarying costume she was as chic as any of the girls who model today for the fashion magazines. Her chic seemed always surprising to me, for a wind was constantly blowing through her head. It was surprising to see a coiffure so neat on a noggin so stormy.

Her name was Margaret Anderson (no kin of Sherwood) and she was the editor of *The Little Review*, or, as it seemed to me in that time, Keeper of the Literary Heavens.

The Little Review was a deceptively thin and modest-looking magazine published from a cubbyhole in the Fine Arts Building on Michigan Avenue. Its innocuous title and its wrenlike tan covers have remained in my mind for thirty years as a piece of the True Cross, glimpsed by a pilgrim in his youth. It was Art. I have met many things in my life that were Art, but they were always Art plus something else—Art plus fame, money, vanity, success, politics, complexes, etc. *The Little Review* was, nakedly and innocently, Art.

There were, and still are, scores of art periodicals in our Republic, but Miss Anderson's publication was like none of them. Unlike *The Dial, The New Masses, The New Republic, Poetry, Others, The Mercury, The Bookman, The Little Review* never found an audience. It found only writers. Its continued emergence off the press seemed always a miracle, and I used to hold my breath from month to month in fear that it would vanish, genii fashion, from the earth.

It paid no money for contributions. Its lovely pilot spent half her time charming printers and paper salesmen into sheathing their claws and swallowing their bills. Occasionally its staff was unable to find money for food or lodging. They fled the city, then, and pitched three tents on the beach near Lake Forest. Here, apparently, the ravens fed them, and inside the leaky canvas shelters Art was served and the Land of the Philistines laid low.

To this harum-scarum, bankruptcy-haunted and unsalable publication, manuscripts poured in from all the geniuses of the world. So it seemed to me then and so it still seems when I remember its electric pages. James Joyce's *Ulysses* ran as a serial in them. Ezra Pound, still blond and sane, flooded them with his bright parrotings of ancient Greeks and Chinese. In them appeared the first trumpet calls of Wyndham Lewis, T. S. Eliot, Carl Sandburg, Jules Romains, Jean Cocteau, Sherwood Anderson, André Gide, Carlos Williams, Djuna Barnes, Edgar Lee Masters, Amy Lowell and platoons of similar moon-shooters.

None of them received a dime for his work and, as often as not, had his manuscript returned with a disdainful line from Miss Anderson, "I don't like this," or "I couldn't read this." Nevertheless, Miss Anderson's desk (or tent) was always heaped with copy signed by names agallop to fame.

It was youth that spoke in *The Little Review*, sometimes even *juvenilia*. Between its covers flared an arrogance now gone out of the world. Each issue was full of the only battle bulletins to be read in that day—triumphant communiqués from all the advancing art fronts.

Why a magazine with so many geniuses writing so brilliantly in it should fail to attract any attention to speak of was never a mystery to me, as a contributor, or to Miss Anderson, or to most of the new Byrons and Dostoevskis who panted to get into its unread pages. We would all have regarded the success of *The Little Review* as a blow to our prestige. We were dedicated to rescuing the art of writing from the latrines of popularity. We considered the approval of either the crowd or critics a mark of final failure. To fascinate "the mob" —as we dubbed the distraught and troubled millions of our neighbors in that day—was proof of having fallen to its canned-soup level. Art was not a thing to sell or to offer for applause. It was the individual's lonely response to the mysteries of man and nature. It was to be enjoyed chiefly by the artist making it, and by a handful of other artists who might weary for an hour of admiring themselves.

This love affair between oneself and one's mind was endangered by any public. It ran the risk of becoming a love affair between oneself and such a public, and we all knew where this led—to fame, fortune and the respect of one's fellows. I am not being facetious. What I write is true. We held Art to be, like Virtue, its own riches.

A ringing line was its own reward. And having written it and had it printed without pay in a magazine nobody read was the finest triumph in the world. We left the Fine Arts Building with fresh copies of *The Little Review* under our arms—we who were lucky enough to be in it—and felt big in the street, anointed but unknown, which was the Shekinah of the True Artist.

I smile as at a thing dead as I put down this concept of Art, which got me into *The Little Review* and, also, into fist fights in saloons where poetry that did not rhyme and prose that was "half cat-fit" were regarded as a menace to the Republic by my lower-level drinking companions.

It is possible that I never had any such concept of Art and that only Miss Anderson did. This theory could explain in part the phenomenon of *The Little Review*. Miss Anderson's genius consisted of making young writers want to please her rather than a larger, more lucrative public. It was a genius that demanded Art of its admirers as some pretty girls demand jewels and love nests of them. It was a genius, also, for filling others with a vision which it was unable, itself, to express. In a similar manner an evangelist evokes delusions of heaven and hell-fire in the bosoms of hitherto rational folk and prods them into hallelujahs of faith.

I have, since, often met this genius for making others create. Theater and movie producers occasionally have it, and editors and, most frequently, women smitten with dreams. Their demands are like an applause that will not subside until one performs for them.

In Miss Anderson's case the demand and applause were more impersonal. It was Art before which she sat uttering her flushed bravos. I was young, without direction or aesthetics, and it may be I saw no Art. But it is certain I saw Miss Anderson. Thus the Art I served in *The Little Review* may have been only Miss Anderson in her robin's-egg blue suit. And the firecrackers I set off in that magazine may have been actually valentines composed for Margaret Anderson.

MY FRIEND, SEÑOR DIOGENES

I WAS TWENTY. The Michigan Avenue windows flashed with early summer sun. I walked its bright stretch with my friend, Wallace

Smith. I was en route to *The Little Review* office, to which I was bringing a literary piece called "Decay."

An afternoon promenade in Michigan Avenue had become a routine for Wallace and me. We sauntered and discussed the characters of our fellow pedestrians. We admired female legs, bosoms and buttocks, criticized the fine ornamental masonry that was beginning to stud the wastes of Grant Park, which Wallace said looked like a row of Etruscan shit houses, and played a game. The game was to identify the profession of a given male approaching.

Wallace studied our next case. He was a dapper fellow in a black and white checked suit, patent leather shoes, holding gray gloves and a Malacca cane, with a jaunty green fedora, a green handkerchief cascading out of his breast pocket and a waxed mustache like a miniature canoe under his nose.

"Your turn," I said. "What is he?"

"An Idea Man in a French whore house," said Wallace.

We walked on.

"Or possibly a writer for *The Little Review*," Wallace added. "I understand that most of its contributors are reformed masturbators."

"Who isn't?" I said. "You'll like Margaret."

"And a cup of coffee," said Wallace, for whom this was always a crushing remark; this, and the words that accompanied his mocking, startled look at all ugly, overfat women—"Ah, my first wife."

We had become what Wallace called "*compañeros*," for he was bitten by the faraway romanticism of "Mehico." He had ridden as a Hearst correspondent with the turbulent Pancho Villa in the great days of La Cucaracha, and attended the overthrow of the whiskered tyrant, General Carranza. He had drunk with the silver fetishist, Fierra, the Butcher—Pancho's personal executioner. And, arrested once as the notorious Colonel Lopez, wanted by the Federalistas as a firing-squad target, he had lain silently in jail for a week rather than speak out and reveal himself an Americano. His arrest as a Mexican and his near execution as the devilish Lopez left its mark on him for all his life. He dreamed always of being mistaken again for a Mexican and in his later years he roamed that country with silver pistols and sombrero and was known in all the cantinas from Mazatlán to Acapulco as the "*grande señor*."

In our youth, Wallace was tall and dark, foppish and athletic. He was cynical as a coroner and disdainful of all humans except Mexicans. Handsome and hard to please as the most fretful of hidalgos, he held to a code that seemed half jest and half mania. Artists were impostors, poets were fakes, actors were idiots, politicians were doormat thieves, women were Delilahs, poor people were bums and rich folk were degenerates. Nobody was worth a damn and that which was not daffy was phony. I have never known anyone more contemptuous of existence. Life seemed to have imprisoned my bold-hearted *compañero* and all who crossed his path were enemies responsible for his incarceration.

This fastidious and sharp-tongued Diogenes flattered me by exempting me, along with the population of Mexico, from the undesirables of the world. His friendship was flattering, also, because he was one of the crack reporters of the town. I regarded him as the best of my rivals and the most stimulating of my newspaper contemporaries. I thought him a touch too critical, too angry and too florid in his manners, which swung from hidalgo to Prussian uhlan, and included bows, heel clicks and a scented handkerchief in his cuff.

But there was more to Wallace Smith than smart journalism and a wisecracking neurosis. He was a black and white artist of high talent. He drew like Heinrich Kley, Aubrey Beardsley and Félicien Rops. From his drawing pen flowed a precise anatomy, tortured and ornamental.

His drawings spoke elegantly of an inner writhing. They were drawings without art, meaning or character. They teemed solely with muscles and joints as correct and humanless as arithmetic. They were muscles and bones distorted on an unseen rack. Their torture wore always perfect draftsmanship. Wallace looked on "bad drawing" as a sin against the Holy Ghost and he felt genuine pain and contempt in the presence of all modern art from Cézanne to Weber and Braque.

Unable ever to add any personality to his work, Wallace remained until his death a man turning out drawings that were like charts, blank of life. He turned them out blindly and perfectly and was content to have his remarkable drawings seem to critics like doodlings on the edges of art.

We entered the Fine Arts Building and *The Little Review* office. Margaret reacted instantly to my *compañero*. She looked at him for a moment and despised him forever. Wallace's response to my Keeper of the Literary Heavens was equally spontaneous. He referred to her always thereafter as "your friend, the idiot Sappho."

But there was another visitor in the office who stirred a different feeling in Wallace. He sat on a cot against the wall, his long-nosed face pale, its cat's eyes half shut. His chin was resting on a heavy walking stick. His brown hair, straight and long like the bob on a medieval page boy, curtained the sides of his face. He was my own age, with a strongly muscled body and a grace dominating his half-shabby clothes. I introduced Stanislaus Szukalski, sculptor and artist.

"Excuse me for not standing," Szukalski said. His voice was purring and nasal and Polish-accented. "I fainted in the street an hour ago. Now I feel better."

"Are you sick?" I asked.

"No," said Stanley. "I am not sick. I am hungry. I have not eaten for several days. Only tea. Now they are bringing me more tea."

Wallace was silent. He stared at Szukalski's powerful hands.

"My friend Wallace is an artist," I said. Stanley looked at him. His eyes were still dizzied with hunger but he managed to get a sneer into them.

"Everybody who can draw better with the right hand than the left hand is an artist today," Stanley said. His face grew paler. It looked up mockingly at me. "You are very lucky to know an artist," he continued. "I do not know one—anywhere in the whole world."

Caesar, the office boy ballet dancer, brought plates of cakes and sandwiches into the room. Szukalski ate sparingly.

"I thought you fainted with hunger," Caesar said.

"Hunger and other things," said Stanley. "Maybe anger. Besides I do not want to spoil my stomach. It is now shrunk to the right size for an artist. It is happy with one sandwich and one cooky. Thank you."

The sculptor stood up, regarded Margaret, his hostess, with distaste and walked out of the office. He walked with long, graceful strides that made him seem almost to be skating. He held his face raised and the heavy stick in his strong hand curbed any snickers his long hair might have aroused.

We went with Szukalski to his studio, which was an unused loft in a Wabash Avenue building whose windows looked out on the thundering elevated cars.

A LOFT ON WABASH AVENUE

WE ENTERED a dimly lighted barren room that looked big enough to house a regiment. And a regiment seemed to be in it, lined against its shadowy walls. They were Szukalski's statues in plaster, bronze and clay.

I had never seen any statues like them, nor have I yet after thirty-nine years. They were like a new and violent people who had invaded the earth. They seemed to be without skins, and their sinews writhed like imprisoned serpents. Torment and grandeur were in them, and a mysterious shout seemed to hang over their heads. It was the shout of Prometheus from his rock. Lucifer and Christ were there and the wrath of God. Hypocrisy, valor, despair and rapture gestured commandingly in the shadows. There were figures that cringed with withered hands held out for alms, and heroes who seemed strangled by their own strength. Secrets animated all the statues, and I was bewildered looking at them those first fifteen minutes.

My friend Wallace had not moved from the first statue—the Aesop. He seemed to be reading it. He pondered on each of its sinews, joints, drapes, folds of flesh, fingers and features. His own face had lost its mockery. I became aware that Wallace was looking at his own talents turned into genius, his own fanatic draftsmanship made alive by art.

"Where did you learn your anatomy?" Wallace asked.

Szukalski began talking softly, his cat eyes half shut. "I used to go walking every Sunday with my father. We would meet in the park in the morning and walk together all day. I loved my father very much, more than anybody in the world. He was a fine man. One Sunday morning I came to the park where he is supposed to be every time. He is not there. Down the road there is a crowd. I go look and it is my father. He has been killed by an automobile. I drive the crowd away and I pick up my father's body. I carry it on my shoulder a long time. We go to the county morgue. I tell them this is my father and I ask them this thing which they did allow. My father is given to me and I dissect his body. I study him carefully. You ask me where I learn anatomy?"

Szukalski looked at us with pride.

"My father taught me," he said.

I remember another speech from Szukalski. We were sitting in a restaurant.

"What would you say makes an artist?" I asked him.

"If you can work for food, love a woman, fight all your troubles and then have something left over, something unused, something that you have to put to work—then you are an artist—maybe."

Two weeks later Wallace and I returned to Szukalski's loft. We brought with us an elegant character named Count Monteglas. He was the art critic for Hearst's *Examiner*, and the most important art voice in the town. Art patrons opened their purses under his guidance, and his favor was secretly dreamed of in the beleaguered ateliers.

Count Monteglas was a Belgian with a monocle and a waxed mustache. He dressed always like the Best Man at a wedding and he carried a cane and a pair of fine yellow gloves.

We had filled Monteglas with tales of Szukalski's genius and fable-like existence.

"You keep writing about Rodin," said Wallace as we approached the loft. "Here is an artist right under your nose who is worth a wagonload of Rodins. And the nice thing about it is, you can discover him, Monty. Not a line has been written about him by anyone."

The Count nodded courteously.

"He's as unknown as a bear in a log," said Wallace. "After you wave your wand over him he'll be the new Michelangelo."

"I value your opinion highly," said Monteglas. "You are yourself an excellent artist."

"Thank you," said Wallace. "But alongside Szukalski I am totally invisible."

We walked up the stairs to the loft. Szukalski's days of poverty and oblivion were over, if our guest subscribed to our opinion. A Monteglas ballyhoo would flood the barren loft with commissions.

Szukalski turned on all three of the electric bulbs in the loft, leaving it more shadowed than lit. Critic and artist shook hands, Szukalski bowing stiffly, as was his habit. Monteglas then started his tour of the statues. He paused, as Wallace had done, before the Aesop. He fixed his monocle firmly and remained staring at it.

"Very interesting," Monteglas finally said and raised his cane. He poked Aesop's torso gingerly with the tip of his cane. "Very strong. Very well done. And there, too, great feeling." Count Monteglas poked Aesop's shoulder with his debonair stick.

"Excuse me," said Szukalski, purring and nasal, "but people do not look at my statues with cane. They look with eyes."

He stepped swiftly up to the critic, snatched the cane from his hand, broke it across his own knee and flung the parts out of the door. This done, he collared Count Monteglas and shoved him violently forward.

"Outside, please!" he said.

Our critic went staggering toward the doorway. He continued down the stairs in a panic.

"There goes fame—and some meat and potatoes," Wallace said.

"You will forgive me if he is your friend," Szukalski said.

"No friend," said Wallace, "just a critic."

"Then no harm has been done," Szukalski smiled.

I invited the sculptor to come to the theater with us. We had passes from our drama editors.

"I cannot," Szukalski said, "not tonight. Tonight is military practice." He smiled and spoke softly. "I am training twenty Polish boys to be soldiers. We drill three nights a week. I teach them the manual of arms. So when the time comes they will be ready to go back and fight for the freedom of Poland."

"THE GREATEST LIVING ARTIST"

FOR TWENTY YEARS my friend Stanislaus Szukalski experienced disasters which would have killed off a dozen businessmen. Sickness, hunger and poverty yipped everlastingly at his heels. Defeat stood constantly in his doorway like a sheriff with a subpoena. And during his struggle he heard only the catcalls of critics and the voices of derision. Yet when I saw him in 1934, twenty years after the day

Wallace and I first visited his studio, I saw a man who had feasted on power and whose eyes smiled with triumph. He had been sent for by the Poles and he was on his way home.

Szukalski became a great artist, not only to me but to a nation that was to hail him as the greatest of living artists. Yet his name is today unknown. His works are vanished. He is without public, without critics, and so complete is the world's ignorance of him that he may as well never have existed.

"I put Rodin in one pocket and Michelangelo in the other and I walk toward the sun," Szukalski said in his powerful youth. And he did, toward a sun that was to illumine him and all his greatness for an hour and then black out forever.

Szukalski, in his own soul, was a country called Poland. I do not understand the process by which an egomaniac such as Szukalski can transform himself into the colors of a flag. But such he was— patriot, chauvinist and lover of Poland, blind with the homesickness of a fish for water. No other history, problems or people existed for him than those of Poland.

He had attended art school in Cracow, and that name was to him greater than Paris or London. His father, a blacksmith, had brought him at sixteen to the U.S.A. and settled in Chicago.

Szukalski owned a trunk which he never unpacked, for he held himself for twenty-five years a man in transit. He spawned a thousand statues and drawings which he never sold or exhibited. He smiled with his cat eyes at the indifference of the world around him as a man might smile at the unawareness of a railroad junction at which he waited for the next train.

He waited, trunk always ready, to return to Poland.

"I make these statues for my people," he said. "It is just as well that Americans do not buy them. There will be more for Poland."

After twenty-five years Szukalski returned to his native land. With him went a wife and a cargo—all his amazing statues, all his undepleted portfolios of marvelous drawings.

And a wonder happened. As Szukalski had loved the Poles, so did the Poles love Szukalski. The sun came out. Honors overwhelmed him. The Polish government of that time embraced him as the Finnish government had embraced the composer Sibelius. The government gave him a studio, the largest in Warsaw, and proclaimed it a national Szukalski Museum. The critics of Warsaw pronounced him the greatest living artist. He was given a commission to erect a statue in the center of Warsaw, one that would blazon Polish valor and genius to the world. Other commissions were given him, more than any one sculptor could execute in three lifetimes. Szukalski statues were to rise in Cracow, and all the cities of Poland. A triumph as unique as the love and glory that once surrounded Michelangelo beat around him—and vanished.

The first Nazi *Luftwaffe* bombardment of Warsaw scored several direct hits on the Szukalski National Museum. It was destroyed. In the rubble that remained lay pulverized and burned to ash every statue Szukalski had ever hewn and every drawing and painting he had ever made.

After two years of underground wandering Szukalski returned to his railroad junction again—the U.S.A. We met. I listened to his story. I remembered his statues and recalled them by name—his Aesop, his Homer, his Man with a Worry. He smiled as I spoke of these and of his scores of other works.

"I am pleased you remember," he said. "They are all gone. I am going to start over again."

His cat eyes continued to smile. His voice purred nasally as it used to. His manner was graceful, his words soft. But of all the refugees from Europe I met in that day, none seemed to me so terribly denuded. Szukalski was an unlisted empire destroyed by the Nazis.

In 1949 I received a long letter from Szukalski. He was living in Hollywood. He was engaged in manufacturing "historical tiles." A sample tile came with the letter. A seven-branched candlestick and other Hebrew symbols ornamented the tile. He was able, wrote Szukalski, to produce these fine tiles for as cheap as two dollars apiece. He asked my help in peddling them to rabbis and synagogue congregations.

"LONG ERE ROME RANG OF HIM"

IT IS STILL SUMMER, 1914. It is still a world given only to minor killings—some Greeks and Bulgarians, some Armenians and some

Jews—just enough for an occasional headline. There is very little even for a philosopher to worry about, except his rent. So I am informed by my elders. To judge from the talk in Mangler's, Stillson's, Vogelsang's and other saloons which are, as far as I have been able to determine, the centers of the world's wisdom, all the Problems have been solved. The Trusts have been busted. Judge Kenesaw Mountain Landis, parchment-faced and steely-souled, has fined the Standard Oil Company twenty-nine million dollars for behaving in an un-American fashion. Our Lieutenant Governor, Barrett O'Hara, has battled unsuccessfully to remove vice from the city. Youth has nothing on its agenda but girls, gab and tomorrow.

In this fine time there sat in Chicago's County Building pressroom a half-dozen young men, of whom I was one, with nothing more to do—it being working hours—than play rummy, listen to Ernie Pratt practice his banjo and to Spike Hennessy hold forth on the advantages of buying an orange grove in Florida and going there to live like a gentleman.

Studying their hands were three of the most lameduck card players I knew and with whom I, a cardsharp trained by a dozen aunts and uncles, was always happy to be engaged. There was Charlie (Vincent Emerson) Starrett, budding essayist, bibliophile, and at present covering an erotic divorce trial two floors above. There was Ronald Millar, graduate of Oxford, ex-oarsman, with bulging head full of profound scholarship, editor-to-be of *Liberty* magazine and author-to-be of a children's encyclopedia which he was to write with hardly a reference book at his elbow. At present Ronald was worried over the mood of his city editor, who had refused to believe that he had signed a sobriety pledge with his Episcopalian pastor. There was Tom Kennedy, with the look of a farmer boy on his face and a new sonnet always in his pocket, and at present on the trail of the murderer of a cornet player, found stabbed and rolled up in a bedroom rug in his North Side home.

The pressroom door opened and the familiar, rakish figure of Jack Malloy appeared, as Irish as Sean O'Casey could write him and with no remote hint of his grand newspaper publisher future about him. He was unusually lyrical for three P.M. and he wore his handsome sneer like a matador's cape.

Malloy had a stranger in tow who from his slouch and rig and the shy and smoky look of his face appeared to be a cowhand. The stranger wore a celluloid collar and had an arc of stiff hair slanting across his forehead and sticking into one eye.

The rummy game halted. Malloy was wont to appear with curious companions, having recently brought Gene Geary into the press-room at a time when the entire city police force was hunting him for the murder of a popular bartender. At another time he had appeared among us with the great actor, Arnold Daly, at his side, each supporting the other.

"I want you to meet my friend," said Malloy, glowering at us, "who is a great genius and too fine a man for these precincts. Kindly arise!"

We remained in our chairs, and Malloy sneered to the heavens.

"Just what I expected," he said. He added to his sober and smiling companion, "Forgive these parasites. They are the untutored scum of letters and unable on a clear day to distinguish their asses from their elbows."

Malloy sat down, closed his eyes and dozed.

"My name is Carl Sandburg," said the stranger. "I'm a reporter on the *Day Book*. Malloy said I could use one of your telephones."

"Go ahead, help yourself," said Charlie Starrett.

Sandburg called his office. The *Day Book* was a daily newspaper of a most unprofessional look and equally strange content. It was the size of a Pierre Marquette Railroad timetable, and you could almost put the whole newspaper in your handkerchief pocket without fold-ing it.

It was full of news stories about the sins of Capitalists and the gallantry and wisdom of labor leaders. Although the only "radical press" in the city, it was nevertheless almost unread. The working-man for whose rights it battled preferred the journals that scorned their cause, for in these they could read of fancier figures than themselves—of boudoir adventures and of love-maddened trollops shooting down their errant sweethearts. The history of radical jour-nalism in our Republic has remained full of rue. Today, as yester-day, the working classes, from the bindle stiff to the top artisan, look for escapism in print rather than for champions. They will give their pennies and loyalties to the comic strip, the cheese-cake photos and the sports section. Karl Marx or Tom Paine playing publisher can seldom coax enough clientele to survive.

I seldom read the *Day Book*. It was known to me chiefly because of a lad of noble soul who had worked for it. His name was Dan MacGregor. He was a lanky, rumple-haired Scot with a long-nosed, jester's face, and a fire burned in him. I had covered stories with him and felt a thing in him rare among newspapermen of that day. His mind was a whip against injustice and it lashed away at the ruthless industrialists of the time. And ruthless they were, running their mines and factories like pirate captains, and cowing the unorganized toilers with bought jurists and National Militia regiments.

Covering a strike of copper miners in Ludlow, Colorado, Dan MacGregor had watched and reported the pitiful battle between a few hundred unarmed workingmen and a fully equipped regiment of National Guardsmen. He had stood by for days while soldiers "defending" the fat profits of the mineowners banged away with their rifles at the infuriated workers and their families, killing and wounding scores. And then MacGregor found his reporter's pencil too little for the rage in him. He jumped into the fight and joined the hunted workers who were throwing rocks at the lines of blazing rifles.

When the strike was broken, the victorious mineowners, eager to teach not only labor but literature a lesson, engineered the arrest of the man who had harried them with contemptuous words. MacGregor was named by a Colorado grand jury as a murderer. He skipped the country and turned up at Pancho Villa's side in Mexico, sending back reports of that peons' champion who was knocking over the tyrants below the Rio Grande. But again MacGregor found his pencil insufficient. And when the battle of Chihuahua was over and the Villistas were singing with triumph, MacGregor lay dead in the road, ripped by a dozen bullets.

Sandburg had written his obit in the *Day Book*, and we had all read it:

> He had no mother but Mother Jones
> Crying from a jail window in Trinidad,
> 'All I want is room enough to stand
> And shake my fist at the enemies of the human race.'

We resumed our rummy play as Sandburg used a telephone, and a summer rain began to hit the pressroom windows.

Malloy woke up, much refreshed and in a lighter mood.

"I would like these gentlemen to hear your poetry," he said to Sandburg, who sat watching our cards.

Poetry reading was no novelty in the pressroom. I had often recited my doggerel to my colleagues. Tom Kennedy had read us only yesterday a sonnet on the death of Julius Caesar. And Starrett was waiting for the right moment, when he was a big enough loser to have a claim on our sympathy, to read a ballad he had written about the "Peacock-Souled Scheherazade." I had already heard it.

Sandburg was reluctant, but Ernie Pratt's banjo at work on "Won't You Come Home, Bill Bailey?" loosened his poet's tongue. Ernie pulled Bill Bailey down to a faint obbligato and, with the rain and its soft drum roll on the windows, we listened to a poem Sandburg said would be called "Chicago" when it was finished.

"It begins like this," Sandburg went on, and started reading from some copy paper in his hand.

> *Hog butcher for the World,*
> *Tool Maker, Stacker of Wheat,*
> *Player with Railroads and the Nation's Freight Handler,*
> *Stormy, husky, brawling,*
> *City of the Big Shoulders . . .*

We listened to "Chicago" and to another poem,

> *Three muskrats swim west in the Desplaines River.*

I was to hear this voice for many years, in the streets during long walks, in the *Daily News* office at the desk beside mine. To this day I remember it as the finest voice I ever heard, reading or talking, better even than the remarkable voices of Paul Muni, Jack Barrymore and Helen Hayes. In Sandburg's voice lived all his poetry. It was a voice of pauses and undercurrents, with a hint of anger always in it, and a lift of defiance in its quiet tones. It was a voice that made words sound fresh, and clothed the simplest of sentences with mysteries. I had heard a cousin of this voice speak out of Sherwood Anderson, but Sherwood was garrulous and many-mooded. There was never garrulity in Sandburg and there was only one mood in him—a measured passion. Whether he chatted at lunch or recited from the podium he had always the same voice. He spoke always like a man slowly revealing something.

That evening an important event occurred in Mangler's barroom

—a fist fight between Ronnie Millar and Jack Malloy. A number of other journalists were drawn into the fracas. A few goblets were broken and a few noses bloodied. Mr. Mangler himself charged our corner and brought us to order by threatening to cut off the credit of all the combatants, whichever side they were on.

We returned to our crowded booth and continued the argument without fisticuffs. The argument was about Sandburg. Malloy had filled Ronnie Millar's scholarly head with anger by contending that what we had heard in the pressroom that afternoon was fine poetry.

"Choctaw!" Millar had cried. "Rhymeless, witless, pompous Choctaw! If those stuttering syllables uttered by that ignoramus in the celluloid collar are poetry, then I am the Nabob of Pasoda."

"Better poetry than Browning or Algernon Swinburne," was Malloy's answer, "and any man who doesn't think so has an ass hole for a brain."

After the blows had been struck and the table top tidied up, Ronnie Millar called for a bottle of rye, breaking his pledge to his Episcopalian pastor. We sat for hours with Millar hurling pages at us from Milton, Horace, Arnold, Keats and Wordsworth.

"Here," he cried, "is poetry! Epithet, rhyme, cadence and beauty." And we heard the "Ode to a Nightingale" and "Intimations on Immortality," and other high reports from bards of old.

I recall Ronnie Millar's last midnight blast at the *Day Book* reporter's poetry. It gave me an understanding of Sandburg that I had missed in the pressroom and that has remained with me since.

I had been pulled to the Sandburgian lines like a fish yanked to a pier. I had fallen in love that first half hour with all the poetry Sandburg was ever to write. Whether it soared or stuck to a dog trot, Sandburg's poetry always vibrated my heart. Ronnie Millar, inveighing against it, first told me why.

" 'Three muskrats swim west in the Desplaines River,' " Millar quoted, mocking the Sandburg voice. "A pretentious statement about nothing! An inarticulate concept of our sewage system—nothing more! Let me tell you once and for all, there is only one definition for the kind of stuff this fellow Sandburg writes. It's called commonplace!"

My friend Ronnie spoke the truth, but his back was turned to it. Commonplaceness is the soul of Sandburg's genius. The commonplace is the nightingale that sings in his poetry. Out of him the

ordinary look of life spoke with sudden, vivid meanings, as if someone had washed the staleness from its face and uncovered its deeply
human gleams.

His own soul was full of wonder at small things. He let these
small things speak for him. Broken factory windows, policemen's
shoes, white curtains fluttering in the steel-mill shanties, a farmer
sweating and smiling, a darkened electric sign, a crowded streetcar—
these and thousands of the unmysterious surfaces of farm and city
recite only their names in Sandburg's poetry and grow mysterious,
as do all things that are loved deeply and spoken of softly.

"My heart is empty," sings Sandburg's lover, "empty as a beggar's
tin cup on a rainy day."

ANOTHER SMITH

"There's a good reporter you ought to hire," I said to my managing editor on the Chicago *Daily News*. "He's as good as Dan Mac-
Gregor was and he's been out of a job since the *Day Book* folded."

"We're overstaffed," said my editor.

"His name's Sandburg," I went on, "and he's not only a good reporter but he writes superb poetry."

"What kind of poetry?" my editor asked.

"The new kind," I said. "Like Walt Whitman. Wonderful stuff.
If you don't believe me ask Jack Malloy."

"Tell him to come around," said my editor curtly, and with a
scowl on his lean dark face such as he always put on when granting
a favor. And Henry Justin Smith walked stiffly to his roll-top desk
in the center of the long, gloomy, neverswept, floor-sagging local
room whose dust-caked windows looked out on the roaring Wells
Street elevated trains. It was a roar that nobody in this local room
ever heard, any more than a sailor in a storm hears the hullabaloo
of the waves.

I doubt if in all the newspaper offices of the land there was ever
such a managing editor as Henry Justin Smith. So odd a newspaperman was he, that no hint of him has ever appeared in any fiction
I have read, or play or movie I have seen—but once. I wrote him
myself, borrowing, however, only his exterior for the look of my
first novel's hero, Erik Dorn.

Tall, thin and fastidious, with flushed lean cheeks and a royalist droop to his mouth and thin-lined mustache (I used to think of him as Henry of Navarre); scanty-worded, hiding a childlike sensitivity in a chronically fretful air so that he might seem like an executive rather than a moon-struck wonderer; bending over to pick up pins from the floor as he walked; incapable of oath or obscenity, scorning liquor and personal scandal and passionately in love with a newspaper—these were some of Henry Smith's qualities.

His love of our paper, the *Daily News*, had little to do with any interest in its circulation figures or editorial policies. He saw the paper as a daily novel written by a score of Balzacs. Its news stories were reports of life to him. Bent over his ever-fresh pile of proofs, he smelled humanity in their printer's ink. He read each story avidly, as if his desk were a prison cell and tales of the outside world were pouring in upon it.

And a prison cell or hermitage this tall, roll-top mahogany desk actually was, for Smith had never ventured beyond it. He had gone nowhere, mingled with no one, known neither adventure nor even disturbances. He had come to work on the *Daily News* after graduating from the University of Chicago with high honors as a Greek scholar. Mr. Stanley Fey, the snorting managing editor of that day, had almost immediately appointed Smith city editor for the sole reason (as given by Mr. Fey) that Smith was the only sober man visible in the local room. This was in the time when the poet, Gene Field, employed on the paper as a columnist, used to stir the Fey bile by arriving at his desk in a striped prison suit and anchoring himself in his chair with a ball and chain.

Smith had never covered the "beats," never known the smell of police stations, flop houses, crowded courtrooms; or ever seen the inside of a saloon, brothel, factory or political caucus. At his roll-top desk, as managing editor, he met the only life he knew—its report.

A CIRCUS ASSIGNMENT

BUT THERE WAS MORE to Smith than this surprising innocence. There was no ingénue in his mind, which was informed and alert. He was

a sharp-nosed editor and he could smell stories from afar with the
best of his colleagues, who included the redoubtable Hearst bloodhound, Walter Howie.

"The Hagenbeck-Wallace circus was in a big wreck last night,"
he said to me when I came in one morning, and city editor Beitler
had figured out no assignment for me. "A lot of its performers were
killed. But the circus is opening today in Beloit, Wisconsin. There
ought to be a good story in the circus performing—with half of its
clowns and acrobats dead."

There was a story, and I was the only reporter whose editor had
assigned him to go look for it. It was the story of Lola, the lion
tamer.

Lola had an assistant named Franz, a tall Swiss who was her lover.
His duties required him to remain outside the cage while Lola
worked with her beasts and be ready with loaded gun to come to
her rescue if there were any mishap.

Lola was in one of the burning wooden circus cars. She lay crushed
in the flames with a wooden beam through her middle. Her lover
found her and she moaned to him to finish her off with a bullet. He
looked at his doomed and tortured sweetheart, drew the gun he had
been given for her rescue and fired a bullet into her head.

At the matinee in Beloit, Franz insisted on entering the cage and
taking Lola's place. He had never worked with the big cats and
he knew nothing of the moods and tricks necessary. But Lola's soul
was in him, he said queerly. The grieving management gave the
heartbroken Franz his way.

I sat in the sawdust outside the cage as Franz entered it and I
watched him stand as Lola had done, imitate her way with a long
whip and repeat her commands. But there was a weakness of grief
in Franz that the beasts could smell. No sooner did he move toward
them with whip cracking than two of the tigers leaped on him and
brought him to the ground. His arms were ripped and his sides laid
open before he could be pulled out of the cage. He died in the
Beloit Hospital.

Wiring the story to the office, I felt that Smith in his wisdom had
foreseen the entire tragedy. But I felt more for him than a reporter's
pride in his boss. He was a continuation. He had succeeded Duffy,
Doc Yak and Finnegan. In the time of the *Daily News* they seemed
at first to have vanished—only to return, and stay.

ORPHEUS IN THE LOCAL ROOM

GEORGE WHARTON, whose A.P. representative's desk was next to mine, said to me after I had returned from Beloit, "That was a fine circus story you wrote. Several people spoke to me about it. They all had the same reaction—pains in the lower abdomen followed by nausea. I took an enema before going to bed and feel all right this morning, fully able to continue as a reader of the *Daily News*." He looked across the gloomy room and added, "I see there is a new addition to the staff."

Sandburg was sitting at a desk. He was removing old pie plates, limp card decks and bits of haberdashery from its drawers and filling them with scores of pamphlets.

"Sandburg?" Wharton repeated. "Never heard of him. But he looks peculiar enough to work on this paper. Where's he from—the Ozarks?"

"He's a Radical and a poet," I said, "and he used to be a semi-pro baseball player in Galesburg."

"You don't say?" Wharton nodded slowly and soberly. "A good spotted terrier would round out the staff."

Smith had not only hired Sandburg as a reporter but had also instructed our city editor, Brooks Beitler, not to burden the new man with any trivial chores. For Smith had read a few pages of Sandburg's poetry and he knew that genius was among us. Smith's love of good writing was almost as deep as his love of the *Daily News*. Succinct or well-turned phrases in a news story sent him to his suburban home glowing with a selfless pride. The thought that he now had a man on his staff who could write like Walt Whitman straightened his spine.

The matter of Sandburg, however, became a problem for editor Beitler. No fancier of poetry was Beit, no coddler of talent, but a realist with his eye on deadlines and the columns of our socking contemporaries. Day after day, he watched the smoky-faced Sandburg come snowshoeing to his desk—it was thus Wharton described his gait—sit down at it and, like some sea squid, seemingly vanish in a cloud of mood. The Sandburg aura disturbed the Beitlerian cosmos.

Our Beitler was used to reporters tapping out novels and sonnets under his nose—used but unapproving. A literary renaissance is of small use to a city editor. Beitler began to glare at his crack reporters hunched over first editions of Arthur Symons and George Moore. He glared worse at the stories they wrote for his front page. They were remarkably fancy stories. No reader could find out who had been murdered or how or why until he had waded through several moody paragraphs of high-class prose. Smith, although a little disturbed by the growing mysticism of his staff, insisted that our copy be run as written. Noble man. "They'll calm down pretty soon," he assured Beitler. Beitler nodded and pointed to the lead story on page one. I had written it. It was a report on an important murder case.

"Well, we got a big scoop today," he said, and coldly recited my lead. "Outside, the pizzicato of the rain . . ."

Sandburg's presence in the local room was a new cross for Beitler. Until now, his reporters had been characters partly intelligible to him as an editor. He had even joined their Anti-Gonorrhea Club, the members of which had to perform a violent five-minute jig each morning before settling down to work. But Sandburg was different. He had refused not only to join our club, he had refused to participate in any manner in any local room activities. Added to this was the open veneration with which Beitler's boss, Smith, said good morning to this new and immobile reporter. And doubly disturbing was the faraway look in the Sandburg eye, and the odd sartorial getup, which included an old Galesburg cap. Wharton had identified this headgear as a "herring catcher's cap." He had also pointed out that Sandburg wore stub-toed shoes with half outside laces, a type of footwear that had not been seen, Wharton insisted, since the Haymarket Riots.

I tried to win Wharton over to my admiration of Sandburg, and read one of Carl's manuscript poems to him, imitating as well as I could the poet's all-important voice. It was a poem that told of the sweat and grinning curse of a ditchdigger. When I had finished Wharton arose and left without making comment. I had not fetched Sandburg an admirer but I had won him a nickname. Wharton always called him, thereafter, "John Guts."

Sandburg's single brief conference with Beitler had left our city editor blinking. The Sandburg pockets were always stuffed with newspaper clippings, usually old ones, often dating back ten years.

He was forever studying these crinkled pieces of print and wagging his head over them. During the flurrying hour in which the Home Edition was being assembled one noon, Sandburg had walked to the City Desk and thrust one of the clippings at the perspiring Beitler. It was from a Dakota paper, eight years before.

Beit stared at the clipping a moment, noted its date line and looked blankly at the mysteriously excited Sandburg.

"What about it?" he asked finally.

"The people of Fargo have got something," said Sandburg slowly and resonantly. He took the clipping back and restored it to his pocket.

Beitler, in his laconic fashion complained to Malloy and me one afternoon.

"I understand this fella's a genius," he said. "You got any idea what a genius can do?"

"The A. F. of L. convention is opening in Minneapolis tomorrow," said Malloy. "Carl's an expert on labor affairs. Why don't you send him up to cover it."

"Good idea," said Beitler.

In the hole in the wall cigar store adjoining the paper where we used to sit on a wall bench and gabble a bit after lunch, Beitler broke the news to his boss.

"That fella Sandburg," he said.

"What about him?" Smith scowled, ready to protect our poet against all crudities of judgment.

"I sent him to Minneapolis," said Beitler. "Labor convention."

Smith smiled.

"Very good idea," he said.

"Not my idea, Malloy's," said Beitler. A defiance suddenly rose in him. "Personally, I wouldn't send him across the street," he said. Muttering the word "poetry," he stepped out of our cigar store wigwam. Smith blushed but forgave the Philistine.

The next day Smith inquired of Beitler during their pre-Home Edition conference, "How much space you giving the Sandburg story?"

"No space," said Beitler, "no story."

Smith scowled. Sandburg's oversight as a staff correspondent in not sending in any story put him in a slight hole.

"Use the A.P. today," said Smith.

"Using it," said Beitler.

A second and third day passed without communication from our staff man in Minneapolis. Smith's scowl grew, but his loyalty to the stonily silent correspondent never wavered.

"He's probably gathering a lot of material," he said to Beitler.

"If he's there," said Beitler. "Who knows?"

On the fourth day a hair-raising story came over the wires from Minneapolis. It was not from Sandburg. It was from the A.P. It announced that an embittered labor delegate had drawn a gun during the forenoon session of the labor congress and opened fire on an orator, severely wounding him. Other guns had been drawn and the fire returned, and a number of labor's champions were now battling against death in the Minneapolis hospital.

This was a story of size and import—but Smith's heart was heavy as he took charge of the paper's remake for it. Not a word had come through from Sandburg.

"Any instructions for our staff correspondent?" Beitler asked.

"Tell him to come home," Smith said.

The order to return was sent to Sandburg, still silent, in Minneapolis.

An hour later a wire from Minneapolis was handed to Smith. He stared at it with blushing face. It read:

"Dear Boss. Can't leave now. Everything too important and exciting."

It was signed "Sandburg."

THE DEATH OF HENRY SPENCER

A HOT SUMMER AFTERNOON was ending in the small town of Wheaton, Illinois. The thermometer outside Crowley's Drugstore registered ninety-two degrees. The sun blazed as it slid down a sky, white and smooth as a bed sheet.

Shirt-sleeved, without collar and tie, fanning themselves and mopping their faces with large handkerchiefs, the townspeople dreamed of evening shadows and a prairie wind. Merchants sat in the awning shade of their empty stores. They dozed, gossiped and read the Wheaton *Daily Journal*. There was always news of interest to home folks in the *Journal*, but on this day the editor seemed to have lost his native bearings. The front page was full of tidings that meant nothing to Wheaton. The German Kaiser was acting up again, and Britishers in striped pants were full of alarms—dim and faraway matters, these, to offer Wheaton, Illinois, on a blistering summer day.

The merchants idled, and housewives were busy with suppers in houses that looked as if they had been abandoned. The deserted streets were full of glare and silence. Only such things were moving as make no noises—bugs and butterflies, sparrows, robins and orioles, the heavy leaves of the maple trees changing positions, and a cat that had remembered something.

I entered the Wheaton jail, and the sheriff recognized me and was pleased to see me.

"Go right on upstairs," he said and then made a joke. "He's still there."

The sheriff's assistant led me to a large cell and opened its barred door. Three people were inside. A man and a woman were singing hymns, accompanied by a melodeon which the man was pumping. Another man, in shirt sleeves, tennis shoes and gray flannel trousers, was listening with a tender look on his square blond face. I knew the listener. His name was Henry Spencer, and he was going to be hanged the next morning between six and nine o'clock.

When the music had ended Spencer introduced me to the hymn singers.

"I want you to meet my spiritual brother and sister, Mr. and Miss MacAuslin," he said. The MacAuslins beamed. They looked alike, lean, short, reddish-haired and a little witless.

"My brother and sister in God." Spencer beamed back at them. "I'm very glad to see you. Sit down. Your friend Wallace Smith interviewed me this morning. He got here ahead of you, evidently. How have you been feeling?"

"Fine," I said.

"It's a very hot day," said Spencer. "I imagine this is about the coolest place in town."

He chatted on and I listened, fascinated by a new voice he seemed to have acquired since I had covered his trial a few weeks before. At that time Spencer had spoken in a half-cockney voice, coarse, sneering and illiterate. He was quite the grammatical gentleman now, and like his two other visitors he seemed idiotically cheerful.

"The sheriff kindly sent me a pitcher of ice-cold lemonade," he said. "Would you care for some?"

I took a glass and marveled at Spencer as I drank. This was the worst murderer I had ever yet encountered, a sly, humanless killer.

He had come to Wheaton and sniffed at the town like a wolf looking for easy and harmless quarry. He had found what he looked for—a lonely, aging woman with a bank account. Her name was Allison Rexroat. She was a spinster who went to lectures and studied dancing. Spencer wooed and seduced her and filled her life with matters of which she had foolishly dreamed in all her lonely years—sex and love. He was a juicy fellow with a catlike body, thick in neck and ankles and with large, fluttery hands. Miss Rexroat sinned with him and bought herself new clothes for the wedding he promised. She gave him her suddenly crazed heart and inexpert body and lastly her bank account.

A week after her money had been put in Spencer's name, he took her on a picnic in the woods beyond Wheaton. After wading in the creek and eating the picnic lunch Miss Allison had prepared with doting hands, Spencer insisted that his sweetheart lie down under a bush and allow him to enjoy her sexually. Miss Rexroat lay on her back, her eyes closed, her heart beating with sin and trusting love. Spencer approached her and cracked her skull with a hammer he had brought along for this purpose. He continued to pound her head until it was well bashed. He had also brought to the picnic a small shovel. He dug a grave with this, and after removing two diamond rings from his sweetheart's fingers, he buried her in it.

The next morning Spencer drew out Miss Rexroat's savings, now in his name. He was waiting for a train to take him out of Wheaton and to fresh hunting grounds when the banker and sheriff of Wheaton arrived at the depot. The banker had known Miss Rexroat all her life. He did not believe she would leave Wheaton, as Spencer had said she was doing, without saying good-by to him.

Spencer was arrested. Miss Rexroat's two diamond rings were found in his pocket. A farmer had seen them entering the woods—carrying a picnic basket. After several days of search, Miss Rexroat's fresh grave was discovered and her body dug up. There was the question, then, of the murder weapon. Spencer roared and cursed for a week that he was an innocent man and the victim of diabolical coincidences. The sheriff's assistant finally lost his temper, listening to the prisoner's stupid denials and contradictory statements, and hit Spencer in the mouth. At the sight of blood dripping from his broken teeth, Spencer became pale and fearful. This man who had smashed a live head into a pulp with a hammer was terrified of pain. To avoid a second blow, he confessed, and there was one detail in his blurted-out confession which he could not undo in his desperate court battle a few weeks later. In the presence of witnesses Spencer told where he had buried the murder weapon, and a half-dozen men went with him to the spot he named and dug up the blood-, hair- and flesh-caked hammer.

The confession offered in court by the state had been beaten out of him, Spencer's lawyers proved to the jury. And Spencer on the witness stand had denied everything, cursing his tormentors and oafishly crying out his innocence.

The evidence of the hammer brought him a death sentence, however, and he was returned to his cell to wait execution on an August morning. This had happened in July. I had left a surly Spencer, still cursing the world, and its sheriff and jury. This happy fellow pouring me a second glass of lemonade and smiling gently at me was, in truth, a thing to marvel at. Not only his voice but his soul had changed.

"I can see how surprised you are," he said. "But I am glad you are not sneering as your friend Wallace did this morning. He got angry when I tried to tell him about certain things and said to me, 'Cut out the act.'"

"What were you trying to tell him?" I asked.

"About God," said Spencer. The MacAuslins nodded like two happy children in a nursery. "And how my brother and sister brought me to him."

"Have you admitted the killing?" I asked.

"That's not important anymore," said Spencer. "I was a sinner. A black sinner. I did evil. Evil was in me. Now it's gone."

"Did you kill Miss Rexroat?" I asked.

The MacAuslins kneeled in the hot cell and began to pray. Spencer joined them on his knees and prayed with them. Then he stood up, dusted his new flannel trousers and said, "Yes, I killed her. I have no secrets from God. He knows me. I am a brand snatched from the burning. I have repented. My soul is washed of all wickedness. God can look into it and see there is nothing evil left. That's why He will let me into Heaven. Because there is not a single lie in me—only truth."

"God forgives those who come to Him with the truth," said one of the little MacAuslins. "Sinners and liars are barred from His grace."

"I'm washed clean," said Spencer and began in a soft voice to tell me the story of his evil doing. He described the picnic, the love-making, the vicious preparations of hammer and shovel and the ugly killing.

"I'm talking to you and to God," he said. "He listens to me and hears every word just as plain as you do."

I stayed another hour while the MacAuslins played their melodeon and sang more hymns. I asked them questions about Spencer, but they were like children too full of some mysterious joy to talk. They could only beam, sing and pray. They had been with Spencer for ten days and ten nights, filling the death cell with hymns, psalms and incantations.

I sat marveling now not only at Spencer but at the miracle of religion. The talk of divine grace and divine forgiveness was meaningless to me. Yet it had worked a miracle. Faith in God had altered a man's soul, diction and vocabulary, drained his nerves of panic and given him a serene face for death.

At dinner in the Wheaton Hotel I talked with Wallace about this miracle, and our friendship felt a strain. We were for the first time since we had met of different minds.

Spencer, said Wallace, was a fraud. His whole mumbo jumbo about God and repentance was an act. The man's soul was unchanged and as sly and rotten as ever.

"The sonofabitch," said Wallace, "is providing himself with his own hop. He's scared pissless and he's found something that he thinks will keep his knees from buckling when he starts up the gallows' steps. There's no faith or repentance involved."

"I think there is," I said. "Montaigne writes that philosophy prepares a man for dying as well as living. Religion is a philosophy of an emotional sort. And its history is full of stories about people who have gone to their deaths exalted by something they called God in their hearts."

"Not hammer killers," said Wallace. "Our boy is a murderer and if he wasn't hanged tomorrow he would go on being a murderer. He'd forget all about God and go after another spinster with another hammer. He's picked up religion out of terror."

"Don't most people?" I asked. "I'm only saying that a belief in God has changed a man vitally. He not only talks different, he looks different. He's got a vision in him."

"And a cup of coffee," said Wallace coldly. "I'm only two years older than you and I shouldn't know so much more than you. Makes me feel like I had a long white beard, talking to you." He looked at me queerly and added, "Nothing can change a man. It's all fake. You are what you are. And you can only pretend to be something else. Henry's a rat and he'll die like a rat. I'll give you three to one on it."

We walked through the summer night to the sheriff's house adjoining the jail. We wanted his opinion on Spencer's new soul. But the sheriff had gone to bed early and left word that no one was to disturb him.

"Another frightened man," said Wallace. "I talked to him this morning. He was shaking like a mongoose. He's not only never hanged anybody but he's never even seen a hanging. The whole thing is very upsetting to him."

The sheriff's daughter was sitting on the front porch. She was a girl of seventeen. Her young face looked tender and romantic in the moonlight. She seemed almost nude in her thin summer dress through which the white of her breasts glinted. A large coil of rope was at her feet. She held one end of it in her hands and was busy rubbing vaseline in its fibers.

"It's the rope they're going to hang Henry with," she said, "and my pa said it'll work better if it's softened up."

"Doesn't that upset you?" I asked. "Fixing up a hanging rope?" I looked at her intent face. "Come on, we'll take a walk," I added.

"I got to finish this."

"I should think your pa would have gotten somebody else to grease it."

"I wouldn't let him," the girl smiled. "He isn't going to let me see the hanging, so I said, anyway, I ought to have some fun out of it. I mean, excitement."

I picked up the rope to examine it.

"You're doing a good job," I said.

The girl frowned. "If you'd lived in Wheaton all your life," she said, "maybe you wouldn't stand there looking so sarcastic. And please go way. I don't want to be bothered."

We left the girl and the hanging rope and walked toward the stockade that had been built on the edge of the town for the execution. The night was thick and without movement. No prairie wind had come. Bugs chirped and made little spatters of sound as they leaped in the shadows. The music of the melodeon rose thinly, pensively, persistently. Frogs grunted. A dog bayed. The heat stirred sweet odors from the earth, its bushes, grass and trees. Overhead the sky sparkled with starlight and billowed with infinity. I wondered that a night could seem so beautiful that promised death in the morning. When I mentioned this to Wallace, he said, "People die all the time. Very nice people. And everything stays just as beautiful."

There were a dozen reporters already in the stockade. They were sitting at the moonlit press table, drinking. Most of them were from Chicago.

I drank and looked admiringly at the stockade. It was almost a Colosseum. Its fence rose fifteen feet in the air. Fifty rows of empty picnic benches faced the gallows. And this, too, was an astonishing structure. It was twice as high as any gallows I had ever seen. The gallows' platform was some thirty feet above the ground. A dangerous-looking, unbroken flight of small steps led up to it.

"Graft," said the Wheaton *Journal* reporter. "This whole hanging is shot through with graft and corruption. Here's a story for you fellas. I can't print it because my editor's a pal of the sheriff. They've got something on each other. But you fellas can spill it. The sheriff's running for re-election next month. That's why this stockade is five times as big as it ought to be. He's given out tickets to every political worker in the county—and he had to make it big enough to hold them all. Some of them got as many as five tickets apiece. Not only that, but the whole stockade is a swindle. The sheriff's brother-in-law owns the Wheaton Lumber Mill. He got the construction job and put in three times more lumber for everything than required. He soaked the county plenty. That's why the gallows is so high up. A guy could get dizzy just standing on it. The stairs, the fence, the gallows—everything is graft."

We drank and told stories of other events we had covered. New booze bottles appeared and were emptied. The smells of a woodland midnight filled the stockade. Owls hooted and a horse neighed from a distant barn. The maple trees towering above the stockade shook with a breeze arrived from the prairie. We lay in the grass in front of the gallows and a reporter named Woody, whom we called Kentuck, produced a pair of dice. We gambled for a while, but after lighting several boxes of matches to see the dice and denouncing each other as crooks miscalling the numbers rolled, we abandoned the game.

"Here's a game we can play without any daffy cheating," said Wallace. "Let's bet on those gallows' stairs. Everybody put up ten bucks and the winner take all."

"How come?" Kentuck asked.

"We'll bet on which step Spencer's going to trip when he starts up to the gallows in the morning," said Wallace. "Three of us will have to stay out of the betting and be judges."

We looked at the tall flight of gallows' steps with new interest.

"Wallie's right," said Kentuck. "No man alive can walk up those steps without trippin'. They're built too small."

"Spencer won't get farther than the fifth step," said the Wheaton reporter. "He'll go right on his ass."

"Place your bets," said Wallace. "And put them in writing so there'll be no humpty-dumpty arguments afterward."

"Hold your horses," said Kentuck. "Before I put up ten bucks I got a right to have a look in the paddock."

"Look all you want," said Wallace.

"I've had a little liquor," said Kentuck, "but I'm no dizzier than Henry will be when he starts climbing those steps in the morning. So I'll just check."

Kentuck started briskly up the stairs to the gallows' platform. A third of the way up his foot slipped.

"Never seen such stairs," said Kentuck, "a man could break his neck easy on them. I'll take steps twenty to twenty-five. Here's my ten dollars."

Seven other reporters entered the "stair pool." We took turns running up the steps to see how far we could go before tripping. I went the farthest, coming within five feet of the gallows before missing a step and almost toppling to the ground. I bet on the last five steps.

The seventy dollars were handed to three reporters who, as judges in the morning, would note without prejudice on which step the murderer of Allison Rexroat came a cropper on his way to the dangling rope.

The night, full of stars and silence, moved toward the dawn.

Sweet night in the shadow of death, night of crickets chirping and a clover-smelling breeze, night of heedless youth and bawdy tales, of young breasts glinting over a hanging rope, of a darkness full of little things—starlight and owls and weather reports and a melodeon playing for the salvation of a man, and haphazard human doings eerie and unpolitical and with the sap of life in them—that night is gone. And none like it was ever to be in my time again. For on this August, 1914, night, an innocence was departing the world.

GOD LOSES A GUEST

THE PICNIC BENCHES were jammed, and another thousand men lined the high fence. The reporters sat at the press table in front of the silent crowd. Telegraph operators and their instruments also occupied the table.

The early morning blazed with sun. Light filled the stockade like a presence. A blue-rinsed sky glared above us.

I was writing and handing my copy to Jimmy, the telegraph operator beside me. His leathery face nodded admiringly as he worked the key and sent my words clicking into the Daily News office. I was writing to please my editor, Henry Smith, who looked for Victor Hugo and Dostoevski in his reporters' copy. I did my best to outshine those gentlemen.

I described the crowd sweating in the bright morning—the lean farmers in from the fields around Wheaton, the plump merchants, the tobacco-chewing artisans, the hail-fellow officials with small jobs and large manners. They were a long-boned people with humor wrinkles in their faces, with shaggy eyebrows and a prairie twang in their voices—a harder "r" and a nasal "n." The country lawyer, doctor and local atheist were there; the horse breeder, the political loafer, the retired locomotive engineer, the wise bartender, the young-buck real-estate dealer. They were my America, unchanged by a single expression since my earliest memories. I thrilled to their galluses, frayed straw hats, blue cotton shirts and steady eyes as if my family were around me. They had come to watch death with shy and frowning faces and they would be ill at ease when they saw that the murderer was a human being like themselves. They were law-abiding. They believed in justice but found no secret pleasure in its exercise. No sadism was visible in them and little morbidity, and they all seemed depressed by the thought of evil in the world. They had come to watch stoically its removal. And on their faces was an American look that has since vanished, the self-contained, untaxed look of a people whose only business was their own.

The sheriff and his aides appeared, entering importantly through a special door in the rear, and I fell to describing them. Then I put down the hush and the sigh and the tension that stiffened the crowd as Henry Spencer appeared.

I described Henry. He was in freshly pressed gray flannel trousers and with a pair of white sneakers on his feet. He wore gray socks. His white shirt was opened at the neck and a red carnation was pinned on it. He was smiling, and his step was light as he walked between the little MacAuslins, who seemed dressed up as if for a wedding.

I stopped writing then and watched, as did ten other reporters—for Henry had reached the gallows' steps and was starting up. Wallace, next to me, his ten dollars at stake, was staring intently at Henry's feet.

Henry Spencer started up the steep, towering steps as if taking part in an athletic event. He went up swiftly, with the agility and eagerness of a man in a track meet. He reached the gallows' platform without missing a step or tripping once.

"Nobody wins," I said to Wallace.

"I should have figured on the hop," said Wallace. "A man full of hop can do anything."

I resumed my writing. There was much to describe now—the fumbling hands of the sheriff fixing the rope around Henry's neck and trying to get the noose's knot in the right place under the ear, and Henry's steady smile during these operations. And the sheriff's aides strapping Henry's arms to his sides and hanging the white robe on him that reached from his neck, covering the noose, to the gallows' floor and hid his feet. I kept watching, listening and writing.

"Have you anything to say, any last words?" the sheriff mumbled. "Yes," said Henry, "I have."

His voice was firm, and the glow in his face deepened. He looked in his white robe against the pure sky like a Crusader holding his head high after some royal blessing.

Henry's eyes looked down at the mob in the sun-drenched stockade. Then they looked up slowly at the green treetops around the gallows. Birds had started singing. Scarlet-winged tanagers flew through the little world of maple leaves. The summer morning rustled, glowed and capered around the gallows.

Then Henry's eyes left the bright earth and looked up at the shining sky. A look so deep and tender filled his face that all who watched held their breaths, and there was a long pause without sound or movement. Then Henry spoke.

"This is the happiest moment of my life," he said. The little Mac-Auslins standing beside him were looking upward, but their beam was less than Henry's. "I have never had a mother or father. Now I have a Father. He is up there waiting to receive me—waiting to welcome me home to a place beside His eternal spirit and His great kindness. My heart is full of happiness because I have made my peace with God. I have given Him the truth of my soul and truth unlocks the gates of Heaven. I can see my new home. Its streets are golden. Its houses are white and pure. I never knew any home before. Now I have one finer than any in the world—with its doors open and waiting for me and God holding out His hand to me. And my soul is clean and happy. And I give thanks to this wonderful thing. I give thanks to God. The Lord is my shepherd, I shall not want. He maketh me to lie down in green pastures—"

I wrote the psalm out as Henry's voice, throbbing with love, recited it high on the gallows. And I wrote also that the mob in the stockade stood bareheaded and weeping and that the busy chirping of the birds in the maple trees sounded like a music behind Henry's voice.

The psalm ended and Henry was silent. His head remained raised, but there were no more words. The silence, the pause, the waiting face with the hidden rope around its neck smiling up at the sky became unendurable. The time had come to kill Henry. The sheriff moved over to him and in a lame voice asked, "You finished talkin'?"

Spencer's eyes came down from the sky. He saw the sheriff raise his hand to signal the man who was to open the gallows' drop.

"No, wait!" Henry Spencer cried out. His voice had lost its sweetness. It was hoarse and full of panic. "I ain't through. I got something else to say! Something else!"

The white robe rose and fell as Henry panted with terror. He was going to die. He wanted to live longer, to look at the summer morning another few moments.

"I got this to say." He looked with horror at the sheriff's lifted hand. "Wait a minute!"

The sheriff stayed his signaling hand.

"What I got to say," said Henry, "is that I'm innocent of the murder of Allison Rexroat! I never killed her! It's a lie! You're all dirty bastards! You got no right! I never touched her—so help me God! I never harmed a hair on her head—so help me God!"

And with this mighty lie on his lips, Henry Spencer went through the suddenly opened gallows' drop. It banged down. The white-robed body fell through space and was arrested in mid-air. The figure started spinning, its head bent to the side, its mouth open and tongue sticking out. The sheriff had forgotten to put the white hood over the head, and the noose knot had been inexpertly placed. The neck had not broken, and we watched Spencer spin on the humming rope, his chest heave, his face blacken as he choked to death for twelve minutes.

Wallace nudged me as I started to describe the torment of the hanging man.

"I told you," he said, "like a rat! In order to live an extra forty-five seconds he spit in the eye of God and the truth and squealed out a lie for a finish."

"Yes," I said, "he gave up his chances of Heaven for another minute of life."

But my heart was heavy. I had heard this all once before in the county jail hanging room when a brother had cried out, "Hang Manow!" Was life so precious that it was dearer always than all honor and future blisses? Was God smaller than the birds in the maple trees and Heaven less than a gallows' platform with its smell of freshly cut lumber?

Jimmy, the telegraph operator, handed me a message. It had come over the wire for me. I read: "Keep story of hanging brief. Omit all gruesome details. The world has just gone to war." It was signed "Smith."

I sent a petulant reply to my editor: "Will try to make hanging as cheerful and optimistic as possible."

Spencer was still choking to death, but I stopped writing. It was August 14, 1914, and a bigger gibbet had risen in the world. The Kaiser's legions were goose-stepping through Belgium.

When I look back today on that hour, I see more than Henry Spencer dying in the sunlight on the end of a rope, with his immortal soul damned and Hell in his blackening face. A civilization hangs in the Wheaton Stockade.

I WRITE OF GERMANS—AGAIN

I HAVE ENJOYED recalling my past. But I come now to the most dramatic time I had yet lived, and my impulse is to avoid its telling. This was the time I spent in Germany as a foreign correspondent from December 1918 to early 1920.

The Germans are guilty of a special crime against my century which makes me a reluctant journeyer among then—even in retrospect. They slipped out of the human mask in 1938 and murdered six million Jewish men, women and children. The mask is back on them again. They look quite like other people now—like Frenchmen, Turks, Montenegrins—like voters, churchgoers, bipeds. Hollywood, which is run by Jews, is making movies about their pathos and their problems. The world, which is run by crime, greed and amnesia, considers bitterness against the Germans unsportsmanlike and eccentric. The Germans, says the world, looked at coolly, are no worse than anybody else.

Are they not a people full of troubles, says the world, and entitled to Christian mercy? Everybody makes a mistake, says the world, nations as well as individuals. The Germans made one. Let's give them a chance to recover by forgetting old grudges. Besides, the Germans are going to make fine, valorous allies for us against the Russians, who are monsters all and constitute a horrible threat to civilization. A beautiful thought, this—Germans, our noble allies! *Hoch, mein Kamerad!*

I am not surprised. I knew when the Germans were committing their crime, murdering the six million Jews, that they would neither be punished for it nor held in any way unworthy because they had done it. I wrote a book during the massacre, A *Guide for the Bedeviled*, in which I pointed this out.

My knowledge of the world's future indifference to the German as a mass murderer was based on the fact, to be noted during the extermination of the Jews of Europe, that it was not an unpopular crime. The governments of the United States, Great Britain and Russia, in fact, officially ignored its raging existence.

I remain today a critic of the Germans, for I have my own logic and my own knowledge of what has happened and is happening. I have no wish to see Germans exterminated in retaliation. I was, in fact, irritated by the postwar execution of the dozen or so German "villains" who were tried in Nuremberg. Their killing was a cover for a lack of conscience, and a pretense of indignation. Worse, it was a sly ruse to make continued indignation against the Germans unpopular. How bloodthirsty to remain angry at a people after they have "paid" for their crimes! How un-American!

There appears now and then a book to fumble with the tale of the ugliest crime in modern history. And there are survivors who speak falteringly of the black years of German slaughter, for they have learned that their anecdotes are irritating and oddly impolitic. And thus the matter rests. The Germans got by with their mass murder of the Jews. No obloquy dishonors their future. They took a physical battering in the war but they have emerged from it with their name mysteriously free of the blood of the six million Jews they butchered, and their hands mysteriously white, and no mark on their forehead. Neither is there shame in their souls, for there is no voice crying shame at them.

All this is not a victory over Jews or a proof that Jews are too unimportant to make their extermination a crime. It is a victory over human destiny and a proof that human values are less than political ones—in a politicalized world. It is a proof that human morality is a flaccid weapon, and a proof that aversion to evil and all the pious outcries against it are tenuous and spurious matters. It is a victory that has given a sad and fraudulent sound to the word "humanity" and will cause it to ring counterfeit for a long time.

I am reluctant to remember the Germans and relate my adventures among them, for it is less the past that comes into my head when I think of them than the present. They remind me of the darkest fact I have learned in my life—that the decency and sanity of the human race is a small mask.

THE BROTHERS—YESTERDAY AND TOMORROW

I HESITATE, also, to write of Europe, no less than Germany, because it is a topic so belabored today that the very name of that disintegrating continent is a synonym for wanton loquacity. Never has there been such a twaddle loosed as rises from everywhere to circle the European twilight, never has there been heard such a goose-headed babble of economic and political debate. Right or wrong, I dislike adding my voice to this haphazard stream of sound which is called history today, for it is a shallow and unclean stream, and whoever enters it must stand amid muck.

But as an individual betrayed and a human being flouted, I owe a protest to this evil history of my time. I have sounded it already in these pages. I sound it again, before packing my trunk for one of the prime breeding places of Evil, Berlin.

All the inhumanity I note today as history, I saw in Germany in 1918 to 1920, except that I saw it then with a youthful delight for the preposterous. Political zanies, quibblers and adventurers—mindless and paranoid—performed around me in that time in Germany as if I had blundered into a side-street Grand Guignol Playhouse. I had no notion that its humorless and macabre atmosphere was to become the air of the world. I considered the antics I witnessed purely German phenomena. And I reported them with the enthusiasm I had brought in Chicago to four-eleven fires, basement stabbings, love-nest suicides and all the other hi-de-ho doings outside the norm of living.

I have decided to write of the Germans because I have an eyewitness account to offer of a year of European history, the sort of history that always escapes the history books. It is a long-ago year, but the pattern of the chicanery that distinguished it is as modern as the portrait of the latest world figure on the cover of *Time* Magazine.

It is a pattern of events that has since bamboozled the world over and over again. Our present shouting up of false boogiemen, our cynical dealings with enemies, our secret betrayals of our friends are all in the tale which the Germany of 1919 dramatized for me.

I was a youth of twenty-four when I entered Germany. When I emerged from it my young cynicism had lost much of its grin.

BERLIN—1918

IT WAS SNOWING. The night was blue with moonlight. I registered at the Adlon Hotel desk. A frock-coated gentleman bowed, shook my hand stiffly and hoped I would be comfortable. He was the hotel manager. He was to remain in the lobby for a year while revolutions, bombings and street *Putsches* disturbed the avenue outside, and he was to continue bowing, shaking hands and hoping for the comfort of his guests. He was a "kind" German. Tears filled his eyes when he saw me. I was the first American in since the war. He had always felt very warm toward Americans. Had I had difficulty getting into Berlin? Not much. I had met a redheaded girl in an Amsterdam café full of correspondents drinking and waiting for visas to enter Berlin. I bought her several drinks. It developed that she was Count von Bernstorff's mistress and a woman of unique influence. She put me on a train an hour later, kissed me goodnight and asked me to be kind to Germany, and here I was.

A fine girl, said the Frock Coat. A true German soul, helpful, hospitable.

Would he mind giving me an interview?

An interview with a hotel manager! That would be of no value. Please, tomorrow he would introduce me to a general.

I had to write a story tonight. What one German thought of the German defeat, what his hopes were, what he thought was now going to happen. The whole world was eager to hear one German speak. And my first German straightened in his frock coat and spoke.

"*Ich stehe auf den Standpunkt*," he began. "Excuse me—you do not understand German."

"A little," I said. "That means you stand on the standpoint."

The Frock Coat corrected me politely.

"You say in America, 'I stand on the platform' or 'My platform is.' I stand on the platform that the Kaiser will return and restore peace and happiness to our country."

I ate blue-tinged potatoes, a bright bluefish and a piece of cheese for dinner. The cheese was a gift from the Frock Coat. The waiter whispered as he placed it in front of me, "This is a very important night."

"What's going on?"

"At ten o'clock Karl Liebknecht is going to attack the Kaiser's *Schloss.*"

"Who is Karl Liebknecht?"

"He is leader of the Spartacus Party."

"Bolsheviks?"

"No, Germans. It is a German revolution. *Ich stehe auf den Standpunkt*—You understand German a little?"

"Yes."

"The *Standpunkt* that Germany's only hope lies in rule by the proletariat."

"Are you going to be in the fight for the Kaiser's *Schloss?*"

"Yes. I get off duty at nine-thirty—in fifteen minutes."

"Mind if I go with you?"

"I'll submit your request to the Central Bureau. What are your politics in the United States?"

"I haven't any. I'm a reporter."

The waiter poured my coffee and said quietly, "Be on the corner by the *Tiergarten* in twenty minutes."

I was on the corner. Three marines in pancake hats with ribbons dangling from their brims greeted me. They were carrying carbines. They were blond, well fed and cheerful. I went with them in a taxi. The snowfall grew thicker. We came to a crowded street. Two hundred marines, armed like my hosts, and a few hundred civilians were standing on the sidewalk in front of the Kaiser's palace. I recognized the little balcony on which Emperor Wilhelm used to be photographed speaking to his people, or reviewing a parade of his invincible legions. The crowd on the sidewalk was silent. The falling snow seemed to muffle them.

A cheer sounded. I watched a black-eyed, quick-moving little man get out of another taxi and walk through the snow to the palace entrance. The tall, rosy-cheeked marines stood at salute as he passed.

At the entrance the little man turned and made an address. His voice was sharp and wild. He spoke too quickly for me to follow, but the phrase "*Ich stehe auf den Standpunkt*" echoed through the snowfall.

This little man was obviously Karl Liebknecht. I had heard of him only an hour ago (although among politically-minded folk he was world famous) but I watched him with excitement. He was my first glimpse of Brutus, Robespierre, Garibaldi, Bolivar, Washington— a leader of revolution, a stormer of kings' palaces.

He entered the *Schloss*. A hundred of the marines followed him. The civilians remained standing in the snowfall. There were no orders given. It looked like a revolution in which anybody could do what he wanted. Ignorant as an Igorot of politics, I was, nevertheless, a good reporter and, as on this night, nearly always a lucky one. I asked no questions and followed Liebknecht.

The tall palace rooms were deserted except for a bewildered elderly fellow in a leather apron. He stood in the corridor watching the invasion. With an eye to all the details of this "historical event" into which I had happily blundered, I stopped to ask him questions. He spoke English. Were there any defenders in the *Schloss*? Only himself. Was he a faithful servant of Kaiser Wilhelm? *Ja, Ja*—since a child. What was he—the janitor? Oh, no. He was the Kaiser's wood-supply man. His duties were, or rather, used to be, to keep the Kaiser supplied with short wooden logs. Each log had to be sawed three-quarters through and put on a pile. The Kaiser came out every morning, sometimes with photographers, sometimes without, and swung the ax with his one good arm and split each of the sawed logs with a single mighty blow.

I hurried on after Liebknecht and his marines, guided by Liebknecht's voice. He was making a speech.

I arrived in a large bedroom. The tall marines stood lining its walls. Their carbines were grounded, their faces raised in stiff attention. Liebknecht's sharp voice was crying out strange phrases in an emperor's bedroom. I recognized some of them—"freedom for the proletariat has come—workingmen are the new dynasty—"

The speech done, nobody moved or made a sound. Liebknecht started undressing himself. There was a fierce, lyric look in his black eyes. Liebknecht, the little workingman with a gift of gab, was undressing himself in the bedroom of a Hohenzollern emperor—and about to lie down in an emperor's bed!

After several minutes, Liebknecht stood barefoot in a suit of long winter underwear. Some of its buttons were missing and the flap seat was baggy from too much laundering. He picked up his bulging brief case and four large books. With these under his arms, he approached the Kaiser's bed. Someone turned off the ceiling lights. A lamp was left burning on the spindly-legged bedside table. The large room became shadowed. The white snow falling was like a face in all the windows.

The marines had stiffened. They stood watching the little man in the homely suit of long underwear approach the royal bed, and I felt that a queer sort of battle was going on—one of which I had never yet read in the histories of revolutions. Things in the shadows were giving battle to the hundred ribbon-capped marines standing against the walls. I could almost see the enemy—a line of kings from the bearded Barbarossa to the gimpy-armed earth shaker, Wilhelm; Black Eagles and Court Balls, and the gonfalons of ghostly guardsmen. Not only the walls and furniture were breathing these phantoms into existence, but they came even more vividly out of the stiffened faces of the revolution's shock troops—the mutineers of the Royal German Fleet.

Liebknecht, the People's Leader, placed his bulging brief case and four reference books on the small bedside table and crawled in between the cold royal sheets. The room had become heavily silent. I heard the royal bedsprings creak as Liebknecht stretched out his legs. Then, as he turned to reach for a book, there was a sudden sharp noise. The spindly-legged bedside table, an antique, had collapsed under the unaccustomed weight of revolutionary literature. The lamp hit the floor and one of its bulbs exploded. And the Soldiers of the Revolution fled. To a man, the hundred marines rushed in half panic out of the bedroom, routed by more ghosts than I had been able to imagine.

I began my first cable to the *Daily News* syndicate of seventy American newspapers with the information—"Kaiser Wilhelm returned to Berlin last night—"

A LIE, A SECRETARY AND
A BOMBING PLANE

LIEBKNECHT and his beribboned *Matrosen* exited the *Schloss* two days later and went on to capture other strongholds. My chief sources of information remained for several weeks the frock-coated manager of the Adlon, the waiter who had tipped me off about Liebknecht's great hour in the bedroom of the Hohenzollerns and a group of homosexual aviators whom I had met in an Officers' Club. These were elegant fellows, perfumed and monocled and usually full of heroin or cocaine. They made love to one another openly, kissing in the café booths and skipping off around two A.M. to a mansion owned by one of them. One or two women were usually in the party —wide-mouthed, dark-eyed nymphomaniacs with titles to their names but unroyal burns and cuts on their flanks. At times little girls of ten and eleven, recruited from the pavements of Friedrichstrasse, where they paraded after midnight with rouged faces and in shiny boots and in short baby dresses, were added to the mansion parties.

I attended nervously. Drugs and perversions were no lures for me, but the tales I heard were. I heard tales of the Kaiser's idiocy, of his amours, his atheism and his cowardice; tales of strange love between generals and lieutenants that had resulted in the losing of battles, of plots to kill off Ludendorff and his chancellor, von Bethmann-Hollweg, and of new plots to assassinate all the canaille who had seized power in Germany.

And there was one tale that came from all three of my "sources," the Frock Coat, the waiter and the hop-leaping pansy merrymakers. This was the tale of the Russian invasion that was coming. Trotsky, on a black horse, was going to lead a million Bolsheviks into Germany, burn it to the ground and sweep on with his Muscovite hordes into France. There was no army in Germany to stop this conquering Trotsky, and the Allies assembling in Versailles to dictate peace terms to Germany were going to bring ruin on themselves by disarming Germany. Germany was the one bulwark against the Oriental conquest of Europe.

Two things amazed me about this tale. One was the fact that the Germans who told it to me did not believe it. They told me the story wantonly and illogically like so many transparent con men making a pitch. They did not even pretend to believe it. They repeated it gleefully, hopefully and with a cynical shrewdness. It was their last weapon against the victorious Allies.

The other fact that amazed me was that everybody outside of Germany seemed to believe it. My chiefs of the *Daily News* Foreign News Syndicate—Charles Dennis in Chicago and Edgar Price Bell in London—believed it. They demanded stories of me about the German fear of the coming Russian invasion. The Allied statesmen in Paris appeared to believe it. And the American spies in Berlin, gathering data for Army Intelligence, sent in reports about Trotsky and his Bolsheviks ready to overrun the Continent.

I cabled no such stories as were demanded. I sent private messages to Dennis and Smith trying to convince them that the Bolshevik invasion was German propaganda. My knowledge was skimpy, my political insights almost nonexistent and my sources of information limited at the time to drug addicts, nymphomaniacs and a waiter. But the Lie about Russia was as obvious to spot as a sheiss house in a fog.

I wrote no such stories, but others did, and the Lie was to grow and become the obsession of the Allied World, injected into it partly with a German syringe and partly by Capitalism's own fear of Marxist boogiemen hovering over its Profits. It was this Lie, wantonly and cynically launched in Berlin, that was to bring back the German infantry, the German tank, the German *Luftwaffe* and finally the original war itself under a new name—World War II.

I disdained not only this Lie but I began also to suspect the German revolution. I hired an interpreter to help me out and read the daily papers for me. The interpreter was Count Erik von Mathis. He had called on me offering to sell me an ivory chess set, three race horses and a Rhineland castle. I needed none of these things, I told the count, but what I would like to buy was an airplane. There were no railroad trains running to speak of and I would be unable to cover Germany properly unless I secured myself some personal means of travel.

Von Mathis brought me two visitors the next day who were in later years to become famous as Marshal Goering's assistants—Ernst Udet and Franz Knerr. After Richthofen, they were the second and third ranking air heroes of Germany. They appeared in uniforms covered with medals. Udet offered to get me an airplane but he wanted fifty thousand dollars cash in advance. Knerr was more reasonable. He was willing to steal his old bombing plane from the army hangars and permit me to pay for it later. I would, however, have to supply food and lodging for him and his mechanician. This was easy. I called the Frock Coat and had him give War Ace Knerr and his aide a suite of rooms adjoining mine.

"You can eat at the hotel and sign the checks," I told Knerr. I cabled Mr. Dennis that night a request for fifty thousand dollars for the purchase of a bombing plane, explaining how invaluable it would be to my work. An answer came ordering me under no circumstances to use any sort of plane for story coverage, as the *Daily News* did not want to be held responsible for any accidents that might befall me.

But Mr. Dennis, despite being a world-thinker, righteous editorial writer and passionate grammarian, was not without a touch of newspaper larceny in his soul. He never questioned in the year that followed my weekly mysterious expense account item—"For upkeep Franz Knerr, etc., $200."

Knerr stole the bombing plane a few days after our first conference and ferried me through the skies during the rest of my stay in Germany. I felt grateful to Count Erik and hired him as a man who could get things done.

REVOLUTION IN A TEAPOT

VON MATHIS wore a monocle, carried a silver-handled trick cane with a thin sword in it and was a fierce anti-Royalist. He had joined the proletarian revolution, monocle, sword cane, title and all. He was slightly built, with a thin face and reddish hair, smelled of cologne but was not a homosexual. Nor was Knerr, a fact I mention for its novelty.

Count Erik kept me informed of the revolution's victories. Garrisons, government buildings, arsenals and cities were falling hourly into its hands. There had never been such a successful revolution, said his lordship, even in Paris in 1793. It was a clean sweep. Socialism was triumphant everywhere, and Germany belonged hook, line and sinker to the masses.

I remembered the lost battle of the Kaiser's bedroom and, shaking loose from the Carlylian von Mathis, went prowling on my own.

I met another count. He was sitting alone and pensive in the bar-room of the Hotel Esplanade, wearing a leather huntsman's jacket, striped pants, a pair of American moccasins and an attractive orange silk muffler. He introduced himself to me in English as Count Russworm von Gleichen. He was a grandson of the poet Schiller and wrote books himself. He was a sad, dark, handsome young man with a soulful face, married and the father of two children. I dined the next day at his fine home, bringing along loaves of white bread, cans of American beef and a dozen bars of chocolate. I had filched these items from the American Military Commission Headquarters.

My new count was sad about the revolution. It was a mistake, he said. No good would come of it.

"What *Standpunkt* do you stand for?" I asked. "The Royalist one?"

"No," he smiled, "the *Standpunkt* of truth."

He was not opposed to the revolution. He was opposed only to the fact that there was no revolution.

"It is a farce," he said, "and farces are bad for a nation—and for the world."

Von Gleichen introduced me to two of his friends.

"You will understand this farce better," said von Gleichen on our way to the Esplanade Hotel, "if you meet some of its authors. My friends are fine Germans but they no longer live in reality. They live in propaganda."

The two friends were Dr. Fritz von Berg, head of the Anti-Bolshevik League of Germany, and General von Hoffmann. Von Berg was highly respected by the Ebert-Noske government. He busied himself, with his many cohorts, slapping up enormous posters on the brick walls of Berlin. The posters were anti-Bolshevik propaganda. They were covered with boldly drawn, highly colored pictures. One of the most interesting of the posters showed a huge and maddened gorilla holding an infant by one leg, as he hungrily devoured its arm. The infant's blood ran from the gorilla's mouth. The poster carried the information in large, blood-dripping letters, "The Spirit of Bolshevism." I was surprised to find the leader of this fearsome anti-Bolshevik propaganda a bland and smiling man.

I was more interested, however, in von Gleichen's other friend—the tall, portly and uniformed General von Hoffmann. Von Hoffmann had been Generalissimo Ludendorff's Chief of Staff on the Eastern front during the last year of the war. He had been the general who had signed the separate German peace treaty with the Russians at Brest Litovsk.

A bottle of cognac was produced. Von Gleichen had brought me here to "see through" the farce of German propaganda. Instead, I was bowled over by the propaganda—and sat listening to the "best" story I had yet come upon as a foreign correspondent.

It was the spring of 1918, the general began his tale. Ludendorff was preparing for the offensive against the Allied armies of the West. It was the drive that was to be Germany's last bid for victory. Ludendorff had ordered von Hoffmann, at the long-dormant Eastern Front, to sign a peace with the Russians. He needed the seventy-five German divisions under von Hoffmann to be moved into vital battle in the West.

Von Hoffmann had answered, "Russia is in chaos. There are a number of governments and it is difficult at this hour to select the most important one."

Ludendorff had replied immediately, "Sign peace with any Russian who can write his name."

General von Hoffmann had signed the peace pact at Brest Litovsk with a Russian named Leon Trotsky who could not only write his name but was eager to yield to all the German requirements.

The Prussian general scowled as he talked. The scar on his cheek reddened.

"We were all fools," he said, "and we still are."

I fancied he was brooding about the lost war and said politely, "The Germans were outnumbered. And with the Americans joining against them, they had no chance."

"The Americans did not defeat us," said von Hoffmann, "nor the French or British."

"Who defeated you, then?" I asked.

"The Russians," von Hoffmann answered promptly. It was an odd answer. It made not only the front pages of the next day but entered the history books. The word of von Hoffmann was expert testimony. He had been with the mighty von Hindenburg in front of the Tannenberg Marshes. He had helped wipe out the valorous, stoical and almost weaponless armies of the Czar. His artillery had filled the eastern bogs with a half-million Russian corpses. He had become, next to von Hindenburg, the German hero who had vanquished the Muscovite Colossus. These facts in my head bewildered me.

"In what way did the Russians win the war?" I asked him.

"When I received my orders from Ludendorff," said von Hoffmann, "we had more than a million troops on the Eastern Front. They were well fed, well equipped and victorious. They had rested in the trenches for six months with the exhausted Russian divisions in front of them. Hardly a shot had been fired. The Russians had neither food nor munitions. They lay facing us awaiting only extermination. We let them live. We wasted no shells on them. The shells were needed in the West. And after six months we signed peace with them, with this man Trotsky. Our plan was to move thirty divisions immediately into the Western Offensive. We were unable to move a single regiment. In the six months that our men had stood on guard over the exhausted Russians there had been constant fraternization. The Russians had been talking to them for six months, singing songs and drinking together. We considered the fraternization harmless, and it was saving us shells.

"We found out suddenly, after signing the peace, that our men were no longer German soldiers. They were lunatic Revolutionists. They did not believe in the Fatherland. They believed in something else—a world brotherhood or some such nonsense. They had become infected by the Russians. We started weeding out the worst of them. But there were too many. There were hundreds of thousands. We held our own patriotic rallies. We addressed our Russian-rotted troops. They argued back! It was dangerous to move these traitors to the Western Front. They would be certain to infect our thinned and suffering but ever-loyal western divisions. Ludendorff's heart broke. He ordered a reorganization of my shameful divisions. A reshuffling of a million men and officers takes time. We courtmartialed thousands. Nothing helped. The Russian lunacy had ruined our German strength, as the Allied guns had never been able to do. We sent no soldiers to the Western Front.

"Ludendorff made his last drive without my once fine divisions. They would have won the war for us had we been able to use them. Their absence from the Western Front cost us the victory. It is therefore I tell you that the Russians won the war for the Allies, and this you may publish as my statement."

Von Berg tried to continue the interview with some information about the present activities of the Spirit of Bolshevism. He offered me another drink, which I swallowed hastily, eager to be on my way with my big story. I could think only of Mr. Dennis and his gratitude and excitement.

I hurried to my typewriter in the Adlon, irritated by my moody shadow, von Gleichen. He was not to be shaken off. In my room he demanded preposterously that I kill the story.

"Don't you see," he said, "this is what we have been talking about for a week. The Lie of the Russian menace. I brought you to von Hoffmann to show you one of the places where the Lie is born. There was a little truth in his story. A few pennies' worth. Yes, there was a little trouble with Russian ideas. But nothing so big, so clear. There were a hundred other bigger reasons why the Eastern Front troops could not be moved. Believe me!"

My friend, von Gleichen, grew eloquent. He spoke of the complex German soul, greatness brought to nothing; of chauvinism and despair plotting a new nationalism.

"You have understood the situation so far," he said. "I will prove to you that you have been right."

I listened impatiently. The facts that von Hoffmann had given me were aching to jump from my fingers to the typewriter. My "lead" was in my mind and all the fine paragraphs of my scoop were already assembled and waiting to follow.

"I can't kill the biggest story I've run into in Berlin," I said.

"It is not a story," von Gleichen pleaded. "It is part of the machinery of the Lie. There was no Russian menace at Brest Litovsk. There is no Russian menace in Berlin. There is no Marxist menace. There is no German revolution. My dear American friend, I will give you a bigger, truer story than von Hoffmann. And I speak the truth. One month ago General Ludendorff issued a General Staff order to all the garrisons of the Reich and all its officers and police chiefs. Here is a copy of that order."

He handed me a telegram which he carried in his pocket. It read, translated, "To All Loyal German Officers and Officials. Great confusion is ahead of us. A new government is appearing in Germany. I order that no matter what happens there must be no shooting. Yield all military posts and government buildings without bloodshed. Ludendorff."

"That's another story," I said.

"No, the same one!" von Gleichen went on a little hysterically. "Ludendorff and the General Staff considered it necessary to have a revolution. They believed the Allies would offer better peace terms to a Socialist Germany. It was for this reason Ludendorff persuaded the Kaiser to flee to Holland. Von Hindenburg wanted the Kaiser and his sons to join him in the front lines and fight and, if necessary, die in the last battle as soldiers. But Ludendorff's ideas won.

"They were Machiavellian but brilliant. Look how brilliant! They are taking you in now! The revolution you are witnessing could still be crushed in a day by our German military. Our military was never routed by the Allies. It is still loyal and intact. It obeys the General Staff."

"I believe you," I said, "and it's a big story and I'll write it. They're encouraging a fire. And today for the first time I believe that there's a fire there. General von Hoffmann convinced me."

"No," said von Gleichen sadly. "No fire. They are fooling the world. But it is worse than that. They are playing with a people's soul."

Alas, von Gleichen. He had imagined he had flushed a fellow philosopher, and a soul, like his own, devoted only to truth. Truth and great insights were one thing, a big story was another. So it is to newspapermen, and so it was to me when I was one of them. I would as soon have thought of not sending in my expense account as of not sending in this startling interview for the world's front pages given me by General von Hoffmann.

But the congratulations I received from the home office failed to quiet the voice of von Gleichen in me and my own growing knowledge of the truth. I saw, in the midst of the praises arrived from Chicago and London, that I had helped the German Military Staff in its plan to restore the old German order. And I became a one-man propaganda front against that plan. It was my first emergence as a political thinker, and I felt somewhat lonely. Outside of von Gleichen, it seemed I had no one on my side in the whole world.

I confronted my secretary and political guide, Count von Mathis, with von Gleichen's tidings.

"But of course, it is true," von Mathis said. "The General Staff has planned it all. But they have underestimated the freedom-loving soul of the German people. I assure you the revolution will succeed anyway."

I demanded that he help me get proofs of the manufactured revolution. We dined with Spartacists, Capitalists, Generals, Firebrands and Important Homosexuals. Proof poured in.

I cabled these matters to Chicago, including Ludendorff's Order to the Officers of the Reich. My cabled stories were spiked. Mr. Dennis wired me, "Your surmises both wild dangerous to President Wilson's work for just peace. Confine yourself solid political facts."

I cabled back, "All my information solid not surmise."

A few days later a new correspondent arrived from our London office. He was a dashing, demobilized flying ace named Gordon Stiles. He informed me at once that he had been sent to replace me. He told me, also, that he had a silver plate in his head as a result of a skirmish with von Richthofen in the air, and that he hated all Germans and was going to treat them severely.

At two A.M. von Mathis telephoned me that my successor, Gordon Stiles, had barricaded himself behind two couches in the lobby of the Kaiserhof Hotel and was trying to pick off the hotel staff and guests with a pair of blazing pistols. I arrived at the Kaiserhof ahead of the police and had a talk with Stiles behind his couches. He agreed to leave Berlin and press on to Russia, whose inhabitants he hated even more. At four A.M. Stiles drove off in a rented taxi for the Russian border. I remained head of the *Daily News* Foreign Staff in Berlin. Some five years later Stiles fired a bullet into his silver-plated head and died in Greenwich Village, New York.

STANDPUNKT CHASER

Standpunkts bombinated around me like strings of firecrackers. Trotsky on his black horse was now hourly expected with his million ravening Bolsheviks—not by me but by a Lie that seemed to be replacing the sanity of Europe. Every day that dawned was like a presidential pre-election eve at home. Nobody seemed to have any personal business or personal thoughts. All was politics, revolution, antirevolution. Every conversation was a political plot. Even the pansies, nymphomaniacs and cocaine addicts, the streetwalkers in

Friedrichstrasse, the sadists in the Kurfürstendam mansions, the battered droshky drivers, the beggars in Alexanderplatz—all I met had at me with *Standpunkts*.

I wrote to Smith, "Germany is having a nervous breakdown. There is nothing sane to report."

A revolution had overturned the city of Düsseldorf, and the Spartacists were reigning in it. A former streetcar conductor named Eichhorn occupied the Burgomeister's office as Dictator of the Soviets of Düsseldorf. Knerr flew me to the outskirts of the town, and I walked with him and von Mathis through the lines of Spartacist troops protecting the city. Nobody fired at us, and Dictator Eichhorn received us eagerly. He wanted the world to know that he had boosted the wages of the streetcar conductors of Düsseldorf one hundred per cent. And that all other workingmen were going to receive similar increases in pay.

"Where is the money coming from for these wage boosts?" I asked.

"From the exchequer of the city of Düsseldorf—and from the banks," said Herr Eichhorn.

"But after you use up the money in the exchequer and the banks, what then?" I asked. "How are you going to continue paying everybody double wages?"

Dictator Eichhorn was not floored by my question.

"By the time the money is used up," he beamed at me, "I will no longer be dictator."

I flew to Stettin and interviewed the Kaiser's war chancellor, von Bethmann-Hollweg.

"All is lost," he told me, "art, nobility, beauty, all that was fine in Germany is destroyed."

He sat at a grand piano and moodily played me a famous composition that bore his name as composer—"The Bethmann-Hollweg March." It had been ghost-written by the pianist Josef Hofmann, whom the chancellor had employed during the war to ghost-compose music for him, and whom I had put on the *Daily News* payroll to play piano for me and teach me chess.

We flew to Kattowitz in Silesia near the Russian border. The revolution was about to establish some more German Soviets there. The shooting had started when we arrived. We walked through the embattled mining town and came upon a troop of marines. They were standing at ease in a side street, their carbines grounded. They were the same type of rosy-cheeked, blondheaded, ribbon-capped gladiators I had seen with Liebknecht.

"What side are you on?" I asked their leader. He was eating an apple. He answered in English.

"We don't know yet. We're waiting to see which side starts winning. That's the side we'll join. We are an independent unit."

Knerr and Braun returned to our plane to stand guard. Von Mathis and I went into a basement restaurant to get out of the way of the shooting. An American was having an early lunch at one of the tables. He was a tall, dark-haired man with an Abraham Lincoln look to him.

"I'm Bob Minor," he introduced himself. I knew who he was, a talented anti-Capitalist cartoonist who had worked on the New York World and then moved on to more radical publications.

"I heard you were in Russia," I said.

"I was," said Minor. "And I've just managed to get out with my ass intact."

"I thought you were a Radical," I said.

"I am," said Minor. "But Russia is no place for Radicals. There are too many of them there. They're all shooting and stabbing each other. Even Emma Goldman can't stand it. If you're heading for Russia, take my advice and stay out. The whole place has gone crazy."

"So has Germany," I said.

"No," said Minor. "I know the Germans. They are a cool, reticent people."

"You're mad," I said.

"Don't argue with me," Minor grinned. "I know the Russians. And I tell you that the Germans are a fine, sane people—by comparison."

I interviewed Generalissimo Ludendorff in his Berlin apartment. The interview was brief, and during most of it I kept staring at von Mathis. My fanatic proletarian secretary was stuck in the doorway and seemed unable to enter the room. He stood sway-backed, his head raised and his hand held stiffly to his brow in a salute.

"Come on in and translate for me," I ordered him. But the ever-obliging von Mathis failed to hear me. He remained like a man paralyzed in the doorway.

Ludendorff sat behind a desk. He was a round-faced, watery-eyed man and looked like a heavier H. L. Mencken. He spoke a single English sentence to me.

"If these are President Wilson's Fourteen Points," he said slapping a piece of paper, "then America can go to hell."

He stood up and added sharply, "That's all!"

Von Mathis executed a sort of military pirouette and marched into the hallway. I asked a number of questions, received no answers from the glowering pale blue eyes—and followed von Mathis, civilian fashion.

I interviewed Admiral von Tirpitz, Commander of the German Royal Navy, also in a Berlin apartment. The admiral was in uniform. His white forked beard fascinated me. He had a finely modeled head and an imperious eye. I was thrilled to be in the presence of the mighty sea warrior who had won and lost an epic victory in the Battle of Jutland. I began with questions about the battle. The admiral waited until I ran down and then spoke in an irritated voice.

"I am not going to answer any questions," he said in English. "I have written my memoirs. I just finished them last week. All the answers to all the questions about Germany's sea power are in my book. I hereby offer it for sale to you for fifty thousand dollars, payable in United States currency."

"I'll notify my office and advise them to buy your memoirs," I said. "In the meantime—if you could tell me—"

"No meantime," the admiral said firmly. "I do not speak a word. Only my memoirs will speak—when you have bought them."

I interviewed Philipp Scheidemann, the Premier of the new Socialist German Republic. Mine was the first interview Scheidemann gave after the war. Mr. Bell was greatly disillusioned with my copy and again demanded my removal. I had written a long description of Scheidemann sitting in Bismarck's chair in the Wilhelmstrasse Chancellery, comparing him to Buffalo Bill. He had the same dandyish goatee and mustachio. I had been trained in Chicago (by myself, possibly) to make hay out of any hirsute or sartorial oddities offered by politicians I interviewed. The evasive Scheidemann, refusing to answer my questions about the German revolution, refusing to discuss the flock of Junker officers who were taking over the Socialist Army—chief among them the pre-Hitlerian Hitler, General

Noske—seemed fair game to me. I reported his whiskers, his evasions, his con-man airs and the frowning face of Bismarck in a gold frame over his swivel chair. I omitted informing the world about his *Standpunkt*'s.

This time I was packed and ready to leave when a cable reinstating me as head of the Berlin office arrived from Mr. Dennis. I decided to reward my kindly chief and his faith in me by getting an interview with Fritz Ebert, President of the German Republic. Herr Ebert had refused to talk to any foreign newspapermen.

"I know him slightly," von Mathis explained. "He used to be a harness maker and is very shy. He doesn't speak English. He's a fairly decent fellow, despite the things Noske is doing in his name. A real Socialist."

"Is he very poor?" I asked.

"He hasn't a kopeck to his name," said von Mathis.

"Can you get to him personally?"

"Yes."

"Go ahead, then," I said, "and offer him five hundred dollars in American money as a bribe." I turned over my last American currency to Count Erik. "Tell him it's his if he'll give me an interview."

Four days later I interviewed Herr Ebert. He was dark-haired, red-cheeked, plump and pear-shaped.

Von Mathis translated his *Standpunkt*'s as he read them off to me from a sheet of paper. I was permitted no questions. In thirty minutes I was back in the Adlon at my typewriter. Despite editor Smith's warnings against my "irresponsible" attitudes, I considered the fact that the new president of Germany had accepted a five-hundred-dollar bribe a newsworthy matter. I made it the lead of my story.

The next day a group of American and English correspondents cornered me in the Adlon bar. A London reporter named Rennick, who was baldheaded and full of high-class journalism, informed me that I had violated all civilized newspaper ethics in my story about Ebert and that I was being dropped from the Berlin Foreign Correspondents' Club.

I had not been aware of any such club, but the news, nevertheless, depressed me. But I had an unexpected cohort. Sitting with me was Duffy's great friend, Richard Henry Little of the Chicago *Tribune*, a veritable Knight of Journalism, with China, Russia, Siberia, Africa, the Philippines all in his past as date lines.

"Consider me also no longer a member of your pusillanimous organization," said Dick Little. "I herewith hand in my official insignia."

And my friend from Chicago sketched a picture of a braying jackass on a piece of copy paper, arose and tendered the drawing to Mr. Rennick with a bow.

A SWORD FOR A CORPSE

THE ALLIED PAPERS continued to discuss the "tragic" collapse of Germany. I remember one pensive headline, "A Great Nation Dies."

I stood by and watched the lamented "corpse" get to its feet and start shining its sword buckles and polishing its military boots. The old German militarism against which most of the outside world had victoriously hurled its manhood was marching furtively again, planning again and muttering hope and obedience into the Teutonic ear. Behind the harmless mask of the new German Socialist Republic, the great munitions factories in Spandau, Essen and Munich were sparking again. The goose-stepping legions were being reforged.

I was no longer "alone." The plot peeped out, and a great many Germans spotted it and set up an outcry. The Allied statesmen and Allied press ignored this outcry and supported the Ebert-Noske government, put together by churchgoers and trade-unionists as it seemed. All the disasters the Allies were to meet in the next twenty years were the grim offspring of this first stupidity.

Looking on Germany in 1919, the Allies beheld a plump little burgher in silver-rimmed spectacles and a shabby coat trying to open a new kind of Socialist state. And they saw only one boogieman— Russia.

The Allied peacemakers in Versailles were stern with Germany on paper. They made staggering demands for indemnities.

The Germans were never to pay these sums. Instead they started almost immediately rebuilding their country with private capital that flowed in from England and America. But the talk of huge fines and horrible indemnities to be paid had given the Teutons a cause.

The cause was enough for the German General Staff. Craftily and brilliantly it worked on the rebuilding of the German army. And the harmless Ebert and the palavery Scheidemann stood in front of the secretly growing arsenals. With them stood all the churchgoers and trade-union members. And all pleaded with the Allies to be allowed to stamp out the fearful Bolshevism in Germany, to be allowed to stay in power as an amiable and Christian state. For this a "Police Army" was needed. Otherwise Germany would go Red, despite all the fine character of its churchgoers and trade-unionists. And the "Police Army" grew.

What the Germans did in 1919 as humble-pie-eating Socialists was done sincerely by a handful of them. This handful even died doing it. But the great body of Germans participated in these humble-pie days because they were ordered to do it. Their gift for obedience made them idealists for a time. They had no interest in the ideals waved over their heads. Their interest lay in obeying. The General Military Staff, command barker for the German soul, was busy preparing other orders to be obeyed. The General Staff was not disturbed by the new German "anti-military idealism." It knew the German soul too well. It knew that this soul of Germany was marking time in silver-rimmed glasses and a burgher's coat. It was waiting for a strong whip to crack over it and give it something more interesting to serve than goodness and idealism.

I was present at none of the secret meetings of the General Staff but I can imagine its debates. They centered on Ludendorff's faith in the slavishness of the German soul. There was nothing to worry about. When the time came, the Germans would show the sort of leaders they really loved—not the comic and shabby puppets like Ebert and Scheidemann, but fine snorting fellows in shining boots like von Hoffmann and all the Junker officers.

Meanwhile the comic puppets continued to reign, either aware or unaware of the strings attached to their heads.

And there were men in Germany like the cultured von Gleichen. Their civilized hearts winced at the spectacle of a people being used, using themselves and whimpering in their dark corner like a dog waiting for its master's return.

THE PLOT GOOSE-STEPS

THERE WERE two German groups who fought against the farce of 1919 Germany. One was the Communists, a minority with hardly enough membership to get out a single newspaper. The other group was the Independent Socialist Party, which believed honestly in the possibility of a German democracy.

The most notable of these honorable men was Hugo Haase, leader of the Independent Socialist Party. He was to be assassinated a few years later on the Reichstag's steps, as were thousands of Germans in whom sanity was stronger than servility. The assassinations, however, did not wait for the coming of Hitler. They had already begun. Liebknecht had been polished off. The fiery Rosa Luxemburg had been shot and killed while "escaping from her captors." Scores of other Radical leaders were being done to death in the prisons of the new Socialist Republic.

But new leaders of revolt appeared to expose the truth of the Junker renaissance taking place. They announced as if gifted with second sight that Germany was being made ready for another World War. Every argument they spoke was to be proven accurate within fifteen years. Every prophecy they voiced was to come true.

"The Junker army is being restored." Haase spoke in the Reichstag, the same words that were later to bring death to him on its steps. "We are not building a new Democratic Germany. We are restoring the old Germany and helping the officer class lead us into disaster again."

The Spartacus-Communists, whose leaders in Prussia did not live long enough to achieve prominence, were protesting with guns.

In March of 1919, a revolution appeared in Berlin. Having constantly reported that the revolution was a fake invented by Ludendorff and his co-plotters, I felt unhorsed.

The revolution was there. I visited it in Alexanderplatz and interviewed it behind its barricades. Nine thousand men, women and boys, armed and full of fierce proletarian vows, were bivouacked in and around the Platz. They had captured the *Polizeipräsidium*. They sent an airplane into the sky to bombard Wilhelmstrasse. Nine thousand grim faces waited behind barricades to do or die for the revolution.

The battle that routed the do-or-die Spartacists from Alexander-platz was the weirdest of which I know. Dick Little, who observed it with me from behind a cathedral pillar, had seen scores of battles, including the almost unbelievable sinking of the Russian fleet by the Japanese at Port Arthur. He watched this one goggle-eyed and assured me that no battle like it had ever come to his notice before.

We stood together watching the enemies facing each other across a two-block no man's land. On one side were the nine thousand Spartacists. The other side consisted of four hundred German officers, most of them overweight and over sixty. The four hundred were in full uniform. They had marched down Unter den Linden in the morning. General von Hoffmann and Admiral von Tirpitz were among them. There were a dozen other generals and admirals. The rest of the four hundred were colonels, majors and captains.

The Spartacist army of German workers stared at the glittering officer ranks drawn up before them. They fired a few volleys. No officer was hit. The fire was not returned. Walking boldly into the Spartacists' midst, twenty-five generals, admirals and colonels demanded that the rebels surrender in the name of the Fatherland's honor.

And, as the hundred marines had bolted before the ghosts in the Kaiser's bedroom, the nine thousand embattled German Revolutionists laid down their arms before these other ghosts of German grandeur—the Prussian officer class. No guns had been fired at the Revolutionists, but a whip had cracked.

THE WHITE TERROR

THREE WEEKS LATER I dropped into the Adlon bar for a drink before going to bed. It was two A.M. The bar was empty save for Heinrich, the bartender, and a lone drinker. A young German in an infantry lieutenant's uniform was propped over the bar, emptying a bottle of cognac. He gulped down glass after glass. I had never seen a German drink in this fashion, and out of curiosity I asked the strange drinker to join me. At the sound of my voice, he burst into tears and collapsed. I helped him up to my room, doused him with cold water, fed him black coffee and before long he had told me the story of the White Terror.

Two hours ago he had been in command of a machine-gun crew in the yard of Moabit Prison near by. Between ten and twelve o'clock his machine gun had assisted in the killing of two thousand men, women and boys. The victims were Germans who had been rounded up after the Spartacus surrender in Alexanderplatz. They had not fired a shot but they had made the gesture of revolution. They had, accordingly, been court-martialed for treason by Socialist army officers, and their mass execution ordered by the General Staff —and officially signed by the shy ex-harness-maker Ebert, and the palavery and harmless Scheidemann.

My lieutenant described the Moabit massacre. Units of twenty-five men, women and boys chained to one another were marched across the prison yard. Three machine guns opened fire on them and kept up the firing until the bodies had stopped moving.

"It is still going on," he wept. "Thank God, they let me go after an hour."

I hurried off to Moabit Prison and was refused admission. Hysterical guards ordered me from the gate. I climbed a tree a block away and sat in its branches with a field glass listening to machine guns still going in the prison yard. It was dark, but I could see an awful movement of dying, of chained human masses falling before gun fire; and I heard shooting and wailing.

My story of Germany's White Terror, of the Socialist government's murder of the two thousand men, women and boys in the Moabit Prison yard was printed the next day in London and Paris, as well as in the United States. At four in the afternoon, a group of soldiers and a government official named Stengel knocked on my door in the Adlon. Herr Stengel was one of Count von Rantzau's war department secretaries. He informed me that I was officially expelled from Germany. I had until midnight to clear out.

I asked on what charges I was being kicked out.

"For reporting lies," said Herr Stengel.

"Does the government deny that it executed two thousand political prisoners last night, several hundred of them women?" I asked.

"That is a dirty propaganda lie," Herr Stengel answered violently. "Our country does not want newspaper liars blackening its name. If you are in Germany after midnight you will be arrested."

Herr Stengel and his soldiers marched off down the Adlon corridor. But I did not leave Germany for another year.

A GERMAN HERO

I WRITE the above caption without sarcasm, for the hero of the story I have to tell was a genuine man of honor.

The Germans have always been capable of group heroism. Put a hundred, a thousand or a million of them together and a spirit is forged among them. They fight well and die well—in clusters.

But of that valor of the mind which a man must feel by himself out of his own righteousness, the Germans are less capable than other people. Fewer of such lone men of honor are to be found among the Germans than among other nationals. But those that do come to bloom are, by reason of the difficulty and rarity of such blooming, of the finest of heroes.

I met a number of such fearless and honorable souls in Germany, of the quality if not the genius of Thomas Mann. I knew three of them well, the aristocrat von Gleichen, the brilliant painter and caricaturist George Grosz and the stocky man from the factories of Spandau—Hugo Haase.

It was to Hugo Haase I went after the ordered expulsion. His broad face listened to me without expression. I had small respect for politicians, even for such as might help me. But there was a quality to Haase that had touched me at our first interview. Party leader though he was, he had seemed the opposite of a politician— a philosopher in pain, without actorish dream of applause.

He said to me now, "Instead of leaving Germany, would you care to come with me to Weimar next Tuesday? I will hide you until we leave. In Weimar I shall be able to straighten out your situation."

I arrived in Weimar Tuesday noon alone. Deep snow was on the ground and on the cozy old houses that lined the friendly crooked little streets. And a great stir was in the air, a great massing of fedoras, mufflers and mustachios on corners and in *Weinstuben*. The first Peoples' National Assembly in the annals of Germany was to open in the Stadt's Theater after lunch. Such an assembly had opened in Philadelphia in 1776 and in Paris in 1794. Now the ancient city of Weimar, archaic and pretty as a museum piece, was to witness the birth of a new freedom in the world.

I mused as I walked the snowy streets:

You say there is no new Germany, no new Freedom—that all is fake and cynicism? Then look at these bustling figures in their seedy overcoats on this 1919 winter's day in Weimar. Frostbitten faces glowing with hope, a little pompous, for the eyes of the world are on them. Besides which, history is always a little pompous. And these men with icicles stiffening their whiskers are walking not through snowy streets but in history pages. All the *Standpunkt*'s from all the villages and cities of Germany wait for three o'clock. At three o'clock a bell will toll, as once in the belfry of Faneuil Hall, and generations to come will look back on this hour and say, Look at that noble little scene. There in Weimar not only Goethe, but German liberty and humanitarianism were born. At three o'clock.

The church bell tolled. It was three o'clock and the Stadt's Theater was jammed. Four hundred Peoples' Delegates sat in chairs on the large stage. The other thousands of delegates filled the auditorium. There was no room for an audience. Everybody in the theater had to be a history maker to get a seat.

I sat with the press in the first row of the balcony, cursing my ignorance of the German language. A new constitution was to be drawn up, laws of the new freedom were to be voted into existence. An event, pregnant and immortal as the one Carlyle described in his great book *The French Revolution*—the launching under Marat and Robespierre of the National Assembly—was to happen before me, and I would understand only one historical word out of ten that were uttered.

Seven history makers had thundered from the stage by four-thirty, waved their arms in fearless and dramatic gestures, stood the house on its feet with cheers, and I knew less of what was going on than a stowaway in a boiler room. The eighth history maker who walked out of the wings and took his place, stage front center, was Hugo Haase. A loud applause greeted him, for all was love of liberty in this Stadt's Theater, and party lines did not dictate cheers. A new Fatherland was being forged by many elements. Diverse though the elements were, they were all admirable and on this day all eager to admire one another.

My ignorance of the German language seemed to leave me as Haase spoke. Oddly, I understood almost everything he said. He spoke slowly, without oratorical flourishes. He spoke of the crime that was being committed against the new German dream of liberty.

He recited calmly the facts of the German General Staff's plot to take over the new Socialist government through the control of its army. He told the facts of the Ebert-Scheidemann government's surrender to this plot. He said that German Socialism was not a reality but a mask behind which the nation played beggar for better peace terms from the Allies.

There were mutterings in the theater. Hisses and cries of "Traitor!" began to sound. The history makers fidgeted and scowled. This stocky man on the stage was robbing them of their roles as history makers and calling them clowns and cat's-paws. Such a thing should not be permitted, at such a place, after a bell had tolled and men had cheered and wept with the joy of freedom in their hearts.

Abruptly, the stocky man began to tell the story of the mass murder in the yard of Moabit Prison a week ago. The crime had been boldly denied by the government. It was unthinkable, the government's spokesmen had pronounced, that German Socialists should kill two thousand Germans who had not been tried openly by any jury! It was an Allied propaganda plot to crush Germany further, to keep food out of its kitchens!

The history makers stood on their feet and began to shout. The traitor must be stopped! Arrested! Removed! And above the bellowing and rage of his audience, Haase's voice continued to sound. Only the fine acoustics of the Stadt's Theater were on his side— but they were ally enough. His words remained ringingly audible. The mass murder had been done! Here were the *names* of the German men, women and boys who had been executed without trial, shot down in chains and shoveled into the ground like refuse. The audience roared and the names of the dead came whipping from the stage. A hundred names, five hundred names, Haase kept reading them from the paper in his hands relentlessly.

I wrote them down as Haase called them out and then I stopped writing. Haase was no longer audible. The history makers had conquered the acoustics. Their shouting erased the unbearable voice and its unbearable roll call. A voiceless man was left standing on the stage. His mouth kept moving but he was no longer to be heard. In a few years this roar was to become a single pistol shot, and Haase was to lie on the steps of the German parliament—rendered permanently inaudible.

A stagehand came to the rescue of the outraged history makers. He pulled a lever in the wings and the great curtains of the Stadt's Theater swept out of the proscenium. The stage and the stocky man with the moving lips vanished.

The press of Germany reported the "scandal." Herr Haase's effort to "ruin Germany's new democracy and blacken its name in the eyes of the world" was angrily chronicled. Brave Hugo Haase's only victory that I could detect was the fact that I was allowed to remain in Germany. But I was barred from all the government offices in Wilhelmstrasse.

I am suddenly aware that my whole story of this German has a mistake in it. I have remembered a forgotten fact about him. Haase was a Jew.

CONCERNING A SUITCASE

I ATTENDED another major event which left me with a permanent cynicism toward history. It was the Bavarian Revolution in April, 1919, and the brief fling of Munich as a Communist state.

I was unable to get all of it into newspaper print. My editors often deleted from my cabled reports of the revolution what I insisted was its truth.

I report this truth now, a generation after its happening, aware that it is no longer quite a "scoop." But it is still a timely tale. In 1953 the American wooing of the Germans as a bulwark against Communism is much as it was in 1919.

Thus I offer this Munich revolution of 1919 as a peep into today as well as yesterday.

The first news of the Bavarian story was brought me in Berlin by Count von Mathis.

"Kurt Eisner has just been assassinated in Munich," he told me. I asked who Kurt Eisner was.

"He was the leader of the Bavarian Workingman's Party," said von Mathis, "and a man of great dignity and spirit. He was beloved by everybody."

"Who killed him?"

"It is not known yet, but we can guess," said von Mathis. "The Munich Junkers, a few unscrupulous adventurers. But this time they have signed their own death warrants. There is certain to be a people's uprising in Bavaria, a genuine proletariat revolution."

"There is no German proletariat revolution," I said. "We've been over that a number of times. The thing is a fake."

"Not in Bavaria," said von Mathis. "In Bavaria there will be no *Schweinerei*. The Bavarians have always hated the Prussians. I am a Prussian myself, but I admit the Bavarians are a more emotional and sincere people. I think we should go there."

I waited a few weeks until more positive news of the impending Bavarian uprising reached us. On an April morning I asked Knerr to fuel up our plane.

"It will take a few days to steal the petrol," Knerr said. "I will let you know as soon as the tanks are full."

The next evening I had five visitors at the Adlon. Dr. von Berg, head of Germany's Anti-Bolshevik League, brought two friends. One was Colonel Bartholdi of General von Hoffmann's staff, the other a member of the Ebert government named Dr. Schmidt. Von Berg had heard I was flying to Munich. Since a railroad strike had isolated all of Bavaria, he asked to be taken along in my plane with his two friends.

As we were talking, the doorbell rang. Two more visitors appeared. One was a Russian called Dr. Bezsmertnii, a word meaning "deathless" in his language. He was known as one of the most important Bolshevik agents in Berlin. The other was an official of the Spartacus Party named Breitman.

"You don't need to introduce us," said Bezsmertnii, smiling at my other three guests. "We know each other."

"Yes, indeed," said von Berg. He bowed and shook my hand in farewell. "We will be at Tempelhof Field to join you."

The anti-Bolshevik trio departed and the Bolshevik duo sat down. To my surprise, Bezsmertnii and Breitman also wished to fly with me to Munich. I reminded them I had just agreed to take along their three enemies.

"That does not need to matter," Bezsmertnii smiled. "There will be no trouble in the plane."

Bezsmertnii was a short, bald-headed man with a long, yellowish face, a constantly smiling mouth and a pair of expressionless watery blue eyes. He was in his fifties. I had met him at his home in Kurfurstendam. He lived in an apartment without furnishings.

There was a single cot in his bedroom, the walls of which had been plastered to resemble a prison cell. The cell, I was told, was a replica of the one occupied by the Marquis de Sade during his imprisonment in France.

In this room Dr. Bezsmertnii officiated over Communist destinies and sadistic revels. The night I had attended, two German girls and a fat boy of fourteen had been chained nude to the wall. Several of the guests had amused themselves whipping them. Bezsmertnii had sat on his cot smiling and playing moodily on a guitar.

"This is just a little impromptu gathering," Bezsmertnii had apologized. "You must come sometime when we have a real party."

My five passengers were on the flying field waiting when von Mathis and I arrived.

I had not notified them of the hour of departure, certain that von Mathis, who seemed to be in everybody's pay, would take care of that behind my back. I noticed that only one of my guests had brought any luggage. Bezsmertnii stood with a large suitcase in his hand. As we waited for the plane to be wheeled out of the hangar, Bezsmertnii held on to the suitcase, refusing to rest it on the ground.

The plane noises and the worry that always attended its sorties into the air kept us silent during the first part of the flight. After an hour we arranged a poker game. Bezsmertnii's suitcase served as a table.

During our poker game I watched von Berg and Bezsmertnii. They had the same sort of witty faces, each with a superior smile at the world. It seemed odd that their beliefs should be a world apart. Odder was the fact that though they were going to Munich to join the opposite sides of a bitter revolution, they did not mind each other's presence in the plane.

When we had landed outside of Munich, Bezsmertnii spoke quietly to me. His suitcase, he told me, contained a million gold German marks, the kind not yet devaluated. He was delivering the money to certain Radicals in Munich. With it they would buy the Munich garrison, which consisted of four regiments of well-equipped Ebert-Noske government troops. With the aid of these four regiments, the proletariat would be able to capture Munich and turn Bavaria into an independent Soviet state.

"I am telling you this," said Bezsmertnii, "because I want you to do me a favor. I want you to carry the suitcase past the government White Guards on the field. You will tell them it is your suitcase, and because you are an American correspondent they will not open it to examine what is inside."

I looked at von Berg. He was smiling, as were Colonel Bartholdi and Dr. Schmidt. Another sort of poker game was going on among my passengers. I became aware that von Berg no less than Bezsmertnii was eager for me to bring the million marks safely into Munich. I said to von Berg, "You know about what's in this suitcase, don't you?"

He shrugged.

"We are your guests," he answered, "and whatever we know, we cannot interfere with anything you choose to do."

Von Berg and Colonel Bartholdi had Lugers bulging their pockets. Knerr, who was standing beside them, was also armed. There were no bulges in the Bezsmertnii and Breitman pockets.

"Please," Bezsmertnii said, "there will be no trouble, I assure you. Take the suitcase, sir, I beg you."

I remained in the plane a few minutes thinking the thing over. The anti-Bolshevik leaders knew that a Bolshevik agent was bringing a million gold marks into Munich. They knew he was going to buy their own troops with the money and overthrow their own government in Bavaria. They had only to draw a gun and put an end to this Lenin-Trotsky plot and, also, enrich their own cause by a large sum. Yet none of them made any such move. Instead they waited politely for me to pick up the suitcase and step out of the plane.

I had been prepared for their attitude by what I had learned in Berlin of the German Communist revolution. Here was concrete proof of what I had believed. Obviously, the Ludendorff plan for a "people's revolution" was now erupting in Bavaria. Faced with the "fact" of a new "great Communist uprising," the Allies would allow the German government to increase further its military power as a bulwark against the Red Menace.

The only confusing element in the plot was Bezsmertnii. Dr. Bezsmertnii was no German militarists' cat's-paw. He was a genuine Red agent. I had met Radek, the lupine friend of Lenin, in his company.

Yet Bezsmertnii had come along, certain that he would not be stopped by his sworn enemies, my anti-Bolshevik passengers. He had known they would let his million marks through. Therefore he must know what I knew—that the German militarists were as eager for a Communist uprising in Bavaria as he was. He must know also that they were certain that they could stamp it out the minute it had served their ends as propaganda to frighten the Allies. And, still, Bezsmertnii was willing to finance a revolution he knew could not win; willing to help fool his own followers and let them be killed.

It came to me, however, that Bezsmertnii was also investing in something. The Russian Communists in Moscow, from whom the million marks came, hoped to attract and excite the Radical sympathy of the world by showing it a heroic Communist outburst in western Europe. As for the Bavarians themselves, the men who were to fight and die for the "great dream of freedom," these were propaganda puppets and nothing more.

Von Berg interrupted my musings.

"You had better get started," he said. "The guards are coming."

It was Dr. von Berg who lifted the suitcase and handed it to me. The cynicism of this action was beyond anything I had as yet met in the world. It said—go hire killers to kill my own people. When the time comes we will kill those killers. And out of all this killing we will win a point. We will convince somebody that the lie we are telling is the truth that the Russians and not we are a menace to their safety.

I carried the suitcase across the field. We paused as three soldiers approached us. They wore the white arm bands of the Ebert-Noske government army. I identified myself as an American correspondent. The three soldiers beamed and waved me on courteously with my unopened piece of baggage.

"HOCH DIE SOVIETEN VON BAYERN"

MY PASSENGERS went their different ways in Munich, Bezsmertnii with his suitcase; von Mathis and I went to the Park Hotel.

Nothing happened for three days. Von Mathis introduced me around, taking me to the suburb of Schwabbing which, I was told, was the center of Munich's highest intellectual life. I met there a number of odd and garrulous folk, among them a shapely young woman called "Countess Sophie."

The countess wore a clinging Grecian robe over her nude body and was barefooted. Like my secretarial count, she was a devout Communist. She told me that Bavaria would soon cast off its Capitalist shackles and squeezed my hands gratefully. "I know what you have done for our cause," she said. "You will be rewarded."

I was taken that evening by the countess and a group of intellectuals to the Bonbonnière Café. Here I witnessed a dance performed by a lean, hollow-eyed homosexual in black tights. He danced with a four-foot phallus for a partner. It was carved out of wood and painted realistically. His coy acrobatics as he manipulated the lifelike prop brought cheers from the café. A woman singer followed him, and I heard the theme song of the revolution—the song I was to hear hummed and whistled in the streets of Munich for the next month. It was called "*Ich weiss auf den Weiden.*" Its chorus, translated, ran:

> *I know in the willows a little hotel,*
> *In a forgotten little street,*
> *Where the night is too short,*
> *And the dawn comes too soon—*
> *Come with me, my little Countess,*
> *Why worry what tomorrow will bring?*
> *The world holds but sunshine and song,*
> *And once you have spent the night kissing*
> *You'll never do anything else.*

From the Bonbonnière we went to the Café Stephanie, rendezvous of Munich's artists. Here I met a poet with pale eyes and a pointed red beard. He was introduced to me as the great voice of the Bavarian proletariat. His name was Eric Mühsam. He was persuaded to recite his famous revolutionary poem, which had stirred the soul of the Bavarian masses. It began, "The sun of liberty is red on the morning horizon—" He followed it with the recitation of more personal strophes beginning, "A rat of pain gnaws at my soul, but does not injure it."

Muhsam reminded me of my friend Bodenheim in Chicago, except that there was a madder light in his eyes. They had the look of tenderness and innocence gone wild. Poet Muhsam squeezed my hand as we parted and he too whispered to me I would be rewarded for my great service to the peoples' cause.

We went next to the Kindle-Kellar, which I was told was a rendez-vous for chimney sweeps, beggars and underworld characters. It was noisy, dirty and jammed with "types." We joined a group of four men and a girl. One of the men was Dr. Max Levien, a professor of zoology at the University of Munich. The girl's name was Ma-thilde. She was the professor's sweetheart. Both of them wore belted bright red Russian tunics. Levien was a dark, thin-faced Jew with glittering black eyes. He was a chain cigarette smoker. Mathilde kept lighting fresh cigarettes and thrusting them between his lips. I thought she did this because Levien's hands jiggled with a tremor.

My hostess, Countess Sophie, was nervous in the professor's presence. She spoke anxiously of her dear friend Walter Rathenau, one of Germany's richest industrialists. Walter, she said, was heart and soul with the revolution.

I had interviewed Rathenau, president of the German Electric and Power Industry, in Berlin. He was called "the Jesus in a frock coat." Leftists and rightists both derided him for his Socialistic dabblings. It was felt that the richest man in Prussia had no right to stick his nose into radicalism. Rathenau had told me he was happy with the wonderful people's government Ebert and Noske had estab-lished. I thought him, at the time, either a fool or one of the Luden-dorff cynics. It turned out, a few years later, that Rathenau was something worse than either of these. He was a Jew and he was shot and killed in the first Hitler days.

"Herr Rathenau will give us his Bavarian coal mines," said Count-ess Sophie, "particularly when he hears we are using his wonderful book on the socialization of industry as a blueprint for our revolu-tion."

The glittering-eyed Levien said nothing. His silence, his immobil-ity and his constant smoking impressed me.

"Do you think there will be a revolution?" I asked him.

"You will interview me later," Levien answered.

The revolution woke me in the morning. There was roaring and rifle fire in the streets below. I dressed and hurried out for a look. The street in front of the hotel was filled with running men. They carried red flags and waved guns in the air and fired into the distance ahead of them. I could see no enemy and there was no return fire from the distance. Roaring and shooting, the revolution charged forward. There were thousands on thousands. Most of them were workingmen, and I saw boys of fifteen and old men of sixty and seventy charging forward together.

Von Mathis joined me. He was full of news. The Munich "white" garrison had gone over to the Red proletarian cause. The running men were munitions workers and coal miners chiefly. They had already captured the munitions works. They were heading for the railroad station to capture it.

We trotted with the mob, whose shouts alone seemed enough to tumble buildings. We reached the Bahnhof. The workers surrounded it. The empty Bahnhof Square became no man's land. A thousand rifles ripped bullets across it. The shooting lasted for an hour. During the first five minutes some answering shots came from the station. Thereafter the shooting was all done by the revolution. At the end of the hour the happy workers stormed the Bahnhof. I went inside the station with them. It was empty. Not a dead or wounded body was to be seen, but all the windows had been shot out and the walls looked like used up punchboards.

The new red flag of the Soviets of Bavaria went up on the Bahnhof flagpole. The square resounded with a long roar of triumph.

The great mob of men started running again, von Mathis and I with them. We were headed for the Wittelsbacher *palais*, ancient home of Bavaria's royal line.

The noise around me suddenly swelled. A regiment of uniformed soldiers came in an orderly trot around a corner. They had exchanged their white sleeve bands for red ones. The cry of joy that went up from the workers at the sight of their new soldier allies rattled the windows overhead.

The siege of the palace lasted till noon. I lay behind a parapet of sandbags and watched the revolution bang away at the elegant buildings. I was unable to detect any return fire. Nevertheless the bombardment continued. A number of trench mortars were put into action. They kept shooting holes in the roof. At noon the revolutionists leaped from behind their sandbags and stormed the *palais* itself.

I had come on the poet Mühsam during the siege. I stuck to his side as the fighters of the revolution made way for their leaders to enter the "fallen" palace.

Escorted by a dozen red arm-banded soldiers, the leaders walked slowly through the high-ceilinged rooms. The palace was completely deserted. Its fine furniture and chandeliers were covered with netting. Its parqueted floors were bare.

The men with whom I walked were the new Communist government of Bavaria. At their head was a thin, blond youth. He was Ernst Toller, a student from the University of Munich. He was also a literary man of some note. He had written a number of plays. He was as nervous now as on an opening night. He kept saying to his colleagues when they spoke to him, "Please—not now. Don't talk to me now."

Beside him was a tall, lanky professor of English named Landauer. He was also from the Munich university. He was introduced to me as the German translator of Walt Whitman. He threw his legs out as he walked and seemed to strut and stumble at the same time. With Landauer were two other men who were to become important Soviet officials. One was Franz Lippe, who looked like a traveling hypnotist. He had a gaunt face and a mop of long straight black hair that hung to his collar.

The second was a good-looking, dark-haired youth of nineteen. He was Rudolph Hise. He spoke good English and had a strong, eager smile. He asked me to call him Rudy and told me he was a poet from Frankfurt. He had seen my name in a copy of *The Little Review*, a periodical he highly esteemed. He was the only member of the new government who was in uniform and armed. He carried a carbine, and a half-dozen hand grenades were in his belt. He also wore side arms. He showed me a small bottle.

"It's full of nitroglycerin." He smiled. "Enough to blow up this whole palace and everybody in it, if I threw it on the floor."

I thought Rudy was a harum-scarum youth tagging along on our historic march through the palace of the Ludwigs just for the hell of it.

"Are you going to write some poetry about this?" I asked.

"No more poetry for a time," said Rudy. "I am going to be very busy. I am head of the Committee for Public Safety."

The title confused me.

"We take care of traitors, cowards and saboteurs," Rudy explained. "We liquidate them." He smiled at me and added quickly, "I am your friend. That was a real sporting thing you did at the air field. I'll remember it."

The slow march through the *palais* continued. A crowd of soldiers and workingmen with guns had joined it. They lagged respectfully behind the little knot of men who had become their new masters.

"They are looking for a room to use as government headquarters," Rudy explained. He waved at the maze of high-ceilinged chambers through which we kept walking.

"Too big," he whispered. "The workers would not like such ostentation."

Toller, the dictator of Bavaria since noon, paused in a doorway. "This will do," he said.

We entered a commodious bathroom. In a corner was an oversized zinc tub. The floor was covered with worn linoleum.

"We will use this as our headquarters," said Toller. "Have some workmen board over the bathtub and bring a big table and some chairs in."

The new government agreed. They would find cubbyholes of their own in the palace, but this bathroom would be the headquarters of Herr Toller, Bavaria's new dictator.

Rudy considered this a fine symbolic gesture. Under the proletariat rule, ruler and people were one, he said. I remembered the marines I had seen run frightenedly out of the Kaiser's bedroom in Berlin, and I had another theory. Bavaria's new people's leaders were frightened of the ghosts in these ballrooms, of the long history of German autocracy that stared stiffly out of the massive chandeliers and the large carved furnishings.

I sat with Toller in his bathroom as he started on his dictator's job. He was a bookish-looking type of writer—blond, slightly built and with a soft, hesitant manner. I wondered how such a fellow had got to be a dictator.

His first gesture as dictator consisted of copying something out of a book. The book was Walter Rathenau's *Tomorrow's Socialization*.

"We are going to use this book as our guide for the redistribution of Bavaria's wealth and industry," Toller said. "I am going to present my plan at a meeting at five o'clock. You may attend, if you wish."

"Could you give me an estimate of how many have been killed and wounded in today's fighting?" I asked.

"I have not heard of anyone being hurt," Toller said. He sighed. "Thank God for that. Let us hope that it may continue like that.

A revolution in which no one is hurt." He smiled. "That's a very good story, isn't it?"

I wrote a full account of the day's excitements to cable to Chicago. It contained all the facts of the von Berg-Bezsmertnii arrival, the smuggled-in million and the mock battles for the capture of Munich. It explained the purpose of the revolution and prophesied that as soon as the German militarists had frightened the Allies into allowing them to increase their German army, they would remove the revolution as one removes scenery from a stage. I wrote that the workers taking part in the revolution had no knowledge of the sinister forces that were pulling the strings; that they were honest human beings who were running amuck. The real power of Germany would speak up at the proper time and put them all back where they belonged.

This was one of many stories that was spiked by my editors.

Rudy read my copy in the telegraph office.

"I have to read it because I'm the censor," he said. "It was arranged this afternoon."

After reading my copy he sighed.

"So you don't believe in our revolution," he said. "Just because there was no one killed. Be patient. We are only in power one afternoon." He smiled. "I will pass this. Because it is actually an attack on our enemies, the militarists, isn't it? It exposes them, not us?"

COMIC-OPERA REVOLUTION

Franz Lippe had been made Foreign Minister of the Soviets of Bavaria. His first action had been to rip out all the telephones on the third floor of the Wittelsbacher *palais* where he had established himself. He had a bell phobia. The ringing of a phone bell brought on a sort of epilepsy. He permitted one bell-less phone to remain on his desk.

As Foreign Minister, Herr Lipp spent most of his time trying to get Clemenceau on the phone in Versailles where he was busy on the writing of the Allied Peace Treaty.

"Inform Monsieur Clemenceau that I wish to speak to him about arranging a separate peace for Bavaria," he kept announcing into the phone. As far as I could make out he was talking to some telephone operator. He continued for days to argue with various telephone operators. Clemenceau never came to the phone.

Landauer, appointed Minister of Education, occupied the palace library on the second floor. He was a restless man, unable to stay at his desk. He kept visiting the other government departments. As he strode through the palace he kept crying out, "Here comes Landauer!"

I interviewed him every day, fascinated by his mannerisms. He would pause during his talk and call out his name in a sudden shout. The interviews were mainly discussions of Walt Whitman.

"Every Bavarian child at the age of ten is going to know Walt Whitman by heart," Landauer told me. "That is the cornerstone of my new educational program."

The oddest of the lot was Mühsam. Dictator Toller was worried about him.

"We have been discussing whether we should arrest him," said Toller, "for his own good. I decided against it—for the time."

Mühsam was in disfavor because of the trouble he created in the streets. He had commandeered a small motor lorry for his personal use. In this he toured the Munich streets. Whenever he saw a crowd, he stopped his lorry, stood up on its seat and started an address. He usually began with a recitation of his famous revolutionary poem, "The Sun of Liberty."

Thousands of workers were still idling in the streets as if a picnic and not a revolution were going on. They took an aversion to their lyrical spokesman, Eric Mühsam. As soon as he started reciting his poetry, they would start yelling and waving their guns. Several times they had stormed his lorry and pulled him off his stage. Once shooting had started and he had had to run for his life.

Dictator Toller finally hit on the idea of appointing Mühsam the Bavarian Minister to Moscow.

"That will get him out of town," Toller said. "It is better than arresting him."

Mühsam was delighted with the appointment but refused to budge out of Munich. He went home instead and started writing long idolatrous letters to Lenin. He signed them, "Mühsam, Poet of the Revolution and Bavarian Minister to Moscow."

Rudy, as censor, confiscated the letters and tore them up.

"I'll let the idiot stay free," Rudy said to me, "if you promise on your honor not to send any of his poetry to America. It would disgrace our revolution."

Mühsam's troubles could not touch his happiness. The people were free. The sun of liberty was shining on them. Justice had come into the world. Mühsam walked in Utopia and his heart overflowed.

His happiness only increased when he found a postal card under the door of his attic room, reading: "Mühsam must die." It was signed, "The Society for the Abolition of Monstrosities."

Mühsam beamed over the postal card as over a great diploma.

"It's from the enemies of the people," he said. "They fear me."

Thereafter he walked the streets, flaunting his black fedora and red beard as a target. He addressed the roof tops as he moved, "Shoot! Why don't you shoot? I am here! Mühsam, the lover of humanity is here! Kill Mühsam—his cause will live on!"

Mühsam's defiance of the roof tops further irritated the proletarians in the streets. They took to chasing him whenever he appeared.

"You must stop behaving like a child," Toller reprimanded him. "If you don't, I shall have to remove you from your post as Minister to Moscow."

The threat subdued Mühsam for a few days.

I reported these doings as Munich's "comic-opera revolt." These amateurs of revolution and death touched my heart. My favorite of those crazy days was Rudy. He was the first German I had met who laughed. Rudy presented me with a specially built Mercedes automobile. It had belonged to Prince Ruprecht of Bavaria and had a bed in the tonneau on which you could stretch out and sleep while riding. It was the only pleasure car to be seen in Munich. No more than a dozen broken taxis were in the streets and a few motor lorries. Even Dictator Toller had no automobile and walked every morning two miles to his dictator's office. I suggested to Rudy that I share the car with Toller.

"He needs exercise," said Rudy. "Besides Comrade Toller is going to resign—very soon."

"Does he know it?" I asked.

"I think he suspects it," grinned Rudy. "You remember Mirabeau and Kerensky?" I nodded. "Toller is another historic stopgap. Yes, he is playing in a little curtain raiser."

Dictator Toller seemed uninterested in his impending doom when I questioned him. "A revolution is always full of rumors," he said. He had become very busy. He sometimes stayed in his bathroom all night working.

He was sending agents into Bavarian towns to spread the revolution. The Countess Sophie, disguised in shoes and a normal street suit, started for Berlin to persuade Herr Rathenau to send coal into a now shivering Munich. The spring days were chilly. The food supply was also worrying the dictator. Farmers arrived in town with wagons full of vegetables and fruits. They refused to sell them for money. I watched citizens in the street exchanging chairs and linen for cabbages and potatoes. The manager of the Park Hotel swapped a lobby couch for a dead pig.

The dictator also supervised an extensive inventory being taken in Munich. Men with red arm bands stood in the city's stores and wrote down every object on their shelves and its value. Nobody knew what Dictator Toller was going to do after the inventory was complete, but everyone in town, except the shopkeepers, was hopeful. The citizens waited for the "redistribution of wealth" to begin.

At the Bonbonnière the lean homosexual in black tights still danced with his phallus partner. In the streets the square-faced Bavarian burgher still walked, humming of the little hotel he knew in the Weiden. Shooting was still going on but after two weeks of it no one had yet been hit. To date the revolution had been much safer than an American Fourth of July celebration.

The only near-casualty was the Rembrandt Museum, which housed Europe's most famous collection of Rembrandt's paintings. A young artist named Titus Tautz had been made Dictator of Art for the Soviets of Bavaria. Tautz was a fierce modernist. He was one of the founders, with George Grosz, of the Dadaist movement in Germany. He had long yellow hair, buck teeth and a voice given to screaming.

"I am going to clean out all bad German art and literature," he yelled. We sat in the Simplicissimus Café. Artists and poets crowded the tables. At Tautz's side was Georg Kaiser, one of the leading young dramatists of Germany.

"I am going to do for the Soviets of Bavaria," Tautz hollered, "what Kandinsky has done for the Soviets of Russia—clean out all the slop, best sellers and dead classical paintings."

On his third day as artistic adviser of the revolution, Tautz organized a midnight parade of Munich's modern artists, poets and their sweethearts. Some two thousand turned up. They were armed with rifles and revolvers and half of them carried red flags and torches.

Tautz addressed them from a stand in front of his headquarters. He announced that the days of talk were over, the hour of action had come.

"We begin at the top," he cried. "We begin with Rembrandt, the King of Kitch. We march tonight to the Rembrandt Museum. We burn it down. We shall have the honor of destroying all the so-called Rembrandt masterpieces in Germany." He raised his torch and his voice. "Rembrandt is the dead past. Only by removing the corpses of the past can we make room for the new and living art of the revolution. Hurray for the Soviets of Bavaria! Down with all decadent Capitalists! Forward, Comrades!"

Singing and waving its torches, the parade started. It moved slowly and solemnly. I walked beside Rudy and Tautz. Almost immediately the parade started thinning out. With every block another hundred of the artists, poets and their sweethearts seemed to melt away in the dark. There were only thirty of us left in line when we reached the Rembrandt Museum. And there was only one torch left. It blazed in Tautz's hand.

Art Dictator Tautz mounted the museum steps, his torch held high, and faced the loyal handful. He made a second speech. He announced he had changed his mind about destroying the Rembrandts. As art they were trash and cliché and fit only for burning.

"But they have a certain historical value," he spoke. "As historical relics on a par with suits of armor and old bedsteads, the revolution will allow them to remain!" With a shout of "Hurray for the Soviets of Bavaria!" he headed for the Simplicissimus Café.

THE RED MENACE STRIKES

RUDY WOKE me early the next morning.

"Get dressed," he said. "There's another revolution today."

Knerr drove us out to the great meadow outside of Munich. All of Bavaria seemed heading for it. Instead of hissing us as the only pleasure-car-owning nabobs in town, the mobs in the streets eagerly opened passage for us and cheered us as we rolled by. I had a feeling they were disloyally cheering Prince Ruprecht.

A hundred thousand people were massed in the meadow. A high speakers' stand was in the center of the throng. Soldiers kept a lane open to the stand. Rudy, his two guards and I walked down the lane. We were hoisted up to the high platform. A dozen men and a girl occupied it. The girl was Mathilde, the red-tunicked cigarette lighter for Dr. Max Levien. I had not seen the zoology professor since I had met him in the Kindle-Keller, and I had wondered what had become of him.

He was visible enough now. He wore his Russian tunic and stood facing the mob with his right arm raised in a Bolshevik salute. He was the new dictator of Bavaria.

He spoke for an hour in a voice that barked and threatened. The crowd cheered at every other sentence. I could understand nothing of what he was saying but I knew Levien was a man of different mold than Toller. Not being a student of Communist religion, I had no inkling of what this mold was. Years later I was to learn that the man I saw in the meadow had been one of the writers and prophets whom international Communism worshiped. In his book of confessions, the renegade Commie, Whittaker Chambers, misspelling his name, names Max Levien as one of the seven great men he had worshiped.

"Now it begins," Rudy whispered to me. "You thought we were fooling, eh? You will see something now. You will see puppets become men." He listened to Levien and interpreted for me. "He is calling on the proletariat to die. He is promising them agony, torture and victory."

We reached the Wittelsbacher *palais* in the afternoon. Toller was out of his bathroom. All the other government officials also had vanished, except Mühsam. The red-bearded poet welcomed Levien with a new ode. Levien and his Mathilde stood in the palace ballroom and listened scowlingly to the recitation. At the conclusion of the ode Levien announced sharply, "There will be no more poetry!"

The new dictator scorned the bathroom headquarters. He set up shop in the largest of the ballrooms. Desks and chairs were lugged in, red flags and large posters of Lenin, Trotsky, Liebknecht and Eisner were nailed up. During the hullabaloo, Levien sat staring in silence and smoking Mathilde's cigarettes. I interrupted his meditation.

"I'd like an interview, Mr. Levien."

His eyes glittered at me.

"What's become of Toller, Landauer, Lippe, Nikish and all the other members of the ousted government?" I asked.

"They are in custody," said Levien.

"Are they going to be executed?"

"No," said Levien.

"Do you expect this revolution to succeed?"

"It has succeeded," said Dictator Levien. "Our proletariat has freed itself from Prussian militarism and stands beside the workers of Russia."

"In what way will the workers be freer if they do what Russia tells them to do, instead of Prussia?"

"They are not obeying Russia," said Dictator Levien. "They are obeying the cry in their own souls—the cry for proletarian freedom." The obsessed thin face smiled. "The Noske government army will start toward Munich in a few days. They think they will be able to walk into Munich and say, 'Enough revolution! You have served your purpose! Back to your kennels, German dogs!' They think this. They are wrong."

Dictator Levien stood up in dismissal.

The tone of my cabled stories changed. A new air was in the streets of Munich. The city had become afraid. During the day the streets were almost bare. A seven o'clock curfew denuded them completely after twilight. The dark city became hollow and silent.

The Park Hotel guests were chiefly people of the upper classes. They sat in the lobby waiting for tumbrels to take them off to some guillotine. No tumbrels came. After two days the tension began to ease. People had errands again in the night. This was a mistake. Motor lorries full of soldiers roared suddenly into the streets. Their machine guns fired at figures breaking the curfew law. There was no preliminary questioning.

Rudy brought me the casualty list—four killed, eleven wounded.

"I saw some of it," I said. "It was outright murder."

"When you enforce a law you do not commit murder," said Rudy. "I suppose you are going to write something about the Red Terror now."

"We have four murders a day in Chicago," I said. "You'll have to do better for that sort of write-up."

Rudy looked around the lobby at the well-dressed burghers. He removed the bottle from his pocket and fingered it, laughingly.

"Have you told them I carry a bottle of nitroglycerin?" he asked. I said no. "Tell them," he grinned. "I hate their fat faces. Pork faces and sausage necks. Tell them. I'd like them to enjoy my company fully when I appear."

The next morning Rudy arrived early. He was on a special mission. Dictator Levien had ordered him to capture the old King Ludwig of Bavaria, whose hiding place in the forests outside of Munich had been discovered. The dictator wanted the king as a hostage. Rudy needed my Mercedes for the kidnaping.

I went with him and his three soldiers. It was raining heavily when we entered the forest. As we approached a small inn, named as the hiding place, an open carriage clattered out of a barn. Two men were in it. One was the white-bearded King Ludwig.

The carriage horses dashed off down a narrow forest road. Our Mercedes was too large to follow. Rudy jumped out of the car and opened fire.

A girl of eighteen came running toward us in the rain, her long blond hair loose on her shoulders. Rudy stopped firing.

"That's the Princess Gundelinda," he said.

The rain-soaked girl stopped a few feet in front of our car. She stood shaking a fist at us and denouncing us savagely. I asked Rudy what she was saying.

"She hates us," said Rudy. "She says we are lower than the lowest of beasts and that God is going to wipe us off the earth."

The speech seemed to depress Rudy. He stood looking moodily at the ranting beauty in the rain, and then ordered his soldiers back into the car.

"What about the princess for a hostage?" one of them asked.

"We do not fight women!" Rudy answered. He walked up to the fierce aristocrat.

"Go back to your house," he said to her. "You'll catch cold in the rain."

He bowed and turned away. We started back for Munich.

Rudy was silent.

"She was like a young Valkyrie," he said after a long time. "Did you notice her face? Like a little fire burning in the rain."

He appeared to have forgotten about the kidnaping.

At the hotel, von Mathis had news for me. Dictator Levien was looking for me.

"I'll take you over," said Rudy.

We drove to the *palais*. Things had happened during our day's absence. Cannon had been set up in the plazas. They pointed in all directions. Soldiers guarded them. Other soldiers were building munition dumps near the artillery.

Dictator Levien looked unpleasant behind his table desk. The red-tunicked Mathilde still sat beside him, lighting fresh cigarettes for him. Military officers filled the ballroom. They were clustered around the large maps of Munich on the walls.

I sat down facing the dictator.

"You are a very superficial young man," he said. His glittering eyes watched my face. "You have no concept of the proletarian revolution. You think it is a game that is being played."

"I brought in some of the chips for the game," I said.

"I have read your dispatches," Levien said. "They are too facetious."

"I wrote the truth," I said.

"Not our truth," said Levien. "You do not know our truth. Our truth is the Future of the World. Here are your dispatches."

He handed me several dozen sheets of paper.

"Your newspaper did not receive them," he said.

I stood up and began complaining wildly.

"We have not stopped your dispatches," said Levien. "Our communications are cut off. There is no telephone or telegraph service going out of Munich. I return you your dispatches because you will try sending them from some other town. It is important that the world know what we are doing, even from your bourgeois point of view."

"How soon do you expect Noske's army to attack Munich?" I asked.

"Not for several weeks," Levien answered.

"I'll be back then," I said. "Do I have to have some permit to get out?"

"Comrade Hise will see to you," Levien said.

"How big do you think the Noske army will be?" I asked.

"Not big enough," Levien answered.

"How many men have you got in your army?" I asked.

"Enough to win," said the dictator.

He stood up and held out his hand with its jiggling fingers.

"A professor of zoology is not a zoo keeper," he said. "Kindly make that correction in your dispatches."

Rudy called for us at the hotel early in the morning. He drove us to the hangar where Knerr had parked our bombing plane.

"I'm going to Berlin, file all my stories from there and then come back to Munich," I promised Rudy.

"I'll be always glad to see you again," said Rudy. "I'd like you to take this," he added. "It's a poem in English. I wrote it last night. It's about the Princess Gundelinda. I thought maybe when you are back in America you can ask *The Little Review* to publish it."

"I certainly will," I said. "But I'll see you before that."

"In case you don't." Rudy smiled.

FINALE—WITH FULL CHORUS

OUR PLANE made a crash landing a few miles outside of Coburg. A wild rainstorm knocked us out of the air. We landed in the deep mud of a cabbage field. The nose of the plane was broken. None of us was injured.

We went to a hotel in Coburg. I was without money. Von Mathis found out by nightfall that no trains were running, that there was not a single automobile to be borrowed or rented, that all the banks were shut down and that it would take five days to repair the plane.

We ate and drank pleasantly for the five days. I was certain the hotelkeeper would throw us all into jail when I told him we were broke and had no money to pay for our keep. The Coburg police department had not closed down.

On the fifth day the brilliant von Mathis reported he had found a possible source of income. Ex-King Ferdinand of Bulgaria was a refugee in Coburg. Ferdinand had been called "the Moneylender of Europe."

"We'll see if he's changed," said von Mathis.

We called on His Highness in the morning. He lived alone in a small house with one servant, a tall man in a leather coat. Von Mathis acted as interpreter. I asked for the loan of a thousand gold marks. The king sat regarding me heavily and silently. After von Mathis had finished talking, His Highness and the Leather Coat conferred. A few minutes later we were dismissed. We seemed to have struck out.

That evening the Leather Coat appeared in our hotel lobby and bawled out my name. He removed a bundle of money from a brief case with a royal monogram on it and handed me a thousand gold marks.

"I'll give His Majesty an I.O.U.," I said.

"His Majesty requires no written acknowledgment," said the Leather Coat. "The word of an American is sufficient security." Happy days of America's debut as a world-saver.

A pile of cables from Chicago was waiting for me at the Adlon. They inquired if I were sick, dead or alive—no word from me had come through for two weeks; there were also the usual number of complaints and warnings concerning the cynical nature of my stories. And there were a number of grateful and congratulatory communiqués. One wire from Editor Smith read, "Stories on Rudy, Mühsam, Tautz, etc., great. Send all feature stuff you can. Glad you're having good time."

Von Mathis arrived for lunch. He was pale and intense.

"Did you file the stories?" I asked. "And where's Knerr? We've got to get started back to Munich today."

"Please," said von Mathis, "let me speak first. It is over. I have brought the papers."

He handed me a sheaf of clippings.

"You know I can't read German," I said.

"I am sorry. I forgot," von Mathis said. "Noske's army entered Munich three days after we left. It overthrew the Soviets."

I stared at the small German headlines.

"How long did the fighting last?"

"A day," said von Mathis.

"They couldn't have taken Munich in a day," I said, "with all those cannon in the streets."

"There were only a thousand men to defend Munich," said von Mathis.

"What of the hundred thousand we saw on the field cheering Levien?"

"They stayed home," said von Mathis. "Levien fought—and a few others. They were killed."

"Levien is dead?"

"It is reported so in the Berlin papers."

"Any other report about people we knew?"

"Yes," said von Mathis. "Landauer is in jail and Toller was executed."

The second fact turned out to be untrue. Toller was alive. He was to spend five years as a prisoner in a Bavarian fortress, come to New York to have a play produced and commit suicide shortly thereafter.

"The Spartacus paper, *Rote Fahne*, has news of Eric Mühsam," von Mathis went on. "It reports that he was tortured, his fingers broken and one of his eyes put out. He was the most severely treated of the Spartacists."

A line of Mühsam's poetry sounded wildly in my memory—"A rat of pain gnaws at my soul, but does not injure it."

"About Rudy Hise," von Mathis paused. "I will read you the story, slowly. Please tell me if there are words you don't understand."

Von Mathis read me an account of "the death of Rudolph Hise, head of the Terrorists of the Bavarian Soviets." On the second day of the Noske occupation of Munich, with the revolution already crushed into silence, Rudolph Hise had leaped in through the window of General Noske's headquarters. The room was crowded with officers. Holding a small bottle aloft in his hand the Terrorist had shouted that it contained enough nitroglycerin to blow up the entire hotel. As the officers stood appalled and motionless, the Terrorist had then made a brief speech announcing that here in this room the proletarian revolution was to win its victory. Rudy Hise had then hurled his nitroglycerin bottle to the floor. It failed to explode. A dozen revolvers sent bullets into his body in the next few moments.

When von Mathis had finished I started looking through my pockets for the poem Rudy had given me to have published. I looked in vain. Rudy's poem was lost.

HOW THE GERMANS LOVED THE JEWS

I HAVE another bit of history to relate. It is as curious as the harlequinade of the German revolution. It is my history of German anti-Semitism.

These Germans in whose midst I lived and traveled and with whom I consorted for almost two years were the same Germans who were to murder six million Jewish men, women and children. They were the Germans who were to build lime kilns in which to dissolve myriads of live Jews and dynamite dumps which were to blow up other myriads. They were the Germans who, in a few years, were to foam at the mouth with anti-Semitism and proclaim that their destiny was to cleanse the world of Jews, who were the fountainhead of all its evils.

The strange bit of history I have to report is that in my two years in Germany, I, a Jew, saw and heard no hint of anti-Semitism. Not once in the time I spent in Germany did I hear the word Jew used as an epithet. No Radical or Capitalist was "accused" of Jewishness in the many wild political debates I heard.

I, the only Jewish correspondent at the time covering Germany from the outside world, was never called Jew by the government officials who denounced and barred me from their offices. There was less anti-Semitism to be heard, seen, felt or smelled in that postwar Germany than at any time in the U.S.A. Berlin was as innocent of aversion or even consciousness of Jews as had been Racine, the city of my boyhood. Even the pansy officers, the drug users, the nymphomaniacs, the gaunt, queer noblemen who staged orgies in empty warehouses, spoke never of Jews, for or against. At this time of its greatest travail, of hunger, of no milk for its children or tobacco for its men, there was no voice in Germany to be heard blaming the Jews for anything.

The only time I was made conscious of the fact that Jews lived in Germany as a separate statistic was during an automobile tour with von Gleichen. He stopped the car in front of a cemetery gate on the outskirts of Berlin.

"This is the cemetery for Jews who were killed at the front in the war," said von Gleichen. "Perhaps you would like to see it."

We went in. It was a vast place—acres on acres of earth covered with rows of little marble slabs.

"Were these all soldiers?" I asked.

Von Gleichen answered, "Yes. They fought bravely for their Fatherland. More Jews were killed in battle than Germans—compared to the percentage of Jews and Germans in the nation. The Jewish population of Germany was one half of one per cent. The Jewish deaths in the war were three per cent."

I know now that all those, or nearly all those, with whom I spoke, dined, played and adventured in that land were the murderers of the Jews. They did not hide their Jew hatred from me. They had no Jew hatred to hide. But they had something worse—a genius for servility that could turn them less than human when the whipcrack of authority sounded.

I had seen a 1918-1920 Germany without a Master. Dreams had flickered in the hearts of its people. Precious hopes for democracy had come to life. With a Master gone, the evil obedience of the German went on a small vacation. He was a man of the world for a day— a dizzy and desperate day. He joined a hundred causes, including that of humanity. He sprouted *Standpunkt*s hourly and tried out odd battle cries.

But it was no moral renaissance I saw. It was a recess. The war defeat had not altered a single German characteristic. It had suspended a few, briefly. In defeat, the secret leaders of Teutonia knew that the Germans were still among the best and quickest builders in the world. They knew they were still among the world's nimblest mechanics, scientists and logistics experts. And they knew also that the tribal trick of obedience found only in savages had survived in this technically civilized German. In him all morality was secondary to this morality of obeying a leader.

Today the Germans are back in the brotherly guise in which I once knew them in 1919. They are again the confused, pathetic and disarmed losers, scratching for a meal and searching for a human sort of government. The language of democracy is again on their lips.

I know little of their present political parties or of their new *Standpunkt*'s. But I know that basically nothing has changed since 1919. I know that as of old there is a Plot going on—the Plot of German world conquest, of Germany taking its "rightful" place as the Master Race of civilization. There is also the Plot of the German soul that waits for the whipcrack, that is darkly, furtively ready to fling all its humanities into a garbage can for the illusion of tribal power.

I add my voice to the prophets of tomorrow's history. We do not need so much to beware of the Russian Bear That Walks Like a Man as of the German Who Talks Like One.

I GO HOME

I NEVER WENT BACK to Munich. In Berlin I watched the army grow, the officers take over the cafés and streets—and the government. I felt no call to issue any further warnings. A distaste for all politics filled me. My editors were very pleased. I sent them long-winded pen pictures of Germany's industrial and social activities. Then one day I wrote Henry Smith that I was bored and asked to be called home.

Henry wrote back, "Go visit Italy, France and Spain and send us feature stories about what you see. Write them any way you want to. And don't forget Africa and China. Have a look around."

I carried the letter from this prince of editors in my pocket for two weeks. I sat most of the time in the Adlon bar staring at a future full of bullfights and pagodas—and other alien barrooms. And politics! *Standpunkt's* in velvet pants and padded silken jackets.

Pondering my future, I became aware of likes and dislikes in myself I had not known before. I had never thought I "preferred" anything. Good and bad food, books, people were much alike to me, as were riches and poverty, importance and unimportance.

Now I discovered that I definitely did not want to see Seville, Milan or Peking. I liked Chicago.

I returned to the sloping-floored, dusty-windowed local room of the *Daily News*. What I had learned in Europe dropped out of my head. Within two weeks I was as much a part of Chicago as if I had never left it. Mr. Dennis honored me by asking me to contribute editorials to his editorial page. He suggested that I interpret some of the events in postwar Germany. I begged off.

During the three years that followed, I wrote a column for the *News* called "1001 Afternoons in Chicago." I wrote five books, many short stories and two plays. I published a newspaper of my own called

The Chicago Literary Times, to which I was the chief and sometimes sole contributor. I went into a high-finance publicity enterprise on the side. Also I fell in love, left my wife and daughter, my grand piano, cloisonné floor lamps, Lillehan rugs and three thousand books, to go away with "the other woman."

This was 1920-1922, among the three most favorite years of my life.

One of the major influences Europe had worked on me was to rid me of what small financial realism I had had before visiting the Old World. When I left Chicago for Berlin my salary had climbed to seventy-five dollars a week, but my hope of solvency had almost vanished. Mysteriously, I owed eleven thousand dollars to innumerable tradesmen.

My assignment to Berlin saved me from the financial debacle that threatened. Out of the eight thousand dollars advanced me for expenses, I paid most of my Chicago debts. I arrived in Europe penniless. During my stay I was unable to reopen the fine Unter den Linden offices of the *Daily News* because I had left the money for its refurnishing and upkeep with my Chicago creditors.

My two years abroad removed any trace of money logic left in me. I lived in Europe on an expense account that ran from five hundred to two thousand a week. I returned to Chicago a pauper confirmed in the ways of a millionaire. Six months after my return I was again in debt. From the confusion around me I could make out I owed some twenty thousand dollars to various people.

Marie had bought a four-storied house that looked like an impressive summer hotel and was filling its eighteen rooms with storeloads of furnishings. She, or we, had also bought an automobile and engaged three servants to keep things going properly in our turreted manor. There were almost nightly parties to which coveys of theatrical people I had never seen before came and emptied pantry, ice box and liquor cellar.

The money situation grew daily more inconvenient. I was forced finally to keep two hats and two overcoats in the *Daily News,* one at my desk, the other a floor below in the advertising department. Thus I was able to walk away from bill collectors sent by my creditors without rousing their suspicions. Having tracked me to my desk, they would remain sitting patiently next to my hat and overcoat while I made off in the second set of garments ready for me in the sad-faced Johnny Weaver's office.

This small ruse provided no permanent solution for the riddle of how to live on a thousand dollars a week while earning a hundred, and stay out of jail.

My confusion was beginning to make inroads on my writing, most of which now had to be done in speak-easies and other sanctuaries, when great fortune suddenly came to me. There appeared in my life the first of the Sindbads I was to meet ever after when financial disaster threatened me.

So in the nick of time has been the arrival of each of these fortune-bearing strangers throughout my life, that I have been almost persuaded some friendly eye is watching over me, and that I need in times of stress only to wait idly and have faith, and a man with a map of a diamond mine will come into my room.

TALE OF MY FIRST SINDBAD

HE WAS a thin-faced, brilliant, gin-drinking young Southerner named Grady Rutledge, freshly come to town from Atlanta, Georgia. I met him in a saloon where he was defending the virtue of Southern womanhood under libel by several Northern drinkers. He was a young man of temper and had prepared himself for argument by tucking an opened penknife into his fist. The first words I heard him speak were:

"I will kill you, suh, unless you apologize to the women of the South."

I persuaded Messrs. Jack Malloy and Ronald Millar to make the apology. An hour later Grady Rutledge and I were partners in a National Publicity Enterprise which he had come North to form. We were within two weeks fantastically successful. Publicity accounts came clamoring to our office, which, after the first month, consumed an entire floor in the Frances Willard Building.

We handled, chiefly, J. P. Morgan's China Famine Fund, Herbert Hoover's Near East Relief and a project to spread the Baptist faith. This was called "The Northern Baptist Drive" and was out to despoil the populace of twenty-five million dollars. Our firm covered the fourteen Midwestern states with mimeographed and oratorical propaganda. It was difficult for me to believe that our services were of any value to anyone, and I remained astonished at the money we earned.

How these matters befell, how our accounts and our income increased I never quite knew, Grady being usually too deep in his cups to explain business details to me. Nor did I have much time to listen. Despite my name on the door of our sweep of offices and the hundred employees buzzing under my new business baton, I continued to write my daily stint for the *News* and to work on stories, plays and novels. I was only a part-time tycoon.

Meeting Dick Little one day and learning he was out of work after forty years of brilliant service as a newspaperman, I persuaded him to join our firm.

"What will my duties be?" Dick asked.

"You can be a full partner," I answered. "The firm sort of runs itself. You can make a fortune."

"Does the fortune you speak of include a weekly drawing account?" asked Dick.

"It does," I said. "Also, if you have any relatives you can put them on the pay roll. Grady likes a big staff."

"I have no relatives," said Dick. "I am alone and an orphan. But I will not let that stop me. I see no reason not to become your partner unless you are lying like a bastard."

Grady was delighted with our new partner and consumed a quart of liquor toasting him.

"I don't know a God-damn thing about publicity work and care less," said Dick. "I have always despised the craft, and both Mr. Duffy and I are shocked to see our friend Ben involved in it."

"Spoken like a true genius, suh," said Grady, "which is the only kind of puhson I like. I drink to your health, suh, and hope we see you again after your name has been added in gold paint on our doors."

Dick became a pillar of our firm. He and I did a deal of curious work. We gave bazaars, staged street carnivals, promoted beauty contests (one of them called "The Boudoirs of Nations" was raided by the police), we promoted lotteries, cotillions and costume festivals, all in behalf of the starving millions of Europe and Asia.

I do not know how much food our activities brought to those empty bellies. I know only that helping the world's needy was part of the American picnic spirit in 1921. The untaxed and idle rich were eager to prance around dressed up as mandarins, friars, Marie Antoinettes and Salomes in the interests of humanity.

I feel no remorse for the antics of those days. It was a pleasant and wanton time, and I doubt if its merry mood will be ever in the world again. As for "saving" China and the Near East by Tag Days and Charity Balls, I find our present Marshall Plan and Military Conquest schemes just as idiotic, and less diverting.

THE KING HAS NO CLOTHES

OF MY OWN ACTIVITIES as a fund-raiser, I remember two chores. One was the "Life of Christ" contest which I arranged. I persuaded the Baptist synod employing us to offer a prize of five thousand dollars for the best biography of the Savior sent in to a jury of leading Baptists.

Hundreds of threadbare clergymen, missionaries and theological students sent in manuscripts. Lured by the princely prize, I also submitted an entry. In order to have a "fair" chance with the Baptist jury, I signed the name of a needy Baptist pastor to whom I promised a fourth of the prize money if I won it. It came to pass that my gaudy tale of Christ was selected by the Baptist jury as the winner. A million copies of this "Life" were printed and distributed, bringing fame to the parson whose name I had signed to it.

The other chore was the affair of Dr. Sze, Chinese Minister to Washington.

Dr. Sze arrived in Chicago accompanied by a score of Chinese and American statesmen. He was to speak in the evening in Orchestra Hall on the aims and ideals of the great new Democrat of China, President Sun Yat-sen.

Our firm was entrusted by Thomas Lamont of the House of Morgan with the job of making Minister Sze's visit to Chicago a triumph.

The Morgans were angling at the time for vital trade concessions from the new China. The Famine Fund publicity we were peddling to the U.S.A. was a grandiose sales campaign for this purpose.

And Dr. Sze was important to our employers. His friendship and gratitude would help greatly the acquiring of financial toe holds in China.

We had printed and given away enough tickets to fill Orchestra Hall several times over. Nevertheless, we were full of alarm when we met the great Chinese diplomat at the train. It was raining, lightning and thundering. A gale was blowing. At five o'clock we knew that we and Minister Sze were facing a debacle. The rain had become almost a cloudburst. The streets were flooded. The wind screamed around the skyscrapers. The prospects of an audience arriving in Orchestra Hall to listen to an itinerant Celestial talk politics were horridly thin.

John J. Abbott, who was a Chicago bank president and related in some fashion to the House of Morgan, appeared at our offices in a rubber coat and cod-fisherman's hat. He was winded and full of panic. His bank had been telephoning friendly depositors all day long and managed only to extract a few unreliable promises of attendance.

"What's more, we can't postpone it," panted Mr. Abbott. "Dr. Sze has to start back to Washington tomorrow morning."

"Does he have to speak at all, suh?" Grady asked.

"He does," affirmed Mr. Abbott. "I have sounded him out. He insists on making his address. He calls it one of the most important moments in modern Chinese history."

At seven o'clock Mr. Abbott and his staff of vice-presidents were still in our offices. Grady had had liquor and food brought up. Mr. Abbott was on the phone speaking to Mr. Lamont in New York.

"Good Lord, Tom!" he cried. "I tell you it's a cloudburst. There's not a human being in the streets. You can't stand up—let alone walk. There's nothing to do but cancel."

He paused and listened for a time and then said crisply, "Very well, sir," and hung up.

"Mr. Lamont says Dr. Sze must deliver his address as scheduled," Mr. Abbott said. He stared at our firm and went on. "The House of Morgan has been paying you five thousand dollars a week, gentlemen. It expects some service in return."

"Good God!" Grady said. "You can't buy miracles, suh!"

An idea came to me.

"Do you mind what kind of audience appears?" I asked Mr. Abbott.

"We wouldn't want all colored people," Mr. Abbott answered moodily.

"I wasn't thinking of colored people," I said. "White ones."

"White ones will be fine," Mr. Abbott said, hopefully. Putting on his fisherman's hat, he went off into the storm.

I telephoned Colonel Wheeler, a retired army officer and head of the Boy Scouts of Chicago. Dick and I talked to him.

At eight o'clock six large automobiles drew up in front of Orchestra Hall. Dr. Sze and his entourage of statesmen came out of the cars and scuttled through the downpour toward the doors of the building. Mr. Abbott emerged from the hall ten minutes later to report that he had put the statesmen on stage, that Dr. Sze was bound to speak at eight-thirty and that not a solitary human being was in the auditorium.

We looked northward and southward down the storm-lashed avenue. No theatergoers were visible. We remained peering into the empty, rain-beaten street for the next twenty minutes, with Mr. Abbott at our elbows demanding action. Suddenly a new sound came out of the storm.

"More thunder," Mr. Abbott groaned as sound filled the storm.

"Not thunder," said Dick. "Drums. They're coming."

"By God, suh, look at those fine little shavers!" said Grady.

A line of small boys, four abreast, turned into Michigan Avenue. They were covered with oilcloth hats and ponchos. To the beating of drums and tooting of fifes, twelve hundred Boy Scouts ranging from nine to thirteen years came slogging through the rainstorm in splendid formation. Colonel Wheeler and several other adults marched with them.

We stood watching happily as wave on wave of these juveniles kept turning the corner. Dripping and silent, the little martyrs entered Orchestra Hall and were ushered efficiently into the rows of seats.

At eight-thirty the curtains parted. A stage filled with statesmen was revealed. Applause and cheers came from the darkened auditorium. The stageful of statesmen rose to their feet and bowed gratefully.

Dr. Sze came out of the wings and began his address. He spoke in English for a full hour without incident. The passion in his voice, the eagerness in his soul, held the twelve hundred small boys silent and orderly. They understood hardly a word of what the Chinese minister was saying. Yet the twelve hundred rose dutifully to their feet, cheering and applauding when Dr. Sze was done with his mysterious oratory.

We closed the stage curtains immediately and emptied the theater as quickly as possible. By the time Dr. Sze and the statesmen came out of the place the last platoon of poncho-covered little boys was turning the corner out of sight, taking home with them the message of the new China.

When I inquired later of Colonel Wheeler what his Boy Scouts had had to say about the event, he told me they had enjoyed every minute of it. Thus I was introduced to a cultural secret which I was to see function often in the arts—it is not necessary for an audience to understand something in order to enjoy it. Once, a year later, I thought to expose this snobbery and to prove to an audience that the king they admired had no clothes. I was running *The Chicago Literary Times* when the Moscow Art Theater Company came to town.

I went to the Auditorium Theater and sat through a performance of *The Brothers Karamazov* by Stanislavsky's actors. The theater was packed. Along with three thousand others, I stared at the stage and watched a dozen men and women sit in chairs for three hours and talk in Russian. There was almost no walking or any other form of movement. A duller three hours could not be imagined, or more meaningless ones.

Yet at the end of the performance a fashionable first-night audience, ninety-eight per cent of them Americans, stood up and cheered, as loudly and rapturously as our twelve hundred Boy Scouts had cheered the incomprehensible Minister Sze.

Irritated by this exhibition of mass snobbery, I asked my friend Rose Caylor to write the review of this performance in Russian. Many of the art lovers who had cheered the Muscovites would be sure to be readers of my *Times*. I thought it would be a good joke to offer them a criticism as unintelligible to them as the play they pretended to adore.

Rose Caylor wrote a thousand-word essay in Russian. I had it set up in a Russian print shop. An accident happened as Renshaw, my printer, was sliding the pan of Russian type into the front-page form. Mr. Renshaw, in the grip of a hang-over, allowed the column of Russian type to slide out of the pan to the floor. We were going to press and there was no time to rush a linguist over from Chicago's West Side. We stuck the scattered type lines back into the pan. The lines were scrambled and the review would make no sense. But I was determined to print it anyway. I argued with Mr. Renshaw that if the audience could cheer Dostoevski played in Russian, they could "read" a pied review as well as an unpied one in a language foreign to them.

If the point of my joke was to expose the audience to themselves as fakes, I failed. Miss Caylor's Russian review appeared on our front page. It received more congratulatory letters from our readers than any other feature in the issue. Not one of the scores of reader communiqués mentioned the fact that the review was scrambled beyond all intelligibility.

THE CHICAGO LITERARY TIMES

I PRINTED and published the newspaper called *The Chicago Literary Times* by myself for a year and a half. I also sold and wrote the advertising copy and helped distribute the paper. The policy of my paper was to attack everything. I enjoyed myself perhaps more than my readers. Here are a few excerpts from my 1923 mind:

ESSAY ON RADIO

Each new triumph over the laws of nature seems inevitably to become a further means for the dissemination of folly and boredom. The radio is already established as a full sister of the movies in the business of emptying American heads.

EDITORIAL

People resist having their eyes opened out of fear that they may despise themselves.

UNCHANGING JOURNALISM

Whythe Williams, employed by a Northcliffe newspaper in London, said to me in Berlin in 1919, "I'm leaving for London because Lord Northcliffe insists that I write of Germany in his own house. His idea is that I will not be under the influence of the Germans if I do this."

THE WORLD'S 22 WORST BOOKS

1. *Pilgrim's Progress*—John Bunyan
2. *Paradise Lost*—John Milton
3. *Ivanhoe*—Sir Walter Scott
4. *Adam Bede*—George Eliot
5. *Les Miserables*—Victor Hugo
6. *The Bluebird*—Maurice Maeterlinck
7. *Clayhanger*—Arnold Bennett
8. *What Is Art*—Leo Tolstoy
9. *Mr. Britling Sees It Through*—H. G. Wells
10. *As You Like It*—William Shakespeare
11. *The New Freedom*—Woodrow Wilson
12. *Peter Pan*—James M. Barrie
13. *The Christian*—Hall Caine
14. *Uncle Tom's Cabin*—Harriet Beecher Stowe
15. *Robert Elsmere*—Mrs. Humphrey Ward
16. *Das Kapital*—Karl Marx
17. *The Life of Christ*—Giovanni Papini
18. *Pendennis*—William M. Thackeray
19. *Virginibus Puerisque*—Robert Louis Stevenson
20. *Women in Love*—D. H. Lawrence
21. *The Rise of Silas Lapham*—William Dean Howells
22. *The Americanization of Edward Bok*—Edward Bok

ON POLITICS

Politics breeds the lowest type of thinkers. A successful politician good-naturedly mumbling his platitudes is a tolerable nuisance. The unsuccessful politician however, yammering on the wrong side of the payroll for Justice, Liberty and Brotherhood, is an irritant. His attacks against American Institutions are a product of the same opportunism out of which these institutions grew. He lays claim to higher aims and deeper intelligence by virtue of his defeat and unpopularity.

ON POLITICIANS

The American politician is bound to discover that his yapping against Communism is ill-advised. The average politician is an incompetent, a wind bag and a parasite. In Communistic Russia he is now king. As soon as American politicians realize that Communism offers a thousand political jobs for every one political job in America, they will in some way start imitating our Russian brothers.

Democracy offers a fairly good meal ticket to the politician. Communism has it beaten 40 ways from the jack.

LITERARY REVIEW

The Gertrude Stein hoax is assuming proportions. The culture bounders who like to be seen eating caviar are pouncing upon Gertie and indulging in exclusive grimaces of pleasure. Sherwood Anderson proclaiming Gertie Stein's genius is Sherwood Anderson trying to chin himself over the heads of the mob whose growing adulation has irritated his sense of superiority. This adulation frequently upsets a successful author. For example Joseph Conrad, when he became a success, found solace in telling interviewers that two London magazines had gone out of business shortly after printing his work.

ON WAR

Idealists always like wars. They cherish the spectacle of millions of able-bodied young men going out to risk their lives to prove that they, the idealists, are right. The only way to prevent further wars that I can see is for the U.S. to build up an overwhelming army, navy and air fleet and conquer the world. Once conquered and made vassals of the U.S., Europeans, Asiatics, Africans and South Americans would be in no position to declare wars—that we couldn't win.

DOSTOEVSKY

Dostoevski's is the most powerful mind that has left its record in the novels of the world. Beside him such intelligent men as Conrad, Dreiser, James and Balzac grow puny and incomplete. There is no pity, no moral or political attitude of any kind in Dostoevski. He wrote with an almost intolerable understanding of human beings.

REPORTER'S MEMOIR

Most of the great authors I have interviewed talked like idiots. John Cowper Powys told me he was heartbroken because out of the window in the Auditorium Hotel he could see railroads, automobiles, steel girders, but not a single violet.

Arnold Bennett told me that Chicago and London should ultimately produce the same sort of writers because they had the same sort of weather.

Maurice Maeterlinck told me for two hours that American movies (he was on his way to Hollywood to write one for Samuel Goldwyn) were more spiritual than any other nation's.

Sir Oliver Lodge told me that if I would read his book *Raymond* out loud and sit still in the dark for an hour I would see my dead uncle.

Blasco Ibañez raved for an hour to me against the insult Charles MacArthur had offered him by writing an article about his toes.

W. L. George told me that American women are sixty-five per cent less sexual than European women.

Georg Brandes told me that he could not stand America because of its smells.

Tagore told me that the only way to improve the world was to teach people to speak in rhyme.

John Masefield told me that any woman who came to hear him lecture must be half idiot.

Hugh Walpole told me that American women were fifty per cent more sexual than European women.

PROGRESS IN ART

In 1913 Americans thought that Art was men who wore long hair and talked like sissies; naked women in a garret; something J. P. Morgan was interested in; a Chinese kimono thrown over a chair in the vestibule; something they had in Europe; any statue in a public park.

In 1923 Americans think Art is something that doesn't look like a photograph; marrying a negro in the South Seas; anything a Russian does; turning colored lights on the orchestra in the movie palace; a rape scene in a moving picture.

CONCERNING A FINE SICKNESS

The mob tabus, idealizations and tyrannies are phenomena under which the egoist ever finds himself struggling to exist. It is his inability to annihilate the obscene realities of his time that turns him toward the minor anarchy of evading them, denouncing them or sometimes merely hopelessly cataloging them; in short, that turns him into an artist.

The errors of the mob have been always the fertilizers of literature. Without them there would be no sickened individuals—and no art.

ON JOURNALISM

Trying to determine what is going on in the world by reading the newspapers is like trying to tell the time by watching the second hand of a clock.

NEWS FROM OUR RUSSIAN PROVINCE

Arthur Hopkins' fine production of Gorki's *The Lower Depths* grossed $1,800 for its week's run in New York and died. It was in English.

Morris Gest produced the same play and grossed $30,000 a week for a run. Mr. Gest's production is in the original Russian.

THE "CHICAGO SCHOOL" SITS FOR SOME PORTRAITS

Maxwell Bodenheim, in manner and appearance, is the ideal lunatic. He is bowlegged and has pale green eyes. While uttering the most brilliant lines to be heard in American conversation he bares his teeth, clucks weirdly with his tongue, and beats a tattoo with his right foot. He greets an adversary's replies with horrible parrot screams. Having finished an epigram of his own he is overcome with ear-splitting guffaws.

Sherwood Anderson has the garrulity of a small-town barker. He accents his talk by lowering his head, half closing one eye as if he were taking aim at the listener, and waving a hand under the listener's nose like an amateur hypnotist. When discussing politics he pronounces Russia "Roosha."

Carl Sandburg's manner is as distinct as a caricature. He draws his breath in between his teeth before speaking, inflates his chest, lifts up his shoulders, wags the upper part of his body from side to side, and talks with the brevity and importance of the Ten Commandments.

Outwardly his senses are as blind as a bat. He sees black hair as green, looks at a young woman and says her age is fifty, reads preposterous meanings into handbills and colorless phenomena, and emerges from situations with humorously inaccurate memories of them.

But Carl's inner response to life is a beautiful emotion—a fellowship set to music.

ON LITERARY GREATNESS

When an author comes to the end of his creative rope, when he is able no longer to uncover new paths in his mind; when, in short, his originality, style and iconoclasm become a rubber stamp—his "greatness" begins. D. H. Lawrence ceased thinking nine years ago after the appearance of his excellent book *Sons and Lovers*. He started imitating himself. In his new book, *The Captain's Doll*, the imitation has grown banal.

ON PUBLIC GOOD-DOING

The conscience-stricken impulse toward grandstand philanthropies plus the advertising value of spotlighted deeds of nobility sent a fleet of aeroplanes to rescue some starving men trapped in the ice floes of Lake Michigan. I read of the expedition with indifference. I find little excitement in the circus gestures with which my unscrupulous and predatory fellow citizens keep alive from time to time the delusion of Christian love and human fellowship.

ON HENRY FORD

Henry Ford's qualifications for the job of President of the United States are basic and incontrovertible ones. He is the perfect flowering of democratic Americanism.

Mr. Ford thinks history "the bunk." He pronounced William Hodges' play *For All of Us* the greatest drama he has ever seen. He thinks Eddie Guest the greatest American poet. He regards literature as "highbrow, vicious and unnecessary." He is proud of his ignorance and succumbs quickly to hysteria. He is afraid of Jews, afraid of foreigners, afraid of Wall Street, afraid of radicals and equally afraid of conservatives. He is ready to tremble before a new menace every day.

It is the height of anti-Americanism to inveigh against Henry Ford as presidential timber.

THEOLOGICAL NOTE

It is generally felt that when William Jennings Bryan dies there will pass from the earth the last man who believed with his whole heart and soul that Jonah was swallowed by the whale.

I feel that the world will be no brighter when this delusion has vanished.

NEW YORK ART NOTE

A lowbrow renaissance is being drummed up by the lads who do the heavy aesthetic thinking in New York. The pages of the art-enfevered periodicals are full of hallelujahs for Ring Lardner, Joe Cook, Rube Goldberg, Ann Pennington, jazz ballads, Jack Dempsey, Charles Chaplin, etc.

I find in these eastern essays small enthusiasm for the subject under discussion, but a large boast of the writer's ability to enjoy things you might think out of his line—he being so fancy minded and high falutin' a fellow.

I am annoyed at these falsetto cheers set up by our eastern cognoscenti for rough-and-tumble entertainment. They are certain to hurt the robust talents by identifying them as art.

SINDBAD'S FAREWELL

SUMMER CAME, my debts were paid off. I now visited the firm only a few hours a week. But Grady's enthusiasms, unlike mine, continued. He organized two new national fraternal lodges. He explained his ideology to me and Dick in a single sentence—"A million members, a dollar a member, a million dollars."

One lodge was the Anti-Intolerance League, an organization pledged to fight for civil rights of the Negro. The second was the National Order of Camels, meant to overthrow prohibition. It was launched at a mass meeting in the La Salle Theater at which thirty girls in tights served free bathtub gin to a cheering constituency.

Thousands of envelopes full of contributions came to our desks in the Frances Willard Building. Grady emptied the envelopes, stuffed his pockets with greenbacks and sailed off for afternoon barroom revels. He was neither thief nor swindler, but a man of childlike dreams. He explained to me that his great-grandfather had signed the Declaration of Independence and that the U.S.A. owed him—a true Rutledge from Georgia—an eternal debt. Grady collected it out of the envelopes.

I argued nervously that the money was being sent to us to stamp out intolerance and prohibition and that we should use some of it for these ends. Said Grady:

"Suh, when people send us in money to battle intolerance we have already scored a great victory. As fo' stampin' out prohibition, I am doin' all I can puhsonally."

Not a penny of the money that flooded us ever got into the Rutledge bank account. On moody days he bought page ads in the newspapers proclaiming our crusade against the evils of the Republic. What remained, Grady either spent or gave away.

When I dropped in for a conference now and then with my partners, an exuberant Grady, aromatic with gin and cologne, greeted me and thrust hundred-dollar bills into my pockets.

"A dividend, suh," he said.

"How much money came in today?" I asked.

"God only knows, suh," Grady said, "but we are doin' very well. You need feel no concern on that score."

One summer afternoon Grady said to me, "If you want any money fo' anything just ask me."

He looked at me proudly.

"I would like fo' you never to have to do any work, suh, but just sit and write immortal prose, suppohted by our organization. Heah, suh." And my partner placed a thousand dollars in my hand.

"Another dividend, suh."

This was the last dividend. Grady got too drunk that night. His wit, his gaiety, his many graces deserted him. He went home and stuck his head into the kitchen gas oven. He was dead when his beautiful wife woke in the morning.

Thus my first Sindbad came and went.

MY HUNDRED FRIENDS

WHAT FUN living would be if all our friendships survived! If all the chums and partners we had still clamored to see us, and we them! How rich our existence would be were it full of that fine cast of characters with whom we played the many scenes of our lives.

But we must grow old on an emptying stage, and in a corner of it, usually. And if anybody speaks our name we are likely not to know theirs. It is a lucky man who after fifty-five can call anyone "old friend."

Our friends vanish with the events that produce them. I look back on a hundred friends, each of them a fellow who once seemed a vital part of my day and is no part of it now.

This is not as depressing as it sounds. I, for one, have never regretted vanished friendships. They are like money happily spent.

I know men who make a career of not permitting friendships to lapse. They keep telephoning, writing, getting together. But when I look closely at the continued friendships of such men I note that it is with "important" people the friendship is kept going. This is the thing that keeps "celebrities" knowing one another longer than people of no renown. Long after their intimacies have ended, celebrities continue to pool their fame. Being together is no longer friendship for them but something almost as important—good publicity. The cafés of New York and Hollywood are filled nightly with a comradeship more for the camera than the soul.

Obviously when I think of how pleasant life would be if our friendships survived, I am not thinking of my old friends alone, but of my own vanished enthusiasms. It is in their air that my old friends breathed and it is for those heady atmospheres I mourn.

I can see now that any time I loved anything, friends bloomed magically around the thing loved. If it was only walking or playing cards, friends appeared to share and increase my pleasure. They stepped out of limbo and became my fellow dreamers. And there were times when it was I and not my activities that lured partisans. These were times when I loved myself.

Out of many friendships I have learned a few unvarying qualities. Most important of them is the quality of impermanence. Friendship is the thinnest of cements. A change of job or a move to a different street can break the pleasantest of friendships. Marriage can put an end to a dozen of them without a word being spoken. Success requires us to change our friends, as does failure. Persistent calamity is also fatal.

Loyalty and sacrifice, if called on too much, destroy a friendship quickly. It is possible to love a woman who has only troubles to give us. But a friend with similar impedimenta ceases to be an equal and thus, automatically, ceases to be a friend.

I have noted that the best and closest friends are those who seldom call on each other for help. In fact, such is almost the finest definition of a friend—a person who does not need us but who is able to enjoy us.

I have seldom suffered over the troubles of a friend. Are his mishaps short of tragedy, I am inclined to chuckle at them. And he is seldom serious in telling me of his misfortunes. He makes anecdotes out of them, postures comically in their midst and tries to entertain me with them. This is one of the chief values of my friendship, as it is of his. We enable each other to play the strong man superior to his fate. Given a friend to listen, my own disasters change color. I win victories while relating them. Not only have I a friend "on my side" who will believe my version of the battle—and permit me to seem a victor in my communiqués—but I have actually a victory in me. I am able to show my friend my untouched side. My secret superiority to bad events becomes stronger when I can speak it and have a friend believe in it.

Another asset a friend has to offer is the fact that he is a soothing fellow—always half a bore. There are no mysteries to him. He may think he has secret characteristics that are hidden from me. But this is literally impossible. Whatever secrets in the way of hidden personality or sex aberration my friend may have, I have guessed at them—for it is the mark of friendship to imagine the worst possible things about a friend. An enemy is a sealed arsenal of vices, a friend is an open clinic.

In fact, I have thought more downright scandal about friends than about any enemy. The fact that I can see his failings so plainly is one of the things that makes him my friend. I note that he lies, drinks, falls down manholes, is a secret bounder and makes a fool of himself over idiotic women. I am daily aware that he brags, forgets, is as blind as a goat toward his own lapses, and I feel often that only a miracle can save him from disintegration.

Yet my friend's faults never alienate me, for I am, somehow, never their victim. In a mysterious way his friendship keeps him from directing his faults at me. He will point them at his wife, his paramour and his enemies. That is why his faults are comic to me. He is Harlequin and never horror.

There are many other qualities to friendship, such as the absence of competitiveness. A friend is a rival whom I wish well, whose success does not irk me but adds almost as much to my importance as to his. There is also the quality of love, an odd, unsensual love, a love without greed or possessiveness (as I have written some pages back), the sort of love one has for liquor or an infant or a book or life itself.

Such brotherhoods, dead and alive, hold in them most of my history. While writing this book I have looked forward to telling the stories of my friends, not alone because I desired to meet them again but because I hoped to recapture the happy things in my life that produced them.

HOW WE RAISED A SMALL FLAG ONCE

IN WASHINGTON STREET between Clark and La Salle was a large store window reading, "Covici—McGee—Booksellers." This was one of my Chicago homes.

How such a stock of books as cluttered the rambling main floor and basement catacombs of this store ever got itself assembled is still unknown to me. Thousands of books as unreadable as if printed in Turkish were on the long, rickety shelves. Philosophers with two heads and both of them empty stood beside necromancers, statisticians, astrologers and erotomaniacs. God, sex, economics and the Spirit World were represented by those addled sages who seem to wander into print and remain lost forever in it as in a limbo.

Brooding in the gloomy cul-de-sacs of this book market were creatures as preposterous as the volumes they gently fingered. They did not come and go like customers in other stores but took up positions and held them through the day. Broken umbrellas dangled from their forearms like folded bat wings. Mufflers as big as bed quilts wrapped their pipestem necks.

Once a week or so one of these pointed-nosed, nearsighted browsers, overcoated like a snow man, would approach Mr. Pascal Covici and hand him a volume bulging with drivel. Mr. Covici would look at the price mark on the back cover and then leaf soulfully through its pages and say, "Seventy-five cents, sir, and a very fine book, too. Full of provocative ideas."

And Mr. Covici would stand beaming not over the seventy-five cents in his hand but at the wonderful lot that was his—the privilege of spreading beauty and learning in the world.

The daft and endearing secret of my friend Covici's charm was that he opened a book—the shabbiest and dreariest of them—as if he were looking into a ruby. I have known other men who watered at the mouth over first editions, collector's items or merely favorite authors. But my friend Pasquale, as I once called him, was not of these limited connoisseurs. He crowed like Chanticleer because there was light in the world. His soul was full of the genius for applause. I never quitted his store as less than Balzac.

In that time Pasquale was a tall shapely man with a Punchinello handsomeness. His chin quivered, his nose twitched, his pale eyes popped like a baseball fan's and his hair stood up in a turkey crest of excitement. And when he became a publisher, with his day full of authors and artists and galley proofs, with press notices covering half the book counters and a Midwestern literary renaissance whistling around his ears, Pasquale still stood in the middle of his store selling books to the frostbitten-looking strays in quest of the latest news from Spirit World and the Fourth Dimension. He had no office from which to operate, and the desk that had been wedged into the basement catacombs was of no service to him. He was too excited to sit down, and too fearful of missing some foot-loose literary genius to leave the front of his store.

I unloaded all my literary-minded friends on Pasquale. He welcomed them all and, to their amazement, published them all. In this he had the eager co-operation of his partner Billy McGee, a gentle and scholarly man.

The Covici-McGee bookstore became swiftly a Mecca of the arts. The stormy and derisive Bodenheim nested there like a happy hen.

He fitfully helped me fill the pages of *The Chicago Literary Times*, which Covici financed under the delusion he was investing in a house organ.

Ashton Stevens unloaded his knapsack of epigrams there, and Gene Markey, renowned as the only Chicagoan to wear a maroon velvet collar on his tuxedo, brought in his unexpected artist's portfolio. Lloyd Lewis, antic as a colt, joked the afternoons away there. Szukalski, Wallace Smith and my editor, Henry Smith, Sandburg, Lew Sarett, bard of the Indians, Sherwood Anderson, the two moody barristers Edgar Lee Masters and Clarence Darrow—and a rash of essayists and poets—occupied counters and crannies, and two collegians who were cutting their eyeteeth as newspapermen—John Gunther and Vincent Sheean.

Pasquale rushed manuscripts into print as if they were a new issue of greenbacks. J. U. Nicholson, who had left a warehouse business to become "King of the Black Isles," arrived with a new translation of François Villon and a carton of his own bellowing sonnets. There appeared also the mysterious William Saphier, a South Side machinist who was a cubist painter and a writer of mystic verses on the side; and the sick and doomed Italian boy, Emanuel Carnavelli, who was our local entry for Baudelaire.

Sam Putnam's pale, triangular face, with a sinus operation remaining like a watermelon plug in his forehead, appeared, bringing in new versions of Rabelais, Chaucer, Huysmans and other purple stylists.

And a young master of the arts, Herman Rosse, set a standard for book illustrating never to be surpassed in my time. Tall, black-haired and with a curious medieval look to him, Rosse, the Dutchman, had come from quests in China, Java and Bali to fall in love with the skyscrapers, crowds and bridges of our town. The Rosse genius that embraced architecture and the history of culture brought an electric professionalism to the catch-as-catch-can publishing boom in this store.

The most beautiful-looking book I have ever seen was my own *1001 Afternoons in Chicago*, designed and illustrated by Rosse. True, it contained some hundred and five typographical errors, including the printing of whole paragraphs upside down, but it was nonetheless a book of wonders to behold.

J. P. McEvoy, who looked like a sturdy cherub, brought his chor-

tling anecdotes to our Washington Street roost and engaged with
Rosse and me in the cooking up of a musical show. And Keith
Preston, Professor of Latin at Northwestern University, arrived with
the ghosts of Martial and Petronius in his pen.

Keith, small of stature and large of eye and heart, came among us
like a princeling fleeing the dull throne of learning. His wit was like
none I had heard before. Had he survived these Washington Street
days, Keith would have added a quality to our national letters that
is still missing from it—a disillusion made serene with culture. As it
was he left its promise behind in some too-brief books of poetry.

Bartlett Cormack, the dramatist-to-be, and Johnny Weaver, lyre
already in hand; Eunice Tietjens, abubble with Japanese mysticism,
Robert Casey, the itinerant stylist; Junius Wood, Flying Dutchman of
foreign correspondents, Phil Davis, the troubadour lawyer, were
there. And there was one already a legend at twenty-four, Charles
MacArthur.

There also were often the literary critics of the town, Henry
Blackman Sell, Harry Hansen, Llewellyn Jones and Burton Rascoe,
the brilliant high-strung young Tory of letters.

OUR CRITICS AND CLAQUE

THE LITERARY CRITIC has been always a citizen of glamour in my
eyes. I have embraced them all—with two exceptions. The professor
critics who write with coy punctilio and the band-wagon critics who
whoop for winners as if they were an advertising department are unreadable fellows. But as for the rest of them, may their tribe increase.

In my youth there was no finer mental sport than could be found
in the pages of Huneker, Brandes, Pollard, Hazlitt, Taine, France,
Vance Thompson, Mencken, Francis Hackett, Arthur Symons and
their like. The novelist and storyteller wrote out of a score of different moods, most of them sour. The literary critic wrote out of
only one mood, an enthusiasm for literature. He spoke nearly always as a lover. His essays were bright with the graces of courtship. And when he turned his disdain on a man of letters, as did
Anatole France on Émile Zola or Arnold Bennett on Kipling, the

performance was equally graceful. For in such critics there were seldom present the qualities of envy and boastfulness which make critical writing tawdry. These qualities are to be found more often in
the critics of the theater. The theater is as much an industry as an
art and its impurities inspire comment often more worldly than aesthetic.

Our literary critics in Chicago were not all men of style. But
without exception they were giddy with a love of books. The giddiest
of them, in fact, was a young man who was almost entirely inarticulate as a critic. This was Henry Blackman Sell.

To the book reader who lived in Chicago in that day the *Daily
News* Wednesday Book Page was the biggest literary show in town,
and possibly in the U.S.A. Beside it, the New York book sections of
the press were colorless and old maidish. Henry Sell invented our
News Book Page.

Henry had tried unsuccessfully to get a job as reporter on the
News staff. After a number of rebuffs, he popped up in 1918 suddenly on the third floor as the paper's new literary editor. There had
been no such high-sounding character on the *News* before him. We
had had book reviewers whose little comments were to be found
tucked away in back-page corners along with feature stories about
exotic fish and oldest living citizens. But despite a reportorial staff
that was half daft with literary dreams, literature had never rated
serious notice in the columns of the *News*.

Henry Sell changed the paper's anti-literature policy overnight. A
Book Section as large and prosperous looking as our Real Estate
Section leaped into existence. It covered two full pages. The business
office was delighted with it, for it flaunted a great unprecedented
show of ads which Henry somehow had wangled out of New York
publishing houses.

The literary content of this new Book Section was even more
startling than its wealth of advertisements. It consisted of reading
matter as beyond the ken of the *Daily News* readers as if it had been
printed in Chinese, and it continued to offer such similar confusion
to its readers with each issue. Articles on Proust, Huysmans, Sandburg, Gide, Anderson, Dostoevski, Dreiser and Nietzsche appeared
each Wednesday. Beside them were fierce attacks on most of the
popular fiction beloved by *Daily News* readers.

Yet with all its antisocial violence and its contempt for the tastes of our paper's multitude of readers, the Book Section flourished. It sold books and excited talk. It may be that its popularity was of a kind with the pied Russian review of the Moscow Art Theater Company I ran in my *Literary Times*. If so, Henry proved again that there is as much money to be made appealing to the fakeness of people as in catering to their low tastes.

The success of Henry's Book Section inspired the Chicago *Tribune* to imitate it, and another civilized literary forum came into the field. With the existing Book Supplement run by Llewellyn Jones in the Chicago *Post*, this made Wednesday, Friday and Saturday three red-letter literary days for the town.

Burton Rascoe was put in charge of the *Tribune*'s Section. It was with Burton I usually battled in print. At one time we waged war over the merits of James Joyce's *Ulysses*, which was running serially in *The Little Review* before its book publication. I defended Joyce, Rascoe attacked. Hardly a hundred people had read the *Ulysses* installments in *The Little Review*. Nevertheless, the myriads of *News* and *Tribune* readers followed our controversy like a bleacher full of Joyce *aficionados*.

In one of these duels, I give myself the palm. Rascoe, in an effort to prove his superior culture and knowledge, had put in evidence a short story I had written in which the hero, a violinist, "played a Beethoven concerto." Rascoe wrote that this reference to "a Beethoven concerto" was typical of the ignorance of the young writers of this day. Beethoven, he pointed out, had composed only one concerto, and thus a violinist, fiction hero or not, would be playing "*The* Beethoven Concerto."

In riposte I entered Covici-McGee's bookstore, where my detracter was holding forth, and played Beethoven's concerto from beginning to end on my fiddle—with every cadenza and double stop sounded. I considered this a victory. I wish I could always answer critics as well.

Henry Sell and Burton Rascoe left us for New York, but the book sections they had launched boomed on. Harry Hansen took over the *News* Book Section. Hansen was a more literary fellow than Sell. The circus excitements of our Book Section subsided a bit under his editorship. There came into it, however, a more solid literary quality. Hansen wrote well, but more important was that he, too, loved books. He lived among books like a pilgrim in a rain of manna. With the erudite Llewellyn Jones, who was our European fisherman waving a weekly catch of Proust and Gide in our eyes, he kept our high and incomprehensible literary standards alive in Chicago's press for another few years.

In addition to critical opponents, we who wrote had, also, our followers. Surrounding us in Covici's bookstore or in Schlogl's wooden-walled and expensive barroom were a dozen or more lively spirits with no manuscripts to submit to Pasquale. The all-knowing Dr. Morris Fishbein, newly made head of the American Medical Association, was one of these. Morris was a medical savant with a passion for oratory. His pale bald dome gleamed at our table like a beacon of knowledge. He was a man of many charms, high among them being his inability to win at any card game.

The actor Leo Dietrichstein, performing in my first full-length play, *The Egotist*; the comedians Joe Laurie, Jr., Ed Wynn, Julius Tannen, Dick Carle and a perpetual Halloween called the Marx Brothers; the eccentric dancer, and even more eccentric reader, Harland Dixon; the flower-loving killer and gangster, Dion O'Bannion; my favorite detective from the Homicide Bureau, Specs Mac Farlan; Dr. Jake Buchbinder, the softly smiling surgical wizard; George Wharton and Duffy; and the tall and bellowing Scot raconteur and insurance magnate, Alfred MacArthur—all these were there. They attended us not as trainbearers or disciples but as friends produced by the common cause of youth.

I doubt whether they always read what I wrote and I can recall none of their opinions of my work except Alfred MacArthur's, who held that I wrote the "sort of stuff I did" because I was unable to write "popular stuff." I asked Alfred how long it took him to read a popular book.

"Two days," boomed the lyrical Scot defiantly, "and what's more, I enjoy it!"

Whereupon I bet Alfred two thousand dollars that I could write a popular book in two days that would be praised by the critics and sell more than twenty thousand copies. I won the bet. The book was called *The Florentine Dagger* and it was dictated in thirty-six hours. The job was a bore, and I never dictated writing again except once when, in a pet, I dictated a movie overnight for Samuel Goldwyn. It was produced as *The Unholy Garden* and starred Ronald Colman.

Of the "fans" of that time I remember most vividly a Mr. Emanuel Sklartz. Mr. Sklartz appeared briefly one lunchtime in Schlogl's restaurant as a stranger in a slightly shabby overcoat.

Our large round table was crowded with novelists, poets, medicos, barristers and journalists. We were deep in our chopped herring and anecdotes when Richard, the lean-faced waiter who loved us all like a mother hen, came excitedly to our table.

The gentleman sitting in the corner by himself wished us to order some wine, said Richard, and it would be his pleasure to pay for it. We looked and saw the somewhat seedy-looking stranger. He was a small man with a round face. He beamed back at us and nodded eagerly.

We ordered three bottles of Liebfraumilch, causing Mr. Schlogl to raise his eyebrows for he had long looked on our *Stammtisch* as a total loss financially.

A half hour later three more bottles of Liebfraumilch were brought us by Richard.

"With the compliments of the same gentleman," he said.

"Tell the gentleman to join us," Sherwood Anderson said. "We can make room for one more."

"He does not wish to," said Richard. "He wishes only to sit and listen to you gentlemen talk and laugh, and buy wine for you."

We were still "talking and laughing" at four o'clock with eight emptied bottles on the table, when our Liebfraumilch Maecenas stood up. We had almost forgotten him, and I caught only a moment's look of him leaving. He stood in the doorway smiling at us, and his smile was so deep and eager that it lingered in my mind like a benediction after the doors had closed behind him and he was out in the gloomy autumn street.

"Who is he?" I asked.

"I don't know," said Richard. "He has never been in here before."

The next morning I spotted a photograph of our admiring stranger in the news columns. His name was given—Emanuel Sklartz. The story related that Mr. Sklartz had embezzled four thousand dollars from the West Side box factory where he was employed as cashier and that the police had been searching for him.

At five o'clock of the previous afternoon Mr. Sklartz had ended his life by jumping into the river from the Clark Street bridge.

His body was recovered several hours later. A search of his clothes revealed pockets and wallet empty.

I looked at the picture and remembered the vivid, eager smile that Mr. Sklartz had flashed at us from the doorway. And for many years afterward, when I fancied myself unhappy, Mr. Sklartz's smile would come drifting back into my mind to tell me I had once been part of a wondrous world glimpsed and applauded by a man in darkness.

The "Chicago School" produced a number of books of varying merit. Would that our writing had been as fine as our lunches! No common art concept brought us together, nor were we animated by any notions of being "modern" or "different." But in all those who brought their talents to my friend Pasquale to delight and eventually bankrupt him, I recall one quality in common. We were landlocked. There were no other cities in our cosmos than Chicago. Fame began and ended at our lunch table, and Pasquale was claque enough.

We were as unaware of the doings in New York, of its critics, columnists and pundits as if that city were a village in the Carpathians. We aspired to no national magazines as outlets and we had no interest in best-seller lists and book clubs.

This tribal egoism did not make us better writers and artists. But it made us happier ones. I have never known the world to seem as small as it appeared in that time—almost as small and enchanted as it had been in the days I sailed "The Seabird" out of its little cove in Racine.

A GAME OF PINOCHLE

I DINED in my parents' home on Fridays. There were never any other guests. My mother cooked a milk sauce fish or sweet and sour meat balls wrapped in cabbage. After eating, my mother, father and I played auction pinochle (for cash). I preferred them as card companions to anyone I knew. They were as concentrated as tightrope walkers when they played, and as explosive as Puerto Ricans.

It was a windy, rainy autumn night. The familiar cookery, furniture polish and soap smells filled the cozy flat with its Turkish bath temperature and overbright lamps. My mother was partial to strong electric globes. They kept her apprised of any dust anywhere.

I had a cold and my mother was worried.

"I'm quite all right," I said.

"You look tired," my mother said. "I wish you wouldn't work so hard."

I looked at the always shining furniture, glistening floor and woodwork, all scrubbed and polished after she had come home from a ten-hour shift in the neighborhood store they had opened. It was still called "The Paris Fashion." My mother clerked and "did the alterations."

"It's you who should stop working so hard," I said. "You're older and you've got dizzy spells. At least you should get a maid."

"A maid!" my mother snorted as if I had advised her to invest in a crocodile. "They're no good. They're all lazy."

"How do you know?" I asked. "You've never had one."

"I've seen them in other people's homes," she answered.

"Your mother is too particular to have a maid," said my father. "She is too particular in everything." He looked at her with the air of wonder, pride and revolt that I remembered since childhood.

My father reached toward a bulging coat pocket. I knew it was stuffed with reviews and press items of my work.

"Joe!" my mother cautioned him. "I told you not to."

"You're not a law," said my father. "Maybe he hasn't seen some of them. There's one from a Los Angeles paper. A fine piece Chasha sent me."

My relatives had become busy sending one another all mention of me in print.

"I got one also from New York," said my father, "from a Yiddish paper." He looked shyly at me. "Maybe you'd like me to read it to you."

"No, thanks," I said.

My mother sneered at him in triumph. My indifference to "fame" pleased her almost as much as the "fame" itself.

"He isn't interested in such things," my mother said. "Who cares what strangers write about you."

"A bad write-up, eh?" I grinned at her.

"Not at all," said my father. "They would like you to be a Jew —that's all."

"I thought I was," I said.

"What they mean is they think you should write about Jewish problems," said my father.

"I don't like to hear such stupid talk repeated," said my mother. "Deal the cards, Joe."

We played for a time, lost our tempers, accused each other of stupidity and underhandedness. The rain grew heavier on the windows. I had a sneezing fit.

"I'll get you some hot tea," my mother said.

"I don't want any," I said.

"You don't change," said my mother. "You always refuse what's good for you."

She went to the kitchen. My father quickly handed me his pocketful of clippings.

"You can read them afterward," he said, looking nervously toward the kitchen.

I thought of the thing I had come to do this evening. I also looked nervously toward the kitchen.

"I met a professor of English in the park last week," said my father. "I explained to him who I was and we had a discussion about Anatole France."

My mother entered, bustling, a tray in her hands.

"Joe!" she said. "I can't stand it when you talk like that."

"She don't believe me," my father smiled. "She thinks I'm making it up about the professor."

"It's embarrassing," said my mother.

"We talked for three hours about literature," said my father defiantly. My mother filled the tea glasses in silence.

"I've got something to tell you," I said. "I've left Marie. She's keeping Teddy and the house and everything. I'm living in a rooming house. My new address is 610 Astor Place."

My parents drank their tea and said nothing. No comment or question came from them. But I could feel their alarm and bewilderment. They had had no hint of "trouble" between me and Marie. They had been to my home for dinner only two weeks ago and had been full of pride for my fine white elephant of a house, for the two servants who waited on the table, for the beautiful, velvet-gowned Marie who spoke always a bit condescendingly to them and for the loveliness of their grandchild, Teddy.

My parents continued sipping their tea in silence. Tears came to my eyes as they asked no questions. They were afraid I was hurt, and their concern was deeper than their curiosity. I had intended to lie to them about my reasons for leaving Marie, so as not to disturb them too much. But this time I found lying to my parents oddly difficult. There was too much love and loyalty in their silence.

"I'm very happy," I said. "I've been in love with another woman for almost two years. Her name is Rose Caylor. I'm going to live with her."

My father paled and looked anxiously at his Sarah. Her face had become purpled and her eyes were wide with shock.

"I'm sure she's very—" My mother was unable to finish the sentence. Tears appeared in her eyes and she made an angry face. She was thinking of the sadness of breaking up a home. The pain and guilt I had lived through stirred again in me.

"Excuse me," said my father. "You've already left—or are going to? I didn't understand."

"I've already left," I said. "I moved out this morning."

The rain beat more loudly on the windows.

"Joe, I think I left the bedroom window open too much," my mother said. "Go see, please."

My father walked out of the room. My mother busied herself with the emptied tea glasses. She put them on a tray, wiped the moisture from the table under them, looked at me suddenly with a smile and carried the tray from the room. I sat alone. My parents returned together.

"Come on," my mother said, sitting down, "it's your deal, Joe."

We played cards for another half hour. It was the happiest half hour I had ever spent with them. I had violated all their conceptions of decency without lessening for a moment their faith in me. Sinner, home-wrecker, I was still their good son whose actions were not to be pried into or judged. Pride in their love and strength overcame me. I felt that no one had ever had finer parents.

I stood in the doorway saying goodnight.

"I'd like you both to have lunch with me on Sunday and meet Rose," I said.

"We'll be very glad to," said my mother, her face purpling again and a pulse beating in her neck. A sneezing fit delayed my exit.

"I think you should stay here, son," my mother said. "You may have fever, and it's pouring outside. I don't like your being alone in that rooming house."

"I'm not alone," I said.

I walked grinning in the rain, my thoughts repeating themselves like a happy litany—"Not one question about Marie. Not one word about abandoning a child of four. Not one criticism of the never-before-heard name of Rose Caylor. Not one question about her. How sweet to be loved like that here on the West Side—and in Astor Place, too."

A LITTLE ABOUT ROSE CAYLOR

IT IS DIFFICULT to write of unended things, at least for me. I am at my nimblest as a composer of epitaphs. A vanished friend, a dead love come easily to my page. But that which is still alive yields itself reluctantly to embalming anecdote.

It is for this reason, mainly, that I hesitate to write of my relation to Rose Caylor. I would rather continue to write out of it, as I have done for almo . thirty years, as if it were the ink and not the subject. Much of what is in these pages is as much part of Rose as of me. The I who wrote them is a collaboration that began in Astor Place, Chicago.

The Rose Caylor who waited for me while I played pinochle with my folks on that rainy Friday night in 1921 was twenty-two. She had ash blonde hair, oversized brown eyes, and a lithe, quick-moving body of excellent shape. When thoughtful she held her chin tucked down and her eyes a bit upturned, like a matador contemplating a bull. When alert she might pass for an Indian uprising. Behavior of this sort could be embarrassing on windy street corners, where for a time most of our meetings and partings took place. The worldly young man who had existed before encountering Rose Caylor would have been thus embarrassed on those windy corners. But worldliness no longer occupied him after his encounter. He was a traveler come to Arcady and he forgot the ways of other lands.

Among the many novelties Rose Caylor had for me was the fact that she was the first Jewess I had ever known outside the members of my own family. It was, however, a Jewishness with which I was completely unfamiliar, being compounded of politics, learning and elegance. A hundred and eleven rabbis, so I was told, had bloomed on the family tree, the last of them a fiery grandfather who had kept the whole Russian village of Dubinki trembling with worry over its sins.

Rose had come to Chicago from Russia with her mother and two sisters. Her father had come there two years before. In Russia the family name had been Damie, and the fine Spanish grandee face of Rose's father looked more native of Seville than Vilno, the city he had departed. It was in Spain, in fact, that the D'Amie ancestors had flourished for many centuries, and in a fashion undreamed of by the barefoot and unrabbinical hatchers of my own family.

Although young Moishe, my father-in-law to be, had refused to become the one hundred and twelfth rabbi of his line (an office which in later years I used to accuse his daughter of having willy-nilly taken over), he had given a vow to his father, the fierce Rov of Dubinki, to observe always every tradition of the Hebrew faith. And so he did to the end of his days. He was inclined to be more critical than proud of his fellow Jews. But his devotion to their God was persistent and intense.

As is the habit of Jews come to a strange land, Moishe Damie had cast about for a name that would make him sound more American. He had come up with the title Morris Libman.

Lise Libman, the mother, was an equally unfamiliar type of Jewish relative to me. She was openly unreligious and considered the traditions of the Jews a sort of ancient foolery. Nevertheless she dutifully humored her husband in his insistence on eating only kosher food and keeping a multitude of holidays holy.

Not Abraham and Moses, but Marx, Bakunin and Herzen were Lise's idols. She was, it was explained to me, a 1905 revolutionist, although by the time I met her her activities had subsided to attending lectures. In her youth the forceful Lise had not only toiled for the overthrow of Capitalism, but studied medicine. She had been graduated by the University of Warsaw as an obstetrician, and she was practicing this art when I met Rose.

In my first evenings among Rose's kin in their Windsor Avenue apartment, I heard many strange tales, a world apart from the Jewish saga of my own people. They had mostly to do with secret revolutionary meetings in the Vilno home; of pike-staffs, pistols and pamphlets kept hidden in chandeliers and behind the nursery stove; of bold young men the children called "uncles," who wore dashing student caps and played the guitar as they plotted the liberation of the oppressed, and vanished, one by one, into the dreaded tundras of Siberia.

It appeared that Moishe Damie had disdained all these revolutionary dreamers, preferring to play poker with his capitalistic cronies. But then, one day, he had found himself drawn into Lise's revolution. Walking peaceably on a Vilno street, he had come on a funeral parade. It was the sort of parade common in those days when hundreds of young students would appear to escort to his grave any martyr who died for "the cause." At this moment, the tyrannical governor of the province came riding into the street in a carriage surrounded by a troop of Cossacks. The governor gave the order to fire at the mourners. Young Moishe had jumped on the step of the governor's carriage and denounced him for his inhuman conduct. Thereafter, despite his capitalistic views, his striped trousers, frock coat and natty beard, Moishe had been a marked man. He had had to flee Vilno as a "revolutionist" wanted by the police.

Two years later Lise followed him reluctantly, for she was loath to lay aside the task of liberating Russia. With her went Anita, aged ten; Rose, nine; and Minna, born between classes in the Warsaw University, aged four.

Standing at night in the railroad station waiting to leave her native land, Rose had called out to the figures in fur coats and caftans come furtively to see them off, "Russia, I will never forget you!"

A snow-covered land where plum trees bloomed in the summer, a land where gleaming-eyed "uncles" played guitars and sang forbidden songs, was my wife's first love.

I learned of Rose's farewell to Russia long after we were married. Her book containing an essay on Chekhov and a translation of "Uncle Vanya" was dedicated to her mother with the vow at the Vilno station wistfully re-echoed.

On her arrival in the U.S.A. in her ninth year, Rose's accomplishments included the ability to sing the *"Marseillaise"* (in Russian and French) as well as many other revolutionary songs. She could recite also from memory entire chapters of Karl Marx's *Das Kapital*.

In Astor Place I still heard her favorite songs of the workers, among them *"Dubinushka,"* forbidden by the Czar. I heard from her, too, the "Pochoronni March": "You fell as sacrifices in the terrible battle, with a love for the people still unrequited in death"; and "Varshavianka," which promised bloodily, "This shall be the last and decisive battle. With the 'Internationale,' the human being will arise."

I heard these songs not as politics but as sweetly sung memories. They are mingled in my own memory with other of her favorites—the poetry of William Butler Yeats, "I will arise and go now, and go to Innisfree"; the poems of James Joyce, "Love, hear thou, how desolate the heart is, ever calling, ever unanswered"; a stern quote from Montaigne advocating either revolt or suicide, "No man suffers long but by his own fault"; a wistful line from de Gourmont, "Success is daylight to beauty"; and an Arabian proverb of great importance to her, "He who does not resent an insult has deserved it."

Rose's early years in Chicago were stormy ones. Time and again, overcome by some piece of sordidness or injustice, she would arise, usually on top of her desk, and denounce the teacher in three foreign languages. After that, the family would move to another neighborhood.

I am impressed by the fact that one of Rose's first American enemies had been a Miss Heuerman, Principal of the Schley School—a grim-visaged woman who strutted to her office in a form-fitting, waist-length sealskin jacket. Some six years before Rose had been driven from this institution, I, too, had been expelled from it by this same Miss Heuerman. She had struck me with a ruler and I had struck her back. My family, thereupon, had moved to Kedzie Avenue and a new school district, and subsequently to Racine. Many years later Miss Heuerman, possibly overcome by her sins, committed suicide.

At ten, with the aid of Charles Dickens' complete works, Rose learned the new English tongue required of her. She was thus able to organize her fellow pupils into strikes and protest parades, which on one occasion included a march of the mothers of the neighborhood. Thereafter she spoke English without a trace of foreign accent, adding to it, in fact, a fastidious enunciation missing on the Northwest Side of Chicago.

At eleven Rose experienced a deep political upheaval. She resigned formally from the Socialist Party. Her reasons for this drastic move were expressed in full in a signed letter on the front page of the Chicago Socialist newspaper. This farewell address exposing the "fatal ineptitude of Socialists" brought great trouble to her mother, who was believed to have ghost-written it. Both mother and daughter considered this charge libelous. From that time on, their politics remained divorced.

Rose's family were not only novel Jews to me, but Rose was completely novel as a young woman. I had met a few intellectual girls in my tours of Chicago but had shied from them as being deficient in charm or shape—a deficiency which in later years I noted to be usually either the cause or result of intellectuality in most women. The young, swift-walking, flashing-eyed reporter I met in the local room of the *Daily News* one morning had no aura of intellectuality about her. I stared, as I was to write in my first novel, at a face of stars.

I became aware of her peculiar roster of accomplishments later. They included higher mathematics (a wild mystery to me), physics, a thorough knowledge of the banking business, astronomy and medicine.

In the years that followed, she was to publish two excellent novels, edit a banking magazine and a scientific journal; and to preside, under Dr. Morris Fishbein, as the first press agent for the American Medical Association. She was, also, when I met her, a fine professional actress who had toured the country from coast to coast in several road shows, and she was a first-rate newspaper reporter. She read hungrily and was as in love with good writing as most girls of her age are with fine clothes.

These many talents might have irritated or depressed me except for a quality that made them seem a lesser part of her nature. This was a depth of emotion, and it brought me wonderingly to her side. I had never met an emotional woman before. I had even come to believe that emotions were not to be found in women—that they were a sex given rather to minor sentimentalities. The women I had known had been void of tempest. Tempest was the climate of my new friend's heart.

So much I am able to write of Rose Caylor without hesitation. Toward the rest I have a reticence as toward a performance still in progress.

Nothing basic has changed since the first days of this performance, a fact I look on with continuous surprise. I am surprised that a character as wanton, stubborn and articulate as myself has failed to alter by a shading the nature of a woman with whom he has shared his life. And I listen to a similar surprise, sometimes indignantly voiced by my companion, concerning my own unyielding characteristics. But her charge is not quite true. Changed or no, I have been seduced by my companion into enterprises from which I might have remained apart without her. Among these was my emergence as a propagandist for the Jews of Europe and Palestine.

Oddly, though we have remained for decades our separate selves, with usually opposite moral values and emotional responses, people who have known us have looked on us as a sort of Siamese character called Rose and Ben. This twinship we seem to have offered our viewers was based not on our similarity but on the fact that we remained, outwardly, noisily unrelated. In our many homes, crowded with many talented disputants, it was usually with Rose that I debated, and always with violence. Yet in the eyes of those who knew us casually or well, we were always a Rose-Ben unit.

Such twinship is the result of two people remaining alive and separate in each other's presence. It comes of there being not one who rules the roost and arouses interest, but two. It is not a usual thing to find in marriage, which has the trick of reducing one or the other of its participants—more often the wife—to a hazy appendage.

I may write more of this later, but for the present I am content to sum up my many years of love and marriage in a single fact. Just as Rose Caylor sat, in her twenties, reading my manuscripts, belaboring and amending them and at times crowing over them, so she sits today reading copy on the penciled pages of this book.

The room in Astor Place to which I came when I freed myself of my first marriage had gray plaster walls. A casement window looked out on the roof tops. There were few visitors, chiefly Rose's laughing and spirited younger sister, Minna, who was to give up a dream of piano virtuosity for an equally talented practice of medicine as psychoanalyst.

Books were read and written in Astor Place, and tunes that were ever after to make me sigh sounded gayly there.

And then, suddenly, I found that a new freedom had come to me. I could pack my bag and wander. My world was no longer in Chicago's streets and friendships. It was at my side and I could carry it away with me. One summer day Rose and I left Chicago.

More a city never gave a man. I remember out of its many gifts one that still says to me that I did not love that city in vain. It is a press notice that has smiled on me through the many years since it appeared. It was printed on the front page of the Chicago *Herald-Examiner*—a "rival" paper—on the morning I said good-by to the Redcaps in the La Salle Street Station.

It was written by Ashton Stevens, and I recall it, still grateful and not ashamed to boast, just as my friend Ashton typed out its largess without shame. He called on Chicago to fly its flags at half-mast because Ben Hecht was leaving town.

NEW YORK FACES

My publisher, Horace Liveright, with chin line intact.

A. Aubrey Bodine

H. L. Mencken, my alma mater.

Charles MacArthur and Helen Hayes, who charmed an era.

Rose Caylor, my Cis-Alpine Legions.

My father-in-law, Morris.

My mother-in-law, Lisa, and her not-yet-famed psychoanalyst daughter, Dr. Minna Emch.

My daughter Edwina (Teddy), who once introduced me to a friend as "the author of my being and other dubious works."

Marian Stephenson

Henry Varnum Poor, who soothed my Rockland County *Welt-schmertz*.

Dr. Samuel Hirschfeld, who cured all ills but his own.

Herman J. Mankiewicz in the days before his Voltarian exile in Holly-wood.

My daughter Teddy in a rare pose (off a horse).

Gene Fowler, the troubadour from Colorado, in one of his homespun suits.

Leland Hayward, the Ivan Skavitzky Skivar of agents.

Irgun Comrade, Kurt Weill. © *Karsh*

Charles Samuels, my Florida cohort.

Billy Rose raises a strong arm for the cause of Palestine.

One of New York's immortals—Fanny Brice.

If I am ever reincarnated I shall start hunting for Constance Collier immediately, with a box of orchids under my arm.

HOLLYWOOD FACES

My favorite Hollywood artist, Lee Garmes.

My favorite Hollywood boss, David Selznick.

Mr. Mankiewicz and the author as comedian and hero of a silent little-known movie, *More Soup*, produced at Paramount Studios as a Christmas present for Adolf Zukor. (He paid for it.)

My
favorite
actor,
John Barrymore.

Charles Lederer, brooding before a tennis game.

Charles Lederer gladdening the world.

My favorite Hollywood agent,
Myron Selznick.

John Decker and his death profile
of John Barrymore.

Charles MacArthur in a brief bid for movie stardom.

A photograph of his wife taken by
the author.

MGM *Photo by Ted Allan*

Harpo Marx, Hollywood's happiest man,
and his wife Susan.

COMMITTEE FACES

A man of history—Peter Bergson.

On the propaganda barricades, S. Merlin.

The third Palestinian musketeer, Mike Ben Ami.

The hero, Abrasha Stavsky.

Our Irgun art department, Arthur Szyk

A yacht I never rode on.

NYACK FACES

The author with thinning hair and sharpened pencil.

Mother and child.

Manny Fuchs

Halley Erskine

Jenny in a scene from her first show, *Midsummer*.

Jenny entering a ballroom.

Our Gertie.

To whom I dedicated my book.

Roy Schatt

Maurice Seymour

Nanette Herbuveaux before her debut as "Desdemona."

Book Five

ARTIST, FRIEND, AND MONEYMAKER

N. Y. C.

IT IS DIFFICULT to remember the New York I found in 1924. It did not look much different but it had quite a different soul than it has in 1953.

New York in the twenties was a bold town with much the same attitude toward political reformers that the Far West once had toward cattle rustlers. It was devoted to pleasure, particularly to the pleasure of not giving a damn. Seriousness was an un-New Yorkish quality. It stamped the hinterland do-gooder, the rogue with a political ax to grind, the social wallflower and the aged. New York insisted that all its idols wear a grin. It regarded all foreign events, including the first World War, as entertainment. It believed that any war could be won by writing the right songs for it, and not losing your sense of humor. Its patriotism consisted of admiring itself ardently. It doted on its own charms—its chorus girls and Mad Hatters, its bootleggers, its sports and its wags. A bon mot was the town's signature.

It was fascinated, also, with its criminal element. Bootleggers, cardsharps, shakedown gangsters were *personae gratae*, and the town felt a real loss when, in the course of their glamorous occupations, one of them was slain.

The insularity of New York was as deep as its buildings were high. Beyond its confines lay, to the best of its knowledge, a region over-run by cowpunchers, religious fanatics and old ladies. It was a bold town, indeed, sharp-tongued, and individualistic. Its credo had it that New Yorkers were a master race.

I am always amused when I read such argument as the above, pronouncing that a city has changed. There are nine million people in New York and I am sure that ninety-eight per cent of them are as unchanged since the twenties as the squirrels in their parks and the lampposts on their corners. I see these unchanged masses in the subway studying the same comic sections and ball scores. I see them on the curbings beaming on the same parades. They still swarm in and out of little stores and littered streets in the same indecipherable scribble. Occasionally one of them turns a familiar face toward me. This is usually a relative, in from the Bronx.

When I follow him home and sit at his crowded supper table, I discover always the same fact. He has not changed in the last thirty years. It is easy to deduce from this that the other millions of rela-tives in New York have failed also to change.

My relative has the same dim notions of the world beyond his work and family he has always had. Nothing has happened in thirty years to alter his concepts—with one exception. Being a Jew, my relative has a shadow in his heart that was not there before. The massacre of the Jews of Europe has left him wondering whether life is as safe and people as human as he had once fondly believed. But even this shadow is no new thing. His father had it before him.

My diagnosis that New York has changed applies, obviously, to no more than a handful of its people—its upper crust of rich ones and clever ones. This sort of snobbery is natural to historical think-ing. The novelist, concerning himself with three people, will fill his book with confusions and contradictions. The historian who concerns himself with supposedly millions of human beings is never bewil-dered. In his books the world is small, neat and sharply patterned, and thus easily written about with authority. I shall ape his trick —for this chapter.

At the time I entered it, the word to use to describe New York was "sophisticated." There you have the change I write of in a word.

I cannot imagine anyone today writing of a "sophisticated New Yorker." The phrase sounds as archaic as a "noble Roman."

The New Yorker today (my colleague, not my uncle) is a character so different from yesterday's New Yorker that it is hard to believe he lives in the same town. It is even harder to believe that he is often the same fellow—with thirty years on his head.

Out of his laughter at reformers and fanatics has come an odd finale. Reform and fanaticism have become his identity. His joke has vanished. Gone also are most of his cynicism and superiority. He is as tame as a white mouse, and as given to running in circles.

He is not to be called a New Yorker unless you wish to insult him. He is a World Citizen with a grown-up soul. He can prove this by the fact that he has given up all selfish thinking. The adult mind, he will tell you, knows it has a big job to do—nothing less than to straighten out the world.

His head is full of political echoes. Say hello to him and he answers with what "we" should do about China. Buy him a drink and you get an essay on Yalta.

I note that my New Yorker's clothes have become duller, and that his haberdashery has dimmed from Charvet to washable nylon. He has also put on weight. I attribute this to his loss of ego. An inner emptiness creates a hunger which the victim tries blindly to appease by stuffing himself with food.

With his second helping of goulash, my New Yorker takes up the problem of India. His small talk embraces seldom less than a continent. I remember a dinner party in the twenties when a famous lady novelist said to Michael Arlen, who had affected a shepherd's crook for evening wear, "You look almost like a woman." And Mr. Arlen, studying her for a moment, answered, "So do you." New York thrived on this mot for a week.

My New Yorker today has no time for such trivia in his eagle thoughts. The world, he explains, has become a small place and nations can no longer live separately. I am aware as I listen to his premise of the world's having shrunk that my New Yorker knows less of the world's activities than has any New Yorker since 1800. Half the world is masked by a Communist censorship. The other half is equally masked by an anti-Communist censorship. An unvarnished fact has no more chance of reaching my New Yorker than a message from Mars. Nevertheless, he is full of rounded phrases about our duty as a nation to help the peoples of Europe and Asia (he is getting around slowly to Africa). He dreads being called an "isolationist," as the New Yorker of yesterday dreaded being called a bounder. He is either terrified of Communists or terrified of being mistaken for one.

After a third drink, his tax troubles float into my New Yorker's head, and he lowers his voice to inquire gloweringly why the Europeans have to be bribed to save themselves from the slavery of Communism. You would think they would want to do that sort of thing by themselves. A thought comes to him, a horrid thought out of the selfish past—"To Hell with Europe and all its God-damn panhandling governments!" He closes his mouth quickly. That way lies a Senate Investigating Committee.

There you have him. This pale-minded worrier is today's New Yorker—a fellow with a small appetite for life and a great hunger for statesmanship. His soul hovers kibitzer fashion wherever "history is being made."

With this depersonalization, a quality has entered the New Yorker never there before; in fact, never much to be noted in any American. It is timidity. In the twenties my New Yorker had ten times more ego as a fellow to whom headwaiters bowed than he has today as a fellow to whom nations bend the knee.

A PAUSE—FOR REVOLUTIONS

IT WAS actually the world that changed, and its changing reshaped the nature of my New Yorker. I was aware of the change, but I remained untouched by it. The Russian upheaval, the Chinese upheaval and the political din everywhere seemed to me faraway matters.

The upheavals contained a few fugitive tableaux of evil vanquished and the oppressed triumphant. Villains of long standing bit the dust and the disinherited were fed and given songs to sing. I enjoyed the toppling of the villains but my enjoyment ended with the end of this first act.

The finest of these first-act climaxes was the collapse of the toothless medievalist Chiang Kai-shek and his being tossed out of China. I had followed the gallant fight of Mao Tse-tung and his ragged army against the might of the Chinese overlords, the Long March of Mao and his dwindling heroes, and their rise out of near annihilation to run an arrogant and vicious dynasty off the continent. No curtain ever came down on a happier finale—bloated tyrants stripped of power and cast out naked, and the long-suffering, famine-gutted masses of Chinese nobodies showered with chicken, justice, music and love.

But act two was as sad a let-down as act two of the Russian Revolution had been. Again the victorious underdog-hero turned into a politician. The cries of nobility that had sounded during his struggle vanished in his triumph. He was no longer interested in the humanities for which his soul had thirsted. He was interested only in achieving power. And he proceeded to achieve it exactly as the toppled villains had achieved it—by becoming insensitive to every human quirk that stood in the way of his dominance. He whose cry had been, "Am I not a human being entitled to food and justice?" became a politician with another cry—"Who does not obey me will be starved and killed."

This change in my hero's character was not unexpected. What I had read in history and noted myself informed me that the poetry of revolt does not survive into its triumph. In revolt people become individuals stronger than authority. When their revolt is over they become authority again. The individual human spirit, always full of bright vision and hope, becomes the mass human spirit, always muddle-headed and cruel.

WE ALSO HAVE A REVOLUTION

THE revolution that began changing the American scene in the thirties had no Russian or Chinese first acts to offer. There were no long-standing villains to topple or masses to rescue from oppression. Actually it was a revolution by contagion. There being little to purge in the U. S. except human nature itself, it was a movement *in vacuo*. It had more psychiatric than political meaning. It provided disturbed personalities with outside targets for love and hate, gave opportunity to the neurotic to ease his inner guilts by playing Christ toward all the world.

It spent itself quickly as an economic movement. It survived, as a political trend and is still at grips with our nineteenth century concept of Americanism. Although lacking in firing squads and mass murders (as yet), it is basically the same sort of thing that produced Fascism and Communism. It is the increase of government and the decrease of the individual.

In our century of over-population and mechanization, all revolutions have had the same ending, whatever were the slogans that animated them. They produced, if successful, a state with god-like authority and a citizen with none.

I have no guesses to make about the success of this revolution in the U.S. Nor have I much of a call to combat it. The fact that my country along with the rest of the world is busy figuring out how to give the coup de grace to all individual enterprise has little importance to an honest individualist.

In reality the world revolution is a small fact, as I look at it. The business of being myself (with nothing howling me down from the outside) is an almost impossible task. A thousand alien winds are forever inside my head, blowing it out of shape. Being an artist, a fellow who is more fascinated by his own powers than those of any group around him . . . is doubly difficult. Such powers are never too strong in the most peaceful of worlds. They glow now and then for an hour. They are seldom around when I want them.

Thus the fact that a government is seeking to come into existence as my enemy is one of my smaller worries. I have been battling worse enemies since I can remember—age, ennui, fumble-headedness and folly.

I NEVER HAD A POLITICIAN
FOR A FRIEND

I HAVE gone through scores of presidential, senatorial and mayoralty campaigns without ever, but once, feeling or expressing a preference for one candidate over another. My only political activity until the Second World War was to try to make money by betting on a winner. I can't remember ever losing an election bet.

I write of politics now, however, as a vital part of my life. My mind went to school in its many campaigns.

The revolution that came to the U.S. from Russia and China expended itself quickly among the intellectuals. Among the poor in whose name it was presumably being waged it found no partisanship ever. The American poor were too engrossed trying to turn into Capitalists to be interested in the destruction of Capitalism.

The revolution abandoned by intelligentsia and proletariat did not die, however. It was taken over by a large group of supernumeraries—the politicians.

There may be potent causes underlying the business of turning government into dictatorship elsewhere, but they do not operate our American politicians. Our politicians are excited by only one factor to be found equally in Fascism or Communism—the more important the government is, the more powerful and eagle-headed the politician becomes.

In the past fifty years the U. S. has developed a large reservoir of potential politicians. This reservoir consists of men unfit in one way or another for the bumpy roads to professional success. Not quite actors, not quite lawyers, not quite gamblers, and not quite ignoramuses, these loafers and misfits head instinctively for politics.

There is another quality that determines the politician. He is usually a man with a weak interest in living—a weak love life and vapid responses to this, that and the other. Just as his talents and ambitions are not quite formed, so is the rest of him vague. With no insides to stimulate him a man is always ready to stick his nose into outer excitements. This automatically makes a man a politician. Disaster is not disaster to him. It is existence, and opportunity.

There are many exceptions but I have noted a rule that can be applied to nine-tenths of the political species. Just as a man of muscle may be attracted to pugilism, so a man without character is drawn into politics. It is a calling that turns his flaws into assets. It demands of him that he wear his passions like detachable cuffs, that he be spurious and pompous, and that he make himself heard—like a firecracker under a tin can. His chief intellectual equipment is a weather vane sewed to the back of his collar. And he must be as fearless as a pyromaniac. He must also share with the crowd its mysterious faith in calamity—as if calamity alone could solve the confusions of economics, religion and philosophy.

Politics is the only profession in which a man improves with age. This is not because he grows wiser but because a man with one foot in the grave has the ideal political attitude of "to hell with tomorrow."

The crowd has a giddy faith in the aged politico. It knows that a dying man is least worried about disasters and will, therefore, shy less at them. But it is not only insensitivity that makes the venerable beloved. Power is the only immorality possible to old men. History-making is the only spree on which the doddering may embark. And history is the great diversion of the crowd.

MORE ON WHY PEOPLE LOVE POLITICIANS

THE politician is the only American whose work consists almost entirely of bragging. If he would remain on the voters' payroll, he must continue to boast constantly of how all-wise and all-noble he is.

A sensitive man would collapse in the midst of the outcries of self-adulation that must rise from the politician. A politician seldom runs for office. He must pose for it like an exhibitionist.

I am able to understand the oddities of the politician when I inspect his origins. He is a civilized version of the tribal witch doctor.

The sound of this ancient magic-man lingers only faintly in our medical and science clinics. In the political arena it is still boldly evident. Politics itself is not much more sensible than the anthropological double-talk of the tribal medicine man and its objectives are much the same. It was the medicine man who put curses on the enemy, who brought blessings to his constituency, and who solved all problems by howling in public.

Today's human tribe still hungers for magic, and this hunger is sated chiefly by the politician. The crowd prefers sonority to reason in its witch-doctor politicos. The nearer to incantation the politician comes the deeper and wilder is the tribe's faith in him.

Thus the seemingly senseless fellow roaring from the political podium, full of passion and unfinished sentences, fulfills an ancient human need for miracle workers. That the only miracle he seems able to bring about is to set civilization burning like a hayrick is no drawback to his devotees.

WHAT I THINK OF COMMUNISM

IN THE twenties and thirties most of the New Yorkers I met were full of purrs for the new Russia of Lenin and Stalin. I used to feel out of it at the literary dinners and confabs I attended. My lack of love for the Bolsheviki and all their noble slogans made me seem very callous.

My non-Communism had nothing to do with the prospect of the Russians conquering Europe, Asia and the world, or with their Marxist notions of how to run factories. It was founded on the single personal fact that in a Communist state I would be either jailed or shot for speaking my mind. I could understand almost anybody espousing Communism except a writing man or a man of active intelligence.

My aversion to Communism has remained unchanged since that time. I have no patriotic conviction that the economics of my country is any prettier than that in Communist countries. The only vital difference I know is that in the U. S. I can speak what I will, and that in all the mighty land of Russia there is no single human being who can do the same.

OUR EMBRYONIC POLICE STATE

THIS privilege of saying what I think is under attack in the U. S. as I write. It is a small attack thus far, but it marks definitely an advance in the American revolution.

The American politician eyeing his colleague, the Russian politician, feels an obvious wince of frustration. The Russian chair warmer is able to frighten poets, playwrights and philosophers out of their wits. He is able to make them bend their superior minds to his own pool-table level. And he is able to make them line up in long queues waiting eagerly to kiss his ass.

What a fine, powerful fellow this Russian politician is, and how different from the pusillanimous American politician, who, if he wishes to get anywhere, has to do all the ass kissing himself. This Russian example has turned the heads, and the behinds, of several of our American politicians. But their bared political rumps are still collecting as many boots as busses. It is still a toss-up whether a politician will be able to shut up an American, or an American will continue able to shut up a politician.

In the meantime, as is usual in the beginning of revolutions, some damage is being done. A number of writers, teachers, parsons, actors, etc., who have indulged in exotic political gabble have been exposed by a fellow who may turn out to be the American Lenin and Trotsky. He is Senator Joseph McCarthy. The exposures have resulted in some of the victims dying of social shock, others taking to beggary, and the most of them skulking around like a new batch of Hester Prynnes—only with a scarlet *T* for traitor on their foreheads.

McCarthy's chief weapon is neither savagery nor cunning. It is no more than the round heels of the victims. McCarthy needs only to stare at his victims with a slightly queer pair of eyes, and over they go.

These round-heeled American intellectuals depress me more than does McCarthy. They are like soldiers who throw their guns away at the sound of a hoot owl in the night.

I am aware that the terror felt by these soul-baring witnesses (against themselves) is no terror of McCarthy. It is a terror of losing jobs and social status. I find myself without sympathy for them. If a fellow is so afraid of getting kicked off a radio program or out of a Hollywood studio that he must start drooling *mea culpas*, he seems to me as much an American turncoat as does McCarthy. In my eyes he mis-serves his country by his cowardice fully as much as McCarthy does by his power-hungry bulldozing.

For a human being to apologize for any ideas he may have sported with is to deny more than his American rights. He denies his human rights. Americans who are guilty of flushes of anarchy, atheism or Karl Marx are guilty of nothing. Thinking, right or wrong, is the chief business of a human being. As we used to say, free speech is America's most priceless heritage.

In my youth this last sentence was a cliché without which a politician could not get elected anything, from dog catcher to President. Today it is a statement that, likely as not, can fetch a voter a small jail sentence. Thus I can see that our American revolution, although colorless and even a mite comic, has made some progress.

THE MIRAGE OF FREE SPEECH

THE deepest American fear has not been fear of censorship as much as fear of being censorable. I can illustrate this by a brief sortie into Hollywood, which is always a few steps ahead of the rest of the nation in matters of cowardice.

In Hollywood beginning in the forties men and women who challenged, however feebly, the anti-Communist hysteria of the land were booted out of their jobs. The artists who were, or pretended to be, scared to death of Communism, took over the studio plums of the town.

This political purity demanded by the movie bosses of their employees was a small matter compared to the intellectual ninnyism that had long been required of them. From their infancy the movie studios had elected themselves guardian of all American buncombe.

No government censorship brought the movies prattling to their knees. The censorship that removed the movie brain was no work of law. Look at it and you look at the phenomena that in this century have made free speech in the U. S. more daydream than fact.

These phenomena consist of hundreds of private anti-free speech cliques—religious, social and racial. They cover the country. There is even a "Nobleman's Society of America" ready to battle any unfavorable depiction of dukes, earls and kings on the screen. There is an Audubon Society that once rallied its membership to boycott a movie that revealed a mean eagle snatching an infant from its crib. It held that this screen drama was unfair to eagles, and would also hurt our prestige abroad since the eagle was our national symbol. The movie was reshot with an escaped lunatic snatching the infant. The analytic and psychiatric societies had not yet been organized, so there was no further protest.

And there are social clubs, Catholic clubs, Jewish clubs, Rotary, Lion, Kiwanis and all manner of lodges and societies and associations. All these cliques bombard the studios with commands to put nothing on the screen that will irritate them.

The commands are, actually, wasted postage. The studios already know what is right and what is wrong—from every point of view except that of the art of drama. There are boards of experts in the studios who ponder each script for violations of any cliché. Even these boards of experts are unnecessary, for the men who make movies are already experts at saying nothing. No censorship rules laid down by the anti-free speech Russian government surpass the thought strangulation of the movies' own movie code. In it everything is forbidden.

Even innocent words are forbidden because they may have a double meaning or because they are distasteful to the paranoid nice-nellyism of the American.

"You are nuts" is a forbidden phrase. Nuts might mean testicles to some sensitive masturbator.

"You're a bum" is forbidden because to an Englishman "bum" means ass.

"You're lousy" is forbidden because the movie-goer who sits scratching his bum and picking his nose while watching the films might consider it vulgar.

The movies are not alone in this social servility. The radio and television programs are equally given to a sort of passionate proof that the stupidity of the audience is a finer (more lucrative) thing to serve than truth.

The thousands of associations and committees, which are constantly meeting in every city and village of the Republic, have for their common goal the subjugation of free speech. They offer so large and united a front against it that its practice becomes not only unpopular, but economically dangerous.

An American police state may be nearer than I have imagined. That it will come is almost a certainty. Americans are already an anti-individualistic lot. The word "American" that, presumably, once stood for independent thinking is today a synonym chiefly for conformity.

My countrymen think actually in the same manner as do the conforming Russians. Americans think what they are told by their politicians. On their own, they think what is good for the protection of their delusions and preservation of their myths. They need no policemen to club them into line, as do the stormier-minded Slavs. They are already there.

The move from suppressing thought by innumerable little cock-eyed vigilante groups to suppressing it by one large dignified body called the U. S. Government is not likely to be an involved or dramatic one.

A HANDFUL OF PATRIOTS

I AM as certain that a war is coming as that it's going to rain. War is the weather of humanity. It surrounds the human soul as winds and dusts do the earth.

I am not as certain who will be our enemy. At present it looks like all of Red Asia, most of Europe and a large section of Africa. So I imagine we will be dodging their atom bombs, and they ours. When such a day comes I shall be quick to concede that the Reds are disturbing the peace (if it is they) and must be destroyed for the good of civilization—us.

But I am not living in tomorrow. I see no sense in borrowing its fears. Nor do I care to prepare myself for it by making myself into a calamity howler incapable of enjoying today. It is today I live, and today the only disturbers of the peace around me are the Red hunters.

These Red hunters are of no more help to our military forces who may someday be hunting Reds in earnest than a barking dog is to a deer stalker. They are nothing but a nuisance. Their hysteria serves only to give our nation the pop-eyed look of a gent who has lost his way to the water closet.

The fiercest of the Red hunters among us nowadays is the ex-Red who has turned his coat. This fellow is usually a dollar chaser. The worse he can make out the Red menace in our midst to be, the more important and expensive are the revelations he has to sell.

As for the "good" he might do us by awakening us to the Red menace among us, it is the same good an idiot boy might accomplish by yelling "fire!" while watching the movie *Quo Vadis*.

Next in line among our Red hunters is the American of German sympathies, still smarting over the German defeat. This is usually a fellow who had to keep his German love fairly well hidden during World War II. He can come out now with his hatred of one of Germany's conquerors—Russia. He is also able to throw mud at those Americans who once worked side by side with the Russians to help crush the Germans. This Red hunter is not hunting Reds. He is avenging himself on all who hurt him, all who helped knock out his world champion—Beau Hitler.

Another of this rabble of Red hunters is the citizen with a load of troubles in his psyche. His sex is off, his wife sets his teeth on edge, his business is driving him potty, and at night dark things twist at his innards. Not so long ago such a fellow was eager to pounce on the Jew as the son of a bitch responsible for everything wrong in his world. But, dim-witted though he be, he has noted that the Red has become for the time a more socially rewarding scapegoat. There is a raised eyebrow, here and there, to stay the anti-Semite in the U. S. There is almost nothing to unnerve the most cringing of the anti-Red soldiers.

Present in this army of Commie hunters is the fellow who likes to feel heroic but has not enough mental courage to sass a waiter. This wallflower who would be Richard Coeur de Lion is eager to believe all the looney cries of phantom dangers set up around him. He adds to them excitedly. The government is overrun by Reds. Reds are skulking everywhere. Reds are threatening to take over his very home. And so he takes his place in the thin ranks that are ready to give battle to this Red menace. The thin ranks consist of ninety-nine per cent of the hundred and sixty million Americans around him.

The Red menace before him being actually as dangerous as a June bug makes everything perfect for the coward who would play hero. He marches daily in battalions of millions against this June bug, and thunders daily against it. He goes to bed glowing with a sense of courage. His generalissimo is Senator McCarthy.

—WHERE WAS I?

I RETURN to the New Yorker of the twenties. He was no great philosopher in his distaste for politics. He bumbled away inanely enough on a hundred major topics (see the works of H. L. Mencken). But on the most major of them—whether he preferred to bray as a lone jackass or as a herd of jackasses—he had a little more sense. He was inclined to go it alone. The politicians had not yet lured him into being more interested in their souls than his own, or in their jobs than his own. He was still a selfish fellow busy with his own world centers. And a series of world calamities (and the threat of worse calamities coming) had not yet given him the feeling of guilt toward being a human being.

Thus he lived in a city and not on a slippery globe. He sharpened his mind (when he had one) with a hone of anarchy and a strop of egotism. I put down his battle cry years ago—about the time he was beginning to vanish.

I quote from *A Jew in Love*, published in 1931, specifically from my hero, Jo Boshere. This worthless fellow, who cost me much trouble with Jews who do not like the word "Jew" used in a title, said:

> "I'm in accord with nothing. I don't give a good God-damn what happens. I'm not interested in industrialism or how Ford or Stalin or anybody else runs his factories. All I know is that factories have nothing to do with life. And that the whole business of making more shoes, selling more shoes, wearing more shoes is a stupid cul-de-sac into which the human race has run itself by inventing machines."
>
> "Well, what are you interested in, then?" asked Mark. "Art?"
>
> "No," said Boshere, "I don't give a damn about art. I'm interested in myself, in human relationships. I'm the boy who's going to preserve what little of value there is in the race. A hundred years from now, you see, there'll be a few Bosheres in the world who will keep psychology alive just as the monks kept culture alive during the dark ages. You fools look down on me as a futilitarian, a man of waste, a fellow who isn't part of the big throb of progress. Well, the true progress of man is in our keeping, in my keeping. We develop ourselves. We sensitize ourselves more and more. We pull ahead of the God-damn dithering crowd of workers and politicians and factory heroes and public-spirited oafs. All we do is feel and analyze our feelings and, little by little, century by century, pull the human idiot out of the swamps into which he was born. We don't serve governments or charities or theories or factories. What we serve is evolution."

MY GROTTO IN FOURTEENTH STREET

IT WAS autumn in New York. I lived on West Fourteenth Street on the top floor of a tenement with a fine aromatic stairway. Around me whirled the spokes of a new city. It had a foreign air. Its people sauntered. A thing strange to my Chicago eyes—antiquity—marked its scenery.

There were more stores, more enterprises and larger crowds than in Chicago, and, surprisingly, there was a greater friendliness in the streets. The people seemed to look on their city as half playground. They strolled its busiest sectors with an air of diversion. The city entertained them.

The real strangeness of New York for me lay in things you could not see—the fact that there were theatrical seasons and music seasons; and that the skyscrapers were full of magazine offices and publishing houses. There had been only one Covici in Chicago. New York seemed to swarm with Covicis—all clamoring for works of art to launch. At times I felt I had come to no city at all but to a bazaar in which I and a few thousand like me were for sale under the loose stock label of artists. Confronted by this suction pump of publishers, producers, editors and agents, I struck my colors and wrote not a word for a year. I felt annoyed by so much "opportunity." At times the day that leaned into my Fourteenth Street window seemed like a fretful customer, and the blaze of electric signs at night were sales rung up on a cash register.

A quartet of old Chicago friends appeared in the loftlike apartment in which Rose and I, as nude of possessions as monkeys of top hats, had come to roost. There appeared again Herman Rosse, the Dutch Marco Polo—tall, black-haired, full of ambassadorial politeness and a thousand schemes. There came to our door again J. P. McEvoy, short and solid as a wrestler, with an electricity-filled crop of hair streaming from his cherub's head. He was as top-heavy with projects as Rosse—except that Mac's projects usually increased his bank balance. The third was Henry Sell, already become a magazine editor for Mr. Hearst and whirling about among duchesses. The fourth was Charles MacArthur, the musketeer from Chicago's Madison Street.

On my first day in the city I had run into Gene Markey, one of Chicago's most elegant exports. Hearing that I, too, was to become a New Yorker, Markey, who had already flaunted his velvet-collared evening jacket in all the highty-tighty places, briefed me loyally on the social mysteries of our new bailiwick.

"And if some important hostess with a diamond stomacher invites you to a party," said Markey in conclusion, "and promises you that you'll meet the most captivating, thrilling, faunlike charmer of our time, don't get your hopes up. It's always that sonofabitch, Mac-Arthur."

Some New Yorkers also appeared in Fourteenth Street. Among them were the publisher Horace Liveright, gaunt and sparkle-eyed; Herman Mankiewicz, the Central Park West Voltaire; the artist Bob Chandler, a tall, bushy-haired, white-overalled millionaire, boisterous and incoherent; the whiskered essayist Ernest Boyd, booming sacrilege out of a Christlike face; the poet Sam Hoffenstein, a man full of eerie problems; and Alex Smallens, the Mephisto-faced conductor.

Of these, Liveright was a new sort. I was to meet many versions of him later, but none had crossed the prairies to Chicago. He was the ego with no tune of its own, in love with the songs of others. No writer could admire himself as much as Horace admired him. His publisher's office—a foolish-looking Florentine chamber—was overrun with cadgers, fakers and ingrates who, being writers, were all geniuses in Horace's eyes. He pressed money on them, wined and coddled them like some daft Maecenas. A mysterious luck and the Sancho Panza eye of his business manager, Arthur Pell, kept the firm's head above water.

I remember one of the Liveright authors, the best-selling historian Hendrik Van Loon, complaining at the Liveright dinner table in New Rochelle.

"You don't run your business right, Horace," he said. "A publisher should have dignity. Instead, your sanctum is always full of rag-bag creatures. You waste most of your time on nobodies with holes in their pants."

Horace answered, "It's not always a waste of time. I recall one nobody with holes in his pants—a dishwasher from Greenwich Village—who got in to see me. His name was Hendrik Van Loon, and

I published his thousand-page manuscript and made us both rich."

They were all young who came to Fourteenth Street. There were no chairs for visitors and insufficient crockery and cutlery for serving them. I had left all my possessions in Chicago to solace Marie. Funds were also lacking for the purchase of food or payment of rent, for I had come to New York without a dollar in my pocket, an aversion to all employment in my soul and a sunny feeling that I could live by borrowing money from rich people or by concocting schemes to bamboozle coin out of them. I borrowed, but only from fellow paupers, and my schemes turned into comic anecdotes instead of paying swindles.

There were parties, and songs rang out from our windows. Music also entered them after midnight—ascending raucously from a dance saloon below. No lovers were ever more violently serenaded.

Through our windows we could survey, across the alley, the back porch of an institution called "Home for Unmarried Mothers" and behold each day a half-dozen blown-up pregnant girls, knitting away sullenly in rocking chairs. Rose, not yet married to me, beamed and waved at these unfortunate sisters of romance, proving how futile is moral propaganda to a happy sinner.

We lived for a year without thought of time in these near-barren rooms. There was no dream of fame in them or any plan for tomorrow—but only a stretch of secret hours more vividly lit than all the streets of the city.

Ever since these days I have had a nostalgia for poverty, and I am sure I wasted the fortunes I subsequently earned in the hope of coming on it again, as upon a halcyon friend. To have no coin for restaurants or theaters or taxicabs and to be independent of all store fronts; to have no money yardstick with which to measure, to want nothing, to have nothing, and hunger only for what can come out of one's own mind or the heart of another—to live in such a fashion outside of greed and the economic system—is to know the only joy of life that is without taint.

These days in Fourteenth Street were the days of love, too deeply lived to be recalled by anything less than a poet's magic. Sitting now at my writing, a little less than poet, I can remember but vaguely the intense and inexhaustible relationship between Rose and me. Like the stone caissons of a great bridge, those memories are out of sight. But the bridge, now thirty years long, still rests firmly on them.

MANHATTAN SEDUCTION

BEFORE COMING to New York I had written books and plays and thus come head on with that moody tyrant, the Public, and with the Fu Manchus who served it as critics. Neither had made any impression on me. I used to feel a distaste when I saw my name in print, but my curiosity about what the print said was small. I seldom read more than a few lines. I felt I knew the merits and demerits of my work well enough. Outside information was unnecessary.

This immunity began to desert me in New York. I started responding to criticism, oral or printed, and it was many years before I recovered my shell.

Responding to criticism is a foolish thing for a writer to do, and an unpleasant one. It is much better to read only the advertisements of your work and to note, briefly, your royalty reports. These will tell you how popular you are. How good you are, or are not, is a thing you know only too well yourself.

Criticism can never instruct or benefit you. Its chief effect is that of a telegram with dubious news. Praise leaves no glow behind, for it is a writer's habit to remember nothing good of himself. I have usually forgotten those who admired my work, and seldom anyone who disliked it. Obviously, this is because praise is never enough and censure always too much.

My social habits also changed in the new city. I had had none before. In Chicago I would as soon have thought of rowing across Lake Michigan in a hollow tooth (as Ring Lardner once cried out) as of visiting anyone for "social reasons."

This aloofness began to leave me in New York. I started going to florid places, fishing for importance and, worse, feminine applause. I joined, gingerly, the café parade of personalities who lived each day so that they might merit an item in some gossip column.

I trotted after social literary groups who played charades, who coquetted with radical causes, who called all famous people by their first names and managed somehow to be snobs and artists both. I was pleased to find myself in some demand at week ends full of ping-pong and headliners. These celebrity get-togethers were a sort of proving ground for wit, alcoholism and prestige—a *La Vie de Bohème* with butlers. They were duller than the drinking rallies I had known in Chicago. But their function was less to entertain than to confer a sense of superiority on their participants. If you felt bored, you could look forward to boasting of having shared a week end with these famous ones. A little Sunday boredom was a small price to pay for Monday's strut.

This liking for people loud with personality and success surprises me as I look back. I have no such liking now. A roomful of celebrities today depresses me, possibly because I have learned at first hand the wretched things that make a celebrity—the pain of almost constant defeat, the arrows of a thousand critics forever sticking out of your rump, the fact that your name has become a magnet for irritation, malice or calumny. And worst of all, the fact that a celebrity cannot, like luckier folk, drop out of sight when he is ripened with age. He must stay on the vine and rot—for all to see and disdain.

But in those other years I was not depressed. A roomful of braggarts, wits and poseurs, of literary kings and stage queens, all bursting with talent and press notices, delighted me. I made few friends among them, for I was not looking for friendship. They were like troupes of actors among whom I, too, could perform.

If I seem to sneer at these glamorous parties now, be assured I did not in the days I yielded them my social virginity. I had a good time and was a good actor. I repaid all my hostesses by exuding a string of anecdotes like a prose barrel organ.

THE KANGAROOS I MET

THERE WERE many curiosities in New York. Nearly all the "Radicals" I met were extremely rich. Its poets were ambitious and worldly fellows. Its finest ladies, including happily married ones, engaged in promiscuous sex as if they were college boys on a spree. Conversation consisted mostly of offering clever insults to your fellow guests. Every other celebrity was being either psychoanalyzed or having his glands tinkered with. You never had to pick up a check in the expensive restaurants. There was always a millionaire in the group waiting to assert himself by seizing the bill.

But these were minor oddities, along with the strange odor of streets and the Turkish-bath smells of the subway, to which I became quickly accustomed. There were other strange matters, however, which continued to keep me wondering. One of these was a new type of male fornicator whom I had met nowhere before. They were men who made seduction their chief activity.

I had known lusty fellows in Chicago, including our local Charlemagne—the immortal Harry C.—who had futtered twenty-five whores in a single night in Minnie Shima's House of All Nations. Reliable newspapermen had kept the score. Bawdiness, in fact, had been a natural atmosphere since boyhood. But in Chicago I had come on no Don Juans. In New York they appeared to be blocking traffic.

As a psychologist I was pleased, for these were the first men I had known who were eager to relate the ins and outs of amour to me. I was introduced conversationally into dozens of interesting bedrooms and given play-by-play accounts of sexual maneuvers. I was privileged, also, to watch the Don Juan at his preliminary chores, for he was a fellow who craved publicity with his courtships. I wondered which was more the object of his desires—the woman he cooed to bed or the men before whom he performed most of his amorous rites.

I needed no help from Freud to understand this Eastern fornicator. He wooed his quarry with a sort of female silliness. He talked as women did, giggled like them, was ruthless and snippy as are flirtatious girls. He was full of a feminine talent for dancing, gossiping, cooking, giving parties, overdressing and idling. He was able to flit from one pair of thighs to another with no sense of proprietorship and a minimum of romance.

Listening to the Don Juan's bedroom anecdotes, I sometimes thought my informants were lying their heads off. How was it possible for a man to meet a famous actress at lunch and have her undressed in his bed by four o'clock? And how could you cohabit with a ballerina in a taxicab, or seduce your hostess with her husband playing backgammon in the next room? Such speed and hazards would have nipped romance for me. But I learned that, for the most part, the Don Juans did not lie. They told all the truth they knew.

The fact that I had never discussed a woman I knew with any man made this spate of confession doubly surprising. I became aware that my appeal to the Don Juan was a fatherly one. Despite my youth (I was usually a good ten years younger than my confidant), I appeared to offer a sort of fatherhood to lean on. I hesitate to say motherhood. If it was "mama" rather than "papa" to whom they brought their problems, the shoe was on their foot, not mine.

I discussed this "new" gentry with Liveright, who was one of them. He pursued women as openly as a small boy running down the street after a fire engine—and this, despite the fact that he was greatly devoted to his wife. In fact, most of the Don Juans I met were doting husbands, and a half of their confessions was concerned with how terrified they were of bringing pain to their spouses.

"I'd die if she ever found me out," Horace used to say a little sadly of his mate. "She's the most wonderful and sensitive woman in the world."

He had a long-nosed, eighteenth-century face. It was a masklike face that became alive only when a smile lit it or drunkenness elated it.

"What fun is there in laying a woman you hardly know?" I asked.

"You use crude words," said Horace. "One doesn't lay a woman. One loves her."

"A stranger?"

"No woman is a stranger," said Horace. "I mean that a beautiful woman is somebody you know with one look. You know she's meant to be loved—and expects it. Not to make love to a beautiful woman is to insult her. And yourself, too. It's like refusing a challenge."

One night in Long Island we were guests at Otto Kahn's country estate. I had retired at one A.M., leaving Horace in deep talk with a young woman he had met that afternoon. I was unable to sleep, for the deep talk continued in a grotto under my window. At four A.M., irritated by the Liveright phrases that kept floating into the magnificent guest room, I walked into the night. It was raining.

Soaked to the skin, Horace was still bombinating in the grotto. As I approached, I heard him saying, "God, it's wonderful to be real! I'm glad we stayed out, because I can see you now, as you really are."

I interrupted. Pulling Horace around a Kahn castle buttress, I pointed out he would get pneumonia if he stayed out in the rain all night, particularly since he was not an outdoor type.

"The girl is obviously mad about you," I said, "so why the hell don't you bring her in the house?"

"I can't," said Horace. "If I go in the house I'll have to take her to bed. And I'm impotent."

"How do you know you're impotent?"

"I always know when one of these impotent spells hits me," said Horace. "Always the same symptoms. An apprehension, a fluttering in the lower bowel region and a dryness of the mouth. She'll be sleepy in an hour or so. So kindly beat it and let a lack of nature take its course."

Though he seemed to do nothing but pursue women and drink himself into nightly comas, Liveright was actually a hard worker and a brilliant one. He published scores of fine books and produced a number of successful plays. He loaned courage and money to many fumbling talents. He fought ably against censorship and was one of the chief forces that freed the literature of the Republic from the strangle hold of its old maids. He launched the Modern Library—the first introduction to the larger public of the world's fine writing. There was in New York no more popular and exciting figure than Liveright. Beauty, success and admiration attended him like a faithful retinue, and hundreds of hangers-on were proud to boast of his friendship.

I was in Hollywood some ten years later when Beatrice Kaufman, who had once worked as a reader in the Liveright firm, telephoned with the news that Horace was dead. He had died broke and full of debts.

"I wonder if you could come to his funeral," Beatrice said. "I've been on the phone all day. So far I've only gotten six people to agree to come."

I was unable to leave Hollywood. On a drizzly day, Beatrice Kaufman and five other New Yorkers accompanied the forgotten pauper, Horace Liveright, to his grave.

In later years I came upon the true hearth of the Don Juan, a place where he not only flourished but set the standards of love and social behavior. This was Hollywood, to which impotence of every sort was drawn as by a wondrous magnet.

JUDEA'S ANONYMOUS KINGDOM

THE GREATEST ODDITY in New York was its Jews. Within a month after settling in Fourteenth Street I had met more Jews than I had run into during my entire preceding existence. They were Jews without accent, and not remotely connected with tailoring—a novelty to me who had known only the Jewish voices and needle-ish activities of my family. And, as in some fairy tale written by some pale ghetto dreamer, they were among the elite of the city.

I felt some confusion. I had always considered myself as un-Jewish. My un-Hebrewizing had been achieved without effort or self-consciousness. I would have said in the days before I came to New York that I was a Jew by accident, and that I had shed this accidental heritage as easily as ridding myself of some childhood nickname.

It had been normal to look on one Jew, myself, and consider him un-Jewish. But it was difficult to look on a swarm of Jews and accept them similarly as un-Jewish. It took me a long time to stop counting, furtively, how many Jews were at a dinner table, and how many famous Christians had intruded. The score ranged from two-to-one to ten-to-one in favor of Judea.

I felt a pride in this Semitic ascendancy that seemed little shared by the ascenders. I noted that my colleagues were no prouder of being successful Jews than they would have been of being unsuccessful ones. Their pride began where their Jewishness left off.

And "left off," their Jewishness had, amazingly. Twenty-five centuries of identity are a lot of baggage to unload overnight. But outside of family names, to which they clung with a subterranean Jewish stubbornness, my New York Jews seemed to have managed the unloading with dispatch. No one could be less religious, less tradition-ridden, less inheritors of broken accents and social obloquy than these celebrities and celebrity fanciers into whose midst I had come. The fact that their parents, like my own, had usually been shawled and yarmulka'd immigrants, made this mass un-Judaizing seem more a piece of legerdemain than cultural evolution.

Although I was one of them, there was little in common between me and most of these New York changelings. I was to find nettle-like proof of our different psychologies as un-Jews in the events that awaited in Europe and Palestine. But before proof fell on me, I had studied it leisurely.

My colleagues had discarded their Jewishness out of the belief that as Jews they could line up only for a snubbing. As Americans or, more particularly, as egoists and talents, they could step forth as superiors and even as snobs.

In this we differed. The menace of being snubbed as a Jew was no part of my renegadism. The snub menace felt by these superior Jews surprised me when I first met it, for it did not exist for inferior ones I had known. A wagonload of Popes, backed up by the entire Four Hundred all pointing belittling fingers, would have fetched only sneers from the souls of my uncles, tantes and parents.

Having got this whiff of anti-Semitism, I looked around vainly for the anti-Semites. They were possibly under my nose but they remained shy in my presence as stupidity usually does when confronted singly by its betters. Thus I met anti-Semitism only through the Jews who were more open to its distress.

I understood what the trouble was with these colleagues. They were full of a pretense missing in me. To become un-Jewish involves no pretense. The pretense lies in the delusion that, having ceased to be a Jew, you have become something else.

Also, my colleagues had become un-Jewish out of fear, rather than out of sacrilege or indifference; and this fear stayed in them. It kept them as vulnerably Jewish as if they attended their First Nights and Croquet Tournaments with talliths around their shoulders. Their pretense that they were something else made my New York un-Jews easy victims for any hostess who chose to stare at their origin rather than their billing.

Perversely, in this center of un-Judaizing, I began to turn into a Jew. It took many years, and I am still uncertain whether it was actually a Jew I became or a humanist. But in those early years in New York I began to look with pride on what was obviously a Jewish-dominated culture. In this world's tallest city, most of all that was entertaining came from Jewish talent. Most of its theaters and many of its publishing houses were run by Jews. Most of its songs were written and sung by Jews. Jews gave most of its concerts, wrote a good share of its plays and poetry. The most elegant parties were as likely as not to be hosted by Jews, and the most exclusive emporia whose labels were symbols of fearless extravagance were more often Jewish than not. There was even a noticeable percentage of Jews writing in its newspapers—among them the new tribe of columnists who were refashioning journalism. Finally, that which was most distinctive about this world center was almost entirely Jewish—its laugh-makers.

Behind the footlights capered a great Jewish cast of clowns and troubadours. They were not only entertaining a nation but shaping its wit and its rowdy flair of dialogue.

I had always, since my first day in Chicago, been lured by the vaudeville theater. In New York, I attended all the Palace Theater shows, all the musical shows and, still unsated, dragged Rose into neighborhood theaters where the lesser acrobats and warblers were on view.

Twenty-five years later most of these antic performers are still the singing, talking and dancing stars of the nation, for they are a hardy lot—these gay Semites. But what a troupe they were in their heyday! What a wild yap of wit and sweet burst of song came surging out of the Jewish slums in the twenties! The Marx Brothers, Al Jolson, George Jessel, Fanny Brice, Eddie Cantor, Jack Benny, Jack Pearl, Benny Fields, Lou Holtz, Ed Wynn, Joe Laurie, the Howard Brothers, Julius Tannen, Phil Baker, Phil Silvers, Milton Berle, Belle Baker, Harry Richman, Ben Bernie, The Ritz Brothers, Smith and Dale, Ben Welch, Harry Green, Ray Samuels, Jackie Osterman, George Burns—these are some of them. There were others.

I was not content to sit out front enjoying them. I joined them in their clubs and hotel rooms, and they became in my mind a second set of relatives. In their presence Jewishness was not Jewishness. It was a fascinating Americanism.

I JOIN A PARTY

THERE WAS A MEANING to the hullaballoo that embraced me in New York. I write of it now with a survivor's understanding. But I had inklings of the truth when it was exploding around me, as had many of my fellow celebrants of the twenties.

This truth was that our twentieth century, inheritor of the budding charms of humanity, never got fully started. It died young in

its second decade, just as a person sometimes dies young. As a time
of human growth our century came to an end in its teens. I had
arrived in New York in time to join a wild and premature *fin de
siècle* party.

Before the sadder years to come made all this plain, we had a
sense of it. We were, in the twenties, a disaster-haunted society.
Ideals had entered oratory. We knew that the more idealism a country pumped up, the more politicians would be necessary to "imple-
ment" it. And the more politicians there were, the more trouble
must come. We busied ourselves putting up the only show possible
against doom, which is to seize all the fun there is.

Thus people sang louder, drank deeper, danced longer and
squandered themselves in every direction. They fornicated in caba-
ñas, in rumble seats, under boardwalks. They built love nests like
beavers and tripled their divorce rate. High, and many of the low,
gave themselves hedonistically to the pleasures of the hour. In the
background, demagoguery, the foulest of the arts, was fingering its
kettledrums and its megaphones. Pleasure was not long to remain
the simple objective of humans. The age of large individual diversion and small mass problems was marked for disposal. The democracy that ate only cake and piped all hands to a continuous picnic
was going to "grow up." Knowing all this in their bones, the people
of the twenties put on paper hats and blew New Year's horns.

The century's farewell party to the pleasure principle of existence
lasted fifteen years. It kept going through a depression and a near
panic. Our *fin de siècle* ball lit up all the cities of the U.S. Anarchy
was its password. The citizenry turned its back on tomorrow, and on
the politicians who were to hand them over soon to experiments in
power.

Crime came to our party. Crooks and hop-heads toting machine
guns became the national idols, for all such hooligans had one honorable thing in common. They risked their own lives in their bid for
power. Politicians were ready only to risk everybody else's life in
their scramble for high places.

There was more than drinking, fornicating and Mardi Gras tumult
to this party. Hedonism is the finest of climates for the arts. Thus
there was also a last stand of poetry and eloquence.

Death had not yet become too common for awe, nor sacrifice too
trite to make a ballad of; nor peace too improbable to inspire its

minnesingers. Those of us who glimpsed what was coming drew the blinds on tomorrow and enjoyed ourselves without its shadow on us.

I sometimes think of the people I knew who died while this party was in progress. How they must have hated to quit a world so promising, so full of gallantry, charm and mirth!

OUR PARTY'S HISTORIANS

A NEW SPECIES of writers and reporters appeared in the New York newspapers. I found their work more interesting than that of most of the current novelists. They chronicled a larger love affair—the one between the nine million human wallflowers of the town and its hundred headliners.

Men with a sharp, taciturn style to whom a full-blown "scoop" consisted of a line or two of trivia dominated the press. The leader of these café Prousts was Walter Winchell—but I read them all. Part of my interest was due to the fact that my name was likely to appear in the "columns"—for no reason at all, except, possibly, to chronicle that I had said "hello" to somebody. I found such appearances meaningless but pleasant—as if I were a showcase object at which a finger pointed occasionally.

My favorites among these floorwalkers of Broadway were Winchell, Leonard Lyons, Ed Sullivan and Louis Sobol. Winchell wrote like a man honking in a traffic jam. His energy was amazing, and his style was as arresting as a café brawl. In the twenty years I have read him, Winchell has not yet written a sentence I didn't understand—which is some sort of a literary record.

Lyons was the Scheherazade of the cafés. His opinions were rare, and, unlike Winchell, his ego almost invisible. He wrote (and still writes) the tale of the town's wit. His heroes are epigrams, his heroines (a minor group) bons mots. Scandal seldom intrudes in the Lyons column, or controversy. Come rain or snow, come hell or high water, my friend Lyons writes only as if the world were full of flashing repartee.

Ed Sullivan's history of the town is a more human one. Occasionally the half-glamorous appear in it, and, at times, the totally unglamorous. This is in a way a violation of the trivia-historian's code.

But Sullivan makes up for it by throwing in an Irish heart, full of Tom Moore truculence and tenderness.

More faithful to the code is Louis Sobol, whose daily column is like a Santa Claus pack full only of glamorous names. The names sometimes wear quotes or minor activities, but more often they are the pleasant gifts of names unadorned.

In Chicago our chief columnists had been sports-page writers and the great wags. Among them had been Gene Field, George Ade, Dick Little, F. P. A., B. L. T., Keith Preston, Hugh Keough, Ring Lardner, Charles Collins, Charles Dryden, Jack Lait. Their New York colleagues struck me as a lesser crew. But there were three of the lot that were prime, Jimmy Cannon, Bill Corum and Bugs Baer.

Corum's sports-page column was a running tale by Dumas. Jimmy Cannon's had more variety. Dostoevski and Schopenhauer took it over, and occasionally Villon and Byron sounded in it. In fact Cannon had (and still has) more the air of a literary renaissance than a columnist.

But the marvel of all columnists (of Chicago or New York) remains Bugs Baer. I read him with daily astonishment for twenty-five years. This king of zany metaphor is without rival anywhere, including between book covers. His long-labored picture of our country is as ribald and powerful a caricature as ever put down.

The city's intellectual ferment went on in another sort of column that I usually skipped. The ratiocinations of Heywood Broun, Walter Lippmann, Samuel Grafton, etc., were a shade fancier than the anonymous print of the editorial pages, but there was much the same drone of politics in them. Occasionally their writers let go with a piece of pixyish fiction, as if to prove that even a great journalist philosopher has his human side. I found the proof usually unconvincing.

One of them, however, held my eye and has kept holding it year after year. This is Westbrook Pegler. I had known Pegler *père* in Chicago and listened with young ears to the snort and crackle of his barroom talk. Son Westbrook had brought his pa's epithets to New York. His bulging portmanteau contained also some dornicks and dead cats of his own. In fact, the lethal verbiage I had admired in Mencken echoed in Westbrook Pegler.

The new thunderhead was not as informed as Mencken. He was, apparently, too busy chasing scoundrels up and down alleys to sit down and read a book. And unlike Mencken, he fell into the error of making friends and handing them candy. This was as disturbing as seeing the young Jack Dempsey take time out to kiss the referee.

I usually skipped Pegler's infatuations and took note only of his honest brutality. He often clouted at targets dear to me. But I was rewarded for my occasional dismay when Pegler aimed his haymakers at chins I disliked.

I found in Pegler, however, more than an attractive rage. He was a sort of one-man counter-revolution going on in the U.S. He fought the mushrooming statism of the Republic and another concentration of power—its labor unions. He took swipes at the Catholic Church and even at a few Jews. He slipped occasionally, for he fought on muddy ground. And when his eyes fogged he was apt to knock over a few innocent bystanders.

Pegler's small cheering section is shy of people I admire. But when he finishes his stint in the land and the editorial shears take him over, he will emerge as one of the brightest of the prose lighthouses in a time darkened by the pall of government.

EXILE IN CLOVER

MY NEW YORK activities were many and varied. I lived for years in a shower of anecdotes. But I have small impulse to relate them. I would like, rather, to write of the lonely fellow who sat in his Nyack room and wrote books, mooned in a garden and studied the Hudson River. This was the self I had brought to Gotham, and preferred to all the other selves that kept appearing and elbowing it into a corner.

> *I came to town like Galahad,*
> *I wandered in like Don Quixote,*
> *With a pencil and a writing pad,*
> *A suitcase and an overcoat—*
> *Pensive and a little mad,*
> *And hungry as a nanny goat.*

Such a fellow continued to exist, despite all the fanfare of Manhattan. He wrote some eight books and a half-hundred short stories. Of them, he preferred the volumes *Count Bruga*, *A Jew in Love*,

A Book of Miracles, A Guide for the Bedeviled and the *Collected Short Stories.* He was proudest of the Miracle book. The critics praised it greatly. But hardly anyone read it. Even in London, where it was identified as one of the important books of our time, it remained unread.

My lack of readers never bothered me. Reading the critical praises my prose usually stirred, I was able to fancy myself an author of enormous prominence and was thus happier than my publisher—who read the royalty statements as well.

My ability to please literary critics and yet fail to attract many readers was due, possibly, to what I wrote and the way I wrote it. Had I written thirty books in New York instead of eight, I would likely have lost what readers I had. For it was my pleasure to write with a whip as much as a pencil. I disliked social or historical themes. I shied from the problems of "little people." I frowned on heroics; and I had a distaste for heroes who represented anything but themselves.

I wrote of people as if I were a doctor in search of their diseases. However lively my bedside manner (I rarely pulled a long face), I was never much welcome. For it is people's conviction that they have no diseases, that their clichés are all symptoms of roaring health and that their virtues are all there is to them. I was a diagnostician with another report. Hearing my knock, customers turned their backs.

At least, such is my picture of my unpopularity as a book writer. But there is more to the picture. The fact that the very critics who acclaimed me forgot me—that was as much my fault as theirs. How could they continue to look on a man as an ironical intellectual who seemed loudly and persistently to be the opposite of such an ivory-tower resident?

This other fellow who got in my way was a self that competed with the literary con men called entertainment makers. He wrote plays and dashed off movies. He scribbled away as rapidly and expertly as a gambler shuffling a deck of marked cards.

I smile at this fellow tossing off manuscripts, attending rehearsals, bombinating through studio conferences, launching producing companies and, without pausing ever to catch his breath, signing more and more contracts. And why?

The money I earned meant almost nothing. I was no more interested in money than in cigar bands, even when it came in in huge sums. I never hid it, invested it or even spent it. I allowed it to blow away—while I sat for six months or a year doing what I liked—writing a book, mooning in the garden and studying the Hudson. What with taxes, dependents, alimony and an ever-growing menage, I sometimes had to earn two hundred thousand dollars during the first half of the year in order to be able to sit out the second half as a prose writer.

The tax-hungry government was a large factor in my literary problems. But my own nature was equally to blame. There had been in me always a duality often to be found in writers. I was eager to write like a beggar but live like a king. I managed to do both for a long time, sliding constantly from penury to riches in a fashion often startling. The move back to riches has grown more difficult of late. Age has put sand on the slide.

Now that I am approaching elderly years of bankruptcy, I look back on my improvidence a little wryly, but still tenderly. It was a sensible improvidence. I never stored money away for future use because to have money in the bank worried me too much. I feared it might keep me from working. I was certain that six months of idleness would destroy me.

I feared idleness as some men fear a contagious disease. My book written, I could never lie around waiting for another volume to burgeon in me—even if the bank balance permitted. A week of doing nothing found me moping and fearful. Traveling was small help. A month in Mexico or South America was all I could endure. The mope would hit me while flying over the Andes or basking in a Mexican fishing village. Without a task to do, I became convinced I would expire of ennui.

It was this menace of ennui that propelled me into the theater and the movies. As a man, slightly demon-driven by melancholy, seeks the cure of liquor and gay parties, I went after tasks. Work itself, swift, half mindless and exhausting, was a happy drug.

From what was I fleeing—hiding? Perhaps from age and death. Or from bitter and untenable angers at the world. Or perhaps from other things. Whatever it was, I need never know. I kept too busy for it to catch up with me.

FANNY

AMONG THOSE who offered parlor space to the windjammers of the town was Fanny Brice. This was in the time when Fanny's name was like a Christmas tree. There was no one like her on the stage. She was Bernhardt, Yvette Gilbert and Toto, the clown. She also danced, hilariously.

Off stage she doted on poetry. She knew a whole volume of Paul Géraldy by heart. She stood spellbound before paintings and was the first of the theater's stars to turn Rembrandt after hours. All the arts were in Fanny, even the Black One. She could do telepathic and Yogi tricks, hypnotize people and, in a pinch, foretell the future.

Theater audiences never adored any performer more than Fanny. I used to sit among them. It would be impossible for an audience to laugh louder, weep more copiously and applaud more violently than Fanny's audience did—and all in thirty minutes.

There was still another response in Fanny's audience—rarer than any of its noisier ones. This was respect. I have known only one other actress who could arouse so remarkable a feeling of homage in an audience—Helen Hayes. The air of human dignity had something to do with it. Behind Fanny's zaniest antics, as behind her saddest ballads, there was always an air of pride. It was not the pride of the comic evoking laughter or of the Thespian stirring applause. It was a pride that was not given her by audiences, but existed mysteriously in this lady out of nowhere.

In her home Fanny was as vivid as she was on the stage, but vivid without jokes or routines of any sort. There was not even the aura of theater about her. No memories of glamour or success were in her talk. But her vividness glowed in a room as if all the Ziegfeldian arcs were still aimed at her.

Fanny died a few years ago (1951), but her features and personality remain more alive for me (and many others) than all her great performances on the stage. Fanny, who could stand like a queen and smile like a clown, who contradicted you as fiercely as a cop with a rubber hose; who, when pleased, turned into a kitten on a couch with a beam like the Hatteras lighthouse—her postures and grimaces remain in my mind because they were rare in the world. Fanny was the individualist whom artists dream of being, sometimes become and seldom remain. Success destroys ego, wealth washes away personality, and the society of other successful people will flatten an anarchist into an amateur butler. None of these things happened to Fanny. The opinions of mankind, the two wars that smote her time and their attendant revolutions, were to Fanny as nonexistent as the doings on the moon. As soon as a war convulsed the nation, Fanny cancelled her subscriptions to all newspapers and magazines. She knew on which side she was—and that was enough politics for Fanny.

Fanny lived her life among people—a thing so rare as to make her seem off another planet. Like some fanatic at an easel, she was interested only in the sitter's face before her—the face of another human being. Into this face she stared with all her art and mysticism. On it she smiled. At it she cursed. Her love and hate were for the human face only. What went on behind such a face was Fanny's idea of the world.

Reading this Fanny would have said, "You write it a little fancy, kid, but you've got some of it straight." And she would have asked me to mention how she disliked fourflushers; except that Fanny never disliked anything. She either hated or she loved. Her hate was hot but seldom enduring. "You hate somebody because they've hurt you," said Fanny, "and nobody can hurt me—long."

Off the stage for fifteen years, with most of the Fanny Brice band wagons returned to their garages, Fanny died intact. The last time I saw her she was still enthroned in the realm of Fanny Brice. She was still unrelated to all the problems of the world, still aware only of self.

She was tall, well shaped, fastidiously rigged out and bejeweled, manicured, scented and as vivid at fifty-nine, when I said good-by to her, as she had been at thirty, when I met her.

MACARTHUR

MY MOTHER-IN-LAW, Lise, a woman of soul, will sit in a theater, laugh and deeply enjoy herself. But she comes out of the theater usually with a shrug and a sigh. "What did it give you to take away?" she asks. "Nothing. It leaves nothing in your mind or spirit. An evening wasted."

But I am wiser than my mother-in-law. Although an unused self stands in the way of half my memories of New York, it does not do all the sighing and shrugging for me. I retain a part of the enthusiasm for the show I enjoyed. And the most fun of the show was those with whom I shared it.

Of these, my friend Charles MacArthur was the most active. We wrote plays and movies together. But our literary work was only a sideline of our relationship. Even the adventures we shared in Mexico, and other spots of the earth, were a lesser factor.

Our friendship was founded on a mutual obsession. We were both obsessed with our youthful years. I had no more interest in Charlie's past than he had in mine. But for twenty-five years we assisted each other in behaving as if these pasts had never vanished. We remained newspaper reporters and continued to keep our hats on before the boss, drop ashes on the floor and disdain all practical people.

But it is difficult for two grown men to continue playing games and palavering as if they were marking time in some pressroom. Thus, since MacArthur (the non-reporter) was hotly in love with the theater and I was ready to work on anything, we added playwriting to our relationship and later movie writing.

We finished only a few of the plays we started, *The Moonshooter, The Front Page, Jumbo,* and *Twentieth Century.* I sigh, remembering the first acts we threw away, the merry plots we lost and forgot. We were lavish fellows and we gave no damn for anything except our youth, and how to keep it going in the teeth of bald spots and graying sideburns, and, God forgive us, even paunches.

It was Charlie who lured me to Nyack. He had been raised on a hill outside the town where his father had tended a sort of tabernacle. The elder MacArthur was a handsome man with the Bibles (both of them) roaring in his head.

Looking around for some place where we might write a play without city interruptions, Charlie remembered Nyack. In Nyack, he said, we would find peace and inspiration. We went there and rented a girls' college that had recently gone bankrupt. Here we lived in some fifty bedrooms for the summer.

Helen and Rose were allowed to interrupt us on week ends. It was on one of these Sundays when the four of us were eating a picnic lunch on a hilltop that we all decided to move permanently to Nyack.

MacArthur was a man of quicker perceptions than anyone I have ever known. He seemed without psychological attitudes and yet he was as aware of people as if he had eavesdropped on them in an analyst's office. The same paradox marked his allure. He seemed never interested in attracting anyone, yet people scampered toward him as if pulled by a magnet.

Alec Woollcott, who loved him, said to me once, "What a perfect world this would be if it were full of MacArthurs."

I knew what he meant. It would be a world in which people charmed each other and let each other alone; in which people knew each other's secrets but never intruded on each other.

I had been used to living in many worlds but beside MacArthur my life seemed almost parochial. He was a fellow with a genius for living everywhere. No place ever quite seemed his home except the past. Murger wrote of Rudolf in *La Vie de Bohème*: "He walked backward through life looking at the day he was twenty-one." MacArthur is still something like that.

One of the many attractive things about my friend was his modesty. In the many years I have known him, I have never heard him utter a boast on any subject.

I never tired of playing games with MacArthur. He was an inept player at cards or sports. The only physical activity at which he was expert was fist fighting. There he was savage and graceful. Had he trained for it at the proper time, he could have been a ring champion of the sort that earns himself the sobriquet of K. O. or Wildcat.

I liked to play games with Charlie because he brought a fierceness to them of a pressroom reporter with a dime left in his pocket. He brought this same fierceness to all thumb twiddling. We never argued through the writing of an entire play. But any game of chance was attended with shout and accusation. A game was the only side of life to which Charlie could give full concentration.

Whatever he did, except play, he did half abstractedly, as if he were thinking of something else. The importance of the work or the danger of the deed never robbed him of this faraway look. He brought it to my Nyack room where we worked together and to the parties he loved to attend. He carried it into wars and wild adventures. I knew its meaning early. It was MacArthur's unused self, smiling gallantly on a world that would never know him.

MANKY

MY FRIEND Herman Mankiewicz died while I was writing this book —and I lost its best reader. But Manky offered me a greater loss. He never wrote a book of his own. What a book that would have been, if only a third of Herman's hilarious and fearsome meditations had gone into it.

I met Herman when he was young, but the doom of unproductivity was already on him. I knew that no one as witty and spontaneous as Herman would ever put himself on paper. A man whose genius is on tap like free lager beer seldom makes literature out of it. In Chicago, the brilliant George Wharton had remained the same sort of unbottled fellow.

I have sat in a room filled with writers of every kind and there was only one to whom we listened—the "non-writer" Mr. Mankiewicz. Beside Manky, the famous people among whom he buzzed all his life like a hornet or gadfly seemed pale-minded.

What did Herman Mankiewicz say? What were his observations, his jokes, his tirades? It is hard to remember. There were too many. They were on every topic. They snarled and lampooned and laid bare sham and roguery. They revealed that all the stupidities of successful people only increased their success, and all the wit of unsuccessful people added only to their failure. They examined the art output of New York and Hollywood, and hundreds of dinner parties quaked as they laughed at Manky's reports.

Manky had no wish to be a funny man. He would have shuddered more at the name "comedian" than he did at any of the others hurled at him by his enemies. (A man cannot hold his world up to caricature for thirty years without a yip out of some of his subject matter.)

Yet most of Manky's utterances, including his deepest philosophic ones, stirred laughter. Even his enemies laughed. He could puncture egos, draw blood from pretenses—and his victims, with souls abashed, still sat and laughed. The swiftness of his thought was by itself a sort

of comedy. Never have I known a man with so quick an eye and ear—
and tongue, for the strut of fools.

Manky died in his fifties, still writing movie scenarios. That he
lasted as long as he did surprised me. To own a mind like Manky's and
hamstring and throttle it for twenty-five years in the writing only of
movie scenarios is to submit your soul to a nasty strain. Manky wrote
good movies. One of them, *Citizen Kane*, won him an Oscar. But all
of them put together won him an early death.

When I remember the dull and inane whom Herman enriched by
his presence, and his numskull "betters" who tried feebly to echo his
observations; when I remember his thrown-away genius, his modesty,
his shrug at adversity; when I remember that unlike the lords of success around him he attacked only the strong with his wit and defended
always the weak with his heart, I feel proud to have known a man of
importance.

A NEW CAST OF CHARACTERS

THERE ARE still parties to go to, and I attend occasionally. Youth is
present at these get-togethers but it makes small noise. What racket
there is comes mainly from the elderly. Bald heads and graying faces
sing the old songs and uncork anecdotes of the past.

The young ones listen agape but with some disbelief. It is difficult to
imagine the world was so different so short a time ago. It is hard to
picture saloons overrun with young Napoleons, parlors teeming with
egomaniacs who wore the future like a posy in their buttonholes, who
plotted over their *canapés* how best to become millionaires and earth
shakers. Our *fin de siècle* ball seems further away than the days of
D'Artagnan. But it was only a couple of wars ago.

In that fabled time, there were countless rallying places for our
pleasures. I remember them, happily.

It was with Manky and MacArthur I did most of my social explor-
ing and met the tops of the town. I list them as I might recite the
cast of a play seen long ago.

Herbert Bayard Swope ran a talkfest in his Long Island keep. Otto
Kahn's castle, not far off, sounded with poets, painters and houris.
Liveright and Bob Chandler and Louise Hillstrum spread Lucullan

wines for wagonloads of Balzacs and Villons. Alexander Woollcott, master of bons mots, presided over a court of croquet players and epigram fanciers. A persnickety fellow was Woollcott, with more fizz than brain. But there was a snap of dialogue in him and he animated a room like a scandal.

Alice Duer Miller, erect and fastidious, crowded her manor with clowns and bombinators. She was a lady with aspic manners and a poet's heart, and she made the arts seem a little more gallant than they are.

Ernest Boyd sat amid his whisky bottles, bearded and erudite, flinging the accents of Dublin at a moony Bohemia.

And on view among the calliope noises were Moss Hart, full of *Weltschmerz* and learning to drink out of an oversized brandy glass; George Gershwin, looking like an eager, youthful rabbi; Oscar Levant, lean, snarling and unpsychoanalyzed, turning a piano keyboard into a string of firecrackers; Helen Hayes, with the wings of Bernhardt in her young and blazing eyes; Sam Harris, who walked backwards through thirty years of theatrical success, looking at his champion Terry McGovern in the ring; the water-whistle laugh of Bob Benchley; the Indian-faced Ring Lardner, gayest of writers and most melancholy of drinkers; Don Stewart, the pixy revolutionist; Dorothy Parker, with a pretty garrote of phrases in her reticule; the collaborators George Kaufman and Marc Connelly, who had wrestled George M. Cohan's mantle partly off his back; F. Scott Fitzgerald, with his sophomore face and troubadour heart; the baggy Heywood Broun, snowshoeing his way toward some Utopia; Dick Maney, crackling with language and high disillusion; George Antheil, driving the music critics out of Carnegie Hall with his airplane propellers and mechanical pianos; Harland Dixon, prince of hoofers, with Nietzsche dancing in his head; Max Anderson, shy and full of rhymes, shedding his schoolmaster shyness on Broadway; the waggish Howard Dietz, with his Packy MacFarland strut; Harold Ross, looking like some stranded cowhand, ringing doorbells and asking for funds to start *The New Yorker*; the tall, comic Muscovite Gregory Ratoff, filling the town with love bellows for his goddess Eugénie; Red Lewis, the Babbitt scalp fresh in his belt; Jack Kriendler and his ever-growing troop of brothers bowing us into our favorite oasis; Walter Wanger, the most elegant and learned of the movie satraps, toiling to make New York a cinema center—God forgive him; Bill Gropper, happily sketching the collapse of the Capitalist system; Mike Gold, the Greenwich Village Marat; Leland Hayward, tall, pale and prowling the backstages, breathing hard; Frank Case, extending credit to a swarm of literary paupers in his Algonquin Hotel; Conrad Bercovici, the one-man gypsy encampment. And there appeared, also, the first run of camel's-hair coats out of a Neanderthal Hollywood; Myron and David Selznick, zigzagging through the town to throw creditors off the scent; the ex-Berlin tap dancer Ernst Lubitsch, who brought a fleeting grace into the movies; the portly Hitchcock, beaming amid his nightmares; Leo McCarey, larkish as an O'Casey character; the mysteriously romantic Howard Hawks; the brooding Basque Harry D'Arrast—and—and—

JED

ONE OF the theater people I came to know well was Jed Harris. He was a graceful and cadaverous young man who looked part matador and part Talmudic student.

Before it became penny doctor for the world's ills, New York was given to finding its great among the arts, mainly the art of the theater. In the twenties, Jed Harris was one of these great ones. Although he seemed to have no friends, he was one of the topics under constant discussion at all the places I stopped.

Jed was gifted with a genius I had not encountered before. It was a genius for boasting. He spoke of himself with a tender passion, as if a hero were under discussion. He moved among writers and actors with the air of a Socrates among his disciples. His superiority was baffling and provocative. He was not overattractive physically, being underweight, unshaven and with the look of caricature to his face. He cared nothing for adventure and lived as cautiously as any office worker.

Yet out of this man of small equipment arose an overpowering air of genius. Nor was he alone in proclaiming himself Caesar. Nearly all who came within sound of his purring voice, and looked into his flat, motionless eyes, were ready to echo his pretensions.

Good luck had something to do with his realistic success. For a time, Jed produced only successful plays. Their success created a legend that Jed Harris could not fail. The legend turned out to be non-sense. Jed failed again and again. He fumbled and guessed wrong like the most inept of showmen.

It was in the time of his unsuccess that I came to understand the thing in Jed that I had often railed against—the "genius" compounded of nothing. When this genius was gone I saw that it had once actually existed. I felt lessened by its vanishing and was aware that a remarkable quality had dropped out of the world in which I moved.

Jed's genius had been the genius of certainty. His were not the pumped-up certitudes of one who hopes for success. They were as much part of him as his features. He never had doubts. His opinions arrived suddenly and permanently. Quietly, never raising his voice above the purr that compelled listeners to lean toward him as if they and not he were a bit deaf, Jed spoke always like an oracle. To contradict him was an almost sacrilegious act.

Such certainty is usually found in preachers and politicians. It is rarest among theater folk. However large their egos are, they are inclined to be lame with doubt toward the world.

In Jed this certainty glowed and never wavered. I used to think it was a sort of egomania, a narcism, a step removed from the hamminess of the worst type of actor. I saw soon that I was wrong. Behind Jed's certainty there was actually a swift and mystic superiority to life. He was right when he boasted he would have made as successful a financier, statesman or scientist as he was theatrical producer had he turned in those directions.

I used to stare at this genius in Jed as at mysterious riches, wondering out of what glands or delusions it came. Though I quarreled with Jed, I nevertheless found writing for the theater easier in his presence, and I even wrote better. I was able to borrow some of his certainty.

I remember it with envy and have thought often how much easier my life would be if I had a half of that talent which was Jed's. How lighter the task would be if certainty were part of it—how enjoyable all the toothachy business of writing! But it is not a quality that can be borrowed or invented. I have been stubborn and even dedicated to a job, but I have remained always a stranger to certainty, whether it was the certainty that led a panic or a battle.

TROUBADOUR BILLY

THERE HAS BEEN always in New York a small band of city *aficiona-dos*. Their faces put together in a photograph spelled out the name of New York. I had belonged to the city *aficionados* of Chicago, which handicapped me from joining the New York chapter. My psychology as a city lover was fixed.

In Chicago the small band who were official Chicagoans by virtue of talent, publicity and a special dash of personality shunned all popular rendezvous. Our swank lay in concealment.

In New York I found an opposite *aficionado* credo. Invisibility was as painful to a New Yorker as a quinsy sore throat. He had a buglike tropism for publicity. To be seen was as important as to be. There is a nervousness that goes with fame in New York. The celebrity is haunted by the fear of waking in the morning and, like an inverse Byron, finding himself unknown.

Of the New York *aficionados* I met, Billy Rose, song writer, café keeper and fame hunter, was the most authentic. He was at the time in his twenties, as who was not? He had a winsome look and reminded you of the hero of certain photographs they hawk in Mexico as "artisticus."

Billy loved many things, but the deepest of his loves was the city of New York. Fame lay hidden in it, to be gone after with pick and shovel. Billy had a residence and an office, but his true home was the cacophonic street, and the café in which he sat all night—without drinking. He was never lonely, for he had a larger family than any patriarch. All celebrities were his relatives.

Billy was a new sort of dreamer to me. Nothing like him had been on display in Chicago. We had press agents and showmen there, but beside Billy they were furtive fellows with their heads in a sack. They felt always a mite embarrassed in their scramble for newspaper plugs. Billy knew no such embarrassment. Without his name in the paper, Billy felt nude.

From the time he moved uptown, as unknown as a locust, Billy Rose, in his own eyes, was a public figure. All that remained was to fit himself with a proper wardrobe of headlines and walk with New York on his arm.

The New York press, unlike the press of any other American city in that time, had a soft spot for publicity seekers. It supplied Billy with the wardrobe he desired, and long before he had done much to merit attention, it began calling him the "pint-sized Barnum" and the "Midget Maestro of Broadway."

The newspaper insistence on Billy as a "pint-sized" character always surprised me. I was never conscious of his shortness until I read about it. This was due to the way he walked—with the bounce of an overwound toy; and to the way he stood still, head raised, face expectant, like a man about to climb a flagpole. And also to the fact that he was no shorter than half the men in town.

The outside layers of Billy Rose the showman are made of neon lights and the best Bessemer steel. Within exists a man of deep modesty and astonishing sensitivity. Before any evidence of talent Billy is as wistful as a June bride. Genius holds him spellbound. The secret of his keen showmanship is that he himself is full of applause for every human performance of merit.

His enthusiasms have carried him from Gyp the Blood to Stravinsky, from carnival alley to Rembrandt. And he has remained after thirty years of showmanship his own best production. He lives like a fanatic and does all his thinking in high. Not a day passes but finds him jumping off Brooklyn Bridge with Steve Brodie. Yet this jackpot of projects is never preoccupied. Through the years I have known him he has seemed always the idlest of fellows. Success and wealth have failed to change him an iota. He is as important only as the current idea in his head, and as in love with life as if he were yet to meet it.

When I walk of an evening down Broadway with Billy Rose, I become aware of its lights and many signs as if I hadn't quite marked them before. The Broadway that is always a dusty, half-slatternly amusement park in my eyes, changes for me as Billy looks at it. It is the bride as beautiful as an army with banners.

"I WROTE A LETTER TO THE WORLD THAT NEVER WROTE TO ME"

IN THE MIDST of those days of Broadway parading I wrote a curious letter to myself. I copy it here:

"No song rises from me. The days play dully on my senses. My heart and hopes are mute. I have no island of secret delight in my soul. I wonder if most people are as I am—with nothing to keep them going but the inane habit of living. The death in me is not disturbed by memories—for the things in me that made me able to achieve memories are part of what has died.

"My chief delight was always the thought of being loved. Now I am no longer loved, although words of love are still offered me, and arms of love and even its familiar vows and tears. But my heart lies unfed amid this seeming feast, and knows it is no feast. Love is real only for the young. The mature must look at it with wiser eyes, and see it for the many other things it is—selfishness, robbery and the desperate hiatus between deceits.

"About those around me—hardly any have ever given me anything I could use as a human being—love, understanding or comfort. They have masked their enmity in pretended and pawky admiration that my most idiot self could see through.

"After my own people died, I saw why this was. It was because others resented me, and because, in a curious way, I never belonged among them. They had no place for children in their hearts—or for me.

"Now, as I grow old enough to know definitely what I have had in life and what I have not had, I see that among the missing things have been routines—plans, prospects, relationships to contribute to my entertainment or to bring air into my life. I never bothered to establish them. I have always neglected my own diversion. Now everyone neglects it.

"In my youth, I was served and loved like a child. Now I am ignored like a child. My throat is sick with too much living, as if I had swallowed a long stove pipe. I write because my head grows calm when I see words appear on paper. This is familiar and I don't feel frightened. I am all the words—and all the words are my family—the only surviving ones.

"My chief memory of life is the ingratitude of those to whom I have given myself. It is only toward what they cannot have or own that people feel grateful. Give them something, and contempt for the gift grows in them.

"I have usually picked out people to serve and enrich who were incapable of making the slightest gift of themselves—rigid, feverishly self-centered people nearly all of them—"

The letter to myself surprises me a little. Apparently I had a worse time than I remember.

MEN OF SPIRIT

GENE

THE WILDNESS of heart that was in Gene Fowler was visible for a long time only in his deeds. He was well matured before it erupted in a succession of fine novels and biographies.

MacArthur and I used to bore our womenfolk at home with tales of the Homeric doings of our friend. The name Gene Fowler became a synonym among us for life undaunted. Charlie's bride, Helen, used to say, "There can't be any Gene Fowler. You've made him up—both of you."

Fowler's arrival at my home for the first time took place at night. He came in through our small greenhouse and threw the manuscript of his first novel, *Trumpet in the Dust*, on the nearest bed. He roared hoarsely that I had seduced him into becoming a novelist and demanded liquor. He then explained to Rose that he kept one shoe on all night to stamp out cigarettes with, and had never set fire to a bed. Thereupon he fell asleep. "He came in like Taras Bulba," said Rose.

Gene was no part of New York's world of arts and letters. He was a newspaperman who had refused to mix with the *Schöngeisten*. There was a larger gaiety in him than the punster wit of the town's litterateurs. He favored the stamping grounds of sportsmen, athletes and crackpots of all trades. His eye was for the lowly and the confused. He brought to them a great compassion masked in jests. All this appeared later in his writing—a lust for existence void of the affectation that often marks the professional "life lovers" who take to fiction. Gene wrote as he had lived. No self-laudation, no hammy posturing as the authority on manly pursuits that he was, disturbed his prose.

After twenty years in New York, Gene retained the gusto of the outlander. His clothes stamped him a man who had never sunk to an interest in tailoring. He was tall, lanky-legged and with a slow Western yodel in his speech as if he were echoing out of a cave. He was a drinking man, with hard fists and a righteous eye, a heller with a parson's frown.

Wherever we went together there were people who loved him. In his company I felt at times as if I were attending a senatorial nominee on a triumphal tour. Bartenders, prize fighters, bicycle riders and wrestling champs; millionaires, promoters of every sort, journalistic stumble bums, waitresses, con men, panhandlers and lonely aristocrats from far away (a queen among them) greeted him with happy fellowship. He had a talent for stirring good will in people.

In the days when MacArthur, Fowler and I spent much time together, he was managing editor of Hearst's New York *American*— a waste of fine material, for Gene was one of the half-dozen great reporters of his era.

The most startling evidence of a man's popularity in the newspaper world that I have ever witnessed occurred during his editorship. Gene had lost William Randolph Hearst's personal brief case containing scandalous documents about a senatorial pet of Mr. Hearst's. Gene had been entrusted with the job of memorizing and destroying them. On hearing of their loss another of Mr. Hearst's personal emissaries fainted over his breakfast. Any rival newspaper finding these documents could blast the Hearst political empire. In this impasse, Gene summoned reporters from all the rival newspapers, told them the truth and organized them into a corps of sleuths to tour the city's taxicab garages. Gene's rival reporters found the documents in a taxi driver's home, where they were being used as drawing paper by his talented six-year-old daughter. They were returned to Gene and no hint of them appeared in the violent anti-Hearst press of the day.

Gene had made his way East originally from Denver, riding free on the train as an escort for a dead whore in the baggage car. Keen on seeing the arcs of his native land, he had zigzagged across the Republic with the corpse, stopping over at many towns. It was at the beginning of the war with the Kaiser, and Fowler, aware of his country's growing idealism, had promoted the whore in the coffin to a captain of French *Chasseurs*. He had wrapped French and American flags around the casket and thus assured himself free patriotic entertainment in Memphis, Louisville, Kansas City, Chicago and other ports.

My first meeting with Fowler was in his Chicago stopover. Mac-Arthur had telephoned me with the news that a Western journalist was captive in the Harrison Street police jail and suggested we get him released. We learned from the desk sergeant that the prisoner had broken the peace in the lobby of the Morrison Hotel. He had taken offense at the sight of a huge American flag made out of red, white and blue electric lights that stood in the center of the lobby. Denouncing the exhibit in words that filled MacArthur and me with envy when we heard them related, Fowler had picked up a large gold fish bowl that was part of the décor and hurled it at the colored lights. We effected his release, and he moved on with his embalmed Magdalene to New York and a bristling career.

HERMAN AND HENRY

OUT OF DIFFERENT WORLDS and of different nature than Fowler were my two friends Herman Rosse and Henry Varnum Poor, yet they were somehow related to him in my mind. Fowler in New York looked like a fellow newly in from the wilderness. Herman and Henry actually lived in the woods. Their houses were in the forests of Rockland County some thirty-five miles beyond New York.

I went often to the home of the tall Rosses. It was a happy house. New infants were constantly appearing in it. Eventually there were nine Rosse children. I was astonished at the way they grew. They turned, in practically no time, from infants into brides and bridegrooms, and looking on them, I sighed and knew that the years were passing.

The child that did not change was Herman. It is never easy for a scenic artist and architect to make a living. Such an artist, with nine children to rear, and in a wilderness to boot, would seem to be a man with problems. But there were no problems to be noted in Herman. He remained serene, learned and full of dreams. The tensions of poverty, of great aspiration and small success, never touched the Rosse manners. There was no calmer place to sit than in the woodland studio where Herman kept his thousand art books and his paintings.

Talking to Herman, I had always the delusion he was a bachelor of great wealth. His wife, the tall and smiling Helena, furthered this delusion when she appeared. Helena was also an artist. She was a landscape gardener. In her youth in Holland she had laid out the gardens for the Queen. In her wilderness, rearing her nine children, she seemed as unpreoccupied as Herman. She looked fondly on her husband as if he were the most charming of guests, happy to inform him that high tea was ready.

Many pages back I wrote of husbands—that I had never known one faithful to his wife. In putting down this finding, I forgot about the Rosses.

Henry Poor lived on the other side of the Rosse woods. Henry was a painter and pottery maker. He was a well-muscled Kansan with a blond, squarish face. He had the snub nose and twinkling silence of a Tolstoy moujik. As artist, he was sired by Cézanne and the fogs of San Francisco.

Henry had been a good athlete in his youth, with strong hands and a flair for troublesome romance. He walked gracefully and worked like a cart horse. Among his productions was a stone house he had built in the woods. It was one of the most beautiful houses I ever knew. Henry put it up stone by stone, toting them out of distant fields. He chiseled out a kitchen sink of stone, hewed and hammered beams into place. He dug a well and a swimming hole. Yet, heavy with tiredness and bitten by field frosts, Henry managed to look in his few tatters of clothes like a woodland fop. Despite his constant toiling, he managed to seem always as free as a forest animal.

I used to seek out Henry not to talk to but to sit with. He had the secret of living without effort. No echoes of any outside world were around him. When things were mentioned that were happening in New York, Henry listened with a sort of gentle surprise as if he were some native hearing tales of a distant civilization.

For many years when the deviltries of my world would jangle me too much, I would go to Henry's house as to a lamasery. On a winter's evening in his candlelit stone house, the dark fields and woods through its windows were the most luring places I had ever seen. Henry offered no other entertainment than the night outside his windows, the fire burning in the big fireplace, a bottle of wine and a composure of soul.

HARPO

ANOTHER FRIEND who was equally a cure for the ills of civilization was Harpo Marx. Like Henry and Herman, Harpo had the gift of relaxing anyone who looked at him. Harpo was many other things, but his peacefulness was the quality most remarkable in him. There are many exciting personalities to be found who can stimulate you, but I have come on few who make you feel content, as if some human sunlight were warming you.

There was nothing naïve about Harpo, as in my other three friends. Harpo's worldly activities had embraced pimps, thieves, whores, dowagers, royalty and statesmen. He had come out of the early vaudeville circuits which were the slums of entertainment. His cruise upward from these lowest of stage alleys to a place among the theater's elite had been full of bawdy adventure. Yet there had come out of it a man mysteriously innocent.

You saw this innocence when Harpo performed on the stage in his red wig and yellow tramp overcoat racing fiercely after blondes.

This same innocence that endeared him to his audiences, Harpo brought off the stage and offered to his friends. It was an innocence that rose out of Harpo's good will toward people. No envy or worry was to be noted in him. He enjoyed all he met, even fools. There were no bad meals, bad ball games, bad shows or bad people in his world. There were a few outside of it, like Nazis and bigots. Harpo went after them with the ferocity that marked his chase of villains on the stage.

But in his private world all was pleasant. If he felt displeased by anything going on in front of him, he smiled, closed his eyes and fell asleep. He was able to fall asleep in a dentist's chair and remain asleep while having a tooth filled.

An insistent stomach sometimes bothered Harpo. His greatest hungers came on him while sitting in the theater. He prepared himself for such seizures by keeping his pockets always full of apples, peanuts, zwieback and hard candy. While watching a show he consumed often the equivalent of a five-course meal. Often he slept the full two hours he was in the theater. He never gained weight and was never ill. In his sixties today, he is still roller-skating, climbing poles, falling off roofs and eager to play baseball.

Unlike Henry, Harpo was not a silent soother only. He could fill a room with cheer by merely sitting in it, but he was also a remarkable storyteller. He told tremendous hair-raising adventures involving murderers and Jezebels. I have sat an entire night listening to a single story from Harpo, for when he spoke it was usually at novel length.

I remember Harpo also as a musician making people laugh with his clarinet and holding them awed as he improvised for hours on his harp.

I remember a scene at the wedding party of his brother, Groucho Marx. It was in Harpo's home. Groucho, philosopher and wit of the family, stood at the piano singing with his new bride, younger than his daughter. A grin was on his face, and his voice made mock of the love ballad he was executing. Suddenly the tune changed. Groucho had taken over the piano. An ancient vaudeville ditty—"*Ist das nicht ein Schnitzelbank?*"—came merrily out of him.

From the four corners of the room the other four Marxes joined in —Harpo, the exuberant Chico, the dashing Zeppo and Gummo, man of business. It was the number they used to sing in their vaudeville act when, under mother Minnie's guidance, they had trouped in their boyhood through the hinterlands. It rose gayly again in voices as fresh as they had been thirty years before. The wedding vanished out of the room. The saga of gay talent and family love that was the Marx Brothers turned us from a wedding party into a happy audience. But happiest of all was Harpo. Looking at him as he stood singing in his corner, I understood my friend in a phrase. It was Harpo who was the bridegroom, here and everywhere else.

SAM

WHEN I LOOK now on life, it is not only the living that I see. In the last twenty years a country has grown up mysteriously around me. It is the homeland of the dead. My parents, relatives and most of my friends occupy it. I journey often to its borders and stare at its population. It is not a mournful journey I make, nor even a moody one. I peer over the borders of their homeland to refresh my knowledge of life.

I have never grieved long for intimates who have died. But I have remained interested in them as if death had made no change in our relationship. I have continued their attitudes and voices in my mind. Because of this, I am often startled by the fact that the friend of whom I am thinking is dead. One of those whose absence continues to surprise me is Dr. Samuel Hirshfeld.

Sam was the most unchanging man I knew. In the twenty years of our friendship I found only a single mood in him—a concern for his fellow man. He busied himself almost the full twenty-four hours of each day with this concern. His work as physician and surgeon was a small part of his activities. Through with his hospital rounds and his professional calls, Sam would dash off to some laboratory where he pursued the secrets of longevity and cancer cures. At midnight Sam would enter his home, stretch himself in his bed and read until dawn. He devoured books with a never-lessening hunger. His mind poked into all the corners of science and psychology, and mysteriously found time for poetry and novels.

But Sam's chief activity was neither medicine nor research. It was his side line of good Samaritanism. His patients were always his friends. In addition to curing them of their real or fancied diseases, he got them jobs, nursed them out of drunks, picked out babies for childless couples to adopt, induced roués to marry girls they had made pregnant, restored the egos of defeated writers and suicidal wives.

Sam spent the last twenty years of his life in Hollywood. He became its leading father confessor and employment bureau. He found his chief happiness in the success of others. When something good happened to me, Sam would sit and beam at me as if the fine fortune were more his own than mine.

I used to argue with Sam about the time he wasted running errands for fools and ingrates, and fixing up the careers of incompetents who had come a cropper. How the hell was he going to find a cancer cure if he spent half his days straightening out the lives of his daft Hollywood patients? How, in fact, was he going to have time for his medical practice if he didn't stop wet-nursing drunks and hysterics? Sam's answer was to find time for everything.

When Sam died, his wife asked me to deliver the oration at his funeral. I sat in Oceanside for a day writing it. As I wrote I became more and more astonished. What astonished me as I examined his life was the enormity of his virtue. I had always known it but never summed it up. Looking now at Sam, my mind held not a single memory of a mean deed, a selfish word or an act of vanity. I was overcome by the modesty of my friend who for a quarter of a century had somehow managed not to call my attention to his virtues.

As I wrote of him, I saw again his wide grin, his tense eyes full of eagerness and wisdom, his trim and tireless body. He was one of my few friends who could beat me at badminton and beach racing. If not for his eyes Sam could have passed for a prize fighter. His eyes were too bright with intellect and his brow wore a constant pucker, like a plume of thought.

Looking on my friend who seemed to be posing good-humoredly for the eulogy I was writing, I thought, "How wonderful it is that there was such a man." I stopped writing and stared at the ocean. I suddenly felt his death as if a robbery had taken place and a large part of my life had been stolen.

But at his funeral I recovered from this feeling of loss. Hundreds of men and women sat in the funeral chapel. There were scores of famous people, of Hollywood's geniuses and sophisticates; and scores of people nobody knew, and scores of people once known and long forgotten. But all of them turned the same eyes to where I stood making my funeral speech. Their faces shone with love for the man who was being buried, and all of them wept.

An odd thing happened to me as I addressed Sam's mourners. I found myself looking at them with Sam's spirit more than my own. Most of them were the fools and ingrates against whom I had argued with Sam, the incompetents who had helped drain his health too early. I saw them now as shy and gentle people, full of hurts. I felt that I had somehow inherited a part of Sam's job—to praise and to love.

His life of good doing fetched Sam little happiness and less money. For several months after his death hundreds of people talked of erecting a monument to Sam, of building a great modern hospital that would bear his name. We went so far as to appoint a committee. We held meetings and made plans for the Samuel Hirshfeld Hospital. It was to be like Sam and to give the best of medical practice to poor people, without charge.

Nothing came of our plans. No monument rose to Sam. As it had during his life, fame continued to elude him after his death.

CHARLIE

I WIRED Rose from Hollywood in 1924, during one of my early sorties into movieland, "I have met a new friend. He has pointed teeth, pointed ears, is nineteen years old, completely bald and stands on his head a great deal. His name is Charles Lederer. I hope to bring him back to civilization with me."

For many of the years that followed into the present time I was to look on my new friend as the last of the world's young men. My first description to Rose was accurate. Although still a stripling, Charles was bald, as befitted the last of a line. He had a solemn, large-eyed, pointed-chin face and looked like the early science-fiction illustrations of a Martian. Shortly after our meeting he entered our life in New York as if the stork had brought him. He entered at the same time and with the same filial completion the homes of Alec Woollcott, Alice Miller, Bob Benchley, Howard Dietz, Moss Hart and the Mac-Arthurs.

He brought into these busy literary households a soothing lack of ambition. It surprised all of us that so excellent a critic and appreciative an audience should have no competitiveness secreted away somewhere in his psyche. But Charles had no time to waste on his own success. In an odd way Lederer, the persistent juvenile, treated us all as if he were a doting parent who would keep us all forever infants.

Charles' chief compliment was his presence. He never went anywhere except with love. Arrived in the household he had chosen as the object of his deep affection, he behaved in a manner seldom seen in literary circles. He heckled, moped or turned people purple with rage during all serious discussions. The smallest departure from modesty or truthfulness by any of his hosts drew from him fits of contempt. Stuffiness also angered him unreasonably. He had, in fact, an allergy toward most adult characteristics. In his presence adults of determined poise often felt as if they had been butted by a goat.

This was a mission in our guest's heart that made him the idol of our families. He had come among us as an evangel dedicated to keeping the world from growing old. This he did in many fetching ways: by sneering at all philosophies—he could prove by reading any page of them aloud that they made no sense; by standing on his head, executing sudden somersaults, swimming underwater for amazing distances, inventing new games to be played in the parlor with a football and baseball bat; by deriding pomp, playing savagely at cards or trapping pedants into losing bets on literary arguments—he always looked up a half-dozen literary facts in the encyclopedia before lunch; by dancing hornpipes anywhere, singing in a piercing tenor voice

———his mother, Reine Davies, had sung the lead in many operettas, including *Madam Sari* (I mention this fact to refute the theory of inheritable musical talent); by sleeping till noon, reading for hours in a hot tub and spending the first part of his day plotting a new practical joke. He refused to work at his chosen calling of literature because of a sinus pain that set in when he so much as wrinkled his brow.

His talent for ridiculing life developed early in Charles. In college he felt a disgust of learning. The professors seemed to young Charles to be engaged in a plot to bore him to death or addle his brain forever. As a protective weapon against them he practiced going into a coma. He came out of college with this talent fully perfected. Always thereafter he was able to stare without seeing, listen without hearing and to fall asleep at will in any position.

My friend's jokes always delighted me, for they were more than jokes. This enemy of philosophy was the finest practical philosopher I had met. He was engaged in a philosophical war to caricature adults. The cruelty of their ideas and the absurdity of most of their convictions were his targets. He chose his own weapons, however. In a Hollywood movie studio where the blown-up strut of his bosses had brought a frown into his soul, he set off the fire-extinguishing pipes in the ceiling and flooded a score of offices. Several of his arthritic superiors were almost drowned. Dining one day in the elegant Colony restaurant in New York, with a musical-comedy star who was his sweetheart, he sat listening owlishly to a lecture from her on how to live properly. It was necessary, she said, to get up before noon and find some work to do. As the lovely girl came to a finish in her discourse on right living, Charles, who had sat seemingly spellbound, arose and handed her his trousers. He had removed them surreptitiously during her lecture.

"Here," he said, "you wear these," and walked coldly out of the restaurant in his shorts.

Years later, as Major Lederer fighting the Japanese in India, Charles spent an evening dining in Calcutta with a rich and high-born English lady. She spoke chiefly and adversely of Jews. Charles, half Jewish and half Irish, listened with his comalike stare. After an hour he went to the antique liquor cabinet in the room to fetch a fresh bottle. The most valuable of the lady's possessions stood on top of it—a beautiful jade vase. With a hand on the cabinet door, Charles smiled at his hostess and said, "I am interested in your dislike of Jews. Could you tell me just what you've got against them?"

"Oh, I've got nothing against the Jews, really," began the lady, and stopped with her mouth agape.

Major Lederer had yanked open violently the door of the liquor cabinet, causing the expensive jade vase to teeter, tumble to the floor and smash into bits.

"You have now," said my friend Charles.

My friend's disillusions were the deepest and most numerous of any I had met. They embraced religion, history, politics, drama, fame and most of the human family. They were more informed and articulate than the disillusions in my other world-hater, Wallace Smith, but the two were much alike in their genius for distaste.

But in my friend Charles, this deep distaste for many things found cap and bells for expression. It was neutralized, too, by an ever-active compassion. This young man who was inclined to despise almost everything not only spent much time playing jokes, but a great deal of time helping people find jobs and shake off melancholia. He pauperized himself for two decades showering presents and lending money. He was almost as busy with good deeds as Hirshfeld.

What happens to an evangel of this sort when the years pile up on his head? At forty, Charles, due chiefly to his early baldness, has changed little in looks, and nothing in disposition. He has learned, however, that nine tenths of the world is incapable of laughter or sanity, that it prizes only ugliness and bitterness. My friend Charles looks on this portion of human beings with an air so sneering as to make him seem the sourest of men. To the other tenth, however, my friend Charles still brings his gift.

A HAPPY SUMMER—AND A SEQUEL

WE LIVED in a house loaned us by McEvoy. It was in a field adjoining a forest outside the village of Woodstock, New York. It was summertime. The roads were dusty, the fields were full of sun, the forest was cool and shadowy. A brook was near our house. It led to a waterfall and a swimming hole. The houses in the neighboring fields and hills were occupied by old farmers who no longer worked the land, and by young artists—who seemed also unemployed.

I lived idly in the house. I was too happy to do any work. At night we lit kerosene lamps and listened to phonograph music and forest sounds.

After a few weeks we ran out of money. Luckily, Woodstock was an artists' community and its village merchants were used to insolvent customers. We were able to buy food on credit. There was no rent to pay and no servants' salaries. Rose cooked, cleaned and washed dishes.

Our ménage expanded. There appeared a girl of eighteen named Ruth and a collie dog named Sandy. Ruth's father was a country doctor and lived in a large old house down the road. But Ruth seldom entered it. She wandered the countryside all day with Sandy at her heels.

Ruth and Sandy seemed more like twins than girl and dog. They had the same color hair, walked alike and were equally graceful and silent. They sat in our living room in the evening. Neither spoke. Both smiled at us. After a few hours they walked off together. Ruth went into the hills. She slept often in the branches of a tree, and Sandy curled up on the ground beneath her.

One sunny afternoon, MacArthur arrived with a suitcase and a harmonica. We were pleased to see him for many reasons, among them the prospect of now being able to pay some of our bills in the village butcher shop and grocery store. But Charlie had come with empty pockets. He had spent his last ten dollars getting to Woodstock. His play *Lulu Belle*, written with Edward Sheldon, was to be produced by Belasco in the fall. On this promise of prosperity, Charlie had flourished for some time, but had finally exhausted all his borrowing sources. He was surprised to hear I was broke, but settled down, nevertheless, to spend the summer with us.

We played endless games of horseshoes and croquet, and hung around the swimming hole. When the kerosene lamps were lighted we started telling stories to Rose. We were polite and took turns. The storytelling lasted each night almost to dawn. It began at the dinner table, continued in the kitchen while Rose washed dishes and went on as she sat in the shadows exhausted by a day of unaccustomed scullery work and cleaning. She was also writing her first novel.

For a time Ruth and Sandy were our only guests. They took to coming in the daytime and watching Rose write in the bedroom. They also watched her wrestle fearlessly with the gasoline stove that was forever sputtering like a bomb about to go off. Here, Rose, giddy with new talents, cooked blueberry muffins, a cake known as The Royal Tropicaroma, and fried steaks and chickens and potatoes—all commodities obtained free from the trusting village merchants.

Ruth and Sandy switched their loyalty to Charlie and me sometimes and watched us play games. Chiefly, they liked to stand on the edge of the woods at twilight and watch my friend wander off into the shadows, playing his mouth organ. He knew only one piece—"The Missouri Waltz." MacArthur was young and lithe. His face was whimsical, his dark hair curled on his skull. His hands were large, his arms heavily muscled. But there was a grace in him equal to that of Ruth and Sandy. His eyes had a distant look in them. He moved vaguely, as if there were never destination in his mind. Ruth and Sandy would watch him wander off into the forest shadows as if they were certain he would never come back—but disappear into the hills to play "The Missouri Waltz" forever.

Another native appeared, named Conklin. He had a home somewhere in the mountains. He wore overalls, a pair of white gloves and he explained that he ate only cake. Rose fed him The Royal Tropicaroma and respected his oddity too much to inquire into it. Noisier visitors began arriving. Bob Chandler and his Mardi Gras entourage, fell in love with Rose's cooking and songs. Our village credit was strained and Rose's kitchen feats doubled by these dinner parties, but Charlie and I were grateful for an enlarged audience.

Harpo, Groucho, Chico and Zeppo Marx, their wives, sweethearts and children appeared. Rose's sister, Minna, arrived with trunks full of pretty dresses. Minna was now a medical student, but her love of music and gaiety seemed only to have been increased by her studies of cadavers. And then one sunny afternoon, Herman Mankiewicz appeared in the road in front of our house—as Jimmy Durante would say—unannounced. He carried two suitcases. He had decided to spend his vacation from The New York Times drama section with us.

We discovered after several days that Herman's larger suitcase contained sixteen bottles of Scotch and nothing else. Herman refused to join in our horseshoes, croquet or swimming-hole activities. He refused, in fact, to leave the house. He sat in a corner of an old couch for two weeks without moving. Here he slowly and happily did away with his sixteen bottles.

Ruth and Sandy were fascinated by this molelike newcomer. They sat in a corner for hours staring at him.

Herman presented other problems than his immobility. He had arrived without a dollar in his pockets, explaining that at the end of his two weeks of healthy basking in the country, his wife, Sarah, would arrive with the money necessary to fetch him back to New York. He had not been allowed to bring any money with him because of Sarah's certainty that he would spend it on liquor, and thus impair the influence of country air and sunshine.

"Poor Sarah is an honest woman," said Herman, "and doesn't understand that liquor can be begged, borrowed or stolen by a man of firm character."

Herman's immobility failed to lessen his appetite. He ate like a platoon of marines, thus putting further strain on our village credit. But worse was his announcement that while guest he desired equal talking privileges with MacArthur. As a result, Charlie and I had to share our audience with Mankiewicz. There were added to our lamp-lit sagas of Chicago, Berlin and Château-Thierry, tales of New York, Far Rockaway and Belleau Wood. The kerosene lamps burned now till breakfast.

A young and ravishing Sarah finally arrived and carted her Herman off. The summer deepened. The days grew too hot for horse-shoes and croquet. We lay in the swimming hole and tried to catch frogs. One day a thunderstorm drenched the morning, and Rose and Charlie and I were forced to remain indoors.

The storm reminded Charlie and me of a number of anecdotes that had slipped our memory, but Rose refused to listen until the lamps were lit. Charlie and I had read a book on Hindu magic. We discussed it for a while and then spent several hours practicing levitation. Nothing came of our efforts. It was still raining. After lunch Charlie and I decided we would try writing a play together.

We finished it in a few weeks and Charlie wrote to a friend for funds to take us into town to sell it. Our play was called *The Moon-shooter.* I have always thought it the best work MacArthur and I ever did together. Unfortunately, we lost it—both copies—before we were able to give it to anyone to read—except Sam Harris.

I read the play to Sam in his Long Island bedroom. He was much impressed by the first two acts and chuckled away during the reading. But when I finished the third act, Sam shook his head and said the last act had confused him.

The play was a loud and comic work, but in its last act the hero was suddenly shot to death. The hero's name was Enoch, and of the hundreds of heroes I have written, or helped to write, Enoch, the Moonshooter, is my favorite. In act three, looking up at the foolish people who had brought him low, Enoch sighed softly, "I didn't mean to die like this," and expired.

"You can't kill a hero like that in a comedy," said Sam. "That's a very funny play there, and you can't stick a death in it for a finish. If you boys will rewrite the last act and bring it back to me, I'll put it on."

MacArthur and I returned to the hot summer night in New York. We encountered Mankiewicz, who was occupying Prince Bibesco's grand suite in the Plaza Hotel while His Highness capered in Long Island. His wife Sarah, our friend explained, had taken the children to Far Rockaway to escape the heat, leaving him to his lonely toil in the city and to come to her on week ends. We moved in with him, there being no rent to pay. We discovered, while helping Herman to undress the first night, that his torso was bound with yards of adhesive tape. He had slipped while trying to get out of the bathtub and lamed his back. When Herman was asleep, MacArthur and I rolled him on his stomach and with an indelible pencil wrote ardent and obscene love messages on his taping. We signed them Gladys and chuckled over the impending moment in Far Rockaway when Herman would undress before his keen-eyed Sarah. During these and other occupations, MacArthur and I forgot *The Moonshooter*. The two copies had disappeared. We were unable to recall in what hotel or on what train we had left them.

Somewhere in some wistful traveler's home, Enoch, our Moonshooter, lies tucked away—his third-act death scene vindicated by time and history. No more than Enoch "meant to die" as he did, were the peace of that summer and the happy-go-lucky charms of existence meant to pass out of the world.

I returned alone to Woodstock and wrote a novel, *Count Bruga*, to pay all our bills in the village.

Such, as I have written in the foregoing pages, was my New York of the twenties, a town bold with self and stormy with selfish ambitions.

Our social consciousness consisted of scorning slogans and politicians. We looked on government as a hideaway for boodlers. We ran from orators and we took our good will for granted. We chased its exploiters from our doorsteps. We spoke our minds on all subjects, and each of us felt more vital to the world than all its political philosophers. Our tongues were our only leaders and our wits the only architects of tomorrow.

We did not know this Enoch of a world was to die young, and we listened happily to its jokes and its music.

THE GENTLE PEOPLE

I HAVE SKIRTED writing about the theater in these many pages. It is one of the few subjects about which I feel diffident. This is odd, for from the time I was seventeen and knew almost nothing, I knew the theater, wrote plays, directed them, watched them open and stood in the rear of the house fascinated by the puppet faces of the audience and the real ones of the actors.

My hesitation in telling of the theater is based on the fact that I have no point of view toward it. There are times when I have thought the theater an important form of human expression. At other times it has seemed to me a sort of enlarged nursery for playing games.

My most consistent impression of the theater is that its art lies chiefly in its audience. Poetry, painting, music, etc., flit haphazardly across the stage. But they are only hints of the arts. The finished job is always the audience. Its response is not only evaluation—but most of the play itself.

Like the telegram, drama is constricted to a few cautiously chosen words of information. Delivered to the right address it may arouse violent emotion. At the wrong address it will be stared at blankly.

There is one side of the theater, however, toward which I have a point of view. This is its actors and actresses. They have always pleased me. One of the few things I would like to be, other than I am, is an actor. Much of my writing has been an actor reciting lines in the private auditorium of his skull.

But my fondness for actors is not only that I am secretly one of them. I admire them because they are the only tribe of people whose relation to the world is always admirable. They are occupied with diverting it.

Before coming to New York I had had the misconception of actors that they were rich and busy people, always hurrying to dressing rooms and make-up boxes, always facing audiences with their talent. I had met no other kind in Chicago.

Now I found that so negligible a part of them was to be seen behind footlights that you could almost say the actors of New York were perennially and totally unemployed. There were hundreds of them for every role to be acted, and as many dancers and singers for every lone spotlight.

The saddest place to see actors is in producers' offices. Here the hundreds come for the single job that is never to be landed. Of many such scenes I recall one that tells this story wryly. It was in a producer's office in Hollywood, not New York. But the helplessness of the actor is the same in either place.

Julius Tannen, after a long fame on the stage, came on hard times in Hollywood. For a number of years he was unable to get a job acting. Tannen's friends were unable to help him. Something always slipped up, and the witty Julius found himself finally in a desperate way. His friends persisted, and after much intrigue a part was secured for Tannen. He was to play an editor in a newspaper drama. All that remained was for the producer to see him and pass on him.

Tannen dressed himself carefully that morning. He was completely bald and wore a toupee which he stuck on his head each morning with a special mucilage.

After studying him for ten minutes and listening to his nimble speech, the producer shook his head and said, "I'm sorry, Mr. Tannen. But I don't think you'll do for the part."

Julius inquired quietly in what way he was deficient. Was he too tall, too thin, too old, too young?

"No," said the producer. "You could act it very well. But I have always visualized a bald-headed man for the part."

Julius smiled and slowly pulled his toupee off his head.

"I think I can satisfy you on that score," he beamed. "I happen to be completely bald."

The producer sat studying the polished Tannen skull and then shook his head again and pronounced, "I'm sorry, Mr. Tannen. I simply can't visualize you as a baldheaded man."

Yet with such scenes as this happening daily in the actor's life, the producer is never a villain in his eyes. The producer can do no wrong, for he is never quite a man to the group sitting proudly and bright-eyed in his waiting room. He is the door to the theater. Thus he is always part of the dream that keeps them coming to his waiting room. This dream of acting is a desperate thing that never leaves the actor's soul. Neither defeat nor incompetence can knock it out. It stays unwaveringly in its place and continues to peer with eager eyes out of cruel and dreary hours.

I have often envied the courage of actors—not only in their unemployment but in their ability on the stage to pick themselves up after having been mowed down. With the boos of critics still burning in their hearts, they face dwindling audiences, they perform gayly in the teeth of disillusion and hostility.

This is a heroism beyond me. Had I had it, I would have written a hundred plays instead of ten. The fear of defeat has halted me a score of times in the middle of act one. Unlike the actor whose mind treasures the few hours of bliss success has brought him, I remember of the theater chiefly its wounds and battles lost. The several successes I have had are vague and unsolacing. The failures remain vivid.

This is one of the oddities of the theater to be found in no other institution—its capacity for bringing pain to its chief servitor—the playwright. I have read quite savage criticism of my published books without feeling the slightest twitch of defeat. It is otherwise in stage-land. Critical attack on a play has left me as battered as after a mugging.

There is a feeling of shame attached to failure in the theater that can become as heavy as an illness. A sense of being cruelly belittled and cast out lays low the playwright's spirit. I have known playwrights to hide in dark rooms after a flop, to sob for days on end, to go without food, to become sexually impotent or to hurl themselves into exile in some foreign land.

I have not experienced quite this much grief, but enough not to criticize when I hear of such a smitten colleague. The chief reason for such collapses is that plays are written not to express oneself but to please an audience. Thus the slap from the critic and the nonappearance of an audience become social snubs—human repudiations

—that leave the playwright bleak and lessened. Seldom can he look to the future for solace. He is no artist writing for the birds and for posterity. He is, much like the actor, dependent on the quick sale of his wares—or none at all.

Many of the actors I knew have died and many have tottered off to limbo. Yet they all seem still to be sitting in the waiting rooms, almost with the same faces, the same tones and gestures. They are a never-changing people, and the charms I saw in them in my youth have not lessened in our uncharming day. The patience of actors, their incorruptible belief in themselves in the face of no one else's interest; the good manners of actors that never leave them in hunger or defeat; their eternal air of expectancy, as if a Christmas Eve were always coming—these qualities are still in them.

I have seldom known a greedy actor or a snobbish one. The most famous of them are no more stuck up than a taxi driver. They will throw fits over their insufficient billing, but socially they wear their names in small letters.

This all may be due to the fact that the actor is trained to live in a world of unreality. The villains and heroes of life are usually vaguer to him than those of drama. Ask him to name a scoundrel and he will name Iago rather than Hitler. And he would rather play Hamlet than be the most fortunate of men—if such a character still exists. Good thoughts and kindly feelings are natural to actors because their souls are full of a single aim—to please. To charm a producer, a playwright—to arrive behind the Promised Footlights and charm an audience—is their dream.

In our present world in which nearly everyone else is loud with hatreds, the actors continue to toil at their ancient craft of making themselves lovable and attractive. Crime is rare among them, and despite their constant nearness to hunger, thievery is almost unknown in their annals. Evil is something to be performed on a stage for the pleasure of an audience.

I have thought of actors as the Gentle People. And I have thought that if the millennium ever comes and Utopia spreads its charms over the earth, then all its inhabitants will be very much like actors.

ACTORS AND ACTRESSES

FAME is as much a part of an actor's equipment as elocution or gesture. An unfamous actor may please an audience but he can rarely excite it. In this fact lies one of the major secrets of the theater— the secret of the audience's presence. People are content to live drearily and anonymously. But they insist on the most splendid of dreams. Their favorite area for dreaming is the theater and their favorite dream selves are its actors.

The proscenium is a peep hole into our own imaginations. When we read books, the generalities of our mind remain thoughts. In the theater these same generalities become people. Nobility, deceit, passion, greed, loyalty, wit, hatred wear human faces, and perform for us. We can close our minds entirely in the theater, and usually do, and enjoy a sort of external thought. We sit relaxed for two hours and a cast of actors carries our burden of living.

Our applause as audience is a somewhat mystic matter. We applaud because the actor has excited us, just as we cheer when a home run or a triple somersault has excited us. The difference is that the ball player and tumbler are outsiders. The actors are as much ourselves as the figments we see at night in our sleep. When we applaud them we do not say, "How wonderful you are!" We say, "How wonderful I find you!" If you listen attentively to an audience's applause, you will hear it boasting more than praising. "How sensitive I am," says the applause. "How emotionally responsive, how full of rapture and largess. What a superb connoisseur I am! By God, that great actress never met anybody as brilliant as us! We'll make her take another bow to prove it."

Most admiration of others contains in it some boast of our ability to admire. In the theater actor and audience are so closely related that there is almost no objectivity in our applause. Just as the tears we shed are not for a stranger on the stage, but for our own dreams wearing a stranger's mask, so our cheers when the curtain falls are for ourselves. The actors come out and take the bows, but you may note that they bow humbly and gratefully and even cautiously. If they are good actors they know they are not yet separate figures—not until the house lights go up. They are still the dream puppets of the half-visible audience. They bow a sort of mystic thanks for having been allowed to occupy the reality of our skulls for a while.

Since boyhood I have applauded thousands of actors and actresses. I have been carried away by their genius, and talked of little else for days. Yet when I try to remember them I can recall almost nothing about them. They are as difficult to remember as my own moods of yesterday.

Dimly such names as Otis Skinner, David Warfield, Henry Irving, Holbrook Blinn, Richard Bennett, E. H. Sothern, Robert Mantell remain alive in the back of my head. Louis Mann is there and Arthur Byron, Cyril Maude, A. E. Matthews, John Drew, George Arliss. They sit in no Pantheon crowned with laurel, but seem rather to be hanging around in an Old People's Home—myself. Unlike famous authors, generals and other heroes, their greatness keeps growing less and less in my mind. They decline, alas, with me.

The more recent actors seem, however, much too vivid in my thought. They are insistent, overlit. Their tones are stuck in my ear, their mannerisms haunt me. No face is more familiar to me than Walter Huston's, no voice has a more personal sound for me than Joseph Schildkraut's zitherish phrases. Alfred Lunt is my favorite uncle whose every deft grimace I know by heart. Laurence Olivier keeps flinging up an arm and announcing it is St. Crispin's Day at least two or three times a week. The electric-voiced Lee Tracy, that Sousa's Band of an actor, Orson Welles, the cello staccatto of Edward G. Robinson, the moody snarl of John Garfield, the intellectual bark of José Ferrer, the lyric mind of Paul Muni—all these qualities are as familiar to me as if they were living in my house.

More vivid than the actors are the actresses, even the ones of long ago. Laurette Taylor's eyes are brighter than Holbrook Blinn's. Mrs. Fiske, Francine Larrimore, Pauline Lord, Julia Marlowe, Nazimova, Jeanne Eagels, Ethel Barrymore, Laura Hope Crewes, Lenore Ulrich, Sara Allgood, Estelle Winwood, Rose Stahl—each of these ladies keeps her looks and shape in my head, and hardly any I ever applauded has become only a name.

As for the still-active ones, they have become almost the only ladies I know, despite my never having met most of them, and being no more than a vague acquaintance to nearly all the rest. When I think idly of women and reach a hand to haul some tender friend out of the past, it is usually Tallulah Bankhead, Margo, Katharine

Cornell, Barbara Bel Geddes, Julie Haydon, Lynn Fontanne, Uta Hagen, Vivian Leigh I come out with. These are more alive in my mind than women I once knew infinitely better.

I have admired many actresses, in fact, nearly all I have seen. My head is almost as full of their gestures, chest tones and flashing eyes as it is of literature and politics. While reading Colette, I suddenly hear Florence Reed reciting the Odyssey of Mother Goddam; or the glittering Emily Stevens whisks her gold gown across a page of De Gourmont; or I hear Jessica Tandy going mad in the New Orleans railroad flat.

The actress who most stirs my mind is Helen Hayes. Unlike other fine players, she does not remain in my head for the parts she played. I see her not as *Coquette*, Maggie Wylie, Queen Victoria, Mary of Scotland or any of her other footlight avatars. I see her always as Helen Hayes. The characters she evokes are always less than her own.

And what a character that is! It is possible all the great ladies of the theater were of this mold. But since Helen is the only one of them I have actually known, she remains unique for me. Slight of build, modest spoken, as untemperamental and polite as an usherette, with a touch of humility towards intimates as well as strangers, Helen Hayes fills the stage with a spirit more potent than any I have ever beheld. Her dominance has nothing to do with the character she is acting. It surrounds her like a secondary costume. A human nobility radiates from her and I have come away from watching her act always with the same conviction. Loose in Paris in 1793, Helen could have won the French Revolution single-handed.

Neither rant nor vocal volume are the secret of her power, yet her voice could hold a regiment at bay. It is the power of seeming more human than humanity, more regal than royalty, and more truthful than gospel. Laurette Taylor had it to an extent, but to me there was a little less magic in her. The pride that led her out of the wings seemed less than Helen's, and the head she raised seemed less high. In one respect, the Misses Taylor and Hayes were one. They could both make an audience cry by merely standing still and smiling at it.

TWO MORE STAGE FAVORITES

I never understood what quality it was that made an actress until a recent night in Hartford, Connecticut.

It was New Year's Eve, 1952. Heavy snow was falling. I joined some two thousand frost-bitten New Englanders in the barn-like New Parsons Theater to witness the opening of a play, *Midsummer*. One of the "on stage" participants was to be my daughter Jenny, then nine years old.

I had kept away from the play's rehearsals and had never heard Jenny "do" any of her lines at home. Jenny's theatrical debut was entirely under her mother's management, with Constance Collier guiding. Whether these two excellent mentors could turn my young harum-scarum friend Jenny into a concentrated thespian I left up to them. Had they been preparing her for a performance on the trapeze or trampoline I would have felt a bit more certain of the results.

Nevertheless I was not much alarmed as I sat this snowy night in the theater. There was about Jenny at nine a curious pride and fearlessness that would keep her back straight anywhere she walked. The curtain went up and I watched the brilliant Geraldine Page flutter happily about in her old New York hotel room. After a few minutes another character appeared.

I could have sworn it rose out of the stage, for it seemed so much a part of it. The character was Jenny. She moved toward Geraldine with feet that seemed not to touch the boards, and with one arm floating lyrically in the air. And around her was such an aura of happiness that no sooner had she spoken her first lines than the audience let loose a thunder of applause. At this stirring sound, my friend Jenny, who had never faced an audience before, paused, considered briefly what was the correct thing to do and decided on a small, friendly bow. Straightening, she returned to her work.

Jenny's performance was excellent. But it was not her performance I watched as much as her happiness. It was the sort of happiness I had once felt when Dick Finnegan had given me my first assignment on the *Journal*.

Between acts I remembered what one of Jenny's predecessors had once told me thirty years ago, and the pronouncement suddenly became the entire secret of acting. The predecessor had been Sarah Bernhardt.

"Go see what you can get out of the Divine Sarah," Editor Henry Smith said, and I bounced off to the Congress Hotel in Chicago where Bernhardt had agreed to meet the press. I found a wrinkled old lady sitting in a wheelchair. Her face was lavender, her hair was orange and a white tulle scarf billowed around her neck. She had a wooden leg. She had just finished a matinee at the Majestic Theater playing the seventeen-year-old boy L'Aiglon.

My fellow reporters asked innumerable questions and I hung back. I knew nothing of Bernhardt except one fact. I had read it a few weeks ago in Vance Thompson's delightful book, *Parisian Portraits*. One of the portraits had been of Jean Richepin, the French playwright and African big game hunter—a powerful heller of a man.

My silence finally attracted Bernhardt. She pointed a finger at me and inquired of the interpreter in French if that young dummy had any questions.

I answered in English that I had one, and asked it.

"Is it true," I asked, "that Jean Richepin playing opposite Miss Bernhardt in the play he had written for her, *Miarka, the Bear*, tried to lay her during their love scene at the end of Act Two so that they had to ring the curtain down?"

The one-legged old lady in the wheelchair listened to the translation of my question and then stared at me. Tears filled her eyes. She reached her arms up and embraced my neck. And a voice shaking with tears and chuckles spoke in my ear. "Yes, yes, it is true! It is true! I loved the big Richepin. I loved many people, many things. But all I can remember now is that I loved the stage. Write of me only that —please, young reporter, that I loved the stage."

SIGH FOR AN ENEMY

OUTSIDE, the ocean lies. It looks like the back of a great animal wrinkling its skin of water. The night comes, and with it bits of "science" stir in my mind. I have heard recently some bad news about the night, and the universe it veils. The earth is tipping and may soon fall over like a spinning top. A new star is being put together somewhere in the dark. This may change the gravitational pulls and send our globe shooting off into space, to burst like a skyrocket.

I wonder if our scientists will have their Space Buses ready to embark us in time for Mars or the moon when these cosmic mishaps first signal. Possibly the signals are already sounding among us. We have an old habit toward disaster signals. Ignore the signals and the disasters will go away.

Thus the signals fall out of my mind and I return to the human race, most of which in my vicinity is obliviously asleep at this hour. Whatever I think of this race in the daylight, I look on it with respect when I see the night. It is as brave as it is puny. Its weapon of thought is like a paper spear against the mighty enemies of Time and Space.

Though poets have murmured of its charms, what else is the night but the dark banner of these enemies? And what else is the God who operates the unimaginable traffic system of the heavens, but an enemy? A kindly One, perhaps, since He allows our planet to travel toward some destination at the rate of eleven million miles a minute, without turning into a spray of dust or bumping into anything. But still an Enemy, for He is as unknown as He is mighty. The heart of man may surrender to Him and seek to disarm Him by loving Him wildly. But our mind must continue to look for His measure, to send its spies out to gauge His strength and identify His armament.

Being no scientist, I am inclined to regard the night and its God-maker with words of love rather than face infinity with a pair of three-inch calipers. But, as I wrote many pages back, my love is not wild. It contains a few wistful similes. It salutes the Enemy-God pensively and with a proper antlike humility. If when I die this Enemy has time amid His incalculable labors to take some vague note of me and continue the mysterious existence of my soul in some guise or other, I shall be surprised and apologetic. And sing my first hymn.

A fine bit of Ring around the Rosie, this—when I have sat down to write of actors. Luckily, it is not a play I am writing for them. Such extraneous monologue as the above would be enough to sink any drama—if it survived rehearsal. But in a book it is different—I hope. Particularly in a book a man writes about himself. For it is a small sidelight on how a man thinks, especially with an ocean at his elbow.

CONSTANCE

ROLL ON, dark sea full of whales and flowers and wondrous fetuses. Roll on, dark Time and Space above the waters. A pair of eyes are not enough to know you. I turn my littleness toward my own kind, who are as little as I am. And I shall write of one of them who is sound asleep in New York at this hour. Her spirit comes to my mind as a bright answer to the mysteries outside my window. It is an undaunted spirit. It wears the name of the actress Constance Collier.

In her youth, in a previous century, Constance was one of the beautiful women of the world. Her eyes blazed, her wit flashed, her slow, wide-lipped smile could send a harpoon into a male heart. She was tall, lithe, shapely as a belly dancer. Her black hair was half coiffeured and half wind-blown. Her voice could pierce an audience without rising above a whisper. It was a voice born of passion and poetry—and a great deal of practice.

Young Constance was a wench to make a lover dream and an audience cheer. Fame attended her, as the bright fishes followed Venus on her sea shell.

The bright fishes are gone, and a number of other things with them. The eyes that flashed can barely see. The legs that danced find walking difficult. But I take my oath on it, Constance is unchanged. There is no old Constance. Beside me when we dine sit Viola, Cleopatra, Thaïs, Juliet, Desdemona and all the Constances who once enchanted the world. There are other less-publicized Constances still present. Their slow smile still throws a harpoon—halfway across the table.

Women sometimes preserve a caricature of youth in their faces and manners when they grow old. They dress "young," they talk gayly, they overpaint and diet. And they manage to achieve the useless look of some overrepaired toy. There is no caricature in Constance. Summer has left the garden, but autumn finds it still glowing with life, though half its flowers are dead. And there will be roses coming through the snow.

I write a bit emotionally about Miss Collier because she represents for me the lyric side of existence—its prettiest charm, its most engaging valor. To face adversity and age is not enough. To ignore it, to continue as one was, to perform when there are no longer stages left, to keep alive under a picture hat the courage of vanished youth—there's a deed worthy of matching against the mysteries of my ocean and my night.

WHY I SELDOM GO TO THE THEATER

I WAS NEVER a true playwright, for I never felt the lure or need of the theater. Its dusty backstages became familiar places to me, but never places of magic. When I have had plays running I rarely came to see them after the first two nights.

Before going to the theater to see any play I have to overcome an aversion. And finally arriving, I feel out of place in the audience, as if I had intruded on an alien house of worship.

Expecting to write of the theater fully, I have made a pile of notes on the subject. They bristle with derogatory remarks about audiences and sour findings on the art of the drama. There is also a dossier on drama critics. Studying these notes, I am aware that they are neither original nor even interesting.

Of drama critics, the truth is that, like most writers for the theater, I have two opinions. As a playwright who occasionally has submitted his fortune into the hands of drama critics, I have regarded them always as the Opposition. They seemed mainly an Opposition of parasites and fatheaded sophomores. And I have wondered at the general cowardice of theater people in not tracking them down and punching their noses.

As a daily reader of their columns, however, particularly in New York, I have a different view of them. They are the most literate of journalists and they often add the graces of civilization to the press. They are mostly men of courage who protect their culture from the current hysterias. I am impressed also by their ability to turn neat phrases in the face of an always driving deadline.

Reading their columns, I am aware that they are no Opposition to the theater but the custodians of its ideals. Even the most butterfingered of them are full of yearning for playwright Messiahs. Never having approached the stage in any such white robes, I have never met the finer side of these pernickety fellows. But as their reader I am able to enjoy their highfalutin outcries. In fact, ninety per cent of my theatergoing has been confined to reading their columns.

Another reason for discarding my theater notes is that they avoid glibly the truth about my aversion to seeing plays.

I tell it now. I have shied at theatergoing because I am in the theater—and almost nowhere else—the sport of overpowering emotions. The smallest unhappiness behind the footlights fills my eyes with tears. The hardships of hero or heroine, including even financial quandaries, depress me and leave me full of gloom for days. I cry when children are mistreated, when anyone is misunderstood, when a heroine can't go to a party because she hasn't a proper dress to wear. As for plays in which someone is unjustly accused of some crime and suffers in a corner despised by all, such works send me running from the theater.

The spectacle of injustice seeming to triumph on the stage upsets me much more than do most of its real triumphs in the world. I am able to turn my head from reality, it being usually further than thirty feet away. I am able to turn on, also, a minor katatonia. When it comes to realities, I never suffer. I only think about them. This was true even of the Jews of Europe.

As a reporter I once stood in a train shed beside a locomotive. I was waiting for a statesman to arrive on another train. While waiting, I idly watched a workman who lay on his back under the engine and tinkered with its interior. His legs protruded from the thighs down. I noted that the locomotive had steam up and that its bell was ringing. As I wondered if the half-hidden workman knew of this, I saw the locomotive start. A few seconds later the workman's long legs were lying on the platform in front of me. The rest of him had remained between the tracks.

I left the crowd that rushed to the bloody scene and hurried to buttonhole my statesman, whose train was coming in. I had felt no shock at what had happened under my nose, and by the time I interviewed the statesman I had forgotten it. Two nights later I woke out of a bad dream and found myself shaking and sweating. I sat up and wrote out a detailed report of the incident as a macabre fiction story to be printed in *The Little Review*. The writing done, I returned peacefully to sleep.

Such katatonic armor has served me frequently in my living. Whether it served me well or not, I have sometimes wondered. But in the darkened theater auditorium my katatonia fails to work. Everything that happens on the stage rushes, with no barriers, into me. Faced by the disorderly exercise of my emotions which I know to be in store for me, I avoid the theater. I have nothing against drama as an art form. What I am averse to is being harried and set to blubbering in public by plays of small or large stature.

Attending comedies, I have often found myself no better off than if I had gone to the soggiest of dramas. At the first sign of gallantry on the stage, particularly the gallantry of a loser—a football player or anybody—congratulating the winner on his fine game, the tears I despise start rolling down my cheeks. One of the worst shames I have felt is to find myself at a comedy weeping like a fool in a theater rocking with laughter.

THE PLAYWRIGHT PERI

THE truth is that a playwright is seldom part of the theater. Watch an old stage doorman permitting the author to enter backstage and you can see how dubiously *persona grata* he is.

The playwright is actually a separate theater by himself made up of phantoms and daydreams. In his chair writing his play he casts, acts, directs, paints scenery, runs the lights. He weeps, chuckles, takes bows, writes dramatic reviews of his play in progress, organizes second and third companies, makes curtain speeches.

At night before going to bed he fondles the little batch of manuscript that grows daily thicker, and pretends to reread it for correction, and sits beaming like the mad King Ludwig in a theater all his own.

The manuscript through which he riffles is the only stage he ever really gets to know. When his play is put on it enters a world in which he has the small, moody existence of a Peeping Tom watching his sweetheart in the arms of another.

I have sat through rehearsal weeks, lunched with the casts, shared eagerly in all the pre-opening excitements of a play I have written— and become daily more and more an outsider. By the time the play opened it belonged to everyone connected with it more than to me. Chiefly it belonged to the actors.

MY TROUBLES AS AN ACTOR

OF THE dozen one-act plays I wrote with Kenneth Sawyer Goodman in 1914, I recall mainly what a good time the actors seemed to have playing in them. My first three-act play, *The Egotist*, was performed by Leo Dietrichstein in 1922.

Dietrichstein was the first important actor I knew. Henry Kolker and May Irwin had played sketches of mine in vaudeville, but they had regarded me as a back-stage alien. Dietrichstein had an old-fashioned European respect for playwrights and allowed me to watch the mysteries of production.

He was a silent, humorless man, who on the stage came to life as a shining, witty fellow. His social life seemed to be only with audiences. He loved literature and spent most of his life in hotel rooms like a hermit.

I said to Leo one night in his theater dressing room in Chicago, "Actors are the happiest people I've seen. I'd like to try and become one. Would you let me play the part of the press agent in our play?"

"Yes," said Leo, "on one condition. You must rewrite the first act so that you and I are not on the stage together."

I rewrote the act and a few days later made my debut in the La Salle Street Theater as an actor—my debut and my swan song. Having recited my stint of dialogue in the opening scene I headed for one of the two doors at the back of the office set to make my exit. I picked the wrong door and collided with an actor making his entrance. Recovering from this head-on collision, I made for the other door and again fell into the path of another character—the heroine—sweeping onto the stage.

The second collision unnerved me and left me with a bruise on my temple from the heroine's umbrella. I looked toward the wings, caught a glimpse of Dietrichstein convulsed with laughter, and retired into a telephone booth on the set. There I stood pretending to telephone until the curtain came down on the scene—and released me from the stage.

I never thought of acting again until some ten years later when George Abbott, directing the play *Twentieth Century*, which MacArthur and I had written, offered me the lead of Oscar Jaffe to play.

It happened in this fashion. We were without a leading man on our fourth day of rehearsal and Abbott asked me to read Jaffe. I read it, giving an imitation of David Belasco's sibilant, breathless way of talking. At the end of an hour Abbott insisted excitedly that I play the part. I didn't want to turn into an actor without consulting Rose, and I asked him to call her up and discuss it with her.

"Did he read the part sitting down?" Rose inquired. Abbott said I had. "Have him stand up and read," Rose suggested, "and then please let me know if you want to engage him."

I returned to rehearsal on my feet, and again I started bumping into actors—this time demoniac ones like Matt Briggs, Bill Frawley and Eugenie Leontovitch. No matter where I moved or when, one of these three thespians came at me like Red Grange and sent me staggering. In addition to this drawback I was able to recite only if my hands were in my pockets. *Twentieth Century* opened with a less handicapped actor in the lead.

A LAST PERFORMANCE

As a writer I consider the many tricks and technical proficiencies that go into acting not too important. But there is one side of acting that has always stirred me as much as any literature has. This is the superiority of the actor over reality. I sit grateful before an actor or actress who can remove the mechanics of the play being performed and present me a brief poem of self—and turn an entire audience into a ghost haunting the footlights.

Of the few actors I have known who had that genius I admired most Jack Barrymore. And the performance he gave that I applauded most was his appearance at his last birthday party.

There is so little to keep the fame of an actor alive, once he is dead, that perhaps I should restate who Barrymore was. He was the greatest actor of my time, and he was a witty, learned, wonderfully handsome fellow, to boot. As an actor, he had a genius for converting himself into different personalities that was only a step short of magic. I always felt that with a little practice Barrymore could have equalled the djinns of the Arabian Nights who were able, at will, to turn themselves into scorpions or seraphs.

Barrymore's acting had many facets. It had strut and oratory in it, and it had naturalness and the tones of commonplace life. Usually it contained both. Although he was master of vocal tricks and mannerisms, Barrymore's acting did not depend on these. It was actually a talent for painting on the air the soul of what he was playing, for writing it on the moment as if every part of him were a pencil.

There are some fine actors who, like magicians, need lighting and distance to make their illusions successful. Barrymore was not of these. I have sat beside him in his garden on a bright morning and listened to him discuss and recite Shakespeare's *Richard the Third*. Before me in the sunny garden Richard appeared, and it required an effort of the imagination *not* to see him.

It was not only for the stage that Barrymore could create characters. Dozens of different Barrymores appeared in his life. During the years I knew Barrymore I met many different men who bore his name. The most brilliantly performed of them was the last—the Barrymore in collapse; the bankrupt, disheveled and forlorn Jack who kept dying slowly in Hollywood.

Barrymore's performance as a dying man lasted several years. It was played chiefly for the actor himself, as all great acting is done. A few cronies were privileged to watch it from the wings and help carry the performer on and off. The birthday party of which I write took place toward the end of the performance.

Barrymore had already been to the hospital twice to die. He had recovered each time and gone teetering back into the world. With each return to life, Barrymore's mind grew vaguer and more disordered.

His idolatrous friend, the artist John Decker, was forced now to give all his time to watching over his hero. For among the deteriorations that befell Barrymore was the fact that he had become again as he was in his first years on earth—unhousebroken. His language, always spectacular, had become a stream of sexual obscenity and invective. Doctor Sam Hirshfeld told us this was due either to the encroachments of senility or to the dissolution of the frontal brain lobe.

"He isn't responsible for what he does," said Sam, "any more than a child of two is."

This was sad news to hear of one of the few men in the world I admired.

Barrymore's decline increased after his divorce. His troublesome marriage to Elaine Barry had helped tip reason in his head. His continued love for the luring Elaine kept sounding out of him.

We sat one evening in Barrymore's last home—a claptrap little bungalow in a suburb. Gene Fowler, on whose gaiety and wisdom Barrymore had thrived for years as on a medicine, had summoned up the usual quorum of Barrymore admirers. This consisted of Fowler, Decker, a muscular young German who was introduced always as "Mr. Barrymore's keeper," MacArthur, Thomas Mitchell and myself.

We had finished eating when the telephone rang. A smile lighted Barrymore's face and he leaped as spryly as a boy from the table to the telephone in the hallway.

"He has a newspaperman's nose for disaster," said Fowler. "That will be Elaine."

It was. She had called to straighten out some post-divorce financial problem. We sat glumly around the rickety dining table and listened to Barrymore talk to the woman who had left him forever and for whom his dying senses continued miserably to cry out.

"Anything you want," Barrymore's voice came rich and purring to our ears. "There's nothing I have I wouldn't give you. All I ask is one favor in return—don't hang up. Tell me how much you hate me, but keep on talking so I can hear your voice. No, I'm not drunk, my dear. I am a man at the bottom of Hell—please keep on talking— tell me anything—about the man you're with, how much you love him—anything, just as long as I can hear your voice it doesn't matter what it says. Darling—"

Elaine had hung up.

A few weeks later I received a call from Decker.

"I wish you'd come over to Jack's house," he said. "I've just brought him home. He's a little off his feed."

I found Barrymore asleep in a chair. His eye was blacked, his nose bloodied and his clothes torn. Decker and Fowler were still applying cold compresses. They told me what had happened.

Barrymore had decided to attend the grand opening of Earl Carroll's night club. He had eluded his German "keeper" and sneaked off to the revel. Not wishing to arrive alone at so gala an event, he had gathered up a colored girl in his street wandering.

The café doorman had refused the couple admission. Colored people were not allowed inside. Barrymore had won the first round. Bellowing that his companion was an Hawaiian princess, descended from the demigods who had first inhabited that blessed island, he had shamed doorman, ushers and assistant managers. He was permitted to enter with his colored lady.

The sudden heat of the crowded café interior affected Barrymore's kidneys.

"I'll be with you in a moment, my dear," he said to the dark lady. And pushing an assistant manager aside with a lordly "pardon me," he had stepped up to a pair of new orange velvet drapes and started pissing on them. A half-dozen Carroll minions leaped at him.

"How dare you interrupt a man at such a moment," Barrymore's voice rang out. "Even the lowest of savages respects the human bladder!"

He was battered down while still roaring, rushed out of the door and tossed into the street. A telephone call by an onlooker had brought Decker to the rescue. No report was available on the "Hawaiian Princess" who had dreamed of an evening in Hollywood society on the arm of the famous John Barrymore.

"I'm going to have to keep a closer eye on him," said Decker. "A man who will piss at an opening is a great problem."

"Or a great critic," said Fowler.

Some months after this event, I called on Decker in his home. Barrymore was to be found there now as an almost permanent house guest. This was before Decker's paintings had hit a Hollywood jackpot and enabled a long-ragged Decker to blossom out in lavender chamois pants and enjoy a florid year or two as one of Hollywood's lavish hosts, before his own death.

The Decker home was in a straggly suburb. The parlor was knee-deep in paint rags and overrun with dismal-looking cats and chickens. The furniture was half unstuffed.

Here Barrymore, in the sad time that was on him now, sat slumped in a chair, silent and befogged for hours, but when he spoke, the brightest of maledictions rolled from him in a voice still full of caper and thunder.

The doctors had forbidden liquor, and Decker, a hearty drinker, had rid his premises loyally of every bottle of it and painted with parched throat and the shaking fingers of sobriety.

Nevertheless, there was usually a drunken air to the dying actor, and Decker was certain he prowled the city at night and broke into saloons to steal the stuff.

"The man has no money to buy a stick of lemon candy with," said Decker, "and his friends have all pledged themselves not to supply him with a drop of anything. So how else can he be getting it except by thievery? He's a much cleverer man than you think."

I was not as baffled as Decker. I could have sworn that Barrymore pretended much of his tipsiness because he preferred to be decried as a sot rather than clucked over as an invalid.

Not that there were many people to do either. This once most alluring of men was almost alone in the last year of his dying. Decker nursed him and Fowler was ever present to help the great actor continue to make his exits and his entrances, and to roar back at him as if a world were still responding to the wild Barrymore sallies. Thomas Mitchell and Roland Young continued to track him down wherever he lay cursing or sleeping and speak to him as if he were still the great man of years before. There were few others.

Of the millions of dollars Barrymore had earned in Hollywood, no penny remained. His estate had been looted and all his pockets turned inside out. And of the once great court of admirers, none but we remained. In fairness to their unmentioned names, I must write that it was difficult to stay a Barrymore admirer during the days of his decline. Missing brain lobe or no, the man's wit flung itself like hot water in your face. And here, too, I would have sworn Barrymore was acting. I could understand that there was small pleasure having a court around when a king had only bruises to put on display.

Decker, this afternoon at his easel, kept an eye trained on his idol. Barrymore's toilet habits had regressed further since the Earl Carroll opening.

"The bastard is sometimes too quick for me," said Decker. "He'll start pissing on the floor before I can say Jack Robinson. And, by God, it's too late to chase him into the can."

"A lie!" came a throaty shout from the broken chair. "You lie, you Kaiser-loving syphilitic!" The syllables hit the air like hammers, and the voice, full of curses, seemed on the verge of song.

"He's going to take his nap now," Decker calmly went on. "We'll be able to talk better as soon as the monster's asleep."

Another roar came, this time from the lumpy couch on which Barrymore had stretched himself. "God-damn your arse hole of a house, Decker! This shambles of a couch is not fit for a pair of midgets to fuck on! Out of what swill barrel do you furnish your disgusting habitat?"

"He'll be asleep soon," said Decker, continuing his painting. A few minutes later he added, "We can talk now."

I looked sadly at my sleeping actor hero.

"I'd like to give a birthday party for Jack," I said.

"In some sewer, I hope." Decker grinned.

"In my home," I said.

Looking on Jack lying on the lumpy couch as in some grimy rehearsal for his dying, a wish had come to me. I wanted to see my friend once more in the mantle of his talent. I have never protested the death that strikes down its victim at once, but the death that comes in stages, that cripples and decays first, has seemed always a wretched thing. That this ignoble sort of demise should come to my friend, Jack, pained me and made me want to dream, as if with Barrymore's mind, that it was not true.

"I'd like Jack to be as he once was," I said to Decker. "He can, too. I'll give a party in my home. Black ties and silk gowns. I'll hire a couple of butlers and an orchestra."

Decker sighed.

"It's a nice notion," he said, "but I can't let you in for it." He looked moodily at the sleeping Barrymore. "He's the sweetest sonofabitch in the world, but you can't depend on him any more. He'll soil your best carpets and send women screaming out of the room. My God, the other evening at a hamburger stand there was a waitress —a blowsy bitch with a wart on her nose. Jack looks at her and starts climbing over the counter, yelling, 'My last Duchess! Hoist your dresses, Madam, and let me see Epping Forest again!' We had to run for it."

It took a half hour to persuade Decker that our friend was still a social human being.

On the night of Barrymore's birthday our elegant rented house was festive with flowers, candlelight and ornamental guests. I always enjoyed the spectacle of a Hollywood social evening launching itself— the celebrities casually nosing each other out; the meaningless topics pulled out of mental nowheres for discussion—like bets against boredom; the drone of ineffectual anecdotes by guests eager to talk to other, more important arrivals. And the look of the party, still assembling, with the bejeweled ladies moving idly back and forth as if they were pickets in front of an unfair diamond shop; the under-forty wives bare to their coccyges and matching tits for an evening with all comers; the over-forty wives bedizened and stranded on couches; and the tuxedoed males of all ages, smiling like Casanovas and looking lonely and constipated. And out of the flash of diamonds, powdered skins and insincere grimacing, as out of an orchestra pit, the rising, tuning-up chatter of stray human beings struggling to become a glamorous ensemble.

I stood with a few family friends, disguised for the night as guests, watching the door. A Spanish orchestra was playing in the patio. Marcel, the handsomest butler in Beverly Hills, borrowed from Fanny Brice, together with a wheelbarrowful of her royal silverware, was presiding over the entrance. New arrivals swept in, took a quick glance around to see if people as important as themselves were present—for in Hollywood this is the essential of a successful party—no underdogs—and joined happily the excellent guest list.

As the party grew and settled down, the bad news percolated through its little groups that they had been assembled to celebrate the birthday of Jack Barrymore. Embarrassment and irritation seized the more important guests—the movie moguls I had drawn. Only a month before, Fowler and I had solicited most of them for contributions to a Barrymore-sustaining fund, asking money for his increasing medical expenses. Not a dollar had come out of their pockets.

Barrymore's antisocial habits were known also to all those present. They began to buzz with tales of his misbehavior on movie sets, of his foul language and crazed antics. The fear smote most of them that the evening to which they had innocently come was sure to produce a scandal such as constantly breaks into the press out of Hollywood.

The family friends around me grew nervous while waiting for Barrymore to arrive.

"It's a sadistic thing to do," said Sam Hirshfeld, "to expose him to a thing of this kind. He's completely irresponsible." He looked at the glittering Hollywood array. "They'll crucify him."

"I don't think so," I said. "I think Jack will have a good time."

"It depends on what you call a good time," said Herman Mankie-wicz. "If you consider rape, vomiting and public pissing diversion, I'm sure your guest of honor will enjoy himself."

"I hear Jack's frightfully ill," said Constance Collier. She sighed and added with a voice almost as rich as Barrymore's, "He always had a demon in him, even in the days he was a great artist. Poor Jack."

Fanny Brice, who knew Decker and Barrymore well, attempted a last warning.

"If you're smart, kid," she whispered to me, "you'll yell 'Fire' and get them all out of the house before that poor crazy guy comes. Once he's inside, it'll be too late."

The front door opened and Marcel ushered in two arrivals. They were Barrymore and Decker. Decker's face was red and his small eyes were squinted with tension. Beside him stood a relaxed and smiling Barrymore in an impeccable tuxedo. The death-marked face was somehow as handsome as in the days of his great fame.

His entrance shocked the room into quiet. It was an entrance as undramatic as the appearance of a smiling child. Some of the company pretended indifference, but most of their eyes were drawn to Barrymore and remained staring at him as if waiting for something more. This graceful, shy man, with a curious air of beauty about him, seemed to deny all the wild gossip of beachcomber and town drunk. Slowly a few of the older guests came forward to greet him. Barrymore smiled back gratefully at them as they spoke his name.

Decker whispered to me, "He's been all right, so far. But it can't last. For God's sake seat us next to each other at the table so I can act quickly."

I caught Barrymore's eye for a moment and I knew that I needed to tell him nothing of what was in my mind. He understood my reason for giving him the party. I had said to him a few years ago in one of our long talks, "An actor is the only man in the world who can do anything. Because his art is to use emotions rather than be used by them."

Barrymore had answered, "Acting is not an art. It's a junk pile of all the arts. But in behalf of my scavenger profession I'll make this boast. An actor is much better off than a human being. He isn't stuck with the paltry fellow he is. He can always act his better and nonex-istent self."

As plainly as if he had repeated these words aloud, his eyes spoke them again to me.

The guests, full of chatter and strained laughter, took their places at the several tables. I led Barrymore to the head of the largest of the tables, at which some half-dozen movie caliphs and their glittering ladies were seating themselves. Decker took a chair at Barrymore's right. The music from the patio drifted into the large room full of candlelight and shadows, and the Birthday Party was on.

Barrymore sat like a man forgotten. No one spoke to him. He remained silent and pale over his untouched soup. I felt a misgiving for my friend whom I had summoned to perform once more in a world he had once enchanted. My guest of honor was obviously going to fall asleep before the soup course was over.

A voice came across the table. A great movie caliph was speaking to Barrymore. The caliph was head of a studio, and his voice always silenced any area around him.

"Do you remember the time you ran out on your contract, Jack, when you were working for me? And cost us a fortune? Those were the days, eh? People can't do things like that in Hollywood, anymore."

"Yes, I recall the incident," Barrymore answered. "It was the time I went to India."

"He could have waited till the picture was finished," the caliph explained to an area of silence. "Most actors would. But not the mighty Barrymore."

Barrymore looked at his old enemy, top man still in Hollywood, and his face became awake.

"No," he answered mockingly, "not the mighty Barrymore. Always a selfish rogue and a blundering ass! Mark you, he'll come to no good end!"

The Barrymore chuckle sounded its full scale. Decker nervously studied the exits.

"What did you have to go to India for?" the caliph demanded.

"I went to meet a saint," Barrymore answered. "I was seized with a great desire to meet a man named Krishnamurti. I had been told he was a saint who could command the ear of Heaven. Have you never in your life yearned to meet a saint?"

"I can't say I have." The caliph considered this a witty answer and laughed loudly at it.

"Pah!" The exultant Barrymore snort that was the vocal trade-mark of his heyday smote the air. It was part sneer and part howl of triumph that only one actor since Barrymore has ever had wind and soul enough to bring out of his throat—Laurence Olivier.

"We are made of different stuff, sir," Barrymore went on. "I always dreamed of meeting a saint and learning from him the true secrets of Heaven."

"Tell us about Krishnamurti," asked one of the young actresses, employing her best enunciation. "I've heard so many wonderful things about him."

"I know nothing of Krishnamurti," Barrymore answered with a great and unexpected sneer. "I never met him. On the morning I arrived in Calcutta, eager for spiritual communion with the young saint, I was picked up by a pimp and led to an amazing whore house. The most delightful I have ever seen to this day. I speak as a devoted student. I would like to describe this pelvic palace so that you will not think me totally an idiot for giving up my saint in its favor. It had a great central room with a floor of pink and white marble which was covered with fleets of pillows. You have never seen such pillows. They cooed at your buttocks. There were tall silver columns, and clouds of colored silks ballooned from the ceiling, giving it the look of a heaven of udders. Incense pots gave forth smells capable of reviving the most dormant of Occidental phalluses. And music came from somewhere—much as now in this room. Gentle music that went directly to the scrotum and cuddled there."

Decker looked nervous. A young woman giggled.

"A gong sounded," Barrymore went on, and he imitated a great gong, struck and vibrating. "Bong! Ahzee-zee-zee. Beautiful women appeared in twos and threes. They moved slowly and their bellies were like serpents. I recall that they were hung with little bells and when they moved they made a noise like a swarm of bees. These delightful creatures sang and danced for me and then draped themselves around me in artistic clusters until I felt like a pubic chandelier.

"Pah!" the snort sounded. "I saw no one else in India. I saw no India. I saw no saint. I saw only Hindu whores. I remained on the pillows for four busy weeks, never leaving them except to make use of a small plumbing contrivance within staggering distance. I lived and slept on those wonderful pillows and was fed like Elijah, but by ravens bearing a superior type of food. I would be happy to describe the dainties that were supplied me—but there are ladies present."

"It's unbelievable," Hirshfeld whispered to me. "How can a completely shattered mind talk like that?"

The cunning of the parable sobered us. As this traveler in quest of a saint had found himself sprawled in an exotic brothel, so had the artist Barrymore once in quest of his art landed and lingered in Hollywood.

We ate, and Barrymore talked on and there was no other sound than the soft music from the patio.

"And so," Barrymore said as the meat course was removed, "I never met my saint. I met only dancing girls and singing girls, all of them devout students of the Kamasutra, which teaches that there are thirty-nine different postures for the worship of Dingledangle— the God of Love."

The symmetrical face, the large eyes, the snorting, cadenced voice, the heavy-fingered hands full of witty gestures, continued the performance. As the coffee arrived the glow in Barrymore's face increased. He had started talking of Shakespeare.

"In my early years," said Barrymore, "when I was still callow and confused, and still a-suckle on moonlight—I used to prefer *Romeo and Juliet* to all the other plays. But, as my ears dried, I began to detest the fellow, Romeo. A sickly, mawkish amateur, suffering from Mogo on the Gogo. He should be played only by a boy of fifteen with pimples and a piping voice. The truth about him is he grew up and became Hamlet." A heavy scowl covered his face. "There, if ever, was a scurvy, mother-loving drip of a man! A ranting, pious pervert! But clever, mark you! Like all homicidal maniacs! And how I loved to play him. The dear boy and I were made for each other."

"I saw you play Hamlet in London," several guests spoke out. "Greatest performance I ever saw."

"Yes, I was a triumph in London," he smiled. "I have never kept a scrapbook of my questionable activities as a man of grease paint. But there's one set of dramatic notices I have saved. I still have them, unless my good friend Decker here has sold them to keep himself in liquor."

He glared at poor Decker, who was sharing his few desperately earned dollars with his idol.

"Go on with your tale, Mr. Barrymore," said Decker stiffly.

"Thank you," Barrymore said. "My *Hamlet* notices are the only criticism I have ever hoarded. I've kept them to read on the day I might become vain and fancy myself a man of artistic qualities."

"But they were marvelous notices," Sam Hirshfeld said. "You showed them to me."

"So they were," Barrymore smiled. "The notices every artist dreams of. The little pieces of yellowing print that testify he once had a soul. I would like to tell you how I earned them, which is something I have never told anyone this side of the Atlantic before."

We were as quiet as our brandy glasses.

"A few days after arriving in London to do Hamlet," Barrymore resumed, "I fell madly in love with a duchess. Pah! I have forgotten her historic name. But, it doesn't matter. I can get it from Winnie Churchill, who, I understand from my friend Decker, has become a great man—and is saving the British Empire singlehanded. Winnie will recall my duchess. But I seem to have gotten ahead of my story. I fell madly in love with the lady whose name I have caddishly forgotten, on the day we started the *Hamlet* rehearsals. And I spent every hour I could steal from my chores trying to seduce the lady, who, it developed, was a human icicle. That's the only thing I've ever held against the British—the semi-lunatic virtue of their women. The duchess over whom I found myself swooning was one of the worst examples of that strange English blight of female chastity. Pah! I sang for her. I danced. I dropped to her feet. I recited from the poets. I plied her with wine laced with Spanish fly. I wept and pawed her hour after hour. To no purpose. Her clothes were glued to her body. I could get my hand under her dress no further than her kneecap—one of the least interesting of the female outposts. And, mark you, I was young and full of juices. I had practically despaired of mounting this aristocrat when a messenger arrived at my lodgings one morning with a note. My duchess awaited me alone in her castle for lunch.

"*Hamlet* was opening that same night, but this was the first murmur of surrender from my lady of ice. I weighed the matter carefully and decided if I used a fast automobile I could ride to her castle, a distance of thirty miles, and be back in time for the opening night of *Hamlet*.

"It was a memorable afternoon. The duchess lowered the drawbridge and your actor, with gonfalon high, marched in. At seven o'clock I was lying exhausted in the lady's bed and trying to revive myself with bottle on bottle of the castle's wine. The more I drank the sleepier I became. But being a man of resource, I switched to Scotch and, with the help of two servants, was finally dressed and on my feet.

"I arrived at the theater a half hour before curtain time and passed out cold in my dressing room. My man revived me as he put me into Hamlet's clothes. He whacked me with wet towels, shoved lumps of ice into me and poured pots of coffee down my gullet.

"I was the first American to play Hamlet on a London stage—and I was also the first drunk to play it on any stage in the world. I reeled out of the wings barely able to stand on my feet. The heat of the footlights made me dizzy. I had to lean on Polonius to keep from falling on my face. I had to make several unrehearsed exits in order to vomit in the wings. I returned once barely in time for my soliloquy. Unable to stand, I sprawled in a chair and recited the God-damn speech sitting down and trying to keep from blacking out.

"Mark you, I was drunk as a fiddler's bitch all through the five acts. But I missed no word of Will Shakespeare's and I missed no cue. So much I will say for myself.

"The dramatic reviews the next day were, as you say, Dr. Hirshfeld, marvelous. They praised me as the greatest Hamlet of the age. Every one of my drunken staggers, my exits to vomit in the wings, my reeling into a chair to recite 'To be or not to be,' were hailed as brilliant artistic interpretations of Hamlet's role.

"As I told you, I've kept those notices as a reminder of the foolishness of fame—and the lunacy of life in general—'A song sung by an idiot running down the wind.'"

Barrymore's voice stopped abruptly. The guests remained silent and waiting. But there were no more words. Barrymore shut his eyes and whispered to Decker, "You better take me off, Johnny. I've gone up in my lines."

We helped Barrymore to his feet. The shy smile was back in his face and he walked gracefully between us out of the room.

A few minutes later the birthday cake with which I had refused to interrupt Barrymore's storytelling was brought in. Its many candles blazed like a triumphant row of footlights.

AHOY, ELDORADO!

THE ADVENTURES I now have to relate have to do with money-making. Since this is a topic of superior interest to my fellow citizens, I shall preface my exotic financial dealings with a small discussion of our economic system.

Next to God, economics produces the dullest of writing. This is because both subjects are treated only with dignity and importance. A ponderous manner is best for the concealment of error and inanity. I may be as full of errors as the next economist but I promise they are not errors which the reader will find impossible to understand.

Money-making is, if anything is, our national soul. It is the one thing on which all Americans think alike. At least I have met only a few extremely eccentric people who were not interested in making money. I have met a larger number who were tired of making it, but not tired enough to stop. High and low Americans alike look on our economic system as one of the wonders of the world. They are proud of it and unwilling to exchange it for any other sort of system.

I share their attitude. It is not because I have, at times, prospered under Capitalism that I applaud it. It is because I have almost a mania for working hard. Until recently, the harder I worked the richer, apparently, I became. This made the system pleasing to me.

I imagine my fellow Americans admire it for the same reason. Capitalism hangs up a pot of gold for every man to go after. As a result, more people die from overwork in the U.S.A. than died under the whips of the Pharaohs. But Americans are proud to die from overwork. It is almost as fine a distinction as dying in battle. They regard perishing from ulcers, high blood pressure and coronary thrombosis as one of the great privileges of our free economic system.

The largest death rate is among our minor Capitalists, called affectionately "little business." In my youth I witnessed most of my relatives turn into Capitalists of this sort. Nearly all of them ended up exhausted and bankrupt. As Capitalists they worked twice as hard and staggered under twice as many burdens as in their wage-slave days. They waited on customers, trimmed windows, operated sewing machines, stoked furnaces, swept sidewalks, ran errands, pleaded for credit extensions and came home for supper too tired to eat with their shoes on. But they fell asleep at night proud of being their own boss.

My relatives, of course, were not true Capitalists. The true Capitalist is a gentleman whose money does all the work for him. Such nabobs occupy ornamental offices, live long, are seldom tired and are able to travel and divert themselves to their hearts' content. What the Plantagenets, the Tudors, the Hohenzollerns and Romanoffs were to their lands, these Capitalists are to the U.S. They are the group which alone is able to use and enjoy the real blessings of our free-enterprise system. They number less than one fourth of one per cent of the population.

When Radicals write against American Capitalism, they attack the handful of money aristocrats who do nothing and own almost everything. The denunciations omit the point that it is an aristocracy open to all. True, few get into it, and thousands expire ahead of their time trying to achieve it. But it is not an aristocracy apart. Given a little luck, even with dice, anybody can join the exploiters. Thus the millions who live on crumbs are ever ready to defend the feast with their lives. It may be theirs some day.

When most Americans read about the corruption and ruthlessness of the rich, they are inclined to grin. These malefactors are their dream selves. The American does not aspire to overthrow the thieves and oppressors half as much as he does to become one of them.

To the Communists such feudal dreams seem witless and ignoble. Of the two—the American and the Communist—it is the Communist I find witless. In Russia the millions of workers support a system which they fancy protects them from exploitation by individuals. No tycoon or sharp promoter can wring power and fortune out of the worker's honest toil. Only the State can do that. To the State all belongs.

Since the toiling Russians believe with a new and foolish mysticism that *they* are the State, there is no defeat in being its undernourished aggrandizers. They are proud to sweat for it, sing of it and to build it bigger and bigger—for it is their riches. Their ownership of "their" State is no more concrete than was the ownership of Heaven by the lowly of the Middle Ages. But the Russians are an extremely spiritual people. This spirituality of the Russians enables them to enjoy and worship unreality, whether it be the unreality of a Father in Heaven or of a Father State.

Americans are deficient in such mystic talent.

Having cleared my head of these economic musings, I am ready to stand again on the ship outside the City of Miami in 1925. I am about to meet the free-enterprise system in one of its most hooligan hours. Three miles beyond where this ship, the S. S. *Alexandria*, carrying me, rides at anchor, the great Florida land boom is on.

I FIND A VALLEY OF DIAMONDS

IT WAS DAWN. We were waiting to be taken ashore in launches, there being no harbor in Miami capable of accommodating any vessel larger than a canoe.

Around us in the pink light and tropic heat of a November morning, a hundred other ships rode at anchor, steamships and sailing ships. I looked at this flotilla of funnels and masts and wondered what in God's name they were doing there.

A passenger in a wrinkled white suit had joined me at the rail. He told me the fleet of ships was loaded with lumber and other building materials. They were waiting to dump their cargoes on Miami's non-existent docks. Hundreds of other ships were heading for Miami with similar cargoes. It would take months before all the lumber, cement, tools and machinery could be taken ashore.

"It's a damn shame," said the passenger, "because if we had a harbor here the damn boom would go twice as fast. But there's always some damn bottleneck when it comes to progress."

"Who's running the boom?" I asked.

There were no plans in my head, but I found the spectacle of a hundred steamships and sailing ships riding at anchor exciting. The money I had earned after Woodstock by writing a novel and selling a dozen short stories was all gone, and I was again without income or bank balance. McEvoy had invited us on the trip as his guests. In return for this largess I was to help him write a movie for the Hollywood actor Thomas Meighan.

Neither Mac nor I had any knowledge of movie writing. But I had seen a few movies and I assured Mac that writing one would be easy.

"Anybody with a good memory for clichés and unafraid to write like a child can bat out a superb movie in a few days."

This was my first pronouncement on the subject of movies. It was among the most prophetic statements I have ever made.

The passenger in the wrinkled white suit failed to understand my question about who was running the boom.

"Why, everybody's running the boom," he answered. "There're about a hundred thousand people over there buyin' and sellin' and buildin' like beavers."

"I mean," I said, "who are the men at the top? The big operators with millions of dollars to spend?"

"Oh, those," said the passenger, and recited proudly a dozen names. I put them in writing. Among them was the name of Charles Ort.

We went ashore after lunch. A group of newspaper reporters were on hand to interview any remotely celebrated arrivals. I was pleased to be singled out for questioning. I spoke glowingly of Miami.

We took in the sights on the way to the inland hotel Mac had selected for our housing. The City of Miami had turned itself into a real-estate cornucopia. A hundred thousand people were getting rich selling building lots to each other. They raced up and down the hot sidewalks in bathing suits, bathrobes and jiggling sweaters. A colored boy had sold his shoeshine stand for ten thousand. The news of great profitable sales spread like the arrival of a Messiah. Straw-hatted salesmen waved "new development" maps in the air and chanted the names Silver Heights, Coral Gables, Picture City, Montezuma Manors, Sea Cove Crest, Biscayne Bay, like the signal towers of a Promised Land. Symphony orchestras played in salesrooms. Buses full of bonanza-hunters roared through the streets and down the coral dusty roads. Tumbling out of their tallyhos, these Argonauts looked at rubbish heaps and reeking swamps and visioned the towers of new Babylons.

Everybody was trying to get rich in a few days. Nobody went swimming. Nobody sat under the palm trees. Nobody played horseshoes. Seduction was at a standstill. Everybody was stubbing his toe on real-estate nuggets. People who had been worth only six hundred dollars a few weeks ago were now worth a hundred thousand dollars —not in money but in real estate.

You could hardly move in the main streets. They were choked with fortune-hunters. These were not gamblers or adventurers. They were chiefly people from nowhere who had come to Florida for a two-weeks' tan. Groggy with our first tour of Eldorado, we arrived at our hotel after dinner.

"The whole thing's mad," said Mac. "It doesn't make sense, financially. A lot of poor people can't make each other rich—by cheating."

"Every one of them," said Rose, "will lose every penny they have, poor things. I studied it in economics."

I heard someone playing a ukulele across the hall and singing. I crossed the hall and looked into an open room.

A dark-haired Irish-featured young man was sitting on a bed strumming and singing, "So Mister Engineer Open Up the Throttle, I'm Gonna Throw Away My Hot-Water Bottle, We'll All Be in Miami in the Morning."

"You sing like a professional," I said.

"Thanks, stranger, you'll find a drink on the dresser," he said. "The name's Walter O'Keefe."

"Glad to know you. Are you singing anywhere in Miami?"

"Texas Guinan's Silver Slipper," said O'Keefe. "I also tell jokes. You in show business?"

I identified myself as a novelist.

"Do any of these men ever come to the Silver Slipper?" I asked. I showed O'Keefe the list of names the *Alexandria* passenger had given me.

"A few." O'Keefe studied them. "They stagger into our café now and then to make googoo eyes at the girls. Why do you ask?"

"I just arrived tóday," I said, "so I haven't had time to figure out something definite. But I have a few notions. I'd like to meet one of those names I showed you. But I want to meet him after a proper build-up. If you'll get me a private session with any one of those nabobs I'll cut you in for ten per cent of everything I make in Miami."

"I've got to run along now to sing songs and make jokes," O'Keefe said. "But you'll be hearing from me, partner."

CAPITALIST OR CON MAN?

Two DAYS LATER O'Keefe led me to an office in the Flagler Building Arcade and introduced me to one of my list of names—Charles Ort.

Mr. Ort was president of the Key Largo Corporation, a ninety-million-dollar group of pioneers.

He sat behind his desk looking at a copy of the Miami *Herald* when we entered. It carried a seven-column headline proclaiming that I, a "prince of litterateurs," had arrived and envisioned Miami as the new Paris of the South.

Mr. Ort looked up eagerly from a study of my prophecies. He greeted me as if I were royalty. I knew at once that the less I said the more potent I would remain.

The tycoon O'Keefe had landed for me was a short, reddish-faced man who spoke with an Ohio twang. He was as shy as a small freckled boy on all subjects but one—Key Largo.

After some difficult small talk, I asked my tycoon to tell me something about Key Largo. Modesty fled his tongue and I listened for a half hour to a Barnum outside the gate of Paradise. Key Largo was the future playground of America—and Europe. On its shores the finest hotels and casinos in the world would arise. Yachts would glitter in its coves. It was a fisherman's Eden. And it offered the only beaches in this part of the world not infested by the man-eating barracuda. Mansions would dot its beautiful acres in a fashion that would put to shame the European Riviera. Within one short year, Key Largo, only a few minutes' flight from Miami, would be the pleasure center of the entire world.

As Mr. Ort spoke, his face grew redder and he kept twirling an old-fashioned gold watch on the end of a vest chain. He punctuated each of his purple passages with the sternly voiced sentence, "And I'm talking facts, sir!"

When he finished, I said I had sought him out because I, too, was fascinated by the great future of Key Largo and had thought of something that might help sell its ninety million dollars' worth of building lots. Mr. Ort said quietly that the board of directors would be honored to have me present any helpful ideas I had. An appointment was made for me to talk to this board the next afternoon.

I sat in our shabby hotel room the next morning and scribbled notes to myself. McEvoy came in and thought we ought to start discussing the movie plot for whose invention he was paying my room and board. I told him of my appointment in an hour.

"What's your plan?" he asked.

I told it to him.

"Sounds pretty good," he said. "How much are you going to ask for working it out?"

"Twenty-five hundred a week," I said, "for ten weeks, minimum."

"I might be of some help to you," said Mac. "Will you let me in?"

"I'd like to keep the twenty-five hundred to myself," I said.

"I wouldn't think of taking a nickel of it," said Mac. "I'll take as my share all we get over twenty-five hundred."

"That's fair," I said.

There were a dozen fine-looking men in the board of directors' room. Most of them wore white suits and looked like distinguished coffee planters. A few nationally known names were among them. I was introduced by Mr. Ort. No attention was paid to McEvoy. It was presumed that like all important men I kept a sort of umbrella carrier at my side.

I stood up and explained my project. Key Largo had a distinction on which no one had yet touched, I said. It was in the heart of the Spanish Main, and directly in the track of all the pirates who had once sailed these waters. As was known to all students of pirate history, these sea robbers had been wont to bury their loot for safekeeping on the various Florida Keys. Key Largo, as the most attractive of these coral strands, must obviously have been one of the most favored hiding spots. Millions of dollars in doubloons, emeralds, diamonds and gold vessels must still be buried and unclaimed on Key Largo.

As I made these fantastic statements, I watched the listening Capitalists apprehensively. My knowledge of Capitalists had a wobble in it. I was unsure of how far they would go in "misrepresentation" to make money. I half expected one of my rich listeners to rise and denounce me for my bouncing lies. None stirred.

My plan, I said now, was to organize a treasure hunt, starting from New York City. I would rent the ex-Kaiser's black yacht, now idle in Long Island, invite fifty leading American society women and famous stage and sports personalities on board as guests, hire Paul Whiteman's band to come along, and then, with the aid of an old pirate map, dig up a great trove of treasure on Key Largo. I would, of course, see to it in advance that this pirate treasure was buried in the proper place. Its discovery would inflame the nation and bring thousands of other treasure hunters to Key Largo and make the sale of its lots as easy as if an oil strike had occurred on the little isle.

I was done. I scanned the happy faces of the assembled tycoons and knew that I had not offended their concepts of the American free-enterprise system.

One of the millionaires spoke up.

"How much will all this cost?" he asked.

My answer was cut off by McEvoy.

"I'm the business side of this outfit, gentlemen," said Mac in an arresting voice. "This operation will cost your company five thousand dollars a week for a minimum of twelve weeks."

The Capitalists sighed with relief.

"That sounds all right," a silver-haired gentleman said.

"Of course," Mac added quickly, "that does not include the per diem expenditures of the treasure hunt Mr. Hecht has outlined. Yacht rental, entertainment, food and all that sort of thing."

"Of course," another of the Capitalists nodded.

"Nor does it include," Mac went on, a little recklessly I thought, "office rental and office equipment. We will need a great deal of floor space in some top Miami Beach hotel—desks, couches, carpets, mimeograph machines, et cetera."

"Naturally," a third Capitalist agreed. "I think we can get together on this."

Mac and I walked into the street an hour later with the first draft of a contract in our pockets. I was a little depressed. I could have had the whole five thousand a week for myself.

But I recognized the fairness of Mac's getting half. In the free-enterprise system which I had boarded, cutlass in hand, the chief thing that paid off was the ability to "think big." Obviously Mac was a better Capitalist than I. He was able to think twice as big.

MY GOLD RUSH

WE FITTED UP an office in the Fleetwood Hotel in Miami Beach. It was about a half acre in size and contained twelve desks and innumerable leather couches and chairs. The office door bore the single word "Press."

On learning from Mac, however, that our contract required us to pay all wages out of our own take, I engaged only a staff of two— a stenographer and a newspaper reporter.

The newspaperman was the one who had interviewed me on my arrival and fervidly described me as "visiting royalty from the land of literature." His name was Charles Samuels. He had vividly blue eyes and blue-black hair. His pointed nose was slightly askew and he hailed from Brooklyn.

Although he was still in his twenties, his life had already been rich with mishaps. In his tales, related in excellent language disguised by a Brooklyn snarl, he was ever the butt of poverty, injustice or woman's wiles. He had once been falsely accused by a lady midget whom he was giving a lift from Coney Island of knocking her down and trying to rape her. Samuels explained that midgets were all publicity hungry. He had traveled and been touched by the wonders of life, which included a Southern lady with two vaginas.

"I would have married her," said Samuels, "but I figured I could never trust her."

I noted that he wrote well and quickly, that he had, despite his ruffian look, a boyish heart and was ready to be as loyal as a Knight Templar. I doubled his newspaper salary and gave him six of the twelve desks as his own.

Mac left for New York to dicker for the ex-Kaiser's yacht and get together a troupe of society ladies for our treasure hunt. Having nothing to do, I wrote a rococo essay about Key Largo. It was printed as a brochure on wedding invitation stationery. Mr. Ort was overcome by this work. He read it aloud a number of times to the thousand salesmen employed by our company.

Rose and I moved into a Fleetwood Hotel suite, bought tropical garments, went swimming, practiced tumbling on the beach and picked up a score of millionaires as friends. Mr. Ort owned an airplane to whisk investors quickly to and from Key Largo, a twin-engined speed yacht and a houseboat with ten large staterooms. This craft, the *Altamaha*, loomed on the waters like a Noah's Ark. Mr. Ort gave it to me to use as my own.

Mac's telegrams from New York grew less and less hopeful. Despite his most lyrical arguments, he could induce no society ladies to sign up for our treasure hunt. Samuels, whose chief duty was to spy on Mr. Ort and his fellow tycoons and bring me word of their mood, reported that there were grumblings among them.

"They are beginning to talk of you and McEvoy as if you were common swindlers," said Samuels, and guffawed as was his habit when he had ill news to tell. "They are creatures of no faith. But what can you expect from millionaires? They're all sick and frightened people."

I wired Mac to quit fishing for dowagers and went to work on a more practical version of the great treasure hunt. I hired a man named Keating, who was head of the Florida Ku Klux Klan, to go to Havana and see if he could find some old Spanish doubloons and also an antique treasure chest. Mr. Keating said he was highly connected in Cuba, where he was organizing, with President Machado's help, a Cuban chapter of the Ku Klux Klan.

He returned in a week with a satchel full of real doubloons loaned him by President Machado. But he had been unable to find an antique treasure chest. Samuels and I went shopping in Miami and flushed a pair of vases five feet tall and weighing a hundred pounds each. They were eighteenth-century Spanish pottery. I had never seen them pictured in any drawings of buried pirate treasure but I assured Samuels a little novelty wouldn't hurt.

I then sent Samuels to fetch a native hero for our project and to prospect out a place for our buried treasure. He returned from a day in Key Largo with tales of searing hardships, as if he had fought his way on and off the moon. But he was a fellow given to dressing up a story and I ignored his bellows. He told me that no human being could live on Key Largo, but he had found a Floridian who was a beachcomber on a more habitable shore.

His name was Cap'n Loftus, and he was one of the native Conchs, so called after the shells whose beach life they emulated.

Cap'n Loftus had a lean corrugated face, a drooping tobacco-stained mustache and he carried a .48 Colt revolver in his belt. His colorless eyes rolled when he spoke and he seemed a bit touched by the sun. Samuels assured me he had passed all the tests—didn't know who was President of the United States and was unable to read or write.

Cap'n Loftus was given a hundred-dollar bill and the plot was explained to him. We were going to dig a big hole in the interior of

Key Largo and announce to the world that he had unearthed a pirate treasure. I gave him the treasure map I had prepared and explained he was supposed to have found it while cleaning out his grandfather's sea chest. I explained also what we were going to do with the vases.

Cap'n Loftus accepted the project solemnly and showed no further curiosity—a fact that worried me.

In the morning we rolled the two massive jars aboard the *Altamaha* and set off for Key Largo. Our houseboat was a maritime snail, and it was late afternoon before we made the island cove. Rose, Samuels and I rolled the jars ashore.

My first view of Mr. Ort's pleasure center of the world astonished me. We had been telling bigger lies about Key Largo than I had imagined. A few beach acres had been cleared and a long wooden "construction headquarters" put up. It was unpainted and its roof was incomplete. There were several shacks standing with piles of garbage around them. A two-hundred-foot stretch of cement sidewalk had been laid down and a dozen ornate lampposts erected. The sidewalks led nowhere. It gave the premises a forlorn and heartbreaking look. A sign attached to one of the lampposts read "Gold Coast Plaza."

Several disabled pieces of machinery, including a steam shovel, lay about as if abandoned by a routed army. There were a few small piles of lumber and some overturned picnic benches. The whole effect was as if one had come on a bit of defunct civilization.

We started our trek inland, rolling the two jars before us. Samuels had told no tall tales. Beyond the pathetic clearing a jungle began. Snakes hung coiled from tree branches. Monkeys or worse animals screeched overhead. A swarm of bugs, some as large as frogs, darkened the air and endangered our lives.

Cap'n Loftus, not a stranger to Key Largo, had provided us with mosquito-net bags to put over our heads, hip boots and heavy mittens. Despite this armor, the fearsome bugs continued to ferret out our flesh and draw blood.

Due to the elephantine vases, our progress was slow. Dusk came. The sinister jungle grew black. We moved in a prehistoric world.

"Can you imagine the poor bastards who buy lots on this pleasure island," Samuels croaked. "Even the lowest of savages wouldn't live here. A human being would be destroyed overnight."

After two hours of struggle we reached a spot I considered sufficiently inland. The Cap'n passed out the shovel he had brought, and we took turns digging a hole large enough to bury us all in. We cracked the vases and posed them on the edge of our crater and scattered a few doubloons in the ooze. I foresaw that the press would want photographs of the spot.

Our preparations done, we returned to the *Altamaha*. Morning found us back in Miami. Samuels was too swollen with bug bites to be of any further use. He seemed also sun-struck and kept snarling of the horrors of Key Largo. I put him to bed and proceeded with the Project.

I wired two hundred city editors asking them how many words they would take on the finding of a half million dollars worth of pirate gold by a Florida native named Cap'n Loftus. A hundred replies asked for stories of various lengths. I wrote out a dozen different yarns and filed them at the Western Union office and then spent the night coaching Cap'n Loftus in what to say to the reporters who would soon be arriving. He was an eager pupil.

The reporters arrived the next day from a dozen Florida towns and a few came from Georgia and Louisiana. They interviewed Cap'n Loftus and examined the portion of his find he had brought to town. He said threateningly that the rest of his pirate gold was hidden and he would kill anyone he caught snooping after it. Listening to the Cap'n, I felt grateful to Samuels. He had, somehow, stumbled on the greatest natural liar I had ever seen in action. It was a fine and exciting press conference.

The story appeared in scores of newspapers all over the country. Within twenty-four hours, craft of all sizes were chugging down the Florida coast for Key Largo. The flat tropic sea was dotted with treasure hunters heading for that sinister isle as for a new Eldorado. They carried tents and provisions, spades and dynamite sticks.

Mr. Ort rushed a hundred of his crack salesmen down by sea and air. In order to dig in Key Largo and not be ousted as trespassers, the Argonauts had to buy lots. In a week the Key Largo company had sold more than a million dollars' worth of snake-covered, bug-haunted jungle land. Each purchase required a down payment of ten per cent, the remainder to be paid in installments.

Mr. Ort and his fellow Capitalists presented me gratefully with a new contract. It extended my services for another twelve weeks.

There followed days of leisure. Mr. Ort invited us to dine at his home. We met his wife, a silent and pretty brunette who spoke but once during the meal.

"I dislike Florida more than any other state in the Union," she said in a mild voice. "And I regret very much that Mr. Ort insisted on coming to it."

Mr. Ort patted her hand gallantly.

"I arrived in Miami eight months ago," he said, "with nine hundred dollars in my pocket. Today I'm worth ninety million dollars. I don't say that as a boast, sir, but just as a vindication of my coming to Miami against Mrs. Ort's wishes."

"I can always imagine a rich man getting richer," I said. "Once you have a million, a second million seems inevitable. But how does a man with nine hundred dollars make his first hundred thousand? That always baffles me."

"It's an interesting story, I think," said Mr. Ort. "The second day I was in Miami and saw the tremendous opportunities for business advancement the city had to offer, an idea came to me. I looked around for a woman fortuneteller and found one called Madam Zubedaya. I made a deal with this lady, sir. I offered her twenty-five per cent up to ten thousand dollars of any money I would make with her assistance. All she had to do was tell each of her clients that she saw great fortune coming to him from a man wearing a black derby hat and smoking a big cigar. Well, sir, after we had agreed on all the details, I took up my stand outside of Madam Zubedaya's place and waited for some rich-looking man to come out.

"Well sir, the very next day a gentleman appeared in a chauffeured limousine. After he came out of Madam's fortunetelling den, I followed him to the beach and watched him go for a swim.

"Soon as he came out of the water, I moved up to him while he was taking the sun and started talking to him about the fine opportunities Miami had to offer. I was wearing a black derby hat, rather unusual on the beach, and, contrary to my habits, holding a big cigar in my teeth. Not smoking it, though. I don't believe in the use of tobacco in any form, sir.

"Well sir, remembering what the fortuneteller had told him, this gentleman became very interested in everything I had to say. Before the day was over I had sold him a hundred thousand dollars' worth of land called Silver Heights. I had put down a five-hundred-dollar option on it, against a five-thousand-dollar purchase price. So that was how I made my first hundred thousand, which is what you were asking about, sir."

I GIVE A PARTY

I FILLED Mr. Ort's cup of happiness by launching a newspaper called *The Key Largo Breeze*. It was an eight-page tabloid relating events supposedly taking place in Key Largo. Mr. Ort, inflamed by these stories to be read in honest print, hired a cast of aristocratic-looking girls and sent a camera crew with them. Movies were taken of the beauties sunning themselves (heroically) on the Key Largo "Gold Coast." Thousands of feet of film were shot of the company's salesmen standing around, monkeying with the disabled machinery and singing lustily on the picnic beaches.

I became Charlie Ort's friend, and as far as I could make out, the only one he had. We talked chiefly of Key Largo, but despite his eloquence, I remained without faith. I had refused, from the beginning, to put any of the money I received in a bank. I was certain that the boom was due to collapse at any hour and take everything down with it, including the bank.

I kept my money in my pockets and by February was walking around with twenty-two thousand dollars on my person. At this point I remembered my wife, Marie, who was in Chicago. I wired her asking if she would give me a divorce in return for ten thousand dollars in cash. The divorce papers came a week later, containing a codicil requiring me to pay alimony for the rest of my life. I was, nevertheless, happy to sign them.

I remained a bachelor for half an hour, after which Rose and I were married by a woman judge in her office. Rose looked young and radiant after the months of sunning and swimming, and wore, unaccountably (unless she had carefully planned the whole matter), a black hat and a black French gown.

The end of February found me bored with sun and idleness. I told Mr. Ort I was quitting.

"You need a change," my friend said. "You've been working too hard." He tried to press on me again, as often before, a bonus of a large section of choice Key Largo property. I refused, as always, for I had now almost a phobia toward Key Largo.

"I'll tell you what we'll do," said my friend. "We'll have a party in Havana. Invite anybody you want up to fifty people. It's on me."

I invited forty people, most of them strangers loitering in the Flagler Arcade, and sent Mr. Keating, the Ku Klux Kleagle who had become devoted to me, ahead to make arrangements.

Two days later we boarded ship. Mr. Ort's airplane escorted us in the skies and a number of blond singing and dancing girls were with us to provide entertainment. Our guests were forty husbands on the loose. Rose was the only wife on the junket.

Our arrival in Havana deflected the town's interest from the revolution building up against the tyrant Machado. All forty of our guests were drunk an hour after disembarking. They stormed the Sevilla Biltmore Hotel and took over its elevators. They played "stump," climbing up and down the elevator shaft. Fist fights broke out on a dozen street corners. Cafés were raided and native female entertainers were carried off. Most of our guests were ex-members of the A.E.F. and, finding themselves again in a foreign town, considered themselves its benefactors and saviors. This being in a time when Americans were still loved and grinned at by foreign eyes, there was a minimum of broken heads.

Hoping to lower the bellicosity of our troop, I organized an international dance contest between "America's leading dancers" and the pick of Havana's terpsichorean talent. I was unable to line up any Cuban dancers but, with Samuels' help, managed to lure a dozen whores out of the local brothels and induced them to compete against our vaudeville blondes. The contest was staged on Marianao Beach. The whores won the grand prize.

Eight days of such doings finally sapped the *élan* of our party. I decided it was time to return to Miami. Mr. Ort was reluctant. He had taken not a single drink, being an Ohio teetotaler; and had dallied with not a single native belle, being a man of high morals. He had tagged along watching the revelry from the side lines and beaming, peri-fashion, on it. Yet he was the most reluctant of us to go.

"Best time I ever had in my life," Mr. Ort said. Shaking my hand, he told me he had brought no cash with him and that the hotel would not honor his check for the large sum we owed. The sum was eleven thousand dollars. It included food, drinks, lodging, wreckage and police fines.

Mr. Ort, who knew I carried thousands on my person, suggested I pay the bill. He would refund me the money as soon as we got to Miami. I paid and was left with a few hundred dollars in my pocket.

THE CLOCK STRIKES TWELVE

As OUR SHIP neared Miami, Mr. Ort took me into his confidence.

"I've had some private information," he said, "that things have slowed down a little in Miami. But you can put that down as foolish talk."

I wondered nervously about the eleven thousand dollars Mr. Ort owed me. My apprehension increased as we stepped ashore. Gloomy faces were on the pier. Worse, the hundred and more pleasure yachts were all at their moorings. Not one had been rented for the day.

Arrived in Flagler Street, I noted that a panic was on. Crowds were screaming around the real-estate offices, waving documents in the air and shouting for their money back. Angry faces were offering thousand-dollar lots for a hundred dollars cash, with no buyers. Police were pushing people out of arcades. Women swung umbrellas and desperate old men tried to use their fists. I said good-by to Mr. Ort in his overcrowded office without mentioning my eleven thousand dollars.

The newspapers held off for a few days but finally the headlines joined the shambles. The banks were tottering. The big companies, including the Key Largo Corporation, were collapsing like financial card castles. Thousands of abruptly unemployed salesmen roamed the streets looking for handouts to get them out of town.

The ball was over. The symphony orchestras no longer played. And the weather joined the grand finale. A high wind was blowing and a hurricane threatened. The air became thick with coral dust and it was difficult to breathe. Then it began to rain. A gale-battered Miami kept yelling for its money back. Eldorado had disappeared like a gaudy tent blown down.

I pushed my way through the embittered crowd in the Flagler

Arcade one day to Mr. Ort's office. I banged on the door for some time before it opened. A red-faced Mr. Ort peered out.

"Oh, it's you," he said. "Glad to see you. Come right in."

I entered and he closed the door quickly against the menacing crowd.

"It's very hot for this time of the year," Mr. Ort said, and sat down behind his president's desk. It was blanketed with documents.

"I was looking over these real-estate contracts," my friend said. "We're not in bad shape at all. There's thirty million dollars due our company in the next two months. Here are the sales. You can see for yourself." He indicated the top of his desk.

"I don't think the company will get another thirty cents out of those sales," I said. "I talked to a dozen Key Largo land buyers. They're all tearing up their land deeds and going home."

"In that case," Charles Ort beamed, "the land reverts to the company. And we'll be exactly where we started—with ninety million dollars' worth of choice property to offer the public. My partners have liquidated their interests—which makes it all the better for me."

"Then you're the entire Key Largo Company," I said. My friend nodded modestly. "How much money have you got left?" I asked. "I mean cash money."

"We're in excellent shape," said Ort. "I have six hundred thousand in the bank. My expenses are down to fourteen thousand a week. So you see we'll be able to weather this flurry with no trouble."

"I suggest," I said, "that you give me five hundred thousand dollars and that I go to New York and put the money in a vault for you. That'll leave you a hundred thousand to operate on. And if everything flops here, as it certainly is going to, you'll have half a million clear to live on when it's over."

Charlie Ort frowned at me.

"I couldn't possibly do that," he said. "If I strip myself of money in that fashion, I'm bound to get caught."

"Caught how?" I asked.

"When the boom comes back," said Charlie Ort, "I won't have the money on hand to swing my deals. And it's coming back, sir. Just as sudden as it went. I know these market fluctuations. No, sir, I'm not going to take any chances on being caught without proper funds."

I put in no bid for my eleven thousand. My friend had too odd a look in his eye.

I decided to avoid him and assigned Samuels to bring me a daily report of Mr. Ort's activities.

"He's standing like General Custer surrounded by desperate Key Largo landowners howling for their money back," said Samuels, the next day. "All the other tycoons have decamped, fearful of being assassinated."

"Did you talk to Ort?" I asked.

"Yes," said Samuels. "I told him how much I admired his mad courage."

"Did he say anything about me?"

"He sends his best regards," said Samuels.

"Did he mention the eleven thousand he owes me?"

"No," said Samuels, "he was silent on that subject." And my staff guffawed.

"I want you to keep telling Ort what a great honest soul he is," I said. "And I want you to tell him I'm going back to New York Saturday on the one-fifteen train. And say I'll try to get to see him before I leave."

"Shouldn't I touch on the subject of the eleven grand?" Samuels asked.

"Not a word," I said. "Everything depends on your not referring to that. I've got a plan."

We were packed Saturday morning. After paying my hotel bill and buying railroad tickets, I had thirty dollars left.

Rose smiled.

"That's three times more than we had when we came here," she said. "In addition to which we're married."

Samuels arrived and I outlined my last Florida project to him. It was my plan for getting the eleven thousand dollars Charlie Ort still owed me. I explained that Mr. Ort was a combination Mad Hatter and Church Deacon. Buried in his booming lies was a man of religious honesty. We had to reach the honest Mr. Ort.

"Here is our psychological approach," I said. "The bank in which Ort keeps his money is directly across the Arcade from his office. It's a minute walk from his desk to the teller's cage. And today is Saturday, which means the bank closes at exactly twelve. At ten minutes of twelve you rush into Ort's office out of breath and tell him I've sent you for the eleven thousand dollars. Tell him I couldn't come myself because I had some last-minute business with my publisher to transact. And tell him I'm on my way to the station and that I'm catching the one-fifteen train for New York. Talk fast and be out of breath. At five minutes to twelve stop talking suddenly and look at the clock on the wall and say, 'My God, I was almost too late. The bank closes in five minutes.' "

Samuels was fascinated. "What'll happen?"

"If my psychology works," I said, "you will have flushed Ort the Deacon. By giving him so easy and open a chance of swindling me, we make him definitely conscious of the fact that he *is* swindling. He knows I'm leaving for good. He knows the bank will be closed in five minutes. He knows he has only to stall for those five minutes—and he won't have to pay the money he owes. But he knows also that his dishonesty will be obvious to me. More important, there isn't time for him to fool himself. The honest Ort, the Ort who doesn't drink or smoke or commit adultery will have to function."

"Very interesting," said Samuels and, after another rehearsal, departed.

At twelve-thirty Rose and I sat in the station waiting room, our bags around us, our eyes on the entrance doors. Mr. Ort's office was five minutes away. No Samuels appeared. At a quarter to one a bleak thought came to me. I had been so concentrated on my Ort psychology that I had forgotten to consider entirely the fact that I had entrusted eleven thousand dollars in cash to a young, irresponsible fellow named Samuels whom I barely knew. It would be a fine blow to psychology if this foot-loose Samuels made off for Mexico with Miami's last bonanza cash.

At one-five I was certain that was what had happened.

"I think we'd better start for our train," I said. "Mr. Samuels has probably been run over and taken to a hospital." I picked up two suitcases, and Samuels appeared. He came toward me weaving and hiccuping and holding out two fists full of greenbacks.

"I stopped over at a couple of speak-easies," said Samuels, "to celebrate good old psychology. Bought everybody drinks. Here's your change."

He handed me ten thousand, nine hundred and sixty dollars.

FAREWELL OF ANOTHER MOONSHOOTER

ON A SNOW-FILLED NIGHT in New York eight months later Rose and I were on our way to a theater. A traffic jam stopped our taxi. Knuckles rapped on the cab window and I saw a blurred face beaming through the glass. It was Mr. Ort. I opened the door and invited him in.

"Haven't got time," Mr. Ort said. "Mighty glad to see you both again."

He shook hands eagerly. I felt sad to see him. Charlie Samuels, who had returned to his newspaper job in Miami, had kept me informed of the disasters that had come upon Ort. He had plunged heavily in an advertising campaign, filling the press with full-page ads and hanging Flagler Street with scores of banners, all proclaiming the return of the boom. Six weeks after I had left, Mr. Ort had hit bottom, and Samuels had reported that he had found our tycoon in a motel eating beans out of a can. A few weeks later the ninety-million-dollar Key Largo Corporation had wound up with its president and his wife sleeping in a parking lot.

"Come in the cab, you'll catch cold," Rose insisted.

"Thank you very much," Mr. Ort beamed, "but I've only a few minutes." Standing in the falling snow with horns honking impatiently, Mr. Ort continued. "I'm here on Key Largo business. It's coming back, you know. Yes, sir, Key Largo today has a tremendous future, bigger than ever before. And I'm talking facts! I'm showing motion pictures of Key Largo tomorrow night at eight-thirty to a group of powerful financiers. They're keen as the dickens on our project. Mr. Childs of the Childs restaurants and a half-dozen leading bankers and a lot of big industrialists. We're going to make Key Largo the pleasure center of the world."

He stopped for breath and added, "I'd be very glad to have you and Mrs. Hecht attend the showing."

He gave us an address on Tenth Avenue, waved goodnight, and our taxi left him behind in the falling snow.

I was against going. I argued with Rose that our presence would be useless to Charlie Ort and a bore to me. There would be enough people without us. Ort wouldn't even notice our absence. Besides, I disliked the pathos of our disinherited tycoon fighting cheerily for a new foothold.

"You'll feel twice as conscience-ridden if you don't go," said Rose.

We arrived at the Tenth Avenue projection room fifteen minutes late. Mr. Ort was standing in the doorway. The projection room was empty.

"I'm expecting Mr. Childs," said Ort after greeting us, "and a number of other very distinguished businessmen and investors."

We stood chatting for a half hour. Or rather Rose and Mr. Ort chatted. I was too depressed by the empty corridor, the empty room and Mr. Ort's idiotic cheeriness to talk. At nine-fifteen, Mr. Ort took another look at his totally vacant room and said, "You folks might as well sit down. Take any seat you want. I think those in the first row are best. And I'll close this door so there won't be any draft on Mrs. Hecht."

Rose and I sat down in the empty little theater. Mr. Ort signaled the projectionist to start the movie and then walked briskly to the proscenium. The film started. Mr. Ort began to address us.

We sat for an hour looking again at the strip of cement sidewalk with its string of forlorn lampposts, at the unpainted shacks, the disabled machinery. Lovely girls in bathing suits basked on the mosquito-infested beach. And the familiar Flagler Arcade salesmen appeared, gesticulating passionately to one another.

And over these shabby Key Largo scenes came the voice of Mr. Ort. It informed us of the four casinos that were going to rise on the island's shores. It indicated the spots and asked us to note their natural beauty. It told us of the wide boulevards, the mansions, fountained plazas and gay yacht clubs that would, in less than a year, convert Key Largo into the pleasure center of the world. Broke, with not a dime remaining of the Great Jackpot he had hit, Mr. Ort sang his siren song of Key Largo to Rose and me and the empty room. Not once did our Moonshooter falter. Hope and good cheer lifted his voice, and the armor of conviction clanked in his words.

When the lights went up again Rose's eyes were tearful.

"You talk to him," she said.

I told Mr. Ort he had made a very impressive talk.

"I use a lot of the things you wrote about Key Largo," said Mr. Ort. "I hope you don't mind, sir."

"Not in the least," I said. I told him I was sure he would put Key Largo over before he was through.

"No question of it," said Mr. Ort. "It's a natural. And now is the time to buy. You can pick up the finest Gold Coast property on Key Largo today for a song. Do you remember that acreage near the Main Casino site? That whole section can be bought for a few dollars. If you recall, it was priced at seven hundred thousand. Think of it!"

I nodded and thought of the eleven thousand dollars I had won out of the Florida boom. Had I had any of it left I would have bought the Main Casino site. Instead, I invited Mr. Ort to join us for a bite.

"I'd come along with you," he said with a glance down the empty corridor, "but someone might show up and I wouldn't want to disappoint them. You'd be amazed, sir, at the number of important men who believe in Key Largo today."

We shook hands. He stood twirling his old-fashioned watch by its vest chain and beaming after us as we left.

A few years later Charles Ort died. I heard no details of his death except that it happened in Miami, Florida—a few minutes by air from Key Largo.

Capitalist or con man, I was never certain which of these Charlie Ort was. But since knowing him, I have looked with some respect on his colleagues of the free-enterprise system. And I am pleased to believe that the great business enterprises of my country are often run by Diavolos on a high wire.

A MONSTER CALLED OPPORTUNITY
KNOCKS

I LIVED in a new home, a top floor in Beekman Place. Its windows looked out on the East River. I could watch the boats passing. Rose and my mother built a garden on the roof, with awnings over it. I was full of peace and lassitude.

One evening in early summer Rose and I walked the streets whose lights were unshadowed by ideologies or age. We were still young and mildly troubled over the fact that our money had given out. The Florida loot and all my other earnings were gone. We were two months behind in our Beekman Place rent. Luckily the building was owned by a family of actors—John Daly Murphy, his brother Frank Conlan and their beautiful old mother, Mrs. Murphy. They set up no clamor for rent. Their only clamor was over the faraway doings of Parnell and the perfidious British. When I knocked on their door to apologize for our unpaid rent, they chuckled and loaned me eggs and other groceries.

We counted our money as we walked the evening street. Twenty dollars left. I spent the twenty in a bookshop and toted home a twelve-volume set of Gibbon's *Decline and Fall of the Roman Empire*.

I took to bed to read of Rome and remained motionless and spellbound for three days.

On the fourth day the Christians had overrun Rome, and the Emperor Julian was making a last brilliant stand against them. But I knew what was coming. I had watched Julian before. Rome would vanish and all the wonders celebrated by Gibbon would be no more. The pleasant gods invented by poets would never again ornament the temples of the world. In their places a god of love was to appear. And what a love! A love served by torture, bigotry and unending wars.

I read on sadly. My own financial collapse seemed too unimportant to discuss in the same breath with such a fall as Rome's. My fatalistic attitude relaxed me. Money would always appear if you forgot about it.

Our doorbell rang during Volume Twelve. It was a Western Union messenger, come to prove again my theory of money-making. The telegram he delivered on this spring day in 1925 came from the unknown Scythian wastes of Hollywood, Calif. It read, "Will you accept three hundred per week to work for Paramount Pictures. All expenses paid. The three hundred is peanuts. Millions are to be grabbed out here and your only competition is idiots. Don't let this get around.

"Herman Mankiewicz."

ENTER, THE MOVIES

FOR MANY YEARS I looked on movie writing as an amiable chore. It was a source of easy money and pleasant friendships. There was small responsibility. Your name as writer was buried in a flock of "credits." Your literary pride was never involved. What critics said about the movie you had written never bothered you. They were usually criticizing something you couldn't remember. Once when I was a guest on a radio quiz show called "Information Please," the plot of a movie I had written a year before and that was playing on Broadway then was recited to me in full. I was unable to identify it.

For many years Hollywood held this double lure for me, tremendous sums of money for work that required no more effort than a game of pinochle. Of the sixty movies I wrote, more than half were written in two weeks or less. I received for each script, whether written in two or (never more than) eight weeks, from fifty thousand to a hundred and twenty-five thousand dollars. I worked also by the week. My salary ran from five thousand dollars a week up. Metro-Goldwyn-Mayer in 1949 paid me ten thousand a week. David Selznick once paid me thirty-five hundred a day.

Walking at dawn in the deserted Hollywood streets in 1951 with David, I listened to my favorite movie boss topple the town he had helped to build. The movies, said David, were over and done with. Hollywood was already a ghost town making foolish efforts to seem alive.

"Hollywood's like Egypt," said David. "Full of crumbled pyramids. It'll never come back. It'll just keep on crumbling until finally the wind blows the last studio prop across the sands."

And now that the tumult was gone, what had the movies been? A flood of claptrap, he insisted, that had helped bitch up the world and that had consumed the fine talents of thousands of men like ourselves.

"A few good movies," said David. "Thirty years—and one good movie in three years is the record. Ten out of ten thousand. There might have been good movies if there had been no movie industry. Hollywood might have become the center of a new human expression if it hadn't been grabbed by a little group of bookkeepers and turned into a junk industry."

"I'm writing a book about myself," I said, "and I keep wondering what I should write about the movies, which are, in a way, part of me."

"Write the truth," said David, "before you start bragging about your fancy Hollywood exploits, put down the truth. Nobody has ever done that!"

I doubt if the truth about Hollywood is as novel as my friend, in his new disillusion, believed. It is novel enough, however, and I shall try to put down as much of it as I know.

WHAT THE MOVIES ARE

THE MOVIES are one of the bad habits that corrupted our century. Of their many sins, I offer as the worst their effect on the intellectual side of the nation. It is chiefly from that viewpoint I write of them —as an eruption of trash that has lamed the American mind and retarded Americans from becoming a cultured people.

The American of 1953 is a cliché-strangled citizen whose like was never before in the Republic. Compared to the pre-movieized American of 1910-1920, he is an enfeebled intellect. I concede the movies alone did not undo the American mind. A number of forces worked away at that project. But always, well up in front and never faltering at their frowsy task, were the movies.

In pre-movie days, the business of peddling lies about life was spotty and unorganized. It was carried on by the cheaper magazines, dime novels, the hinterland preachers and whooping politicians. These combined to unload a rash of infantile parables on the land. A goodly part of the population was infected, but there remained large healthy areas in the Republic's thought. There remained, in fact, an intellectual class of sorts—a tribe of citizens who never read dime novels, cheap magazines or submitted themselves to political and religious howlers.

It was this tribe that the movies scalped. Cultured people who would have blushed with shame to be found with a dime novel in their hands took to flocking shamelessly to watch the picturization of such tripe on the screen.

For forty years the movies have drummed away on the American character. They have fed it naïveté and buncombe in doses never before administered to any people. They have slapped into the American mind more human misinformation in one evening than the Dark Ages could muster in a decade. One basic plot only has appeared daily in their fifteen thousand theaters—the triumph of virtue and the overthrow of wickedness.

Two generations of Americans have been informed nightly that a woman who betrayed her husband (or a husband his wife) could never find happiness; that sex was no fun without a mother-in-law and a rubber plant around; that women who fornicated just for pleasure ended up as harlots or washerwomen; that any man who was sexually active in his youth, later lost the one girl he truly loved; that a man who indulged in sharp practices to get ahead in the world ended in poverty and with even his own children turning on him; that any man who broke the laws, man's or God's, must always die, or go to jail, or become a monk, or restore the money he stole before wandering off into the desert; that anyone who didn't believe in God (and said so out loud) was set right by seeing either an angel or witnessing some feat of levitation by one of the characters; that an honest heart must always recover from a train wreck or a score of bullets and win the girl it loved; that the most potent and brilliant of villains are powerless before little children, parish priests or young virgins with large boobies; that injustice could cause a heap of trouble but it must always slink out of town in Reel Nine; that there are no problems of labor, politics, domestic life or sexual abnormality but can be solved happily by a simple Christian phrase or a fine American motto.

Not only was the plot the same, but the characters in it never varied. These characters must always be good or bad (and never human) in order not to confuse the plot of Virtue Triumphing. This denouement could be best achieved by stereotypes a fraction removed from those in the comic strips.

The effect on the American mind of this forty-year barrage of Mother Goose platitudes and primitive valentines is proved by the fact that the movies became for a generation the favorite entertainment of all American classes.

There are millions of Americans who belong by nature in movie theaters as they belong at political rallies or in fortuneteller parlors and on the shoot-the-chutes. To these millions the movies are a sort of boon—a gaudier version of religion. All the parables of right living are paraded before them tricked out in gang feuds, earthquakes and a thousand and one near rapes. The move from cheap books to cheap movie seats has not affected them for the worse.

But beside these grass-root fans of platitude sit the once intellectual members of the community. They are the citizens whose good taste and criticism of claptrap were once a large part of our nation's superiority. There is little more in them today than the giggle of the movie fan. Watching the movies, they forget that they have taste, that their intelligence is being violated, that they are being booted back into the nursery. They forget even that they are bored.

In the movie theaters, all fifteen thousand of them, the U.S.A. presents a single backward front.

There is a revolution brewing and movie audiences are beginning to thin out. I shall take up this revolt later and mention here only that it is not an intellectual uprising. It is a revolt downward.

THE CAPTIVE MUSE

THE PERSISTENT banality of the movies is due to the "vision" of their manufacturers. I do not mean by manufacturers, writers or directors. These harassed toilers are no more than the lowest of *Unteroffizieren* in movieland. The orders come from the tents of a dozen invisible generals. The "vision" is theirs. They keep a visionary eye glued to the fact that the lower in class an entertainment product is, the more people will buy it.

Since their start, the movies have been, practically, in the hands of this same dozen. A few have died, to be replaced by men of identical indifference to every phase of entertainment save one—its profits.

These dozen Tops of the industry have nothing to do with the making of movies. They have to do only with the *sort* of movies that are to be made—commercial ones. There is no murmur of revolt. Only hosannas rise from the movie slave pens.

In no industry into which I have peered have I seen the wanton boss flattery that is normal in movieland. Proud and wealthy men of intelligence are not ashamed to prostrate themselves publicly before the hollow-headed big boss—the Owner. They will gasp with wonder over his dullest droppings and see in his fumbling efforts to understand what is going on the constant mark of genius. No workman I have ever seen is as afraid of a boss, no servant as aquiver before a master as are the movie factotums who come near to the golden throne of the movie-company Owner.

The fear that inspires this kowtowing is as deep as religious fear.

It rises from the same source—guilt. Nearly all who work in the making and even selling of movies are guilty of distorting, constantly, their minds and in one way or another of violating their tastes and their instincts.

The only movie figure exempt from such guilt is the company Owner. He is usually a man who has no taste to be violated or intelligence to be distorted. He admires with his whole soul the drivel his underlings produce in his factory.

This boss fear-adulation is the chief color of movieland. My contacts with the studio Owners and their viziers who ran the studios for them informed me early in my movie service that most of them were nitwits on a par with the lower run of politicians I had known as a reporter. Yet they all moved in an aura of greatness, and the reports of their genius would have embarrassed Michelangelo.

In addition to the guilt of violating their culture, which brought these courtiers to heel, there was a money guilt. The greater were the sums these underlings received, the more fearful of the boss they grew. When you overpay small people you frighten them. They know that their merits or activities entitle them to no such sums as they are receiving. As a result their boss soars out of economic into magic significance. He becomes a source of blessings rather than wages. Criticism is sacrilege, doubt is heresy.

In the court of the movie Owner, none criticized, none doubted. And none dared speak of art. In the Owner's mind art was a synonym for bankruptcy. An artist was a saboteur to be uprooted as quickly from the company's pay roll as a Communist with a pamphlet.

Whenever the movie-company Owner found himself with three or more employees at his feet he made a pronouncement. "I'm a Showman," he said, "and as long as I remain a Showman all you geniuses who work in my studio don't have to worry. You will have jobs—and big wages."

The movie company Owner was and is no more Showman than he is a pilgrim bound for Mecca. His single objective as Owner is to see that his movies make profits. He asks nothing else of them. He has no more instinct to gamble with the contents of his product than have the makers of Flit. What the public wants, he proclaims, is "solid entertainment, and for God's sake, Ben, don't stick those ideas of yours into this film. You want to help make a successful film, don't you? A picture people will be glad to see? All right then—don't insult the things they believe in. Make 'em realize how wonderful life is, and what a fine fella this hero of yours is, so that everybody will be glad to have him elected senator."

The movie Owners are the only troupe in the history of entertainment that has never been seduced by the adventure of the entertainment world—by the dream of diverting people with something a "little better," or a "little different." Their fixation on peddling trash has many causes. For one thing, they are further removed from the creation of their product than any showmen have ever been before.

Showmen in the theater read manuscripts, interview actors, select out of their tastes the product on which they put their names. The gypsy aroma of entertainment goes to their heads, however hard they are. And however greedy they are, the tinkle of show bells becomes as winsome to them as the tinkle of money. The movie showmen, however, read no scripts, consort with no actors. They have no ideas to offer. They stick no finger in the pie. Thus they have no spiritual or mental stake in their product. No show bells tinkle in their counting rooms.

Their product, also, is a more expensive one than any heretofore peddled by showmen. Millions of dollars and not mere thousands are involved. Men who manipulate the spending of millions must put aside enthusiasm for anything but money. The artists they employ may bask in press notices. The Owners can afford to bask only in box-office returns.

The fame of the movie-company Owners is small in the public eye. It is even small in movieland, where the movies are made. In my years in and out of the Hollywood studios I have not managed to learn all the names of my true bosses—the "men of vision" who dictated my work. I have encountered some of them. L. B. Mayer, Howard Hughes, the Schencks, the Cohens, the Warners, the Balabans. There are others as unknown to me as to any outsider.

The major triumph of the movie-company Owners lies in this fact—The barrage of movie trash has conditioned the public to the acceptance of trash only. A "different" movie is usually scorned by Americans. They will sneer and catcall during its showing, and leave the theater with cries of having been cheated.

Yet the movie Owner's victory is not a solid one, and here I come to the little revolution that stirs among the sixty million movie fans.

The movie industry is beginning to wobble. The sound track is beginning to echo cavernously in its theaters. Although the American
will still run from a "different" movie as from a small-pox sign, he has
shown a mounting aversion to the hog feed he has hitherto gobbled.
The studios continue to manufacture this mush with undiminished
cunning and largess. No sum is too vast for the making of a Great
Epic of Roman History, or of the Indian Wars or of the Song-
Publishing Business. Nevertheless the movie fan has begun to stay
away from the movie palaces that cater fiercely to his love of trash.

Surveying their sagging box-office charts, the movie Owners point
wildly to television as the villain responsible. I have a notion that my
old bosses are wrong.

Put a squirrel on a treadmill and he will run gayly and happily for
hours on end. But there comes an hour when the squirrel's soul feels
the falseness and insufficiency of the treadmill as a road for travel.
The squirrel begins, then, to twitch, to roll its eyes, to chatter fren-
ziedly. And if not removed from the treadmill the bewildered little
animal will fall dead.

The American moviegoer, experiencing these squirrel-like twitches,
is removing himself from the movie-trash treadmill. Confronted by
the double problem of being unable to enjoy any longer the dime
novel movie, and of disliking angrily still any departure from it,
the American has retreated into his parlor to stare at another
national eruption of trash on his television set. And acquire another
set of twitches.

MONEY IS THE ROOT

As a writer in Hollywood, I spent more time arguing than writing—
until the last four years when the British boycott left me without
much bargaining power. My chief memory of movieland is one of
asking in the producer's office why I must change the script, evis-
cerate it, cripple and hamstring it? Why must I strip the hero of his
few semi-intelligent remarks and why must I tack on a corny ending that makes the stomach shudder? Half of all the movie writers
argue in this fashion. The other half writhe in silence, and the psychoanalyst's couch or the liquor bottle claim them both.

Before it might seem that I am writing about a tribe of Shelleys in chains, I should make it clear that the movie writers "ruined" by the movies are for the most part a run of greedy hacks and incompetent thickheads. Out of the thousand writers huffing and puffing through movieland there are scarcely fifty men and women of wit or talent. The rest of the fraternity is deadwood. Yet, in a curious way, there is not much difference between the product of a good writer and a bad one. They both have to toe the same mark.

Nor are the bad writers better off spiritually. Their way is just as thorny. Minus talent or competence, the need for self-expression churns foolishly in them and their hearts throw themselves in a wild pitch for fame. And no less than the literary elite of Hollywood they feel the sting of its knout. However cynical, overpaid or inept you are, it is impossible to create entertainment without feeling the urges that haunt creative work. The artist's ego, even the ego of the Hollywood hack, must always jerk around a bit under restraint.

The studio bosses are not too inconvenienced by this bit of struggle. Experience has proved that the Hollywood artist in revolt is usually to be brought to heel by a raise in salary. My own discontent with what I was asked to do in Hollywood was so loud that I finally received a hundred and twenty-five thousand dollars for four weeks of script writing.

APULEIUS' GOLDEN STOOGE

I HAVE TAKEN PART in at least a thousand story conferences. I was present always as the writer. Others present were the "producer," the director and sometimes the head of the studio and a small tense group of his admirers.

The producer's place in movie making is a matter that, in Hollywood, has not yet been cleared up. I shall try to bring some clarity to it.

The big factory where movies are made is run by a super-producer called Head of the Studio who sits in the Front Office and is as difficult of access as the Grand Lama. He is the boss, appointed by the studio Owner himself. Thus, despite the veneration in which he is held by the thousand studio underlings, he is actually the greatest of the movieland stooges. He must bend his entire spirit to the philosophy of the movie Owner—"make money." He must translate this greedy cry of the Owner into a program for his studio. He must examine every idea, plot or venture submitted to him from the single point of view of whether it is trite enough to appeal to the masses.

If he fails in this task, he is summoned from his always teetering studio throne to the movie Owner's New York Office, in which nothing ever teeters. Here he receives a drubbing which the lowest of his slaves would not tolerate. He is shown pages of box-office returns. He is shoved into the presence of homicidal theater Owners snarling of empty seats. Proof is hurled at his head that he has betrayed his great trust, that he is ruining the movie industry, and that he is either an idiot or a scoundrel.

Shaken and traumatized, he returns to his throne in the studio. Here he must wiggle himself into the Purple again and be ready to flash his eyes and terrorize his underlings with his Olympian whims.

His immediate underlings are the producers. He has hired them to do the actual movie making for him. After all, no one man can weigh, discuss and manipulate fifty movie plots at one time. He has to have lieutenants, men who will keep their heads in the noisy presence of writers and directors and not be carried away by art in any of its subversive guises.

ILLUSTRATIONS BY DORÉ (GUSTAVE)

THERE ARE different kinds of producers in the studios, ranging from out-and-out illiterates to philosophers and aesthetes. But all of them have the same function. Their task is to guard against the unusual. They are the trusted loyalists of cliché. Writers and directors can be carried away by a "strange" characterization or a new point of view; a producer, never. The producer is the shadow cast by the studio's Owner. It falls across the entire studio product.

I discovered early in my movie work that a movie is never any better than the stupidest man connected with it. There are times when this distinction may be given to the writer or director. Most often it belongs to the producer.

The job of turning good writers into movie hacks is the producer's chief task. These sinister fellows were always my bosses. Though I was paid often five and ten times more money than they for my working time, they were my judges. It was their minds I had to please.

I can recall a few bright ones among them, and fifty nitwits. The pain of having to collaborate with such dullards and to submit myself to their approvals was always acute. Years of experience failed to help. I never became reconciled to taking literary orders from them. I often prepared myself for a producer conference by swallowing two sleeping pills in advance.

I have always considered that half of the large sum paid me for writing a movie script was in payment for listening to the producer and obeying him. I am not being facetious. The movies pay as much for obedience as for creative work. An able writer is paid a larger sum than a man of small talent. But he is paid this added money *not* to use his superior talents.

I often won my battle with producers. I was able to convince them that their suggestions were too stale or too infantile. But I won such battles only as long as I remained on the grounds. The minute I left the studio my victory vanished. Every sour syllable of producer invention went back into the script and every limping foot of it appeared on the screen.

Months later, watching "my" movie in a theater, I realized that not much damage actually had been done. A movie is basically so trite and glib that the addition of a half dozen miserable inanities does not cripple it. It blares along barking out its inevitable clichés, and only its writer can know that it is a shade worse than it had to be.

DIAVOLO, AGAIN—

Such is half of my story of Hollywood. The other half is the fun I had—during the heyday of the movies—1925 to 1945. There was never a more marzipan kingdom than this land of celluloid.

There was only one factory rule. Make a movie that went over big at the preview, and the town was yours. You could be as daft as you wanted, as drunk and irreverent as Panurge, and, still, the bosses bowed as you passed. The bosses were all earthy fellows with the smell of junk yards, tire exchanges, and other murky business pasts clinging to their sport ensembles. Though we wore their yoke, we were nevertheless literary royalty, men of grammar.

In the time when I first arrived in it, the movie world was still young. Jhinns and ogres, odalisques, Sindbads and earth shakers were still around in wholesale lots, especially the ogres. And whatever the weather elsewhere in the world, it rained only gold in Hollywood.

Mankiewicz's telegram had told the truth. Hollywood, 1925, was another boom town, and my nerves were alive to its hawker's cry an hour after I had left the train. It reminded me happily of that other Eldorado—Miami. Miami had run up the price of its real estate. Hollywood was doing the same thing for talent, any kind of talent, from geese trainers to writers and actors.

Hungry actors leaped from hall bedrooms to terraced mansions. Writers and newspapermen who had hoboed their way West began hiring butlers and laying down wine cellars. Talent, talent, who had talent for anything—for beating a drum, diving off a roof, writing a joke, walking on his hands? Who could think up a story, any kind of story? Who knew how to write it down? And who had Ego? That was the leading hot cake—Ego or a pair of jiggling boobies under morning-glory eyes. Prosperity chased them all. New stars were being hatched daily, and new world-famous directors and producers were popping daily out of shoe boxes.

I went to work for Paramount Pictures, Inc., over which the Messrs. Zukor, Lasky and Schulberg presided. They occupied the three Vatican suites on the main floor of a long, plaster building that looked like a Bavarian bathhouse. It still stands, empty of almost everything but ghosts.

Most of the important people got drunk after one o'clock, sobered up around three-thirty and got drunk again at nine. Fist fights began around eleven. Seduction had no stated hours. The skimpy offices shook with passion. The mingled sound of plotting and sexual moans came through the transoms. It was a town of braggadocio and youth. Leading ladies still suffered from baby fat (rather than budding wattles as today) and the film heroes had trouble growing mustaches.

Nor was the industry yet captive. There were as many wildcatters around as bankers. And the movies, God bless 'em, were silent. The talkies had not yet come to make headaches for the half-illiterate viziers of the Front Office. In fact, to the best of my recollection, there were no headaches. There were no unions, no censor boards, no empty theater seats. It was Round Three and everybody looked like a champion.

Movies were seldom written. They were yelled into existence in conferences that kept going in saloons, brothels and all-night poker games. Movie sets roared with arguments and organ music. Sometimes little string orchestras played to help stir up the emotions of the great performers—"*Träumerei*" for Clara Bow and the "Meditation" from *Thaïs* for Adolphe Menjou, the screen's most sophisticated lover.

I was given an office at Paramount. A bit of cardboard with my name inked on it was tacked on the door. A soiree started at once in my office and lasted for several days. Men of letters, bearing gin bottles, arrived. Bob Benchley, hallooing with laughter as if he had come on the land of Punch and Judy, was there; and the owlish-eyed satirist Donald Ogden Stewart, beaming as at a convention of March Hares. One night at a flossy party Don appeared on the dance floor in a long overcoat. "That's silly and showing off to dance in an overcoat," said the great lady of the films in his arms. "Please take it off." Don did. He had nothing on underneath. F. Scott Fitzgerald was there, already pensive and inquiring if there were any sense to life, and muttering, at thirty, about the cruelty of growing aged.

Listening to Mankiewicz, Edwin Justus Mayer, Scott Fitzgerald, Ted Shayne and other litterateurs roosting in my office, I learned that the Studio Bosses (circa 1925) still held writers in great contempt and considered them a waste of money. I learned, also, that Manky had gotten me my job by a desperate coup. The studio chieftain, the mighty B. P. Schulberg, smarting from experience with literary imports, had vowed never to hitch another onto the pay roll. Manky had invaded the Front Office, his own two-year contract in his hand. He had announced that if his friend Hecht failed to write a successful movie they could tear up his contract and fire us both.

I was pleased to hear this tale of loyalty and assured Manky *The New York Times* would be happy to take him back on its staff if things went awry.

On my fourth day, I was summoned and given an assignment. Producer Bernard Fineman, under Schulberg, presented me with the first "idea" for a movie to smite my ears.

An important industrialist, said he, was shaving one morning. His razor slipped and he cut his chin. He thereupon sent out his butler to buy an alum stick to stop the flow of blood. The butler was slowed up by a traffic jam and the great industrialist, fuming in his onyx bathroom, had to wait fifteen minutes for the alum stick. The movie I was to make up was to show all the things that were affected in the world by this fifteen-minute delay. I recall of the details only that something went wrong with the pearl fisheries. The whole thing ended up with the great industrialist's mistress deserting him, his vast enterprises crashing, and his wife returning to his side to help him build a new life.

I relate this plot because my distaste for it started me as a successful scenario writer. I had seen no more than a dozen movies but I had heard in my four days in Hollywood all that was to be known about the flickers.

"I want to point out to you," said Manky, "that in a novel a hero can lay ten girls and marry a virgin for a finish. In a movie this is not allowed. The hero, as well as the heroine, has to be a virgin. The villain can lay anybody he wants, have as much fun as he wants cheating and stealing, getting rich and whipping the servants. But you have to shoot him in the end. When he falls with a bullet in his forehead, it is advisable that he clutch at the Gobelin tapestry on the library wall and bring it down over his head like a symbolic shroud. Also, covered by such a tapestry, the actor does not have to hold his breath while he is being photographed as a dead man."

An idea came to me. The thing to do was to skip the heroes and heroines, to write a movie containing only villains and bawds. I would not have to tell any lies then.

Thus, instead of a movie about an industrialist cutting his chin, I made up a movie about a Chicago gunman and his moll called Feathers McCoy. As a newspaperman I had learned that nice people—the audience—loved criminals, doted on reading about their love problems as well as their sadism. My movie, grounded on this simple truth, was produced with the title of *Underworld*. It was the first gangster movie to bedazzle the movie fans and there were no lies in it—except for a half-dozen sentimental touches introduced by its director, Joe von Sternberg. I still shudder remembering one of them. My head villain, Bull Weed, after robbing a bank, emerged with a suitcase full of money and paused in the crowded street to notice a blind beggar and give him a coin—before making his getaway.

It was not von Sternberg who helped me put the script together but another director, Arthur Rossen. Art Rossen was the first of these bonny directorial gentlemen with whom I was for many years to spend happy days locked away in fancy hotel rooms sawing away at plots. Art was one of the best of them, but, with a few nightmarish exceptions, they were all good. They were the new sort of storyteller produced by the movies, and, to this day, they remain the only authentic talent that has come out of Hollywood.

The Paramount Viziers, all four of them including the ex-prize fighter Mr. Zukor, listened to my reading of *Underworld*. It was eighteen pages long and it was full of moody Sandburgian sentences. The viziers were greatly stirred. I was given a ten-thousand-dollar check as a bonus for the week's work, a check which my sponsor Mankiewicz snatched out of my hand as I was bowing my thanks.

"You'll have it back in a week," Manky said. "I just want it for a few days to get me out of a little hole."

My return to New York was held up for several weeks while Manky struggled to raise another ten thousand to pay me back. He gambled valiantly, tossing a coin in the air with Eddie Cantor and calling heads or tails for a thousand dollars. He lost constantly. He tried to get himself secretly insured behind his good wife Sarah's back, planning to hock the policy and thus meet his obligation. This plan collapsed when the insurance company doctor refused to accept him as a risk.

I finally solved the situation by taking Manky into the Front Office and informing the studio bosses of our joint dilemma. I asked that my talented friend be given a five-hundred-dollar-a-week raise. The studio could then deduct this raise from his salary and give it to me. Thus in twenty weeks I would be repaid.

I left the Vatican suite with another full bonus check in my hand; and Manky, with his new raise, became the highest paid writer for Paramount Pictures, Inc.

THE CLOWNS: PINK PERIOD

MAKING MOVIES is a game played by a few thousand toy-minded folk. It is obsessive, exhausting and jolly, as a good game should be.

Played intently, it divorces you from life, as a good game will do. For many years I was one of the intent, though part-time, players. I paid some twenty visits to Hollywood and remained there each time only long enough to earn enough money to live on for the rest of the year. This required from two weeks to three or four months of work. With my bank balance restored, I would seize my hat and fly. Nearing penury again, I would turn again to Hollywood. There went with me, usually, Rose, a relative or two, two or three servants, many trunks and suitcases, all my oil paintings and whatever animals we possessed.

I remember, along with my indignation, the sunny streets of Hollywood, full of amiable and antic destinations. I remember studios humming with intrigue and happy-go-lucky excitements. I remember fine homes with handsome butlers and masterpieces on the walls; vivid people, long and noisy luncheons, nights of gaiety and gambling, hotel suites and rented palaces overrun with friends, partners, secretaries and happy servants. I remember thousands of important phone calls, yelling matches in the lairs of the caliphs, baseball, badminton and card games; beach and ocean on diamond-sparkling days, rainstorms out of Joseph Conrad and a picnic of money-making. More than all these pleasant things, I remember the camaraderie of collaboration.

Although I wrote most of my sixty movies alone, all my movie writing was a collaboration of one sort or another. The most satisfactory of these were my actual literary collaborations with MacArthur, Lederer or Fowler. The Hollywood party grew happier at such times.

But even without collaborators, the loneliness of literary creation was seldom part of movie work. You wrote with the phone ringing like a firehouse bell, with the boss charging in and out of your atelier, with the director grimacing and grunting in an adjoining armchair. Conferences interrupted you, agents with dream jobs flirted with you, and friends with unsolved plots came in hourly. Disasters circled your pencil. The star for whom you were writing fell ill or refused to play in the movie for reasons that stood your hair on end. ("I won't do this movie," said Ingrid Bergman of *Spellbound*, "because I don't believe the love story. The heroine is an intellectual woman, and an intellectual woman simply can't fall in love so deeply." She played the part very convincingly.) The studio for which you were working suddenly changed hands and was being re-organized. This meant usually no more than the firing of ten or twenty stenographers, but the excitement was unnerving. Or the studio head decided it would be better to change the locale of your movie from Brooklyn to Peking. You listened to these alarms, debated them like a juggler spinning hoops on his ankles, and kept on writing.

Of the bosses with whom I collaborated, Selznick and Zanuck and Goldwyn were the brightest. David, in the days he loved movie making, was a brilliant plotter. He could think of twenty different permutations of any given scene without stopping to catch his breath. Darryl was also quick and sharp and plotted at the top of his voice, like a man hollering for help. Goldwyn as a collaborator was inarticulate but stimulating. He filled the room with wonderful panic and beat at your mind like a man in front of a slot machine, shaking it for a jackpot.

Of the directors with whom I collaborated, most were sane and able fellows. I remember them happily—the young, piano-playing Leo McCarey, with a comedy fuse sputtering in his soul; the ex-clog dancer Ernst Lubitsch, who loved rhythm and precision in his scripts; the drawling fashion plate Howard Hawks, a-purr with melodrama; the moody and elegant Harry D'Arrast; the gentlemanly Alfred Hitchcock, who gave off plot turns like a Roman candle; the witty and Boccaccian Otto Preminger; the antic Jack Conway; the hysterical Gregory Ratoff; the chuckling, wild-hearted Willie Wellman; the soft-spoken, world-hopping Henry Hathaway; the aloof and poetical Victor Fleming. These and many others were all men of talent with salty personalities. Working with them was like playing a game—"Gimmick, Gimmick, Who's Got the Gimmick?"

There were directors, however, who added some depressing rules to the game and made collaboration a messy affair. These were the humorless ones to whose heads fame had gone like sewer gas. They resented a scenario writer as if he were an enemy hired by the Front Office to rob them of their greatness. They scowled at dialogue, shuddered at jokes, and wrestled with a script until they had shaken out of it all its verbal glitter and bright plotting. Thus they were able to bring to the screen evidence only of their own "genius." This consisted of making great psychological or dramatic points by using props, scenic effects or eye-rolling close-ups instead of speech. Knowing these pretenders well and the foolish egomania that animated their work, I managed to avoid most of them. A few, however, fell like rain into my life and darkened some of my days.

This sickly "greatness" is, however, rare in Hollywood. I remember little of it. At dinner parties where all the guests were famous movie stars and directors, none acted famous or even felt famous. Their world-known faces were full of shyness or sociability. The enormous publicity that flared around stars and directors seldom touched their inner personalities, which were as modest and eager as those of factory workers on a picnic. The only strut I remember was the strut of power. A few of the studio caliphs were inclined to make lordly entrances and to relish a bit of homage.

My favorite collaborator in Hollywood was neither writer, director nor boss, but the cameraman Lee Garmes. It was with Lee as a partner that I made all my own pictures, starting with *Crime without Passion* and *The Scoundrel, Specter of the Rose* and *Actors and Sin*. Lee introduced me to the real magic of the movie world—its technical talents. He was not only one of the finest camera artists in Hollywood but more learned about movie making than anyone I met in movieland. The camera was a brush with which he painted, but in his painting was the knowledge of the hundred hazards of a movie set. Nothing I ever encountered in the movies was as uniquely talented as the eyes of Lee Garmes. I prided myself on being an acute observer, but beside Lee I was almost a blind man. Driving his car at fifty miles an hour he would inquire if I had noticed the girl in the back seat of a car that had passed us, speeding in the opposite direction. What about her, I would ask. Lee would beam, "We ought to put that in a picture sometime. She was using daisies for cuff links, real daisies."

Standing on a set, Lee saw a hundred more things than I did. He saw shadows around mouths and eyes invisible to me, high lights on desk tops, ink stands and trouser legs. He spotted wrong reflections and mysterious obstructions—shoulders that blocked faces in the background, hands that masked distant and vital objects. These were all hazards that no look of mine could detect. He corrected them with a constant murmur of instructions. While ridding the set of its wrong nuances of light and shade, Lee also watched the grouping of figures and carried the cutting of the picture in his head. He knew the moods of space, the value of planes, the dynamics of symmetry as well as any painting master. And all this wisdom went into his pointing of the camera.

Working with Lee, I became aware of the other fine talents that are part of movie making. The gaffer, or head electrician, taking his orders from Garmes was a fellow as fond of his work and as full of technical skill. Carpenters, prop men, painters, special-effects men all moved about with quick and economic gestures. They were as removed from laborers as the master craftsmen working beside Cellini in his silver smithy. As director of the movie being shot, I was the final word on all matters. But I would sit by silent and full of admiration as Lee and his overalled magicians prepared the set for my "direction." My job seemed to me little more than putting a frame on a finished canvas.

A FEW TEN PER CENTERS

I HAD ANOTHER SORT of company in my Hollywood work. This was an over-energized and exasperating fellow known as my agent. During my years in Hollywood I employed dozens of them. There was little variation among them. When my fortunes were high, they swarmed around me like Oriental courtiers. When my fortunes were low, they clapped on their turbans and bolted. But high or low, they continued to detach ten per cent from my earnings and harass me with charges of infidelity and duplicity. It was the theory of each of my agents that he alone was entitled to nab ten per cent of my studio checks. I saw no sense in the entire agency business. But I took no stand against them. Most of them were good companions, and their preposterous existence was, somehow, a natural part of the movie scene.

The first and most important of my agents was Leland Hayward. Leland had launched himself as a ten per center by sneaking a manuscript from my desk in Beekman Place and selling it to Metro behind my back. The manuscript was a short story I had discarded as unfit for publication. (It was produced as *The Green Ghost*, with Lionel Barrymore directing it.)

Leland's immediate demand for a cut of fifteen hundred dollars startled me. It was the first time such inroad into my earnings had been attempted. I hurried indignantly to the Metro office in New York and insisted on an extra fifteen hundred dollars for my story, and sent this added boodle to Leland. Thereafter I became reconciled to paying over great sums to men who seemingly did nothing but notify me they had secured a task for me which either I did not want or had already finished.

Leland had become an agent out of a boyish veneration for writers. This mood deserted him early in his agent's career. He became disdainful of writers and easily irritated by them. He said they had disillusioned him—"So help me God, they're more hammy and hysterical than even actors, and more ungrateful." But the truth was that Leland had become disillusioned with writers because of their eagerness to throw away their high talent and turn into movie hacks. Although he made his fortune out of this flaw in the literary soul, Leland was complex enough to sneer at it. He was always more perked up over my refusing to do a movie chore than over my having done it. A good part of my reputation as a troublesome fellow in Hollywood was based on Leland's happy pronouncements to the studio caliphs—"You can't get Hecht. He read the story and thinks it stinks. I tried to argue with him, but all he said was you haven't got enough money to get him to do such kind of crap."

Leland shuffled 'between New York and Hollywood like a man in a fever, sometimes flying his own plane and getting lost for days. He was continually vanishing, becoming involved in mysterious enterprises, flying into hysterics and losing total track of who his clients were and what they were doing. Yet in the midst of more confusion than all his secretaries could untangle, Leland managed to unload millions of dollars' worth of talent a year on the studios. Unload was Leland's own concept of his activities. He came away from a studio deal grinning like a con man who had disposed of a hole in the lake.

Among Leland's partners was an even eerier businessman than himself. This was Myron Selznick. They were partners only briefly, for not even a movie agency could house two such exotics long.

Myron's attitude toward writers was different from Leland's. Not that he loved writers, but to Myron the writer was an important weapon in his war on the movies. Myron considered the movie owners as his enemies. They had brought low his father, Lewis Selznick, who had been among the first of the great movie showmen, and Myron had sworn in his soul to avenge him.

His work of vengeance changed the Hollywood climate. It doubled and quadrupled the salaries of writers, actors and directors—myself among them. Myron making a deal with a studio head was a scene out of Robin Hood. He was not only dedicated to the task of bankrupting the studio, but ready to back up his sales talk with fisticuffs, if the discussion went not to his liking. Brooding in his tent after a sortie on a major studio, Myron would chortle, "I'll break them all. I'll send all those thieves and fourflushers crawling to the poorhouse. Before I'm done the artists in this town will have all the money." Myron rose to great riches in Hollywood before his untimely death. But even the respect of the bosses failed to win him over against the artists or dim his personal courage in their behalf.

A VISIT FROM SCARFACE

MY FIRST DEALING with Myron involved going to work for Howard Hughes. I told Myron I didn't trust Mr. Hughes as an employer. I would work for him only if he paid me a thousand dollars every day at six o'clock. In that way I stood to waste only a day's labor if Mr. Hughes turned out to be insolvent.

Myron was pleased by my attitude and put the deal over with dispatch. The work I did for Hughes was a movie called *Scarface*. News that it was a biographical study of Al Capone brought two Capone henchmen to Hollywood to make certain that nothing derogatory about the great gangster reached the screen. The two henchmen called on me at my hotel. It was after midnight. They entered the room as ominously as any pair of movie gangsters, their faces set in scowls and guns bulging their coats. They had a copy of my *Scarface* script in their hands. Their dialogue belonged in it.

"You the guy who wrote this?" I said I was.

"We read it." I inquired how they had liked it.

"We wanna ask you some questions." I invited them to go ahead.

"Is this stuff about Al Capone?"

"God, no," I said. "I don't even know Al."

"Never met him, huh?"

I pointed out I had left Chicago just as Al was coming into prominence.

"I knew Jim Colisimo pretty well," I said.

"That so?"

"I also knew Mossy Enright and Pete Gentleman."

"That so? Did you know Deanie?"

"Deanie O'Banion? Sure. I used to ride around with him in his flivver. I also knew Barney."

"Which Barney?"

"Barney Grogan—Eighteenth Ward," I said.

A pause.

"O. K., then. We'll tell Al this stuff you wrote is about them other guys."

They started out and halted in the doorway, worried again.

"If this stuff ain't about Al Capone, why are you callin' it *Scarface?* Everybody'll think it's him."

"That's the reason," I said. "Al is one of the most famous and fascinating men of our time. If we call the movie *Scarface*, everybody will want to see it, figuring it's about Al. That's part of the racket we call showmanship."

My visitors pondered this, and one of them finally said, "I'll tell Al." A pause. "Who's this fella Howard Hughes?"

"He's got nothing to do with anything," I said, speaking truthfully at last. "He's the sucker with the money."

"O. K. The hell with him."

My visitors left.

SOME GILDED ASSIGNMENTS

WRITING under handicaps of one sort or another—deadlines to be met, censors to be outwitted, stars to be unruffled—was normal procedure. Writing to please a producer who a few years ago had been a garage owner or a necktie salesman was another of the handicaps. But given a producer literate as Anatole France, there was still the ugly handicap of having to write something that would miraculously please forty million people and gross four million dollars. The handicaps, including this last Liverpool Jump, only added bounce to the job. They made it always a half-desperate performance. If there was little excitement in the script, there was more than enough in its preparation to keep me stimulated.

Goldwyn, Selznick and Eddie Mannix of Metro were my favorite handicap makers. I wrote million-dollar movies for Mannix in a week each. They had to be rushed to the camera to catch release dates set long in advance. For Goldwyn I rewrote an entire script in two days. It was called *Hurricane. Nothing Sacred*, done for Selznick in two weeks, had to be written on trains between New York and Hollywood.

One of my favorite memories of quickie movie writing is the doing of half the *Gone With the Wind* movie. Selznick and Vic Fleming appeared at my bedside one Sunday morning at dawn. I was employed by Metro at the time, but David had arranged to borrow me for a week.

After three weeks' shooting of *Gone With the Wind*, David had decided his script was no good and that he needed a new story and a new director. The shooting had been stopped and the million-dollar cast was now sitting by collecting its wages in idleness.

The three of us arrived at the Selznick studio a little after sunrise. We had settled on my wages on the way over. I was to receive fifteen thousand dollars for the week's work, and no matter what happened I was not to work longer than a week. I knew in advance that two weeks of such toil as lay ahead might be fatal.

Four Selznick secretaries who had not yet been to sleep that night staggered in with typewriters, paper and a gross of pencils. Twenty-four-hour work shifts were quite common under David's baton. David himself sometimes failed to go to bed for several nights in a row. He preferred to wait till he collapsed on his office couch. Medication was often necessary to revive him.

David was outraged to learn I had not read *Gone With the Wind*, but decided there was no time for me to read the long novel. The Selznick overhead on the idle *Wind* stages was around fifty thousand dollars a day. David announced that he knew the book by heart and that he would brief me on it. For the next hour I listened to David recite its story. I had seldom heard a more involved plot. My verdict was that nobody could make a remotely sensible movie out of it.

Fleming, who was reputed to be part Indian, sat brooding at his own council fires. I asked him if he had been able to follow the story David had told. He said no. I suggested then that we make up a new story, to which David replied with violence that every literate human in the United States except me had read Miss Mitchell's book, and we would have to stick to it. I argued that surely in two years of preparation someone must have wangled a workable plot out of Miss Mitchell's Ouïdalike flight into the Civil War. David suddenly remembered the first "treatment," discarded three years before. It had been written by Sidney Howard, since dead. After an hour of searching, a lone copy of Howard's work was run down in an old safe. David read it aloud. We listened to a precise and telling narrative of *Gone With the Wind*.

We toasted the dead craftsman and fell to work. Being privy to the book, Selznick and Fleming discussed each of Howard's scenes and informed me of the habits and general psychology of the characters. They also acted out the scenes, David specializing in the parts of Scarlet and her drunken father and Vic playing Rhett Butler and a curious fellow I could never understand called Ashley. He was always forgiving his beloved Scarlet for betraying him with another of his rivals. David insisted that he was a typical Southern gentleman and refused flatly to drop him out of the movie.

After each scene had been discussed and performed, I sat down at the typewriter and wrote it out. Selznick and Fleming, eager to continue with their acting, kept hurrying me. We worked in this fashion for seven days, putting in eighteen to twenty hours a day. Selznick refused to let us eat lunch, arguing that food would slow us up. He provided bananas and salted peanuts. On the fourth day a blood vessel in Fleming's right eye broke, giving him more of an Indian look than ever. On the fifth day Selznick toppled into a torpor while chewing on a banana. The wear and tear on me was less, for I had been able to lie on the couch and half doze while the two darted about acting. Thus on the seventh day I had completed, unscathed, the first nine reels of the Civil War epic.

Many of the handicaps attending script writing I invented without anyone's aid. I often undertook to do two or more movies at the same time. Once I did four simultaneously, writing two of them with Lederer, one with Quentin Reynolds and one by myself. The house in Oceanside where this mass composition went on swarmed with secretaries, and producers motored down from Beverly Hills to spy on me. Lederer and I had small time for our favorite diversions, which were Klabiash, badminton, horseshoes on the beach and cooking up Napoleonic schemes for getting rich without effort.

MY POVERTY ROW

WHEN I CAME to Hollywood alone I usually stayed in a Beverly Hills hotel. One of my favorite memories of my hotel existence in Hollywood is of the "breakfasts" over which I presided in the Beverly-Wilshire Hotel.

My activities and social duties had made it impossible for me to see the innumerable people "of no standing" whom I still knew. Unemployed and often hungering writers and actors kept my telephones ringing constantly. I decided to consort with them at breakfast, from seven to ten. Accordingly, each morning my suite filled up with raucous and embittered fellows—newspapermen who had turned up only cinders in Eldorado, actors whose bad luck was as fantastic and inexplicable as the good luck of the movie favorites. They drank up bottles of champagne each morning, emptied tins of caviar and filled the air with calumny of Hollywood's Fortunatuses. I was pleased to offer them behind-the-scenes tales proving their contentions that the town was run by cretins and monsters. There was little more I could do for them. Despite their wit and even talent, unsuccess was in their eyes. The need to be underdogs and rail against existence was as strong in them as their lust for fame and money. You could see it not only in their faces but hear it in the gloat with which they detailed their misfortunes.

There is little that can be done in Hollywood to alter the status of its indignant misfits. Jobs obtained for them, lyrical introductions written out for them, are valueless. They fall out of jobs overnight and the high prose commending them brings only a frown to the boss's face. He knows their real objective, which is to add another sonofabitch to their roster of employers who misused and misunderstood them. Occasionally one of these Has-Beens or Never-Weres erupts into fame. But much more frequent in Hollywood than the emergence of Cinderella is her sudden vanishing. At our party, even in those glowing days, the clock was always striking twelve for someone at the height of greatness; and there was never a prince to fetch her back to the happy scene.

SEX IN HOLLYWOOD

THE SEXUAL ACTIVITIES of Hollywood have a vast number of kibitzers, most of them waving pennants. There are some necks straining here and there for a peek that disapproves. But this is an old moral trick that even the clergy has begun to see through. Denouncing sin is one of the few ways open for virtuous people to enjoy it. A sermon against the evils of promiscuous sex indulgence can send a congregation home to masturbate as quickly as a reading from Fanny Hill.

Not many years ago the sex life of Hollywood would have stirred thunder from the pulpits of the land and set the vigilantes riding. In fact, it did. But something has changed—sex, of course. The Devil is out of it. It has almost the status of a game. And as in all games, the public looks toward champions.

Thus Hollywood is to sex what the major leagues are to baseball. The glamorous Hollywood figures perform in a sort of World Series sex match. The public rises to its feet with a happy roar when another one of its marriages is wrecked by a great base-running siren. A celebrated cocksman batting four hundred against the curves and inshoots spreads joy in the bleachers.

Hollywood's love-making is as spotlighted as its movie making for its insiders as well as outsiders. Much of the conversation in movieland is concerned with the venal doings of the ladies and gentlemen of the screen. A great star returning from her honeymoon to start her divorce proceedings told of her first night with her new, third, husband. He had asked her for an unnatural caress. "And I said to him," the beautiful young bride related, " 'nix, I don't have to do that any more. I'm a star now!' "

A male star hosting a party at Chasen's Restaurant asked for advice. He was starting a picture in the morning. He had reason to believe that his director was his wife's lover. What was the best way to handle the situation? His own paramour, beside him, spoke up. "Have her come on location with you. In that way it will seem that she's devoted to you, and all the columnists will write about your happy home life. And she'll be able to be with the director. And so everybody will be happy." The star took the suggestion and his movie was shot in Arizona with happiness enow for all.

In movieland fidelity is as passé as sideburns. Boccaccio would have delighted in its parties. Crébillon would have found among them a perfect cast of lewd and witty duchesses and nimble chevaliers.

The chief advance (or backslide) the movie people have made is freeing sexual activity from social censure. A woman who is known to change her lovers five times a year is as acceptable socially as any virgin—a meaningless statement, that, that marks my age. Virgins have never been acceptable in Hollywood. In all the time I spent there I never heard virginity discussed any more than the canals of Mars.

Even married women who are known to be betraying their husbands with chauffeurs, actors or salesmen are under no cloud. Friends may caution such a wife about running into a blackmailer, but no door closes against her, and there is amusement rather than sting in the gossip she stirs. Men who have been the targets of rape and bastardy charges and who make seduction a profession remain honorable figures in Hollywood society.

I have sat at a dinner party of twelve, knowing that my host, in the last two years, had seduced all six of his feminine guests. There was no hint of tension at the table. No memory of love or sin put a stutter in the talk. Similarly, I have sat in a room where one of the lady stars present had bedded with five of the men chatting around her. She could not have been more at ease had they been five beaux who had taken her canoeing and no more.

News that a group of stars and caliphs have been engaging in orgies is received casually by the movie dinner parties. Information from a qualified source that a certain great star is perverse in her love-making and will engage in amour only in a bathtub full of warm milk, or that a local Casanova has taken to substituting electrical appliances for phallic attentions makes the smallest of ripples. You will see the lacteal siren and the sexual Edison at dinner the next evening and there will be no nudging or winking. People's sex habits are as known in Hollywood as their political opinions, and much less criticized. In fact, they are hardly noticed. In a world of tigers it is difficult for a stripe to stand out.

The absence of moral censure makes gossip depend on its wit or freshness. My friend, on the verge of getting married, told this anecdote about himself. "What can I do? She's cold, and difficult to get along with. Her last husband refuses even to come to the United States as long as she's here. And she's going to drive me crazy with her idea that she's an actress. But on the other hand I am only potent with her. Since falling in love with her, I have tried five other girls. Nothing! With my fiancée, I am like a lion. Of course I had to tell her this. My mistake. As soon as she found it out she insisted on marriage."

Men embarking on love affairs seek counsel with their predecessors on the quickest way to gain entry into the bedroom of the mutual friend. "Don't boast to her of how successful you are," said one Don Juan to the other. "She hates Hollywood success. She says it's a sign of stupidity. Attack Hollywood, the studio, the movies. Tell her they're eating up your soul. She's very artistic."

A friend said to me, "You know, she was my mistress for four years. We were as close as any husband or wife. She cooked me dinner sometimes, rubbed my back. Suddenly she announced, 'I don't love this man I met, but he's a railroad vice-president and rich. And he's asked me to marry him. I told him I would see you first. He's waiting in New York right now for me.'

"I said to her, 'Darling, you're wonderful. I can't ask you to marry me. I wouldn't be sincere. So—go to him. And be happy.'

"Well, we got undressed, went to bed for an hour. She was so wonderful, I cried. Both of us cried. At three-thirty she jumped out of bed. 'Darling, I must hurry. I'll miss the train to New York. It leaves at five. Don't get up. You don't have to take me to the station. I'd rather remember you lying in bed like that—smoking a cigarette.' I asked her if she had her ticket and drawing room. Yes, she had them. The railroad vice-president had taken care of that. She walked out. And I lay there on my bed. At first I was just numb. Then I began to suffer. At four o'clock I was like a man being choked to death. I wanted to get down on the floor and cry. I did. I wanted her back. I kept looking at the clock. I could call her at the station. It's easy to have somebody paged. At four-thirty I grabbed the phone. I thought I would die, I was suffering so. And I called. I had her paged. I couldn't live without her. The thought of her going to bed with this railroad vice-president was like a knife in my heart. The voice on the phone said to me, 'Sorry, sir. The train has already left for New York.' I told him he was stupid and crazy. It was only twenty minutes to five. He tells me it is five minutes after five. My clock is twenty-five minutes slow. I hang up. My God, that was the greatest moment of my life. Such a relief came over me, I wanted to yell. I felt suddenly twenty years old, new, fresh, saved!"

Unmarried women discuss their lovers openly, concentrating usually on their sexual failings. "Good God, a man with his reputation. You'd think he'd know something! All I can tell you is we got to the bedroom at exactly two-thirty. We went straight there from Romanoff's. At exactly two-forty-five we were dressed again and leaving. How do you like that for a big lover! No more actors for me."

"Well, lay off producers. They're worse. I said to Joe last night at Chasen's, 'For God's sake, everybody thinks we're mad lovers and we haven't been to bed for three weeks!' He answered me, 'Don't be selfish, darling. We're having a shake up at the studio.' "

At a dinner table once in a movie caliph's home, I showed surprise at the recently publicized infidelity of a movie star whom I and the public had considered always a chaste wife. All fifteen of the diners turned on me with derision. They supplied me with a list of ten men with whom my heroine had copulated in the past two years. My delusion about the lady seemed a larger flaw in their eyes than her ten defections. When I riposted with this, one of the other famous ladies present said, "What's so wrong about a woman having ten lovers, if they don't interfere with her career or make her unhappy?"

Concealment is not only passé in Hollywood but the publicizing of sin is actually the rule, as much for the girls as the men. Actresses and near actresses hire press agents to notify the newspaper columnist of their new love affairs. Or else they call up the newspaper themselves—"Oh, darling, it's the greatest love of my life! He's so wonderful! Oh, no, that affair is over. I haven't seen Mr. J. for God knows how long. But this time it's real, darling! I'm swooning so I don't know if I'll be able to act in my next picture. No, not *Hold Me Forever*. That's been postponed. I'm playing the feminine lead in *Lady of the Swamps*. Thank you, darling. I wanted you to be the first to know how happy I am."

Items that a starlet (which in Hollywood is the name for any woman under thirty not actively employed in a brothel) has hit the hay with a new glamour boy are an important aid to her career. The movie caliphs are averse to hiring unknowns. In the caliph's eyes any reputation is better than none. A girl who has figured in a dozen "romances" with men of any sort of prominence (even prominent drunkards will do) has proven she is a good prospect for further exploitation. The phrase is—She's star material.

As I hinted a few pages back, it was otherwise once. In the twenties, women's clubs boycotted actresses who changed husbands. Civic organizations picketed theaters in which some recently exposed fornicator was cooing on the silver screen.

Movie stars whose sexual activities slopped over into print were actually dropped by the studios. In fact, the moguls were so intent on keeping their stars sexually pure in the public eye that they did their best to suppress the news that an actress was honorably married. How expect the public to buy a heroine fighting to preserve her virginity when it knew she was being bounced every night in a marital bed?

It was the theory of the studio caliphs in that time that the public demanded purity above all other things in an actress, and that its absence was punished with artistic as well as box-office failure. There was no middle ground between virgin and vampire.

The switch to selling strumpets instead of pure girls to the public was a gradual one. No one press agent or studio philosopher merited an Oscar for the deed. As with other Hollywood trends, it was actually what the public wanted. It wanted no ladies with their legs nobly crossed. It wanted bacchantes and satyrs chasing them, or vice versa.

The moguls have as yet been unable to cater to this great boxoffice yen for immorality. The churches and the civic leagues still stand guard against the art of underpants. The movie censorship code still demands that no woman shall sleep with a man unless married to him, and that if she seems to be sleeping with any man to whom she is not married, she shall be either sent to jail or killed at the end of the film—as a lesson.

The movie makers have not been too stymied by this part of their self-imposed curbs. They have learned how to hint at fornication in a hundred masterful ways and so much so that I, for one, watching a movie, am ready to believe that all its males and females fall to fut-tering one another as soon as the scene "dissolves."

A rash of Bible pictures has recently solved the fornication problem for the major studios. Although the historian Cecil B. De Mille pointed the way decades ago, the movie makers hung back, dubiously. But, no longer. Immorality, perversion, infidelity, cannibalism, etc., are unassailable by church and civic league if you dress them up in the togas and talliths of the Good Book.

DON JUAN IN HOLLYWOOD

DON JUANISM is part of society everywhere. In Hollywood it is the standard. Love and marriage are secondary matters there to sexual excercise. And oddly, it is my impression that there is less successful sex in Hollywood than in Wichita, Kansas. I have no five hundred fieldworkers to bring me morning reports on the situation, as the good Professor Kinsey had, but I have my own accumulation of data. It convinces me that Hollywood, uninhibited center of venery, is more headquarters for impotence than stallion play.

I have known a number of Don Juans who were good studs and who cavorted between the sheets without a psychiatrist to guide them. But most of the busy love-makers I knew were looking for masculinity rather than practicing it. They were fellows of dubious lust.

And their conquests were most often ladies of similar lack. Their female sexuality was nearly all in their clothes, their mannerisms and their reputations. The glamour girls of Hollywood number many an honest set of glands among them, and there are even some nymphomaniacs of note to be met. But, as with the male Don Juans, the ladies hopping from lover to lover brought more ambition to bed than passion.

On this subject my friend Fanny Brice used to say, "Men always fall for frigid women because they put on the best show."

I can add little to Fanny's observation—except that Don Juan is apt to prefer the hullaballoo of spurious passion to the simpler noises of honest sex. His own love racket is also more windy than seminal.

With all the infidelity going on in movietown and with its large sexual turnover, you would expect much smolder and violence. There is some alcoholic torch-carrying to observe and an occasional explosion to read in the papers. But pain and explosion are rare in the love annals of Hollywood. Marriages break up with a minimum of emotional pother. What bitterness appears has usually to do with property division. Great romances, which have kept the public shaking with vicarious passion, collapse suddenly and usually their only epitaph is a new Great Romance, announced in the press on Monday.

This is one of the reasons for the human feebleness of the movies. They are made by these same folk. Most movies deal with matters foreign to their makers—the agonies of love, the miseries of infidelity and the wonders of a safe and loyal marriage that lasts till "death do us part."

The movie makers are able to put more reality into a picture about the terrors of life at the ocean bottom than into a tale of two Milwaukeeans in love. They know more about the former matters.

I remember a phone call to Nyack from the M-G-M Studio in Hollywood. Bernie Hyman, then the studio head, wished my help on a plot problem that had arisen in a two-million-dollar movie being prepared for shooting.

"I won't tell you the plot," he said. "I'll just give you what we're up against. The hero and heroine fall madly in love with each other—as soon as they meet. What we need is some gimmick that keeps them from going to bed right away. Not a physical gimmick like arrest or getting run over and having to go to the hospital. But a purely psychological one. Now what reasons do you know that would keep a healthy pair of lovers from hitting the hay in Reel Two?"

I answered that frequently a girl has moral concepts that keep her virtuous until after a trip to the altar. And that there are men also who prefer to wait for coitus until after they have married the girl they adore.

"Wonderful!" said the Metro head of production. "We'll try it."

FAREWELL, SOLDIER

I KNEW few actors and actresses well in Hollywood. Adventures and work shared with actors are not enough to make friendships. Actors are modest and warmhearted but they remain stubbornly in their own world. One of the few exceptions was Jack Gilbert. He became a friend, suddenly. We met at a dinner party and Jack came home with me and talked all night.

In the time of Hollywood's most glittering days, he glittered the most. He received ten thousand dollars a week and could keep most of it. He lived in a castle on top of a hill. Thousands of letters poured in daily telling him how wonderful he was. The caliphs for whom he worked bowed before him as before a reigning prince. They built him a "dressing room" such as no actor ever had. It was a small Italian palace. There were no enemies in his life. He was as unsnobbish as a happy child. He went wherever he was invited. He needed no greatness around him to make him feel distinguished. He drank with carpenters, danced with waitresses and made love to whores and movie queens alike. He swaggered and posed but it was never to impress anyone. He was being Jack Gilbert, prince, butterfly, Japanese lantern and the spirit of romance.

One night Jack sat in a movie theater and heard the audience laugh at him in a picture. It was his first talkie. His squeaky boy's voice accompanying his derring-do gestures turned him into a clown.

After the preview the Metro caliphs decided not to use him again. His contract for ten thousand a week still had many years to run. He would draw his salary and remain idle.

Jack called in three vocal coaches. He worked two hours a day with each of them. He started breaking into the front offices crying out, "Listen to me now. I can talk." And he recited passages from Shakespeare and the poets. The caliphs remembered the laughter in the theater and waved him away.

One day he entered Walter Wanger's office, fell on his knees and pleaded for the male lead in *Queen Christina*. Garbo, one of his former leading ladies, was being starred in it.

"Listen to me talk," said Jack. "It's a real voice, a man's voice." Tears fell from his eyes.

Wanger gave him the lead. Gilbert played it well, but the movie failed to bring him back to fame. The Gilbert voice no longer made audiences laugh. It left them, however, unimpressed. Jack played in no more pictures. He became a ten-thousand-dollar-a-week beachcomber. He strutted around the movie lot and gave drinking parties in his Italian-palace dressing room. There was no gloom visible in him. He played Jack Gilbert to a small audience of masseurs, fencing and boxing instructors, vocal coaches, barkers, whores, hangers-on and a few friends.

One rainy afternoon I called on him in his dressing room. He was lying down on one of his five-thousand-dollar beds reading one of my books. He asked me to autograph it. I wrote in it, "To Jack Gilbert—Dumas loaned him a mustache." I regretted the sentence as soon as I put it down. Jack grinned as he looked at it. "So true," he said. "Can you have dinner with me tonight?"

The rain became a tropic storm. Four of us drove out to Gilbert's house on Malibu Beach. MacArthur was one of the guests. Another was one of Jack's staunchest friends, Dick Hyland, the athlete and sports writer.

We drank and told stories after dinner. The wind howled in the night and the dark sea came crashing almost up to the windows. Gilbert was silent. He sat drinking and smiling at us. At eleven o'clock he sprang to his feet.

"I've got a date," he said. "I'm swimming out and returning a mustache to Dumas. Good-by—everybody—sweethearts and sons-obitches, all."

He waved a bottle of liquor at us and was gone. We saw him for a moment racing in the storm toward the roaring ocean. No one moved.

"For God's sake!" young Hyland said. "He's gone to drown himself!"

Hyland watched the storm for a few minutes and then left to find Jack. He returned in an hour, drenched and wearied. We were still drinking and talking.

"I couldn't find him," Hyland said. "He's gone."

I looked at MacArthur and asked, "What do you think, Charlie?"

"I don't know," said my friend, "but if a man wants to kill himself that's his privilege. Everybody destroys himself sooner or later."

MacArthur stood up unsteadily. He had remembered a phrase out of the Bible, which was always half-open in his head.

"A man fell in Israel," he quoted, and resumed his drinking.

The noises of the storm filled the room. The door opened suddenly. Rain and wind rushed in. A dripping Jack Gilbert stood weaving in the doorway. He grinned and tried to speak. Instead he vomited, and fell on the floor.

"Always the silent star," said MacArthur.

I thought of the Hans Christian Andersen tale of the Steadfast Tin Soldier. He had been swept away to sea in a paper boat, and in his ears as he was drowning had sounded the voice of one he loved.

Farewell, soldier, true and brave,
Nothing now thy life can save.

A few months later Gilbert went to a gay Hollywood party. While he was dancing with a movie queen, his toupee fell off. Amid shouts of laughter he retrieved it from under the dancers' feet. He was found dead the next morning in bed—in his castle on the hill.

AT HOME ON MISTY MOUNTAIN

EACH TIME we went to Hollywood we took with us most of our Nyack ménage. Lester Bartow, our driver, rode them across country in the car. Lester is now in his forties. He became our driver in his teens. Being the only member of our household who could drive a car, repair electric lights, remember appointments, understand plumbing and mail letters, he posed during these years as an admirable Crichton and fancied himself the keystone of my existence—which, possibly, in sundry ways he was.

With Lester on the coast-to-coast treks went my strongman trainer, Elmore Cole, under whose eye for twenty years every morning at eight I punched the bag, did mat work and grunted lifting weights; our French poodle, Googie, named after the fine Russian writer Nikolai Gogol; and our three old ladies, Gertie, Jo and Hilja. Twenty suitcases, six trunks, oil paintings, our radios and phonograph records, and favorite window drapes went each time by freight. Rose and I took the train.

Lying in a drawing room for three days reading mystery books, having neither to bathe, shave nor dress, and without the Homeric Elmore and his punching bag to torment me, without telephones, pencils or problems, was always a time of fetal bliss. Nevertheless, I often flew to Hollywood—a mode of travel that has never failed to terrify me.

Roaring through the sky in the always precarious plane, I would wonder what perversity or weakness it was that made me risk my life and sweat nervously through a dozen hours in the air instead of riding peacefully and lethargically in the drawing room of my dreams. Once, waiting for my plane to take off in Buenos Aires and fly over the Andes to Santiago, I was given insight into what sent me off on trips through the sky.

I had thought before that it was the cowardice of conformity. Most of the people I knew flew to and from Hollywood. Obviously, I did not want to stand out as someone fearful of flying. Rather than have people think that of me, I submitted myself to the bumps and palpitations of aerial transport.

I became aware in Buenos Aires that I had explained myself incorrectly. Sitting in the plane that was going to hop over the Andes —in that year still an enterprising thing to do—the word "jeopardy" came to me. I was not in the plane because of social fears. I was in it because of the lure of jeopardy, the same jeopardy lure that makes men risk their well-being on the roll of dice or fall of cards.

The small boy, ancestor of such jeopardy hunters, likes to see how close to the railroad track he can stand without being run over by the train. The engine roaring past him, spraying his face with cinders but leaving him still in one piece, fills the small boy with a sense of victory. He has tested his courage and won. He has also done something else. With his feat of daring and danger, he has atoned for certain boyish sins. By offering himself as a possible sacrifice to the thundering locomotive, he feels himself punished for those sins, and thus cleansed of them.

I am willing to believe that to rid myself of the guilt of going to Hollywood I punished myself by flying there.

I return to Lester and his non-perilous cavalcade. The ménage he transported made movieland more palatable to me. Magically, my home and its many familiar faces appeared there.

Gertie was the oldest lady of our ménage. She was in her seventies and was one of our cooks and cleaners. She was five feet tall, deaf, red-cheeked, weather-beaten and radiant-eyed. She teetered and clomped through the day like a redskin on the warpath. Dust was the enemy.

Gertie had been a scrub lady and washerwoman since her childhood. At eight she had begun to clean floors in Germany. Come to Brooklyn, she had been early widowed and left with five small sons. Of her husband she said, "Ooh! He wash no goot! All the time drink. Und he was hit me, too. He died in Bellfew Hoshpital. No goot, dat feller."

Left alone, she had toiled eighteen hours a day bringing up her five sons to become policemen. They ate well in their boyhood. She had never made complaint and had worshiped God amid her scrub pails and washtubs.

She was in her fifties when we found her "schroobing" in a Henry Street house where we had gone to live among the noises, smells and hazards of the slums. I had induced Rose to move to Henry Street after a year in New York. I thought it would be good to taste the city's squalor.

Gertie, discovered in this squalor, was to remain with us until she died in her eighties, never to stop teetering and clomping, whooping and schroobing till she was ridden off to the hospital to die. "Gott ish goot zu me," she announced proudly when in a reminiscent mood. "He always gived me woik to do."

She went to church once a year on Christmas Eve and contributed ten cents toward the maintenance of the Catholic faith, which she revered. "Ish enough fer dem. Dem priests got lotsh money. Oho!"

Rose sat beside Gertie in the hospital when she was dying and told her she would ask the priest in St. Patrick's Cathedral to say a mass to take away the pain. Gertie was dying of cancer. "A high mass," said Rose, weeping. "No Mish Heck," Gertie gasped, "high mass cosht ten dollar. Too much. Better make low mass. Cosht one dollar." She held up a gnarled finger. "Must nit t'rown money away."

"No, Gertie," said Rose. "It will be a high mass, for ten dollars."

In St. Patrick's Cathedral the priest refused the money, after hearing the story of Gertie. He said a high mass for nothing. A stranger was found to light the candles in front of St. Anne, Gertie's favorite intercessor. The stranger in the big cathedral whispered, "Tell her I will know her when we meet in Heaven."

Gertie's stinginess was deep and touching, to friends as well as to priest and stranger. It was like a battle trauma. It told of the days of eighteen-hour toil, of penny by penny earned over her scrub pails to feed her sons. In Nyack her hand would reach into the bathroom and switch off the light while I was shaving.

On her first trip across the country with Lester she demanded each night before retiring that he fetch her a pail of water, soap and brush. She scrubbed the floors of each of the motels in which she slept. During the day she whooped with anguish at the prices charged by restaurants. Lolling in the back seat of the Cadillac she would look for poor people all along the way to California. A dusty figure in the road would set her to clucking, "Poor people. All alone und so hungry."

Rose gave her fancy hats and silk dresses and sent her off with Lester to the theater. She returned always with a drunken air and whooping that she had seen, "Lots fine t'ings. Lobely goils! All neked! Whee! Real lobely! But nit so goot like the Mish Heck! No, neber! The Mish Heck ish the best von all of them!" And she would push her head against Rose's head and laugh boisterously. A portrait of Gertie painted by Billy Brice hangs in our entrance hall in Nyack. Gertie looks moodier on canvas than she did in life, but her small deep eyes still twinkle on our home.

Our second oldest lady, Jo, was Gertie's relative. Their children had married each other. Jo was also cook and cleaner. She had come out of the same Henry Street basement that had given us Gertie. When we had lived in Henry Street, Gertie and Jo used to wait for us on the curb to come home in a taxi. They would stand surrounded by howling kids and neighborhood toughs, their arms loaded with apples and flowers.

Jo's voice was hoarse and to be heard frequently in moans of despair or foghorn sighs of such sadness as to tear the heart. She mourned some mysterious past. Yet Jo loved lively doings. When guests were laughing and music played in our house, she would seize her friend Gertie and waltz with her in the kitchen. In her seventies Jo was not quite as powerful as Gertie, due to a trouble with her hip. Her toil was less demoniac. But when she was unable to walk up the stairs she continued to polish the woodwork as high as she could reach on tip-toe. Gertie and Jo loved each other with sneers and grimaces, and they loved the home in which they worked as if it were a roost in Eden.

Hilja, our third old lady, was from Finland. She was a gentle and mystic figure with a canary-bird tweet for a voice. Her face was white and childlike. She would stand for an hour in front of the sink, motionless and smiling into space, and attentive only to the dream in her head. The dream was divided between Jesus and the snails, bugs and birds in the garden. She spoke to Jesus in silence, but addressed the little garden life openly, kneeling before snails and beetles and speaking sweetly to them in Finnish. Hilja had been a hotel chambermaid before joining our home, where she was to live till she died many years later. In her girlhood in Finland she had written poetry, dreamed of becoming an actress and come upon a great grief. The grief, never known to us, had left her gentle and abstracted all the rest of her life.

Lester and his troop arrived at the newly rented Beverly Hills *palazzo* on the day Rose and I got there in May, 1939. So did a van full of suitcases, trunks, paintings and other impedimenta. Credit for this fine timing was shared between Rose and Lester. We all started poking into new rooms and uncovering fresh wonders, for we had come this time on an actual castle. It had been built by Fred Niblo, one of the early geniuses of the town. Old palace rooms had been brought from Italy and reassembled inside it. There were carved beams and carved and painted high ceilings, ancient panelings, antique stairways and stained-glass windows. A large Roman pool with arbors at each end lay beyond the house. Sweeping lawns and curling driveways were in front of it. But most exciting about our new abode was that it was built on top of the highest hill in Hollywood. The hill was called Misty Mountain. A perilous and winding road called Angelo Drive, after climbing Misty Mountain, ended in our wide driveway, lit by old Italian lanterns. Toward evening a mist sometimes covered the hillsides ending a few yards below our buttressed stone house. On such evenings we seemed to perch over a vanished world. Inside the house we felt ourselves drifting away in an extravagant balloon.

Glass walls enclosed half the dining room. From our table we saw far below the lighted city of Hollywood that looked no larger than a blazing chandelier.

As we were sitting down to our first meal, our Western retainers began to appear, having read of our arrival in some movie column. There was no question of whether or not they were to work in our new home. They had bolted whatever jobs they had, appearing with bulging suitcases like relatives moving in.

The most constant of our Western retainers was Lucy, who was tall and in her seventies. She was as proud as a top sergeant, bold-eyed and noisy with dreams of love. She was a Croatian and spoke an English too incredible for recording. Her happily squealing voice filled the kitchen like a calliope. She stood over stove and sink swooning with anecdotes of life undaunted, of lovers entwined in each other's arms leaping to their deaths, of murders and suicides rising out of thwarted passions. Her tales of Croatian, Bulgarian and Egyptian romances held Jo spellbound. Jo would stand motionless with a broom in her hand for an hour listening agape and crying out hoarsely at intervals, "Balogny!" Hilja, who heard nothing but the sounds of Heaven and the converse of snails and beetles, was unable to make head or tail out of Lucy's high whistle of talk. But Gertie, who could hear nothing lower than a yell, nevertheless got the sense of it. She would swing a wash rag at Lucy and scold, "Dosh aber terrible! An olt lady mit a big nose talkin' doity talk! My Gotness!" Lucy would answer in her lusty squeal, "Oh mine soul! Mine body ees olt—but mine heart ees yoong!"

Lucy brought her tales into the dining room. She would stand near the table while we ate, her ancient face aglow, and tell us of men and women she had seen die of love. "Love ees only t'eeng in woild, Mahdam. Ees wonful! Oh, oh, mine Heaven, when I was yoong— when I was yoong!" One day she asked in a solemn voice, "Mahdam, weech way ees dot Alatzka? You know, Alatzka, weet bears, the white ones?"

We pointed to the north. Lucy darted to a window, crying out, "Mahdam, mine man ees gone Alatzka! I meet him by park. He has beautiful eyes! I love heem! But he go Alatzka. I waiting now. Ooh, mine God in Heaven, how I love heem!"

We asked his name.

"What I want name for?" Lucy cried. "He is Irishman. Ees enough for me!" Her seventy-five-year-old face flushed with romance and she blew a kiss to the north.

When alone with her Mahdam, Lucy would offer to make her love spells. She had two spells she eagerly recommended. One was done with the aid of a piece of knotted string. It guaranteed my impotence while away from home. The other spell would make every man who looked at Mahdam quake with sexual desire and sink to the floor to kiss her feet. This one was made with herbs. Rose scorned both spells and Lucy, hugging her, cried out, "Mahdam, you yoong! Beaudeeful! You no need spell. I make spell for the Esther. He need." Esther was Lester, whose name, along with a thousand other names, she always mispronounced.

Screams from Lucy's room roused the house often in the middle of the night. No one ever moved to investigate, for we all knew it was Lucy wrestling with the Devil again. In the morning she would say, "He come to me last night thot Deevil! I fight weet heem for whole hour. Today I go in church, make novena."

I sat one evening in the kitchen of our *palazzo* on the Misty Mountain and watched our three cooks and their helper Hilja prepare a dinner party for twenty. Gertie was cooking her favorite veal stew, a dish she always brought to the table regardless of what had been requested. She was also preparing her favorite salad ("cosht notting"), which I never tasted for twenty years. Jo was tending ducks in the oven. Soup was steaming on the stove, a soup that took almost forever to cook but when eaten was guaranteed to double male virility, according to Lucy. The smells of seven different desserts baked by Lucy—cakes, tortes, strudels and *dampfnudels*—filled the mountain air. Lucy was making chicken sausages for appetizers. She had ground up the meat of five chickens into a paste and was stuffing them into skins of dough.

"I cooka for Kaizer thees sausagen in Port Said," Lucy cried out.

"Go wan!" Jo pushed her. "You never seen no Kaiser. Balogny!"

"What you talk! You crazy!" Lucy squealed rapturously. "Before Heaven, I see heem! He say to me, 'Lucia, you best cook in whole Europa. You come home by me.' I tell him, 'You fine man. Fine eyes. I like your eyes. But I no like work for Germans.' Ho, ho, thot Kaizer! He squeazie mine hand."

Gertie heard nothing. Her eyes glared again at the shelves piled with cakes and strudels. She shuddered and cried out, "You aber crazy! Truly Gott, you verrickt! All dot stuff! The Mish Heck gonna holler, you t'rowen away the money!"

"On me, holler! Who? Never! I love mine Mahdam. I love her with mine soul!" Lucy yelled in rebuttal.

"Mish Heck ish best woman in the woild," Gertie retorted. "She nit shmoked und she nit goed out mit oder man. I cut mine head off on dat!"

Lucy was reminded of a story. She had worked once for a Croatian general. One night the general had come home unexpectedly and discovered his young bride being kissed by a colonel of hussars. The general had drawn his sword and run the colonel through. Then with one swoop of that weapon he had cut off his wife's beautiful head. A moment later the general, still madly in love with his bride, had picked her head up off the floor and sat weeping and kissing it. The colonel had revived for a moment, screamed with jealousy at this sight, and shot the general dead. Then he had uttered a last cry of love and fallen dead himself.

Jo listened with her mouth open in wonder, crying out hoarsely now and then, "Balogny!" Gertie had dropped to her knees unexpectedly and was giving the floor a schroobing. Hilja sliced vegetables and smiled dreamily into the sink. I left to get dressed for dinner.

We had no butler, Rose having decided it would be an affront to her retainers to introduce one into the house, let alone the impossibility of finding a butler who would tolerate our kitchen circus. As a result, despite our numerous staff, there was never anyone to answer the doorbell or the telephone. None of our ladies could speak over the instrument. They usually unhooked it slyly and let the receiver lie untouched till it had stopped rumbling.

This night, as on other nights, our guests let each other in and ultimately came to the dining table. One of the guests was Charles Chaplin, at the time under a cloud of unfavorable publicity.

I had always considered Chaplin the best actor, the best scenario writer and one of the best directors in the movies. The fact that he had never received or even been mentioned for any sort of an Academy Oscar was a measure of the sad cowardice of the movie people. They were afraid to honor the great artist among them because the press called him wicked or traitorous. I have never known a less wicked man than Chaplin (in Hollywood, at least) or one who contributed more riches to the country in which he lived.

Socially Chaplin lived in Hollywood like a hermit. He was seldom to be seen at any of its cafés or parties. I was pleased to have this moody man at our table. The dinner started. We never had bells on our table to summon servants. Rose preferred to bring them on with a friendly cry that reached the kitchen. Such a cry sounded, the pantry door opened and Gertie and Jo entered. Rose had bought them black taffeta dresses and small white aprons for the occasion. Our two old ladies sidled in like a pair of musical-comedy characters. They carried platters of Lucy's chicken sausages. Beholding the dressed-up guests, Gertie paused to titter and pay homage with a drawn out "ooh." Jo advised her hoarsely to behave herself and they both started around the table with the appetizers.

Gertie suddenly stopped. Her small eyes were peering excitedly at one of the guests.

"Ya, it's der Sharlie!" she cried out, pointing and going into a half-crouch. "Oh mine gotness! Der Sharlie Shaplin!"

Jo, forgetting her social schooling, came running over for a look. Her face lit up as brightly as Gertie's and her voice fog-horned, "God. It's him! Charlie Chaplin. What d'ya know!"

Both old ladies stood beaming and speechless. Lucy, peering in to see how her sausages were going, spied Chaplin and came squealing into the room.

"Ooh, mine Charlie!" she cried. "Oh, how I lovin' thot man! Meester Charlie, you mine sweetheart! I lovin' you!"

Gertie smiled shyly as Chaplin stood up, his hand held out to her.

"Ya," she whispered, "I seen him lotsh times in der nickel shows. Ya, lotsh times. Wonerful! Truly Gott!"

Jo croaked, "How do you do, Mr. Chaplin. We are proud to have you eat from us. Thanks."

She curtsied to him, as before a king.

After Chaplin had shaken their hands, Gertie and Jo returned flushed and giggling to the kitchen. Lucy remained in the pantry doorway wringing her hands and uttering cries of love.

Since that evening I have never worried over the fact that the movies have failed ever to honor their greatest artist, Charlie Chaplin.

MY INFERNO

As I WAS IMPATIENT always after a spell in Hollywood to get out of that town, so I am suddenly impatient now to be done with writing about it. I leave unwritten a hundred tales of stars and factotums, hilarities and mishaps and skip to my last chapter on the subject. It begins in Nyack in 1946.

I came home from Hollywood well off and with many things to do. Chief among them was the business of helping to oust the British from Palestine. Around me in Nyack the Palestinian underground crackled constantly. Russian and British spies pattered through the house and eavesdropped at the swimming pool where the Irgun captains were wont to gather for disputation.

To ease the political tensions of the household I organized a baseball game with Lederer's help. Baseball had always been our chief social sport in Nyack. MacArthur and I had organized our first team in 1935 and played the College Heroes Team, captained by Tommy Shevlin, Jr., and "managed" by Jack Kriendler. On that occasion Jack had contributed four busloads of chorus girls in mink coats as spectators and a fifth bus full of liquor.

We had provided the baseball diamond, owned by my Nyack neighbor, Oom, the Omnipotent, a brass band led by Boris Morros and six elephants to parade before and after the game. The elephants were also part of Oom's Yoga enterprise. On our team, dressed in sailor suits, had played Ed Sullivan, Bugs Baer, Robert Sherwood, Marc Connelly, Harpo Marx, Dennie Miller, Lederer, MacArthur and myself. We held two National League pitchers, disguised in sailor suits, in reserve. With their aid we won the game.

Some of our original team answered the call for this summer's play. Among the new batch of athletes were Norman Katkov and Marlon Brando. It was raining and we played in a field of deepening mud. I pitched. During the second inning I picked up a Charley horse. Worse, for a man in the fine condition I believed myself to be in, I seemed to be sweating unduly throughout the game. The next morning I awoke with a high fever and thought I had caught cold in the rain. It developed, however, to be an acute gall bladder attack.

A few days later I was taken to the hospital and operated upon. It was discovered after I was opened up that I had peritonitis, and my doctors were unable to remove the stones or the affected bladder. I was sewed up again, fed drugs for a month and drained of the peritonitis and then returned to the operating room for another session with the surgical knives. This time the doctors removed the stones and bladder, and I lay around for weeks, after returning to Nyack, waiting for strength to return.

Such was the factual side of my first and unexpected sickness. During the three months of its active presence, however, a number of curious things happened to me. They were things of the mind. To my astonishment there appeared a man I hardly knew with totally alien moods. This man was I.

The changes began when I came back to consciousness after the first trip to surgery. The last thing I remembered before the anesthesia took me off was hearing a loud metallic sound as of a sledge hammer smiting an anvil. The sound and I had vanished together.

When I opened my eyes again I was surrounded by apparatuses filling me with blood and salt water. I learned afterward that I was in a state of surgical shock, with the foot of the bed raised up and my doctors uncertain for several days whether I would live or die. I was surprised to hear that there had been any such concern, for death had never been further from my thoughts than in those precarious days.

My first sensations on opening my eyes were the smells of ocean water and seaweed and an eerie feeling of having been whisked back in a Time Machine to the beginnings of the world. A peace and emptiness engulfed me and my senses seemed to touch a pristine earth and water. I beheld no saurians nor had I any other visions, but I seemed to be looking with eyes I had never used on a planet not yet inhabited. The sense that life was new, and all land and sea were at their beginnings, made me happy.

When I was able to talk I assured Rose I felt good and that she need not worry about me. Her face was the only one I could make out. It floated like a disembodied face into the new world.

At night the sea odors deepened and I demanded of my nurses to be allowed to hold pieces of ice in my hands. In the dark I heard again the sledge-hammer clang ringing on the anvil and wondered what it was. The ice in my hands pleased me, as if I had been given perfect toys to play with. When I awoke at dawn I was filled with a longing to go to the sea and look at sky and water. I felt as if I were some finny creature that had been plucked out of faraway deeps. The desire to return to them was like a powerful homesickness. During the day this need to go live somewhere under salt-smelling waves lessened, and I was able to understand some of its causes. The saline solution being constantly injected into me spread the odors and images of briny seas in my head.

Another series of sensations then occupied me. I had the illusion of being distributed around various parts of the room in which I lay. It seemed there were a number of me's, and try as I would I was unable to assemble them. I was fascinated with being a number of people and discussed this with Rose and her sister Minna. I had no thought for my illness, and the fact that Rose and the doctors believed me seriously ill seemed to me absurd. I had never felt so remarkably alive, nor so full of eagerness. The discomfort of having a Levin tube stuck through my nose into my stomach, of being unable to move because of a belly full of sutures and of having a drain running poisons from my insides into a jar on the floor, appeared a minor matter. I was much more interested in the alien excitements in my head. Even on the third day when I learned, by guessing first from the long faces around my bed, that something had gone wrong, and that I would have to be operated on again in a few weeks, the news seemed of small importance.

The room in which I lay was no longer a mystic place full of sea odors. It was a white, sunlit hospital room in which visitors sat and talked. But I looked on a strange world in this room. I had never known or felt this world before. It was a world of gentleness. My heart ached with happiness as I beheld it. The kindliness of the faces that looked at me, the fine, cool talent of the doctors and nurses that tended me were only a part of the gentleness that embraced me. The gentleness was mostly something within me. I looked on everything with love. As the days passed, each morning became a rendezvous at which I arrived eager and smiling. I needed no visitors, books or music to keep me diverted. The day flying in through the window was enough. The sky darkening, the night coming, delighted me. The word God did not enter my head, but a word that seemed to mean the same was always there. It was the word life.

I felt a gentleness toward people because they were part of a happy mystery of moving and breathing. I was pleased by the way they walked and felt close to all who came into my room, including the hospital barber, as if they were kinsfolk.

I returned to Nyack on the day Jenny was having a birthday party. The garden was filled with the voices of her four-and-five-year-old friends. Their whoops and squeals of joy seemed the perfect sounds of mankind.

Two weeks later it was time to go back to the hospital for the second operation. Before leaving, I walked slowly around the garden. I carried all its colors with me to the new hospital room.

That night while being prepared for the morning's surgery, I thought of the prospect of dying and found myself smiling at the impossibility of such an event. The love that had come to me a few weeks ago swelled my heart and brightened the room. I played cards with Rose and Lederer, and a sense of adventure was in the night. Drugs finally put me to sleep. When I awoke, the second operation was over. Again the odors of ocean water and seaweed filled a new world, and again I lay through dreamy hours, making love to time as if it were a dancing girl.

Only one unhappy experience befell me. I was wheeled out in my bed, after a few days, and taken to the roof to be in the summer sun. The trip had made me dizzy. When I opened my eyes I beheld some twenty fellow invalids basking in beds and wheel chairs. The sight of them shocked me. They were haggard-faced, sunken-eyed. Tubes ran from their bellies to jars on the roof floor. The knowledge that I was one of them, haggard and sunken-eyed as the most scare-faced looking of them, made me miserable. I had not thought of myself as a pathetic-looking invalid, and I had not seen myself in a mirror since the first hospital hour. Seeing myself now in the faces of these fellow invalids, I demanded to be taken back to my room. After a day, the image of myself as a pleasant, whimsical-looking fellow returned, and I was content again.

I said good-by to my doctors, Dr. Harold Hyman, Dr. Henry Cave, Dr. Scudder Winslow and Dr. Sterling Mueller. I had for two months looked on these men as I once had on my parents. They were all-knowing and devoted. I felt saddened to be leaving them, as if I were leaving some loving circle. I looked behind me as I walked off slowly down the hospital corridor. My doctors were already busy entering other rooms, and I thought, "Are there people anywhere more wonderful than doctors?"

With me to Nyack went one of my nurses, Harriet Hayward. I had picked her to come along because she was the youngest of those who had cared for me and the best looking. She had also diverted me with the best anecdotes. Harriet had been an army nurse in India during the war, working in one of the hospitals on the Lido Road.

In Nyack the homesickness for the sea that I had felt some weeks before came to me again, but in a more practical guise. I wished to be on a beach and feel the sun, the salty wind and the hot sand. As soon as I was able to walk easily, our ménage started west again, for my home in Oceanside, California.

SOMETHING ELSE DIES

THE BEACH was wide and empty, the sand white and warm. The sea glittered and the sky was alive with light. Over me on a fifty-foot hill bank loomed my many-windowed house with its friendly walls and roofs. In front of me was the Pacific Ocean. I lay breathing the warm salty air and feeling the pinch of the sun as it burned my skin. I walked the water's edge, and the moist land under my feet felt alive. I sat down and let the waves tumble me up on the beach and pull me back again. Everything I had longed for during my illness was here.

The morning passed like a parade which only I was watching. After lunch Jenny appeared and began running in zigzags in and out of the sparkling surf. She played with the ocean as if it were a pet on a string. Birds circled her blond head, and our black poodle bounced up and down around her and broke into demented sprints over the sand.

Giddy with sun and salty wind, I climbed the wooden stairway to my house, ran fresh water on my skin in the patio, and then stretched out in the great front window and watched the sun set and the colors run from the sky into the sea. I ate dinner in a room lit by a hanging circle of candles. The dim roar of the sea and the soft crash of waves accompanied the talk at the table. The white curtains billowed like little sails in the open windows. After eating, I listened to music over the radio and watched the star-flooded night till Rose announced bedtime. I followed her into the patio. The many-gabled roofs of the house made it look like a sleeping village.

In the bedroom, a wide, carved walnut bed waited for me. The fresh sheets and pillows cooled my sun-warmed skin. I fell asleep and dreamed of the day, the sun, the sea, the sand and wind. There were few thoughts in my head. At times I remembered incidents of past years and made notes of them. The memories were curiously alike. They were all happy. I loved not only what was around me but all that had ever been. Gratitudes I had never felt brought tears to my eyes at night and I wondered what I could do to thank the sea, the stars and the multitude of days through which I had come. After a few weeks I bought a stock of pencils and began to write this book.

When I had written for several months I learned we were out of money and that I would have to go to work in Hollywood again. And here my farewell to Hollywood began. It was to continue for several years. During these years all that I remembered of Hollywood kept vanishing. The movie people grew timorous and cynical. There was no elation to be tapped in the studios. From the Owner to the smallest of his stooges rose a fog of weariness.

I found myself too bored by the tasks I took on to ponder much on the causes of this collapse of movieland. A new fact that was evident was the Hollywood Terror. All the varied neuroses that used to animate the movie makers appeared to consolidate themselves into a single one—the fear that they might seem un-American or pro-Communist.

Patriot committees of actors, directors, producers and writers policed the talk and thought of movieland. These patriots were recruited chiefly from the Boob McNutt personnel of movieland. The dullest actors, the most wallflower social types, the lame ducks of all departments came together vengefully to wreak their will finally on their betters.

Under the threat of these mental hobgoblins, the Hollywood egos struck their colors. I knew as I rode to work in Hollywood that it could never add a grin or a piper's tune to my day again.

During my last stint in Hollywood (1952), the frowsiness and cowardice of the town, and the literary lust that had been growing in me, made me bolt it, leaving half a movie job money uncollected. While walking its familiar streets for what seemed to me a last time, a mild hallucination came to me. I stood in a moldy, once gaudy saloon. A mustachioed barkeep dozed among his bottles. The tables were dusty and deserted. Music started up, and a siren came in through the swinging doors and stood ogling me. I knew her name—Madam Hollywood. I rose and said good-by to this strumpet in her bespangled red gown; good-by to her lavender-painted cheeks, her coarsened laugh, her straw-dyed hair, her wrinkled fingers bulging with gems. A wench with flaccid tits and a sandpaper skin under her silks; shined up and whistling like a whore in a park; covered with stink like a railroad station pissery and swinging a dead ass in the moonlight.

I said good-by to her, and she said, "You don't look so good yourself, fella. I remember you when you had a feather in your hat and took the stairs two at a time." But there was no anger in her eyes. They were weary and kind, for I was as nice a friend as she had ever known.

Book Six

THE COMMITTEE

As a young reporter I used to hang around the Harrison Street
police station in Chicago hoping to pick up some item interesting enough for Mr. Finnegan to put on the front page of the *Journal*. Harrison Street specialized in the judgment of a crime called
Disorderly Conduct. The court clerk would bawl out, "Vi'lation
statue twenty hundert twelve, disorderly conduck. City o' Chicago
versus John Doe. Step up, everybody."

A new cluster of witnesses would rise from the worn benches, push
up to the bar of justice and start giving evidence against a new but
seldom varying culprit. Known as the Defendant, he stood to one
side with a policeman impolitely gripping his arm.

The witnesses would follow each other rapidly until the full tale
of the Defendant's disorderliness was before the court. "Your honor,
he grabbed the stove and t'rew it down the stairs!—He come at me
wit' a brick in each hand!—So then he started kickin' out the plate-
glass window."

The judge, half a-doze through such familiar testimonies, would
finally cock an eye at the rumpled and wistful man in the policeman's grip, and inquire, "All right, John Doe, what have you got to
say for yourself?"

And John Doe, stove thrower, brick wielder, window smasher, would begin nearly always with the same pensive words of rebuttal.

"Well, your honor, I was walkin' down the street, mindin' my own business, when all of a sudden—"

My sympathies as a young reporter usually went to the culprit. The witnesses against him, even the bandaged ones, seemed a smug lot. Also, there was no voice but his own to speak for him, and, alas, when he raised it, it was a faltering and unconvincing voice. Nevertheless I was inclined to feel that the culprit, denounced by everyone as an enemy of society, was somehow in the right, and could the judge but know the real tale back of all the events, he would have changed John Doe's finale—"Thirty days—next case."

It is as a Jewish John Doe under indictment as one of the helpers of the Palestinian "Terrorists," who proudly called themselves the Irgun Zvai Leumi, that I now speak up. All the other witnesses have had their say—the Jewish Zionists, Hebrew statesmen, authors and journalists and the British Empire. I offer my evidence neither as Jew nor propagandist but as an honest writer who was walking down the street one day when he bumped into history.

I had no notion on that April day in 1941 that any such collision was taking place. All that was evident was that I was buying drinks for a pair of male strangers in the Twenty One Club.

One was a tall, sunburned fellow in a sort of naval uniform. He was Captain Jeremiah Helpern, who had recently created a Hebrew Navy for the nonexisting Hebrew Republic of Palestine. The navy had consisted of a lone training ship that had run aground in the Mediterranean a few months before and been put out of service. Captain "Irma" Helpern had come to the U.S. in search of some Maecenas to buy him a new navy.

My other companion was a man in his thirties, of medium height, with a small blond mustache, an English accent and a voice inclined to squeak under excitement. He was Peter Bergson of Warsaw, London and Jerusalem.

I ordered a third round of drinks for my guests, unaware that neither had eaten that day. They kept their eyes firmly averted from the platters of fine food moving to and fro under their noses—for they were Hebrew heroes trained in self-discipline. They praised me for one of my "Thousand and One Afternoons" columns appearing daily in the scrappy newspaper, *P.M.* The column had discussed the attitudes of American Jews toward the new German anti-Semite, Hitler. I had deplored the fact that America's important social, political and literary Jews were reluctant to speak out as Jews under attack and preferred to conduct themselves as neutral Americans.

Bergson admired my point of view rather extravagantly and told me of the fine Jewish renaissance begun by a man named Vladimir Jabotinsky, of whom I had never heard. Being allied with the creator of a Jewish renaissance made me nervous, for I had no such dreams in me. But Bergson spoke the name Jabotinsky with such pride that I asked to meet him and learned he had died recently in New York.

Bergson then spoke of matters in Palestine. I told him that as a Jew I had no interest in Palestine and I felt that its problems confused the issue. In my mind the issue was the cowardly silence of America's influential Jews toward the massacre of Jews started in Europe. Both men smiled politely at my irritation with their Palestine talk, and their sudden silence on the subject impressed me as something more than good manners.

I noted that my guests were a bit mysterious about answering any direct questions I put to them such as, "Where are you living now?" or, "What are you doing in the United States?" I was impressed, also, by a pride in them, as if these two stray "fans" who had sought to meet me were somehow men of importance. They left after asking permission to call on me at my hotel. Rose was writing movies in Hollywood, and I was living at the Algonquin.

I ate my dinner alone, unaware that another Sindbad had entered my life, he of the blond mustache and somewhat squeaky voice—a Sindbad bringing greater riches than any of the diamond-mine peddlers who had preceded him.

"MY TRIBE IS CALLED ISRAEL"

MY MEETING with Peter Bergson was the result of my having turned into a Jew in 1939. I had before then been only related to Jews. In that year I became a Jew and looked on the world with Jewish eyes.

The German mass murder of the Jews, recently begun, had brought my Jewishness to the surface. I felt no grief or vicarious pain. I felt only a violence toward the German killers. I saw the Germans as murderers with red hands. Their fat necks and round, boneless faces became the visages of beasts. Their descent from humanity was as vivid in my eyes as if they had grown four legs and a snout.

I was too old to enlist in the battle in Europe. But I was not too old for anger. I went through the days holding my anger like a hot stove in my arms. There seemed nothing to do with it but carry it and suffer its heat.

The anger led me to join an organization for the first time in my life. It was called "Fight for Freedom" and was dedicated to bringing the U.S.A. into the war against the Germans. Herbert Agar, a handsome and eloquent fellow, was at its head. My work in the organization consisted of writing war propaganda speeches and a pageant called "Fun To Be Free," which MacArthur collaborated on and Billy Rose put on in Madison Square Garden. I wrote and staged other similar shows for the Red Cross and the War Bond Drive.

I was aware that I was doing all these things as a Jew. My eloquence in behalf of democracy was inspired chiefly by my Jewish anger. I had been no partisan of democracy in my earlier years. Its sins had seemed to me more prominent than its virtues. But now that it was the potential enemy of the new German Police State I was its uncarping disciple. Thus, oddly, in addition to becoming a Jew in 1939 I became also an American—and remained one.

I dreamed day and night of a German collapse but I desired something more than their military defeat as a nation. I desired their ostracism from the human family. How could the Germans, in 1940 already methodically launched on torturing and murdering millions of harmless Jews, ever be allowed to sit in the conclaves of men again? I knew, bitterly, that they would be allowed, that their crime against the Jews would be overlooked as if it had been an unfortunate bit of war strategy and not a befoulment of the human spirit.

Another bitter thought was in my head—how could the Jews whose butchery was going on before an indifferent world ever be a people of dignity again?

I knew, and wrote, that the Germans would be beaten in battle if the U.S. joined against them, and I was certain their miserable megalomania would be knocked out of them—for another few decades. But I felt there would be no victory for Jews in this. As I walked the street, a million Jewish men, women and children had been butchered and four million more were yet to be fed to the lime kilns and bonfires. Yet there was no voice of importance anywhere, Jewish or non-Jewish, protesting this foulest of history's crimes.

A people to whom I belonged, who had produced my mother, father and all the relatives I had loved, was being turned into an exterminator's quarry, and there was no outcry against the deed. No statesmen or journalists spoke out. Art was also silent. Was the Jew so despised that he could be murdered en masse without protest from onlookers, or was humanity so despicable that it could witness the German crime without moral wince?

Ten years after the massacre a bitterness still comes to me when I write of it. But I am no longer wholly bitter. I know now that the silence during the massacre was caused by many things other than I thought of then. Chief among them was the indifference to death which an era of wars had bred into the world. The American of yesterday watched American soldiers suffer and die in Korea with the same lack of emotional response he had for the massacre of Jews a decade ago. Individual life is not sacred, death is not important. The modern soul thus conditions itself for the great battles to come, the battles of H-Bombs, which Professor Einstein prophecies will number their dead in the hundreds of millions; a war which William Laurence, science reporter for *The New York Times*, prophecies will count as a casualty not nations but a planet.

These half-understandings were not in me in the years of the Jewish massacre. The silence, then, shamed me. It contained for me an anti-Semitism more sinister than the massacre. I felt the most deeply shamed by the silence of the American Jews. Around me the most potent and articulate Jews in the world kept their mouths fearfully closed.

The unassimilated Jews—the Yiddish Jews—were speaking their horror in the Jewish newspapers. In the synagogues the Jews were weeping and praying. In thousands of homes where Yiddish was spoken the German murderers and their deeds were cursed. But these were the locked-away Jews who had only the useless ear of other Jews and, possibly, of God.

The Americanized Jews who ran newspapers and movie studios, who wrote plays and novels, who were high in government and powerful in the financial, industrial and even social life of the nation were silent.

Talking of these things at home in Nyack one evening, I received an unexpected gift from Rose. She had been conferring with Ralph Ingersoll, editor of *P.M.*, and Ingersoll had agreed to take me on as a daily columnist, at seventy-five dollars a week.

I went to work at once, grateful for a forum larger than my dinner table. I wrote of the city as I had done years before on the *Daily News* in Chicago, but only part of me was a newspaperman now. I was as much Jew as reporter, and I wrote often of Jews. My column reported the incredible silence of New York's Jews in this time of massacre.

I continued the column while writing movie scripts in Hollywood. There the movie chieftains, nearly all Jews, protested that I was on the wrong track with my Jewish articles. They told me that Ambassador Joseph Kennedy, lately returned from beleaguered London, had spoken to fifty of Hollywood's leading Jewish movie makers in a secret meeting in one of their homes. He had told them sternly that they must not protest as Jews, and that they must keep their Jewish rage against the Germans out of print.

Any Jewish outcries, Kennedy explained, would impede victory over the Germans. It would make the world feel that a "Jewish War" was going on.

As a result of Kennedy's cry for silence, all of Hollywood's top Jews went around with their grief hidden like a Jewish fox under their Gentile vests. In New York, the influential Jews I met had also espoused the Kennedy hide-your-Jewish-head psychology. I argued that a moral outcry against the massacre, regardless of who raised it, would fill the Germans with doubts and fears. It would make them realize they were acting outside the human family. Such a single avaunt from the King of Denmark was to frighten off the Germans from murdering the Jews of that land.

I argued too that the sound of moral outrage over the extinction of the Jews would restore human stature to the name Jew. In the silence this stature was vanishing. We Jews in America were fast becoming the relatives of a garbage pile of Jewish dead. There would be no respect for the living Jew when there was no regret for a dead one.

I wrote in a column called "My Tribe Is Called Israel":

I write of Jews today [1941], I who never knew himself as one before, because that part of me which is Jewish is under a violent and apelike attack. My way of defending myself is to answer as a Jew. . . . My angry critics all write that they are proud of being Americans and of wearing carnations, and that they are sick to death of such efforts as mine to Judaize them and increase generally the Jew-consciousness of the world.

Good Jews with carnations, it is not I who am bringing this Jew-consciousness back into the world. It is back on all the radios of the world. I don't advise you to take off your carnations. I only suggest that you don't hide behind them too much. They conceal very little.

It was a few days after the foregoing was printed that the letter from Peter Bergson arrived. The letter contained a mysterious ferment that led me to invite for a drink, unknowingly, the political head of the not yet notorious Palestinian underground called the Irgun Zvai Leumi.

THE COMMITTEE MEETS

I LOOKED with confusion at the three men and a woman who were calling on me in my Algonquin Hotel room that day in the spring of 1941. Peter Bergson, their spokesman, had just stated he wished me to be the American leader of the great cause in which they were engaged. I had not quite understood what this cause was, beyond that it had to do with Jews and raising millions of dollars to improve their status in Palestine, but I felt sorry for my visitors and their cause, both. They could have selected no more unqualified and uninformed and un-Palestine-minded man in the entire land. Their choice of me made them seem naïve and a little overdesperate.

It was not modesty that gave me this attitude but a realistic knowledge of myself. I disliked causes. I disliked public speaking. I could bring myself neither to make orations nor listen to them. I never attended meetings of any sort. I had no interest in Palestine and had always bolted any conversation about a Jewish homeland. My heart had never turned to Jerusalem. Finally, there was nothing more socially distasteful to me than getting involved in a money-raising campaign.

My visitors listened politely as I explained my general unfitness for their project. I became aware as I spoke that I was addressing four as tenacious human beings as I had ever met. My arguments as to who and what I was only made them smile. They continued to look at me knowingly, as if I were a mystery only they understood.

I was to work intimately for seven years with these three young men. (The young woman married and vanished.) Yet I was to find out little else about them than was evident in our first meetings. I looked on my visitors then as perfect Jews, and such they remained to me until we finished our work years later. It was not that they spoke with words of courage. There was, to the contrary, small eloquence in them. Nor were they stormy with ideas.

They were contained, smiling and wary. Their eyes glinted with the mood of adventure. They were unmarked by memories of suffering. The cries of dying Jews seemed not to echo out of their spirits. Instead they sat solemn with energies, like a group of knights dedicated to the rescue of a maiden in distress. The maiden was the Jew of Europe and the Jewish soul of the world.

Although hundreds of active cohorts were to come to this group, the three men who sat in my room that day remained for me always "the Committee." Through all its guises my response was always to these three. I ignored their ramifications—and no committee ever ramified itself more. It took a dozen different forms and titles and busied itself in all corners of the earth. It howled down an empire, saved myriads of Jews and armed a revolution. Eventually four hundred thousand Americans contributed millions and their moral backing to it; and such stalwarts as Senator Guy Gillette, Senator Ed Johnson, Harry Selden, Alex Wilf, Harold Ickes, Secretary Frank Knox, Alfred Strelsin, Will Rogers, Jr., Louis Bromfield and scores of congressmen and officials carried its banners.

Through all the adventures that ensued I continued to regard the Committee as consisting only of Peter Bergson, Sam Merlin and Mike Ben Ami. The young woman who was present that day sitting straight-backed under a large black picture hat was a beauty from Jerusalem named Miriam Heyman. The Committee had brought her along hoping that a look at Jewish loveliness would add to my enthusiasm for the cause.

"THE COMMITTEE FOR A JEWISH ARMY OF STATELESS AND PALESTINIAN JEWS"

SUCH WAS the clumsy-sounding banner we first raised. Its verbiage reflected the single Jewish oddity in my otherwise worldly new comrades. They had a pedantic feeling about titles and were often to spend weeks cooking up the most cumbersome and literal of slogans.

I suggested that we might improve on "The Committee for a Jewish Army of Stateless and Palestinian Jews."

"In what way?" Peter's voice squeaked. He could discuss matters of life and death with calm, I was to learn, but any parliamentarian matter, such as what to put in a telegram, threw him into deep excitement. Titles were parliamentarian business.

"The title reveals the exact nature of our project," he answered me fiercely. "I don't see anything wrong with it. It's a fine title."

"It's unattractive," I said, "and not very inspiring."

"I don't agree," said Peter.

"Would you mind just taking the word 'committee' out of it?" I asked.

"Why?" Peter demanded. "That's what we are—a committee. Why hide the fact?"

We sat again in my Algonquin Hotel rooms where I had hidden myself to write a play. It was our third meeting. Bergson had brought with him this time only Merlin and Mike Ben Ami. Miriam Heyman and her picture hat had been sent off to Hollywood, armed with letters of introduction to all the movie moguls I knew.

Merlin was tall, dark, moody and with a curved pipestem clenched in his teeth. He was a stateless Jew, a man without family, government or passport. His home in Bessarabia had been blasted and his kin wiped out by the Germans. He had escaped being murdered and made his way to Paris to work as a journalist. He was a distant-looking man with a fine vocabulary.

Mike Ben Ami was one of the native-born Palestinians called Sabras after the cactus plant that blooms in that land. His people were well to do. He had attended the Hebrew University in Jerusalem with Bergson. Peter Bergson was then called Hillel Kook. Student Hillel had changed his name so as not to embarrass his family in Palestine by his unpopular political activities. His father was a rabbi in Jerusa-

lem and his uncle was chief rabbi of Palestine and widely regarded
as a saint.

Ben Ami was a cool, square-faced young man with steady eyes and
a fuse of temper under his quiet speech.

My three guests had come to ask me to send out a hundred letters
to important Jews in New York inviting them to join me in promot-
ing The Committee for a Jewish Army of . . . , etc. I asked for
more information to put in the letters. My guests told me there were
two hundred thousand young Jews in Egypt, Syria and Palestine
eager to fight the Germans. The Committee had lists of their names,
which they were prepared to hand over to General Wavell, in command of the African Campaign. I sipped a highball and took notes.
I was leaving in a week for Hollywood, where Rose and Miriam
were plotting to stage a mass meeting of the movie industry's leading
Jews. They had decided that I was to address them. I asked questions
and made notes of the answers, hoping to be able to talk convincingly
to my old Hollywood friends.

"Imagine," said Peter, "the kind of soldiers these Jews will make
against the Germans! They will be like a suicide army. Given guns to
fight Germans with, there is not a young Jew in the Middle East who
would not gladly die on a battlefield. And the fine thing is, these
two hundred thousand don't have to be shipped across oceans to
join the battle. Most of them are in the Near East, only a bus ride
from the front. And they don't need military training. They've already been trained in Germany, Egypt, Russia and Palestine. Do
you realize that an army with such a spirit can actually change the
course of the war in Africa? They can win it!"

I was impressed. I was also confused to learn that the British did not
want such an heroic army helping them in the field. Their not wanting the Jews was no sensitive delusion of Peter's. I learned for the first
time of official and open anti-Semitic laws instituted by the British
in their guardianship of Palestine. One such law was called the Law
of Parity. It stipulated that only one Jew might enlist for every Arab
who volunteered for His Majesty's Army. Since no Arabs were volun-
teering, Jews could virtually not get in.

But what made the tribal mind of Peter Bergson boil over was
yet another matter. Those Jews who had been accepted and been put
by the British into the front lines of Tobruk must fight under the
Union Jack without any private insignia identifying them as Jews.

"The Aussies," he expounded squeakily, "wear turned-up hats, the Canadians have their special regimental insignia. But we are forbidden to wear the Star of David on our sleeves."

I was unaware that the Star of David was a current matter anywhere (or that there existed anywhere any such passion for people to identify themselves as Jews). I knew it only as a Biblical symbol surviving in our time in the *décor* of synagogues and on the trunks of sentimental Jewish pugilists. I had had small reaction to it usually when seeing it in the ring—except one night. I was much pleased to see it on Maxie Baer's pants leg the night he knocked out the German Max Schmeling, and kept the world championship.

My lack of response to the proscribing of the Star of David brought a frown into the faces of Merlin and Ben Ami. I felt that I had come down a little in their esteem. Bergson did not frown. He continued to look at me with the bright and friendly air of a man devoted to controversy.

"I'm not interested in the religious symbols of the Jews," I said.

"There is nothing religious about the Star of David," said Peter. "It is a national symbol, as the eagle is for the U.S.A."

"I've never thought of the Jews as a nation," I said. "And I don't see much sense in mooning about David and Solomon as if they were current monarchs."

"You haven't given the present situation in Palestine much thought, I can see," said Peter.

"Very little," I said.

"I would like to tell you about it," said Peter, "because it is part of the structure of the world Jewish situation. Without Palestine as an independent Hebrew state, the Jews of the world must lose everything they have."

I failed to see the logic of this but remained silent. I had heard similar statements from the speaker's rostrum of the Irish Fellowship Club in Chicago whose luncheons I used to cover—"Without Ireland free, the Irish of the world are doomed."

"At present the situation in Palestine is one of the great crimes of our civilization," Peter continued. "The Jews in Palestine have less political, human or economic rights than Jews anywhere in the world."

"Except in Germany," I said, thinking my friend completely overboard in his briefing of me.

"No," said Peter. "I include Germany—before the pogroms started. The Jews of Germany could own property. Jews in Palestine today are not allowed to own more than two per cent of the tiny strip of Palestine in which they are permitted to live. Also, Jews may be seized on the streets or in their homes, imprisoned, or exiled to concentration camps in Africa without benefit of trial or without even being charged. That is the British law."

"I'm surprised to hear the British are so unfair," I said. "But I guess everybody is always unfair to colonies."

Peter let this reference to "colonies" go by.

"It's not the fault of the British entirely," said Peter. "The Jews have accepted British rule with hardly any protest. Not only that, they bitterly discourage any protest against it."

I said I imagined this was because the Jews did not want to expose themselves to certain defeat, but they must, obviously, resent such laws in their hearts.

"No," said Peter firmly. "They do not. The strongest moral law in existence in Palestine today is 'Look up to the British as superiors.'"

"Well, anyone who looks up to a superior, has got a superior," I said. "Tell me what other peculiar rules the superior British have laid down."

"Hundreds," said Ben Ami.

"For instance," said Peter, cheerfully, "there is a law that says if a Jew is caught carrying arms he is punishable by death or life imprisonment in chains."

I asked if that was to keep Jews from shooting Englishmen.

"That is not the case," said Peter. "It is to prevent them from defending themselves against the Arabs. The law was made during the Arab raids on Jewish settlements."

Ben Ami added quietly, "There is a law also that punishes an Arab for carrying a gun. The penalty in this case is five shillings."

"What's the attitude of the Jews toward the English disarming them?" I asked.

"Their attitude? They approve," said Peter. "They have adopted it as the official Zionist policy of nonresistance."

"The policy is called Havlaga," said Ben Ami. "It is considered a morally superior policy. The Zionists have also pledged themselves to turn over to the British authorities any Jew who does carry a gun."

I found myself too irritated with the Jews of Palestine to ask any further questions about them. I talked, instead, of the British.

"I didn't know the British were so openly on the side of the Arabs," I said. "I suppose it's because the Arabs are potentially a big military help to them."

"To the contrary," Peter answered. "The Arabs have always been, and still are, enemies of the British. You understand, ninety-five per cent of the Arabs are not Palestinians at all. They are from Syria, Morocco, Iran, and so forth. Their leaders, Raschid Gailani Bey of Iraq, Achmed-Abdulla of Trans-Jordan and Fawzi el Kawkji of Egypt, are all high Nazis. The fugitive ex-Mufti of Jerusalem, Amin el Huseini, is hiding with Hitler and has called on his tribes to revolt against Britain. These Arabs from abroad are in Palestine now only for pay, and they are wild beasts and they not only kill but they mutilate and rape their victims. All these incidents are paid for by the British."

I doubted this statement and said so. Merlin and Ben Ami smiled.

"It is quite true," said Merlin. "Not even the Zionists deny it."

"Even the Arab urchins in the streets know it," said Ben Ami. "In the first Arab attacks, which the British said, regrettably, they could not stop, the children yelled 'The British Government is behind us. Kill the Jews.'"

I found Peter Bergson's version of the British disturbing, chiefly because of my admiration of British valor and Churchill's rhetoric. A handful of English and a handful of words were holding the line for humanity in London.

I had no facts with which to counter what Bergson and his friends told me—but one. These British activities in Palestine were possibly out of the same political basket as British activities in India and Ireland. They were the Colonial Office side of Great Britain, a nation inclined to be Dr. Jekyll at home and a fang-flashing Mr. Hyde abroad. I found myself still more admiring of one than critical of the other.

"The British," Peter went on calmly, "have been trying desperately to revive the Arabs as a nation, with the hope that the Arabs would be able to seize all Palestine. The reason is very simple. It will be easier for Britain to hold and rule a backward Arab state than a thriving Hebrew homeland. A Hebrew homeland might ask for independence and even fight for it—as did the Irish. An Arab state would be satisfied to remain a dependent British parasite."

"The British don't seem to have had much luck so far," I said. "From what I've read, the Jews seem quite able to cope with the Arabs."

"The Jews," said Peter, "could run the Arabs out of Palestine in a week if they wished to."

"Absolutely true," said Ben Ami.

"But they don't wish to," said Peter. "The Jews have promised the British not to disturb the peace by hitting back at any Arab attacks."

"But I've read of them hitting back and winning," I insisted. Peter smiled.

"That was us," he said. "The men and women of the Irgun."

"How many are there in the Irgun?" I asked.

"Four hundred," said Ben Ami.

"That is a slight exaggeration," said Peter. "Let us say in the neighborhood of three or four hundred."

"And these three hundred carry guns?" I asked.

"They do," said Peter. "The Irgun policy is we kill two Arabs for every Jew who is murdered. This policy was declared in 1937."

"Since we began," said Merlin, "the Zionists have been of great help to the British in informing against us. They were able to accomplish the arrest of our leader, David Raziel, by revealing his hiding place to the British authorities."

"However, ten per cent of the population is on our side," said Ben Ami.

"Let's say five per cent," said Peter. "You will have a correct picture of Palestine today if you conceive of ninety-five per cent of the population, including all the Zionist officials in Palestine and the outside world, as being eager to believe the British are their friends, and being eager to obey and respect them. And also eager to inform against us and help put us all in prison."

I frowned again at this news. I found the information about Jews and British increasingly uncomfortable. I called down for more drinks.

"I used to think the Irish were confusing," I said, "when my Sinn Fein friends in Chicago used to try to set me right on what was going on. But you Palestinians are worse than the Irish as confusionists. I guess you've had a longer time to get confused—two thousand years, isn't it, since there was a Jewish state?"

"Excuse me, Mr. Ben Hecht," said Merlin. "Since the imperishable **stand** of Bar Kochba it is a little more. But you are nearly exactly right. Since Pompey took Jerusalem from the last of the Maccabees, it is exactly two thousand and three years."

"It is very simple," said Peter, "and not confusing. At one time, the British behaved excellently to the Jews. After the Gallipoli campaign, when England was beginning to run short of man power, they were willing to listen to Vladimir Jabotinsky and permitted the formation of the Jewish Legion, July 27, 1917. They even promised, if the Jews distinguished themselves, their battalions would be given the name 'The Judeans,' instead of Royal Fusiliers, and would be entitled to wear the Menorah as their badge, and have the word Kadima— forward—as their motto.

"Then, a hundred days later, November 2, 1917, they published the Balfour declaration. Don't forget—the Zion Mule Corps had already been fighting at Gallipoli."

"How did they fight?" I asked nervously.

"Nobly," said Merlin. "The Commander-in-Chief mentioned in his dispatches that they were the bravest of the brave."

Ben Ami the Sabra said: "Among them were Captain Trumpeldor, Lieutenant Gorodetsky, Sergeant Rosenberg, and Corporal Groshowsky. You must have read about them."

"I've forgotten," I said.

"The nobility of the Jew is easily forgotten," Merlin said.

"I take it things didn't go so well with the Legion—since they didn't earn their insignia . . . ?" I inquired.

"The Jewish battalions," Merlin said, "had the opportunity to be cast into the final and most ferocious combats on the Palestine front. Lieutenant Colonel Patterson of the Dublin Fusiliers was in charge of them. You will meet him. He is one of us. Under his illustrious leadership, when the word Kadima was given, they drove the Turks before them and took all the important fords over the Jordan River. They conquered Amman, also Es Salt was crushed under Jewish arms.

"Then, on September fifteenth, the Jews were assigned to be annihilated by the Turkish attack in the east, and thus to permit the British advance to the sea. They failed to be annihilated. In three days the Turkish spine was broken, eighty thousand prisoners were taken, ten thousand more surrendered voluntarily. October thirty-first, Turkey surrendered."

"I hope the British proved grateful," I said.

"They were extremely grateful. An order was issued publicly citing every member of the Jewish battalions for valor, and at the same time giving the Jews a chance to be degraded to labor battalions. It made Colonel Patterson extremely indignant, and naturally no one of them volunteered for the labor battalions, which you understand, is a somewhat safer duty."

"The British lost their love for the Jewish Legion rather quickly, I take it."

"It was the end of a certain enthusiasm," Merlin admitted. "The Jews made several small mistakes. For instance they carried off every one of the seven gold medals for prize fighting offered by the British Expeditionary Force. This made for some very poor feeling in Cairo."

"Officially," said Peter, "the attitude of approval continued. The British opened all our ports to the Jews of the world and invited them to immigrate to Palestine. They also, like fine fellows, appointed three of the leading Jews of England to act as administrators of Palestine. The High Commissioner was Sir Herbert Samuel, later a member of the House of Lords."

I was pleased to hear this good news at last about the British.

"The first thing that Sir Herbert Samuel did," said Peter, "was to pardon an Arab who was serving a fifteen-year sentence for murder, the same ex-Mufti who is now hiding with Hitler. This Arab was the most notorious of the anti-Semitic minority among the Arabs. He was a rabid enemy of all Jews. Sir Herbert pardoned him and appointed him Grand Mufti of Jerusalem. And the first thing the Grand Mufti did was organize attacks on Jewish settlements—and devote himself to robbing and killing Jews."

I told my guests they need tell me no more about Sir Herbert Samuel. He was one ingredient in the Palestine situation I knew well enough. Samuel's espousal of anti-Semitism was one of the ways that Jews of small soul and large social bounderism lifted themselves out of Jewry in their own foolish minds. I had met this anti-Jewishness of the Jew often in New York and had written of it as "hiding in the scabbard of one's enemy." I was to meet it still more often after I joined the Committee. The most startling voicing of it was from the movie producer, lately become Sir Alexander Korda of London. Sir Alex, a witty, amiable, if not too talented, movie maker invited Rose and me to dinner in New York. When the talk reached the topic of Jewish troubles then beginning to brew in Palestine, Sir Alexander Korda, born a Jew in Hungary, declared in a Jewish-Hungarian accent, "If the Jews make any trouble for the English in Palestine, we will annihilate them!" At this point Rose and I left.

"Please understand," said Peter. "Sir Herbert Samuel is still very popular in Palestine. He was a great friend of the leader, Dr. Weizmann, and after he resigned from his office, the Zionists named one of their best squares in Tel Aviv after him. It is still there—called 'Herbert Samuel Square.'"

"Let's skip Sir Herbert and his squares," I said, "and tell me how it happens that the Jews are still a minority in Palestine. There were twenty years, it seems, when millions could have gone there if they'd wanted to. I don't see the sense of trying to turn Palestine into a Jewish homeland when the Jews don't seem to care about going to it."

"They did care very much," said Peter, "but they were stopped by the Zionists."

"What!" I cried. "I thought it was the Zionists who were colonizing Palestine. I have a brother-in-law who is always contributing money to the Zionists with which, he tells me, they buy land for Jewish settlers in Palestine."

"Yes," said Peter, "the Zionists have invested millions of dollars into building up a Jewish home there. But they have also done their best to keep immigrants out. During the twenty years when the ports of Palestine were open, the Zionist leaders went up and down Europe pleading with its Jews to stay in their European homes. In 1937, a few years before the Germans started exterminating the Jews, Dr. Chaim Weizmann made a speech to the Jews of Europe. It was printed in the Fall Number of *New Judea*, the official British publication. Would you like to hear it?" I said yes. "Merlin carries a copy of it. Read it, will you please."

Merlin read from a newspaper clipping. "Dr. Chaim Weizmann declared today while on a visit to Poland that Palestine was no solution for the Jewish problem of Europe. 'Palestine cannot absorb the Jews of Europe,' said Dr. Weizmann. 'We want only the best of Jewish youth to come to us. We want only people of education to enter Palestine for the purpose of increasing its culture. The other Jews will have to stay where they are and face whatever fate awaits them. These millions of Jews are dust on the wheels of history and may have to be blown away. We don't want them pouring into Palestine. We don't want our Tel Aviv to become another low-grade ghetto.

I asked what Dr. Weizmann's position was. My guests were pleased by my ignorance.

"Dr. Chaim Weizmann," said Merlin, "is the President of the Zionist Organization of the World. He is, so to speak, the King of the Jews."

"He doesn't quite sound like Saul or David," I said.

"We have men who do," said Merlin.

"Jabotinsky answered Weizmann in 1937 with a terrible prophecy," said Peter. "He told the Jews of Europe that they were all sitting on a powder keg. He said that if the Jews did not leave Germany, Poland and eastern Europe, they would be exterminated by the Germans in the worst massacre of history."

"Pardon me," said Merlin, "but Mr. Ben Hecht made the same prophecy in his *Book of Miracles*. We were astonished by it. Now that I realize you were unaware of Jabotinsky's struggle against Zionism, I am even more astonished."

"Why didn't the Jews of Europe listen to Jabotinsky?" I asked.

"Because the majority of Jews, like the majority of all other people," said Merlin, "venerate respectability more than genius, more than courage, more than anything else. Unfortunately, you might say Dr. Chaim Weizmann is the most respectable Jew in the world. He is immensely rich, he is a scientist, he is treated almost as a social equal by British statesmen. He is invited to tea in the finest English and American homes. The respect which the Jews of the world feel for him is only equaled by the harm he has done them. Even the Jews of Poland who are now being exterminated still respect the man who persuaded them to stay in their homes and be killed—instead of going to Palestine to live."

"In 1939," said Bergson, "Dr. Weizmann was able to end his work of keeping the undesirable Jewish masses out of Palestine. The British took over the job. They reversed all their former attitudes and issued the White Paper, closing the ports of Palestine to Jewish immigration."

"Francis Hackett used to tell me in Chicago, when discussing Irish independence, that the British always had the Long View," I said. "And that the Irish were unable to cope with them because they operated in different generations. They seem to have had their Long View toward Palestine."

My Palestine friends asked what I meant.

"It seems obvious from what you tell me," I said, "that the British used the traitor Weizmann to keep Palestine free of Jews until they found the time right for closing the ports themselves."

My friends shook their heads nervously.

"We do not think that Weizmann was aware of any such plot," said Bergson.

"Why not?" I asked.

"The Zionists and their leaders are not traitors," said Merlin. "They are merely respectable people who are afraid of offending anybody— even their enemies."

"I don't see much difference between traitors and cowards," I said.

"Besides," Bergson smiled, "the British are not exactly our enemies. They are pursuing a political policy which insists that Palestine remain a British possession of one sort or another. And a large percentage of the Zionists are of the same mind."

"I have no yearning to see Palestine a Jewish state," I said. "If I had, I'd be considerably depressed. Altogether it's a rather dismal picture you fellows draw. The only reasonable party seems to be the British. They seem to have capitalized cleverly on the spinelessness and respectability of the Zionists. Having proved now for twenty years that the Jews don't care very much about having a homeland, the British will be able to step in and politely take Palestine for themselves."

"They will never steal Palestine from the Jews," said Ben Ami.

"I don't see why you call it stealing," I said. "If ninety-five per cent of the Jews in Palestine are as frightened and dim-witted as you describe, why should the British present them with an independent Hebrew state? Obviously the Jews are not worthy of having a nation."

"The Irgun Zvai Leumi is ready to fight for the freedom of Palestine on both sides of the Jordan," said Peter.

"All three hundred of them," I grinned.

"There were only fifty men who cried out for the independence of Greece," said Merlin, "and won it."

"Let's forget about the liberation of Palestine," I said. "It's too involved for my understanding."

"It is not involved." Peter's voice went into a squeak. "It is very simple. To date the Jews of Palestine have tried two methods for gaining freedom. They have tried to buy it as if it were a bagel. And they have tried to make the British love them so much as to give them Palestine as a keepsake. There is a third method—revolution."

"I'm not interested in foreign revolutions," I said.

"May I ask, Mr. Ben Hecht," inquired Merlin, "if you are opposed to the liberation of Palestine?"

"I have no interest in it one way or another," I said. "I'm interested only in the status of the Jew."

"Exactly," said Merlin. There was a pause. "Was I correct in observing a short while ago that you did not recognize the great name of David Raziel when we mentioned it? He was our leader in the war of retaliation against the Arabs. I would like you to be informed about him. David Raziel and Peter Bergson were like brothers."

Peter said, "I will get you Pierre van Paassen's book about Palestine. It contains the story of Raziel's death."

I said I preferred to hear the story first hand.

"Raziel was in prison in Jerusalem," said Peter. "He had been informed on by the Zionists and convicted of carrying arms. After his second attempt to escape, he was put in chains. A military situation arose while Raziel sat in chains. The most important oil wells in Iraq were in German hands. They were guarded by a crew of German engineers pledged to blow them up rather than let them fall into the hands of the British. General Wavell was aware that among us were many boys who were trained guerrilla fighters, who spoke Arabic and could pass as Arabs. He also understood that he could trust Jews to fight Germans. Raziel, in chains, was brought to see General Wavell and, naturally, he agreed to lead the suicide mission into Iraq. Twenty-five Irgun boys went with him. They took the Germans by surprise, killed all of the fifty engineers. And the British army was able to move in without losing a single oil well. Raziel and eighteen of his men were killed."

Peter smiled into his drink.

"We are very proud to tell you about our brother David Raziel," Peter said.

"It's curious that this story never got into the news," I said.

"It was not published," said Ben Ami, "not even in Palestine."

"The British suppressed it?" I asked.

"Yes," said Peter. "They buried David Raziel under a stone with a false name on it."

I asked why that was.

"It is part of the British campaign to dishonor the Jew and make him seem in no way worthy of having a country," said Peter.

I changed the subject.

"How big is the Irgun in the U.S.?" I asked.

"We are seven all told," said Peter.

"Who is in charge?" I asked.

"I am," said Peter.

I asked if they had any funds.

"No," said Peter. "We have not yet been able to achieve our personal budget of five hundred dollars a month—for our food and lodging."

"How do you manage?" I asked.

"Merlin and I have a room together," said Peter, "and we do our own cooking."

"Have you an office?" I asked.

"No," said Merlin. "When we wish to give out a statement we invite the press to the lobby of the Hotel Astor. We have had several very successful press conferences there."

A cause without nickels, without cohorts, or a roof over its head, and with an army that numbered six men and a pretty girl! I found myself, nevertheless, eager to belong to it. The talk of the three Palestinians had confused me somewhat. But I was pleased by the personalities of the three men. The fact that they were possibly Mad Hatters was less important to me than that they were Jews of gallantry and good health. They were also Jews who told neither Jewish lies nor anti-Jewish lies. Their sense of reality was as deep as their idealism. And their idealism was devoid of the communistic escape dreams that usually distinguished Jewish idealism. I found even their gloomy pronouncements invigorating, for they were made without fear.

"It's all pretty mixed up," I said. "But the most confusing thing is the British attitude to this Jewish army you want to raise. I can't see why the British should be so pigheaded as to object to being helped by two hundred thousand David Raziels in Africa."

Instead of answering, Peter asked me if I were willing to help bring such an army into existence. When I said I was, he went on quickly. "What we must do is stir up American excitement for such a Jewish army. We will make a campaign first in the press. Then we go to Washington and get a number of senators and congressmen to make speeches in both Houses. After that we tackle the War Department. It will have to do what Congress wishes. And if the War Department acts—the British will have no choice. They must put a Jewish army into the field."

Suddenly the secret of the unaccountable pigheadedness of the British became clear to me.

"I've just thought of why the British are against a Jewish army," I said. I waited for one of my guests to open up and explain the British attitude, now that it had become obvious to me. But they were not lads to give a secret away, even to a friend.

"You've skipped the most significant thing about this Jewish army," I said.

Peter joined the rootless one and the cactus plant in their silence.

"If you get a Jewish army organized," I went on, "you'll have a big military force with which to fight the Arabs, after the war is over. And, who knows, maybe the British, too. Obviously, that's the reason the British are opposed to putting such an ally in the field today. It might mean their losing Palestine tomorrow."

"You have said the truth, Mr. Ben Hecht," said Merlin.

"I'll work with you," I said at the end of this meeting, "if you'll leave Palestinian politics out of the picture. I'd like to help do something to bring respect back to the name of Jew. I think the Jewish army a fine idea—from that point of view. An army of David Raziels fighting Germans under a Jewish flag is something that would thrill all the Jews of the world.

"We'll have to be careful about two things," I added. "We must make it very plain that this Jewish army is not for American Jews."

"Our title explains that," said Peter.

"Titles confuse people," I said. "Secondly, we mustn't let any of your hop-headed Palestinian nationalism creep into our propaganda. That would frighten off large sections of important Jews who don't care to get involved in a Palestine—anti-British row."

"You are completely right," Peter smiled. "One thing at a time. First step—a Jewish army in Africa. Then—next step—the opening of the ports of Palestine and moving in the Jewish refugees from the massacre. Then—third step—Palestine and the liberation."

It was thus that I became cochairman for the Committee for a Jewish Army of Stateless and Palestinian Jews, to be followed by other chairmanships in long-titled committees. My objective in all of them remained the same—to help make a little more impressive the older and simpler title—Jew.

A NEW PLOT FOR HOLLYWOOD

I FELT DUBIOUS about launching the Jewish Army Cause in Hollywood, and by the time I got there early in 1942 I wanted to bolt the whole business. I felt out of character as a man with a cause, and I kept brooding on a thing Mencken had once said to me: "The leader of every cause is a scoundrel." He had meant leaders who use causes to hoist themselves into riches and who wrest medals and honors out of the slick championing of human travail. I was rather certain, and it turned out correctly so, that no personal good would come to me out of my new chairmanship. Nevertheless, Mencken's nasty statement made me cock a wary eye at this new self who had come to Hollywood, a Leader of a Cause.

The sight of my first group of disciples crowded into a rented Hollywood parlor warned me that there would be no wriggling out of the situation—at least for some time. It would take a sturdier spirit than mine to resist the curious blackmail I felt in their hopeful, admiring faces.

I determined, however, that I would resist all the things happening to me that I disliked when they happened to others. I would never stand up in public and accept inscribed plaques. I would never go around making speeches. (In the eight years of propaganda work that followed, I broke this fine, anti-oratory credo only three times.) I would never parade myself socially as a leader, I would avoid taking bows and, finally, looking at my eager cohorts, I made inward oath that I would dodge all banquet hall applause.

I learned that Rose and Miriam Heyman had been busy working to prepare a mass meeting for the cause. They had, with fine cunning, wangled the use of Twentieth Century-Fox's commissary as a site for the first Jewish Army Rally. Now that I had arrived, they were ready to send out a thousand telegram invitations over my name, for which I paid. I told them that my name on a telegram would fetch too small a number to our barricades and that we needed two or three other cosponsors of prominence.

At this point Peter Bergson arrived, having mysteriously raised the fare to Hollywood. He pointed out that I knew the twenty most important Jews in the movie industry and that in a few days I could win most of them over to our Cause. I listened glumly, for I knew these Jewish moguls better than Peter. Nevertheless, to keep our mass meeting from ending up as a fiasco, I went after them as a cause-salesman with small hope of making any sale.

Hollywood's Jews, like rich and important Jews everywhere, are easy marks for Jewish philanthropies. They seldom turn a frock-coated panhandler from their door. They are as eager to support Jewish orphanages, hospitals and other charity projects as the projects are eager to be supported. This eagerness (on the part of my rich landsmen) is the product of a guilt that blooms in the soul of the immigrant Jew who turns into an American nabob.

This ex-steerage passenger who achieves fortune in the U.S. is bothered by a sense of renegadeism. He finds it convenient to forget his Jewishness in the high-class world into which he has vaulted. He is thus eager to prove his Jewishness secretly by donations to Jews in distress. He will support a synagogue with large gifts for thirty years without ever entering it. The nearest he comes to this secret Judaism to which he stubbornly lays claim is observing a few religious principles, such as not going to the races on Jewish holidays, or arranging for a rabbi to officiate (in English) at his funeral.

My twenty Jewish moguls were men much of this sort. Though they seldom turned down a chance to help Jews in trouble, I knew there was small likelihood of their helping Jews make trouble. It turned out there was none. Their answers were quick and loud. Jews fighting as Jews! Was I crazy? If Jews wanted to fight, let them fight as Englishmen or Americans—or Chinese.

I pointed out that they couldn't. The Americans weren't fighting. And I explained to them as best I could the puzzle that even General Wavell couldn't grasp: Why the tens of thousands of young Jews who volunteered to fight in Britain's cause were not being armed, when the enemy was at the gates of Palestine.

My revelations only increased the anger of my prospective converts. What did I want Hollywood's leading Jews to do—criticize England? Did I want the studio chiefs (with a glittering eye always out for the British market) to mix in and tell a great nation like England what it should do in a war? Did I not realize what would happen if Jews began to make trouble for the British? The whole world would get disgusted with Jews, and they would be hated worse than ever. A Jew, each explained in his own way, could do anything he wanted to as an American, but as a Jew he must be very careful of angering people and very careful not to assert himself in any unpopular way. As Americans they could boast and swagger, apparently, but as Jews they must be as invisible as possible.

After a week of darting around I had garnered no important Jewish name for the sponsorship of our mass meeting. My twenty moguls were men loud with ego, but the Jew in them was a cringing fellow almost as frightened of the world as the Jew in a German-policed ghetto. They could not visualize Jews as heroes—only as victims.

I consulted with Ernst Lubitsch, the lone Big Name Rose and Miriam had won to our Cause before my arrival. He was surprised to hear I had not called on David Selznick in my sad efforts to flush a cosponsor. I explained why. I was fonder of David than of the other bosses I had tackled, and I feared finding the Jew in him cringing behind his Hollywood greatness.

I called on David the next day and was happy to find there was no cringing stowaway in my friend. Nevertheless, he was full of arguments. They were not the arguments of a Jew, but of a non-Jew.

"I don't want anything to do with your cause," said David, "for the simple reason that it's a Jewish political cause. And I am not interested in Jewish political problems. I'm an American and not a Jew. I'm interested in this war as an American. It would be silly of me to pretend suddenly that I'm a Jew, with some sort of full-blown Jewish psychology."

"If I can prove you are a Jew, David," I said, "will you sign the telegram as cosponsor with me?"

"How are you going to prove it?" he asked.

"I'll call up any three people you name," I said, "and ask them the following question— What would you call David O. Selznick, an American or a Jew? If any of the three answers that he'd call you an American, you win. Otherwise, you sign the telegram."

David agreed to the test and picked out three names. I called them with David eavesdropping on an extension.

Martin Quigley, publisher of the *Motion Picture Exhibitors' Herald*, answered my question promptly.

"I'd say David Selznick was a Jew," he said.

Nunnally Johnson hemmed a few moments but finally offered the same reply. Leland Hayward answered, "For God's sake, what's the matter with David? He's a Jew and he knows it."

David, honorably, admitted defeat. Apparently in everybody's eyes but his own he was a Jew. His name went on the telegram.

A BRITISH HERO

THE NIGHT WAS BALMY. The Beverly Hills streets were as deserted as the interior of a bank after hours. The mansions and haciendas of the movie makers with their billiard table top lawns and their walled gardens loomed forlornly in the night as if waiting to be occupied.

I looked at Peter Bergson beside me in the car and felt a little weak-minded. Somehow against all my instincts he had manipulated me into some sort of world-bedeviling enterprise. In an hour I would make my debut before a thousand movie folk as a Jewish propagandist.

In recalling that night, which was to alter my life as completely as if I had changed my name and gone to another land, my memory plays me a trick. It is no new trick, for it is the way I usually remember things. I remember more of the night than of the events in it. The look of the star-filled sky comes back to me, the feel of the warm breeze, the smells of jasmine and orange and the great dark glowing silence of the spaces around me. Riding in the night to make my speech about David Raziel, whom I called a Champion in Chains, I knew nothing of where I was heading. The burn of insult in my belly alone seemed to be guiding me. When I breathed, I could feel this burn, and the words in my head became hot.

Beside me, Peter talked, explaining his idea of diplomacy, or possibly of lobbying. I was to hear this theory of his often. He called it his theory of a hundred guns. It meant that he would gather cohorts wherever he might find them and shoot in all directions, so that when the day of victory came, no one, not even he, would know which gun had fired the decisive bullet. He had been busy of late making friends in Washington, and, among other senators and congressmen, had bagged Senator Claude Pepper of Florida by sharing his hobby of dropping into movie theaters of an evening.

We were on our way now to pick up this important solon, for Peter
had somehow induced him to come to Hollywood to address its leading Jews at our meeting.

Peter and I waited in the foyer of the Lakeview Country Club for
the senator to finish his dinner. We were unable to join our champion
at his table due to the Club's strict rule against letting Jews into
its dining room. We spared the senator this information as we escorted him, happily wined and dined, to our Jewish rally.

The large commissary was crowded and festive with bunting. In
front of me were the famous and familiar faces of Hollywood with
an odd expectancy in them. They were not waiting for a horse to
come in, or a gross to pile up or a press notice to appear, yet there was
an eagerness in their eyes, and behind it a furtiveness. I was aware
that they had come to our meeting expecting the thing for which
they dared not ask outright—outlet for the injury in their Jewish
souls. The Jewish massacre story had started coming out of Europe,
and the bellies of Jews everywhere felt the burn of outrage. Even
those who had yelled me down in their offices, including Harry War-
ner, who had threatened me with the police, were here, as was Charles
Chaplin, who had never before attended any "Jewish affair" lest he
give credence to the persistent tale that he was a Jew.

The tricky memory I have owned to excludes almost the whole of
Senator Pepper's speech. It may be that he and Peter had a comradely
fondness for the movies. They did not share any similar passion for
the Jews. I remember the beauty of Senator Pepper's voice, and little
of any good to our cause.

I watched our audience from the speaker's table while Senator
Pepper's fine voice paid homage to the culture and virtues of the
Jews. Some of them were carried away by the flattery of his saying
anything at all. But many stared with a question in their eyes. Were
these foggy words all that we had to offer them when our invitation
had sounded a bugle call of a Jewish army rising out of heaven knows
where?

Our next speaker was Col. John H. Patterson, D.S.O., of the British Army—he who had commanded the Jewish Legion under Allenby
when they crossed the Red Sea and took Palestine. Our audience,
unaware of this bedeviling fact, broke into loud applause, and even
some revolutionary yelling. England was our hero this night, and an
English colonel with decorations in his lapel was a man for cheering.

Besides, never was there a finer-looking old man than this tall straight colonel of beautiful visage. In his youth he had been a famous lion-hunter and bridge-builder in the Uganda, and his book, *Man-Eaters of Tsavo*, was said to be the lion-hunters' bible. This, too, our audience did not know, except perhaps to be moved, experts that they were, by the fine swagger of his bearing.

Our colonel took off at once on what had veered him into our cause in his middle years—a precise and documented account of British mistreatment of Jabotinsky's Jewish Legion.

Here was a fine kettle of fish! He spoke, not of the bravery of the British, but of heroic Jews, of Trumpeldor—"The bravest man I have ever seen"—and of instance after instance of British foul play and anti-Semitism against his beloved Jews. The story Merlin had told me, of the British attempt to degrade the entire legion, after citing it for valor, to a labor battalion—broke about our audience's unsuspecting heads. Catcalls rang out, and cries for our speaker to be seated.

Our speaker did no such thing. He went on. From his personal experiences with British anti-Semitism, he moved to the British betrayal of their promise to the Jews to prepare Palestine for their homeland. They were, said he, doing nothing of the sort. But instead, under the ancient pretext of policing the land, they were preparing the soil to "protect" it by taking it over.

And now people began stalking out of the place. Leading the noisy exodus was a London Jew who had left his beloved (and beleaguered) homeland to direct pictures in Hollywood for the duration. (I spent two hours the next day answering questions from a pair of F.B.I. investigators to whom he had denounced me. He, and several other Jewish lovers of Britain, had also denounced Colonel Patterson and demanded his arrest as a Nazi agent. The colonel was not arrested but permitted to expire, unsung, in his La Jolla home a few years later.)

Good Colonel John H. Patterson, friend of truth, friend of the Jews, and brave in the face of people as he had been in the face of the eight lions whose skins hung in his La Jolla home—an even rarer bravery. Never was an honorable voice more lost in a wilderness than his. But this lion-hunter, expert in bravery, and commander of historic battles, had never employed worse tactics than in his battle of the Twentieth Century-Fox Commissary. It was not the time to introduce the truth about the British and the Jews into our campaign to

put a Jewish army in the field against the Nazis. Time would uncover
the British as an enemy. As for tonight, all that was uncovered was
the enmity of Jews—to Jews.

Our audience of big shots whom we had assembled with such difficulty in the hope of their helping us to arm our champions, the
young Stateless and Palestinian Jews who wanted to fight, had not
only been outraged. Worse, they had been a little bored by the tale
of British skulduggery in a distant desert for which they were in no
mood. It was as if we had asked them to listen to the plot of an old
silent movie starring Lewis Stone.

Burgess Meredith spoke in favor of the Jewish army, and then Peter
Bergson, and Miriam Heyman, and I.

Out of the oratorical free-for-all that started up in the audience
after I had done talking, the voice of Hedda Hopper, the movie
columnist, sounded.

"We're here to contribute to a cause," Miss Hopper said firmly. "I'll
start the contributions with a check for three hundred dollars."

Whereupon, despite the shock of Colonel Patterson's speech, and
the confused objectives offered by Pepper, Bergson and myself, a wave
of largess swept our audience. One after another, its members cried
out their contributions, ranging from a hundred dollars to five thousand dollars. I was chagrined to note that among the five-thousand-
dollar donors were Gregory Ratoff, Sam Spiegel and a few others
whose solvency at that time could be said to be in question.

At the end of an hour, a hundred and thirty thousand dollars had
been pledged to our cause. Of this sum we managed, after two weeks
of grim fieldwork, to collect nine thousand dollars. A great part of
this money was from my friends.

Thus our first Jewish propaganda meeting was a fine success—if you
care to overlook its failure. Money had been raised and partisans won.
Whatever confusions had fetched these partisans, the Committee now
had funds for an American office, a letterhead and a mimeographing
machine.

Once more the night, the sky and the earth welcomed Peter and
myself. This time we were on foot. As we walked in the calming
darkness, we felt far apart. Peter's cause, and the cause I believed I
was serving—the single word Jew—seemed widely separate.

They were. Of the many thoughts that must have been in his head
—the similarity of our experience to a thousand such incidents in the

lives of Herzl and Jabotinsky, he said nothing . . . for he was too wise to speak of failure. Nevertheless he told me without any shame that he had expected, with my help, to raise several million dollars that night in Hollywood. The "high command" of the three hundred Irgunites hiding in the swamps of Palestine had entertained the same childish hope. It was historically impossible. And yet . . .

"They could have easily given us several millions of dollars," he piped. "But they are not going to give it to us. Why did we fail to sell them?"

"The only thing you could sell such Jews," I told him, "is a magic wand to make them disappear, or a Moses named Throckmorton to come and take back the Ten Commandments, the Talmud and the Star of David."

Peter accepted this bit of realism, which he had learned over and over from sterner realists than I was. But I was still dreaming of the strength that could be loaned to the dolorous figure of the Jew by Jews like those I had summoned, unhurt Jews, powerful Jews and Jews with money—those of us who could add our voices to his battle-cry rather than his moan. And I thought it odd that the cause of justice to the Jews should burn so brightly in the heart of a Britisher who was no Jew—Colonel Patterson. It was odd, also, that this Britisher with a lifetime record of service in his country's armies should attack his own people when they were fighting so desperately. Then the thought came to me that it was on this unprejudiced sense of justice that the greatness of the England I admired was founded. There had always been British intrigue and hypocrisy in their dealings with the lands they occupied. But there had always been voices like this to keep justice a part of the Anglo-Saxon record—Patterson, Pitt, Burke.

The day after our meeting, William Morris, Jr., of the famous agency that bore his name, had a dozen of us in his office. He offered to finance the entire project of the Jewish army propaganda out of his own pocket if Peter and I would agree to remove the words Jew and Jewish from our committee's title.

Peter grinned and nudged me to take up the offer.

"You said yourself you didn't like the title when I made it up," Peter's voice squeaked. "For heaven's sake! We'll make up another title."

Again I knew that Peter Bergson and I were facing in different directions. He wanted money for the cause of Palestine. I wanted it for the cause of the Jew. It would be a queer thing to work for this cause if the word Jew had been forbidden it.

And so it was that our letterhead, when the usual polite and congratulatory letter of my Irgunist friends reached me, read:

COMMITTEE FOR A JEWISH ARMY
of Stateless and Palestinian Jews

To which Peter Bergson had added a subtitle. It read:

The Sponsoring Committee of the Proclamation on the Moral Rights of Stateless and Palestinian Jews

UP THE HILL AND DOWN AGAIN

FROM NEW YORK Peter kept me posted on the success of our undertaking. A new cohort was at his side, a hard-muscled advertising tycoon named Alfred Strelsin. Of the fifty men to whom I had written to join our cause, Al Strelsin had been the only one who had accepted. It developed immediately that with Al in the fold the other forty-nine would never be missed. Peter and our convert invaded the nation's capital and in no time were playing poker with Cabinet members. Peter's letters reported victory after victory. Congressman Andrew Somers had introduced a resolution in the House calling for a Jewish army in Palestine. How Peter loved resolutions! Senators Gillette, Thomas and Johnson had espoused the Cause eagerly—and Peter wrote, "When the Jewish army wins its first battle against the Germans you will feel more than repaid for all the work you have done." I went to bed grinning at that historic moment to come. Germans facing Jews with guns as good as their own and with a valor beyond their own! I wrote Peter to hurry up.

It would take another month, Peter answered. There were still barriers to breach. With the redoubtable Strelsin at his side, Peter proceeded to breach them. Assistant Secretary of State Berle had become active in our Cause, and Secretary of State Hull had come out also for a Jewish army. And a bright fellow named Adlai Stevenson, working in the Navy Department, had brought the Cause to the attention of Secretary of the Navy Knox and won him over. New solons and dignitaries were flocking to the Jewish army project every day. All these converts seemed to be Gentiles.

The first important Washington Jew approached gave us our first hint of odd things to come. He was Supreme Court Justice Felix Frankfurter. Professor Frankfurter curtly dismissed our Cause in a letter reading: "It would be improper for a Supreme Court Justice to express an opinion on this issue."

Chief Justice Harlan Stone (of the same Supreme Court) had answered, however, in the opposite vein: ". . . it's a wonderful idea! . . . I wish your program for a Jewish army in Palestine all necessary success. Call on me whenever you are in Washington again."

Thus Yankee Harlan Stone. But with hardly an exception the big Jews of Washington stood shoulder to shoulder with Frankfurter —worldly, able fellows who regarded their Jewishness as if it were a hole in their striped pants that must be kept adroitly hidden.

Escorted by Robert Nathan, of W.P.B., Peter had called on the British Ambassador—Lord Halifax—and on Field Marshal Dill, Chief of the British Staff in Washington.

"His lordship," wrote Peter, "was a little shocked but he could not very well turn us down flatly, for he needs the good will and co-operation of Donald Nelson. General Dill, by the way, is on our side. He came out firmly for a Jewish army."

And now the stirring business had reached the American War Department. With resolutions popping in Congress, and administration leaders lined up behind the project, it was up to the American military to say its yes or no.

Under Secretary of War Patterson, a moody and talented man, listened to Peter Bergson for two hours and approved the plan. Mr. Patterson appointed a group of military experts to work out the project.

"It looks," wrote Peter, "as if by the time you get back to New York the Jewish army in Palestine will be a reality. I think you ought to join me in Palestine as soon as this work starts." I agreed to join him. And then the letters stopped.

Two months later Bergson and Merlin met me at the plane in New York. They spoke sparingly. I was taken to the Committee's new headquarters on Fifth Avenue. Here I met three newcomers from Pal-

estine—Eri Jabotinsky, son of Vladimir, as well as Arieh Ben Eliezer and Dr. Alexander Hadani-Rafaeli. They were young, polite
and taciturn.

"You look like a thriving outfit," I said, "a water cooler, switch-
board and everything."

"Except a Jewish army," said Merlin.

Peter told me the story of the set-back of our Cause. The Zionists,
led by Rabbi Stephen Wise, had come to Washington to scotch our
campaign. The doddering Jewish Congressman, Sol Bloom, had
spearheaded the attack.

I interrupted Peter to ask why the Zionists didn't believe in a
Jewish army.

"It's not a matter of what the Zionists believe," said Merlin.
"They fought the project not because they are against it, but because
they are against us. Stephen Wise will not tolerate any other Jewish
organization working for Palestine and stealing honors and publicity from him."

I had met Stephen Wise once. I went to his synagogue with my
aunt, who was a member, to arrange for the burial of my mother
whose body was being brought east from Hollywood. Rabbi Wise
agreed to officiate but asked me to pay him five thousand dollars in
advance. The money, he explained, would cover the use of a pew in
his synagogue. I said I had not come to join his synagogue but
to have my mother buried. Rabbi Wise answered firmly that he
would not conduct the funeral unless I paid the five thousand dollars
in advance.

I suggested to Rabbi Wise that he hang three gold balls over the
front door of his synagogue.

My mother was buried by Rabbi de Sola Pool of the Spanish and
Portuguese Synagogue. Thereafter, when the name Stephen Wise
came to my ear, I always thought of the name de Sola Pool as an anti-
dote.

Peter resumed—the Jewish army project had entered its final
stages, and Secretary Patterson had decided to place it in the hands
of an American officer. And, presto, a Jew had appeared.

The high-ranking American Jewish officer took a running dive at
the Jewish army project and removed it from the face of the earth.

"It is incredible," said Merlin. "A hundred American statesmen
and high-ranking officials including the British General Dill were

eager for the creation of an Army of Stateless and Palestinian Jews, and a single Jew kills it!"

THE GOODNESS OF A JEW

DR. HAYIM GREENBERG, editor of the *Jewish Frontier*, a New York weekly written in English, removed a heap of papers from his brief case.

"I think these contain the facts you wish to know," he said. "Some are from eyewitnesses and some from underground sources. They come to us through Switzerland."

We were lunching in a crowded kosher restaurant. I had been told that Dr. Greenberg was one of the best-informed people in New York on the massacre of the Jews.

I read the documents he had taken from his brief case. I read of the execution of the Jewish population in Munich, of the extermination camp in Tremblinka. A survivor reported the dark cloud of smoke that hung over the crematorium in which thousands of Jews were being burned alive daily.

I read of the freight cars lined with tons of quicklime into which five thousand live Jews were jammed, and out of which five thousand partially consumed corpses were removed at the end of the trip and dumped into waiting trench graves.

I read of the twenty thousand Jews herded together in a field in Silesia and used as practice targets for the *Luftwaffe* gunners. For a week the Stukas swooped back and forth over the heads of the Jews and improved their marksmanship until the twenty thousand were dead.

I read of the burning alive of the Jewish population of Cologne, of five thousand Jews burned alive in Bavarian towns.

I read of the promotion of Colonel Wolfe to General Wolfe. The colonel had been in charge of the Jewish affairs in Warsaw. Each day his men selected another five hundred men, women and children from the Warsaw ghetto and marched them naked to the incinerator. One day Colonel Wolfe took a hundred soldiers with him and a tank and went on a real Jew hunt. The hunters invaded the ghetto and opened fire on every visible Jew. By sundown, Colonel Wolfe and his men had bagged three thousand Jews. For this feat, the colonel was given his general's star.

I read of the hanging of rabbis, of the rape and torture of Jewish women, of German exterminators forcing old Jews to rub excrement over their heads and faces while they prayed.

The dispatches were terse and lacking in adjectives. One clipping from a Berlin paper boasted that all the three hundred thousand Jews of Germany had been killed and called on all good Germans to rejoice over the fact that their Fatherland was Jew-free.

I read of French, Dutch and Hungarian Jews being transported in freight cars to extermination camps in north Germany and Poland. There were pages of names of Jewish doctors, professors, scientists, writers, actors, dancers, housewives, lawyers, being burned in different crematoriums. I wondered why always to Poland to be murdered? Then I realized that murdering millions of men, women and children was a crime that had to be organized. The German genius for orderliness was necessary, otherwise the dead might get out of hand. They might start rotting in roads and poisoning rivers.

I looked up from the documents at the people in the restaurant. They were unusually silent for lunch hour Jews. I watched their friendly, saddened faces and thought of how these faces had never brought harm to the world; and of how faces like these were being tortured and murdered by the millions.

I turned to my reading. I tried to find in the German clippings some hint of nervousness or reluctance toward the murder of Jews. There was none. The city and village Germans, the farm and factory Germans, accepted the murder of the Jews as a political essential and a spiritual improvement. They felt themselves better Germans after killing myriads of Jews. The German newspapers boasted of the massacre as of some cultural achievement.

I remembered the German streets in which I had walked, the German people whom I had seen daily for two years. I stared at them again in my mind. I watched them killing.

Dr. Greenberg had sat silent as I read the dispatches. He asked me now,

"What sort of an article are you going to write, Mr. Hecht?"

"I'm going to write something about Germans," I said.

"From what point of view do you intend to write of the Germans?" Dr. Greenberg asked.

"From the point of view that the Germans are a nation of murderers," I said.

"I don't think it is wise to accuse all the Germans of being murderers," Dr. Greenberg said. "I would like to ask you to consider carefully before denouncing the German people. To denounce a people is to do what the Germans are doing to the Jews."

"They are not denouncing Jews," I said. "They're killing them."

"I know," said Dr. Greenberg. His eyes looked painfully at the documents heaped on the table. "But, please, may I point out to you that it will be bad for the Jews if you make the Jews seem as cruel and unthinking as those whom you are trying to attack. More than ever before in our history, the Jew today must have a philosophical view. He must keep his mind undarkened by hate and look with clear eyes on the world. He must rise above his bitterness and not fight back only out of his pain. The evil ones should be punished. But, please, let us not become like them. It is not ethical to attack a whole race—even the race of Germans."

I thanked this man whose kindness I understood. But his way was not my way. I was unable to answer his philosophical words. My head was full of faraway screams.

A SEARCH FOR TRUMPETS

THE READER'S DIGEST MAGAZINE broke the American silence attending the massacre of the Jews in February, 1943. It printed my article called "Remember Us," based on Dr. Greenberg's data.

Reading it in the magazine, I thought of a larger idea and set out to test its practicality. Thirty famous writers (and one composer) were assembled at George Kaufman's house by my friend, his wife Beatrice. All had written hit plays or successful novels. Put their names together and you had the box-office flower of American culture. In addition to success, wit and influence, they had in common the fact that they were all Jews.

I had said to Bea that thirty New York dinner guests might save the surviving four million Jews in Europe. The first massacre scores had come in: dead Jews—two million; anti-German-butchery protests—none.

I looked eagerly at the thirty celebrities in Bea's drawing room. Some were friends, some enemies. Some wrote like artists (almost), some like clodhoppers. Some were insufferably fatheaded, some psychotically shy. But such variation was unimportant. Bold, shy, Shakespeare or Boob McNutt—they had a great common virtue. They could command the press of the world.

What would happen if these brilliant Jews cried out with passion against the German butchers? If these socially and artistically celebrated Jews spoke up in rage at the murder of their people! How they could dramatize the German crime! How loudly they could present the nightmare to America and the world!

When we sat with coffee cups, Bea said to me, "Why not talk to them now, before they start playing games or something?"

I recited all the facts I knew about the Jewish killings. I said I felt certain that if we banded together and let loose our talents and our moral passion against the Germans we might halt the massacre. The Germans now believed that the civilized world looked with indifference on their extermination of Europe's Jews. How could they think anything else? Had anybody (but the biased kinsmen of the victims) protested? Had England's great humanitarian, Churchill, spoken? Or our great keeper of the rights of man—Roosevelt? No, nary a word out of either of these politically haloed gentlemen. And out of that third champion of all underdogs—Stalin—no more hint of Jews than if they had all bowed out with Moses.

Consider (this was part of my speech to the thirty Jewish geniuses of New York City), consider what would happen to the Germans if they were to hear that their crime was sickening the world! If a roar of horror swept the civilized earth and echoed into the land that was once Goethe's and Beethoven's! Imagine the effect on the descendants of Schiller, Wagner, Kant, Hegel, etc., etc., were they to hear a universal shout go up! "You are not heroes. You are monsters."

And to back up my theory I wheeled out my sole exhibit—the King of little Denmark. Peter Freuchen, the writer and explorer, had told me the story. He had been in Copenhagen at the time the Germans announced they were going to "clean" Denmark of Jews. The King of Denmark, with the German heel on his neck, had answered that the Danes would never stand for this crime against humanity. He had put the yellow arm band identifying Jews on his own sleeve and requested his people to do the same. They did. The Jews of Denmark went on living, protected by the moral passion of an otherwise powerless king.

I concluded with another argument. I said that an outcry against the massacre would have an important effect on the British. The British were not a bloodthirsty, murderous people. If they heard that millions of Jews had already been murdered, and that the Germans planned to kill the four million still left breathing in Europe, and that most of these still-breathing Jews could be saved if the ports of Palestine were opened, the British, fine, decent people that they were, would certainly not continue to collaborate with the Germans on the extermination of the four million surviving Jews.

There was no applause when I stopped talking. Not that I expected any. The authors of hit plays and novels are more interested in receiving applause than in giving it. But the nature of the silence was revealed to me when a half-dozen of the guests stood up and without saying "Boo" walked out of the room.

"It looks like I struck out," I said to my hostess as the silence kept up.

Edna Ferber's voice rose sharply.

"Who is paying you to do this wretched propaganda," she demanded, "Mister Hitler? Or is it Mister Goebbels?"

Her query started irritated and angry talk. The anger and irritation were against me.

In the vestibule, Beatrice said to me, "I'm sorry it turned out like this. But I didn't expect anything much different. You asked them to throw away the most valuable thing they own—the fact that they are Americans."

How argue with Beatrice, a fine woman with as bright a mind and as soft a heart as anyone I knew? How convince any of her highfalutin guests that they had not behaved like Americans but like scared Jews? And what in God's name were they frightened of? Of people realizing they were Jews? But people knew that already. Of people hearing that they had Jewish hearts? What kind of hearts did they imagine people thought Jews had, non-Jewish hearts? Or did they think they would be mistaken for "real" Americans if they proved they had no hearts at all? Two of the thirty guests came into the vestibule to say good night to me.

"I thought I'd tell you that if I can do anything definite in the way of Jewish propaganda, call on me," said Moss Hart.

Kurt Weill, the lone composer present, looked at me with misty eyes. A radiance was in his strong face.

"Please count on me for everything," Kurt said.

THE HATFIELDS AND THE MCCOHENS

A THIRD JEW soon joined us—Billy Rose. He needed no briefing. He came under his own steam, which was considerable.

Kurt, Moss and I sat in Billy's Beekman Place mansion and discussed a propaganda project I had figured out. It was a pageant about the Jews to be called "We Will Never Die," and it would be put on in Madison Square Garden as a "Memorial to the Two Million Jewish Dead of Europe." I would write it. Kurt would contribute the music. Moss would direct it. And Billy would produce it. I told them about Bergson, Merlin and the Committee, who would dig up the money for it.

"I don't think we ought to tie up with any partisan Palestinian group," said Moss. "I understand there are all sorts of embattled factions over there. Unless, of course, you're pledged to this Committee of yours."

"I think Moss is right," said Billy.

"Our propaganda would be more effective and have more meaning if it came from all the Jews," I agreed instantly, "and wasn't underwritten by a group of Palestinian Sinn Feiners."

I wrote the pageant and called on Bergson, Merlin and Ben Ami in the Committee's headquarters.

"We're going to put on a pageant and troop it around the country," I said. "It has nothing to do with Palestine or the Jewish army project."

"I know," said Peter. "I have read the announcements. The pageant will fit perfectly into our new program."

I asked what that was.

"We have formed 'The Emergency Committee to Save the Jewish People of Europe,'" said Merlin. "You are the cochairman, Mr. Ben Hecht."

I explained my propaganda attitude. I did not want to work for the Committee at present. I admired my new Palestinian friends as much as ever, but I wanted to work for the Jews—all of them. "There must be a number of other active Jewish organizations in New York besides you," I said.

"There are about thirty-three," said Merlin.

"Good. We'll put this pageant on with the backing of all thirty-four Jewish *Vereins*," I said. I gave him the names of our small Broadway unit, which included now the opera conductor Isaac Van Grove and the scenic designer Lemuel Ayres.

"You are seceding from us?" Ben Ami asked quietly.

"No, I'm asking you to join us in this particular job," I said.

"What can we do?" Peter inquired.

"I'd like you to arrange a meeting of representatives of all the Jewish organizations in New York," I said.

Peter grinned.

"I shall be very glad to do that for you," he announced in his special parliamentarian voice.

We set a date and I rented a suite in the Algonquin Hotel.

Thirty-two Jewish presidents, vice-presidents and secretaries crowded into my Algonquin parlor. It was raining outside. My visitors sat down in the folding chairs, removed their rubbers, laid their umbrellas down and said not a word. They represented thirty-two Jewish organizations ranging from the powerful B'nai Brith to a society of Brooklyn rabbis. Bergson whispered to me that the thirty-third organization would be along later. Its representative had taken the wrong subway. He handed me a typewritten list of those present and said, "The meeting is yours."

He retired with Merlin to the rear of the room. Billy Rose and Kurt Weill stayed beside me. I recalled the thirty Jews in Beatrice Kaufman's house. These faces were no more "Jewish looking" than those others, but here were Jews active as Jews. There would be no wounded egos when I addressed them as Jews.

I told my guests much the same things I had said to the thirty literary celebrities. Their eyes brightened and they straightened eagerly in their seats. I then read excerpts from the pageant, and Kurt Weill played the accompanying music on a piano.

The pageant opened with a prayer spoken by a rabbi, in holiday canonicals. I read the prayer to them.

"Almighty God, Father of the poor and the weak, Hope of all

who dream of goodness and justice; Almighty God who favored the children of Israel with His light—we are here to affirm that this light still shines in us.

"We are here to say our prayers for the two million who have been killed in Europe, because they bear the name of your first children—the Jews.

"Before our eyes has appeared the strange and awesome picture of a folk being put to death, of a great and ancient people in whose veins have lingered for so long the earliest words and image of God, dying like a single child on a single bayonet.

"We are not here to weep for them, although our eyes are stricken with this picture and our hearts burdened with their fate.

"We are here to honor them and to proclaim the victory of their dying.

"For in our Testament are written the words of Habakkuk, Prophet of Israel, 'They shall never die.'

"They shall never die though they were slaughtered with no weapon in their hand.

"Though they fill the dark land of Europe with the smoke of their massacre, they shall never die.

"For they are part of something greater, higher and stronger than the dreams of their executioners.

"Dishonored and removed from the face of the earth, their cry of Sh'ma Israel remains in the world.

"We are here to strengthen our hearts, to take into our veins the pride and courage of the millions of innocent people who have fallen and are still to fall before the German massacre.

"They were unarmed. But not we!

"We live in a land whose arm is stronger than the arm of the German Goliath. This land is our David.

"Almighty God, we are here to affirm that our hearts will be a monument worthy of our dead.

"We are here to affirm that the innocence of their lives and the dream of goodness in their souls are witnesses that will never be silent. They shall never die."

I read on for an hour. No words I had ever written had ever been received with such love as beamed on me now. When the reading was done, there was a great deal of nose blowing and tear drying. There was only one face in the room without tenderness—Peter Bergson's. He stood looking at me with an ironic grin that I thought in the worst of taste.

I told my guests then that the pageant they had heard was going to be put on in Madison Square Garden, New York, and, thereafter, in a dozen other cities. We needed no money from any of the organizations present. Nor did we want any work from them. We did not want them to sell tickets for us, or buy tickets from us. All we wished of them was their approval. Our small Broadway propaganda group wanted to work for all the Jews of New York. All we asked concretely of each organization present was its name on our letterhead and the privilege of saying that all the Jewish organizations of New York were presenting the pageant.

As for any profits made by this project, and any other project in which, with their approval, we engaged, they would be divided equally among the societies present. I announced I would call the roll and asked that each official answer yes or no to the question.

The first two names I called answered in unhappy voices, "I pass." The third called was the secretary of the American Jewish Congress.

"I wish to know," he spoke up, "whether you are asking for my personal co-operation or the co-operation of my organization."

"I want the yes from your organization," I said.

The representative of the American Jewish Congress stood up, pointed a finger and cried out, "As an organization, we refuse to work with Morris Goldfarb! Never will the American Jewish Congress join up with anything in which the *Arbeiterring* is involved!"

A man, possibly Morris Goldfarb, was on his feet yelling back, "And we will never work with the American Jewish Congress in a thousand years."

Other voices arose. English and Yiddish outcries filled the room. Within five minutes a free-for-all, bitter as a Kentucky feud, was in full swing. The thirty-two Jewish organizations were denouncing each other as Socialists, as Fascists, as Christians, as undesirables of every stripe.

The door opened and the thirty-third representative—he who had taken the wrong subway—entered. He understood instantly what was going on and began yelling without taking his hat off.

I retreated into the bedroom. The spectacle of Jews comically belaboring each other in the worst hour of their history sickened me.

How could Jews under a load of hate in the world, find time to hate each other?

One by one the battlers stepped into the room where I stood staring at the rain. Each shook hands with me, smiled, shrugged and went away, and each seemed embarrassed. A dozen or so repeated almost the same words of apology. "Don't try to bring us together. We can never work together. It's an old trouble. But go on working by yourself. Please don't let this discourage you."

When I came back into the parlor only Bergson, Merlin and Ben Ami were left. The carpet was strewn with forgotten rubbers, umbrellas and crumpled Yiddish newspapers.

Merlin's face was grim. Peter, however, was still smiling.

"I knew what would happen," he said. "I arranged the meeting just to convince you how impossible your plan was."

"It's extremely sad," said Merlin.

"It is the same old story," Peter declared. "Jews must always battle Jews. It's the only politics open to a stateless people. The only victories they can hope to enjoy are victories over each other."

"What about the pageant?" Ben Ami asked.

"It must be put on—everywhere," said Merlin. "It will change Jewish history."

"I agree," said Peter firmly. "When we go back to the office we will form a special Committee for the presentation of 'We Will Never Die.' Ben, of course, will be cochairman."

OUR CLANS COME DOWN THE HILLS

I SEEM to be offering a picture of myself as a lone righteous fellow battling a world of error. This comes of preferring to boast of enemies rather than friends—an old habit of mine.

The truth is I was never less alone in my life. I had no sooner sounded my first propaganda chirpings than Jews and Gentiles came rushing to me as if I were giving money away. Enough Thespians, acrobats, ventriloquists, opera singers, musicians and spear carriers offered themselves for our pageant to have put on ten separate companies.

Nineteen forty-three brought a February of blizzards and zero weather, yet at eight P.M. each evening our rehearsal hall filled up with thousands of frostbitten applicants. They lined the walls modestly and patiently. They were like strange soldiers come from the moon to help the Jews.

We picked a hundred lads from the Yeshiva College in Brooklyn. I was surprised there was a Hebrew college in Brooklyn attended, apparently, by unaccented young Americans brimming with culture and athletics.

We picked also fifty cantors, each able to sing louder and higher than Caruso. Among our players for this and later propaganda shows were Stella Adler, Luther Adler, Jacob Ben Ami, Edward Arnold, Roman Bohnen, Kurt Baum, J. Edward Bromberg, John Garfield, Paul Henreid, Joan Leslie, David Leonard, Paul Muni, Katina Paxinou, Eleonora von Mendelssohn, Fred Keating, Edward G. Robinson, Spivy, Paul Stewart, Sylvia Sidney, Akim Tamiroff, Blanche Yurka. Later there joined us: Eddie Arcaro, George Baxter, Ralph Bellamy, Mario Berini, Marlon Brando, Sid Caesar, Ruth Chatterton, Rita Gam, Jonathan Harris, Steve Hill, Lou Holtz, George Jessel, Sidney Lumet, Jerry Lewis, Dean Martin, Gregory Morton, Quentin Reynolds, Bill Robinson, Hazel Scott, Phil Silvers, Frank Sinatra, Danny Thomas and Leonard Bernstein.

There were also bevies of stage managers, errand runners and drum beaters. Our spirits were so high that we even made a convert. Fefe Ferry, New York restaurateur and *bon vivant*, wiped tears from his eyes after watching a rehearsal and cried out passionately, "I am ready to admit for the first time in my life that I am half Jewish!"

Nevertheless, we ran into casting trouble. Rose Keane, who bore the new Bergson title of co-ordinator, reported that she had been unable to sign up the fifty orthodox rabbis called for in the praying scene of my script.

"It seems," said Rose, "that it's against the orthodox religion for rabbis to stand on a theater stage and pray."

"Did you tell them they could keep their hats on?" I asked, for I was not entirely without Hebrew lore.

"With or without hats on, they refuse to commit what they say is sacrilege," said Miss Keane. "But I've arranged a luncheon where you can talk and try to argue them into committing this sin."

ORDEAL OF THE HUNDRED RABBIS

THERE WERE at least a hundred of them in the private dining room of Schwartz's Kosher Restaurant. I sat facing them from a sort of speaker's table, flanked by Rose Keane, Sam Rosen, a Jewish journalist who had unexpectedly joined our cause—which at this time was as shy of Jewish journalists as of Jewish millionaires—and several workers from Bergson's office. I had told Bergson to keep away. Despite his descent from a famous rabbinical line, I feared he would sound a wrong note. He was too argumentative. I, on the other hand, knew that if the rabbis were old and wore long beards and smiled with childlike patience at me—I would love them.

Old they were, most of them ancients mysteriously plucked out of the hands of German, Rumanian and Hungarian murderers. How such white-bearded ancients, some in their nineties, could have escaped their young and avid executioners was a baffling thought. But here they were in Schwartz's Kosher Restaurant sitting in black skullcaps and alpaca frock coats, and greeting each one of the courses with some sort of prayer.

Occasionally a few of them stopped eating, conferred among themselves and dispatched a delegate to the speaker's table to shake hands with me. Introduced to Rose Keane, the delegate would remove a large linen handkerchief from his alpaca coat, hand her one end of it and pull on it several times. Journalist Rosen explained apologetically that certain extra-religious rabbis considered it a sin to touch a woman's person except in blessing.

"And you'd better start with your speech," journalist Rosen said. "If you wait for them to stop praying we'll be here till doomsday."

My speech? What could anyone say to such holy men, and how could I ever persuade them to commit a sin? I sat looking at them and smiling, and those who weren't praying over a dish of something smiled back. The sense came to me that here in Schwartz's Kosher Restaurant I was as deeply loved as I had been in my mother's or my Tante Chasha's kitchen. I felt that every one of these ancients had X-ray eyes that saw deep into me—through all sorts of layers of Godlessness and cynicism—and beheld me as I was—a runaway who loved old rabbis—and little else. Which was somewhat true. I would never pray with them, never believe the fairy tales they called the word of God, never have anything but a grin for the thousand and one taboos by which they lived and died—but my soul nevertheless embraced them as if they were all favorite uncles. And my mind informed me proudly that they were superior men.

But still I hesitated to get to my feet. Journalist Rosen kept nudging me, saying he would translate anything I said into the finest Yiddish.

My silence became apparent to the rabbis. They also stopped praying and washing their finger tips and sat in silence. "Good rabbis," I said—to myself, not to them,"why can't you forget God for once. I give you my word of honor He won't mind."

"Don't rush me," I answered Rosen. "I'm waiting for some idea to come to me, or for some miracle to happen."

"Miracles don't happen in Schwartz's Restaurant," said Rosen.

He was wrong. A rabbi, over six feet tall, with a long white beard riding on his chest, came to the speaker's table. He looked a little like Michelangelo's Moses—but older—so old that his pale eyes no longer reflected light, and his long legs shook as he walked. I stood up to greet him.

"I am Rabbi Levin from Czechoslovakia," he said in understandable English, "and if you wish it, instead of your speaking to the rabbis, I will speak." He smiled wryly. "To come on the stage like actors and recite our holiest prayer is a sinful thing in our eyes. But, who knows, maybe I can convince them they should for once in their lives do a sin for the Jews. They've done everything else."

"If it's not too much of a strain," I said.

"Strain." The old rabbi winked at me. "What isn't a strain? It's a strain even to stay alive. However, since you mention it, maybe a few drops of schnapps would help."

I poured the rabbi a drink, which he downed like a veteran bar fly—in a single gulp—and I made room for him in front of the speaker's microphone. Whereupon, the tall, tottering rabbi from Czechoslovakia addressed the other ninety-nine rabbis in Yiddish, which that day I seemed to follow easily.

"Fellow rabbis," he said, "instead of the young man who invited us here, I, Chaim Levin of Podbrodz, am going to talk to you. In a way it's a shame, because the young man who invited us here could tell you things you don't know and things you never heard of because he is a man of such brilliance that the whole world listens to him with its mouth open when he speaks. So you can imagine what a difference it will be for me to speak in his place."

The listening rabbis all seemed to wink at me and pat me on the head.

"And so, fellow rabbis," spoke my tall, bearded proxy, using the plural "rabbonim," which had in it the flavor of Yiddish wryness that makes the Yiddish tongue seem to come always from a comedian, "what can I talk to you about that you don't know already? About Jews?"

Rabbi Levin shrugged hopelessly. "About Jews you know as much as I do," he said. "And about God you know also as much as I do. So I will tell you about the village of Podbrodz. About Podbrodz I know more than you, because it is where I was born, where I grew up, where I studied the Torah and became a rabbi, and where they burned my synagogue and chased me out.

"Well, long ago in Podbrodz I was young and happy," Rabbi Levin went on. "Nobody killed Jews, nobody burned synagogues. With luck you could keep alive from week to week and taste wine on Friday night. Not every Friday night, but who expects to live like Solomon? So in that time when everybody was young and happy, the people of Podbrodz built a theater for themselves—a fine high theater with wide steps on the outside. When the theater was finished, an opening performance was announced. Such excitement nobody ever saw. People came from as far as five miles and everybody in Podbrodz crowded into the theater, except one—our beggar. He was an old beggar with an accordion and he sat on the wide steps of the theater and watched everybody go in. And then he sat alone and waited till everybody started coming out, talking and smiling with happiness.

"So our beggar finally pulled at the sleeve of one of the audience coming out and said, 'Please, happy man, out of the kindness of your soul would you tell me what went on in the theater tonight?'

" 'What went on,' answered the man, 'is we paid two rubles to hear a man sing. And you can believe me it was worth every heller.'

" 'Two rubles to hear a man sing!' The beggar shook his head in wonder at such a thing. 'What magnificent songs he must have sung.

Would you be kind enough to tell a poor beggar the names of such wonderful songs?'

"'Who knows the names of such songs,' said the man. 'He sang beggar songs. That's all I can tell you.'

"'Beggar songs!' cried the beggar—and he gave his accordion a squeeze. 'Did he sing this song?'

"And the beggar sang a line or two from a song he liked to sing in the rain.

"'Yes,' the man from the theater audience answered.

"Then the beggar asked, 'Did he sing this song?' And again he squeezed his accordion and sang a few lines from another one of his favorites.

"The man from the theater listened and said, 'Yes, he sang that also.'"

Rabbi Levin stood still and smiled for the first time on the ninety-nine rabbonim. It was a smile so winning as to have melted the heart of a wild animal.

"Dear fellow rabbis from all over," said Rabbi Levin, "we are the beggar on the steps with the true song, and this young man who sits beside me is inviting us to come inside the theater, and sing it to the world." The rabbis nodded their heads, chuckled to each other and came to the speaker's table to shake my hand—as if it were I who had made this wondrous speech—and all agreed happily to commit sacrilege, to sin against the Torah, to come into the theater and recite the holiest of their prayers.

I have one more memory of our rabbis. In Washington, D. C., where we took our propaganda show to play before the nation's lawmakers and the world's ambassadors, we were unable to get hotel space for our fifty ancients. Hearing that the "Westwood Hotel" (I am renaming the hostelry in question) was run by a fiery Irish patriot, we informed him that a delegation from Dublin had arrived to press for an Irish loan. To this the stormy manager answered he would put them up free of charge if he had to throw out every paying guest in the house.

"Not free," said our emissary, an Irish lad himself, "but for the sake of the freedom which we all treasure in our hearts give us a good rate. And so that there will be no ugly financial deeds to discuss after their arrival, let me pay the whole bill in advance."

"You are a man of fine sensitiveness," said the manager. "I'll take your money."

A week later our fifty white-bearded, white-socked, alpaca-coated rabbis, with curled sideburns from under skullcaps and flattened black hats, filed up to the "Westwood" registration desk and, blindly obeying instructions, signed themselves in as O'Toole, O'Hamilton, Gilhooley, Clancy, O'Casey, Sweeney, Murphy, and forty-three other sons of Erin.

A NEW JEWISH BATTLE CRY

I AM likely to sound rather immodest in this chapter, but truth is truth, and a man should not be afraid to speak it even if it embarrasses him. My activities quickly produced a new Jewish battle cry. And not only in New York but in Chicago, Boston, Indianapolis, Los Angeles, San Francisco and even in London. This new Jewish battle cry was "Down with Ben Hecht." It came roaring from synagogue pulpits (reformed ones). It filled the Jewish press and the Jewish magazines. I can still see the headlines in the *American Jewish Congress Monthly* and other such periodicals. They identified me as the American Goebbels, as Hitler's Hired Stooge, as the Broadway Racketeer Growing Rich on Jewish Misery, and this and that.

The first Jewish outbursts against me remained, actually, unknown to me. I was too busy getting the pageant ready. Besides, I was unable to read Yiddish, and my informants about what American Jews were writing and thinking were Bergson and Merlin, and a few of my uncles.

My two Irgun friends came to me always with glowing faces and the brightest of communiqués. We were, they said, bringing new concepts to Jewry. And they never failed to tell Rose, in my hearing, that my name had been cheered like Patrick Henry's or Abraham Lincoln's at the last meeting they had staged.

I knew in the back of my head that their meetings at this time were more or less lame affairs. But who looks a cheering gift horse in the mouth?

As for my uncles, they were even more full of loyalty and evasions than Bergson and Merlin. They brought me bales of columns cut out of Yiddish newspapers and magazines, and pointed out proudly my name in the headlines and the innumerable photographs of me. When I asked what the columns said, my uncles, long trained in lying by their womenfolk, beamed with pleasure and answered that everybody was agreed I was doing wonderful work for the Jews, and everybody was proud of me, and the Organization of Young Israel in my Uncle Joe's orthodox synagogue in the Bronx had prayed for me at eight o'clock that very morning.

I first became aware that there was annoyance with me among the Jews when Rabbi Stephen Wise, head of the Jews of New York, head of the Zionists and, as I knew from reading the papers, head of almost everything noble in American Jewry, telephoned me at the Algonquin Hotel where I had pitched my Hebrew tent.

Rabbi Wise said he would like to see me immediately in his rectory. His voice, which was sonorous and impressive, irritated me. I had never known a man with a sonorous and impressive voice who wasn't either a con man or a bad actor. I explained I was very busy and unable to step out of my hotel.

"Then I shall tell you now, over the telephone, what I had hoped to tell you in my study," said Rabbi Wise. "I have read your pageant script and I disapprove of it. I must ask you to cancel this pageant and discontinue all your further activities in behalf of the Jews. If you wish hereafter to work for the Jewish Cause, you will please consult me and let me advise you."

At this point I hung up. When I informed Bergson of Rabbi Wise's fatheadedness, he answered moodily, "We'll have to get the spies out of our organization. There are obviously people among us carrying information and documents to the enemy."

I was confused by the word enemy. I had up to that moment been thinking only of an enemy with a swastika.

Another hint of the new battle cry hatching among American Jews came to me during one of the pageant rehearsals.

"We are having a little trouble with the B'nai Brith," Bergson said. "I think you ought to know about it."

"Yes, indeed, Mr. Ben Hecht," Merlin added, at his side.

I knew only of the B'nai Brith that my uncles belonged to it, when they were able to pay dues. And I remembered that my father had scorned it—preferring the Loyal Order of Moose, The Modern

Redmen, The Knights of Pythias and the all-wise B.P.O.E.—the Elks.

"The B'nai Brith," Peter said to my surprise, "demands that we do not place your latest propaganda advertisement in the newspaper —the one attacking the American State Department. They say that if we print such a full page ad in *The Times,* the American State Department will raise Hell with the Jews of America."

The ad under discussion was in rhyme and was called, "Ballad of the Doomed Jews of Europe." Its refrain ran:

> *Hang and burn, but be quiet, Jews,*
> *The world is busy with other news.*

Some further lines stated that by Christmastime all the Christians could enjoy their peace on earth without the Jews, who would all be killed by that time.

"Judge Proskauer, who is president of the American Jewish Committee and a very educated gentleman," said Peter, who had learned wisely never to take my knowledge of Jewish affairs for granted, "states that such an anti-Christian attitude could well bring on Jewish pogroms in the U.S.A."

"What is your opinion of Justice Proskauer's theory?" Merlin asked, puffing aloofly on his pipe.

"You can tell Judge Proskauer for me," I answered, "to go gazump himself."

"Very good," said Merlin. "I think your approach 'is correct, Mr. Ben Hecht."

"We will print the ad and not bother you about it any more," said Peter Bergson.

Standing beside me during this political discussion was a man I had come to admire as much as I did my two Palestinian Sindbads. He was the Polish artist Arthur Szyk, a short, compact, bald-headed fellow who had recently added his wit and genius to our cause.

"You make me wish I had been born in America," said Szyk. "Then I, also, would know the right words to use at the right time. A foreigner like me must always rely on epigrams."

SZYK, MASTER OF LIGHTNING

How OR WHY Arthur Szyk became our one-man art department I never found out. He appeared among us one day like a bonanza on the doorstep. Thereafter, he illustrated all the ads I wrote. He drew program covers for all the pageants I invented. He drew posters and pictures for throwaways at rallies, for invitations to shake-down dinners. He worked for eight years without pause. Nobody paid him anything and nobody thought of thanking him. Nor was he an unknown artist using a Cause to add luster to his name. It was already one of the most illustrious names in international art.

Szyk put away his success and drew pictures only for Bergson and Merlin—and the Irgun. They were as good pictures as Daumier, Rops, or Delacroix could have drawn for any cause.

Szyk's work resembled that of the ancient Persian miniaturists, except that it had power as well as precision, and that it was alive with valor rather than languor. His paintings and drawings were like choruses chanting out of the past. In his early days in Poland, he had lived in a rich house far from the buzz and bicker of ghetto life. He had been one of the handful of fortunate Polish Jews. He had married a young woman as renowned for her beauty as he was for his painting. And in this time Szyk, as an artist, specialized in one subject—the Hebrews of the Bible. He painted their rituals, their lust, their magnificence. He ignored the modernistic revolutions that were turning art into decorative symptoms. He continued to draw with fanatic lyric precision the humanity and pomp of the Hebrew yesterday.

When Poland was conquered by the Germans and all the Jews in it murdered—two million in the first few months—Szyk was in London as a friend of the English Queen and crony with half the British nobility. So witty and talented a man had not been heard in London since Pope or Wilde and so beautiful a consort had not been seen since Lady Hamilton.

Szyk's art lent a nobility to the Irgun cause. His Hebrews under fire, under torture, exterminated in lime pits and bonfires, did not change. They remained a people to be loved and admired. Their faces, fleeing from massacre now, were tense and still beautiful. There was never slovenly despair or hysterical agony in Szyk's dying Jews, but only courage and beauty. If there was ever an artist who believed that an hour of valor was better than a lifetime of furtiveness and cringe, it was Szyk. Just as the Irgun produced the first fighting Jew since Bar Kochba, Szyk put him on paper for the first time. He died still drawing for the Jews.

During the years I worked with Szyk I considered him as much a literary man as an artist. His mind was nimble and relentless in the violent propaganda we shared, and always calm. I knew always that this battle to which he gave his life was as happy a place for him as if he had come upon the jolliest of picnics. It gave him a chance to fight for the Jews with all his wit, genius and manhood.

A folder lies at my elbow as I write looking out again on the ocean outside my Oceanside window. It is a copy of the eulogy delivered by a rabbi at Szyk's funeral on September 14, 1951. In its summation of Szyk's life there is no mention of the word Jew or of the cause for which he worked so passionately—the Irgun Zvai Leumi that drove the British out of Palestine. It is like reading an obituary of Ethan Allen and finding in it no reference to the American Revolution or the Green Mountain Boys.

F. D. R.

I BEGIN my Roosevelt-Jewish story with a footnote. It is his relation to a single Jew whom I knew. Roosevelt's failure to raise one of his humanitarian fingers to prevent the extermination of the Jews, his many sullen statements about the "Jewish situation" and his spiritual anesthesia to the greatest genocide in history, can only be understood, by me, in the light of this anecdote.

My Roosevelt contribution, including this anecdote, is going to be a nuisance to write, for my passions are much cooled on its subject matter, and I wince a bit when I think of all the people it will offend—possibly all the Jews from pole to pole who happen to read it. For if there was one thing of which the Jew of that anti-Jewish time—1933 to 1945—was sure, it was that the great F. D. R. in the White House was his friend. The Germans who hated him called him Rosenfeld, not because they believed he was Jewish but because he was beloved by the Jews.

In my case the only reason I "loved Roosevelt" (for a time) was because he called the Germans names, and because he induced the U.S.A. to join the British in destroying them—for a time. That our beloved F. D. R. did this in defense of the British Empire rather than in defense of Jews made little difference to me. As a Jew I knew that it is always dangerous to examine a hero too closely. I remember a Jewess who adored Chekhov but was careful not to read his story, "The Jew."

But I do not want to do a disservice to the Jews by writing that they all, or nearly all, worshiped the great F. D. R. for the same reasons I did. If they had, they would have quit lighting incense pots under his name when I did. This happened when I found out that Roosevelt, who was a knight against the enemies of the Jews, did not like Jews.

Jews were to him an irritating people. Out of his great humanitarian face there came never more than a sneer for them. Most of the Jews around him didn't mind this. Jews have learned to be broadminded in the presence of a great man. A little anti-Semitism doesn't rule out the fact that the rest of him is very high class. Says the worldly Jew, if the Ship of State is headed in the right direction, you help stoke its furnaces even if the captain doesn't like you.

Of the many Jews around Roosevelt in the White House, there was one I will call Mr. W. Mr. W. was a wealthy merchant. He was a foreign-born Jew and spoke with a Jewish accent.

Mr. W. dined frequently with the President, often at his bedside, contributed heavily to the financial activities of his sons and daughter, Anna, and was called "Popsy" by the entire Roosevelt clan. He was a noisy, witty man and fun to have around, what with his jokes, his questionable English and his fine unquestionable bank account.

So infatuated was Mr. W. with the great man in the White House that he commissioned a famous sculptor to make him a bust of Franklin Roosevelt. This bust Mr. W. kept in his own home, mounted on a pedestal and with concealed lights shining on it as if it were a shrine.

But there was one thing that kept disturbing the happiness of this Jewish Popsy in the White House. Mr. W. was too rich, too successful a Jew, to feel crushed by anything that happened to other Jews.

But still, he was a Jew and he read the papers and he heard people talk. He thought something should be done or at least said about the massacre of the Jews of Europe.

After delighting the President with some jokes in the children's nursery one day, Mr. W. brought up the topic that was beginning to burn like a match in his robust insides—the German massacre of the Jews.

"I don't want you to talk about Jews to me," the President stopped him sharply. "Now or ever. I haven't time to listen to any Jewish wailing."

Mr. W. cracked a few more jokes and retired to one of the historic bedrooms in the White House which he was privileged to occupy. Thereafter, the President began kidding Popsy in a way Mr. W. found a little unpleasant.

"Watch out for Popsy," Mr. Roosevelt would say to his family. "He may turn out to be another Goldman."

"Who was Goldman?" Mr. W. asked. The President refused, archly, to answer. But hardly a week passed in which Mr. Roosevelt didn't point a stern finger at Popsy and say, "Try not to be another Goldman."

Mr. W. finally ran down the abominable Goldman. He had been a friend of F. D. R.'s when the Groton alumnus had run for the governorship of New York. He had been, also, chief financial backer of the campaign. A month before the elections, this Goldman had suddenly switched sides. He had walked out of the Roosevelt camp and smack into the camp of his rival. He had, also, taken over the financing of this rival's camp.

Why he had done this Mr. W. was unable to learn. But done it he had, and on the surface it sure looked like a betrayal.

"But," said Mr. W., talking to me, "it was not Goldman, a political climber, who had betrayed Roosevelt. It was Goldman, a Jew. And I began to realize that whenever President Roosevelt heard the word Jew, he saw this fellow, Goldman. The Jews being massacred in Europe were all Goldmans. The Jews trying to escape getting murdered were all Goldmans, too. And I, who loved him and thought he was a god on earth, I was a Goldman—to be."

Mr. W. was a Jew who loved importance, who thrilled at the thought of being able to eat and sleep in the White House. But there was in him also a thing that has leaked out of most Jews, the righteousness and arrogance of my own favorite ancestor—the Prophet Elijah.

After Roosevelt's death, Mr. W. said to me, "I'm not going to speak against him. He was a great man. And now he's dead. I'm not going to tell you what he said about Jews—except that one night I went home and picked up his bust that had cost me five thousand dollars and threw it out of the window, from the ninth floor. I was glad, despite it was beautiful marble, that it smashed to pieces."

When Mr. W. went home, I sat remembering not him or Roosevelt, but Voltaire. I remembered how Voltaire had given a pair of valuable cuff links to a jeweler in Berlin to have them repaired. The jeweler was a Jew. When Voltaire called for the cuff links, he studied them and set up a cry that the jeweler had robbed him—that the gems in the cuff links were not the same. Whereupon the great philosopher had brought suit against the jeweler. The trial proved that Voltaire was mistaken and that the jeweler was innocent.

The little Berlin Jew won his case, but the Jews of Europe lost it. For after leaving the courtroom, Voltaire added another target for his electric tirades—Jews. He never tired of maligning and ridiculing them, and preparing them as a contemptible people for future abuse.

I have, by the way, never known an intelligent Jew who did not admire Voltaire as one of the great friends of humanity.

THE FURTIVE AMERICAN REVOLUTION

IN THE TIME I made obeisance to Roosevelt, practically all the Jews in the U.S., except those who toiled in Hollywood, were on his side. He had a following there, but not of the Jewish royalty.

In fact, in the Roosevelt-Landon presidential tussle, Beverly Hills, home of the togaed Jews who ran the studios, voted overwhelmingly for Landon. It was the sole community in the U.S. that came up with an Alf Landon landslide.

The landslide was the result of considerable bulldozing in the studios. A Roosevelt man in the M-G-M studio, for instance, where I was working, was likely (if overheard) to be drummed out of that movie compound. The wives and concubines of the movie caliphs also campaigned ardently. They called in their retinues of servants and told them that if Roosevelt was elected, the U.S.A. would collapse and be overrun with weeds. They, the chatelaines, would be forced to shut down their houses and go live in cheap hotels—without servants. Thus all the butlers, cooks, maids and chauffeurs of Beverly Hills rushed to vote for Alf Landon and continued employment around the swimming pools.

I mention this as proof of the sort of humanitarian leader Franklin Roosevelt was believed to be. The Rich quaked before him as before a new and horridly lyrical Robin Hood. The Poor and the Workers loved him as if he were a more informed Christ than the original one, interested in their problems and not merely their souls. As for the Jews, they loved him chiefly as the symbol of a new American obsession called "liberalism." Most of the Jews who give their souls to politics are of this stamp. They are keen for a better world, as who wouldn't be who got snubbed and kicked around in this one.

But Jews have no corner on "liberalism." The Common Man, flattered pink by the Ciceronian love pouring on him from out the White House, was only slightly Jewish. Ninety-five per cent of him was as Gentile as an Easter egg.

Nor was the liberalism that Roosevelt headed up in our country confined to the Poor. A good segment of the Rich fell behind our Prester John headed for the new Holy Land. But it was not the Rich he was interested in. There was a lot of mysticism in Roosevelt. He was one of the best political fortunetellers sitting in high office. He foresaw that the U.S. could not remain an oasis of special privilege for the lucky in a world intent on the rescue of the unlucky. This is not exactly what was going on, but Fascism and Communism both wore a Christ face when they first started in business.

I have a feeling that Roosevelt was not taken in by this Christ face, and that he foresaw that what was striking was not the hour of the Poor but the hour of the Politician. The revolutions that were blowing up nations were to make small difference in the status of the Poor. They were to make a vast difference in the status of the politicos; they were to make czars of all who could pin a political badge on their lapels.

Roosevelt, as bold an ego as the U.S. had produced since Andy Jackson, saw that the new way to power lay in championing the lowly and the unchampioned.

I do not deride the Roosevelt gifts to the Common Man in the U.S.—an unfortunate title which journalist Westbrook Pegler has been more or less correctly belaboring for a decade. Nor do I deride Roosevelt here. That he was a cool, bold boyo, with a realistic rather than a passionate eye for the Main Chance, is no mark against him. If we had to have a revolutionary leader in the U.S., I still thank heaven it was a Walter Pater and not a Gertie Stein.

Looking on the rise of dictators everywhere else in the world, Roosevelt coolly changed the great American concept of life. He announced that it was more important for the Government to have taxes than for the Individual to prosper. He announced that it was more important for people to be protected by government than to be served by it.

This was what Mussolini, Hitler, Bevin, Stalin, and Mao were announcing. There was a difference, however. It lay slightly in the character of the announcement makers, and greatly in the character of the peoples who heard them.

A few months after Roosevelt had entered the White House for the first time, I bet MacArthur (Charlie) a substantial sum that he would be either impeached before the year was over, or that a great counterrevolution led by all the Union League Clubs would sweep the streets with shrapnel. I couldn't imagine that Capitalism would take its first big American licking lying down.

But nothing happened. It is true that the majority of the Rich hated F. D. R. as heartily as if he were conspiring to strangle them in their beds. But the screech set up by the hitherto sacred Profit System was as tempestuous as that of a cat with its tail caught in the screen door—and as powerless. There was no shooting.

THE PINK LEMONADE OF LIBERALISM

Having never been in any political camp before Roosevelt's, I looked around a little ill at ease at my new comrades. I was more used to heaving dornicks at villains than to sitting cross-legged at a Master's feet. I usually came away from such Roosevelt salaamings irritated with most of my fellow head bumpers, especially those Sensitive Souls who went in for a sort of co-suffering with the afflicted of the world—everywhere. Did a Negro get lynched in Alabama, and their own necks felt mystically stretched. Did workmen in Milan or Marrakech raise a cry of an insufficient food supply, then hunger overcame such liberals, as if they themselves were threatened with the closing of the Stork Club.

I know that such sensitivity may often lead to human improvements (usually impermanent) and to lasting first-rate literature. Out of it art, love, grace and Godliness may come.

But I know also there is likely to be a sickness in it that improves nothing and writes nothing and is no more than a poultice for inward guilts. I know that buzzing away sensitively about righting all the world's injustices is more likely the sign that a man is too weak to live than that he is eager to fight.

Put bluntly, sensitivity is more often an illness than a point of view. It is to goodness what brutality is to strength. As a "Roosevelt man," I noticed that around me there were more invalids than Ivanhoes, by a hundred to one. I decided early in the great man's reign to remain his devotee but dodge his other devotees.

On the whole, I fear I was a churlish Liberal, to whom all political leaders of all persuasions seemed no better than gadget peddlers with their foot in the door, whining the sale of their wares. With the politician, the foot stays longer, the whine is louder and the wares on sale more worthless—himself.

Such "Liberals" as myself are apt to be uncomfortable with a friend in power. We prefer an enemy on the throne—an arrogant creature who despises the rights of man, or some paranoid knight of unreason. Then we know where we stand. No sooner does any such devilish fellow come into high office anywhere than we specialized Liberals let go with our howitzers. They are the howitzers of art, and no villain has ever stood up long against them.

Today we are inactive, because there is no such Belshazzar in the U.S.A., not yet. There are plenty of half-assed imps around but the artist is still like Milton. He prefers to do battle with Lucifer. It makes for better writing and for more importance as a writer.

THE HUMANITARIAN WHO SNUBBED
A MASSACRE

SINCE THE ONLY REASON for putting on our pageant, "We Will Never Die," was to call attention to the massacre of the Jews by the Germans, I said to Peter Bergson one day, "We're wasting time doing this pageant. It's actually no more than playing house. What we should do is get President Roosevelt to inform the Germans that if they keep on killing Jews they'll be held responsible and treated as criminals after they're licked in the war. Such a pronouncement from Roosevelt would be worth a thousand pageants."

"It's a sound philosophic idea," said Peter, "but it isn't practical."

I argued angrily. My friend waited till I was done and then, as if he were addressing the House of Lords in London (once his favorite visiting place), said, "The United States has a secret pact with Great Britain concerning the future of Palestine. It is intended to belong to the British. President Roosevelt will do nothing to violate that pact. He will not speak of Jews being massacred because that might excite popular opinion to rescue them—and result in their being sent to Palestine as a haven, which would be a violation of this pact."

"Pact, my eye," I answered. "I'm sick of our theorizing. A single practical gesture can blow theories to hell in a moment."

"It is not exactly a theory," said Peter patiently. "In 1938 the Irgun received secret information of the pact—to keep the Jews out of Palestine. It was then we began to smuggle Jews out of Europe. Abrasha Stavsky was in charge of the operation."

"Who was Abrasha Stavsky?" I asked, pleased by the name.

"The greatest human being I know," Peter uttered a rare chuckle. "You will meet him sometime. He's like a hero out of Conrad or Gogol. He's the Taras Bulba of the Jews—six feet three inches tall, the best sailor on the Mediterranean, and he can throw five men out of a window in a fight. He's afraid of nothing, also he can drink more than anybody I know."

"What's he doing now?" I asked.

"Saving Jews," said Peter. "Do you remember the Free City of Danzig? Abrasha took fifteen hundred Jews out of it, piled them into some sort of a leaky boat and sailed it almost singlehanded to Tel Aviv. He's been doing the same thing ever since then."

"You seem to have lost the thread of your argument," I said to Peter.

"Nothing of the sort," said Peter.

"We were discussing getting a statement from Roosevelt," I said.

"I will come to Roosevelt in a moment," said Peter. "First I must tell you that you have never understood the White Paper. The British White Paper closed the ports of Palestine, openly and officially, to the Jews. All the Jews of the world protested—even the Zionists. When the British refused utterly to listen, every important Jew there was appealed to Roosevelt. He turned them all down worse than the British had done. They were told that President Roosevelt was too busy being the head of a nation to be bothered with saving Jews from a mythical pogrom."

"Roosevelt can't call it mythical any more," I said. "Don't tell me that a man who is the leader of the world's humanitarians is going to turn his nose up at the slaughter of an innocent race."

"I'll check with Washington," said Peter, "and see if Mr. Roosevelt's point of view has altered. I know his chief secretary, David Niles. He's a fine fellow and also a Jew. But don't call off the pageant yet."

Two days later I was informed by David Niles that President Roosevelt would not make a speech or issue a statement denouncing the Germans for the massacre of the Jews.

"Let's forget about Roosevelt and devote ourselves to your pageant," said Peter.

The next morning Billy Rose called up Albany and spoke to Governor Dewey. He asked the governor to declare the day of our pageant an official day of mourning for the State of New York, in memory of the Jews killed by the Germans. Mr. Dewey agreed and said he would issue such a proclamation to the press.

At noon, the next day, Governor Dewey's secretary called up and said that Rabbi Stephen Wise had brought a delegation of twelve important Jews to Albany and obtained an audience with the governor. At this audience, Rabbi Wise had tried to induce Dewey to cancel his "Day of Mourning" proclamation. He had stated, said the secretary, that Governor Dewey was likely to lose most of his Jewish vote in New York City if he did not break with the "danger-.

ous and irresponsible racketeers who are bringing terrible disgrace on our already harassed people." The secretary concluded that we could no longer be certain of the governor's promised action, and hung up.

Billy and I discussed how best to win the governor back to our side. We decided to do nothing and let Dewey wrestle himself out of his dilemma.

Two days later Governor Dewey issued the proclamation declaring the day of our pageant an official day of mourning for the State of New York, in memory of the massacred Jews of Europe.

"We Will Never Die" played two performances in its one night in Madison Square Garden. Some forty thousand people squeezed in to witness it. Another twenty thousand crowded the streets outside and listened to the performance and Kurt Weill's great music piped over loud-speakers.

A few weeks later the pageant played Washington, Philadelphia, Boston, Chicago, St. Louis and Los Angeles. Our victory was more than weeping and cheering audiences. The news and pictures of our pageant in the press were the first American newspaper reports on the Jewish massacre in Europe.

THE UNMARKETABLE JEW

I WALKED an empty wintry Fifth Avenue with Kurt Weill late one night. He was a short man, bald, large-eyed and with an always lighted expression. The pageant business was over. All the cohorts who had helped stage and put it over had, seemingly, melted away— except Kurt. My composer friend was unmeltable. He was a piece of Jewish obsidian.

"The pageant has accomplished nothing," he said as we walked. "I know Bergson calls it a turning point in Jewish history, but he is stage-struck. Actually, all we have done is make a lot of Jews cry, which is not a unique accomplishment."

"There won't be any more silence," I said.

"There is too much silence still," said Kurt. "Let me read you something." We stopped under a street light. "It's a Swiss-German newspaper."

Kurt translated several inches of print. The story said that the

Rumanian government had offered to release seventy thousand Jews in Rumania, including ten thousand children under the age of twelve, in payment of fifty dollars apiece. The fifty dollars were to cover transportation expenses to Palestine.

"We don't want to get rich selling Jews," a Rumanian official was quoted, "but we would like to get them out of Rumania before the Germans come in and start killing them all off and giving us a bad name."

There were, said the report, only one hundred and ten Nazi gauleiters as yet in Rumania. The Rumanian official added that his government had made its offer through Switzerland to the world at large.

I telephoned Peter Bergson in the morning. "It's true," he said. "We have just received reports from our Irgun men in Bucharest. The offer has been made by the Rumanian government to the world at large. I'm leaving for Washington in an hour."

Bergson had become a name in the Capital to which doors opened. His calm and seeming cheeriness, as if he were some school-tie British diplomat, made him a rather unexpected representative of Jews. Neither violence nor hysteria were in him. But there was a quality a hundredfold more effective. He was as persistent as a force of nature.

He was somewhat un-Jewish in another regard. He had no respect for the great men whom he bagged with his persistence. He respected only his cause.

Peter interviewed scores of Government officials. All denied there was such a Rumanian offer.

They were all lying like Russian politicians hewing to a party line. The truth was to come out five years later in a number of published works and documents. Among these were Henry Morgenthau's articles in *Collier's* Magazine, Josiah du Bois' *The Devil's Chemist*, and Ira Hirschmann's *Lifeline to a Promised Land*. Such an offer had been made by the Rumanians. Our State Department, directed by President Roosevelt, had immediately sent a secret and reassuring letter to the Arab leaders, Ibn Saud among them. The President wrote Ibn Saud not to fear an influx of Rumanian Jewish refugees into Palestine.

But in his three-day siege of the State Department, Bergson was unable to uncover a syllable of this truth.

I nevertheless wrote a propaganda ad that broadcast the Rumanian offer. It appeared on a full page in a dozen leading newspapers. Bless the advertising departments of the American press! Peter had discovered that nowhere else in the world could truth and passion speak, unedited—if you could afford the rates.

The ad announced that seventy thousand Jews of both sexes had been offered for sale by the Rumanian government at fifty dollars a head. They were, our ad vouched, guaranteed human beings.

I wrote the ad in bitter phrases. Its object was to shock Jews, infuriate Jews and set them to screaming. This they did, chiefly at me. I was, said the Jewish country clubs, the Zionists, the other Jewish organizations, a liar and a sensation monger, trying to attract attention to myself—and nothing more. I had dragged the name Jew down to a new low. If such an offer had been made, cried the Roosevelt-loving Jews of the land, President Roosevelt would have snapped it up. No decent American could imagine that the American government could let seventy thousand Jews be butchered.

It did. President Roosevelt held the breach, with Lord Moyne, for five months until the Germans swarmed into Rumania. Then our President and his State Department relaxed. The Germans took care of the rest of the job of keeping the Rumanian Jews—including their ten thousand children—out of Palestine. They were all slaughtered.

The "abominable ad," as the Zionist press called it, had not been entirely futile. My bitterness, my certainty and the size of the type in which they were offered won the Committee a large following.

We were creating a new school of Jews in the U.S.—one which refused to believe blindly in the virtues of their enemies in Democracy's clothing.

THE UNMENTIONABLE JEW

It is difficult to get rid of illusions, for they are the product of our deepest hopes. They need no fact to feed on. Worse, fact can rarely destroy them.

All these matters I have recited failed to turn me against Franklin Roosevelt. I remained his ardent drum beater. He was not on the side of the Jews, but he was on the side of the angels. A Jew can imagine this is the same thing.

Besides, what proof did I have other than the logic of events? Believe in logic and your sweetheart is unfaithful every time she lies to you. It's better to wait till you can look in, unexpectedly, through the bedroom window and see something besides logic.

Such a look, a long one—I took in September, 1944. On that day the three Allies issued the Moscow Declaration in which the Germans were informed they would be punished after the war for their crimes against humanity.

This document was called officially, "Statement on the German Atrocities." It stated that Great Britain, the United States and the Union of Soviet Socialist Republics had received indisputable evidence of atrocities and cold-blooded mass executions of noncombatants done by the Germans. It listed the killing of Polish noblemen, Polish workingmen, Polish officers, of French, Dutch, Belgian and Norwegian hostages and of a group of innocent Greek peasants on the island of Crete. The list identified sixty-two different categories of German victims. Every name was listed but the name of Jew.

In this most righteous of humanitarian documents, no reference appeared to the three million murdered Jews, noncombatants of both sexes ranging from infancy to hoary age. And no reference was made to the remaining three millions waiting to die in the German ovens! There was a pretty omission—the greatest race murder in history, omitted from the official Allied statement on German atrocities signed by the Englishman Churchill, the Russian Stalin and the American Roosevelt.

Reading it, I could think of no political gesture in history as hypocritical and repulsive as this silence—a silence that was like a door closing furtively and surreptitiously on the murderer and his victim—the Jewish people.

Reading it I knew, without any further data from the Committee, that British policy preferred that all the Jews die incognito in the German furnaces rather than that a single Jewish refugee enter Palestine. I knew that my American President Roosevelt was of similar mind in the matter. He was on the side of the angels, but he looked now a little too red with Jewish blood for my further hosannas.

The previous Rooseveltian record on Jews might have been

surmise and fog. But here was evidence in print, signed, sealed and delivered to the world.

I wrote another ad for a score of newspapers. It filled a page with large type. It was headlined, "My Uncle Abraham Reports."

My Uncle Abraham, said the ad, was a member in fine standing of the Jewish underground, which consisted of millions of dead Jews, recently murdered by the Germans. He had been sent as a delegate by this underground into the world to see if anybody had as yet shown any interest in their extermination. Pad and pencil in hand, my Uncle Abraham had attended the great Moscow Conference between the three champions of humanity, and he had come away considerably depressed. Apparently, said my Uncle Abraham, making his report to his fellow dead, Jews were not allowed to remain alive in the world, and when they died, nobody was allowed to mention it. But my Uncle Abraham had not given up. He had come to Washington, D.C., and gone straight to President Roosevelt's study in the White House. And there he still was sitting on the window sill, pad and pencil in hand. But he had small hope of hearing anything about Jews dead or alive worth writing down.

F. D. R. RIDES TO THE RESCUE!

BERNARD BARUCH, the venerable counselor of American Presidents, telephoned me two days after the ad appeared. I knew Baruch slightly and had once done him the favor of removing his name from some movie dialogue. I had met him subsequently at dinner parties and been impressed by him as a man who loved life and people more than power. He wanted, this time, another favor.

"I was talking to Mr. Roosevelt," he said, "and he was very upset about your Uncle Abraham ad. He told me he's going on an important trip soon, and that during this trip he will settle the Jewish problems in the Near East to my satisfaction—and yours. In view of this statement, I am taking the liberty of asking you to call off all further criticisms of President Roosevelt and his administration—until you hear from me again."

I went to the offices of the Committee that now had a half-dozen different titles on its many frosted glass doors. I had not been there

for some months. Scores of men and women were racing in and
out of doorways, typewriters and mimeographs were banging, a
newspaper called *The Answer* was being printed weekly. There
were scores of desks occupied by journalists and professors. A multitude of filing cabinets filled all the rooms, and thousands of books,
periodicals, clippings and communications still unfiled were stacked
against the walls.

All the people I saw, including most of the young women stenographers, were working without pay. In fact, this entire teeming
industry was a sort of Capitalism in reverse. At the end of each
working week the workers called on the boss and paid him as much
as they could afford for the privilege of working for him. The Committee kept expanding its activities and the greater its successes the
bigger always were its deficits.

I picked out Merlin, Bergson and Ben Ami out of the hullaballoo
and behind closed doors told them my top secret. After reading
Baruch's statement to them, written down as he made it over the
phone, I said, "Baruch doesn't say it, but what he said can mean
only one thing. What Jewish problem can President Roosevelt solve?
He can make the British open the ports of Palestine—and he can
help save Jews from German slaughter and he can help get them to
their homeland."

"It might mean that," said Merlin.

"It can't mean that," said Ben Ami.

"I think Mr. Baruch believes Roosevelt is going to do all or some
of those things," said Bergson, "but I think Mr. Baruch is wrong."

"Whatever you think," I said, "I'd like all sniping at Roosevelt
and his administration to stop."

My three friends nodded.

"We'll not print or send out a line," said Peter, "until you agree."

A month later President Roosevelt returned from his visit to the
Near East. He had consorted with many leaders, but no Jewish ones.
The most important of his conferees was Ibn Saud, ruler of Saudi
Arabia, and recipient of a hundred thousand dollars a day as royalties
from American oil companies. In addition to being the darling of
American industry, Ibn Saud was, next to Hitler, the most out-
spoken anti-Semite on the world map.

In a statement by Ibn Saud a few weeks before President Roosevelt's conference with him, the dusky and gilded Arab chief had

said, "The only way to solve the Jewish situation in the Near East is to take all the Jews out of Palestine and send them into Central Africa where they won't be able to bother anybody. If they refuse to go, the only other alternative is to exterminate them where they are, and be rid of the Jewish situation for good."

On his return, President Roosevelt made a report to Congress in March, 1945. The report had been written by Judge Rosenman, President Roosevelt and son-in-law John Boettiger. In delivering it to Congress, Roosevelt added an extemporized paragraph that he had never discussed with his collaborators.

Said Roosevelt, standing before the world, "For instance, on the problem of Arabia, I learned more about that whole problem—the Moslem problem, the Jewish problem—by talking with Ibn Saud for five minutes, than I could have learned in the exchange of two or three dozen letters."

In his book, *Working with Roosevelt*, Rosenman, the Jew, comments naïvely, "This was a thought that must have popped into his head at just that moment, for I never heard him say anything like that on the way home from Algiers."

A few weeks after his report to Congress, Roosevelt, writing to the Arabian-Jewish problem solver, Ibn Saud, addressed him as my "great and good friend." I telephoned Bernard Baruch to tell him our little Roosevelt amnesty was at an end.

Baruch answered, "I have had a two-hour talk with President Roosevelt about the Jews and the Jewish problem. I have spoken also to Governor Dewey on the same subject. I can only tell you as a result of these talks that, despite my having been a lifelong Democrat, I would rather trust my American Jewishness in Mr. Dewey's hands than in Mr. Roosevelt's."

Baruch, one of the most esteemed Jews in the U.S., had failed along with Popsy and all other lesser Jewish influences that sought to get the Roosevelt mind off the memory of Goldman.

REST IN PEACE

THE MUTUAL NETWORK, for whom I had done a number of war propaganda radio shows, asked me to do another one. They wanted a curtain raiser for the opening session of the United Nations to be held in San Francisco. Harold Stassen, the dashing politico out of Minnesota, had agreed to be one of the costars of the Mutual show.

I accepted the chore, wrote the show and recruited Edward G. Robinson as Stassen's coplayer. A grandiose propaganda stroke had occurred, simultaneously, to me. I would write and stage another show also while in San Francisco, one that would explode the Jewish issue in the face of the entire United Nations. This one would be put on in a theater and run as long as the delegates remained in session.

I imagined there might be some trouble and that the American State Department might try to raise hell. But I knew the State Department from Stettinius down and had worked for it, and it was not a group of men to stir fear in anyone's heart. A more vacuous wagonload of politicos I had never run into.

I had written a movie for them called *The World of Tomorrow.* Its purpose was to make the citizenry who gaped at it in the movie theaters fall in love with the wonders of the United Nations. What these wonders were no one in the Department seemed to know. I finally put some scraps of information together, larded them with rhetoric and war episodes and sent the script on to Hollywood for production. I came away from a week's toil in the Department stunned by my own naïveté. It was to this group of soupy-brained errand boys that I had appealed over and over to "save the Jews."

Preparing now my secret propaganda play to be played in San Francisco, I grinned at the thought of the State Department attending its opening. The show I was writing was going to be a long one-acter, titled, *Call the Next Case.* Its plot was: Franklin Delano Roosevelt being summoned before the Bar of History to state what he had done to save the Jews of Europe. The jury trying the case consisted of twelve dead Jews from the German crematoriums.

I was writing the script in a Beverly Hills hotel with the radio playing soft music. The music stopped abruptly and a faltering voice announced that President Roosevelt had just died.

That evening I sat listening to the cries of love for F. D. R. that poured out of the radio. No more tear-compelling eulogies had ever hit the nation since the death of Lincoln. There was a sincerity in all the voices that wept, unable to finish their oratory.

The reports of the nation's grief continued to come in like the tale of a spreading holocaust. In their homes, in the streets, in saloons and hotel lobbies, in farm houses, in faraway places and near places, the people of America were bowing their heads and weeping. More than a President had died for them. Some of their own strength and hope had also gone out of the world.

To all this I listened and my own heart remained cool. No humanitarian hero was lying dead for me. A bold and fretful man, an arrogant and lusty man, but a stranger to love and goodness, had died for me. A man with the gift of making himself unreasonably loved, a man who had discovered the poor, like some happy political explorer come upon a hidden continent of voters, was being wept over, and all his great fine deeds acclaimed. In my mind his chief monument remained—the dead Jews of Europe.

I threw away the pages of *Call the Next Case* and, a few weeks later, went to San Francisco to put on the Stassen radio show. After the radio performance, I was summoned to come to the St. Francis Hotel, where the State Department was hacking away at a knotty international problem.

I entered a room full of smokers and drinkers and diplomats all. Secretary Stettinius explained the problem to me. They were trying to decide what piece of music should open the first historic session of the United Nations. Anything by Brahms, Tchaikovsky, Sibelius, Chopin, Beethoven, Mozart, Sullivan, Elgar, Gershwin, etc., was out, because it would then have a nationalistic flavor and thus might irritate the other peacemakers assembled. I left at midnight with the problem still in the air.

But it was neatly solved after my departure. The first session of the United Nations opened with the tune "Lover Come Back to Me."

I knew who the Lover was. Cool though my heart had been for the death of Franklin Roosevelt, I looked at the Opera House stage where the world's leaders were waiting to open the historic session, and I knew that the show would be a flop. The leading man was missing, the crooning lieutenant in the white pants who gets the girl, for whom the script had been written, had left the cast.

MIRAGE OF WORDS

THE COMMITTEE became a force in the world. It had active units in a score of U.S. cities and in London and Paris. It even acquired respectability for a time—among the Gentiles. The Jewish organizations, however, kept their heads. Their choice lay more and more between admiring the Irgun or despising themselves; and they made it without falter. Led by the Zionist Jews, they increased their stone throwing and name calling.

I had made a pact with Peter Bergson early in our work. I had got a promise from Peter that no matter how vociferously and viciously the Jews attacked us we would never attack Jews. We would continue only to attack the enemies of Jews.

Despite the increasing barrage of Jewish brickbats under which we found ourselves, and despite the great Jewish enthusiasm I had aroused for my own scalp, I found it easy to keep this pact. I became aware that one of the chief reasons the Jews had never won out in the world was that they were always too busy fighting each other. It had been always safer for Jews to fight Jews than to turn on any Gentile enemies. Jew versus Jew produced little more than vituperative reading matter in the Yiddish press. Jew versus Gentile could produce exile and pogrom.

The unanswered Jewish attack under which the Committee operated did it small harm—for a time. Its power and prestige kept growing. Guy M. Gillette stepped from a seat in the U.S. Senate to become the Committee's official spokesman. Will Rogers, Jr., and his wife, Collier, came into our ranks with the whoop of a cavalry column. William B. Ziff brought his wisdom and oratory to our camp. Governors, admirals, generals, statesmen, philosophers and even financiers, most of them Gentile, were happy to fly their names from our letterheads.

Our working cohorts, however, remained the Jews. Jews contributed the money we needed to run our propaganda. Millions came in, most of it in dollar and five-dollar bills.

A part of this money was contributed in secrecy. The donors asked that their names not be made public. They were Jews belonging to the organizations of Jewry that were attacking us.

Under this shower of gold, Bergson and Merlin continued to live like a pair of paupers. No new suits bloomed on them. They bought no automobiles and moved into no Waldorf suites. They remained in their hall bedrooms and ate frugally. The other half-dozen Palestinian Irgunists now serving under Bergson practiced similar austerities.

But Bergson, Merlin and Ben Ami were no longer landlocked. They flew often to France. Here they collared more French statesmen for the Irgun and lent a financial hand to the still invisible Abrasha Stavsky.

Stavsky was now loading his cargoes in Marseilles and other French ports. The cargoes were larger but always the same— Jews; the trickle of Jews able to get out of the German extermination zones.

Stavsky's work had become more difficult. His leaky tubs jammed with Jewish refugees must now outwit the Royal British Navy guarding the coast of Palestine against "enemies of the British Crown." Stavsky and his death-haunted Jews heading for their Holy Land came under this classification. Armed to the teeth, British land forces also guarded all the landing points on the Palestinian coast.

But Stavsky brought his cargoes in. He sailed them in under cover of fog and tempest. And when British batteries opened up on Stavsky's tossing, shadowy targets, our Stavsky offered no answering shot. But he knew every shoal and reef off the Palestinian coast, and he would race the British Navy for a storm-whipped line of rocks, wreck his tub on them and swim and wade his cargo to the shore of the Holy Land.

Here, despite British land patrols, Irgunists whisked the sea-sick, sea-battered refugees to safety in the Hebrew settlements. And Stavsky would head back for Marseilles. How? God knows. Several times he remained afloat off the coast on a piece of timber, enjoying the lights of Tel Aviv from afar, until picked up by another Irgun tub. But back he always went, and back to Palestine he always came again, with a new cargo.

All this was a hundred times more than I had wished for when I had first longed to hear an outcry against the German murder of the Jews. The outcry had arisen and grown. There were scores of Irgun mass meetings, rallies, dinners, pageants, ads, brochures and columns and pages of newspaper print. They all made outcry.

But now that it had come, the outcry seemed to make little sense and hold less victory. It had reached German ears and done no good. My theory had been wrong. The Germans, made aware that the murder of the Jews was humanly distasteful to the world, had not stayed their reddened hands. They had continued killing Jews.

But my theory had been, possibly, only half wrong. For there had been only half an outcry against the massacre of the Jews. The political outcry had been missing. With all our mass meetings and stinging propaganda we had managed to rouse no protest against the Jewish massacre from Roosevelt, Churchill, Stalin, or their official governments.

THE JEWS STRIKE OUT

THE WAR for the rescue of humanity from German defilement ended "triumphantly" with all the Jews of Europe exterminated and the great victors still indifferent to that amazing fact. The word Jew lay lusterless in its horrid grave.

I knew now that rhetoric was no better than tears as a solution for my "Jewish Problem"—the rescue of the word Jew from the garbage can into which the Germans had dumped it. I had had faith in eloquence as a historical force. History had disproved my faith. I saw that propaganda was incapable of altering anything around it. It might incubate in time, it might mold the future. But it could only confuse the present or irritate it, or be lost entirely in all the other word noises of its own day.

I began to wonder if the cause I had tried to serve was even sensible. Did such a cause even exist—the salvaging of the word Jew? What did it mean? Obviously one of its meanings was the fact that my ego had identified itself with this historic word. Something in me, as well as in Europe, was being removed and befouled. Since it had been always my habit to answer insults, I had answered back to the Germans. But was an outraged ego a cause?

I kept avoiding something I knew, because it was contrary to my version of myself. In this version I had been always a sort of detached fellow who believed in nothing or, at least, in very little— in a few good human traits, in the charms of love and gallant friendship and in the single dictum—let your neighbors alone as you would like to be let alone. I was, also, a man of much negative kindness. The only prayer I had ever heard that had appealed to me was a line by the Hindu pundit Acharya. He had written, "I pray each day that I may be made strong enough not to hurt anyone."

I found it difficult now to face the all-too-human fact that the "cause" I had tried to serve was not what I had kept telling myself it was. The egoistic concern for the word Jew was there. But the compelling thing that had thrown me into the Jewish fight was that I loved Jews. It may have been mostly the memory of my parents and tantes and uncles that I loved—I find it hard even now to understand where this love came from and for whom it was. But there rose up before the eyes of my soul a world that I loved, that was Jewish; a world of fine-smelling kitchens, fascinating little candy stores, crowded tenement streets with infants crawling over hot pavements; a Jewish world of tearooms, amusement parks, cloak and suit factories, huge holiday dinners, jokes and curses in broken English and even of whiskered rabbis and tiny synagogues smelling of musty books and candle grease.

I had lived in such a world only for the first ten years of my life, but it was as vivid as if I had never stepped out of it.

The fact that the torture and massacre of Jews had failed ever to bring any tears to my eyes, that it was rage against the brute I felt rather than pity for his victim, had helped conceal from me why I was in the Jewish cause. I had looked on myself and seen a man hot with angers. He seemed as lacking in love and sentiment for Jewish memories as if he had been born on the moon, rather than in the New York ghetto.

But when I saw now that the Jews were forever done for, a wail came into my heart. Who could save them now—the dead and dishonored? What words were there that could make the cold world tip its hat to their grave—their disowned and unkept grave?

I looked at the Jews around me still trying to believe themselves intact. But the intactness was gone. However they twisted about to evade the truth, they were members of a race, a tribe, a religion or whatever the Jews are, that had been burned alive in a great public bonfire with no friend in the world to cry "shame" or "stop." They were Americans, too, these Jews around me. But wounded ones. The wound was big.

The American in me came to a painful conclusion: "The Jew isn't much good as a Jew. But he's fine and brave as anything else. The best thing a Jew can do is forget there is any Jewish cause —and stick to causes that he can back up under a flag—and with a gun."

I nodded to my honest American counselor—myself from Racine and Chicago. It was sensible advice. I would go back to being an American, full of American pride and victory. There would remain a small, private area of defeat in me called Jew. On the Jewish holy days that I never had observed before, I would make certain observances now. I would remember that all the people to whom, in a curious way, I belonged had been slaughtered and that they had been too lowly a people for the world to regret. And too spiritless a people to raise a fist or a gun against their enemies.

Except the Jews of the Warsaw ghetto. I would remember them on the Jewish holidays. There had not been many—some thirty thousand. But they had faced the German exterminators with more than prayers on their lips. They had old guns and oaken staves, and iron crowbars, and bombs made out of tin cans. Armed with these almost playful weapons, they had met the German Panzer tanks, the German cannon, gas, machine-gun fire and fought them to a standstill for three very military weeks. During these weeks the Jews of Warsaw had issued their communiqués over a single radio. They were standing firm but the need for guns and bullets was growing. Would somebody in the world drop them some ammunition out of the skies, or perhaps even a cannon or two.

Nobody in the world answered. Not a bullet, a bomb or even a cap pistol fell out of the skies. The day of Jewish manna was a long time ago. Thus the Jews of Warsaw were finally reduced to fighting with stones, hot water and sticks. They continued the battle until they were either all slain or too maimed to move.

The Germans carted the wounded quickly to the always ready lime pits, tossed them in and covered them up; and the slaughter of Jews went on as if nothing had happened. Which was not entirely true. I and many Jews like me would remember these Warsaw Jews on the Pesach and, in the security of our American protected homes, drink to them. They were the little souvenir of Jewish pride that glinted in Europe's garbage can.

THE MISSING BATTLE

BERGSON and Merlin sat in my room in Nyack and talked again of Palestine. We must now concentrate our propaganda on its fight for freedom, they said.

I listened listlessly to my friends' Palestinian flag-waving. But they ignored my indifference. They seemed full of new passion on the topic.

"The Jews of Europe are a dead issue," said Merlin, grimly. "If we continue to discuss and lament them we will be doing only what Jews have always done—concerning ourselves with a dead past."

"The British must be driven out," said Bergson, "and Palestine must become a Hebrew Republic. There is no other solution for the Jewish problem. Only if the Jew has his own nation, will the slaughtering of Jews end. As a nation he can speak to other nations, win allies and have a standing in the world. As a Jew he can speak to no one."

"Except God," said Merlin, grimly.

"How many British soldiers are there in Palestine?" I asked.

"Some seventy thousand," said Bergson.

"The Irgun can put five thousand men and women into the field against them," said Merlin.

"Maybe a few less," said Bergson.

I sat silent. As my friends talked I brooded irritably on the new task they were offering. More words in the papers, this time denouncing the British and ordering them sternly, in large type, to get the hell out of someplace they didn't belong. Which was almost like telling them to get off the earth. The hundred and one British strongholds came to my mind—all the lands of other peoples, all owned or ruled by Britannia. I had never given a damn about the justice or injustice rising out of British empire-building.

The British piously announced plans for fashioning a home for non-Britishers in Palestine had taken a not unexpected turn—for any student of British lore. Pledged to create such a homeland, the British had proceeded to arm the enemies of the Jews, to deprive the Jewish pioneers of all citizenship rights, to hang all who protested and, finally, to close all the ports of Palestine and forbid the Jews to enter it altogether.

All these seemingly underhanded activities were, in British eyes, not wrong at all. It was the way one went about improving civilization, in a world given to all sorts of sentimental bottlenecks.

The British were not a people who did things stupidly out of sexual aberration—as did the Germans. There was little hatred of Jews involved in their sly work of filching Palestine from under the Jewish nose. The theft, after all, was a small one.

Considering the immense benefits to mankind (the British Empire), what were a few broken promises? A Jewish state in Palestine would be obviously worthless to anyone (except a few noisy, foolish Jews). For despite all the noise they made, there weren't enough Jews to make such an ally worth a plugged shilling. Whereas an Arab kingdom under British control could mean an ally numbering forty millions. It might even mean an ally numbering a half-billion Moslems.

"If you want to start a country," I said to Bergson and Merlin, "go find Washington or Bolivar or Garibaldi. And go dig up Nathan Hale and Robert Bruce, Robert Emmet and Joan of Arc. There are no such characters in Nyack. Besides, what's the use of talking about the Jews driving the nasty British out of Palestine when ninety-eight per cent of the world's surviving Jewry, including its Zionists, the Jewish Agency supporters, and the Palestinians themselves, are on their knees to the British? All of them trying to whimper a nation into existence! All of them begging for justice as if their swinish enemies had it to give! I'll write no more propaganda babble about Jews. Let the dead ones keep silent, and the living ones keep on whimpering."

My Irgun friends and I parted ways that night. And I went to bed done with Jews and the empty words of Jewish propaganda.

MY UNCLE ABRAHAM FINDS
A NEW UNDERGROUND

I saw the Committee no more for several weeks. The Jewish Problem appeared to have subsided to some sort of polite discussion between the British usurpers of Palestine and those two great Jewish watchdogs, Weizmann and Ben-Gurion. The Jews were the politer of the disputants, for the British lost their heads and threw all the argufying Zionists into jail—except Weizmann and Ben-Gurion.

But in a short while the Anglo-Saxon manners returned and the Jews were all let out of jail. They emerged a little less eager to argue with the British. Led by Weizmann and Ben-Gurion, they launched the new Zionist and Jewish Agency policy for the Holy Land—no more argument with the British. The British must be trusted. The more soldiers they sent into Palestine, the more they must be trusted. And if they found it necessary to establish puppet Arab kingdoms around Palestine, they must still be trusted. And if all the Jews trusted the British and "co-operated with them," watchdogs Weizmann and Ben-Gurion were certain the Jews would be rewarded in one fashion or another; if not with a Hebrew Republic, then with a British-Jewish Protectorate. And if not with that exactly, then with a British Protectorate for an Arab-Jewish state. And even if this failed and the British remained in a purely British Palestine, they would certainly not injure or confiscate any of the Zionist properties or the Jewish Agency's holdings, or forbid Jews to live in the Holy Land, without citizenship rights, but with the right to pray—day and night.

These Zionist and Jewish Agency pronouncements to be read now in the American press struck me as pure Gilbert and Sullivan. I wished, if the Jews had to keep on argufying about Palestine, they could find some way to keep their arguments out of the papers.

A few more interesting items began appearing under Palestine date lines. Some hotheads in Tel Aviv seemed to be taking pot shots at friendly British officers out for a stroll, or stealing a few British motorcars, or holding up an honorable British bank. There was more disquiet to be read in the morning blotter of any Manhattan police station, however, than seemed to be troubling Palestine. It looked a little less than the revolution Bergson and Merlin had been forecasting.

I called on the Committee in its West Forty-fifth Street Headquarters. There was a new title on the frosted door. The odd thing was that the same title was on all the frosted doors. It read, "The American League for a Free Palestine."

I entered and stood watching the most glowing-faced and busiest Jews I had ever seen, busier even than the ones I remembered in my

Uncle Joe's sweatshop. They were freeing Palestine—with mime-ographs and speakers' bureaus and dinner rallies.

Bergson was in his generalissimo's office, a rare place to find him. Standing facing him when I entered were his Palestinian colleagues, Merlin, Ben Ami, Hadani, Ben Eliezer and Eri Jabotinsky.

"Come in," said Peter.

"You appear just at the right time, Mr. Ben Hecht," said Merlin.

"The Irgun has declared war on the British in Palestine," said Ben Ami.

"Here is the declaration by Menachem Beigin," said Peter.

I asked who Beigin was.

"He is the successor of David Raziel as Commander-in-Chief of the Irgun," said Peter. "The declaration begins: 'Enough! The hand that touches our sister, our father, our child—that hand shall be cut off.'"

"Sounds rather Biblical," I said.

"It is going to be fought by a Biblical people," said Hadani.

"Arieh Ben Eliezer and Eri Jabotinsky are returning to Pales-tine," said Peter, "immediately."

"I'm going too," said Ben Ami with a scowl. "It's my home. I belong in the fighting."

"You have my permission," said Peter, "even though there is a price on your head. Don't go too near the posters." To me, he said, "I would like you to accept your usual post on our new league."

"Cochairman?"

"Yes," Peter said.

"I'll start writing about Jews again," I said. "Imagine reading of a Jewish battle instead of a pogrom!"

It was then that the young patriot Arieh Ben Eliezer, who was to end up in a British concentration camp, betrayed into British hands by the Zionists, said to me, "You will see. The unity of the Jews will come after we have driven the British out of Palestine. Just as the unity of the Americans came after the redcoats were driven from the colonies. And please remember, before that more than two thirds of the American population were on the British side— and don't think too badly of our Jews—no matter what happens."

"As your cochairman," I announced, "I'm going home and sharpen some pencils—not against the Jews but the British."

"FROM THE DEPTHS OF THE UNDER-
GROUND AND FROM THE DEPTHS
OF THEIR HEARTS"

THE IRGUN ACTIVITIES in Palestine increased. They were no longer
a matter of pot shots and stolen motorcars. They included the raid-
ing of British arsenals, the blowing up of railroad communications
and bridges, the delivery of Irgun prisoners from Acre Prison—a
feat of daring and cunning that left the British sputtering.

They were to expand daily and end up including the British
withdrawal from Palestine.

There are in the world many stories of Scotch bagpipes and
British drums and American "yippees" rallying beaten men to
victory; many stories of Frenchman, Magyar, Mexican, Turk, Bo-
livian and a hundred and one other sections of the human family
raising a flag out of disaster and adding a radiance to the chronicles
of man. The Irgun Zvai Leumi added such a Jewish tale to the
sagas of the undefeatable.

The Jews who came out to battle the hundred thousand British
soldiers encamped in Palestine consisted of two groups, the Irgun
and an outfit called, sneeringly, "The Stern Gang." Jointly the two
groups numbered less than three thousand men and women, almost
as primitively armed as had been the Jews of the Warsaw ghetto.

If I discontinue reference here to the Sternists and write now only
of the Irgun, it is not because there was anything less deserving about
the Sternists. They were as valorous and nobly inspired a group of
human beings as I have ever met in history.

But it is the Irgun I know. News of every gun it fired, every barrel
of dynamite it exploded, of every arsenal it looted and railroad train
it tipped over was brought to me in secret communiqués, some of
them hidden in cigarette packages. I never read news with a more
pounding heart. I had had no interest in Palestine ever becoming a
homeland for Jews. Now I had, suddenly, interest in little else.

Here were Jews finally fighting for their own honor and not someone else's—usually their enemy's. You could ask for nothing more
novel than that as a piece of Jewish news.

But the fact that they were willing to fight and die for the liberation of a land they called their own was not the great fact to me. Valor had not been missing in the long tale of the Jews. They had stood up often in alien parts of the earth and died memorably.

The great fact was that here were Jews with a new soul, or, possibly, an old one returned. They did not dream of victory as a thing to be won by a tearful parade of their virtues. (Good God, how tired the goyim of Europe must have become of hearing how good their victim was!) Here were Jews who did not believe in the Jewish master plan of submitting always to injustice and then patiently removing it as one removes burrs from a dog's body. Here were Jews who had broken with the ancient Jewish wisdom of waiting piously and unprotestingly for the rage of their enemies to ebb. And I saw that these new qualities had been always in many of the Jews, but that without a land to fight for, they were like a great musical talent without an instrument for its playing.

But chiefly unwanted Jews had trained themselves for centuries in the business of dying carefully, of taking care never to protest too loudly against the villainy of their destroyer, for their descendants must live on among these same destroyers. Thus to give the destroyer a bad name was to make him look for vengeance against these descendants.

There was a heroism in this long-practiced careful dying of the Jews. But there was also a stupidity in it that kept ruining the Jews. The Jew managed, by his proud and pious silence, to give himself a bad name. He gave himself the name of Frightened Jew. This identity was almost a sufficient lure in itself for any group of Christians wanting to blow off steam in a pogrom.

Now here suddenly in the once miracle-haunted land of Palestine were all these new Jewish miracles. I looked at the finest of them with continued wonder—Jews ready to battle the anti-Semitism of their enemy rather than to bask, a little bruised, under his heel.

MEN STAND UP IN ISRAEL

As THE DEEDS of the Irgun increased, a drama of dual courage came out of Palestine. It was the courage of a handful of young Jews hurling themselves onto the bayonets and gallows of the British. And it was also the courage of standing up against the roar of invective set up by the Jews of all the lands—including the one for whose liberation they were battling. Here, fanned by the Socialist Ben-Gurion and the Zionist Weizmann, the Jewish bitterness against the Irgunists sounded its fiercest snorts.

The astonishing cry of all these Jews was that the Irgun was shaming and disgracing Jewry. What curious things cowardice always figures out as shameful and disgraceful! Organized Jewry had felt no shame in failing to send a dollar's worth of help to the thirty thousand Jews who fought and died for the honor of all Jews in the Warsaw ghetto. But here in the Holy Land where young Jews were bravely standing up to a mighty enemy—here was disgrace!

In Tel Aviv the Socialist Jews led by Ben-Gurion, the Zionists and Jewish Agency-ites, all scampered eagerly to British headquarters to protest their own innocence, and to prove it by betraying Irgun hiding places to British Intelligence. British troops with names and addresses in hand, supplied by these Jewish organizations, arrived at secret stores of Irgun bullets and seized them, marched straight to the hideaways of the bravest and cleverest of the Irgun warriors, and arrested them.

The men betrayed by Ben-Gurion's Socialists and the Zionists were sent off to desert concentration camps or hanged on Palestinian gallows.

Among these exiled was the redoubtable Meridor, military wizard of the Irgun. Meridor and a score of other young Jewish heroes were bagged by the British in a stool-pigeon betrayal recorded at the time in the Palestine *Observer* as Operation Golda Myerson. Golda was high in the councils of the Zionists.

Betraying Jewish fighters to the British was not enough for the Ben-Gurion-Weizmann contingent. The fighters must also be betrayed to the world, before the world took to looking on them as Jewish heroes, and took to looking on the other, non-fighting, back-pedaling Jews as something else. Ben-Gurion launched a rear-guard action at the Irgun. He was the first to denounce the Jewish fighters as a gang of terrorists. They were, he said, a small criminal element that must be stamped out by Jews as well as by the British—or no Jew would ever be able to hold his head up again among decent people. Thus spoke the political boss of Palestine.

The name Terrorists became overnight the favorite epithet that all the Jews of the world took to hurling at the fighting Jewish troops. American and Jewish newspapers alike chronicled the Irgun's deeds of valor as the scurvy antics of hoodlums and gangsters. At last the complications of Jewish thought and argument became quite clear to me. In this year, 1947, their hundreds of arguing schools had dwindled to two simple sects—the Terrorists and the Terrified. Alas, how more numerous and popular the latter lot was!

The British propagandists needed hardly to bestir themselves. The press of the world—Christian, Jewish and Moslem—hailed the Goliath of the hundred thousand British soldiers as the forces of peace and order. The handful of Jewish patriots who moved against the British Giant with hardly more than David's slingshot in their hands were the Terrorists.

This confusion about who was terrorizing whom came out of the British triple position in Palestine. They were there as a burglar might be in another man's house. When the house owner spotted him and called for the police, lo and behold, it was the burglar who was the policeman. And when this burglar-policeman dragged the householder into court to stand trial for kicking up a row, lo and again behold, it was this burglar-policeman who sat on the bench as Judge. The world thus witnessed a due process of law. The verdict of Terrorist handed down by the Burglar-Policeman-Judge seemed a fair example of crime and punishment.

In an odd way, undreamed of by the Jewish and Christian name callers, the epithet Terrorist was to turn out a correct one. The Irgun terrorized the British out of Palestine.

NO GIBBON, I, NOR YET A KLAUSNER

WRITING HISTORY is almost as difficult, I find, as writing successful plays. No matter how much truth you put into a play, there is likely to come out of it only some big lie. The same seems to be true about history.

I look at piles of material surrounding me. An ocean of clippings laps at my feet. It is my data on the Irgun fight in Palestine. Each bit of this data is as true as the label on a catchup bottle. Yet I know that if I put all these truths together they may tell some sort of lie.

The reason for this, I suspect, is not in my clippings but in myself. History, somewhat like poetry, is the tranquil echo of ugly matters. There is no tranquillity in me on this historic topic—not yet. What was ugly yesterday strikes me as no less ugly today. Time has lent no enchantment to the evils committed against Jews—not even to those committed by Jews themselves.

An echo comes to me out of my young reporter days in Chicago. Shmarya Levine, the brilliant Zionist, speaks to me. "You are not interested in the problems of Jews right now. I can only say—I envy you. For a Jew not to be interested in Jewish problems is the same as for a man sitting on a hot stove not to be interested in fire. But I would like you to promise me, if you do become interested in Jews some day and start writing about them, you'll write with jokes. At least here and there, a joke."

And Zionist Louis Brandeis, who sits beside him in the Chicago hotel room, speaks. "He means, he hopes you won't lose your head, when you come to use it for the Jews."

And Shmarya Levine adds, "In history there is very little comedy—even in non-Jewish history. But people are always a little comic. Especially Jews."

The echo dies—"especially Jews." I wish the echo had come earlier into my head. But—it's never too late for jokes. Shmarya, I'll see what I can do from here in.

I write this bit of history—the Irgun's liberation of Palestine—for two reasons. The Irgun was part of my life for eight years. The other reason is that almost no one else has written about it. This is as if no one had ever put down the story of Bunker Hill, and Valley Forge; or as if no one had ever mentioned in print the Irish Rebellion.

The reason for this is that the American Colonists who rebelled became the American Government; and the Irish Rebels became the Irish Free State, and Lenin and Trotsky, who fought in the field, became Russia. The Jewish rebels, the Irgun who liberated Israel, became nothing. The freedom they had won by their fighting and dying was taken over by the Weizmanns and the Ben-Gurions who had been too timorous even to ask for it.

I recall an English ballad about a poor but virtuous family whose daughter had gone off to become a rich gay gal in London.

"They drink the champagne wot she sends them," moaned the ballad, "but they never will forgive."

Thus with the Jews of Palestine (and most of the world) who now drink the champagne of a tiny free state called Israel. But they never will forgive the "sinfulness" of the lads who gave them the wine. (There, Shmarya, is a small joke for you.)

And now, as an historian, I must make an apology. I am going to omit something—the "official" army of the Haganah. This is a bigger omission (in a way) than that of the Sternists, for the Haganah was the large Jewish army that finally entered the battle for Israel— and helped win it. My clippings, documents, telegrams and brochures reveal that the Haganah finally stopped betraying and harassing the Irgunists and fought beside them. Without the Haganah army there might have been no Jewish victory.

I smile as I write the above, for I consider it a lie—one of the kind of lies that becomes history and can never be dislodged. Push it out of one history book and it will pop up in another—even in my own. In the history books the Haganah will have stood on the field of battle and valiantly fought for the establishment of a free Hebrew nation.

Alas, they did nothing of the sort. The truth, that must lie buried, perhaps for ever, in the past that knew it—is this. Without a Haganah army, with only the Irgun in the field, the war for Palestine might have taken a little longer, but it would have ended in victory instead of compromise and tomorrow's defeat.

The bewildered Zionist and Socialist government leaders would have been left chattering like kibitzers, and an Irgun army of Israel's youth would have swept into Trans-Jordan. It would have kicked over another half-dozen British-Arabian suburbs and established an Israel worth looking at. Partition, division, internationalization of Jerusalem and all the other surrenders of the Ben-Gurion government made to the United Nations would never have been.

With only an Irgun army to carry it to an Irgun victory, Israel would have emerged as a proud and healthy young democracy, instead of a harassed little beggar of a nation with its extended hat always in its hand.

The great Hebrew historian Klausner wrote in *The Answer*, on February 7, 1947, during the Arab-Hebrew war:

"If we abandon Jerusalem, Haifa, Bethlehem and Hebron . . . the Mounts of Judah and Ephraim . . . and all those other historic landmarks . . . we abandon our Torah, our history, the whole of our past and our future."

And this is precisely what the victorious Jewish government did.

A MATTER OF JUSTICE

FOUR YOUNG JEWS of Tel Aviv were found guilty of treason in the British court of Palestine in 1946. They had cried out against the British burglar in their home. Whereupon the burglar had arrested them, and then the burglar had given them what the burglar called a fair trial.

It was proved in this fair trial that the four young Jews in the prisoners' dock had escaped "from a true hell in Poland." One of them admitted that "his father, mother, sister and all his relatives and friends—all those whom he had loved"—had been burned alive at Auschwitz, Germany.

It was brought out in the court that another one of the defendants believed that "God had decreed he should not die in the German ovens," but that he should make his way to what he called his "homeland."

It was also proved that the defendants did not like the state of things in Zion when they arrived there "after numberless wanderings." All four defendants stated they did not care for the English policy of closing the gates of the Jews' only home.

The defendants admitted that "it was only now since they had joined the Irgun they felt something like happiness." The nineteen-year-old ringleader declared on the witness stand, "My life is a gift from God, and I am not wasting it in pleasures and egoistic pursuits. I have thrown them off. I have remained faithful to my oath. I will fight for the arrival of the remnant of Europe's Jews to their homeland—till they come all, to the last of them."

All four under interrogation accused the British of the crime of keeping the Jews out of Palestine because the British planned to run the place for themselves.

The British entered no denial to these Jewish charges—unless sentencing the Jews in the prisoners' dock to be hanged can be considered, legally, a denial. I am not sufficiently up on British law to speak out on this point.

On hearing their death sentence, the four young Jews—all under twenty—removed four yarmulkas from their pockets and placed them piously on their heads. They then prayed. They thanked God for having let them remain alive unto this day. Shortly after their prayer, the grateful lads were taken out and hanged.

A British General, running the British show in the Holy Land, commented on the verdict favorably. "The quickest way to put an end to all this trouble in Palestine," said he, "is to hang a hundred Jews." This differed from Foreign Minister Bevin's solution for the same problem of bothersome Jews. Bevin's theory was, "Keep arresting them and fining them heavily. Hit them in the pocketbook. That's the only place Jews can feel anything."

It can be seen from the General's comment that the Jew had risen a little in British eyes since Bevin's declaration that there was no more to a Jew than greed. This elevation of the Jew to a personage fit for hanging was brought about by the Irgun.

The four young Jews were hanged by the British without much trouble. The trouble came in cutting them down, and getting them out of sight and earshot.

Two years later when the hundred and fifty thousand British troops pulled out of Palestine, the four young yarmulka'd Jews were still to be heard and seen. Other tall young Jews hung now by their side, Dov Gruner among them; and all their voices had never stopped chanting from the gallows as their limp figures turned and turned. It was a chant of a love of freedom that drowned out all the other noises of the land.

Dov Gruner, Jacob Weiss, Meyer Nakar, Absalom Habib—these were the last of the Jewish heroes to hang on British gallows for the crime of being soldiers of their land. After them the Irgun had stopped the British hanging of Jews and put an end to British justice in Palestine.

Speaking over the undergound radio as the Voice of the Irgun, Menachem Beigin had warned the British that the Jews had also a code of justice. They never had been in any position for two thousand years to use it. But here in Palestine where it had come to birth, it rose again out of a hidden Irgun radio—"An eye for an eye, and a tooth for a tooth. An English soldier on the gallows for every Jewish soldier who is hanged."

I don't have to tell you that the sound of this old Hebrew dictum frightened nearly all the Jews of the world out of their wits and set them to denouncing the Irgun as if it were a plague. Luckily it also frightened the British—not the warning, but its execution.

The Irgun had stopped the public whipping of its captured soldiers by whipping three captive British officers before an astonished crowd of Jews in Jerusalem. It stopped the hanging of captured Jewish soldiers by hanging two captured British sergeants in a wood beyond Natanya.

The British general's estimate that the hanging of a hundred Jews would put an end to the dustup in Palestine remained unverified. The British had to quit the Holy Land still a little short of the general's quota.

"ONLY THUS—"

THE BRITISH, who love freedom almost as much as they love depriving people of it, departed Palestine in some confusion. Everybody, including the most important unexterminated Jews, had assured them of the basic factor that there was no fight in the Jews; especially in the Jewish patriots who kept talking about a Palestinian homeland. And British experience with such infatuated Hebrews had been that you had only to point a monocle or wave a teacup at them and they begged your pardon. There had been every reason for British Intelligence to believe that all the brave and eloquent Jews lay dead in the Old Testament.

Yet here were the British, now one hundred and fifty thousand strong, leaving the Holy Land they had coveted, beaten by somebody. It was a somebody whose name is going to have trouble getting into the history books. But you can still read this name in the back files of the London press, where it made an almost daily appearance. It is in the largest English type.

"Tommies Drive Out Irgun," "Royal Marine Commandos to Hit Irgun," "British 'Get Tough' Policy to Break Irgun," "Another Irgun Terrorist Hanged," "British Tanks Advance on Irgun at Jaffa," "Gruner Hanged: Britain Fears Irgun Action," etc.

It was not only from the gallows that the Jews of the Irgun had beaten the British. The Irgun had licked them in street fights and on the battlefields of Jaffa and Haifa. It had blown them out of military headquarters, stolen air bases from under their noses and kicked the stuffing out of the British Commandos brought in from Malta. It had played devilish tricks as an army of underground ghosts. Emerging in 1948, they were no longer ghosts but soldiers. They went into battle as if the words of Vladimir Jabotinsky about the first Jewish Legion were written in the sky over them:

"And the boys—'those tailors'—shoulder to shoulder, their bayonets dead level, each step like a single clap of thunder; clean, proud, drunk with the National Anthem and with the sense of a holy mission unexampled since the day when Bar Kochba in Betar, not knowing whether there would ever be others to follow and take up the struggle, threw himself upon the enemy."

At Jaffa the British mask was off and all the flags were up. The Star of David insignia that the British had forbidden on the sleeves of the Jewish defenders of Tobruk had found an even better lodging. It flew over Hebrew heads.

Britain ran up its own mightier if not older ensign. Sounding its bagpipes, the same bagpipes that had screeched so bravely at El Alamein, Britain made its long-planned grab at the Holy Land.

The bagpipes were the same, but luckily for the Jews the soul of Britain was not in them. A British colonial adventure manned by anti-Semitic mercenaries skirled out of them, but there was no cry of St. Crispin's Day to rise with their music.

To the contrary, the voice of Churchill, husky guardian of England's honor, spoke fretfully on the subject. The English must get out of Palestine, he pronounced, before that dubious adventure brought down on their heads the obloquy of the world.

The colonial adventurers, out to bag another colony for the Crown and win a Moslem world for an ally, shook off the Churchillian rhetoric and tooted the battle horns.

The Irgun marched out to the firing line—"in full strength, all of us as one man, to fulfill our duty under all circumstances." So spoke Beigin.

The self-appointed government headed by Ben-Gurion, Shertok and their fellow politicians struck a less military posture. It went straight to its knees and declared that it was "madness" to seek a

Jewish state of any sort, and promised the gallows—a Jewish gallows
—for the Terrorists, if only the British would stop the fighting.

The Irgun took Jaffa. The Jewish Agency politicians offered to give
it back. A hundred thousand Arabs, who had murdered and raped at
will for years, fled before the avenging armies of the Irgun. The
self-elected government of Ben-Gurion begged to be allowed to re-
settle them.

Had the British been in a mood to negotiate with politician Ben-
Gurion, trying to hold on to a job, I am sure they could have gotten
him to settle at this time for a letterhead: "Palestine—Jewish
Chargé d'Affaires—Ben-Gurion."

But the British had already learned that the Ben-Gurion pleading,
though it appeared to come from the most important Jews in the
world, was no voice of the Jews. This voice was at Jaffa, at Acre, at
Pardess-Hannah, at Mishmar-Haemek and in Jerusalem—where the
Irgun fought. The British had both hands full attending to these
Irgun soldiers, whose numbers grew daily greater through the deser-
tion to them of the soldiers of the Haganah.

And the British commanders in the field, Brigadier Glubb Pasha of
Trans-Jordan, Brigadier Norman Lash of the Arab Legion, Fawzi
Bey el Kawkaji, commander of all foreign mercenary anti-Palestine
forces, had their hands full also—making their brave Moslem allies
stay in the fight at all.

Army after army melted as if by magic—Fawzi el Kawkaji's Yarmuk
army, the remnants of Rommel's Afrika Korps, now manned by
many British. It was soon obvious that the British had been fooled
on all sides. They had been fooled about Jews not having any fight
in them. They had been worse fooled about the Arabs. Abdulla, their
costly puppet-king of Trans-Jordan, with an army that had cost
the British almost its weight in gold, failed to break through.

And here another miracle happened. The army of the Haganah,
grown restive under the politicians' rule, and no longer willing to
fight the Irgun, as they had at Galilee, Yehudia, Mishmar-Hayarden
and Tel Aviv, stood in Jerusalem and fought beside the Irgun instead.
And, driven to it by public demand and by the strategy of the Irgun
commanders, the Jewish government received into its army six battalions of Irgun veterans.

But just the same, Ben-Gurion and Foreign Minister Shertok found a way to please the British enemy at the same time. A January 2, 1948, headline reads:

"Jewish Agency Capitulates,
Agrees to Bar More Jews from Palestine."

May 15 approached—the date the British had announced for their withdrawal from Palestine. The secret agreement they had made with the Arab League—that, on the date of the withdrawal, Palestine would be divided among the nominal victors—Lebanon, Trans-Jordan, Saudi-Arabia, Iraq and Syria—this secret proposal could no longer be enforced.

But still the Ben-Gurion government stood firm—against the Jews. With the combined Irgun and Haganah armies near victory in Jerusalem, the politicians accepted a new White Paper—the truce of Bernadotte.

On the same day that an Irgun ship loaded with volunteers—and arms enough to win the battle of Israel—left from Port-de-Bouc in France—on that same June 11, the Ben-Gurion government, having agreed to the sailing of the ship for Tel Aviv, barred all further import of arms. (Shmarya—a man sometimes needs two heads.)

The truce suggested by Bernadotte and the United Nations would be kept. Instead of letting the Hebrew soldiers fight on, the Ben-Gurion government would hew to the white flag and the U.N. order for Jews only—Cease Fire. (Shmarya—three heads!)

And with this battle cry I leave them—to return to the "Second Front," 25 West 45th Street, N.Y.C., home of the Committee and all its brave hopes.

AN HONOR COMES TO ME

THE LITERARY DANE, Georg Brandes, wrote with a sigh one day, "He who writes in Danish writes on water." I had come to feel that propaganda was even less than water writing. It was writing traced on the air with a finger.

But now I knew it was also something else. Propaganda with deeds behind it could echo valor and victory—and raise funds for larger triumphs. It could sustain warriors like a medicine and bewilder their enemy like a plague of locusts. It could confuse the enemy's home front, particularly a British home front as susceptible to phrases as to bombs.

Our Second Front was no longer an impotent yell into a barrel. Propaganda in behalf of dead Jews had been like an advertising campaign minus a commodity. In behalf of live men in whose hands flashed the first steel since Bar Kochba, it was a hell-raising medium. It could sell deeds to the world as lustily as it sold automobiles and hair lotions. It could never knock an enemy soldier down but it could sink the spirit of his home front—and its eagerness to keep him all shined up and shooting.

Thus our Second Jewish Front in West Forty-fifth Street graduated from its long status of shadowboxer and stepped into the ring of world affairs. It was no place of danger such as the one in which the Irgun stood. No blows would blind it or rip out its innards. No last ounce of courage would be asked of it, no last grimace of fearlessness against the snub-nosed figure of Death. These were the sad, wild privileges of the Jews with guns in Palestine.

But there were certain minor privileges for the Second Front— hoarseness, ulcers, bankruptcy, verbal lambastings sufficient to bring complexes out of their holes, social obloquy, broken-up homes and lost sweethearts, voodoo death threats through the mails, fist fights; and finally, arrest, a few bullets and a bitter death for our best one.

There was, also, a special discomfort aimed at my pillow alone. It was the British boycott of my movies, of which I was then writing two or three a year. I felt perked up when word of the boycott first came out of England. I beamed on it as the best press notice I had ever received—a solid acknowledgment of the work I had been doing with all my might.

I had already sipped a little historical fame—the first Jew to be denounced in the House of Commons for five hundred years. It was unfair and even a little embarrassing, for there were Jews a hundred times more active against the Crown than I—Meridor, Beigin, Tamir and all the fellows dedicated to drive Britain out of Palestine or die.

But the boycott put an end to my modesty. An empire hitting at a single man and passing sanctions against him! There was something to swell a writer's bosom and add a notch to his hat size. I could recall in history no other case of a nation's declaring war on a lone individual. I was impressed.

My exuberance waned, however, when I arrived in Hollywood a few months later. My bank balance had melted again and I was looking for work. Ever since the first time I had detrained in Hollywood, a week in that town had seen me always on my way to riches again. But this time—a chill Christmas week—there were no jobs (or parties) for me. The movie moguls, most of them Jews for whose pockets I had netted over a hundred million dollars in profits with my scenarios, were even nervous of answering my hellos, let alone of hiring me.

Hire me and jeopardize their English markets—what movie-making Jew was crazy enough for such a gesture! Besides, they had all disapproved of my propaganda business from the beginning—and warned me against it over many a card game. Our only Irgun cohort of stature in movietown was the effervescent Mrs. Frankie Spitz, wife of Leo, who ran the Universal Studios. I thought Madam Spitz was in enough Irgun hot water without taking on my need for a job as a Cause.

Later some of my former friends agreed to employ me if I would cut my price in half and forgo the "thrill" of seeing my name on the finished product. I wrote a half-dozen movies in this fashion, under the table. I signed my work by various names of good Christian flavor, including the name Robert Emmet. The studio's legal department objected to this alias on the ground that it might irritate the British market from another angle. I withdrew Robert Emmet and substituted my driver's name. It was not too good a movie, and Lester felt little pride in his "credit."

Back in Nyack, I further outwitted the empire that was gunning for me by taking to prose. Ben Franklin's old weekly, *The Saturday Evening Post*, and *Collier's* were not ready to trim their literary policies to British boycotts.

The vitality and endurance of this boycott came to amaze me—as well as make my income a constantly precarious matter. Long after the British had forgiven all the other Jews who had battled them—allowing even Menachem Beigin to publish his memoirs in London—they continued to berate and boycott me as if, God save me, I was busy shelling the coast of Albion with some private cannon. I came to feel less and less flattered by these unprecedented attentions of an empire. A decent man can grow weary of calumny as the sole reward for his labors.

Eventually, after five years, and after I had tired of movie writing for reasons that had nothing to do with England, the boycott was lifted. Peter Bergson, flitting between London and Washington, had prepared the "victory." Spyros Skouras, a Greek, and head of Twentieth Century-Fox, wrote the necessary official letter requesting that England's unfair tactics against an American citizen in good standing be brought to an end.

Lest I seem petulant about the British reprisal, let me write that I never considered it unfair, nor once during the five years did I yell "foul"! Not being a tradesman myself, I even continued using my favorite English soap.

And it was a fine sign of Jewish progress that the British had fastened on me alone as a scapegoat. Usually it is all the Jews who are held responsible and punished for any Semitic restlessness.

Perhaps one reason for this philosophic attitude (above) is that I was too busy dodging nearer brickbats—Jewish ones.

HELLO—MY AMERICAN FRIENDS

THE U.S. JEWS, one would think all six million of them, responded to the opening of the Battle of Palestine as if it had broken out under their bedroom windows. My first impression was that after a horrified look at the fracas, they had all rushed into the enemy cheering section.

They seemed, however, to have enough wind left over after denouncing the fighting Irgun to cry scandal at my name. I heard from a multitude of Jewish sources that much of the trouble going on was due to the fact that I, personally, was a bloodthirsty Jew. "A bloodthirsty Jew"—there was a phrase to startle Jewry by its novelty if nothing else. Blood-covered Jews, blood-emptied Jews—these were identities that had depressed the soul of the American Jew but never jarred his respectability as I had.

My uncles no longer brought their *Zeitungs* along when they visited in Nyack. They looked at me, sighed and squeezed my hand in silence. But I knew what was in the papers they had left on their sideboards. I had been promoted from a wanton, publicity-seeking racketeer to a Fascist out to plunge the surviving Jews into a blood bath.

But I was no longer a novice in Jewish affairs. The cry that had risen so fiercely and spontaneously against the fighting Jew was no Jewish cry. It was the cry of organized Jewry—of the Zionists, the Jewish Agency, the American Jewish Congress—and of the score of other Jewish lodges.

Despite the noise they made, these Jewish lodges had no strangle hold on American Jews. There were millions who belonged to none of them, millions of American Jewish mavericks with no lodge president to guide them.

I watched with awe as they rose out of the stores and work shops and came to our side. Jewish clerks and salesladies, garage workers, plasterers, elevator boys, Yeshiva students, policemen, garment workers, prize fighters, housewives; Jewish soldiers and sailors still in American uniforms, Jews from night clubs, tenements, farm lands, synagogues and even penthouses came boldly to the Irgun banner— a clenched fist holding a gun aloft and labeled, "Only Thus—"

They poured their dollar bills and five-dollar bills into the Irgun coffers, and the coffers swelled with millions. They crowded our rallies and theaters. They cheered with joy and there was no more fear in them than in any other group of humans whooping for victory. They were Americans with no desire to settle anywhere else, but they stormed the Committee's offices demanding to be ferried to Palestine into the ranks of the Irgun.

The Irgun needed men, armaments and medical supplies. Its wounded had to be tended in underground hideouts. The Irgun needed also that shadowy but vital ally all brave men want when they fight—a nod of approval from somewhere. The heart of the soldier is a bit like that of the actor. He performs his death scene better when it isn't hissed.

Our Second Front dispatched most of these commodities to the battle lines. Our propaganda continued to stir the bile of organized Jewry. But the unorganized Jews of the land gave us their hearts and their money, and their Americanism. You couldn't have asked for a better Second Front if you were an Englishman standing at Dunkirk.

THE UNDERWORLD TURNS UP

MICKEY COHEN, then Bookie Emperor of California, arrived in Oceanside one afternoon with his manager and bodyguard, Mr. Howard. Mr. Howard was a small, tempestuous man, a manufacturer from New York.

Mickey had been a good prize fighter in his youth, in the 135-pound division. But he had put on weight as an "underworld king" due to his passion for ice cream and French pastry. He ate little else. Outwardly he was a calm, staring man in a dapper pastel suit.

Mickey had come to my home for two reasons, Mr. Howard explained. First, he wanted to talk to me; secondly, he wanted to be sure it was me he was talking to. Los Angeles, said Mr. Howard, was so full of thieves that Mr. Cohen, who had become interested in the Jewish Cause, was leery of being swindled by phony Jews. This, said Mr. Howard, had already happened. Mr. Cohen had bought a Palestine bronze plaque for two hundred dollars from a "Jewish" patriot who turned out to be a Chicago con man.

"As soon as Mr. Cohen's friends catch this thief," said Mr. Howard, "they will break his head. In the meantime we would like to be of some help to the Jewish situation—if we can be assured we are not goin' to be trimmed. So Mr. Cohen would be obliged if you told him what's what with the Jews who are fighting in Palestine. Mr. Cohen is sorry for the dead Jews in Europe but is not interested in helping them."

Mickey looked coldly at the ocean outside my room and nodded.

I told my visitors what was what in Palestine.

"I can't understand why you are having any trouble raising finances in Hollywood for your outfit," Mr. Howard said, very businesslike. "The movie studios are run by the richest Jews in the whole world. They could underwrite this whole Irgun matter overnight."

I explained that all the rich Jews of Hollywood were indignantly opposed to Jews fighting and were working very hard to keep us from helping them. Mickey Cohen spoke for the first time.

"Knockin' their own proposition, huh?" he said.

They both studied me. It was obvious they had never before made any distinction between upper-bracket Jews. Finally, Mr. Howard asked quietly, "What city were you born in?"

"New York City," I said.

"What school did you go to?" Mr. Howard asked.

"Broome Street Number Two," I answered, "in the ghetto."

A wave of relief seemed to come over them.

"I'd like to see you some more," said Mickey gently. "Maybe we can fix up something."

THE UNDERWORLD KICKS IN

I WENT WITH MICKEY COHEN and his court jester "Neddie" Herbert on all-night drives along the Pacific Coast. These were bad times for Mickey, and there was practically no diversion open to him. Any public appearance he made in Hollywood was sure to draw gunfire. A rival gambling syndicate and some personal upstate enemies were pledged to kill Mickey and all his friends. They tossed bombs into his Westwood home, killed several of his cronies, including his invaluable barrister, and eventually blew "Neddie" Herbert's headful of jokes off and sent most of Mickey's entourage into their caskets. Mickey himself was finally plugged in the shoulder. He lay in the hospital for some time watching his room window for gun barrels. After he came out, the U.S. Government closed in and removed Mickey from further danger by sending him to jail for some tax irregularities. But before all these things happened, Mickey had struck his blow for the Jews.

We drove along the Pacific shore toward an open-all-night ice cream stand that Mickey owned. "Neddie" Herbert made a joke that kept Mickey moodily silent for fifteen minutes. The joke was about Mickey's clothes. Mickey changed his pastel suits three times a day, before any wrinkle or sag could appear to spoil their gluelike fit. Looking at his chief with feigned hunger, "Neddie" asked, "Hey, Mickey, you got an orange on you?"

"This is no time for jokes," Mickey finally riposted. He turned to me. "If you'll make a speech, I'll give a party where you can raise some dough."

The "party" was in Slapsy Maxie's Café. A thousand strangers, some with battered faces, some in society rig, came to the event. I asked Mickey who they were. Mr. Howard, tempestuously in charge of everything, answered.

"You don't have to worry. Each and everybody here has been told exactly how much to give to the cause of the Jewish heroes. And you can rest assured there'll be no welchers."

"Maybe I don't have to make a speech," I said.

"The speech," said Mr. Howard, "is what Mr. Cohen wants to hear."

I addressed a thousand bookies, ex-prize fighters, gamblers, jockeys, touts and all sorts of lawless and semi-lawless characters; and their womenfolk.

At the finish of my oratory, Madam Frankie Spitz took over the hat passing. There was no welching. Each of the bookies, toughies and fancy Dans stood up and called out firmly his contribution.

I stood against the back wall with Mickey. He struck me a stinging blow on the arm and said, "Make another speech and hit 'em again."

I said I was recently out of the hospital and had no steam for a second address. I had spoken for forty-five minutes.

Mickey pushed Mr. Howard suddenly toward the stage.

"You tell 'em," Mickey ordered grimly. "Tell 'em they're a lot o' cheap crumbs and they gotta give double." Mickey pointed to me and his eyes were filmed. "You heard what he said. It's for Jews ready to knock hell out of all the bums in the world who don't like them. Go on—tell 'em."

Mr. Howard roared inarticulately over the microphone for a spell. When he had done, Mickey came to the edge of the stage and stood in the floodlights. He said nothing. Man by man, the "underworld" stood up and doubled the ante for the Irgun.

"You can quit crabbin'," Mr. Howard said, mopping his face. "We raised two hundred G's. Furthermore, we been here three hours and nobody's taken a shot at us."

I wrote Mickey a letter of thanks telling him that nobody would ever forget what he had done for the Jews. A few months later, Mickey, stripped of his home, his hundred form-fitting suits and every other vestige of empire, broke and sentenced to the Federal penitentiary for his tax troubles, telephoned me in Nyack. He needed five thousand dollars to hire some new lawyers to take the place of the

ones who had been shot and killed in his employ. I was broke but
told Mickey I would make some phone calls and call him back in two
days. I made the calls—and called Mickey back.

"I couldn't raise the five grand for you," I said.

"That's O.K.," said Mickey. "Good luck."

JEWS IN A GARDEN

NINETEEN FORTY-SEVEN had been a purely Jewish summer. The front
pages of the New York newspapers looked like house organs for the
B'nai Brith. They were full of news about the war in Palestine. It
was no longer a war being fought (on the Jewish side) by a "bloodthirsty criminal element." The Irgun was in the field as a Hebrew
army. Ace foreign correspondents like Homer Bigart were reporting
its astounding exploits. And the Jews of America felt the joy in their
vitals that victorious armies have brought to their people since the
days of Ulysses.

My Nyack garden had become like unto a hill outside of Canaan.
There were almost as many Jews as flowers in it. (The only Christian in the garden was the gentle flower tender, Almer Lundgren, who
had kept it blooming for twenty-five years.)

Irgun captains flew in from Palestine with curt and hair-raising
tales of matters there. Jewish casualties from the battle of Jaffa appeared—blinded youths of nineteen still clinging to their gun-toting
Yemenite nurse, Malka Haroun. There were some British spies
among the early irises. One, a pretty English-Jewish girl, wept her
way to my side as the daughter of a rabbi and cabled a wildly lying
account of my remarks to the London *Express*.

There were also Russian agents in the garden. One of them, a tall
Frenchman in his sixties, insisted on selling me ten million dollars'
worth of guns.

"Please sign this paper," he said, "and the guns will be sent at
once through Czechoslovakia to the Irgun in Palestine."

"I have no money," I said. "The Committee can't possibly pay you
any ten millions."

"I am not worrying about payment," said the tall monsieur. "Where
there are guns there is money."

"I sign no papers," I said. "Menachem Beigin is running the fight. Get him to sign."

My old *compañero*, Wallace Smith, used to say thoughtfully, at least once a day, "Women are peculiar." So are the Russians. On this summer afternoon they were on the side of Zion, ready to help knock out the Moslem armies.

Odd things determine a man's behavior at vital moments. One of the reasons I refused to buy tanks and cannon for a piece of paper was the voice of Yellow Kid Weill, the best of the Chicago con men, speaking out of the past. His voice echoed in me, "Never buy something for nothing. You'll always end up on your ass."

My Russian agent in the garden snorted at what he called my "insincerity."

"I thought you were a Jewish patriot," he said.

I and the Yellow Kid stood firm.

MY CHEER FOR ULYSSES

THE PLAY I'd written, A *Flag Is Born*, netted the Irgun nearly a million dollars. Bergson bought a fairly large "ocean liner" with some of the money. He put my name on its bows. My namesake craft sailed nine hundred refugees to Palestine. It was captured by the British Navy. Six hundred of the refugees were carted off to the Isle of Cyprus where the British were holding some fifty thousand Jews in escrow. The other three hundred passengers escaped and made, most of them, for the Irgun ranks.

(The Committee repossessed the S.S. *Ben Hecht* from the British and turned it over to the government. It flourished for a time as the flagship of the Israel Navy.)

In the garden we talked Jewish hopes and Jewish strategy as if it were the time of Solomon and there was nothing else worth talking about. I had written a book about Jews—A *Guide for the Bedeviled*. I had written also short stories, ads and pageants about Jews. And I had kept drumming away at the British without much pause.

My bout with the distinguished surgeons Cave and Winslow had hardly interrupted my work. When I had come to under an oxygen tent, the Committee was squatting in my hospital room.

They were smoking pipes and cigarettes despite a large sign forbidding it. An oxygen tank, said the sign, was likely to blow up and destroy half the hospital if a spark came near it. But the Committee was disdainful of explosives, and it had something on its mind. It wanted me to write another ad, an important one.

"We need more money," said Harry Selden. "Millions."

I spoke fretfully from my tent.

"We've raised millions," I said.

"They have been consumed," said Merlin.

"How are you going to pay for an ad?" I asked. "An ad's no good unless it's printed all over."

"We have a man who will pay for ten full pages," said Selden. "A fine fellow named Mr. W."

I emerged from my tent and called for stationery. I quote from the ad I wrote, for in it, in a sort of compressed journalese that has escaped me since I quit writing ads, is the full and honest report of our Committee's fiduciary and spiritual accomplishment.

The ad carried the headline:

"LETTER TO THE TERRORISTS OF PALESTINE"

It read:

"My Brave Friends,

"You may not believe what I write you, for there is a lot of fertilizer in the air at the moment.

"But, on my word as an old reporter, what I write is true.

"The Jews of America are for you. You are their champions. You are the grin they wear. You are the feather in their hats.

"In the past fifteen hundred years every nation of Europe has taken a crack at the Jews. This time the British are at bat.

"You are the first answer that makes sense—to the New World.

"Every time you blow up a British arsenal, or wreck a British jail, or send a British railroad train sky high, or rob a British bank, or let go with your guns and bombs at the British betrayers and invaders of your homeland, the Jews of America make a little holiday in their hearts.

"Not all the Jews, of course.

"The only time the Jews present a United Front is when they lie piled up by the millions in the massacre pits.

"I shenck you this front. I like yours better.

"Brave friends, I can imagine you wondering, 'If the Jews of America are behind us, why don't they help us with their support and money?' This is a legitimate curiosity. I'll try to answer it.

"It so happens that a certain small percentage of the Jews of America are not behind you—yet. Remember, you haven't won yet.

"Unfortunately, this small percentage includes practically all the rich Jews of America, all the important and influential ones, all the heads of nearly all the Jewish organizations whom the American newspapers call 'The Jewish Leaders.' They're all against.

"Every time you throw a punch at the British betrayers of your homeland, nearly all these Jews have a collective conniption fit.

"They rush in waving white handkerchiefs and alibis. They didn't do it—not they!

"Respectable people don't fight. They gabble.

"This exhibition of weak minds and weak spines would be the blackest mark ever pasted on the word Jew, were it only a Jewish exhibition.

"Luckily for the Jews, history tells us, a bit sadly, that respectability and wealth never line up with a revolution—or a fighting minority.

"The American Revolutionary Army under George Washington went a long time without shoes, guns or food. The respectable and wealthy American colonists preferred British admiration to liberty and freedom. They thought it was bad taste to fight for such things —against the British, of all people. And they proved their respectability by playing informer to the British.

"You can see how little respectability has changed since 1776.

"Right now all the respectability of the Jews is handsomely engaged in cooing before the United Nations.

"The British put the matter of who's who and what in Palestine up to the United Nations because they were frightened of you. They were afraid your gallant fight for your homeland would gather to you the sympathy of the world.

"So they took the ball out of play (for a breather) and handed it to the referee—who was a personal friend.

"The British figured the sound of gabble before a world court would drown out the sound of Hebrew guns in Palestine.

"It hasn't and it won't.

"True enough, Jewish respectability is making a bit of noise at the moment. Our 'Jewish Leaders' are pleading for a Jewish sanctuary in fine, measured strophes.

"They are not nearly as hotheaded about it as were the bird lovers of America who a few years ago pleaded for a sanctuary for the vanishing penguins.

"But they are much alike. They want a sanctuary where the Jews of Europe can all stand on a rock and eat philanthropy fish till the Messiah arrives.

"We are ringing doorbells and peddling your cause and passing the hat.

"Forgive us if our take is a little meager—for the time.

"The rich Jews are pouring millions into the business of feeding the survivors of the German massacre.

"Jewish wealth and respectability are fearlessly rushing sandwiches to them.

"But, for a change, the Jews of America hear more than Jewish groans to solace.

"We hear Hebrew courage.

"We hear brave men fighting on despite torture, calumny, low supplies and overwhelming odds!

"We're out to raise millions for you.

"Hang on, brave friends, our money is on its way.

> "Yours as ever,
> "BEN HECHT, *Cochairman*"

The ad appeared in a few days. Some fifteen newspapers printed it at their "usual advertising rates." Hundreds of other newspapers in the U.S., Mexico, South America and France ran the ad gratis. It had appealed to them, apparently, as news.

My second week in the hospital was a lonely one. My New York friends had stopped dropping in or telephoning. The ad had outraged the British and the Jewish respectables alike. My Committee was busy removing checks from the mail brought in by the advertisement.

My friend Charlie Lederer was, for a while, my full list of callers. One day the door of my hospital room opened and a tall white-haired man entered. It was Bernard Baruch, my first Jewish social visitor. He sat down, observed me for a moment and then spoke.

"I am on your side," said Baruch. "The only way the Jews will ever get anything is by fighting for it. I'd like you to think of me as one of your Jewish fighters in the tall grass with a long gun. I've always done my best work that way, out of sight. It's what I told President Wilson when he gave me my first mission."

THE SOUL OF MAN

I SAT in the garden at the summer's end reading letters that had accumulated while I was in the hospital. There were barrels of them, and they were from Jews. They brought tears to me—particularly the misspelled ones full of the sort of odd grammar my parents had favored in their correspondence. The epistles from the educated were almost as moving. The love in all of them was a tonic that made my sawed-up insides feel firm again.

But as I read on under the apple trees, I knew they were written to a me who didn't exist—a leader of Jews. I was no more a leader of Jews than of Kentuckians. Not even of the Jews in West Forty-fifth Street, not even of the Jews in my Nyack garden. To be a leader a man has to learn to stand still, and be content with repeating himself. I was going nowhere that I knew of, and never again might have anything as interesting to utter as I had uttered about Jews. But having said my say, it was my nature to wander off, hoping for other topics.

After the Palestine war, I might try my hand at a type of Jewish writing that had gone out of style with my people. You stood in the wilderness and bellowed about their failings. During my eight years among them I had noted some flaws in their behavior.

But I had no great wish for Elijah's long hair or dusty black robe. At best, I would make a poor (and short-winded) Prophet. Not believing that God had made a Covenant with the Jews, I could not rail long at them for the sin of being like everybody else.

The only thing I had discovered that was unique about the Jews was that they had insisted on remaining a people after losing their homeland and historic right to their name. This was like a man walking around after he had been pronounced dead. People grew interested chiefly in burying him.

These musings under the apple trees were my answers to the piles of mail—to the letter from the "Rabbis' Union of Europe" that

praised me for my "holy work"; to the one from the "Correct Pleat-
ing and Skirt Company," the writer of which was "filled with a glori-
ous feeling" over what I had done; and to the letters from soldiers
and D.P. Jews in Cyprus, and Jews with fine addresses in the U.S.A.
Vale, these letters. And vale all the Jews. They had lost a massacre,
but were winning a war. Their name would be a little brighter—for
how long?

Almer Lundgren looked up worriedly from his garden chores.

"Mr. Peter Bergson is coming," he said. "Should I tell him Mister
Hecht has to be quiet?"

"I'll be quiet," I said.

Lundgren watched me anxiously as I covered my mail with a
blanket—and then I heard again the clip-clipping of the shears that
was part of the summer sounds of my garden.

Peter Bergson was walking down the path. He always had a
springy step and a cheery look as if he had just inherited something.
He usually had—trouble. But he was bringing me no troubles this
time.

Behind him walked a tall man with bulging shoulders, heavy hands,
bushy brows and a smile. I had never seen his picture but I knew
who he was.

"This is Abrasha Stavsky," said Peter.

Stavsky, the Rescuer, stood smiling in my garden. Like all heroes
he looked shy in a peaceful place. He remained standing and silent
as Peter sat down and talked.

Peter had interesting news, but Stavsky was more interesting. His
adventures sounded around him like the echo of horns on a hill. The
Pirate of the Mediterranean! But no pirate had ever looked like this.
His face was a shade brighter than most men's faces, as if his soul
were nearer its surface.

As Peter talked, Stavsky continued to smile some sort of benediction on me and the life to which I had returned from the surgeon's
table. I felt suddenly what it must have been to the poor and frightened ones of Europe to see this rescuer's face.

Peter's news was about the young American war veterans who had
volunteered to fight in Palestine. Barney Ross, ring champion and
Marine hero, had helped recruit them. I told Peter to be sure and
tell them that Ibn Saud had a thousand wives, all young and pneu-
matic.

Stavsky waited until we both had stopped talking and then modestly handed me the front page of a Jewish newspaper. It was a page almost coming apart at its creases.

"I can't read Yiddish," I said.

"It's a foolish old story," said Peter, "but Abrasha insists you ought to know it, so that if you mention his name sometime and somebody says, 'Oh, Stavsky! That's the murderer who was sentenced to be hanged in Palestine,' you'll not be surprised."

"Is this the story of his trial?" I asked.

"No," said Peter. "It's the full account of his final acquittal. But you must have heard the story. It tore all Palestine apart fifteen years ago."

I shook my head. It seemed that however informed I became about Jews, there were always vital matters still strange to me. I write the story now of Stavsky's march to the gallows and down again because I shall have to refer to it, briefly, after Stavsky's return to Palestine.

It was 1933. A Labor Zionist leader named Arlosoroff was strolling along the beach in Tel Aviv with his wife. He was a man little liked in the land, except by labor leader Ben-Gurion. Arlosoroff, representing the Jewish Agency, had signed a deal with the Nazis. (This was before the massacre.) Jews would be allowed to take their fortunes out of Germany in the form of manufactured German goods. Thus Palestine was to become the biggest outlet in the world for Nazi industry. The young Palestinians called Revisionists did not approve of this.

Arlosoroff was shot and killed while strolling on the beach. Madam Arlosoroff ran to the police with the news that a group of Arabs had attacked and murdered her husband.

Abrasha Stavsky was immediately arrested. He was no group of Arabs, but he was a man feared and hated by politician Ben-Gurion.

At the trial, Madam Arlosoroff falteringly changed her story and introduced a tall man as her husband's assassin. The four judges voted a three-to-one verdict. The one Arab and two Englishmen judges were for hanging Stavsky. The one Jewish judge voted that Stavsky was an innocent man. Under British rule, a three-to-one decision of the court was considered unanimous. How else could justice ever have been served in Palestine, with the fourth judge always a Jew?

"Abrasha waited for several months to be hanged," said Peter.

"But the case went to a court of appeal, and he was acquitted. I think the angriest man in the whole Near East on the day of Abrasha's acquittal was David Ben-Gurion."

"Did you kill Arlosoroff?" I asked my tall guest.

"No," said Stavsky. "I have never killed a Jew."

It was growing dark and we went into the house. Stavsky walked up and down in my room, making it look small. I had looked forward for years to hearing Stavsky's stories, but I was not disappointed when he failed to start on a single one of them. You didn't need to hear Stavsky talk. The twenty thousand Jews he had somehow pulled out of the German ovens and taken to Palestine seemed to speak for him—from the crowded decks of the Stavsky fleet. What a fleet it had been! Limping tubs, discarded "bottoms," riffraff hulls with engine rooms steaming like Turkish baths. I had read some of their fine names, for all ships however foolish cling to proud names —*Artemis, Star of Panama, Parita, Columbia, Naomi, Sakarya.*

For fifteen years Stavsky had worked like some Jewish Saint Christopher, ferrying the unexterminated Jews to Palestine—on boats, on rafts, on his broad back. Look at him closely now and you could still feel his passengers watching him. Not the tempest roaring around them, or the British warship firing on them, or the shadows moving in the water that might be mines—but always Stavsky. One frown on Stavsky's face meant that the last hope was gone. I knew where Stavsky had grown his smile.

"I hear Peter's buying a new ocean liner," I said, "and calling it the *Altalena.*"

"It was one of Jabotinsky's pen names," said Peter. "We plan to use it for the Hebrew navy."

At the name *Altalena* Stavsky stopped being a guest. He became a happy man. He poured himself a full tumbler of whisky and drank it thirstily, as if it were pop.

"The *Altalena* will carry a thousand soldiers to Palestine," said Peter, "and millions of dollars' worth of armament."

"For the Irgun?" I asked.

"No," said Peter. "For the combined Hebrew armies of the Haganah and the Irgun." And then Peter uttered the fateful words, "With this cargo the Jews can win a nation—a real Hebrew state. They won't have to stop when they've chopped out a little desert ghetto for themselves."

Peter and I spent the evening in talk. But I watched Stavsky as he stood looking in silence at the moon over the Hudson. He was easier to understand than words. Abrasha Stavsky was dreaming on his feet, as he had dreamed most of his life on slippery decks packed with white-faced Jewish refugees. He was dreaming of a Jewish land, strong and proud as himself. Through its thousand adventures, through all its Homeric tossings, Stavsky's soul had stood on a rock all his life and looked on a land of the Jews.

I shared no part of Stavsky's dream. Beyond my window lay no Palestine, but only the Hudson and the pleasant lights of Tarrytown. "Know you the far land where the lemon trees bloom?" the Jew Heinrich Heine had once sighed. No such sigh had ever been in me. Yet I could feel Stavsky's love of this far land, this nonexistent land, as if it were something in me. An actor can make you feel what isn't yours. So, too, can a hero.

Looking at the tall man smiling out of my window, I knew that patriotism could be as good a dream as any that found lodging in the soul of man.

But, alas, for dreams. For a child of man to look back on them is like looking back on a dog run over on a highway.

We were three bright lads in this room, full of varied information about Jews, past and future. But none of us knew that Stavsky's dream had already been run over on its road. We did not know that the pre-battle surrender had been determined. As the Weizmann-Ben-Gurion government had bowed to the British tyrant, so they knelt now to their new master—the United Nations.

The Jewish government had called for the Irgun to help it stay alive against five enemy armies. But they would never dare welcome an *Altalena* loaded with enough arms to rescue beleaguered Jerusalem or to enable an army of victorious young Hebrews to sweep through Eretz-Israel and win the land on both sides of the Jordan!

There would be no Hebrew nation, no room for cattle and grain, no cities, no freight yards, no ancient capital revived, no space for industry or destiny. There would be a beach head called Israel, to which the Jews could cling, as they had always clung, like castaways.

HOME IS THE DREAMER

ON JUNE 25, 1948, the *Altalena*, commanded by the American, Monroe Fein, cut down its engines as it entered the harbor of Tel Aviv. In the Hudson it would have looked like a lesser craft. Nevertheless, it was the proudest ship ever to enter Jewish history.

Aboard were a thousand volunteers, American veterans among them, come to fight for a Hebrew nation. A first round had been won by the Jews, but the fight was still on in Jerusalem and on all the borders.

Stowed in the *Altalena* was a five-million-dollar cargo of armament. In its French loading port, the *Altalena* had received the waited word from the Israel government. The word had said, "Await your munitions and other reinforcements. Both vitally needed by Israel to win war."

Now in the captain's cabin a conference was in happy swing. Merlin was discussing with his commander in chief, Menachem Beigin, the allocation of the tanks and machine guns, of the four million rounds of ammunition, of the bazookas and cannon the *Altalena* was bringing to the Hebrews. Twenty per cent to the Irgun in Jerusalem and eighty per cent to be divided equally to all Hebrews under arms, including Irgun battalions. With the new supplies, both Hebrew armies would be able to win Jerusalem and push on. As for the volunteers aboard, Beigin agreed they could enter either army they wished—Haganah or Irgun—it was all the same now.

And in the bows of the *Altalena* stood Abrasha Stavsky. No more conferences for him. He had had enough of conferences. Stavsky's conferences had been in Greek, Turkish and Portuguese barrooms, in tropic honky-tonks; on the piers of Brest, and Santo Domingo; in Polish, Rumanian, Czechoslovakian caves, in hide-outs under the Nazi nose. They had been full of fist fights and swinging knives. Out of these conferences Stavsky had wrested his Jews at so much per head and smuggled them off to the Holy Land, and broken all the laws from Riga to Tel Hai.

But that was all over. Here was Israel. He had written his mother in Tel Aviv, "I am coming home, at last."

Merlin came up to the smiling Stavsky and spoke. The cabin conference had ended very satisfactorily, he said. There was only one small piece of business not yet concluded. The Israel government had not sent any stevedores yet to help unload the cargo. But, said Merlin, the representative must arrive any minute. Merlin showed Stavsky the government radiogram received en route and explained its significance. "It means no more treason, no more informers among the Jews. We are all one."

"If not for this cablegram," said Merlin, "I would begin to worry why no one has come out to welcome us yet."

Stavsky saw no cable and heard no word of what Merlin spoke. He kept looking at his dream and his homeland. They were no longer separate things to look at. Turning to Merlin, Stavsky said, "I'll be home with my mother tonight."

A little late but in fine order the Jewish government of the new state of Israel appeared on the beach. Jewish soldiers with cannon and machine guns came marching toward the harbor of Tel Aviv. The blue-starred flag of Israel was over their heads. They opened fire on the *Altalena.*

It was easy target practice—an anchored ship at a hundred yards. Shells struck the *Altalena* as if someone were intent on ringing up a big score in a shooting gallery. A rifle volley killed six men on its decks and wounded twenty. A second volley killed four and wounded fifteen. A third killed four more and wounded thirty.

Stavsky remained standing where he was. But he turned his back to the shooting.

Merlin called to him, "Jump, Abrasha, into the water!"

Bullets caught Merlin in the leg and dropped him to the deck.

Others jumped. Machine guns turned on the swimmers. The Haganah accuracy had improved. Forty swimmers were hit. Six of these drowned.

Below decks on the burning ship Irgun men were having an argument with their commander in chief. Menachem Beigin, like Stavsky, refused to abandon ship. He would remain where he was, said Beigin, and die when the ship exploded.

Beigin was a brave and dedicated man. But he weighed too little. He was easily lifted out of his cabin and carried off to safety by his men.

Stavsky, with his back still turned to the firing squads with the Hebrew flag over their heads, watched the *Altalena* burning. He had seen bonfires on the sea before. A special volley was trained on the tall figure still standing with its back turned to the Jews. He went down full of Jewish bullets.

When Stavsky lay dead, politician Ben-Gurion issued a statement to the world.

"Blessed be the bullets that killed these enemies of Israel," he said. "The cannon that destroyed the *Altalena* is a holy gun and should be placed in the temple."

I leave the bullet blesser with the last word. This little politician with the comic haircut, whose white hair looked always like a chicken with its wings spread, was not only good at politics. He was good at hating. The gallows this little angry man of Tel Aviv had kept in his head for fifteen years—had finally claimed its tall, bright-faced quarry.

But I'll write no more of Palestine. I turned my back on it the same time Abrasha Stavsky did.

GOOD-BY TO SOMEONE

I HAVE WRITTEN more endings than I care to remember—play endings, movie endings, book and story endings and a number of letters that were also endings. Here is another.

When I went to bed last night I decided, if the weather warranted, I would end my book with a lyric description of a day—its sky, sun, soft wind; its always bright and clear face. What is there as friendly in the world as a fine day, or as good a piece of fortune? The memory of a lovely day will last longer than anything that happened in it. This is not true of the night but only of the lighted hours.

Such a day has come again—a summer morning that enters my garden like an orchestra of elves. A screen door bangs and my dog is off to smell the world.

I wish I could trot along with him, not to share his odors but his thoughts. To think like a dog, or even a goose, would be a decided advantage to any writer. He would be observing life without human confusion, and bound to find some wonderful news.

On such a morning as this, long ago, the first restive sea monster must have stuck its horrendous nose out of the water and decided on the earth as a better place of residence.

But I must postpone discussing my best and most constant friend—the day. I shall come back to it, as I planned. But at my elbow is a large basket of Omissions. They are the material that failed to get into my book.

They bother my conscience and vanity. From the look of this basket I have omitted from my book almost as much as I put in. I need no basket to tell me this. I have only to throw an honest glance at my life to know I have written hardly more than a few of its days. But who has ever written more?

Much like my dog who is sniffing at what he possibly calls "life," I am moved to sniff among these basket scraps. Here are a few of the notes I read, idly, and with one eye on the day.

PARABLE

BION, the philosopher, said of a king who tore his hair in grief, "Does this man think that a bald head will assuage his sorrow?"

THE EGO AND ITS OWN

A MAN may be discontented with everything—God, country, wife, art—but he is never discontented with the amount of sense he has. It is always enough.

THE AMERICAN STARE

THE more we let others sing, dance and perform for us, the more empty we become.

BALLET NOTE

THE lesser the art, the more artistic are its admirers.

THE CITY

THERE is hardly one in three of us who live in the cities who is not sick with unused self.

ENEMIES ARE BETTER THAN NOTHING

IT grows ever harder to make friends in a complex world, for friendship requires contact. But one can make enemies of those one has never seen or heard. This lonely enemy-making activity is becoming more and more The American Way.

SCIENTIFIC NOTE

Much of psychoanalytic therapy is based on the theory that it takes a thief to catch a thief.

SOCIETY NOTE

"Light cares find words but heavy ones are dumb," wrote Seneca.

I have found that people who use their griefs as calling cards are not the stricken ones.

USELESS PROGRESS

Our political leaders no longer sleep with their mothers, as in Suetonius' time, no longer skip off into bedrooms with their prime ministers, or relax by ravishing small boys in swimming pools. But it does not seem to have improved them as leaders.

ARGUMENTUM AD HOMINEM

Most writers try to translate themselves into comprehensible and entertaining fellows—except the philosopher. In the philosopher it is the Subject Matter that thinks and seldom the man.

"LOVE THY NEIGHBOR" STILL A SUCCESS

After nineteen hundred years of Christianity it is possible for a nation to exterminate six million non-Christians and still be loved by its neighbors.

WHY WE LOVE WAR

A nation used to war grows melancholy in peace. Its people, robbed of their talent for living, must turn to death for entertainment.

EVOLUTION OF A PARROT

"What if the soul of man keeps on getting worse?" Montaigne asks. It has.

Man is no longer engaged in living but in organizing himself. His sensitivities become more and more useless. Already most of his exaltations have nothing to do with himself. He curses with his state, he exults with his parliaments, he weeps with his ambassadors—and he lies with his politicians.

OUR DUBIOUS TROUSERS

MOST things we consider facts are symbols whose meanings are as variable as those in a dream. The wearing of trousers, for instance, was considered effeminate in the time of the Emperor Trajan. Men in pants were held to be either invalids or homosexuals.

WILL-O'-THE-WISP

PINDAR wrote of the battle of Artemisium between the Greeks and Persians:

There the sons of Athens set
The stone that Freedom stands on yet.

A HISTORY OF POLITICS

JOHN ZISKA, the Bohemian leader, left orders that they should skin his body after his death and make a drum of the skin. He was certain the noise of this drum would be able to defeat his enemies.

SOCIAL AMBITION

A FOOL is always looking for new friends who will see only the part of him that has learned how to live—his pretenses.

WRITERS WITHOUT PENCILS

I VISITED the county insane asylum yesterday. I was impressed most by those inmates who stand like sentinels on the threshold of nightmare and watch warily the dark wonders of their minds.

WORLD WAR III?

THE need to fight Communism with our guns is the result of our stupidity in tackling it with our minds. We lost the political debate with the Communists by imitating their hysteria and mendacity—at which we are comparative amateurs. We have left to us only the chance to prove we are physically stronger than the Red armies—and as eager to die for our muddleheadedness as the Russians are for their fresher lunacies.

AN EARLY HOLLYWOOD GENIUS

THE first drama contest of which there seems to be any full record was "won by Themistocles."

The great man who had never written a line or recited a single strophe placed his name as producer ahead of the author and actor. His marquee reads (says Plutarch):

> *Themistocles is in charge of the show—*
> *Phryrichus wrote it—*
> *Admonatus starred in it.*

The Athenian award for drama was given to Themistocles because he had put his name first.

BUGLE FUN

IN so complex and depersonalized a civilization as ours, war may be a wistful effort to return to the past and its vanished fellowship, and to the importance of being a human being.

NURSERY NOTE

ANGER is increasing in the soul of man, an anger seemingly with itself such as a child feels when it has failed to solve something. What it cannot solve, it breaks.

The unsolvable problem today seems to be the human being himself.

A FUTURE DR. KINSEY

Two little boys were playing on Tenth Avenue.

"What are you gonna do when you grow up, Willy?"

"I'm going to eat candy for a living."

THE HIGHEST ART

THE test of an art is how much it can say itself, and how little it leaves to be said about it. The only art that actually speaks for itself is the art of words.

MY FAVORITE LOVE STORY

A CHINESE woman sat in the graveyard fanning the earth beneath which her husband lay buried.

"What a tender heart that still hopes to comfort him with her loving fan," sighed an onlooker.

The Chinese woman had promised her husband not to marry again until the earth of his grave was dry.

MY OWN "ORIGIN OF THE SPECIES"

THE Finnish people once believed that God molded man's body out of clay and then went to heaven to fetch him a soul. God left a dog to watch His handiwork. The Devil came and seduced the watchdog with the gift of a fur coat. Then the Devil spat upon the clay and beslavered it from head to toe.

When God returned He looked on His handiwork and despaired of ever cleaning it. Instead, He turned the body inside out to hide the dirt.

ESSAY ON HAPPINESS

LOOKING for a me that might be a genuinely happy fellow, I have day dreamed myself into a position of wondrous fame and wealth. But when I had established this Fortunatus in my mind's eye, the dream of him grew restless. The Fortunatus I had evolved began to sigh. Visions of a more spiritual and simple life took to harrying his grandeur.

Whereupon my day dream would make me into a sort of poetic peasant living with senses open to nature, and no disquiet touching my days. But, as I walked the green fields in the guise of this child of nature, a nervousness would come into my dream self, and a new day dream would become necessary—that of a Society favorite, or a glittering man about town in a half dozen fine cities, or of a great statesman, scientist, explorer and even miracle-worker.

In no day dream have I ever found happiness, not even in the especial day dream which I reserve for sick interludes, where I am all things a man can be combined in one. But as poet, athlete, Croesus, statesman, sage, scientist and overwhelming lover, as a man famed for everything and capable of everything, I am still without the reward I seek—happiness. This synthesis of all genius and all activities that I become looks back, sees the glittering dead of a hundred lands and eras, and grows again dissatisfied.

My inability to imagine happiness and find a home for it is brother to my inability to imagine God and seat Him in His proper place. No man who confines his dreams to earth can discover happiness. He must be content with the fugitive warmths of the world and leave the great glow he seeks to that other tribe of day dreamers—the people who can imagine God.

I understand now why I failed to use the dots and dashes of thoughts in my basket. They grow gloomier and unhappier as I paw among them. To run them as a finale of my book today would be to finish my tale with a falsehood.

Tough though I have found the world, and wicked though man is, the story is not bitter and tragic. The ghosts of my mother and father and Tante Chasha hover round it, of Duffy and Wally Smith, George Wharton and Mankiewicz, and the ghosts of many people still alive —of my daughter Teddy—who had to become an adult with a foreign address, and of MacArthur, my friend with whom I made much noise —people dead and still living whom I have loved.

There is a day outside as bright and as gentle as a child's forehead. And all the people dead and still living whom I have loved seem to beam at me in its brightness. The evils that I have faced and fumed at seem less than these smiles. Even the history that has burned my mind with its cruelty, all the barbarism and cant of the century I've lived in—these are less than the others—the tender eyes that looked on me, the strong spirits that wished me well and admired me.

And music is playing—not simile music, but brass bands and pretty fifing. The Volunteer Fire Departments of a hundred towns are parading in Nyack.

GOOD-BY AGAIN

MY FAMILY and friends are squatted on the curb in front of Mrs. Probst's grocery store watching the marchers. I know just where they will be when I walk up Perry Lane for a look at the revels. They have occupied this strip of curbing, like some opera box, for twenty-five years of parading firemen. The group is a little less. Gertie, Jo and Almer Lundgren are no longer in it.

There is a great racket of music all the way from Castle Heights Avenue, where we sit, to distant Main Street. Nanette tells me twenty bands have already passed. Nanette is Miss Herbuveaux, who has been typing and retyping this book for the last four years. She is young and would look well on the stage. Rose and I have often debated whether she would be better as Juliet or Jerry Lewis.

"Have you seen Jenny?" Rose smiles at me.

"I've been writing," I answer.

Jenny, my daughter, is now nearly eleven.

Lester comes up with the news that he saw Jenny racing down the sidewalk beside the parade.

You wouldn't think there were so many firemen or so many towns in and around Nyack—and all volunteers. The parade turns the corner at Castle Heights Avenue and goes up a small hill. There is some disorganization climbing the slope. Hook and Ladders come to a stop. Big red fire trucks roar ahead of the marchers. And some of the marchers sneak a breather in the grass. But we keep our eyes from these backstage confusions.

Approaching us down Broadway all is glitter and grandeur. Each town has its own different uniform for its firemen and their lady auxiliaries, its own banners, mottoes and band. Zouaves swing by, cake-walk dandies in red coats, Gauchos, Chauncey Alcotts in green stovepipe hats, Rough Riders, a contingent of Svengalis in satin capes, etc., etc.

Each troop of volunteers marches behind its own band and is followed by its full quota of fire-fighting vehicles. The great trucks look as red and shining as if they had just come out of a Christmas stocking.

The marchers are fun to watch. Despite their uniforms they are as ill assorted as a crowd on a beach. They are tall, short, fat, skinny, young, ancient—but they all walk with a snap. Their faces are equally varied. Every expression is to be seen in them but one. There is no evil. No hatred marches on this summer day. These are vain, grinning, sometimes giggling, paraders. They are the people who come to fix your furnace, exterminate your ants, patch up your roof or save your trees from dying. They wait on you in stores, or take care of you in banks. They are the television watchers, the bingo players, the breeders. With all their fluttery banners and tooting bands, they seem somehow not to disturb the peacefulness of the street or the languor of the summer day.

I sit on the curbing beside Rose and my heart grins at them. A loyalty fills my spirit. I am loyal to the Volunteer Firemen of Blauvelt, Piermont, Tappan, Hackensack, Saugerties, Pearl River, Congers, Nyack and so forth. I feel proud on this prince of days to tip my hat to the human race.

Then suddenly I hear a new sound in the street. It is a small sound but louder in my heart than the Haverstraw band. It is Jenny come to inform her parents of some new and wonderful thing about to appear.

The Hebrew poet Bialik said of a little girl he had watched all day while traveling in a train that he would gladly renounce all the Nobel prizes in this world and the hereafter in the next, were the mother of this little girl to "give" her to him and his wife. I have given up no Nobel prizes. . . .

Yet here she stands—our daughter—vibrating beside us beneath the pillars of Mrs. Probst's porch. She wears short pants—pedal pushers. Her eruption of blonde hair is slightly checked by a gypsy scarf. Things dangle from her belt, her neck, her wrists—sea shells, feathered walnuts, tops, pocketknives and several watches. She is lean, and built, it would seem, chiefly for climbing. Her eyes are large and glowing. They are eyes meant for loving as well as seeing. Her hands float as if a dream were moving them. A heart with no baggage of yesterdays; a smile that explodes at the touch of sun or the sound of music; a look of mystery and talent—these are Jenny. How bright the world seems where she stands! How wondrous tomorrow!

But now she is gone, racing down the street, leaping into the air at every fifth step.

Watching her, I remember a lad in Racine. My book is done—but it is beginning all over again.

Index

635

About the Author

Ben Hecht, author, dramatist, and propagandist, started his career as a newspaper reporter. From 1914 to 1923 he worked for the Chicago Daily News, *spending two of those years as chief of the Berlin bureau. Meanwhile he had begun to write short stories, books—fiction, non-fiction—and plays. He became one of a well-known group of Chicago literary people that included Sherwood Anderson, Theodore Dreiser and Carl Sandburg. Both in collaboration and alone, he has written such plays as* Front Page, Twentieth Century, To Quito and Back, *and* Jumbo. *Among his books are* 1001 Afternoons in Chicago, Count Bruga, A Book of Miracles *and* A Guide to the Bedevilled. *A few of the movies he has written are* Viva Villa, Scarface, The Scoundrel, Nothing Sacred, Gunga Din, Crime Without Passion, Spellbound, Notorious, Spectre of the Rose, Actors and Sin.